Other Books by S. J. Perelman

THE

MOST

OF

S. J. PERELMAN

SIMON AND SCHUSTER • NEW YORK • 1958

COPYRIGHT © 1930, 1931, 1932, 1933, 1935, 1936, 1937, 1938, 1939,
    1940, 1941, 1942, 1943, 1944, 1945, 1946, 1947, 1948, 1950, 1951,
    1952, 1953, 1955, 1956, 1957, 1958 BY S. J. PERELMAN
COPYRIGHT © 1942, 1943, 1944, 1952, 1957 BY THE CURTIS PUBLISHING CO.
COPYRIGHT © 1957 BY THE NEW YORK TIMES
PUBLISHED BY SIMON AND SCHUSTER, INC.
ROCKEFELLER CENTER, 630 FIFTH AVENUE
NEW YORK 20, N. Y.

SECOND PRINTING

Most of the material in this book first appeared in The New Yorker.
All of Westward Ha!, *the two chapters from* The Swiss Family Perelman, *"I'll Always
Call You Schnorrer, My African Explorer," and "And Did You Once See Irving Plain?"
first appeared in* Holiday.
"Dental or Mental, I Say It's Spinach" and most of Acres and Pains *first appeared in*
The Saturday Evening Post.
One chapter of Acres and Pains *first appeared in* The Country Book.
"The Idol's Eye," "The Red Termites," and "The Love Decoy" first appeared in
College Humor.
"Scenario" and "Second-Class Matter" first appeared in Contact.
*"Strictly from Hunger" is based on a piece that first appeared in the old humor maga-
zine,* Life.
"A Farewell to Omsk" first appeared in the book, Crazy Like a Fox *(Random House).*
"Who Stole That Golden Metaphor?" first appeared in the book, The Road to Mil-
town *(Simon and Schuster).*
"The Pants Recaptured" has never before been published.
The Introduction by Dorothy Parker is based on a piece that ran originally in The
New York Times Book Review.

LIBRARY OF CONGRESS CATALOG CARD NUMBER: 58-10353
MANUFACTURED IN THE UNITED STATES OF AMERICA

For Laura

❦ CONTENTS

❧ *INTRODUCTION*

by Dorothy Parker

IT IS A STRANGE FORCE that compels a writer to be a humorist. It is a strange force, if you care to go back farther, that compels anyone to be a writer at all, but this is neither the time nor the place to bring up that matter. The writer's way is rough and lonely, and who would choose it while there are vacancies in more gracious professions, such as, say, cleaning out ferryboats? In all understatement, the author's lot is a hard one, and yet there are those who deliberately set out to make it harder for themselves. There are those who, in their pride and their innocence, dedicate their careers to writing humorous pieces. Poor dears, the world is stacked against them from the start, for everybody in it has the right to look at their work and say, "I don't think that's funny."

It is not a pleasant thought, though, I am afraid, an unavoidable one, that there cannot be much demand for written humor in this our country today. For the supply is—with one exception—scanty and shopworn. There are quantities of those who, no doubt, if filling out a questionnaire, put "Occupation, humorist," but their pieces are thin and tidy and timid. They find a little formula and milk it until it moos with pain. They stay with the good old comic symbols so that you won't be upset—the tyrannical offspring, the illiterate business associate, the whooping, devil-may-care old spinster (always reliable), the pitiable inadequacies of a man trying to do a bit of carpentry, the victorious criticisms of the little wife.

Over and over and on and on, they write these pieces, in the rears of magazines, in glossy Sunday supplements of newspapers, over and over and on and on, like a needle stuck in a phonograph record. I could name names, if I could remember them. But that would mean nothing. You have seen those pieces, and they were dead before the sun went down on the day on which they were published.

I had thought, on starting this composition, that I should define what humor means to me. However, every time I tried to, I had to go and lie down with a cold wet cloth on my head. Still, here I go. (For the British I had great reverence, until now, when it is so much about how charming Lady Cicely looked when she fell out of the punt.) Humor to me, Heaven help me, takes in many things. There must be courage; there must be no awe. There must be criticism, for humor, to my mind, is encapsulated in criticism. There must be a disciplined eye and a wild mind. There must be a magnificent disregard of your reader, for if he cannot follow you, there is nothing you can do about it. There must be some lagniappe in the fact that the humorist has read something written before 1918. There must be, in short, S. J. Perelman.

Mr. Perelman stands alone in this day of humorists. Mr. Perelman—there he is. Robert Benchley, who was probably nearest to Perelman, and Ring Lardner, who was nearest to nobody, are gone, and so Mr. Perelman stands by himself. Lonely he may be—but there he is.

And here he is in his own words:

"Button-cute, rapier-keen, wafer-thin and pauper-poor is S. J. Perelman, whose tall, stooping figure is better known to the twilit half-world of five continents than to Publishers' Row. That he possesses the power to become invisible to finance companies; that his laboratory is tooled up to manufacture Frankenstein-type monsters on an incredible scale; and that he owns one of the rare mouths in which butter has never melted are legends treasured by every schoolboy.

"Retired today to peaceful Erwinna, Pennsylvania, Perelman

raises turkeys which he occasionally displays on Broadway, stirs little from his alembics and retorts. Those who know hint that the light burning late in his laboratory may result in a breathtaking electric bill. Queried, he shrugs with the fatalism of your true Oriental. *'Mektoub,'* he observes curtly. 'It is written.' "

Mr. Perelman has bounded over continents and seas, and come back to put it all before you—not quietly, not sweetly, nothing about the messes of nations, but just right there. Mr. Perelman, every time he writes, takes a leap that causes you to say, "Now wait a minute," but it is so well worth waiting for. Mr. Perelman went around the world, of course, but he took the world by the tail and slung it casually over his shoulder.

Then there are the remarkable bits called "Cloudland Revisited" spaced through his book. They are his blood-curdling experiences with old-time movies. For six months after seeing Erich von Stroheim in *Foolish Wives,* confesses Mr. Perelman, "I exhibited a maddening tendency to click my heels and murmur *'Bitte?'* along with a twitch as though a monocle were screwed into my eye. The mannerisms finally abated, but not until the dean of Brown University had taken me aside and confided that if I wanted to transfer to Heidelberg, the faculty would not stand in my way."

There are his days as a young rapier-keen cartoonist for a comic weekly whose editors, he complains, were inexplicably unmoved by such masterpieces from his drawing board as one showing "a distraught gentleman careening into a doctor's office clutching a friend by the wrist and whimpering, 'I've got Bright's disease and he has mine.' "

But Mr. Perelman does not tilt at windmills (Dear, dear—is it National Cliché Week already?); he goes after the big nasty ones, the cruel, the ignorant, the mean. He is not frightened by the rich and the idiotic. As he says, "I don't know anything about medicine, but I know what I like."

Some time ago Mr. Perelman had pressed on his humid brow a wreath of laurels for his work as a screen writer. I think I may say that Mr. Perelman never wanted to be a great screen writer, never saw screen writing as a goal. Still, if you're going to be a screen writer, it must be a satisfaction to be the best. And that is also true of a humorist writer.

PART I

1930–1944

THE NEEDLEWORK *in the section that follows—the greater part of it published originally in* The New Yorker, *the balance in magazines no longer extant—was executed in the thirties and early forties. During much of that epoch, I gained my livelihood writing for the silver screen, an occupation which, like herding swine, makes the vocabulary pungent but contributes little to one's prose style. Unhappily, I had few qualifications for Hollywood: I was immoderately slothful, had no facility for salesmanship or apple-polishing, and possessed a very low boiling point. Faced with hallucinatory tasks like transferring "Sweethearts" into a vehicle for Jeanette MacDonald and Nelson Eddy or distilling a scenario from* How to Win Friends and Influence People, *I became inarticulate and disputatious by turns, a square in a hole full of round pegs. As my shortcomings grew obvious to management, I was given more and more leisure, and lacking the agility to wash windows or harvest oranges, I was forced back willy-nilly to my embroidery hoop. While none of these brocades compares with the Coptic work at the Metropolitan, or even the traditional designs on a child's mitten, they may be of trifling historical interest to lovers of good, clean textiles.*

1

❧ WAITING FOR SANTY

A CHRISTMAS PLAYLET
(*With a Bow to Mr. Clifford Odets*)

SCENE: *The sweatshop of S. Claus, a manufacturer of children's toys, on North Pole Street. Time: The night before Christmas.*

At rise, seven gnomes, Rankin, Panken, Rivkin, Riskin, Ruskin, Briskin, and Praskin, are discovered working furiously to fill orders piling up at stage right. The whir of lathes, the hum of motors, and the hiss of drying lacquer are so deafening that at times the dialogue cannot be heard, which is very vexing if you vex easily. Note: The parts of Rankin, Panken, Rivkin, Riskin, Ruskin, Briskin, and Praskin are interchangeable, and may be secured directly from your dealer or the factory.

RISKIN (*filing a Meccano girder, bitterly*): A parasite, a leech, a blood-sucker—altogether a five-star nogoodnick! Starvation wages we get so he can ride around in a red team with reindeers!

RUSKIN (*jeering*): Hey, Karl Marx, whyn'tcha hire a hall?

RISKIN (*sneering*): Scab! Stool pigeon! Company spy! (*They tangle and rain blows on each other. While waiting for these to dry, each returns to his respective task.*)

BRISKIN (*sadly, to Panken*): All day long I'm painting "Snow Queen" on these Flexible Flyers and my little Irving lays in a cold tenement with the gout.

PANKEN: You said before it was the mumps.

BRISKIN (*with a fatalistic shrug*): The mumps—the gout—go argue with City Hall.

PANKEN (*kindly, passing him a bowl*): Here, take a piece fruit.

BRISKIN (*chewing*): It ain't bad, for wax fruit.

PANKEN (*with pride*): I painted it myself.

BRISKIN (*rejecting the fruit*): Ptoo! Slave psychology!

RIVKIN (*suddenly, half to himself, half to the Party*): I got a belly full

3

of stars, baby. You make me feel like I swallowed a Roman candle.

PRASKIN (*curiously*): What's wrong with the kid?

RISKIN: What's wrong with all of us? The system! Two years he and Claus's daughter's been making googoo eyes behind the old man's back.

PRASKIN: So what?

RISKIN (*scornfully*): So what? Economic determinism! What do you think the kid's name is—J. Pierpont Rivkin? He ain't even got for a bottle Dr. Brown's Celery Tonic. I tell you, it's like gall in my mouth two young people shouldn't have a room where they could make great music.

RANKIN (*warningly*): Shhh! Here she comes now! (*Stella Claus enters, carrying a portable phonograph. She and Rivkin embrace, place a record on the turntable, and begin a very slow waltz, unmindful that the phonograph is playing "Cohen on the Telephone."*)

STELLA (*dreamily*): Love me, sugar?

RIVKIN: I can't sleep, I can't eat, that's how I love you. You're a double malted with two scoops of whipped cream; you're the moon rising over Mosholu Parkway; you're a two weeks' vacation at Camp Nitgedaiget! I'd pull down the Chrysler Building to make a bobbie pin for your hair!

STELLA: I've got a stomach full of anguish. Oh, Rivvy, what'll we do?

PANKEN (*sympathetically*): Here, try a piece fruit.

RIVKIN (*fiercely*): Wax fruit—that's been my whole life! Imitations! Substitutes! Well, I'm through! Stella, tonight I'm telling your old man. He can't play mumblety-peg with two human beings! (*The tinkle of sleigh bells is heard offstage, followed by a voice shouting, "Whoa, Dasher! Whoa, Dancer!" A moment later S. Claus enters in a gust of mock snow. He is a pompous bourgeois of sixty-five who affects a white beard and a false air of benevolence. But tonight the ruddy color is missing from his cheeks, his step falters, and he moves heavily. The gnomes hastily replace the marzipan they have been filching.*)

STELLA (*anxiously*): Papa! What did the specialist say to you?

CLAUS (*brokenly*): The biggest professor in the country . . . the best cardiac man that money could buy. . . . I tell you I was like a wild man.

STELLA: Pull yourself together, Sam!

CLAUS: It's no use. Adhesions, diabetes, sleeping sickness, decalcomania—oh, my God! I got to cut out climbing in chimneys, he says—me, Sanford Claus, the biggest toy concern in the world!

STELLA (*soothingly*): After all, it's only one man's opinion.

CLAUS: No, no, he cooked my goose. I'm like a broken uke after a Yosian picnic. Rivkin!

RIVKIN: Yes, Sam.

CLAUS: My boy, I had my eye on you for a long time. You and Stella thought you were too foxy for an old man, didn't you? Well, let bygones be bygones. Stella, do you love this gnome?

STELLA (*simply*): He's the whole stage show at the Music Hall, Papa; he's Toscanini conducting Beethoven's Fifth; he's—

CLAUS (*curtly*): Enough already. Take him. From now on he's a partner in the firm. (*As all exclaim, Claus holds up his hand for silence.*) And tonight he can take my route and make the deliveries. It's the least I could do for my own flesh and blood. (*As the happy couple kiss, Claus wipes away a suspicious moisture and turns to the other gnomes.*) Boys, do you know what day tomorrow is?

GNOMES (*crowding around expectantly*): Christmas!

CLAUS: Correct. When you look in your envelopes tonight, you'll find a little present from me—a forty per cent pay cut. And the first one who opens his trap—gets this. (*As he holds up a tear-gas bomb and beams at them, the gnomes utter cries of joy, join hands, and dance around him shouting exultantly. All except Riskin and Briskin, that is, who exchange a quick glance and go underground.*)

CURTAIN

❦ DOWN WITH THE RESTORATION!

DOES ANYBODY here mind if I make a prediction? I haven't made a prediction since the opening night of *The Women* some years ago, when I rose at the end of the third act and announced to my escort, a Miss Chicken-Licken, "The public will never take this to its bosom." Since the public has practically worn its bosom to a nubbin niggling up to *The Women,* I feel that my predictions may be a straw to show the direction the wind is blowing away from. I may very well open up a cave and do business as a sort of Cumaean Sibyl in reverse. You can't tell me people would rather climb up that Aventine Hill and have a man mess around with the entrails of a lot of sacred chickens when they can come down into my nice cool cave and get a good hygienic prediction for a few cents. So just to stimulate trade and start the ball rolling, here goes my first prediction: One of these days two young people are going to stumble across a ruined farmhouse and leave it alone. . . . Well, what are you sitting there gaping at? You heard what I said. That's my prediction.

Honest Injun, I hate to sound crotchety, and the last thing in the world I want to do is throw the editors of all those home-making magazines like *Nook and Garden* and *The American Home-Owner* into an uproar, but the plain fact is that I've got a bellyful. For over two years now, every time I start leafing through one of those excellent periodicals, I fall afoul of another article about a couple of young people who stumble across a ruined farmhouse and remodel it on what is inelegantly termed spit and coupons. Or maybe it's the same article. I couldn't be reading the same issue over and over, could I?

All these remodeling articles are written by the remodelers themselves and never by the ruined farmer or the man who didn't get paid for the plastering, which accounts for their rather smug tone. They invariably follow the same pattern. A young couple named Mibs and Evan (and if you checked up, I'll bet they were never married at *all!*) have decided to return to the land. I see Mibs as one of those girls on the short side, with stocky legs, a low-slung posterior, and an untidy

6

bun of straw-colored hair continually unwinding on the nape of her neck. Before anyone ever heard of Salzburg, she wore a high-bodiced dress with full skirts, a sort of horrid super-dirndl with home-cooked hems that have a tendency to hang down in back. She is usually engaged in reading a book written by two unfrocked chemists which tells women how to make their own cold cream by mixing a little potash with a dram of glycerine and a few cloves. Evan is a full-haunched young man in a fuzzy woolen suit (I don't suppose there's any such thing as a fuzzy cotton suit, but you know what I mean) who is forever rubbing a briar pipe along his nose to show you the beauty of the grain. He smokes his own mixture of perique, Latakia, and Imperial Cube Cut, for the very good reason that nobody else will smoke it, and he has probably read more of Arthur Machen than any man alive.

Well, as I say, your average remodeling yarn begins with Mibs and Evan stumbling across the most adorable ruin of an eighteenth-century farmhouse. It doesn't *have* to be a farmhouse; it can be a gristmill, or a tobacco barn, or a Mennonite schoolhouse. It can even be an early Colonial hen house, with delightful hand-hewn beams and perfectly sweet old tar paper scaling off the sides. Apparently nobody previous to Mibs and Evan has realized its possibilities, but Evan takes one look at it and says in a guarded tone, "Two hundred dollars would restore that beautifully if you didn't go crazy putting in a lot of bathrooms you didn't need." "Oh, Evan!" breathes Mibs, her eyes shining above her adenoids and her brain reeling with visions of Cape Cod spatter floors. "Dare we . . . ?" That night, at dinner in the Jumble Shop, they put their heads together—Evan removes the pipe from alongside his nose, of course—and decide to jump at the chance. It involves giving up that trip to Europe, a choice the characters in these stories always have to make, but Mibs has always dreamed of a sunny garden filled with old-fashioned flowers of the type her mother used to read about in Max Schling's catalogue. So they bravely draw two hundred dollars out of their little hoard, leaving a hundred in case they ever want to take a really long trip to some place like Bali, and lay it on the line.

After considerable excitement, in which everybody searches the title like mad and Mibs discovers the quaintest old parchment deed describing their land in terms of rods, chains, and poods, they are ready to take the "Before" snapshots. Evan digs up one of the cameras used by Brady at the battle of Antietam, waits for a good cloudy day, and focuses across a mound of guano at the most ramshackle corner of the "manse," as Mibs calls it with irreverent mischief. The article generally carries several gray smudges captioned "Southwest corner of the house before work began," and you can't help wondering where those giant oaks came from in the "After" photographs. Maybe they sprang up from acorns dropped by the workmen while they were having lunch.

The first thing the high-hearted pair decide on is a new roof. This fortunately costs only eight dollars, as they use secondhand wattles and hire a twelve-year-old scab—all right, maybe he only mislaid his union card—to tack them on. The outside walls are a problem, but an amazing stroke of good fortune comes to their rescue. Opening a trap door they hadn't investigated, Mibs and Evan stumble across countless bundles of lovely old hand-split shingles which have been overlooked by previous tenants, like the hens. Two superb Adam fireplaces, hitherto concealed by some matchboarding, now make their appearance, in one of them a box of dusty but otherwise well-preserved pieces of Sandwich and Stiegel glass. "The attic!" shout Mibs and Evan simultaneously, suddenly remembering their resolution to look through it some rainy day, and sure enough, there they find a veritable treasure trove of pewter ware, cherry escritoires, Chippendale wing chairs, sawbuck tables, and Field beds, hidden away by survivors of the Deerfield massacre. "It just didn't seem *possible*," recalls Mibs candidly, up to her old trick of taking the words out of your mouth.

And now, suddenly, the place becomes a hive of activity. A salty old character named Lafe (who is really Paul Bunyan, no matter what *Nook and Garden* says) appears and does the work of ten men at the price of one. He pulls down trees with his bare hands, lays new floors, puts up partitions, installs electricity, diverts streams, forges the ironware, bakes porcelain sinks, and all but spins silk for the draperies. How this djinn ever escaped from his bottle, and where he is now, the article neglects to mention. The upshot is that in a little over two weeks, the last hooked rug—picked up by Mibs at an auction for ten cents after spirited bidding—is in place and the early Salem kettle is singing merrily on the hob. A fat orange tabby blinks before the fire and Evan, one arm around Mibs, is adding up a column of figures. "Think of it, lover," whispers Mibs with dancing eyes. "We did the whole thing for only *fifty-one dollars and eighteen cents!*" "Less than we'll get for that article in *The American Home-Owner*," murmurs Evan exultantly, reaming the cake from his pipe. "Tell me, does oo love its 'ittle—" . . . And now, would you hate me if I stole out very quietly? I'm afraid there's going to be just a wee bit of baby talk.

❧ SCENARIO

FADE IN, exterior grassy knoll, long shot. Above the scene the thundering measures of Von Suppe's "Light Cavalry Overture." Austerlitz? The Plains of Abraham? Vicksburg? The Little Big Horn? Cambrai? Steady on, old son; it is Yorktown. Under a blood-red setting sun yon proud crest is Cornwallis. Blood and 'ouns, proud sirrah, dost brush so lightly past an exciseman of the Crown? Lady Rotogravure's powdered shoulders shrank from the highwayman's caress; what, Jermyn, footpads on Hounslow Heath? A certain party in the D. A.'s office will hear of this, you bastard. There was a silken insolence in his smile as he drew the greatcoat about his face and leveled his shooting-iron at her dainty puss. Leave go that lady or I'll smear yuh. No quarter, eh? Me, whose ancestors scuttled stately India merchantmen of their comfits and silken stuffs and careened their piratical craft in the Dry Tortugas to carouse with bumboat women till the cock crew? Yuh'll buy my booze or I'll give yuh a handful of clouds. Me, whose ancestors rode with Yancey, Jeb Stuart, and Joe Johnston through the dusty bottoms of the Chickamauga? Oceans of love, but not one cent for tribute. Make a heel out of a guy whose grandsire, Olaf Hasholem, swapped powder and ball with the murderous Sioux through the wheels of a Conestoga wagon, who mined the yellow dirt with Sutter and slapped nuggets across the rude bars of Leadville and Goldfield? One side, damn your black hide, suh, or Ah'll send one mo' dirty Litvak to the boneyard. It's right up the exhibitor's alley, Mr. Biberman, and you got to hand it to them on a platter steaming hot. I know, Stanley, but let's look at this thing reasonable; we been showing the public Folly Larrabee's drawers two years and they been cooling off. Jeez Crize— it's a hisTORical drama, Mr. Biberman, it'll blow 'em outa the back of the houses, it's the greatest thing in the industry, it's dynamite! Pardon me, officer, is that General Washington? Bless yer little heart, mum, and who may yez be, savin' yer prisince? Honest old Brigid the applewoman of Trinity, is it? How dégagé he sits on his charger, flicking an infinitesimal speck of ash from his plum-colored waistcoat! Gentlemen, I give you Martha Custis, hetman of the Don Cossacks, her features

etched with the fragile beauty of a cameo. And I walked right in on
her before she had a chance to pull the god-damned kimono together.
But to be away from all this—to lean back puffing on one's churchwarden at Mount Vernon amid the dull glint of pewter, to watch the
firelight playing over polished Duncan Phyfe and Adam while faithful
old Cudjo cackles his ebony features and mixes a steaming lime toddy!
Tired, Roy, I'm tired, I tell you. Tired of the rain, the eternal surge of
the breakers on that lagoon, the glitter of the reef in that eternity out
there. CHRISTIAN! She laughed contemptuously, her voluptuous
throat filling with a rising sob as she faced Davidson like a hounded
animal. You drove me out of Papeete but I'll go to Thursday Island
with my banjo on my knee. Yeh, yeh, so what? We made FOUR pictures like that last year. Oh, my God, Mr. Biberman, give me a chance,
it's only a flashback to plant that she's a woman with a past. Sixteen
hundred a week I pay you to hand me back the plot of *Love's Counter-
feiters* Selig made in 1912! She's who? She's what? What's the idea her
coming here? What's she trying to do, turn a production office into a
whorehouse? No, Miss Reznick, tell her to wait, I'll be through in five
minutes. Now get it, Mr. Biberman, it's big. You establish the mess-
room and truck with Farnsworth till he faces Charteris. I said Sixth
Rajputana Rifles and I don't want a lotta muggs paradin' around in
the uniforms of the Preobazhensky Guard, y' get me? Yep, he's on a
tear, those foreign directors are very temperamental, did I ever tell you
about the time Lazlo Nugasi said he'd buy me a brassiere if I let him
put it on? Fake it with a transparency of Khyber Pass. Now an overhead shot of the dusty tired column filing into Sidi-bel-Abbes. Shoulder
by shoulder they march in the faded blue of the Legion, fun-loving Dick
and serious-minded Tom. Buddies, the greatest word in the French
language, flying to the defense of each other like a homo pigeon. Greater
love hath Onan. Swinging a chair into that mob of lime-juicers in the
Mile End Bar in Shanghai. But came a slant-eyed Chinese adventuress,
and then? Don't shoot, Butch, for Gossake! Heave 'em into the prison
yard, we'll keep the screws out of the cell-block and wilderness were
paradise enow. Stow the swag in Cincy, kid, and go on alone, I'm done
for. Too late, old Pogo the clown stopped it in the sweetbreads. They
buried him outside the town that night, a motley crew of freaks and
circus people. What a sequence! Old man Klingspiel told me he bawled
like a baby. Laugh, you inhuman monster they call the crowd, old
Pogo lies dead with only a bareback rider's spangle to mark his grave
and a seat for every child in the public schools! When tall ships shook
out their plumage and raced from Salem to Hong Kong to bring back

tea. Break out the Black Ball ensign, Mr. Exhibitor, there's sweet music in that ole cash register! A double truck in every paper in town and a smashing drawing by the best artist we got, mind you. Take the kiddies to that colossal red-blooded human drama of a boy's love for his dog. This is my hunting lodge, we'll stop here and dry your things. But of course it's all right, *cara mia*, I'm old enough to be your father. Let me go, you beast—MOTHER! What are you doing here? I ask you confidentially, Horowitz, can't we get that dame to put on some women's clothes, a skirt or something? The fans are getting wise, all those flat-heeled shoes and men's shirts like a lumberjack. Get me Gerber in publicity, he'll dish out some crap about her happy home life. Vorkapich around the room to Dmitri's brother officers as they register consternation at the news. Good chance for some hokey bellies on comedy types. What, sir, you dare mention Alexandra Petrovna's name in a saloon? The kid takes it big and gives Diane the gloves across the pan socko. The usual satisfaction, I presume? Drawing on his gloves as a thin sneer played across his features. Yeh, a martinet and for Crisakes remember it's not a musical instrument this time. But eet ees madness, Serge! The best swordsman in St. Mary's parish, he weel run you through in a tweenkling! Oh, darling, you can't, you can't. Her hair had become undone and he plunged his face into its fragrance, unbuckling his saber and flinging it on the bed beside them. Hurry, even now my husband is fried to the ears in a low boozing-den in Pokrovsky Street. Of course it is he, I'd know that lousy busby anywhere in St. Petersburg. Shoot it two ways, you can always dub it in the sound track. She shrieks or she don't shriek, what the hell difference does it make? Told me he was going to night school at the Smolny Institute, the cur. And I believed him, thought Pyotr pityingly, surveying her luscious bust with greedy eyes. Never leave me, my sweet, and then bejeezus an angle shot toward the door of the General leaning against the lintel stroking his mustache. Crouching against the wall terrified yet shining-eyed as women are when men do gallant combat. Throw him your garter, Lady Aspinwall, throw your slipper, throw your lunch, but for Gawd's sake throw something! *Parry! Thrust! Touché!* Where are they all now, the old familiar faces? What a piece of business! Grabs a string of onions and swings himself up the balcony, fencing with the soldiers. Got you in the groin that time, General! Mine host, beaming genially, rubbing his hands and belching. Get Anderson ready with the sleighbells and keep that snow moving. Hit 'em all! Hotter on eighty-four, Joe Devlin! Are we up to speed? Quiet, please, we're turning! Chicago, hog-butcher to the world, yclept the Windy City. BOOZE

AND BLOOD, he oughta know, running a drugstore eleven years on Halstead Street. You cut to the back of the Big Fellow, then three lap dissolves of the presses—give 'em that Ufa stuff, then to the street— a newsbody, insert of the front page, the El roaring by—Kerist, it's the gutsiest thing in pictures! Call you back, chief. Never mind the Hays office, this baby is censor-proof! Call you back, chief. We'll heave the telephone through the glass door and smack her in the kisser with the grapefruit, they liked it once and they'll love it twice. Call you back, chief. The gat in the mesh-bag. A symbol, get me? Now remember, staccato. . . A bit tight, my sweet? Marrowforth teetered back and forth on his heels, his sensitive artist's fingers caressing the first edition he loved. Item, one Hawes and Curtis dress suit, one white tie, kindly return to Mister Dreyfus in the wardrobe department. What color do I remind you of? Purple shot with pleasure, if you ask me. Do I have to work with a lot of pimply grips giving me the bird? Papa's in the doghouse and keep up the tempo of the last scene, you looked crummy in yesterday's dailies. A warm, vivid and human story with just that touch of muff the fans demand. Three Hundred Titans Speed Westward as King Haakon Lays Egg on Shoe-String. And sad-eyed Grubnitz by the Wailing Wall demands: What will the indie exhibs do? Let 'em eat cake, we're packing 'em in with 29 Garson-Pidgeons in 1944. Ask Hyman Gerber of Waco, he can smell a box-office picture a mile away. In the freezing mists of dawn they gathered by the fuselages of their planes and gripped hands. But Rex Jennings of the shining eyes and the high heart never came back. Jerry got him over Chalons. I tell you it's murder to send a mere boy up in a crate like that! The god-damned production office on my neck all day. It's midsummer madness, Fiametta! You mustn't! I must! I want you! You want me? But I—I'm just a poor little slavey, and you—why, all life's ahead of you! Fame, the love of a good woman, children! And your music, Raoul! Excuse me, miss, are you Fiametta Desplains? I am Yankel Patchouli, a solicitor. Here is my card and a report of my recent urinalysis. Raoul! Raoul! Come quick! A million dollars! Now you can go to Paris and study your counterpoint! Damn my music, Fiametta, my happiness was in my own back yard all the time and I was, how you say it, one blind fool. The gingham dress and half-parted lips leaning on a broom. But why are you looking at me in that strange way, Tony? . . . Tony! I'm afraid of you! Oh . . . You utter contemptible despicable CAD. He got up nursing his jaw. Spew out your poison, you rat. You didn't know she was the morganatic wife of Prince Rupprecht, *did* you? That her affairs with men were the talk of Vienna, *did* you? That—Vanya, is this true? Bowed head, for her man. His boyish tousled head clean-cut against the twilight. Get out. *Get out.* GET OUT! Oh, mumsey, I want to die. That hooker's gotta lay off that booze, Mr. Metz, once more she comes on the set stinking and I take the next boat back to Buda-Pesth. But in a great tangled garden sits a forlorn tragic-eyed figure; the face a mask of carved ivory, the woman nobody knows—Tilly Bergstrom. What lies behind her shattered romance with Grant Snavely, idol of American flaps? Turn 'em over, you punks, I'll stay on this set till I get it right. Cheese it, de nippers! The jig is up, long live the jig—ring out the old, ring in the new. For love belongs to everyone, the best things in life are free.

❧ SOMEWHERE A ROSCOE . . .

THIS IS THE STORY of a mind that found itself. About two years ago I was moody, discontented, restless, almost a character in a Russian novel. I used to lie on my bed for days drinking tea out of a glass (I was one of the first in this country to drink tea out of a glass; at that time fashionable people drank from their cupped hands). Underneath, I was still a lively, fun-loving American boy who liked nothing better than to fish with a bent pin. In short, I had become a remarkable combination of Raskolnikov and Mark Tidd.

One day I realized how introspective I had grown and decided to talk to myself like a Dutch uncle. "Luik here, Mynheer," I began (I won't give you the accent, but honestly it was a riot), "you've overtrained. You're stale. Open up a few new vistas—go out and get some fresh air!" Well, I bustled about, threw some things into a bag—orange peels, apple cores and the like—and went out for a walk. A few minutes later I picked up from a park bench a tattered pulp magazine called *Spicy Detective*. . . . Talk about your turning points!

I hope nobody minds my making love in public, but if Culture Publications, Inc., of 900 Market Street, Wilmington, Delaware, will have me, I'd like to marry them. Yes, I know—call it a schoolboy crush, puppy love, the senseless infatuation of a callow youth for a middle-aged, worldly-wise publishing house; I still don't care. I love them because they are the publishers of not only *Spicy Detective* but also *Spicy Western*, *Spicy Mystery* and *Spicy Adventure*. And I love them most because their prose is so soft and warm.

"Arms and the man I sing," sang Vergil some twenty centuries ago, preparing to celebrate the wanderings of Aeneas. If ever a motto was tailor-made for the masthead of Culture Publications, Inc., it is "Arms and the Woman," for in *Spicy Detective* they have achieved the sauciest blend of libido and murder this side of Gilles de Rais. They have juxtaposed the steely automatic and the frilly panty and found that it pays off. Above all, they have given the world Dan Turner, the apotheosis of all private detectives. Out of Ma Barker by Dashiell Hammett's Sam

Spade, let him characterize himself in the opening paragraph of "Corpse in the Closet," from the July 1937 issue:

> I opened my bedroom closet. A half-dressed feminine corpse sagged into my arms. . . . It's a damned screwy feeling to reach for pajamas and find a cadaver instead.

Mr. Turner, you will perceive, is a man of sentiment, and it occasionally gets him into a tight corner. For example, in "Killer's Harvest" (July 1938) he is retained to escort a young matron home from the Cocoanut Grove in Los Angeles:

> Zarah Trenwick was a wow in a gown of silver lamé that stuck to her lush curves like a coating of varnish. Her make-up was perfect; her strapless dress displayed plenty of evidence that she still owned a cargo of lure. Her bare shoulders were snowy, dimpled. The upper slopes of her breast were squeezed upward and partly overflowed the tight bodice, like whipped cream.

To put it mildly, Dan cannot resist the appeal of a pretty foot, and disposing of Zarah's drunken husband ("I clipped him on the button. His hip pockets bounced on the floor"), he takes this charlotte russe to her apartment. Alone with her, the policeman in him succumbs to the man, and "she fed me a kiss that throbbed all the way down my fallen arches," when suddenly:

> From the doorway a roscoe said "Kachow!" and a slug creased the side of my noggin. Neon lights exploded inside my think-tank . . . She was as dead as a stuffed mongoose . . . I wasn't badly hurt. But I don't like to be shot at. I don't like dames to be rubbed out when I'm flinging woo at them.

With an irritable shrug, Dan phones the homicide detail and reports Zarah's passing in this tender obituary: "Zarah Trenwick just got blasted to hellangone in her tepee at the Gayboy. Drag your underwear over here—and bring a meat-wagon." Then he goes in search of the offender:

> I drove over to Argyle; parked in front of Fane Trenwick's modest stash . . . I thumbed the bell. The door opened. A Chink house-boy gave me the slant-eyed focus. "Missa Tlenwick, him sleep. You go

way, come tomollow. Too late fo' vlisito'." I said "Nerts to you,
Confucius," and gave him a shove on the beezer.

Zarah's husband, wrenched out of bed without the silly formality
of a search warrant, establishes an alibi depending upon one Nadine
Wendell. In a trice Dan crosses the city and makes his gentle way into
the lady's boudoir, only to discover again what a frail vessel he is *au
fond*:

> The fragrant scent of her red hair tickled my smeller; the warmth
> of her slim young form set fire to my arterial system. After all, I'm
> as human as the next gazabo.

The next gazabo must be all too human, because Dan betrays first
Nadine and then her secret; namely, that she pistoled Zarah Trenwick
for reasons too numerous to mention. If you feel you must know them,
they appear on page 110, cheek by jowl with some fascinating advertisements for loaded dice and wealthy sweethearts, either of which will
be sent you in plain wrapper if you'll forward a dollar to the Majestic
Novelty Company of Janesville, Wisconsin.

The deeper one goes into the Dan Turner saga, the more one is struck
by the similarity between the case confronting Dan in the current issue
and those in the past. The murders follow an exact, rigid pattern almost
like the ritual of a bullfight or a classic Chinese play. Take "Veiled
Lady," in the October 1937 number of *Spicy Detective*. Dan is flinging
some woo at a Mrs. Brantham in her apartment at the exclusive Gayboy Arms, which apparently excludes everybody but assassins:

> From behind me a roscoe belched "Chow-chow!" A pair of slugs
> buzzed past my left ear, almost nicked my cranium. Mrs. Brantham
> sagged back against the pillow of the lounge . . . She was as dead as
> an iced catfish.

Or this vignette from "Falling Star," out of the September 1936
issue.

> The roscoe said "Chow!" and spat a streak of flame past my
> shoulder . . . The Filipino cutie was lying where I'd last seen her. She
> was as dead as a smoked herring.

And again, from "Dark Star of Death," January 1938:

From a bedroom a roscoe said: "Whr-r-rang!" and a lead pill
split the ozone past my noggin . . . Kane Fewster was on the floor.
There was a bullet hole through his think-tank. He was as dead as
a fried oyster.

And still again, from "Brunette Bump-off," May 1938:

And then, from an open window beyond the bed, a roscoe coughed
"Ka-chow!" . . . I said, "What the hell—!" and hit the floor with my
smeller . . . A brunette jane was lying there, half out of the mussed
covers. . . . She was as dead as vaudeville.

The next phase in each of these dramas follows with all the cold
beauty and inevitability of a legal brief. The roscoe has hardly spoken,
coughed, or belched before Dan is off through the canebrake, his nostrils filled with the heavy scent of Nuit de Noël. Somewhere, in some
dimly lit boudoir, waits a voluptuous parcel of womanhood who knows
all about the horrid deed. Even if she doesn't, Dan makes a routine
check anyway. The premises are invariably guarded by an Oriental
whom Dan is obliged to expunge. Compare the scene at Fane Trenwick's modest stash with this one from "Find That Corpse" (November 1937):

A sleepy Chink maid in pajamas answered my ring. She was a
cute little slant-eyed number. I said "Is Mr. Polznak home?" She
shook her head. "Him up on location in Flesno. Been gone two week."
I said "Thanks. I'll have a gander for myself." I pushed past her. She
started to yip . . . "Shut up!" I growled. She kept on trying to make
a noise. So I popped her on the button. She dropped.

It is a fairly safe bet that Mr. Polznak has forgotten the adage that a
watched pot never boils and has left behind a dewy-eyed coryphée clad
in the minimum of chiffon demanded by the postal authorities. The
poet in Dan ineluctably vanquishes the flatfoot ("Dark Star of Death"):
"I glued my glims on her blond loveliness; couldn't help myself. The
covers had skidded down from her gorgeous, dimpled shoulders; I
could see plenty of delishful, she-male epidermis." The trumpets blare
again; some expert capework by our *torero,* and ("Brunette Bump-
off"): "Then she fed me a kiss that sent a charge of steam past my
gozzle . . . Well, I'm as human as the next gink."
From then on, the author's typewriter keys infallibly fuse in a lump

of hot metal and it's all over but the shouting of the culprit and *"Look, Men: One Hundred Breezy Fotos!"* Back in his stash, his roscoe safely within reach, Dan Turner lays his weary noggin on a pillow, resting up for the November issue. And unless you're going to need me for something this afternoon, I intend to do the same. I'm *bushed.*

🌸 BEAT ME, POST-IMPRESSIONIST DADDY

ANY of you kids seen Somerset Maugham? I haven't run into him lately, but I'll bet those advertisements for *The Moon and Sixpence* put the roses in his cheeks. In case you've been spending the last couple of weeks underwater, the Messrs. Loew and Lewin have just transferred to the screen Mr. Maugham's novel of the ordeal of Charles Strickland, a character closely resembling Paul Gauguin. Faced with merchandising so spiritual a problem, the producers evidently recalled that Vincent van Gogh had been popularized as a man who mailed his ear to a friend, and decided to sell their boy on a similar basis. The leitmotiv of the campaign was a busty Polynesian hussy in a pitifully shrunken sarong, lolling on her back in considerable abandon and smelling a flower. Peering out of a palm tree above, mighty lak a chimp, was George Sanders in the best beard that money could buy. "I DON'T WANT LOVE! I hate it!" he was declaring petulantly. "It interferes with my work . . . and yet . . . *I'm only human!*" A second advertisement portrayed the painter in an equally disenchanted mood, over the caption "WOMEN ARE STRANGE LITTLE BEASTS! You can treat them like dogs (*he did!*)—beat them 'til your arm aches (*he did*) . . . and still they love you (*they did*). But in the end they'll get you and you are helpless in their hands."

Although Gauguin's journal, *Avant et Après*, and his correspondence with D. de Montfreid are fairly blue in spots, he is not primarily remembered as passion's plaything, and these insinuations may confound the strait-laced. Now that Hollywood has thrown the ball into play, however, the following letters I recently unearthed in my bottom bureau drawer deserve careful scrutiny. They were written by the artist to my father's barber, who lived in the bureau between 1895 and 1897. Here and there I have taken the liberty of translating the rather difficult argot into current idiom, for clarity.

19

MATAIÉA, JULY 17, 1896

DEAR MARCUS,

Well, my old, you must think I am a fine *pascudnick* indeed not to answer you before this, but man is born to trouble as the sparks fly upward and I am winging. The day after I wrote you, who should come mousing around but that little brunette, Tia, in her loose-leaf pareu, which it's enough to melt the umber on a man's palette. It so happened I was in the hut with this tall job from Papeete, dashing off a quick pastel. I told Tia to stop needling me, but she was inconsolable. Distraught, I asked what she required. "Poi," she responded. Poi is one thing I have never refused anybody yet, Marcus, so, brushing off this other head, I made with the poi. The instant we were alone, the pretty trickster revealed her design. "I'm a strange little beast!" she cried. "Beat me 'til your arm aches!" Me, a family man. *Figurez-vous.* Marcus, what could I do? I bounced her around a bit, knocked out several of her teeth, and invited her to withdraw, as I had to complete a gouache by five o'clock. *Dame!*—the next thing I knew, Miss Goody Two-shoes had sealed the door, swallowed the key [*clef*], and I was it.

As to the painting, it goes very slowly. Kindest thanks for your new calendar, which arrived in good condition. Personally, the model is somewhat skinny for my taste and there is too much drapery, but *tiens*, that is the bourgeois style. Tell me more about that youth, the son of your patron. The boy has genius, Marcus; I have an instinct for these things. Mark me well, he will yet be another Piero della Francesca.

I pinch your claws,

PAUL

MATAIÉA, NOVEMBER 12, 1896

DEAR MARCUS,

Life here becomes increasingly tiresome, my friend; the women refuse to let me alone. How I envy Vincent those days at Arles, with nothing between him and his muse but the solar spectrum. I came to this miserable hole surfeited with civilization and its trinkets. One might as well be back in the Rue Vercingétorix. Last night I attended a native fête and, like a chump, neglected to close my door. Returning home about two with a charming person who insisted on seeing my frescoes, I found the wife of the Minister of Public Works concealed under the bed. The old story—I must beat her without further ado, treat her like a dog, else she will stop loving me. *Quelle bêtise!* My arms are so tired from flailing these cows that I can hardly mix my pigments. I sit down in a workingmen's café for an infusion; immediately I am

surrounded by hordes of beauties begging me to maltreat them. I arise each morning determined to spend the day seriously. A pair of dark eyes at the window, a tender glance, and *pouf* [pouf] go my resolutions. After all, I'm only human.

I have a superb conception for a canvas which would be the very antithesis of Manet's "Olympia"—a native girl stretched on the sofa, regarding the onlooker with a mixture of fear and coquetry. At this rate I shall never finish it. Every sketch I begin ends the same. I pose the model on a divan, run my hand lightly over her back to enhance the sheen—*au fond* I am a painter of highlights—and *zut*, we are off on a tangent. For the time, merely to block in the masses, I am using a rolled-up umbrella in lieu of a girl. Actually, an ironic comment on your modern woman—all ribs and cloth. Where are those big, jolly, upholstered girls one used to see?

One fault only I find with your letters: there are too many lacunae. You say your patron's son was surprised embracing his governess. *Et alors?* What ensued? You leave too much to the imagination. Describe the scene with greater fidelity. Send photographs if possible. In any event, I must have a photo of the governess, preferably in her chemise, for a composition I am engaged on. It is an airy caprice in the manner of Watteau, quite unlike my current things—the startled governess blushing profusely, repulsing yet yielding to a diminutive satyr. I call it "Tickled Pink." Don't misunderstand, *mon copain*. This is simply relaxation, a change of pace from everything else I'm doing.

As ever,

PAUL

MATAIÉA, MAY 3, 1897

DEAR MARCUS,

Epochal news! I have arrived! After years of scorn and obloquy, after a lifetime of abuse from academicians and the kept press, I have at last attained official recognition! It came in the person of Mme. Dufresnoy, wife of the new Governor General, just as I was at the lowest ebb of despair. Reconstruct the scene for yourself: I was pacing moodily before my easel, alone, forgotten, attempting to wring some inspiration from the four or five scantily clad houris grouped on the dais. Suddenly, the sound of carriage wheels, and enter a vision of loveliness, a veritable Juno. What fluid rhythm, what vibrations . . . and yet a touch of that coarseness I find so piquant—I trembled like a schoolboy! But the real surprise was still to come. Housed in this ravishing exterior is no sordid Philistine but a delicate, subtle spirit attuned to mine; in a word, a connoisseur. Tales of my work have percolated through her flunkies and plenipotentiaries, and she must see it instanter. In a trice, the details are arranged—I am to bring my best canvases to the executive mansion next Tuesday for inspection. Only one cloud mars my bliss. As the house is being plastered, the view is to be held in Madame's boudoir, a pitifully small room which I fear is hardly adequate to exhibit the larger oils. Perdition! . . . but we shall make the best of it. I am in a frenzy of preparation, varnishing pictures, borrowing pomade for my hair, a hundred distractions—I must fly.

I embrace you, my dear fellow,

PAUL

P.S. One passage puzzled me in your last letter. How could your patron's son have penetrated to the landlady's room without climbing up the airshaft? Curb his exuberance, I implore you, and do not fail to send me a snapshot of the landlady.

MATAIÉA, MAY 19, 1897

DEAR MARCUS,

My decision is irrevocable: I am through with painting. I have a new mission, the extermination of the official class and particularly of its wives. After that, the monastery.

The betrayal was complete, catastrophic. I waited on Mme. Dufresnoy afire with plans—a house in the Avenue Matignon, a summer palace on the Bosphorus, a villa at Chantilly. I am received by my benefactress in a filmy black peignoir, eyes sparkling with belladonna. The room is plunged in shadow; she prefers (sweet tyrant) to examine the canvases by artificial light. I shrug at her eccentricity, swallow a *fine à l'eau* as a digestive, launch into a short preamble about my work. *Basta!* Suddenly we are in Stygian darkness and I am held in a clasp of iron. "Madame," I entreat, "let us at least sit down and talk this thing over." *Enfin*, she reluctantly disposed herself in my lap and we had just arrived at a rationale when the door flew open and the Governor General rushed in. I could have demolished the big tub of tripes with my small finger, but he was escorted by a band of *apaches*, armed to the teeth. I acquitted myself handily, nevertheless, and outside a discolored eye and a trifling greenstick fracture, emerged an easy victor. Thanks to Madame's intercession, I was given the most spacious room in the lockup and the assignment of whitewashing the walls. It is not painting, but working with new textures is good artistic discipline.

Your letters, as always, remain my constant solace. If I may presume on our friendship, though, please to omit all further references to that miserable little brat, your patron's son. I am not interested in his grimy amours, nor anybody else's, for that matter. I have had enough of the whole goddamned subject.

Eternally,

P. GAUGUIN

COUNTER-REVOLUTION

THE OTHER NIGHT a forty-five-year-old friend of mine, after ingesting equal portions of Greek fire and artillery punch, set out to prove that he could walk across a parquet flooring on his hands while balancing a vase on his head. As a consequence, about eleven o'clock the following morning he was being trepanned at the Harkness Pavilion and I was purchasing a bottle of Major's Cement. I had reassembled the shards and was about to uncork the cement bottle when the bold yellow leaflet in which it was wrapped caught my eye. To predict that this small circular will eventually outrank Magna Carta and the Peace of Breda in historical significance may seem audacious. Yet even the most frivolous cannot escape its implications, for in a single decisive stroke it alters the entire status of the consumer.

From its opening sentence, the document was marked by a note of brooding, reminiscent of a manifesto:

> If we could make the cement in liquid form and transparent, and at the same time as strong and as proof against moisture as it is now, we would be glad to do so. But this cannot be done.

A dozen lines further on, the manufacturer was fretting again over the possible imputation that he was holding back on his product:

> If we could make a cement transparent and in liquid form as strong as the way we make our cement, we would do it. There is no material that you could use that would make cement that way.

Obviously an *idée fixe*, I thought to myself, but aloud, I merely said quietly, "All right now, I can hear you. I use Leonard's Ear Oil as well as Major's Cement." My witty reprimand fell among thorns; a moment later the circular was behaving like a regular ogre:

> If you do not succeed the first time in mending an article, do not throw up your hands and go pulling your hair and yell out "I have

been swindled once more"; but have patience, for the Cement is all right.

By now I was thoroughly nettled. Patience, eh? Look who's telling me to have patience. Why, I've got more patience in my little fing—but my words were blotted out in a last echoing apoplectic bellow:

> If, before doing as suggested, you tell others that the Cement is no good, you are saying an untruth and injuring the reputation of Major's Cement. Remember the Golden Rule, "Do unto others as you would be done by."

Since I long ago gave instructions to strew my ashes to the four winds when the hour sounds, this precept left me with only one course open, and I took it.

It is obvious that such a *volte-face* in sales technique is fraught with the most far-reaching implications. There is every chance that Major's plaintive exasperation with the customer may yet be adopted and distorted by other firms. I take the liberty of presenting a few glamorous possibilities in a curtain-raiser, with the hope that it may inspire some fellow-dramatist to attempt a more sustained flight:

SCENE: *The men's furnishing section of a large department store. As the curtain rises, a salesman, Axel Munthe, is waiting on a patron. Munthe is not related to the physician who wrote* The Story of San Michele; *it is simply an interesting coincidence. Enter Leonard DeVilbiss, a typical customer—in fact, a luggage tag reading "Mr. Average Consumer" depends from the skirt of his topcoat. He looks timidly at Munthe.*

DEVILBISS: Do you sell Mackinaws here?
MUNTHE: No, we give 'em away. That's how we stay in business—giving away free Mackinaws.
DEVILBISS: I don't see any around here.
MUNTHE: What the devil do you think those are hanging on the rack—flounders?
(*DeVilbiss meekly takes a seat and, picking up copies of* Click, Pic, *and* Look, *begins to hold the pages against the light to discover possible salacious effects.*)
PATRON (*uncertainly*): I don't know about these shorts. I had in mind something with a banjo seat.

MUNTHE: Banjo seat! Banjo seat! Why don't you wear a banjo and be done with it?

PATRON: These won't shrink, will they?

MUNTHE: Look—Boulder Dam shrank six inches last year. You want me to underwrite a pair of lousy ninety-eight-cent shorts against it?

PATRON: Hmm. Well, I think I'll look around.

MUNTHE: Not in here, you won't. If you want to browse, go to a bookstore. (*Patron exits; Munthe approaches DeVilbiss*) All right, Buster, break it up. You're not in your club.

DEVILBISS: I'd like to try on some Mackinaws.

MUNTHE (*suspiciously*): Got any money?

DEVILBISS: Yes, sir. (*He shows Munthe some money. Latter reluctantly pulls out rack.*)

MUNTHE: Now, let me see. You want something in imported camel's hair, fleece-lined, with a lifetime guarantee, for only five dollars?

DEVILBISS (*dazzled*): Sure.

MUNTHE: That's what I thought. They all do. Well, cookie, you're in the wrong pew.

DEVILBISS (*humbly*): Haven't you any shoddy old blue plaid ones with leatheroid buttons for about fifty dollars?

MUNTHE: To fit a little shrimp like you?

DEVILBISS (*submissively*): It don't have to fit me.

MUNTHE (*bridling*): Oh, you're not going to wear it, hey? Just one of those sneaking comparison shoppers who—

DEVILBISS: No, no—I thought for carrying out the ashes—you know, around the cellar.

MUNTHE (*loftily*): You must be a pretty small-time lug to carry out your own ashes.

DEVILBISS: I am.

MUNTHE (*grudgingly*): Well, all right. Slip this on for size.

DEVILBISS (*after a struggle*): It binds me a little under the arms.

MUNTHE: You're damn right it does. If we knew how to lick that, we'd all be in clover.

DEVILBISS: Could you—I mean, maybe if a seam was let out—that is, the sleeve—

MUNTHE (*infuriated*): See here, chump, if you think I'm going to rebuild a measly fifty-dollar Mackinaw for every stumblebum who mooches in off the street—

DEVILBISS: Oh, no. I wouldn't dream of asking you! I—I was just wondering whether Alberta—that's Mrs. DeVilbiss; she's a regular whiz at things like that—and time, say, she's got all the time in the world—

MUNTHE: O.K., come on. Do you want it or don't you?

DEVILBISS: You bet your life I do! Does—er—does this model come with pockets?

MUNTHE: Yes, and we throw in two tickets to a musical and dinner at Voisin's. (*shouting*) What the hell do you think we're running here, a raffle?

DEVILBISS: Gee, you got me wrong. I wouldn't want anything I wasn't entitled to, honest!

MUNTHE: Next thing I know you'll be chiseling me out of paper and string to carry it home.

DEVILBISS: My goodness, no! I'll put it right over my arm—it's no trouble, really!

MUNTHE (*taking money from DeVilbiss*): Say, if I'd known you had nothing but twenties—

DEVILBISS: Gosh, never mind the change—that's quite all right. Thank you very much.

MUNTHE: Now, listen, chum, watch your step. If I hear any squawk out of you about our merchandise, I'll cool you off fast enough.

(*DeVilbiss exits hurriedly. A moment later Lin Yutang, the floorwalker —also no relation to the author of* The Story of San Michele— *enters.*)

YUTANG (*glowering*): Look here, Munthe, was that a customer I just saw coming out of this section?

MUNTHE (*quickly*): Of course not, sir. It was only a shoplifter.

YUTANG: All right, then, but don't let me catch you selling anything around here. You know the policy of this store. Carry on!

(*Munthe returns his salute and, picking up a bottle of acid, begins to dump it over the goods as Yutang, arms folded, watches him approvingly.*)

CURTAIN

❧ NOTHING BUT THE TOOTH

I AM thirty-eight years old, have curly brown hair and blue eyes, own a uke and a yellow roadster, and am considered a snappy dresser in my crowd. But the thing I want most in the world for my birthday is a free subscription to *Oral Hygiene*, published by Merwin B. Massol, 1005 Liberty Avenue, Pittsburgh, Pa. In the event you have been repairing your own teeth, *Oral Hygiene* is a respectable smooth-finish technical magazine circulated to your dentist with the compliments of his local supply company. Through its pages runs a recital of the most horrendous and fantastic deviations from the dental norm. It is a confessional in which dentists take down their back hair and stammer out the secrets of their craft. But every time I plunge into its crackling pages at my dentist's, just as I get interested in the story of the Man with the Alveolar Dentures or Thirty Reasons Why People Stay Away from Dentists, the nurse comes out slightly flushed and smoothing her hair to tell me that the doctor is ready. Last Thursday, for example, I was head over heels in the question-and-answer department of *Oral Hygiene*. A frankly puzzled extractionist, who tried to cloak his agitation under the initials "J.S.G.," had put his plight squarely up to the editor: "I have a patient, a woman of 20, who has a full complement of teeth. All of her restorations are gold foils or inlays. She constantly grinds her teeth at night. How can I aid her to stop grinding them? Would it do any good to give her a vellum rubber bite?" But before I could learn whether it was a bite or just a gentle hug the editor recommended, out popped Miss Inchbald with lipstick on her nose, giggling, "The Doctor is free now." "Free," indeed—"running amok" would be a better way to put it.

I had always thought of dentists as of the phlegmatic type—square-jawed sadists in white aprons who found release in trying out new kinds of burs on my shaky little incisors. One look at *Oral Hygiene* fixed that. Of all the inhibited, timorous, uncertain fumble-bunnies who creep the earth, Mr. Average Dentist is the worst. A filing clerk is a veritable saber-toothed tiger by comparison. Faced with a decision, your dentist's bones turn to water and he becomes all hands and feet.

28

He muddles through his ordinary routine with a certain amount of bravado, plugging a molar here with chewing gum, sinking a shaft in a sound tooth there. In his spare time he putters around his laboratory making tiny cement cupcakes, substituting amber electric bulbs for ordinary bulbs in his waiting room to depress patients, and jotting down nasty little innuendoes about people's gums in his notebook. But let an honest-to-goodness sufferer stagger in with his face out of drawing, and Mr. Average Dentist's nerves go to hell. He runs sobbing to the "Ask *Oral Hygiene*" department and buries his head in the lap of V. C. Smedley, its director. I dip in for a typical sample:

> Question—A patient of mine, a girl, 18, returned from school recently with a weird story of lightning having struck an upper right cuspid tooth and checked the enamel on the labial surface nearly two-thirds of the way from the incisal edge toward the neck. The patient was lying on a bed looking out an open window during an electric storm, and this one flash put out the lights of the house, and at the same time, the patient felt a burning sensation (like a burning wire) along the cuspid tooth. She immediately put her tongue on the tooth which felt rough, but as the lights were out she could not see it so she went to bed. (A taste as from a burnt match accompanied the shock.)
>
> Next morning she found the labial of the tooth black. Some of the color came off on her finger. By continaully brushing all day with the aid of peroxide, salt, soda and vinegar she removed the remainder of the black after which the tooth was a yellow shade and there was some roughness on the labial surface.
>
> Could the lightning have caused this and do you recommend smoothing the surface with discs?—R. D. L., D.D.S., Oregon.

Well, Doctor, let us take your story step by step. Miss Muffet told you the sensation was like a burning wire, and she tasted something like a burnt match. Did you think, by any chance, of looking into her mouth for either wire or matches? Did you even think of looking into her mouth? I see no mention of the fact in your letter. You state that she walked in and told you the story, that's all. Of course it never occurred to you that she had brought along her mouth for a reason. Then you say, "she removed the remainder of the black after which the tooth was a yellow shade." Would it be asking too much of you to make up your mind? Was it a tooth or a yellow shade? You're quite sure it wasn't a Venetian blind? Or a gaily striped awning? Do you ever take a drink in the daytime, Doctor?

Frankly, men, I have no patience with such idiotic professional behavior. An eighteen-year-old girl walks into a dentist's office exhibiting obvious symptoms of religious hysteria (stigmata, etc.) She babbles vaguely of thunderstorms and is patently a confirmed drunkard. The dentist goes to pieces, forgets to look in her mouth, and scurries off to *Oral Hygiene* asking for permission to smooth her surface with discs. It's a mercy he doesn't take matters into his own hands and try to plow every fourth tooth under. This is the kind of man to whom we entrust our daughters' dentures.

There is practically no problem so simple that it cannot confuse a dentist. For instance, thumb-sucking. "Could you suggest a method to correct thumb and index finger sucking by an infant of one year?" flutters a Minnesota orthodontist, awkwardly digging his toe into the hot sand. Dr. Smedley, whose patience rivals Job's, has an answer for everything: "Enclose the hand by tying shut the end of the sleeve of a sleeping garment, or fasten a section of a pasteboard mailing tube to the sleeping garment in such a position as to prevent the bending of the elbow sufficiently to carry the thumb or index finger to the mouth." Now truly, Dr. Smedley, isn't that going all the way around Robin Hood's barn? Nailing the baby's hand to the high-chair is much more cozy, or, if no nail is available, a smart blow with the hammer on Baby's fingers will slow him down. My grandfather, who was rather active in the nineties (between Columbus and Amsterdam avenues—they finally got him for breaking and entering), always used an effective method to break children of this habit. He used to tie a Mills grenade to the baby's thumb with cobbler's waxed thread, and when the little spanker pulled out the detonating pin with his teeth, Grandpa would stuff his fingers into his ears and run like the wind. Ironically enough, the people with whom Grandpa now boards have the same trouble keeping him from biting his thumbs, but overcome it by making him wear a loose jacket with very long sleeves, which they tie to the bars.

I have always been the mildest of men, but you remember the old saying, "Beware the fury of a patient man." (I remembered it very well and put my finger on it instantly, page 269 of Bartlett's book of quotations.) For years I have let dentists ride roughshod over my teeth; I have been sawed, hacked, chopped, whittled, bewitched, bewildered, tattooed, and signed on again; but this is cuspid's last stand. They'll never get me into that chair again. I'll dispose of my teeth as I see fit, and after they're gone, I'll get along. I started off living on gruel, and, by God, I can always go back to it again.

❧ THE IDOL'S EYE

I HAD been weekending with Gabriel Snubbers at his villa, "The Acacias," on the edge of the Downs. Gabriel isn't seen about as much as he used to be; one hears that an eccentric aunt left him a tidy little sum and the lazy beggar refuses to leave his native haunts. Four of us had cycled down from London together: Gossip Gabrilowitsch, the Polish pianist; Downey Couch, the Irish tenor; Frank Falcovsky, the Jewish prowler, and myself, Clay Modeling. Snubbers, his face beaming, met us at the keeper's lodge. His eyes were set in deep rolls of fat for our arrival, and I couldn't help thinking how well they looked. I wondered whether it was because his daring farce, *Mrs. Stebbins' Step-Ins*, had been doing so well at the Haymarket.

"Deuced decent of you chaps to make this filthy trip," he told us, leading us up the great avenue of two stately alms toward the house. "Rum place, this." A surprise awaited us when we reached the house, for the entire left wing had just burned down. Snubbers, poor fellow, stared at it a bit ruefully, I thought.

"Just as well. It was only a plague-spot," sympathized Falcovsky. Snubbers was thoughtful.

"D'ye know, you chaps," he said suddenly, "I could swear an aunt of mine was staying in that wing." Falcovsky stirred the ashes with his stick and uncovered a pair of knitting needles and a half-charred corset.

"No, it must have been the other wing," dismissed Snubbers. "How about a spot of whisky and soda?" We entered and Littlejohn, Snubbers' man, brought in a spot of whisky on a piece of paper which we all examined with interest. A splendid fire was already roaring in the middle of the floor to drive out the warmth.

"Soda?" offered Snubbers. I took it to please him, for Gabriel's cellar was reputedly excellent. A second later I wished that I had drunk the cellar instead. Baking soda is hardly the thing after a three-hour bicycle trip.

"You drank that like a little soldier," he complimented, his little button eyes fastened on me. I was about to remark that I had never drunk a little soldier, when I noticed Littlejohn hovering in the doorway.

31

"Yes, that will be all," Snubbers waved, "and, oh, by the way, send up to London tomorrow for a new wing, will you?" Littlejohn bowed and left, silently, sleekly Oriental.

"Queer cove, Littlejohn," commented Snubbers. "Shall I tell you a story?" He did, and it was one of the dullest I have ever heard. At the end of it Falcovsky grunted. Snubbers surveyed him suspiciously.

"Why, what's up, old man?" he queried.

"What's up? Nothing's up," snarled Falcovsky. "Can't a man grunt in front of an open fire if he wants to?"

"But . . ." began Snubbers.

"But nothing," Falcovsky grated. "You haven't lived till you've grunted in front of an open fire. Just for that—grunt, grunt, grunt," and he grunted several times out of sheer spite. The baking soda was beginning to tell on Snubbers.

"Remarkable thing happened the other day," he began. "I was pottering about in the garden . . ."

"Why must one always potter around in a garden?" demanded Couch. "Can't you potter around in an armchair just as well?"

"I did once," confessed Snubbers moodily, revealing a whitish scar on his chin. "Gad, sir, what a wildcat she was!" He chewed his wad of carbon paper reminiscently. "Oh, well, never mind. But as I was saying—I was going through some of my great-grandfather's things the other day . . ."

"What things?" demanded Falcovsky.

"His bones, if you must know," Snubbers said coldly. "You know, Great-grandfather died under strange circumstances. He opened a vein in his bath."

"I never knew baths had veins," protested Gabrilowitsch.

"I never knew his great-grandfather had a ba—" began Falcovsky derisively. With a shout Snubbers threw himself on Falcovsky. It was the signal for Pandemonium, the upstairs girl, to enter and throw herself with a shout on Couch. The outcome of the necking bee was as follows: Canadians 12, Visitors 9. Krebs and Vronsky played footie, subbing for Gerber and Weinwald, who were disabled by flying antipasto.

We were silent after Snubbers had spoken; men who have wandered in far places have an innate delicacy about their great-grandfathers' bones. Snubbers' face was a mask, his voice a harsh whip of pain in the stillness when he spoke again.

"I fancy none of you knew my great-grandfather," he said slowly.

"Before your time, I daresay. A rare giant of a man with quizzical eyes and a great shock of wiry red hair, he had come through the Peninsular Wars without a scratch. Women loved this impetual Irish adventurer who would rather fight than eat and vice versa. The wars over, he turned toward cookery, planning to devote his failing years to the perfection of the welsh rarebit, a dish he loved. One night he was chafing at The Bit, a tavern in Portsmouth, when he overheard a chance remark from a brawny gunner's mate in his cups. In Calcutta the man had heard native tales of a mysterious idol, whose single eye was a flawless ruby.

" 'Topscuttle my bamberger, it's the size of a bloomin' pigeon's egg!' spat the salt, shifting his quid to his other cheek. 'A bloomin' rajah's ransom and ye may lay to that, mateys!'

"The following morning the *Maid of Hull*, a frigate of the line mounting thirty-six guns, out of Bath and into bed in a twinkling, dropped downstream on the tide, bound out for Bombay, object matrimony. On her as passenger went my great-grandfather, an extra pair of nankeen pants and a dirk his only baggage. Fifty-three days later in Poona, he was heading for the interior of one of the Northern states. Living almost entirely on cameo brooches and the few ptarmigan which fell to the ptrigger of his pfowlingpiece, he at last sighted the towers of Ishpeming, the Holy City of the Surds and Cosines, fanatic Mohammedan warrior sects. He disguised himself as a beggar and entered the gates.

"For weeks my great-grandfather awaited his chance to enter the temple of the idol. They were changing the guard one evening when he saw it. One of the native janissaries dropped his knife. My great-grandfather leaped forward with cringing servility and returned it to him, in the small of his back. Donning the soldier's turban, he quickly slipped into his place. Midnight found him within ten feet of his prize. Now came the final test. He furtively drew from the folds of his robes a plate of curry, a dish much prized by Indians, and set it in a far corner. The guards rushed upon it with bulging squeals of delight. A twist of his wrist and the gem was his. With an elaborately stifled yawn, my great-grandfather left under pretense of going out for a glass of water. The soldiers winked slyly but when he did not return after two hours, their suspicions were aroused. They hastily made a canvass of the places where water was served and their worst fears were realized. The ruby in his burnoose, Great-grandfather was escaping by fast elephant over the Khyber Pass. Dockside loungers in Yarmouth forty days later

started curiously at a mammoth of a man with flaming red hair strid-
ing toward the Bull and Bloater Tavern. Under his belt, did they but
only know it, lay the Ruby Eye.

"Ten years to that night had passed, and my great-grandfather, in
seclusion under this very roof, had almost forgotten his daring escapade. Smoking by the fireplace, he listened to the roar of the wind and
reviewed his campaigns. Suddenly he leaped to his feet—a dark face
had vanished from the window. Too late my great-grandfather snatched
up powder and ball and sent a charge hurtling into the night. The note
pinned to the window drained the blood from his face.

"It was the first of a series. Overnight his hair turned from rose-red
to snow-white. And finally, when it seemed as though madness were to
rob them of their revenge, they came."

Snubbers stopped, his eyes those of a man who had looked beyond
life and had seen things best left hidden from mortal orbs. Falcovsky's
hand was trembling as he pressed a pinch of snuff against his gums.

"You—you mean?" he quaveled.

"Yes." Snubbers' voice had sunk to a whisper. "He fought with the
strength of nine devils, but the movers took away his piano. You see,"
he added very gently, "Great-grandfather had missed the last four in-
stallments." Gabrilowitsch sighed deeply and arose, his eyes fixed intently on Snubbers.

"And—and the ruby?" he asked softly, his delicate fingers closing
around the fire-tongs.

"Oh, *that*," shrugged Snubbers, "I just threw that in to make it interesting."

We bashed in his conk and left him to the vultures.

❧ TO SLEEP, PERCHANCE TO STEAM

To ANYBODY around here who is suffering from a touch of insomnia these days (surely no more than a hundred-to-one shot), the sequence of events in my bedroom last night may have a certain clinical interest. About nine o'clock, after a brisk session with the newscasters, I shuddered for approximately half an hour to relax my nerves, plugged a pair of Flents into my ears, and tied on a sleep mask. I probably should have waited until I got into bed before doing so, as I took a rather nasty fall over a wastebasket, but in a few moments I was stretched out, busily reviewing the war news and adding up the family bank account, with my pulse furnishing a rich musical background. When this palled, I read several chapters of Durfee's *Monasteries of the Rhône* with no success whatever until I discovered I had forgotten to remove my mask. As soon as I did, I was amply rewarded, for I found that with a little practice I was able to handle the strategy of the war and add up my bank account while vagabonding down the Rhône.

At this point, I regret to say, I tarnished an otherwise perfect record by falling into a slight doze. I must have been asleep almost fifteen minutes when I awoke suddenly and realized I had neglected to take a sedative before retiring. I promptly went out into the kitchen for a cup of hot milk with which to dissolve the nepenthe tablet and found Delia, our buxom cook, seated on the knee of her policeman friend. Actually, we have no cook called Delia, but we do have an impassive Englishman named Crichton and he was seated on the knee of a police-woman. The general effect was the same: a scene of coarse, steamy intimacy rivaling Hogarth's "Gin Lane." Muttering "This rivals Hogarth's 'Gin Lane,' " I stalked back to bed just in time to discover that the annual outing of the Clan-na-Gael was beginning directly beneath my window. Egged on by shrill cries of approval from the ladies' auxiliary, strapping bosthoons executed nimble jigs and reels, sang come-all-ye's, and vied with each other in hurling refuse cans the length of the street. The gaiety was so spontaneous and impulsive that I could not refrain from distributing several bags of water as favors. The gesture moved the crowd deeply, a few of its members even offering to come up and

35

include me in their horseplay. Unfortunately, my good-natured refusal caused considerable pique and the revelers disbanded shortly. The sky and I were turning gray when, without any preamble, a woman in the apartment directly overhead began beating her husband mercilessly. Unable to withstand his screams, I finally gathered up all the available bedding, wrapped my head in it, and lay in a cedar chest in the foyer until routed out by the odor of coffee.

It is the notion of the General Electric Company, as set forth in a booklet I picked up at Lewis & Conger's Sleep Shop later in the morning, that this sordid series of events need never have occurred had I only been equipped with a recent discovery of theirs. Some anonymous genius in Schenectady (who will yet turn out to be Paul Muni, mark my words) has conjured up from his alembics and retorts an electrical comforter known as "The Blanket with a Brain." Just how General Electric came to be mixed up in blanket research is not too clear; perhaps it was one of those accidents we know take place daily in laboratories. I can readily imagine some brilliant young chemist bursting into the office of the head of the division, exultantly waving an Erlenmeyer flask. "What's cooking, Shaftoe—I mean Muni?" inquires his chief irritably. "Another one of those impractical daydreams of yours?" "N-n-no, sir," stammers Shaftoe in his excitement. "Do you recall that precipitate of blanketane, comfortate cellulose, and old voltage I left on my bench last night?" "Yes, it was the seven-hundred-and-forty-fifth combination you and Bazurdjian had tried, and although all the others failed, you doggedly persisted, scorning the mockery of older and wiser heads," replies the chief. "Look here, sir!" cries Shaftoe, holding the flask up to the light. "My God!" exclaims his usually imperturbable senior. "A little electrical quilt! Imperfect, incomplete, picayune, but still a quilt! What formula did you use, my boy?" "A very old one, sir," says Shaftoe quietly. "One part inspiration and ten of perspiration." "Success hasn't changed you, Shaftoe," observes the chief. "You're still a drip." And, pocketing the discovery, he kicks Shaftoe out into the corridor.

Outwardly, the G. E. Electric Comforter is a simple wool-and-taffeta affair which runs on the house current and automatically adjusts itself to the changing temperatures of the night. What emerges from a study of the booklet, however, is a weird complex of thermostats, transformers, and control boxes likely to frighten the putative customer out of his pants. "The heart of the Comforter," states the booklet, "is a web of 370 feet of fine flexible copper wire of low resistance arranged in a zigzag pattern." Set me down as a dusty old eccentric, but frankly, there would seem to be some more ideal haven nowadays than a skein of copper wire, no matter how fine or flexible. Nor it is any more reassuring to learn that "six rubber molded safety thermostats are placed at intervals in this web of insulated wire (you can feel these thermostats with your fingers beneath the cover of the Comforter)." It needs no vivid imagination to imagine oneself lying in the dark with eyes protruding, endlessly tallying the thermostats and expecting at any moment to be converted into roast Long Island duckling. The possibility is evidently far from academic, to judge from the question a little later on: "Can the Comforter overheat or give an electric shock?" The manufacturers shrug aside the contingency in a breezy 450-word essay, easily comprehensible to wizards like Steinmetz but unhappily just out of my reach. One passage, nevertheless, is all too succinct:

> Even if the full 115 volts went through the Comforter, the body would have to be moist . . . a worn spot on the web wire inside the Comforter would have to touch the body . . . and another part of the body, as a hand or leg, would have to come in contact with a piece of metal, in order to get the sensation of an electric shock.

Given half a chance, I know I could fulfill these conditions, difficult though they seem. As one who puts on a pair of rubbers when he changes a fuse, only to find himself recumbent on the floor with his eyelashes singed, I'll go further. I bet I could pass through a room containing an Electric Comforter in the original gift box and emerge with a third-degree burn.

The balance of the booklet, to tell the truth, held for me a purely formal interest, as I had already reached a decision regarding the Comforter. Such questions as "What causes the slight clicking noise in the control box?" are obviously intended to relieve the fears of neurotics, and, thank God, I'm no neurotic. All I know is, when I got that far I heard a slight clicking noise and experienced a distinct tingling sensation which could only have emanated from the booklet itself. Luckily, I had the presence of mind to plunge it into a pail of water and yell for help. Right now it's over at some expert's office, about to be analyzed. And so am I, honey, if I can lay my hands on a good five-cent psychiatrist.

IS THERE AN OSTEOSYNCHRON-DROITRICIAN IN THE HOUSE?

LOOKING BACK at it now, I see that every afternoon at 4:30 for the past five months I had fallen into an exact routine. First off, I'd tap the dottle from my pipe by knocking it against the hob. I never smoke a pipe, but I like to keep one with a little dottle in it, and an inexpensive hob to tap it against; when you're in the writing game, there are these little accessories you need. Then I'd slip off my worn old green smoking jacket, which I loathe, and start down Lexington Avenue for home. Sometimes, finding myself in my shirtsleeves, I would have to return to my atelier for my jacket and overcoat, but as I say, when you're in the writing game, it's strictly head-in-the-clouds. Now, Lexington Avenue is Lexington Avenue—when you've once seen Bloomingdale's and the Wil-Low Cafeteria, you don't go nostalgic all over as you might for the Avenue de l'Observatoire and the Closerie des Lilas.

Anyway, I'd be head down and scudding along under bare poles by the time I reached the block between Fifty-eighth and Fifty-seventh streets, and my glance into those three shop windows would be purely automatic. First, the highly varnished *Schnecken* in the bakery; then the bones of a human foot shimmying slowly on a near-mahogany pedestal in the shoestore; and finally the clock set in the heel of a congress gaiter at the bootblack's. By now my shabby old reflexes would tell me it was time to buy an evening paper and bury my head in it. A little whim of my wife's; she liked to dig it up, as a puppy does a bone, while I was sipping my cocktail. Later on I taught her to frisk with a ball of yarn, but to get back to what happened Washington's Birthday.

I was hurrying homeward that holiday afternoon pretty much in the groove, humming an aria from "Till Tom Special" and wishing I could play the clarinet like a man named Goodman. Just as it occurred to me that I might drug this individual and torture his secret out of him, I came abreast the window of the shoestore containing the bones of the human foot. My mouth suddenly developed that curious dry feeling when I saw that they were vibrating, as usual, from north to south, every little metatarsal working with the blandest contempt for all I hold

38

dear. I pressed my ear against the window and heard the faint clicking of the motor housed in the box beneath. A little scratch here and there on the shellac surface showed where one of the more enterprising toes had tried to do a solo but had quickly rejoined the band. Not only was the entire arch rolling forward and backward in an oily fashion, but it had evolved an obscene side sway at the same time, a good deal like the *danse à ventre*. Maybe the foot had belonged to an Ouled-Naïl girl, but I felt I didn't care to find out. I was aware immediately of an active desire to rush home and lie down attended by my loved ones. The only trouble was that when I started to leave the place, I could feel my arches acting according to all the proper othopedic laws, and I swear people turned to look at me as if they heard a clicking sound.

The full deviltry of the thing only became apparent as I lay on my couch a bit later, a vinegar poultice on my forehead, drinking a cup of steaming tea. That little bevy of bones had been oscillating back and forth all through Danzig, Pearl Harbor, and the North African campaign; this very minute it was undulating turgidly, heedless of the fact the store had been closed two hours. Furthermore, if its progress were not impeded by the two wires snaffled to the toes (I'll give you *that* thought to thrash around with some sleepless night), it might by now have encircled the world five times, with a stopover at the Eucharistic Congress. For a moment the implications were so shocking that I started up alarmed. But since my loved ones had gone off to the movies and there was nobody to impress, I turned over and slept like a top, with no assistance except three and a half grains of barbital.

I could have reached my workshop the next morning by walking up Third Avenue, taking a cab up Lexington, or even crawling on my hands and knees past the shoestore to avoid that indecent window display, but my feet won their unequal struggle with my brain and carried me straight to the spot. Staring hypnotized at the macabre shuffle (halfway between a rumba and a soft-shoe step), I realized that I was receiving a sign from above to take the matter in hand. I spent the morning shopping lower Third Avenue, and at noon, dressed as an attaché of the Department of Sanitation, began to lounge nonchalantly before the store. My broom was getting nearer and nearer the window when the manager came out noiselessly. My ducks must have been too snowy, for he gave one of his clerks a signal and a moment later a policeman turned the corner. Fortunately, I had hidden my civvies in the lobby of Proctor's Fifty-eighth Street Theater, and by the time the breathless policeman rushed in, I had approached the wicket as cool as a cucumber, asked for two cucumbers in the balcony, and signed my name for Bank Nite. I flatter myself that I brought off the affair rather well.

My second attempt, however, was as fruitless as the first. I padded my stomach with a pillow, grayed my hair at the temples, and entered the shop fiercely. Pointing to the white piping on my vest, I represented myself as a portly banker from Portland, Maine, and asked the manager what he would take for the assets and good will, spot cash. I was about to make him a firm offer when I found myself being escorted out across the sidewalk, the manager's foot serving as fulcrum.

And there, precisely, the matter rests. I have given plenty of thought to the problem, and there is only one solution. Are there three young men in this city, with stout hearts and no dependents, who know what I mean? We can clean out that window with two well-directed bombs and get away over the rooftops. Given half a break, we'll stop that grisly *pas seul* ten seconds after we rendezvous on the coping. If we're caught, there's always the cyanide in our belts. First meeting tonight at nine in front of the Railroad Men's Y.M.C.A., and wear a blue cornflower. *Up the rebels!*

❧ WOODMAN, DON'T SPARE THAT TREE!

NOT LONG AGO a landscape architect down my way was retained by a lady who, to put it bluntly, had just fallen heir to a satchelful of the stuff. Instead of the same old flowers and trees, the fair client wanted a garden plan for her country house which would express her own unique personality: something arresting, terribly audacious, yet smart; in short, identifying her unmistakably as a lady who had just fallen heir to a satchelful. The architect smacked his lips in a refined way, like a fox in a henhouse, and went to work. Employing a dozen wooden horses gleaned from a defunct amusement park, and a profusion of the rarest vines, creepers, and bulbs known to man, he created a spectacular floral carrousel that dazzled the countryside. Farmers came from miles around to lean on their manure forks and gape at the horticultural gewgaw, but Mrs. Krebs was clearly disappointed.

"You haven't captured my mood at all," she pouted. "Deep down, I'm really a mystic—haunting, inscrutable. Now this," she went on, waving toward a mournful Chirico which had set her back eleven thousand clams, "this is really *me*."

"You took the words right out of my mouth," agreed the architect, "but I was just interpreting the little girl in you. The spiritual side is on the fire and should be ready any day now."

A week later, wrenched from its native California by political influence plus considerable baksheesh, a gnarled Monterey cypress rolled into the county seat on a flatcar. It was unloaded and borne to the estate, where a gang of workmen sank it in a cement base and sprayed it dead white. One of New York's most recherché decorators then looped smilax and Spanish moss from its writhing limbs, and on the first night of the full moon the result was unveiled to its owner. The effect was so electric that the architect now sends his fees to the bank in an armored car and has taken to wearing pencil-striped pants in the forenoon.

One might be inclined to shrug one's pretty shoulders and dismiss such decadence as isolated were it not for a photograph in a recent issue of the *American Home*. It portrays a lifeless apple tree, hairy with vines and birdbaths, rearing up forlornly in a small patio under the caption "Seeing the artistic possibilities of this dead tree, Mrs. Clyde L. Hagerman, of Bloomfield Hills, Michigan, bought it, had it set in concrete in her outdoor living room, so she can drape it each summer in moonflowers and gourd vines." Here, then, is a trend, as significant as the first shifter pin or the original Eugénie hat. As the hysteria spreads, any number of provocative situations may arise, but one of them seems to fall naturally into the dramatic pattern. Places, please.

SCENE: *A country road toward dusk. A station wagon rounds the bend, in its front seat Mr. and Mrs. Updegraff. The tonneau is heaped high with Chinese-lacquer taborets inlaid with mother-of-pearl, paintings on velvet, and other post-Victorian bagatelles with which Mrs. Updegraff plans to redecorate her home. She is busily examining two yellowed Welsbach mantles.*

MRS. UPDEGRAFF (*exultantly*): They're just like the ones Lilian Gassaway bought at the Parke-Bernet Galleries—she'll be furious! I'll have them dyed dark blue and use them for flower-holders.

MR. UPDEGRAFF (*listlessly*): What are you going to do with that old sewing machine back there—open a sweatshop?

MRS. UPDEGRAFF: No, the feet'll make a lovely coffee table. I saw the very piece of marble in that Portuguese cemetery we passed. Couldn't we sneak out some dark night . . .

MR. UPDEGRAFF (*violently*): Who the hell do you think we are— Burke and Hare? Now, listen, look here, Juanita—

MRS. UPDEGRAFF (*suddenly*): Stop! Stop the car! We just passed it!

MR. UPDEGRAFF: What?

MRS. UPDEGRAFF: The hickory I've been lickory for—I mean the hickory I've been looking for! Oh, Leslie, it's a dream! Look at those great, tormented limbs! Come on! Let's find out how much they're asking!

MR. UPDEGRAFF (*desperately*): Now, Juanita, you know we can't afford—

MRS. UPDEGRAFF (*in another world*): I can just see Myrtle Greneker's face, giving herself airs with that miserable little sycamore of hers.

MR. UPDEGRAFF: But this thing's dead!

MRS. UPDEGRAFF: Of course it is, silly. Do you suppose I'd put a live hickory in our patio? Don't be tacky.

MR. UPDEGRAFF: A zombie, that's what I married. Cemeteries, dead hickories. . . .

(*He moodily throws the car into reverse. The curtain is lowered for a few moments while the scenery is being shifted. Should the audience become restive, the interval can be filled by a ballet, "Six Who Pass While the Concrete Boils," in which half a dozen stocky Bryn Mawr girls in gray jersey stride convulsively from one end of the stage to the other tugging at a veil. This symbolizes the forces of water, sand, and Portland cement at first refusing to work harmoniously, then uniting for the common good. When the curtain rises again it discloses Reuben Hayseed, a farmer with chin whiskers and a linen duster, seated in a rocker tilted against his home, over which towers the dead hickory. One of Reuben's two young sons has hoisted his brother up into the limbs in a fragile box of the sort used for packing eggs.*)

HAYSEED (*thickly*) : Gad, it's murder to send a mere boy up in a crate like that.

(*His words are prophetic; a moment later the boy plummets out of the tree and breaks his neck. He is borne off stage with many lamentations by the six Bryn Mawr girls in a pageant entitled "Youth in the Hands of the Receivers." Enter Mr. and Mrs. Updegraff.*)

MRS. UPDEGRAFF: That tree's unsafe! It ought to be condemned!

HAYSEED (*placidly*) : We like it.

MRS. UPDEGRAFF: You watch, it'll come crashing down through the roof some day.

HAYSEED: That's what makes life at Echo Valley Farm so piquant.

MRS. UPDEGRAFF (*snorting*) : It's just a lot of old firewood to me.

HAYSEED: Really? I can't quite agree. Sometimes, viewed by moonlight, its gaunt agony typifies the melancholy and futility of existence.

MR. UPDEGRAFF: That's pretty dickty talk for a farmer.

HAYSEED: It may interest you to learn that I am one of the few farmers who ever graduated from the Sorbonne.

MR. UPDEGRAFF: No kid? Why, I'm an old Sorbonne man myself! What'd you major in?

HAYSEED: None of your goddamned business.

MRS. UPDEGRAFF: Look here, young man, we may have a use for that old stump. How much do you want for it?

HAYSEED: Sixty dollars.

MR. UPDEGRAFF: Sixty dollars!

HAYSEED: Hear that echo? Clear as a bell. (*proudly*) No wonder they call this place Echo Valley Farm.

MRS. UPDEGRAFF: Isn't—isn't that rather expensive?

HAYSEED: Not for an original. I've got a barnful of copies out there at ten dollars, if that's what you want.

MRS. UPDEGRAFF: No, I couldn't bear anything near me that wasn't authentic. I'm funny that way.

HAYSEED: So am I. I'd just as soon take half the money to have my pieces go into a home where they're appreciated.

MR. UPDEGRAFF: Is that an offer?

HAYSEED: No, simply a manner of speaking.

MRS. UPDEGRAFF: Oh, Leslie, it *is* divine, isn't it? After all, we could economize next month. Spaghetti's cheap, but it's filling.

MR. UPDEGRAFF (*a dead pigeon*): Yes, dear. (*to Hayseed*) Do you mind taking a check? It isn't certified.

HAYSEED: Not at all. What bank?

MR. UPDEGRAFF: Corn Exchange.

HAYSEED: Funny, I'm an old Corn Exchange man myself. How big's your balance?

MR. UPDEGRAFF: None of your goddamned business.

HAYSEED (*folding check*): There. And now can I interest you folks in a plate of Mrs. Hayseed's real country doughnuts, piping hot from the oven?

MR. UPDEGRAFF (*hastily*): Er—no, thanks, we'll just pick up some cheap copies along the road.

(*As the Updegraffs exit, Hayseed resumes his seat in the rocker with a contented sigh and, taking up an old cobbler's bench, begins to convert it into a lamp.*)

CURTAIN

❧ STRICTLY FROM HUNGER

YES I WAS EXCITED, and small wonder. What boy wouldn't be, boarding a huge, mysterious, puffing steam train for golden California? As
Mamma adjusted my reefer and strapped on my leggings, I almost
burst with impatience. Grinning redcaps lifted my luggage into the
compartment and spat on it. Mamma began to weep into a small pillowcase she had brought along for the purpose.

"Oh, son, I wish you hadn't become a scenario writer!" she sniffled.

"Aw, now, Moms," I comforted her, "it's no worse than playing the
piano in a call house." She essayed a brave little smile, and, reaching
into her reticule, produced a flat package which she pressed into my
hands. For a moment I was puzzled, then I cried out with glee.

"Jelly sandwiches! Oh, Moms!"

"Eat them all, boy o' mine," she told me, "they're good for boys
with hollow little legs." Tenderly she pinned to my lapel the green tag
reading "To Plushnick Productions, Hollywood, California." The
whistle shrilled and in a moment I was chugging out of Grand Central's
dreaming spires followed only by the anguished cries of relatives who
would now have to go to work. I had chugged only a few feet when I
realized that I had left without the train, so I had to run back and wait
for it to start.

As we sped along the glorious fever spots of the Hudson I decided
to make a tour of inspection. To my surprise I found that I was in the
only passenger car of the train; the other cars were simply dummies
snipped out of cardboard and painted to simulate coaches. Even "passengers" had been cunningly drawn in colored crayons in the "window," as well as ragged tramps clinging to the blinds below and drinking Jamaica ginger. With a rueful smile I returned to my seat and
gorged myself on jelly sandwiches.

At Buffalo the two other passengers and I discovered to our horror
that the conductor had been left behind. We finally decided to divide
up his duties; I punched the tickets, the old lady opposite me wore a
conductor's hat and locked the washroom as we came into stations,
and the young man who looked as if his feet were not mates consulted

a Hamilton watch frequently. But we missed the conductor's earthy conversation and it was not until we had exchanged several questionable stories that we began to forget our loss.

A flicker of interest served to shorten the trip. At Fort Snodgrass, Ohio, two young and extremely polite road-agents boarded the train and rifled us of our belongings. They explained that they were modern Robin Hoods and were stealing from the poor to give to the rich. They had intended to rape all the women and depart for Sherwood Forest, but when I told them that Sherwood Forest as well as the women were in England, their chagrin was comical in the extreme. They declined my invitation to stay and take a chance on the train's pool, declaring that the engineer had fixed the run and would fleece us, and got off at South Bend with every good wish.

The weather is always capricious in the Middle West, and although it was midsummer, the worst blizzard in Chicago's history greeted us on our arrival. The streets were crowded with thousands of newsreel cameramen trying to photograph one another bucking the storm on the Lake Front. It was a novel idea for the newsreels and I wished them well. With only two hours in Chicago I would be unable to see the city, and the thought drew me into a state of composure. I noted with pleasure that a fresh coat of grime had been given to the Dearborn Street station, though I was hardly vain enough to believe that it had anything to do with my visit. There was the usual ten-minute wait while the porters withdrew with my portable typewriter to a side room and flailed it with hammers, and at last I was aboard the "Sachem," crack train of the B.B.D. & O. lines.

It was as if I had suddenly been transported into another world. "General Crook," in whom I was to make my home for the next three days, and his two neighbors, "Lake Tahoe" and "Chief Malomai," were everything that the word "Pullman" implies; they were Pullmans. Uncle Eben, in charge of "General Crook," informed me that the experiment of air-cooling the cars had been so successful that the road intended trying to heat them next winter.

"Ah suttinly looks fo'd to dem roastin' ears Ah's gwine have next winter, he, he, he!" he chuckled, rubbing soot into my hat.

The conductor told me he had been riding on trains for so long that he had begun to smell like one, and sure enough, two brakemen waved their lanterns at him that night and tried to tempt him down a siding in Kansas City. We became good friends and it came as something of a blow when I heard the next morning that he had fallen off the train during the night. The fireman said that we had circled about for an hour trying to find him but that it had been impossible to lower a boat because we did not carry a boat.

The run was marked by only one incident out of the ordinary. I had ordered breaded veal cutlet the first evening, and my waiter, poking his head into the kitchen, had repeated the order. The cook, unfortunately, understood him to say "*dreaded* veal cutlet," and resenting the slur, sprang at the waiter with drawn razor. In a few seconds I was the only living remnant of the shambles, and at Topeka I was compelled to wait until a new shambles was hooked on and I proceeded with dinner.

It seemed only a scant week or ten days before we were pulling into Los Angeles. I had grown so attached to my porter that I made him give me a lock of his hair. I wonder if he still has the ten-cent piece I gave him? There was a gleam in his eye which could only have been insanity as he leaned over me. Ah, Uncle Eben, faithful old retainer, where are you now? Gone to what obscure ossuary? If this should chance to meet your kindly gaze, drop me a line care of *Variety*, won't you? They know what to do with it.

— II —

The violet hush of twilight was descending over Los Angeles as my hostess, Violet Hush, and I left its suburbs headed toward Hollywood. In the distance a glow of huge piles of burning motion-picture scripts lit up the sky. The crisp tang of frying writers and directors whetted my appetite. How good it was to be alive, I thought, inhaling deep lungfuls of carbon monoxide. Suddenly our powerful Gatti-Cazazza slid to a stop in the traffic.

"What is it, Jenkin?" Violet called anxiously through the speaking-tube to the chauffeur (played by Lyle Talbot).

A *suttee* was in progress by the roadside, he said—did we wish to see it? Quickly Violet and I elbowed our way through the crowd. An enormous funeral pyre composed of thousands of feet of film and scripts, drenched with Chanel Number 5, awaited the torch of Jack Holt, who was to act as master of ceremonies. In a few terse words Violet explained this unusual custom borrowed from the Hindus and never paid for. The worst disgrace that can befall a producer is an unkind notice from a New York reviewer. When this happens, the producer becomes a pariah in Hollywood. He is shunned by his friends, thrown into bankruptcy, and like a Japanese electing hara-kiri, he commits *suttee*. A great bonfire is made of the film, and the luckless producer, followed by directors, actors, technicians, and the producer's wives, immolate themselves. Only the scenario writers are exempt.

These are tied between the tails of two spirited Caucasian ponies, which are then driven off in opposite directions. This custom is called "a conference."

Violet and I watched the scene breathlessly. Near us Harry Cohl, head of Moribund Studios, was being rubbed with huck towels preparatory to throwing himself into the flames. He was nonchalantly smoking a Rocky Ford five-center, and the man's courage drew a tear to the eye of even the most callous. Weeping relatives besought him to eschew his design, but he stood adamant. Adamant Eve, his plucky secretary, was being rubbed with crash towels preparatory to flinging herself into Cohl's embers. Assistant directors busily prepared spears, war bonnets and bags of pemmican which the Great Chief would need on his trip to the "Happy Hunting Grounds." Wampas and beads to placate the Great Spirit (played by Will Hays) were piled high about the stoical tribesman.

Suddenly Jack Holt (played by Edmund Lowe) raised his hand for silence. The moment had come. With bowed head Holt made a simple invocation couched in one-syllable words so that even the executives might understand. Throwing his five-center to a group of autograph hunters, the great man poised himself for the fatal leap. But from off-scene came the strident clatter of cocoanut shells, and James Mohl, Filmdom's fearless critic, wearing the uniform of a Confederate guerrilla and the whiskers of General Beauregard, galloped in on a foam-flecked pinto. It was he whose mocking review had sent Cohl into Coventry. It was a dramatic moment as the two stood pitted against each other—Cohl against Mohl, the Blue against the Gray. But with true Southern gallantry Mohl was the first to extend the hand of friendship.

"Ah reckon it was an unworthy slur, suh," he said in manly tones. "Ah-all thought you-all's pictuah was lousy but it opened at the Rialto to sensational grosses, an' Ah-all 'pologizes. Heah, have a yam." And he drew a yam from his tunic. Not to be outdone in hospitality, Cohl drew a yam from his tunic, and soon they were exchanging yams and laughing over the old days.

When Violet and I finally stole away to our waiting motor, we felt that we were somehow nearer to each other. I snuggled luxuriously into the buffalo laprobe Violet had provided against the treacherous night air and gazed out at the gleaming neon lights. Soon we would be in Beverly Hills, and already the quaint native women were swarming alongside in their punts urging us to buy their cunning beadwork and mangoes. Occasionally I threw a handful of coppers to the Negro boys, who dove for them joyfully. The innocent squeals of the policemen as the small blackamoors pinched them were irresistible. Unable to resist them, Violet and I were soon pinching each other till our skins glowed. Violet was good to the touch, with a firm fleshy texture like a winesap or pippin. It seemed but a moment before we were sliding under the porte-cochère of her home, a magnificent rambling structure of beaverboard patterned after an Italian ropewalk of the sixteenth century. It had recently been remodeled by a family of wrens who had introduced chewing gum into the left wing, and only three or four obscure Saxon words could do it justice.

I was barely warming my hands in front of the fire and watching Jimmy Fidler turn on a spit when my presence on the Pacific Slope made itself felt. The news of my arrival had thrown international financial centers into an uproar, and sheaves of wires, cables, phone messages, and even corn began piling up. An ugly rumor that I might reorganize the motion-picture industry was being bruited about in the world's commodity markets. My brokers, Whitelipped & Trembling, were beside themselves. The New York Stock Exchange was begging them for assurances of stability and Threadneedle Street awaited my next move with drumming pulses. Film shares ricocheted sharply, although wools and meats were sluggish, if not downright sullen. To the reporters who flocked around me I laughingly disclaimed that this was a business trip. I was simply a scenario writer to whom the idea of work was abhorrent. A few words murmured into the transatlantic telephone, the lift of an eyebrow here, the shrug of a shoulder there, and equilibrium was soon restored. I washed sparsely, curled my mustache with a heated hairpin, flicked a drop of Sheik Lure on my lapel, and rejoined my hostess.

After a copious dinner, melting-eyed beauties in lacy black underthings fought with each other to serve me kümmel. A hurried apology, and I was curled up in bed with the Autumn 1927 issue of *The Yale Review*. Halfway through an exciting symposium on Sir Thomas Aquinas' indebtedness to Professors Whitehead and Spengler, I suddenly detected a stowaway blonde under the bed. Turning a deaf ear to her heartrending entreaties and burning glances, I sent her packing. Then I treated my face to a feast of skin food, buried my head in the pillow and went bye-bye.

— III —

Hollywood Boulevard! I rolled the rich syllables over on my tongue and thirstily drank in the beauty of the scene before me. On all sides nattily attired boulevardiers clad in rich stuffs strolled nonchalantly, inhaling cubebs and exchanging epigrams stolen from Martial and Wilde. Thousands of scantily draped but none the less appetizing extra girls milled past me, their mouths a scarlet wound and their eyes clearly defined in their faces. Their voluptuous curves set my blood on fire, and as I made my way down Mammary Lane, a strange thought began to invade my brain: I realized that I had not eaten breakfast yet. In a Chinese eatery cunningly built in the shape of an old shoe I managed to assuage the inner man with a chopped glove salad topped off with frosted cocoa. Charming platinum-haired hostesses in red pajamas and peaked caps added a note of color to the surroundings, whilst a gypsy orchestra played selections from Victor Herbert's operettas on musical saws. It was a bit of old Vienna come to life, and the sun was a red ball in the heavens before I realized with a start that I had promised to report at the Plushnick Studios.

Commandeering a taxicab, I arrived at the studio just in time to witness the impressive ceremony of changing the guard. In the central parade ground, on a snowy white charger, sat Max Plushnick, resplendent in a producer's uniform, his chest glittering with first mortgage liens, amortizations, and estoppels. His personal guard, composed of picked vice-presidents of the Chase National Bank, was drawn up stiffly about him in a hollow square.

But the occasion was not a happy one. A writer had been caught trying to create an adult picture. The drums rolled dismally, and the writer, his head sunk on his chest, was led out amid a ghastly silence. With the aid of a small stepladder Plushnick slid lightly from his steed. Sternly he ripped the epaulets and buttons from the traitor's tunic, broke his sword across his knee, and in a few harsh words demoted him to the mail department.

"And now," began Plushnick, "I further condemn you to eat . . ."

"No, no!" screamed the poor wretch, falling to his knees and embracing Plushnick's jackboots. "Not that, not that!"

"Stand up, man," ordered Plushnick, his lip curling; "I condemn you to eat in the studio restaurant for ten days and may God have mercy on your soul." The awful words rang out on the still evening air and even Plushnick's hardened old mercenaries shuddered. The heart-rending cries of the unfortunate were drowned in the boom of the sunset gun.

In the wardrobe department I was photographed, fingerprinted, and measured for the smock and Windsor tie which were to be my uniform. A nameless fear clutched at my heart as two impassive turnkeys herded me down a corridor to my supervisor's office. For what seemed hours we waited in an anteroom. Then my serial number was called, the leg-irons were struck off, and I was shoved through a door into the presence of Diana ffrench-Mamoulian.

How to describe what followed? Diana ffrench-Mamoulian was accustomed to having her way with writers, and my long lashes and peachblow mouth seemed to whip her to insensate desire. In vain, time and again, I tried to bring her attention back to the story we were discussing, only to find her gem-incrusted fingers straying through my hair. When our interview was over, her cynical attempt to "date me up" made every fiber of my being cry out in revolt.

"P-please," I stammered, my face burning, "I—I wish you wouldn't. . . . I'm engaged to a Tri Kappa at Goucher—"

"Just one kiss," she pleaded, her breath hot against my neck. In desperation I granted her boon, knowing full well that my weak defenses were crumbling before the onslaught of this love tigree. Finally she allowed me to leave, but only after I had promised to dine at her penthouse apartment and have an intimate chat about the script. The basket of slave bracelets and marzipan I found awaiting me on my return home made me realize to what lengths Diana would go.

I was radiant that night in blue velvet tails and a boutonnière of diamonds from Cartier's, my eyes starry and the merest hint of cologne at my ear-lobes. An inscrutable Oriental served the Lucullan repast and my vis-à-vis was as effervescent as the wine.

"Have a bit of the wing, darling?" queried Diana solicitously, indicating the roast Long Island airplane with applesauce. I tried to turn our conversation from the personal note, but Diana would have none of it. Soon we were exchanging gay bantam over the mellow Vouvray, laughing as we dipped fastidious fingers into the Crisco parfait for which Diana was famous. Our meal finished, we sauntered into the rumpus room and Diana turned on the radio. With a savage snarl the radio turned on her and we slid over the waxed floor in the intricate maze of the jackdaw strut. Without quite knowing why, I found myself hesitating before the plate of liqueur candies Diana was pressing on me.

"I don't think I should—really, I'm a trifle faint—"

"Oh, come on," she urged masterfully. "After all, you're old enough to be your father—I mean I'm old enough to be my mother. . . ." She stuffed a brandy bonbon between my clenched teeth. Before long I was eating them thirstily, reeling about the room and shouting snatches of coarse drunken doggerel. My brain was on fire, I tell you. Through the haze I saw Diana ffrench-Mamoulian, her nostrils dilated, groping for me. My scream of terror only egged her on, overturning chairs and tables in her bestial pursuit. With superhuman talons she tore off my collar and suspenders. I sank to my knees, choked with sobs, hanging on to my last shirt-stud like a drowning man. Her Svengali eyes were slowly hypnotizing me; I fought like a wounded bird—and then, blissful unconsciousness.

When I came to, the Oriental servant and Diana were battling in the center of the floor. As I watched, Yen Shee Gow drove a well-aimed blow to her mid-section, following it with a right cross to the jaw. Diana staggered and rolled under a table. Before my astonished eyes John Chinaman stripped the mask from his face and revealed the features of Blanche Almonds, a little seamstress I had long wooed unsuccessfully in New York. Gently she bathed my temples with Florida water and explained how she had followed me, suspecting Diana ffrench-Mamoulian's intentions. I let her rain kisses over my face and lay back in her arms as beaming Ivan tucked us in and cracked his whip over the prancing bays. In a few seconds our sleigh was skimming over the hard crust toward Port Arthur and freedom, leaving Plushnick's discomfited officers gnashing one another's teeth. The wintry Siberian moon glowed over the tundras, drenching my hair with moonbeams for Blanche to kiss away. And so, across the silvery steppes amid the howling of wolves, we rode into a new destiny, purified in the crucible that men call Hollywood.

🌱 FROU-FROU, OR, THE FUTURE OF VERTIGO

JUST IN CASE anybody here missed me at the Mermaid Tavern this afternoon when the bowl of sack was being passed, I spent most of it reclining on my chaise longue in a negligee trimmed with marabou, reading trashy toffees and eating French yellow-backed novels. What between amnesia (inability to find my rubbers) and O'Hara's disease (ability to remember all the cunning things I did last night), you might think I'd have sense enough to sit still and mind my own business. But, oh, no, not I. *I* had to start looking through *Harper's Bazaar* yet.

If a perfectly strange lady came up to you on the street and demanded, "Why don't you travel with a little raspberry-colored cashmere blanket to throw over yourself in hotels and trains?" the chances are that you would turn on your heel with dignity and hit her with a bottle. Yet that is exactly what has been happening for the past twenty months in the pages of a little raspberry-colored magazine called *Harper's Bazaar*. And don't think it does any good to pretend there *is* no magazine called *Harper's Bazaar*. I've tried that, too, and all I get is something called "circular insanity." Imagine having both circular insanity and *Harper's Bazaar*!

The first time I noticed this "Why Don't You?" department was a year ago last August while hungrily devouring news of the midsummer openings in the *haute couture*. Without any preamble came the stinging query, "Why don't you rinse your blond child's hair in dead champagne, as they do in France? Or pat her face gently with cream before she goes to bed, as they do in England?" After a quick look into the nursery, I decided to let my blond child go to hell her own way, as they do in America, and read on. "Why don't you," continued the author, spitting on her hands, "twist her pigtails around her ears like macaroons?" I reread this several times to make sure I wasn't dreaming and then turned to the statement of ownership in the back of the magazine. Just because the Marquis de Sade wasn't mentioned didn't fool *me*; you know as well as I do who must have controlled fifty-one per cent of the

53

stock. I slept across the foot of the crib with a loaded horse pistol until the next issue appeared.

It appeared, all right, all right, and after a quick gander at the activities of Nicky de Gunzburg, Lady Abdy, and the Vicomtesse de Noailles, which left me right back where I started, I sought out my "Why Don't You?" column. "Why don't you try the effect of diamond roses and ribbons flat on your head, as Garbo wears them when she says goodbye to Armand in their country retreat?" asked Miss Sly Boots in a low, thrilling voice. I was living in my own country retreat at the time, and as it happened to be my day to go to the post office (ordinarily the post office comes to me), I welcomed this chance to vary the monotony. Piling my head high with diamond roses and ribbons, I pulled on a pair of my stoutest *espadrilles* and set off, my cat frisking ahead of me with many a warning cry of "Here comes my master, the Marquis of Carabas!" We reached the post office without incident, except for the elderly Amish woman hoeing cabbages in her garden. As I threw her a cheery greeting, Goody Two-shoes looked up, gave a rapid exhibition of Cheyne-Stokes breathing, and immediately turned to stone. In case you ever get down that way, she is still standing there, slightly chipped but otherwise in very good condition, which is more than I can say for the postmaster. When I walked in, he was in process of spitting into the top drawer, where he keeps the money-order blanks. One look at Boxholder 14 and he went out the window without bothering to raise the sash. A second later I heard a frightened voice directing a small boy to run for the hex doctor next door to the Riegels'. I spent the night behind some willows near the Delaware and managed to work my way back to the farm without being detected, but it was a matter of months before I was able to convince the countryside that I had a twin brother, enormously wealthy but quite mad, who had eluded his guards and paid me a visit.

For a time I went on a sort of *Harper's Bazaar* wagon, tapering myself off on *Pictorial Review* and *Good Housekeeping*, but deep down I knew I was a gone goose. Whenever I got too near a newsstand bearing a current issue of the *Bazaar* and my head started to swim, I would rush home and bury myself in dress patterns. And then, one inevitable day, the dam burst. Lingering in Brentano's basement over *L'Illustration* and *Blanco y Negro*, I felt the delicious, shuddery, half-swooning sensation of being drawn into the orbit again. On a table behind me lay a huge stack of the very latest issue of *Harper's Bazaar*, smoking hot from the presses. "Ah, come on," I heard my evil genius whisper. "One little peek can't hurt you. Nobody's looking." With trembling fingers I fumbled through the advertisements for Afghan hounds, foundation garments, and bath foams to the "Why Don't You?" section. Tiny beads of perspiration stood out on my even tinier forehead as I began to read, "Why don't you build beside the sea, or in the center of your garden, a white summer dining room shaped like a tent, draped with wooden swags, with walls of screen and Venetian blinds, so you will be safe from bugs and drafts?" I recoiled, clawing the air. "No, no!" I screamed. "I won't! I can't! *Help!*" But already the column was coiling around me, its hot breath on my neck. "Why don't you concentrate on fur jackets of marvelous workmanship and cut, made of inexpensive furs with incomprehensible names? Why don't you bring back from Central Europe a huge white baroque porcelain stove to stand in your front hall, reflected in the parquet? Why don't you buy in a hardware store a plain pine knife-basket with two compartments and a handle—mount this on four legs and you will have the ideal little table to sort letters and bills on, and to carry from your bedside to the garden or wherever you happen to be?" Unfortunately I had only the two legs God gave me, but I mounted those basement stairs like a cheetah, fought off the restraining hands of voluptuous salesladies, and hurtled out into the cool, sweet air of West Forty-seventh Street. I'm sorry I snatched the paper knife out of that desk set, Mr. Brentano, but you can send a boy for it at my expense. And by the way, do you ever have any call for back numbers of fashion magazines?

❧ A POX ON YOU, MINE GOODLY HOST

A FEW NIGHTS AGO I strolled into our Pompeian living room in my stocking feet, bedad, with a cigar in my mouth and a silk hat tilted back on my head, to find Maggie, with osprey plumes in her hair and a new evening cape, pulling on long white gloves. A little cluster of exclamation points and planets formed over her head as she saw me.

"Aren't you dressed yet, you bonehead?" she thundered. "Or were you sneaking down to Dinty Moore's for corned beef and cabbage with those worthless cronies of yours?" I soon banished the good woman's fears, and in response to my queries she drew from her reticule an advertisement clipped from the *Sun*. It displayed photographs of George S. Kaufman and Moss Hart framed in a family album over the legend "From Schrafft's Album of Distinguished Guests. The parade of luminaries who enjoy Schrafft's hearty dinners includes columnists, sports-writers, stage and radio personalities, football coaches, illustrators, producers. Adding to the glitter of this list are the distinguished names of Kaufman and Hart, who have written many a Broadway hit." Of course, nothing would do but we must dine at Schrafft's that very evening and mingle in the pageantry, so without further ado we set out.

Although it was not yet seven o'clock when our cab pulled up in front of the Forty-third Street branch, a sizable crowd of autograph-seekers had assembled and were eagerly scrutinizing each new arrival. A rapturous shout went up as I descended. "Here comes dashing Brian Aherne!" exulted a charming miss rushing forward. "Isn't it sickening?" I murmured into my wife's ear. "This happens everywhere—in stores, on buses—" "Yes, I know," she grated. "Everybody takes me for Olivia de Havilland. Get out of the way, you donkey. Don't you see the man's trying to get by?" To my surprise, I found myself brushed aside by Brian Aherne, who must have been clinging to the trunk rack. As I shouldered my way after him, curious stares followed me. "That must be his bodyguard," commented a fan. "That shrimp couldn't be a cat's bodyguard," sneered his neighbor. I looked the speaker full in the eye. "That's for the cat to say," I riposted, and as the bystanders roared, I stalked through the revolving doors, conscious I had scored.

Buoyant the advertisement had been, but I was frankly dazzled by the scene which confronted me. The foyer, ablaze with lights, was peopled by personages of such distinction as few first nights attract. Diamonds of the finest water gleamed at the throats of women whose beauty put the gems to shame, and if each was not escorted by a veritable Adonis, he was at least a Greek. A hum of well-bred conversation rose from the throng, punctuated now and again by the click of expensive dentures. In one corner Nick Kenny, Jack Benny, James Rennie, Sonja Henie, and E. R. Penney, the chain-store magnate, were gaily comparing pocketbooks to see who had the most money, and in another Jim Thorpe chatted with Jay Thorpe, cheek by jowl with Walter Wanger and Percy Grainger. Here Lou Little and Elmer Layden demonstrated a new shift to a fascinated circle, while there Ann Corio demonstrated still another to an even more spellbound circle. Irving Lazar, Henry Irving, and Washington Irving had just planed in from the Coast to sign everyone to agency contracts, and now, swept along by sheer momentum, were busily signing each other. As far as the eye could see, at tables in the background, gourmets were gorging themselves on chicken-giblet-and-cream-cheese sandwiches, apple pandowdy, and orange snow. One fine old epicure, who had ordered a sizzling platter without specifying what food was to be on it, was nevertheless eating the platter itself and smacking his lips noisily. Small wonder that several world-famed illustrators, among them Henry Raleigh, Norman Rockwell and Pruett Carter, had set up easels and were limning the brilliant scene with swift strokes. I was drinking in every detail of the shifting panorama when a hostess well over nine feet tall, with ice mantling her summit, waved me toward a door marked "Credentials."

"We—we just wanted the old-fashioned nut pudding with ice-cream sauce, Ma'am," I stammered.

"That's up to the committee, Moozeer," she said briskly. "If we let in every Tom, Dick and Harry who wanted the old-fashioned nut pudding with ice-cream sauce . . . Ah, good evening, Contessa! Back from Hobe Sound already?"

I entered a small room exquisitely furnished in Biedermeier and took my place in a short queue of applicants. Most of them were obviously under tension, and the poor wretch in front of me was a pitiable spectacle. His eyes rolled wildly, tremors shook his frame, and it was apparent he entertained small hope of meeting the rigorous requirements.

"What have Kaufman and Hart got that I haven't got?" he demanded of me desperately. "I bought a house in Bucks County and wrote two plays, both smash hits, even if they didn't come to New York. Why, you ought to see the reviews *Tea and Strumpets* and *Once in a Wifetime* got in Syracuse!" I reassured him as best I could, but his premonitions were well founded, for a few moments later he was ignominiously dispatched to dine at a cafeteria. I was shuffling forward to confront the tight-lipped examiners when a scuffle broke out in the foyer and Kaufman and Hart, bundled in astrakhan greatcoats and their eyes flashing fire, were herded in unceremoniously.

"What is the meaning of this—this bestiality?" sputtered Hart. "How dare you bar us from this bourgeois *bistro*?"

"I've been thrown out of better restaurants than this!" boomed Kaufman, rapidly naming several high-class restaurants from which he had been ejected. The chairman of the board picked up a dossier and turned a cold smile on the playwrights.

"Naturally, we regret any inconvenience to you gentlemen," he said smoothly, "but our house rules are inflexible. You directed a play called *My Fair Lady*, did you not, Mr. Hart?" Hart regarded him stonily. "Starring Rex Harrison, I believe?"

"Yes," snapped Hart, "and he's sitting right up at the fountain this minute having a rum-and-butter-toffee sundae with chopped pecans."

"Why were we not shown the script of that play, Mr. Hart?" The chairman's voice was silky with menace. "Why was nobody in the Frank G. Shattuck organization consulted regarding casting?"

"I—I meant to," quavered Hart. "I swear I did! I told my secretary —I made a note—"

"Thought you'd smuggle it into town without us, did you?" snarled the chairman. "Let 'em read the out-of-town notices in *Variety*, eh?" A tide of crimson welled up the alabaster column of Hart's neck, and he stood downcast, staring at his toecaps. Kaufman would fain have interceded for his associate, but the chairman stopped him with a curt gesture.

"Hamburg Heaven for thirty days," he barked. "Take 'em away."

"Help, help!" screamed the luckless duo, abasing themselves. But no vestige of pity lurked in the chairman's granite visage, and an instant later they were borne, kicking and squealing, from the chamber by two brawny attendants.

And now little else remains to be told. How I managed to elude my captors and steal the superb mocha cupcake the natives call "The Star of Forty-third Street Between Sixth Avenue and Broadway" must be left to another chronicle. Suffice to say that whenever your mother and I pass Schrafft's, she turns to me with a secret smile and we continue right on up to Lindy's. We can still get in there without a visa.

❧ OUR UNBALANCED AQUARIUMS

IF YOU are going to be a smug little purist and agree with the Concise Oxford Dictionary that an aquarium is an "artificial pond or tank for the keeping of live aquatic plants and animals; place of public entertainment containing such tanks," you had better keep your arctics on, because this rookery is not large enough to hold both you and me. There is something about a home aquarium which sets my teeth on edge the moment I see it. Why anyone should want to live with a small container of stagnant water populated by a half-dead guppy is beyond me. Yet figures, which I am making up as I go along, state that one out of every eight people owns and operates an aquarium. It hardly seems possible, does it? Yet that is what figures state.

Fortunately, I have no figures whatsoever on *The Aquarium*, the monthly journal of the fish fancy issued by the Innes Publishing Company of Philadelphia. For all I know, I am its only reader, a rather creepy feeling somewhat like finding out that one is the only passenger on a transatlantic liner. Perhaps "sleepy" is more exact than "creepy," because the next thing I knew after struggling through "Success with *Macropodus cupanus*," by Joseph A. Elam, and "The Dwarf Gourami, *Colisa* lalia," by William T. Innes, in the February number of *The Aquarium,* the sunlight was streaming in and it was Thursday. The only thing that puzzles me is that I started reading these articles in bed at the Brevoort and woke up in a rowboat near Little Egg Inlet. Maybe "creepy" is the word, after all.

I know a man who keeps an ocelot, and I have seen Mistinguette with a sheep on a leash, but if *The Aquarium* really wants to steal into my heart, it will have to stop referring to fish as "pets." No fish ever gave the alarm in a burning building by barking or played with a ball of yarn on the hearth. The most you can say for the fish is that he has a certain icy composure and austere dignity, unlike those who take care of him. Of the several hundred letters which have appeared in the question-and-answer department of *The Aquarium* over a period of three years, not one has ever come from a fish. You don't catch *him* beefing about conditions to the editor or wringing his fins and wallowing in self-pity. Your true aquarist, however, emerges in the magazine as a febrile amateur, a bundle of nervous tics, and a pretty contemptible proposition. Let an unforeseen bubble burst in his tank and he flees to the "Correspondence" column to snuffle weakly and babble out his horrible blunders. The incredible saga of a Brooklyn fancier in the April issue of *The Aquarium* is a case in point:

To the Editor: About eight or nine weeks ago, four small *scalare* which I have raised from small specimens started on a hunger strike which I assumed was nothing out of the ordinary, judging from what you have written on the subject. This went on for about a month, when the smaller of the two original fish suddenly appeared to have a convulsion, swimming wildly along the surface of the water and coming to rest on his side at one corner of the tank with scarcely a sign of breathing. In a few moments he righted himself and then turned bottom side up.

His fins and body appeared to be in good condition. I immediately prepared a salt bath such as you prescribe, watching the proportions and temperature, and transferred him to it. For a while it looked as though he was through, as he spent most of his time on his back. Finally he righted himself and I kept him in the "salt hospital" for a week, freshening the solution every two days as directed.

At the end of the week, and just about as I had about decided to return him to the home tank, the other original *scalare* went through a similar contortion, although he did not seem to have such a bad attack as his smaller brother. I transferred him to the salt and kept both fish in that solution for another week.

They seemed much improved, so I gradually sweetened the water and then returned them to the community tank. All this time they had eaten nothing, nor had the remaining two angel fish been interested in food. (I feed them on Tubifex worms altogether.)

Three weeks ago the two smaller *scalare* recovered their appetites and are now enjoying their meals regularly, but the other two (that had the salt treatment) are still on strike and both appear to be blind. They act very much as though they could not see where they are going and I have tried various tests which seem to bear out my contention that their sight is gone.

They still seem to be in good condition so far as appearance of fins and body are concerned, although the larger fish has three small white spots on either side of his head directly above his eyes. These are easily discernible and regularly placed. Two weeks ago I subjected

him to the HC1 treatment as you suggest, and after four days returned him to the larger tank despite the fact that the spots still
remain.

I have carefully watched the temperature of my tanks and at no
time to my knowledge have they dropped lower than 65 degrees or
gone above 85.

Naturally, I should like very much to save these two pets if possible, and any suggestions you may care to offer will certainly be
gratefully received.—J. S. T.

This amazing tissue of hypocrisy and contradiction made me see red
for days. Such false endearments as "angel fish" and "pets" deceive
nobody. These four fish, brutalized by a starvation diet of Tubifex
worms, with never a finger of grog or a bit of plum duff to relieve the
monotony, went on a hunger strike. Our fine friend, despite his soapy
assurances, behaved with a fiendishness worthy of the notorious Captain Bligh. But where the latter would have had the mutineers seized up
at the forward gangway and given twelve dozen of the cat, this De Kalb
Avenue Bluebeard invents modern refinements for his captives. Deep
in his underground torture chambers he submerges the mute little fellows in diabolic "salt hospitals," performs bloodcurdling "tests" on
them, and altogether conducts himself like a character in a Universal
picture. Pray God that there is still time to circumvent his satanic
schemes. If volunteers will come forward within the next thirty-six
hours, I shall gladly lead a rescue party to his lair in back of the delicatessen store and batter down the steel doors. A fig for his murderous
beta rays and pale-green henchmen; let me once draw a bead on him
with my Buck Rogers pistol and I wouldn't want to be in *his* shoes,
thank you.

ANOTHER pair of shoes I have no desire to tenant are those of the resident of Collingswood, New Jersey, whose quavering letter appeared in
the October number. It painted a pretty picture of suburban life:

> *To the Editor:* I am having serious trouble with the fish in my
> lily pool. For the past three weeks they have stayed constantly at the
> top. Half of them have now died or been caught by cats and birds,
> and the remainder are in very bad condition, with frayed and con-
> gested fins, lice and fungus. The bottom of the pool seems to be
> coated with a layer of black muck having a horrible odor when dis-
> turbed. The only substances I have put in the water are bone meal

and dried blood to fertilize the lilies, about four pounds of rock salt, one-half pound of Epsom salt, and twelve boxes of a popular fish tonic. The pool holds about 900 gallons.

The fact that rains have caused the pool to overflow twice, carrying grass cuttings into the water, and the further fact that a large number of seeds from a nearby white maple blew in this spring, may have a bearing on the case. A number of goldfish fry about three-quarters of an inch long, which were hatched in the pool this year, seem to be unaffected.

If you can tell me the cause of my trouble and how to remedy it, I shall be very grateful.—J. G. F.

The cause of J. G. F.'s "trouble," as he calls it, is nothing more or less than loose thinking. "Lily pool" is no longer the word for the morass of fertilizer, rock and Epsom salts, fish tonic, grass cuttings, and white-maple seeds in his back yard. There are, luckily, two remedies at hand. The first is for him to disappear. I don't mean move to another address or hide; I mean disappear completely, like a puff of smoke. The second is easier, and is my way out. As I sit here watching the last charred embers of the bound volumes of *The Aquarium* glowing in the grate, a hushed peace invades the room. Rising, I cross softly to my own little aquarium, demolish it with a single blow of the hammer, and grind my little pets under my heel. Then, squaring my shoulders and with head erect, I give myself up to the S. P. C. A.

🌿 BUTTON, BUTTON, WHO'S GOT THE BLEND?

ABOUT EIGHT O'CLOCK last night I was lounging at the corner of Hollywood Boulevard and Vine Street, an intersection celebrated in the eclogues of Louella Parsons and Ed Sullivan, waiting for a pert baggage who had agreed to accompany me to a double feature. If I bore myself with a certain assurance, it was because I had chosen my wardrobe with some care—a shower-of-hail suit, lilac gloves, a split-sennit boater, and a light whangee cane. Altogether, I had reason for self-satisfaction; I had dined famously off a charmburger and a sky-high malt, my cigar was drawing well, and the titles of the pictures I was about to witness, *Block That Kiss* and *Khaki Buckaroo*, augured gales of merriment. For a moment high spirits tempted me to invest in a box of maxixe cherries or fondant creams for my vis-à-vis, but after due reflection I fought back the impulse. How utterly cloying, how anticlimactic sweets would be after the speeches I had in store for the pretty creature!

Weary at last of studying the colorful throng eddying past me (I had already singled out Eddy Duchin, Sherwood Eddy, Eddie Cantor, Nelson Eddy, and Eddie Robinson), I fell to examining a nearby billboard. The advertisement was one of that familiar type in which an entire cross section of the population seems to be rhapsodizing about the product—in this case, a delicacy named Hostess Cup Cakes. "You should hear my bridge club rave about those Hostess Cup Cakes," an excited housewife was babbling to her friend, whose riposte was equally feverish: "I wouldn't dare pack John's lunch without putting in Hostess Cup Cakes!" Close by, a policeman smiled benignly at a baby in a carriage, addressing its mother with, "You have a lot of time for 'Precious' these afternoons, Mrs. Jones." The reason for Mrs. Jones's leisure was not unpredictable: "That's because it's easy to plan desserts with Hostess Cup Cakes." The baby itself was making no contribution to the symposium; apparently the kitten had got hold of its tongue, but you could tell from its expression that it would creep a mile for a cupcake. It was, however, with a dialogue between two small boys that the copywriter kindled my interest into flame. "Hurry!" one of them was admonishing the other. "I've got 5c for Hostess Cup Cakes!" "Oh, boy!" chortled his companion. "Do I love that *secret chocolate blend!*"

Although the romantic possibilities of a secret chocolate blend and its theft by the spies of an enemy power are undeniable, I think that behind the phrase there lurks a warmer, more personal story. Naturally, the brief harlequinade which follows can indicate no more than its highlights, but if the Hostess Cup Cake people care to endow me for the next few months, I could expand it into a three-act version, suitable for annual presentation at Hollywood and Vine. I have no further use for that corner, or, may I add, for my *petite amie*, who turned up sobbing drunk with a Marine on either arm.

SCENE: *The office of Dirk van Bensdorp, president and general manager of the Hostess Cup Cake Corporation. As the curtain rises, Dirk, a forceful executive, is reading a lecture to his ne'er-do-well nephew, Jan Gluten, a minor employee of the firm. The latter fidgets nervously with an icing gun. His eyes are puffy with lack of sleep and the little lines radiating from his nose attest eloquently to fondness for the grape.*

DIRK (*warningly*): Now, look here, my boy, I'm going to talk to you like a Dutch uncle. Bakery circles are abuzz with your escapades. You had better mend your ways ere I lose patience.

JAN (*surlily*): Aw, can de sermon.

DIRK: It's a stench in the nostrils of the cupcake trade—throwing away your guilders on fly chorus girls and driving your Stutz Bearcat in excess of sixty m.p.h.

JAN (*lighting a cigarette with nicotine-stained fingers*): I'm getting sick of dis joint. Every time I take a schnapps or two wit' de fellers, some willy boy splits on me to de front office.

DIRK (*severely*): It's your work that gives you away, my fine fellow. That last tray of fig bars you frosted was a botch!

JAN (*lamely*): Dere was a fly in de amber icing.

DIRK: Excuses, excuses! Why, the complaints I've had about your work would almost fill a book. (*He holds up a book almost filled with complaints about Jan's work, a first edition.*) And what's this about the attentions you have been paying a certain raven-haired miss in the custard division?

JAN (*fiercely*): You keep Lorene Flake's name out of dis, d'ye hear?

DIRK (*aside*): I see I have touched the lad in a vulnerable spot. This seems to be more than mere philandering.

JAN: Lorene's decent, and clean, and—and fine! She's straight as a string, I tell you!

DIRK (*who loves a good joke now and then*): That's probably why you're "knots" about her—ha-ha-ha!

JAN: Sharrap.

DIRK (*earnestly*): Why not prove yourself to the girl, Jan? Eschew your dubious associates and turn over a new chocolate leaf.

JAN: Hully gee, I ain't fit to kiss de cuff of her slacks.

DIRK: Do your job and you'll win through. Make the cupcakes fly under your fingers!

JAN (*cynically*): Aw, rats. Youse is attempting to fob off de speed-up system under de cloak of benevolent paternalism. (*He exits.*)

DIRK: Ah, well, there's good stuff in the boy. I was the same at his age. (*Ten Eyck, the shop foreman, bursts in, his face ashen.*)

TEN EYCK (*panting*): The formula—

DIRK: What is it, man? What's happened?

TEN EYCK: The secret chocolate blend—gone—stolen!

DIRK (*sputtering*): Ten thousand devils! But I locked it in the safe myself last night!

TEN EYCK: I found the door wrenched off, beside it an acetylene torch and a complete set of burglar's tools.

DIRK (*instantly*): Someone must have opened the safe by force! (*A heavy footfall is heard on the stair.*)

TEN EYCK: Why, who can that be?

DIRK: God grant that it may be Inspector Bunce, he who gave us such material assistance in that mysterious affair of the oatmeal cookies! (*His prayers are answered; Bunce enters, looks about him keenly.*) Inspector, our secret choc—

BUNCE: Yes, I know. When I find a safe pried open, a series of unfrosted cupcakes, and two middle-aged bakers in a notable state of agitation, the conclusions are fairly obvious.

DIRK: You mean that the finger of suspicion points to Loose-Wiles, the Thousand Window Bakeries, whose agents have recently been skulking about in dirty gray caps and gooseneck sweaters?

BUNCE: This is an inside job, Bensdorp. I should like a few words with your nephew.

DIRK (*paling*): Surely you don't believe Jan—

BUNCE: Please be good enough to call him. (*Dirk, bewildered, presses a button and Jan shuffles in sullenly.*) Well, Gluten, still sticking to your story?

JAN (*sneering*): I ain't got nuttin' else to add, see? I pinched de secret chocolate plans to pay for de extravagances of an actress I was infatuated wit'. It's an oft-told story, rendered none de less sordid by repetition.

BUNCE (*with deadly calm*): One moment. *Why are you shielding Vernon Flake?*

JAN (*roughly*): I never heard of de cove. Come on, clap de darbies on me wrists. I'm ready to face de music.

BUNCE: It won't wash, Jan. You found Vernon, Lorene's worthless brother, crouched before the safe and to protect the girl you love you have shouldered the blame yourself!

JAN (*modestly*): Any bloke in me shoes would have done de equivalent.

DIRK: Hooray! I was convinced of his innocence at all times!

JAN (*producing a cinnamon bun*): And here is de formula inside dis sweetmeat, where de luckless Vernon hid it for safekeeping.

BUNCE: You've a smart cub there, Bensdorp. Nephews of his stripe don't grow on trees. (*reaching for his Persian slipper*) Well, Ten Eyck, what do you say to Sarasate at the Albert Hall tonight, eh?

TEN EYCK: Capital, my dear Bunce. (*They exit.*)

DIRK (*embracing Jan*): Well, you young rascal, you shall have your reward for this. Henceforth our Friday specials will be known as "Cub Cakes" in your honor—and remember, there's always room for brains at the top in this organization.

JAN (*surreptitiously pocketing his uncle's stickpin*): You said a mout'ful, cul.

CURTAIN

❦ A FAREWELL TO OMSK

(The terrifying result of reading an entire gift set of Dostoevsky in one afternoon.)

LATE ONE AFTERNOON in January 18—, passersby in L. Street in the town of Omsk might have seen a curious sight. A young man of a somewhat flushed, feverish appearance was standing outside Pyotr Pyotrvitch's tobacco shop. This in itself was interesting, as Pyotr Pyotrvitch had no tobacco shop in L. Street. Even had he had one, there would have been a large gaping hole in the sidewalk in front of it due to a sewer excavation, so that only the top of the young man's head would be visible. Of itself there was nothing unusual in the spectacle of a young man standing up to his knees in water staring fixedly at the fresh loam piled up about him. What amused the passersby was that any one should want to go into Pyotr Pyotrvitch's shop, since it was common knowledge that Pyotr had died some years before of the bends and his shop had been converted into an abattoir or worse. Indeed, there were those who maintained that the shop had never been there at all—was, in short, a sort of mirage such as is often seen by travelers in the desert. But there was such a look of idealism on the young man's face, of the kind which is so often to be observed nowadays in our Russian university students, that the irreverent titters and cries of "Ach, pfoo!" were quickly silenced. Finally the young man sighed deeply, cast a look of determination around him, and entered the shop.

"Good afternoon, Pyotr Pyotrvitch!" he said resolutely.

"Good afternoon, Afya Afyakievitch!" replied the shopkeeper warmly. He was the son of a former notary public attached to the household of Prince Grashkin and gave himself no few airs in consequence. Whilst speaking it was his habit to extract a greasy barometer from his waistcoat and consult it importantly, a trick he had learned from the Prince's barber. On seeing Afya Afyakievitch he skipped about nimbly, dusted off the counter, gave one of his numerous offspring a box on the ear, drank a cup of tea, and on the whole behaved like a man of the world who has affairs of moment occupying him.

"Well, Afya Afyakievitch," he said with a sly smile, "what can I sell you today? Cigarettes, perhaps?"

"Cigarettes?" repeated the young man vaguely. A peculiar shudder passed over his frame as he regarded the top of Pyotr's head intently. It was just wide enough to fit the blade of an ax. A strange smile played about his lips, and only the entrance of another personage distracted him. This was none other than Alaunia Alaunovna, the shopkeeper's daughter, a prostitute with a look of exaltation on her timid face, who entered and stood unobtrusively in a corner.

"How patient she is!" thought the young man, his heart touched. An overpowering desire to throw himself at her feet and kiss the hem of her garment filled his being.

"Well, well!" exclaimed Pyotr Pyotrvitch, anxious to impress his customer. "Allow me, kind sir, to present my daughter, Alaunia Alaunovna. She is a girl of education—he, he!" A stifling feeling overcame the young man; he wanted to throw himself at the man's feet and bite them. Alaunia Alaunovna dropped a small curtsy. The young man, a pitying expression on his face, picked it up and quickly returned it to her. She gave him a grateful glance named Joe.

"And—and what does your daughter do?" Afya asked with emotion.

"She is a prostitute in a small way of business," replied Pyotr proudly.

"It's great work if you can get it," the young man stammered.

"Permit me, it is the only way to live!" cried the shopkeeper excitedly. But by now Afya was even more excited than he was.

"Ah yes—excuse me—that is to say!" he began confusedly. A swarm of thoughts filled his brain. "I used to know a man, a titular councilor, Andron Andronovitch Pojarsky, in the province of Z——. We were in the Gymnasium together. Well, only fancy, last night I met him at the Petrovsky Bridge, as I was returning from Dunya's where we were having a discussion of certain ideas, I won't go into them, but Pimentov—he is a goodhearted fellow, he had entered into a free marriage with his cousin—*tfoo*, how I wander! Well, this Andron Andronovitch, poor fellow, is in a bad way, in a word is reduced to eating his rubbers, all he has left, in a certain sense. Ach, these Slavophiles!" broke off Afya, taking out some old pieces of cucumber and fish he had been carrying in his pocket and dipping them in his tea. "Just imagine, he has such extreme notions—Utopias, one might say . . ."

"Yes! Yes!" interrupted Pyotr, nodding with great rapidity, almost perspiring with excitement. "But you spoke formerly of cigarettes, did you not? Here is a good brand—fifteen kopecks a package, or two packages for twenty-five kopecks! A brand much favored by the garrison, young gentleman!"

"Fifteen kopecks?" asked Afya slowly. "Then the second package must be only ten kopecks?"

"True, young sir," said Pyotr, screwing up his little red-rimmed eyes in the manner of one who is about to inspect a private vivarium. "But unfortunately I have only one package."

"Pyotr Pyotrvitch," said the young man quietly, "do you know what I think? I think this is a hell of a tobacco shop, in any language."

"You're telling *me*?" inquired Pyotr sadly. "Hey, where are you going? Just a moment—come, a cup of tea—let's have a discussion . . ."

"I'll be right outside in that sewer excavation if you want me," said Afya over his shoulder. "I'd sort of like to brood over things for a while."

"Well, skip the gutter," sighed Pyotr.

"Don't take any flannel kopecks," said Afya gloomily. He dislodged a piece of horse-radish from his tie, shied it at a passing Nihilist, and slid forward into the fresh loam.

❧ *CAPTAIN FUTURE, BLOCK THAT KICK!*

I GUESS I'm just an old mad scientist at bottom. Give me an underground laboratory, half a dozen atom-smashers, and a beautiful girl in a diaphanous veil waiting to be turned into a chimpanzee, and I care not who writes the nation's laws. You'll have to leave my meals on a tray outside the door because I'll be working pretty late on the secret of making myself invisible, which may take me almost until eleven o'clock. Oh, yes, and don't let's forget one more thing. I'll need a life subscription to a new quarterly journal called *Captain Future, Wizard of Science*, a bright diadem on the forehead of Better Publications, 22 West Forty-eighth Street, New York City.

As one who triggered a disintegrator with Buck Rogers and could dash off a topographical map of Mongo or Dale Arden with equal facility, I thought in my pride and arrogance I knew all there was to know about astronomical adventure. It was something of a shock, therefore, to find out several days back that I was little more than a slippered pantaloon. Beside Captain Future, Wizard of Science, Flash Gordon and the Emperor Ming pale to a couple of nursery tots chewing on Holland rusk.

The novelette in which this spectacular *caballero* makes his bow to "scientification" fans opens with no fumbling preamble or prosy exposition. Into the office of James Carthew, President of the Earth Government, staggers a giant ape, barely recognizable by the President as John Sperling, his most trusted secret agent. The luckless investigator had been ordered to Jupiter to look into a complaint that some merry-andrew was causing atavism among the Jovians, but apparently had got badly jobbed. Before Carthew can intervene, a frightened guard drills the ape man with a flare-pistol, and in his dying breath the latter lays the blame for his predicament squarely at the door of a mysterious being he calls the Space Emperor. As you may well imagine, Carthew is all of a tizzy. He immediately instructs his secretary to send for Captain Future in the ringing phrase, "Televise the meteorological rocket-patrol base at Spitzbergen. Order them to flash the magnesium flare signal from the North Pole." Personally, I think Carthew might have

softened this whiplike command with "And just for the hell of it, why
don't you try the Princeton Club?" but perhaps I delve too deeply. In
any event, the perpetual uranium clock has hardly ticked off two hours
before Captain Future (or Curt Newton, to call him by his given name)
appears on the escarpment with one of the most endearing speeches
in my experience:

"You know my assistants," Curt Newton said shortly, "Grag the
robot, Otho the android, and Simon Wright, the Living Brain. We came
from the moon full speed when I saw your signal. What's wrong?"

Fiction teems with sinister escorts and everybody has his favorite,
but Captain Future's three-man mob leaves the worst of them kissed
off and frozen against the cushion:

> A weird shape had just leaped onto the balcony. It was a manlike
> figure, but one whose body was rubbery, boneless-looking, blank-
> white in color. He wore a metal harness, and his long, slitted green
> unhuman eyes peered brightly out of an alien white face. Following
> this rubbery android, or synthetic man, came another figure, equally
> as strange—a giant metal robot who strode across the balcony on
> padded feet. He towered seven feet high. In his bulbous metal head
> gleamed a pair of photoelectric eyes. The robot's left hand carried
> the handle of a square transparent box. Inside it a living brain was
> housed. In the front of the case were the Brain's two glittering glass
> lens-eyes. Even now they were moving on their flexible metal stalks
> to look at the President.

At this juncture I took time out to moisten my lips with the tip of
my tongue, retrieved my own eyeballs, and plunged on. Captain Future
himself was somewhat more tailored than his comrades, in fact quite
swagger. "His unruly shock of red hair towered six feet four above the
floor, and his wide lithe shoulders threatened to burst the jacket of his
gray synthesilk zipper-suit." In pulp fiction it is a rigid convention
that the hero's shoulders and the heroine's *balcon* constantly threaten
to burst their bonds, a possibility which keeps the audience in a state
of tense expectancy. Unfortunately for the fans, however, recent tests
reveal that the wisp of chiffon which stands between the publisher and
the postal laws has the tensile strength of drop-forged steel.

To acquaint the reader more fully with "that tall, cheerful, red-haired
young adventurer of the ready laugh and flying fists, the implacable
Nemesis of all oppressors and exploiters of the System's human and
planetary races," the author interrupts his smoking narrative with a

brief dossier. In the year 1900, the brilliant young Earth biologist Roger Newton, aided by the living brain of Simon Wright ("the greatest brain in scientific history"), had unraveled the secret of artificial life. Now, certain dark forces headed by one Victor Corvo were determined to appropriate Newton's secret. To confound him, Roger Newton proposed to Elaine, his wife, and the Living Brain that they conceal themselves on the moon.

"But the moon!" Elaine exclaimed, deep repulsion shadowing her eyes. "That barren, airless globe that no one ever visits!" Elaine's dainty disgust is pardonable; Far Rockaway out of season could not have been more painfully *vieux jeu*. A few weeks, nevertheless, see the little company snugly housed under the surface of Tycho crater upon the moon, where its number is swelled by the addition of the infant Curt and Grag the robot, whom Roger and the Living Brain construct in their spare time of neurons and nails and puppy dogs' tails. Eventually, still another fruit of this intellectual union—Otho, the synthetic android—is capering about the laboratory. Just as Newton is on the verge of returning to earth, up turns Public Bad Penny No. 1, Victor Corvo, and slays him and his wife. When the Brain assures him vengeance will be swift, Corvo hurls the taunt supreme at the preserved scientist: "Don't try to threaten me, you miserable bodiless brain! I'll soon silence you—" He stops throwing his weight around soon enough when Grag and Otho burst in, and, directed by the Brain, rub him out effectively if none too tidily.

Dying, Elaine Newton entrusts Curt to the care of the trio in a scene which must affect the sensibilities of the most callous:

> "Tell him to war always against those who would pervert science to sinister ambition," whispered Elaine. "I will tell him," promised the Brain, and in its toneless metallic voice was a queer catch.

The guardians justify Elaine's faith in them to a degree; by the time Curt has attained his majority, he is one lovely hunk of boy, a hybrid of Leonardo da Vinci and Dink Stover. From then on, as Captain Future, Curt ranges the solar system with his pals in an asteroidal supership, the *Comet*, avenging his folks and relentlessly waging war on what the author is pleased to call "interplanetary crime."

But to return to our muttons, if so prosaic a term can be applied to the streamlined quartet. Speeding outward into space toward Jovopolis, chief Earthman colony on Jupiter, Captain Future plucks haunting music from his twenty-string Venusian guitar while Grag and Otho tend the controls and the Living Brain burrows into textbooks for a clue to the atavism. Their snug *Kaffeeklatsch* is blasted when a piratical black space-cruiser suddenly looms across the *Comet's* bows and attempts to ambush the party, but Curt's proton beams force the attacker down on Callisto, outermost of Jupiter's four biggest moons. The boys warp in alongside and Grag prepares to rip open the jammed door of the pirate craft so his master may question the miscreants:

> Grag's big metal fingers were removable. The robot rapidly unscrewed two of them and replaced them with small drills which he took from a kit of scalpels, chisels, and similar tools carried in a little locker in his metal side. Then Grag touched a switch on his wrist. The two drills which had replaced two of his fingers whirled hummingly. He quickly used them to drill six holes in the edge of the ship's door. Then he replaced the drills with his fingers, hooked six fingers inside the holes he had made.

The rest is brute strength, a department in which Grag is pre-eminent. Inside are Jon Orris and Martin Skeel, whose names instantly tip them off as wrong guys. Yet it is impossible not to be moved by Orris' pathetic confession: "Skeel and I have criminal records. We fled out here after we got into a murder scrape on Mars." They admit under pressure that they are creatures of the Space Emperor, though actually they have never seen him. "He's always concealed in a big, queer black suit, and he speaks out of it in a voice that don't sound human to me," Skeel says.

Time, even on Callisto, is a-wastin', and nimbly dodging a plague of creeping crystals which bids fair to annihilate them, the space-farers resume their course. On their arrival at Jovopolis, Otho the android disguises himself as Orris and repairs to that worthy's hut to await the Space Emperor and overpower him so that Captain Future can steal up and clap the darbies on him. Arriving at the rendezvous, the Emperor promptly makes himself invisible and Curt leaps through him, only to sprawl on his finely chiseled beezer.

Recovering from this contretemps with his usual sunny equanimity, Curt hastens to the mansion of the governor, Sylvanus Quale, to reconnoiter. Here he encounters the heart interest, a plump little cabbage named Joan Randall, who is head nurse to the chief planetary physician. Lucas Brewer, a shifty radium magnate, Mark Cannig, his mine superintendent, and Eldred Kells, the vice-governor, are also at the mansion. It is apparent at once to the *cognoscenti* that any one of these worthies is the Space Emperor, and with no personal bias other than that his name had a particularly sneaky sound, I put my money on Eldred Kells. Fifty pages later I was proved right, but not before I had been locked in an atavism ward with Curt and Joan, flung into a pit by the green flipper-men, and nibbled by giant six-foot rats called "diggers" (a surprisingly mild name for a giant six-foot rat, by the way). But even such hazards, for all their jeweled prose, cannot compare with the description of the main street of Jungletown:

> Here were husky prospectors in stained zipper-suits, furtive, unshaven space-bums begging, cool-eyed interplanetary gamblers, gaunt engineers in high boots with flare-pistols at their belts, bronzed spacesailors up from Jovopolis for a carousal in the wildest new frontier town in the System.

And so, all too soon for both Joan Randall and myself, comes the hour of parting with "the big red-head," as the author shakily describes Curt in a final burst of emotion. In the next issue, Captain Future and his creepy constabulary will doubtless be summoned forth again to combat some horror as yet to be devised. Meanwhile I like to think of his lighthearted rebuke to Otho the android, already chafing against inactivity:

> "Sooner or later, there'll be another call from Earth, and then I hope there's action enough for you, you crazy coot."

There may be another call, Curt, but it won't come from Baby. Right now all he wants is a cup of hot milk and fourteen hours of shut-eye. And if it's all the same to you, he'll do his sleeping with the lights on.

KITCHEN BOUQUET

YESTERDAY MORNING I awoke from a deep dream of peace compounded of equal parts of allonal and Vat 69 to find that autumn was indeed here. The last leaf had fluttered off the sycamore and the last domestic of the summer solstice had packed her bindle and caught the milk train out of Trenton. Peace to her ashes, which I shall carry up henceforward from the cellar. Stay as sweet as you are, honey, and don't drive through any open drawbridges is my Christmas wish for Leota Claflin. And lest the National Labor Relations Board (just plain "Nat" to its friends, of whom I am one of the stanchest) summon me to the hustings for unfair employer tactics, I rise to offer in evidence as pretty a nosegay of houseworkers as ever fried a tenderloin steak. Needless to say, the characters and events depicted herein are purely imaginary, and I am a man who looks like Prince Philip and dances like Fred Astaire.

The first reckless crocus of March was nosing up through the lawn as I sprang from the driver's seat, spread my cloak across a muddy spot, and obsequiously handed down Philomène Labruyère—colored, no laundry. Philomène was a dainty thing, built somewhat on the order of Lois De Fee, the lady bouncer. She had the rippling muscles of a panther, the stolidity of a water buffalo, and the lazy insolence of a shoe salesman. She stood seventy-five inches in her stocking feet, which I will take my Bible oath were prehensile. As she bent down to lift her suitcase, she picked up the car by mistake and had it halfway down the slope before I pointed out her mistake. She acknowledged the reproof with a glance of such sheer hatred that I knew at once I should have kept my lip buttoned. After all, perhaps the woman wanted my automobile in her bedroom for some purpose of her own.

"You—you can take it up with you if you want," I stammered, thinking to retrieve her esteem. "I've got plenty of others—I mean I've got plenty of nothing—I mean—" With my ears glowing, I attempted to conceal my *gaffe* by humming a few bars of "Summertime," but her cold, appraising glance told me that Philomène had me pegged.

"Whuh kine place *is* this?" she rumbled suspiciously. "You mus' be crazy."

"But aren't we all?" I reminded her with a charming smile. *"C'est la maladie du temps*—the sickness of the times—don't you think? *Fin-de-siècle* and lost generation, in a way. 'I should have been a pair of ragged claws scuttling across the floors of silent seas.' How well Eliot puts it! D'ye ever see any of the old *transition* crowd?" I skipped along doing my best to lighten her mood, carried her several hatboxes, and even proffered a reefer, but there was no doubt in either of our minds who had the upper hand.

That Philomène was a manic-depressive in the downhill phase was, of course, instantly apparent to a boy of five. Several boys of five, who happened to be standing around and were by way of being students of psychopathology, stated their belief to me in just those words: "Manic-depressive, downhill phase." At the close of business every evening, Philomène retired to her room armed with a sixteen-inch steak knife, doubtless to ward off an attack by her Poltergeist. She then spent the best part of an hour barricading her door with dressers, armoires, and other heavy furniture, preparatory to sleeping with the lights on. I say "sleeping" utterly without conviction; she undoubtedly molded lead statues of her employer and crooned to them over a slow fire.

But if her behavior was erratic, there was no lack of consistency in Philomène's cuisine. Meat loaf and cold fried chicken succeeded each other with the deadly precision of tracer bullets. At last, when blood and sinew could stand no more and I was about to dissolve the union, I suddenly discovered that this female Paul Bunyan had grown to womanhood under the bright skies of Martinique, and I knew a moment of elation. I let it be bruited through the servants' hall that I would look tolerantly on fried plantain, yams, and succulent rice dishes. That afternoon the kitchen was a hive of activity. The air was heavy with saffron, pimento, and allspice. I heard snatches of West Indian Calypsos, caught a glimpse of Philomène's head swathed in a gay bandanna. With the care befitting a special occasion, I dressed negligently but with unimpeachable taste in whites and cummerbund, mixed myself several excellent stengahs, and sauntered in to dinner for all the world like an up-country tea planter. A few moments later, Philomène entered with what might be called a smoking salver except for the circumstance that it was stone cold. On it lay the wing and undercarriage of an even colder chicken, flanked by two segments of meat loaf.

After five minutes of reflection, during which, I am told, my features closely resembled a Japanese print, I arose and, throwing out my tiny chest, marched into the kitchen. The maledictions withered on my lips. Seated at the table, my black hibiscus blossom was tucking in a meal consisting of *potage Parmentier avec croûtons*, a crisp *gigot, salade fatiguée*, and *pot de crème au chocolat*.

"You—thing," I said at length, and five minutes later Philoméne was on her way back to St. Pierre.

Her successor was a chapfallen Australian cadaver who had reached his zenith as steward of a country club in Pompton Lakes and treated me and mine with the tired fatalism of a social worker. For some reason I never could fathom, unless it was that I occasionally wore a Tattersall vest, William persisted in regarding me as a racing man. He could recall every entry in the Cesarewitch Sweepstakes since 1899 and did, but faced with a pot roast, he assumed a wooden incomprehension that would have done credit to a Digger Indian. It was William's opinion, freely given, that cooked food was dead food and that I would triple my energy by living on fronds. He knew a hundred different ways of preparing bran, each more ghastly than the last. For an avowed vegetarian (or "raw-fooder," as he described himself), he spent his leisure in a puzzling enough fashion, polishing and whetting the superb collection of Swedish steel carving knives that was the one relic of his former magnificence.

William hadn't been with us long before I began to feel uneasy, but I attributed my disquiet to Edmund Pearson's admirable study of the Lizzie Borden case, which I was reading at the time. And then, on the sultry morning of August 4th—by an uncanny coincidence the forty-seventh anniversary of the Fall River holocaust—I came down to find awaiting me an exact duplicate of the breakfast which had been served on Second Street that fateful morning: warmed-over mutton soup, cold mutton, and bananas. I am not unduly superstitious, but there is no sense flying in the face of history. I left the check and the usual reference on William's bureau and hid in the woods until traintime.

The time had now come, I felt, for plain speaking. I inserted two and a half inches in the metropolitan press setting forth my special needs. I wanted something stout and motherly, with floury hands and a hot apple pie cooling on the window sill. What I got was an ancient Latvian beldam named Ilyeana, who welcomed the idea of living in the country with such alacrity I was convinced she must be a fugitive from justice. Her cooking did nothing to contradict the impression; three nights hand running she served mulligan and coffee made in a tin and seemed strangely familiar with the argot of hobo jungles. How near I was to the bull's-eye was revealed a week later with the arrival of a letter sent to Ilyeana by relatives in Canada. She ripped open the envelope and a newspaper clipping fell to the floor. I picked it up and was about to hand it to her when I saw the sinister heading, "Missing Man Believed Found." The Mounties, idly dragging a lake near Moose Jaw, Saskatchewan, had recovered some parcels which, laid end to end, turned out to be the body of a man. "The victim's sister, whom the authorities would like to question," the account added, "is at present thought to be in Latvia." Far from being in Latvia, the victim's sister was standing at that exact moment peering over my shoulder in good old Tinicum Township, Pennsylvania. I cleared my throat and edged a little closer to the fire tongs.

"What do you make of this, Ilyeana?" I asked. I knew damn well what she made of it, but you have to begin *somewhere*.

"Ah, this happen every time I get good job," she said. "Always pickin' on me. Well, I guess I go up there and take a look at him. I know that head of hair anywhere."

At the station, Ilyeana bought a ticket to Savannah, which would seem a rather circuitous route to the Dominion, but nobody was surprised, least of all the passenger agent. What with people winging through to Martinique, Australia, and similar exotic climes, that little New Jersey depot could give cards and spades to Shepheard's Hotel in Cairo. And speaking of spades, could anybody put me on to one named Uncle Pompey, with a frizzy white poll and a deft hand with grits?

❧ *BOY MEETS GIRL MEETS FOOT*

ANYBODY WHO CHANCED to be flatboating down the Sunday book-review sections lately, poling his way through such nifties as *Bismarck: A New Synthesis*, by Dr. Stauffer, or *A Deciduous Girl of Old Williamsburgh*, by Sara Leamington Latrobe, probably wound up the day in a darkened room applying vinegar poultices freely to his forehead. It would seem from the publishers' spring lists that the entire Hippocratic fraternity had forsworn the art of healing in favor of letters. Possibly because of the general world breakdown, the family doctor whose reticence was celebrated in song and story has suddenly caved in and become a garrulous old chatterbox, buttonholing the passerby and babbling your most cherished anatomical secrets. Since the success of Dr. Victor Heiser, a veritable freshet of reminiscence has been roaring through the bookshops. If turnabout is fair play and a layman may diagnose his physician's complaint, the boys who wrote *The Horse and Buggy Doctor*, *Consultation Room*, and *Doctor, Here's Your Hat* are down with a thundering case of *furor scribendi*. Gone the spatula and the glittering optical mirror, and in their place the quill pen and the purple patch. If you have been looking for a bargain in secondhand scalpels, this is your golden opportunity. But it looks like a hell of a summer for invalids.

It remained for Dr. Dudley J. Morton of the College of Physicians and Surgeons at Columbia, however, to invest the common or garden foot with glamour and employ it as material for romance. In *Oh, Doctor! My Feet!* undeniably the most plaintive title of the season, Dr. Morton sets your foot tapping, if only to convince yourself that it still articulates. Dr. Morton has builded better than he knew; the reader becomes so acutely aware of his feet that he spends his day listening with a rather cunning expression to his toes meshing into gear. My experience has been that although this type of work is not exhausting, it pays very badly.

Dr. Morton, with a sense of dramatic value not commonly encountered in orthopedists, opens his narrative explosively. Into the office of a Dr. Nelson, shouting, "Oh, Doctor! *My feet!*" bursts Mrs. Roberts, an attractive young matron. Conscious of the brusqueness of her words, she adds hastily, "Oh, please forgive me, Dr. Nelson, but my feet burn and ache so I scarcely know what to do." Dr. Nelson soothingly guides her to a chair with, "Well, you have done the rational thing by coming to see me, for I'm certain I can help you." I suppose the irrational thing for Mrs. Roberts would have been to consult a blacksmith, but I myself would have liked her better for it. As a matter of fact, Dr. Morton throughout portrays Mrs. Roberts as something of a creep, which I suspect is a deep-seated conviction among doctors about their patients. She is scarcely seated when her face expresses "a considerable degree of surprise." "Why, I didn't know you were interested in feet, Doctor." By one of those amazing coincidences which happen only in fiction, Dr. Nelson turns out to be the ideal party to whom Mrs. Roberts should have brought her feet. He invites her to relate her symptoms. "Well, Doctor," Mrs. Roberts replies, "they started to bother me about two years ago and since then I've tried almost everything. My closet is so full of shoes I've bought on recommendation or seen advertised that my husband laughs at me and suggests I open a store." You will notice that Dr. Morton, not content with delineating Mrs. Roberts as a simpleton, gratuitously insinuates her husband is a red-faced, bull-necked extrovert who taunts his wife with her malady. Somehow, it left me with the uncomfortable feeling that the author had poisoned a well. Try as I would, I kept seeing Mr. Roberts in my mind's eye as a sort of Dr. Grimesby Roylott, a savage tyrant who goes around kicking open doors and bending pokers double.

Oddly enough, at this very juncture Dr. Nelson puts on a display of scientific deduction that would have done credit to Holmes himself. Ordering Mrs. Roberts to remove her shoes and stockings and stand directly in front of him, he asks his patient, with hardly more than a cursory glance, "Do you have the calluses on the soles of your feet treated often?" If Mrs. Roberts was surprised before, she now is reduced to a stupefaction worthy of Watson. "You haven't even looked at the bottom of my feet," she reminds the doctor faintly. The latter, without even a casual yawn, points out that her second toes are distinctly longer than her great toes. Simpering girlishly, Mrs. Roberts replies, "But I always took that to be an indication of a perfect foot. If you will permit a little confession, I have always been secretly proud of my feet—at least, I have been since I noticed that the short great toe is distinctly shown in Grecian sculpture." Dr. Nelson, in that maddening way doctors have, crushes Mrs. Roberts' pitiful little pride in her feet with the rejoinder, "What was ideal for the women of ancient

Greece is definitely not ideal for the modern woman who wears high-heeled shoes." Of course, old smarty-pants Nelson knows what Grecian women wore on their feet; he was there. Everybody remembers *him* around the agora, arm in arm with Pericles. Oh, you wine-dark, loud-thundering, many-throated Nelson, you!

Well, one thing and another and before you know it Mrs. Roberts is on her way home with orders to stay off her feet and plunge them alternately into hot and cold water, which I could have told her who know as much about podiatry as any wide-awake gibbon in the Bronx Park Zoo.

The next chapter is a colloquy on Mrs. Roberts' feet between the doctor and his nurse. This could easily be lifted in its entirety and put into a revue. The dialogue is crisp and meaty, and Dr. Nelson manages to make quite a fool of the girl with his answers. It would have made an effective blackout had they beaten each other with rolled-up newspapers, but there I go carping again. Early next morning another patient staggers in, a Mrs. Wells. She, too, is having a very thin time with her feet, and the doctor treats her with the tender sympathy of a Torquemada: "He then proceeded to test the movements of all the joints of the foot and ankle, noting that Mrs. Wells was able, when her knees were held straight, to bend her feet upward only slightly beyond a right angle with her legs. [That is, without applying the boot.] Finally he pressed gently but deeply into the center of her instep. She winced and drew her foot back, just as Mrs. Roberts had done the day before." The upshot of this diablerie is one of those superb bits of patient-baiting that doctors excel at: "His patient . . . could no longer suppress her eager curiosity. 'Doctor,' she asked, 'are my arches fallen?' 'No,' he replied, 'they aren't—any more than a person with eyestrain is blind.' " In her place I would have given the doctor a jab in the sweetbreads with my shiv and trusted my feet, however retrograde, to outrun the law. But Mrs. Wells, shaken by her session on the rack, has hardly strength to whimper. With the admonition she is to rest her feet and take contrast plunges—old sure-shot Nelson—Mrs. Wells totters out, her nerves vibrating like mandolin strings.

From this point on, I must confess, the suspense implicit in the characters is not sustained. With all the elements of a corking triangle, two women driven crazy by their feet and their love for a handsome orthopedist, the author does little. True, he has Dr. Nelson afford his patients some relief, but at what a price! In the twelfth chapter, Mrs. Roberts confesses, "Dr. Nelson, my feet are so much better, but I am embarrassed over the ridiculous way I acted the other day." In other words, he has succeeded in substituting a nice expensive neurosis for what is, after all, only a housewife's occupational disease. Moreover, on the very next page is the alarming admission, "The doctor examined her feet again. He noted that the calluses had been removed and the areas covered with moleskin." Is Mrs. Roberts happier with an inferiority complex and feet that look like a pair of old football pants? That's her lookout. Me, I'll string along with hexerei. Where would a man pick up a lucky potato and the hair ball of an ox?

❦ SAUCE FOR THE GANDER

EVERY SO OFTEN, when business slackens up in the bowling alley and the other pin boys are hunched over their game of bezique, I like to exchange my sweat shirt for a crisp white surgical tunic, polish up my optical mirror, and examine the corset advertisements in the New York *Herald Tribune* rotogravure section and the various women's magazines. It must be made clear at the outset that my motives are the purest and my curiosity that of the scientific research worker rather than the voyeur. Of course, I can be broken down under cross-examination; I like a trim ankle as well as anyone, but once I start scrubbing up and adjusting the operative mask, Materia Medica comes in the door and Betty Grable flies out the window.

God knows how the convention ever got started, but if it is true that the camera never lies, a foundation garment or a girdle stimulates the fair sex to a point just this side of madness. The little ladies are always represented with their heads thrown back in an attitude of fierce desire, arms upflung to an unseen deity as though swept along in some Dionysian revel. If you hold your ear close enough to the printed page, you can almost hear the throbbing of the temple drums and the chant of the votaries. Those sultry, heavy-lidded glances, those tempestuous, Corybantic gestures of abandon—what magic property is there in an ordinary silk-and-Lastex bellyband to cause a housewife to behave like Little Egypt?

Perhaps the most curious mutation of the corset advertisement is the transformation, or clinical type, consisting of two photographs. The first shows a rather bedraggled young matron in a gaping, misshapen girdle at least half a dozen sizes too large for her, cringing under the cool inspection of a trained nurse and several friends. Judging from the flowers and the tea service, the hostess has invited her neighbors in to deride her physique, for they are exclaiming in unison, "Ugh, my dear —you've got *lordosis* [unlovely bulge and sagging backline]!" The second photograph, naturally, depicts the miracles wrought by the proper girdle, which, in addition to the benefits promised in the text, seems to have removed the crow's feet from under the subject's eyes, marcelled her hair, reupholstered the divan, and papered the walls.

It strikes me that, by contrast, the manufacturers of dainty under-things for men have been notably colorless in their advertising. The best they are able to afford are those static scenes in which four or five grim-jawed industrialists stand about a locker room in their shorts scowling at ticker tape, testing mashie niblicks, and riffling through first editions. It may be only sexual chauvinism on my part, but I submit that the opportunities for merchandising male lingerie are limitless. I offer at least one of them in crude dramatic form to blaze a trail for future copywriters.

SCENE: *The consulting room of Dr. Terence Fitch, an eminent Park Avenue specialist. The furniture consists of a few costly, unusual pieces, such as a kidney-shaped writing desk, a pancreas-shaped chair, and a spleen-shaped spittoon. As the curtain rises, Miss Mayo, the nurse, is at the telephone-shaped telephone.*

MISS MAYO (*into phone*): Hello, Dr. Volney? . . . This is Miss Mayo at Dr. Fitch's office. The Doctor is forwarding you his analysis of Mr. Tichenor's underwear problems; you should have it in the morning. . . . Not at all.
(*As she hangs up, Dr. Fitch enters, thoughtfully stroking his Vandyke beard. He is followed by Freedley, a haggard, middle-aged patient, knotting his tie.*)
DR. FITCH: Sit down, Freedley. . . . Oh, this is Miss Mayo. She's a niece of the Mayo brothers, out West.
FREEDLEY (*wanly*): How do you do, Miss Mayo? I've read grand things about your uncles.
MISS MAYO: Not mine, you haven't. They've been in Folsom the last three years for breaking and entering. (*She exits.*)
DR. FITCH (*seating himself*): All right now, Freedley, suppose you tell me your symptoms.
FREEDLEY: But I just told them to you.
DR. FITCH: You did?
FREEDLEY: Sure, not ten minutes ago.
DR. FITCH: Well, repeat them. (*Angrily*) You don't suppose I have time to listen to every crackpot who comes in here bleating about his troubles, do you?
FREEDLEY (*humbly*): No, sir. Well, it's just that I have this stuffy, un-comfortable sensation all the time.
DR. FITCH: That's the way a head cold usually starts. (*Scribbling*) You're to take fifteen of these tablets forty times a day, or forty of them fifteen times a day, whichever is more convenient.

FREEDLEY: It's not my nose or throat, Doctor. I get it mostly around the hips and the small of my back.

DR. FITCH (*testily*): Of course, of course. That's where it's localized. Now, I also want you to get hold of a tonic. I forget the name of it, but it's about thirty dollars a bottle. The clerk'll know.

FREEDLEY: Will I feel better after I take it?

DR. FITCH (*coldly*): I'm a physician, Freedley, not an astrologer. If you want a horoscope, there's a gypsy tearoom over on Lexington Avenue.

FREEDLEY (*plaintively*): Gee, Dr. Fitch, this thing's got me crazy. I can't keep my mind on my work—

DR. FITCH: Work? Humph. Most of *my* patients have private incomes. What do you do?

FREEDLEY: I'm with the Bayonne Bag & String Company—assistant office manager.

DR. FITCH: Getting along pretty well there?

FREEDLEY (*pitifully*): I was until this started. Now Mr. Borvis keeps riding me. He says I'm like a person in a fog.

DR. FITCH: That bulging, oppressive condition—notice it mostly when you're sitting down, don't you?

FREEDLEY: Why, how on earth can you tell, Doctor?

DR. FITCH: We medical men have ways of knowing these things. (*Gravely*) Well, Freedley, I can help you, but only if you face the facts.

FREEDLEY (*quavering*): W-what is it, sir?

DR. FITCH: Your union suit is too big for you.

FREEDLEY (*burying his face in his hands*): Oh, my God!

DR. FITCH: There, there. Buck up, old man. We mustn't give up hope.

FREEDLEY (*whimpering*): But you might be mistaken—it's just a diagnosis.

DR. FITCH (*sternly*): The fluoroscope never lies, Freedley. When I looked at you in there a moment ago, I saw almost five yards of excess fabric bunched around the mid-section.

FREEDLEY (*wildly*): It's bound to shrink after I send it to the laundry! Maybe Velma can take a tuck in it!

DR. FITCH: That's only an evasion. (*Pressing a button*) It's lucky you came to me in time. If the public only knew the annual toll exacted by ponderous, loosely fitting underwear—(*Miss Mayo enters*) Miss Mayo, get me a sterile union suit, size thirty-eight, porous-knit.

FREEDLEY (*licking his lips*): What—what are you going to do?

DR. FITCH (*soothingly*): Now, this won't hurt a bit. We'll just slip it on for size—

FREEDLEY: I won't! *I won't!* (*He cowers into a corner, flailing at Dr. Fitch and Miss Mayo as they close in on him. They pinion his arms tightly, thrust him into an adjoining dressing room, and fling the union suit after him.*)

MISS MAYO (*in a low voice*): Do you think he's got a chance, Doctor?

DR. FITCH: Hard to say, poor bugger. Did you feel those enlarged folds of material on his back?

MISS MAYO: He may have a blanket and some sheets hidden on him.

DR. FITCH: You can't tell. They get cunning in the later stages.

(*The door-shaped door of the dressing room opens and Freedley re-enters, a changed man. He is portly, well groomed, a connoisseur of fine horseflesh and pretty women, but withal a man of keen business judgment. He wears a pearl-gray Homburg, Chesterfield overcoat, and spats, carries a gold-headed cane, a hot bird, and a cold bottle.*)

FREEDLEY (*booming*): Well, Fitch, my boy, can't waste any more time jawing with you. I've got to cut along to that board meeting. Just merged Bayonne Bag & String with Consolidated Twine, you know!

DR. FITCH: Er—that was rather sudden, wasn't it?

FREEDLEY: Can't stand beating about the bush. Think in telegrams, that's my motto. Want to know my secret, Fitch? I've worked hard and I've played hard. And I've drunk a quart of whisky every day of my life!

DR. FITCH: Well, remember what I said. Don't overdo it.

FREEDLEY (*roaring*): Stuff and nonsense! Why, I'm as sound as a nut. Got the appetite of a boy of twenty, sleep like a top, and I'll outdance a youngster any day! (*To demonstrate, he catches up Miss Mayo, whirls her around giddily, and, flushed with exertion, drops dead. The Doctor and his nurse exchange slow, sidelong glances.*)

MISS MAYO: Well, I guess science still has a lot to learn.

DR. FITCH (*curtly*): None of your goddamned lip. Drag him out and show in the next patient. (*He turns back to his desk, stroking his Vandyke more thoughtfully than ever.*)

CURTAIN

🌱 THE RED TERMITES

A STORY FOR YOUNG STRIKEBREAKERS

"CENTREVILLE! All out!"

The conductor's voice rang out in the Pullman, and Avid Lissner, her piquant figure smartly attired in the latest Fifth Avenue creation, added a touch of flour to her nose and arose. Old George, the "darky" porter, beamed paternally at her as he scratched his woolly poll.

"Shall I brush yo'all off, Miss Avid?"

"No, George, I shall descend in the usual way," replied Avid merrily. Her jest was not lost on old George, who chuckled appreciatively and flung her baggage out of the window. Avid descended and found old George, the foreman of her father's factory, awaiting her on the platform. He wiped his grease-covered hands apologetically on her underskirt and shook hands.

"Faix, macushla, hit's sho' glad Ah'm bein' at seein' yez back from college," he said respectfully. "Dem cussed Reds has almost got de upper hand, dat dey has! Evah sence yo' poor pappy passed on . . ." He shook his head pessimistically, and several moths fluttered out of it. Avid's lips set grimly and little fires sparkled in her eyes; it was easy to see that her iris was up.

"I'll show those sneaking Nihilists!" she declared angrily. "Coming in here and corrupting our good American workmen with their utopian ideas! If they don't like our country, why don't they go back where they came from? Just imagine, George, they want me to divide everything fifty-fifty with some smelly peasant! That's the trouble with those foreigners, they make all their money over here and then take it back with them to Poland. Hanging's too good for those Socialists!" Unfortunately, Avid's heated words were not lost on a Red spy lurking in the crowd. Bomb in hand, he slunk off sneering evilly and promising revenge.

It was a troubled butler who met Avid at the gates of the Lissner mansion. Old George had raised Avid from a baby he had once had and she had come to love him like a brothel.

"Why, what's the matter, George?" inquired Avid, as she drew off her tight slippers and placed her feet with a sigh in the steaming caldron of soup bubbling on the fire.

"It's those Reds, miss," confided George in an anxious whisper. "They've been leaving notes ordering us to eat only black bread and caviar. Only yesterday they held a meeting changing the name of the town to Centregrad. It's all the doings of that Jake (Soviet) Gold." Avid recognized the name as that of a hulking Bolshevist bully who had been swaying the workers with his insidious doctrines. Late into the night she sat thoughtfully in the library, listening to the crushed levant bindings rustle against each other, and when the first faint flush of dawn and the milkman came peeping into the windows, her plan was ready.

Three hours later, disguised as a workman, a red handkerchief knotted loosely about her forehead and her features thickly daubed with oil, Avid took her place in the swarm of laughing, joyous laborers entering her factory. Soon she was operating a punch-press in a corner of the foundry, keeping her eyes and ears open, you may be sure. Suddenly a hoarse, throaty laugh attracted her attention. Looking up she discerned the lineaments of Jake (Soviet) Gold leering at her.

"Give us a little kiss, comrade," he invited bestially, chucking her under the chin. "A little class-consciousness there, my cabbage!" Avid attempted to repulse him, but he was already crushing her to him. Her shrieks were drowned in the whir of the machinery as his grimy face sought hers. An unexpected blow sent him plunging back. Linwood Flowers, a sturdy young American machinist, was confronting him with doubled fists.

"Tell *that* to your Moscow masters," grunted Flowers, as he drove a telling blow into Gold's solar plexus. "I'll teach you to lay your hands on defenseless American girls!"

But the cowardly Communist was already begging for mercy, albeit he could not resist a final threat to Avid.

"Just wait, your time'll come!" he sneered. "You'll be nationalized the same as everybody else! No marriage, do you hear? If two people love each other, all they have to do is sign a certificate!"

"Oh, so that's it—free love, hey?" demanded Flowers, springing at him. But the skulking bully had fled like the craven he was.

"Oh, Linwood!" breathed Avid, as she felt his muscular arms tighten about her. "It all seems so hopeless! Is this alien within our gates to warp the idealism for which our grandfathers fought at Bunker Hill, Chicken Ridge and Mungerstown? Was it for this that Montcalm faced Wolfe on the snowy heights of Quebec? And, just think, they won't even let you take a bath under Communism! Oh, Linwood . . .''

"There, there, Avid," he soothed her. "We'll win through yet, and when we do . . ." His eyes held an unspoken question. She nodded, a blush tinging her frame. The shrill noise of the noonday whistle interrupted their reveries; together they retired to a grassy spot to share pork pies from their lunch pails and dream dreams. In a few moments Avid fell into a deep dreamless sleep whilst Flowers brushed the swarms of flies from her head and studied the *Harvard Classics*, with which he was improving himself in his spare time.

The witching hour was striking one that night as a hooded figure stole along the waterfront toward the secret subterranean cavern in which the Red plotters held nightly conclave. Disguised in the scowling black beard and astrakhan coat of a Soviet envoy, Avid Lissner's heart was pounding furiously. The surly guard at the entrance of the cave eyed her suspiciously.

"Halt, give the password!" he snarled in Russian.

"Death to all bourgeois aristocrats," replied Avid in the fluent Tartar she had mastered at school. Still suspicious, the Red undesirable attempted to bar her progress.

"One side, dog of a swine!" spat Avid, striking him down with her riding-crop. "Is this the way you welcome a comrade with secret dispatches from the Central Council?" Bowing and scraping humbly, the guard fell back, muttering to himself in an obscure Ukrainian dialect. Gathered around a roaring fire, a score of evil-eyed, dark-skinned Anarchists were scheming the overthrow of U. S. supremacy. Among them Avid recognized many notorious agitators, Single Taxers, liberal readers of the *Nation* and the *New Republic*, World War slackers and other destructive forces.

"Greetings from the Union of Socialist Soviet Republics," said Avid in deep tones, "also from the autonomous republics of Turkmenistan and Uzbekistan. Regards also from the boys in the pool room in Tobolsk. The government sends you this gift." And she laid a tractor on the sideboard. A roar of savage welcome sounded from the throats of the revolutionaries. Seating herself by the fire and swallowing a cup of hot *borsch*, or Russian beet soup, Avid looked about fiercely.

"What news from our beloved fatherland?" demanded Jake (Soviet) Gold, throwing a copy of the American Constitution on the fire.

"Everything is progressing satisfactorily," replied Avid, drawing a piece of sturgeon from her pocket and gnawing it wolfishly. "Last week we shot three traitors whom we found wearing white linen shirts, also a counterrevolutionary girl spy of seventeen who owned two pairs of silk stockings."

"And what about the New York *Times*?" queried a left-wing Socialist from the right-hand corner of the room.

"Bah! One can do nothing with them—they refuse to be bribed," growled Avid. A chorus of hisses aimed at the New York *Times* filled the room.

"We, too, have been active," reported Kalmar and Ruby, the leaders of the central factory committee. "Last night we held elections. Comrade Ryskind was appointed Head Commissar in Charge of Clean Towels."

"You betchum life," chimed in Comrade Besprizorny. "We also elected comrades Oppenheimer and Mankiewicz to the firing-squad."

"In front or in back?" demanded Avid in guttural English, kissing the newly elected members of the firing-squad on both cheeks. It was a rash move, for accidentally Avid's false beard became unloosened and fell to the floor. A yell of rage went up as the plotters saw how they had been duped. In a trice Avid was securely bound and gagged. A hasty meeting of the Committee on Native-born American Spies was convened and she was sentenced to be tortured and burnt. Flaming with vodka the drunken Communists piled wood on the fire and prepared the instruments. Avid, pale but determined, surveyed them contemptuously. At last the hideous paraphernalia was ready; she could hear the hiss of the smoking irons slowly approaching her skin, nearer, nearer . . .

Suddenly the clear call of a bugle resounded from outside; the door buckled, then crumpled like matchwood under the crushing battering ram of a squad of U. S. Marines at whose head Avid dimly discerned Linwood Flowers, saber in hand. Behind them picked units of members of the National Security League, the Boy Scouts, the Girl Guides, the D. A. R. and other patriotic organizations charged in. The discomfited Reds, mouthing coarse Slavonic oaths, were soon overpowered and removed by the courteous but firm captors to serve heavy sentences at Leavenworth.

"Yes," laughed Linwood Flowers, thoroughly enjoying Avid's astonishment as he drew a gold badge from his pocket, "none other than Abe Smolinsky, U. S. Department of Justice, Operative No. 540, at your service. Jake (Soviet) Gold turned stool pigeon just in the nick of time and telephoned me. You are a brave girl."

"Oh, Jake," murmured Avid as she snuggled in the shelter of the repentant Gold's arms, "I knew you were true-blue all the time. And now promise me you won't believe any more of that nasty subversive propaganda, will you?"

"No, Avid," responded Jake in manly tones. "I have learned my lesson once and for all, and should my country need me, I am ready!" And with these words he took his flushed young intended in his arms amid the cheers of the civics class. And here, as their lips met, let us draw the kindly curtain.

Little else remains to be told. The employees of the Lissner Ball-Bearing Works, exultant at being freed from the Red menace, demanded a thirty per cent wage cut and requested to be allowed to work eleven hours a day. Avid and Jake were married and shortly afterward were found murdered in their beds. Luckily, no clues to this ghastly affair were ever found; and it is still spoken of by old-timers as "that suspicious occurrence up at Lissner's."

❦ CAUTION—SOFT PROSE AHEAD

I DON'T WANT to shame anybody, but while you lazy slugs were lying abed this morning, all knotted up in the sheets and covered with a fine perspiration, Mummy had been up for hours in her gardening apron and floppy hat, shearing great, showy blooms from the publishers' fall announcements. Whether it was that rainy spell or what, there has never been a year like this for the giant double-flowering fatuity and gorgeous variegated drivel. Is there anything you can catch from being around too much overripe beauty? I feel a little faint.

It may seem arbitrary to select for one's affection any single title from twenty catalogues full of them, yet there is something so artless, so downright dewy, about G. P. Putnam's Sons issuing a book called *Trout Fishing in New Zealand in War Time* that you want to rush up to their editorial offices, tuck back their beards, and smother them with kisses. It's a pity that so sweeping a title, embracing, as it does, sport, travel, and war, couldn't have sneaked in a romantic complication as well, like *Trout Fishing with Lana Turner in New Zealand in War Time.* Second to Putnam's in my love parade are Farrar & Rinehart with *Sniffy: The Story of a Skunk*, by David M. Stearns, who is also author of *Chuckle: The Story of a Woodchuck.* If Mr. Stearns ever does a book on labor, he could do worse than call it *Finkle: The Story of a Fink.* Another rippling title promised for late this month by the John Day Company is *Piskey Folk,* by Enys Tregarthen. *Piskey Folk* is a book of Cornish legends, the nature of which is extremely vague even to the John Day Company:

> Not all the legends published here are of the Piskeys. The seagoing little people of "Bucca Boo's Little Merry Men" and the gnomes of "The Gnome Maiden" play their parts as well; and "A Brotherhood of Little Shadows" presents no little people at all, but a cast of even more nebulous characters in a tale which for beauty of imagery is perhaps unrivaled in folklore.

Frankly, I got so confused by this dreamy précis that I had to loosen my foundation and pour myself a wee dram before I could continue.

To imply that the John Day list is the only one touched with moon magic, however, would be grossly unfair. Henry Holt & Co. are patting their back hair rather self-consciously over a new book called *Skittles*, by Rosemary Lamkey. Just what Miss Lamkey's book is about is hard to say, but here is the plotkey:

> Skittles, the hero of this story, is fond of wool-gathering, even though he knows it is wrong. And when he is caught bare-handed, he lies. He does that so well, he believes his lies himself! That works until, intent upon some specially lovely wool, he falls *plop*! into a bog, and can't get out. When rescuers ask how he got there, he can't tell the real reason, and each time he lies, he sinks deeper, and his rescuers can't get him out. So they leave him, and after a long time Skittles finally admits the truth to himself, and then the bog releases him. After that, Skittles knows how to tell the difference between the truth and a lie. One of Skittles' friends is a bee, Blzz, and he lives with his mother in a beautiful fairy cottage, and his friends and his house and his rescuers all appear in full colors on the pages of this handsome book.

Maybe it was the sound of the bee's name that got me, but at this juncture a small cloud appeared over my hammock, inside it a log of wood with a saw going through it and the caption "Z-z-z." Had it not been for two comical tramps named Weary Willie and Dusty Rhodes, who stopped by to beg some pie and milk, I should have been sleeping yet.

Probably the most sullen title of the year is that of a shopping guide by Kay Austin, announced by Carrick & Evans: *What Do You Want for $1.98?* I cannot feel that this is the best of all possible titles for a book intended to retail for exactly one dollar and ninety-eight cents, no matter how apropos its subject matter. The average reader, in the first flush of resentment, is liable to turn a dusty pink and pitch the book into the fire before he catches on to the pun (or whatever it is). Of course, the book could be printed on asbestos, but the expense would put it beyond the reach of most readers. Or is that what I had in mind in the first place?

No publishing season passes without its complement of novelty books, but this year such mandarins as Frederick A. Stokes and Appleton-Century have flung discretion to the winds and are kicking

up their heels like colts in a pasture. The former is sponsoring something rather spicy called *Fun with String*, by Leeming, while the latter's
Betcha Can't Do It, by Alexander van Rensselaer, is a cinch for the
curiosa trade, explaining "how to put twelve persons in eleven beds
and numerous other intriguing stunts which will break the ice at any
party." Apparently the feeling around Appleton-Century is that now
is the time for the Piskey folk to come to the aid of the party, for among
other piquant icebreakers in this manual will be found directions on
"how to crawl under a broom" and "how to put your head through a
calling card." If the publishers would like to include an old Creole
recipe, which has been in my family for generations, on "how to go
soak your head in a bottle of milk," I shall be only too pleased to
send it on.

In the field of humor, Frederick A. Stokes is grooming a veritable
pippin in the form of a high-spirited travesty on *How to Read a Book*,
by Mortimer J. Adler. It is called *How to Read Two Books,* by
Erasmus G. Addlepate (get it?), and is obviously the work of Joe, the
stockroom boy. I see Joe as a rather big boy of fifteen whose literary
output to date consists of an unproduced play about the bridge craze
called *The Glorious Fourth* and a hilarious parody of *Gone with the
Wind* called *Come with the Breeze*. The most the Stokes catalogue will
admit to booksellers is this:

> We have been repeatedly foiled in our numerous attempts to dis-
> cover the identity of the famous author, lecturer, numismatist, and
> entrepreneur who lurks behind the pseudonym of Erasmas G. Addle-
> pate.

[How about it? Is that Joe, the stockroom boy, or not?]

> If Mr. Addlepate's skill at lurking exceeds *our* skill at detection,
> you might just as well not bother *your* pretty head about it, but just
> go ahead and sell *How to Read Two Books*.

All right, fellows, that's a deal. Not only won't we bother our pretty
heads about it but we'll go further: the next one who ever mentions
the subject of publishing or publishers is a rotten egg. That is, all except
my dream boys, G. P. Putnam's Sons, who, in their description of Isabel
Paterson's novel *If It Prove Fair Weather*, indulge in one last magnificent orgy of self-analysis. "The new novel," says the blurb, "concerns
Emily Cruger, who loves her man and can't get him. The man is James

Nathaniel Wishart, a stuffed shirt who is also a publisher, a maddening sort of man who nevertheless comes to fascinate Emily as well as to drive her nearly insane with rage and laughter."

Move over, Emily.

♣ ENTERED AS SECOND-CLASS MATTER

WHAT HAS GONE BEFORE: Poultney Groin, disillusioned and middle-aged playboy, member of Manhattan's "upper crust," tires of Simone Dravnik, beauteous model whom he has been protecting. Womanlike, stung to the quick, she stares into her hand-mirror in her lavishly appointed apartment on Park Avenue and asks herself the age-old question: *Finished your dinner? Now it's acid's turn to dine! These small cavities filled with decomposed food morsels rapidly hatch bacteria. In a few hours your formerly healthy system is a mass of putrefaction. Ask Dr. Fritz P. Tanzpalast of the German Deaconess Hospital in Chicago. Or ask Mr. Fred Dahlgren of Norfolk, Virginia. Dog mah cats, folks, jes' give me mah spoon vittles, mah side-meat an' yams, an' dat little blue tin of Edgeworth, sho sho.* Down the dusty Chisholm trail into Abilene rode taciturn Spit Weaver, his lean brown face an enigma and his six-gun swinging idly from the pommel of Moisshe, the wonder horse. I'm curryin' my dogs in a pail of hot H_2O when the ball-and-chain ankles in beamin'. I get the bulge on her both ways from the whistle. Listen, sister, I snarls, Spike McGinnity'll be a push-over for the Kid's meathooks. He'll be kissin' the canvas in two frames. So take a powder. You're slugnutty, grates she, how you gonna do it? Just bend the old auditory apparatus, meanin' ear, I warbles. *Women of America, all you worried fatties, simply apply my marvelous Thinno treatment to that sagging, foolish bosom of yours and in ten minutes you'll be as svelte as a Fifth Avenue model—svelter, by Christ. Vy svelter in the city's heat when poised, self-possessed cosmopolitans rub elbows in the Salon Mixte of the S.S. "Getroffen"? Mingle with courtly diplomats, scintillating stars of stage and screen, and world-famous bon vivants in the spacious, airy playrooms of this floating weekend! Shoot clay ducks in the privacy of your cabin! Roach-ridden, pockmarked, hog-fat, land-poor, nigger-rich, penny-wise and pound-foolish genuine Breton stewards attend to your every want!* Beginning next month: Edith Waterhouse Prattfogle's dynamic novel of human destinies against the brilliant background of a Hawaiian volcano. A tapestry shot through and through with the vivid plumage of pleasure-mad

sybarites. A flaming pageant of a forbidden love. White man . . .
brown girl . . . caught in the volcanic drama of life . . . on the sun-
drenched shores of a magic isle . . . where blood runs hot and the heart
is free and man holds in fierce embrace the alluring image of elemental
woman as the jealous God in the Mountain of Fire sunders the earth
and splits the skies and hurls the sea to a bottomless pit because she
broke the savage taboo! *Shape your nose the new scientific way with
this new device discovered by leading European chemists. Freckles, pim-
ples, wrinkles, blackheads, enlarged pores, pits, pots, pans, abrasions,
painter's colic, trachoma, treachery, and trainman's headache all disappear before this invigorating compound.* Dog of a Christian unbeliever,
know then that in all Samarkand dwells none as lovely as gazelle-eyed
Vashtar. Even the lotus petal fades before her modest demeanor, and
when she walks abroad veiled in her yashmak, foolhardy indeed is he
who would dare gainsay her. But in the crooked Street of Ten Thousand Lanterns wily Ah Gow fingered a jade-encrusted fly worth a
prince's ransom and kept his own counsel. Verily is it written that the
fool has a hundred tongues but the wise man will mother a clucking
hen with soft speeches. Parsley Braddon of the fuchsia eyes and the
storm-tossed curls lounged moodily in her chaise-longue atop Gotham's loftiest skyscraper. Her exquisitely modeled shoulders shivered
disgustedly at the thought of Southampton in August. *Feh! Ptoo!* If
only Roddy Lathrop and Mimi Lubliner would call for her in their
yellow speedster. To feel the giddy onrush of wind in her hair as she
sped down the Merrick Road—free, free! *Lots o' folks figger they're
sassiety fellers becuz they own a claw-hammer coat. Pussonally, I'd be
a dern sight happier a-whittlin' chaws off'n my old plug o' Mechanics
Delight. And Mr. Burns, however homely his philosophy, is right. This
little box of Tasty Chocolate candy . . . collapsible, easily cleaned, fits
into any orifice . . . will blow the bejesus out of your lazy colon. Clean
house! Clear the decks! Clear the courtroom! Open your bowel and
let the sunlight in!* It was glamour that put highlights in her hair, glamour that made him throw back his shoulders like a young Lochinvar
come riding out of the West. Young they were, absurdly young . . .
brave, defiant of the world, lazing the days away. All both of them
wanted was a little nook. Foolish, tender, quixotic, impulsive, generous
to a fault, they called me Aunt Vi, albeit I was scarcely three years
their senior. At times their innocence and gay bravado brought a lump
to my throat. *Take the lump of margarine, whip well with a skein of
gray worsted, roll well in breadcrumbs till your skin gets that tingly*

feeling, and then ask these six questions of your Church toilet seat. My husband was touchy, morose, flatulent. He would leave for his office in the morning, throw himself at his typewriter, and practically tear the clothes off her. I consulted a specialist and together we examined the fine, saw-toothed edges of the tissue under the microscope. Sure enough . . . they were snails. We hesitated at first but after the garçon assured us, we tried them and found them delicious. We also visited La Reine Pedauque, Weber's, the Tomb of Napoleon, the House of All Nations, and many other spots of the City of Light. All in all the trip cost us two hundred and five dollars, including tips. Well, dear Betty, "nuf sed" for tonight and I certainly must say that the Furness-Withy Lines are all a body could want in the way of economical, pleasant travel. Oh, yes, and I musn't neglect to tell you that two seventeen-thousand-ton, steam-heated liners leave every Tuesday and Saturday for Haifa and Smyrna from Pier 89. To Tracy Hand, a formal figure with elegant hands erect by the rosewood spinet, his cravat a white patch of arrogance below his dark, alien face, the futility of life in Salem was a fact, a proved quantity. Poppaea couldn't, he knew, feel the resentment, inevitably, which he had been storing up inside him. The notes died in the twilight and he turned carefully, almost stiffly, toward the gunroom. However brittle his role in the succession of frivolities which he tolerated in this house, the memory of Lily Jastrow's laughter followed him. *Frankly, we're Knox-label-conscious . . . and why not? We'd be dull young moderns not to realize that* après tout *Knox gelatin has that certain* je ne sais quoi . . . *That how you say* élan . . . *That mysterious "spreadable" quality possessed only by this zesty old cheddar dusted lightly over wheaty little Thinsies. You there, Uncle Mose, you black rascal, whuffo' ain't you done bring in de cunn'l's fatback 'n' co'n-pone? Faix an' begorra, Ah's been savoring de delicious odor ob Chase and Sanborn's date-marked coffee, befo' de Lawd! Well, Mose, I certainly can't blame you for that, but where did you get it? Why, Bascom's, just above Forty-fourth Street, you know.* Which explains how Mr. Demosthenes P. Johnson, late Grand Sachem of the Affiliated Sons of the Imperial Order of the Setting Star, happened to be walking down F Street in the Ethiopian quarter of Birmingham, Alabama. He had just passed the tonsorial parlors of T. Agamemnon Snowball (Motto: We shave you, you save yourself) when he was hailed by a familiar voice. Turning, he descried the beaming lineaments of none other than Pericles Q. Shoat, late vice-president in charge of production of the Abyssinian Motion-Picture Studios. *You American mothers, in those intimate little heart-to-heart talks with your daughters, what about this question of* shashlik (*the medical name for soiled stomach*)*? You like to think of yourself as a sister to Mary Ellen, not as a mother, and yet you are allowing the fluff to accumulate in her navel and store up illnesses for later years. You must be a pretty flea-bitten son-of-a-bitch, dash it all! But that's only part of our service! We, the makers of Roylcord-Bounceaway tires, the tire habit of a nation, the tire with the triple suction grips, the double reinforced shock-absorbing cushion-impact, and that modern innovation in tire-engineering, floating shoulder pressure, have posted a bond with 184 of America's leading insurance companies. If any tire bearing our name blows out in less than six hundred thousand miles of use, you can take it and shove it into the nearest post office and receive postpaid an absolutely new one in exchange! Remember it's* shish kebab (*your doctor's name for sensitive epidermic tissue*) *which shortens your shave-life! Boy, you haven't felt shave-ease on your old shave-surface till you've discovered Shav-Komfy, the shave-secret of the Aztecs!* Evening was a bright lasso drawing the sun's red ball behind the ridge when Virgil Spafford stopped the Ford outside Gedney's. Man-fashion, he made as if to pass April, laughing there in the little circle of onhangers. She was a bright lasso drawing awkward young men down from the farms. Virgil snorted; her hand fluttered from his coat, and he entered Gedney's. Gedney's, the bright lasso which drew the main street of Shoreham into a hard, angular knot, was empty, partially through having burned down the previous month, partially because old man Gedney had never set foot in Shoreham. *Brazilian peons, humming their native songs, picked the coffee which flavors this new and startling confection; from the snowy summits of the Andes came long-fibered llama wools to give it body; and from our own Pennsylvania coal fields comes the delicious gritty anthracite dust which is making this obscene little candy the lunch substitute of millions.* A mischievous breeze molded the outline of her figure against the dunes. Cap'n Eben Mushmouth chuckled to himself and relit his pipe. Sairy Ann would have plenty to say about this new arrival in Hyannis. *Forty Fathom mackerel, scales glistening with the still-fresh brine of the Georges Bank, bursting with impatience to leap into your frying pan and treat your palate to a real old-fashioned tummy-fest! In galvanized iron, hermetically sealed pails direct from our cleaning sheds in Gloucester to your doorstep!* And now, dear reader, a final word from Mr. Editor Mans. We have scoured the fiction market to set before you *Three Million Tiny Sweat Glands Functioning* in that vibrant panorama of tomorrow so that *Your Sensitive Bowel*

Muscles Can React to the inevitable realization that only by enrichment and guidance *plus a soothing depilatory* can America face its problems confidently, unafraid, *well-groomed, mouth-happy, breaking the hair off at the roots without undue stench. Okay, Miss America!*

❦ KITCHENWARE, NOTIONS, LIGHTS, ACTION, CAMERA!

To THE CASUAL READER, there was nothing in yesterday's *New York Times* to distinguish it from any normal edition of that newspaper. Caught like flies in the amber of the daily screen jottings, however, were two items which easily outweighed anything on the front page. "Virginia Dale, Esther Fernandez, Dana Dale, and Martha O'Driscoll," ran the first, "have been loaned by Paramount to Harry Donahue, independent producer, to appear in a fashion short, which will be photographed in color in the Grand Canyon . . . the film will be exhibited in department stores throughout the country on a rental basis." Hard on the heels of the first came this second tidbit: "Gloria Jean, child songstress at Universal, will make a personal appearance at Gimbel Brothers at 11 A.M. today to discuss her favorite sports and life in Hollywood."

Aesthetes may decry this *rapprochement* between art and commerce, this spiritual wedding of L. B. Mayer and R. H. Macy, but I feel the match was made in heaven. The day is dawning when film and department store may fuse into a single superb medium, with mighty themes like *Resurrection* and *Gone with the Wind* harnessed directly to the task of merchandising winter sportswear and peanut-fed hams. Once self-consciousness disappears, January white sales, midsummer clearances, and current specials will be neatly embodied in the pictures themselves, and it should surprise nobody to hear Miss Loy address Mr. Powell thus in some future *Thin Man*: "Why, hello, dear, long time no see. Yes, this divine mink coat, tailored by mink-wise craftsmen from specially selected skins, is only $578.89 at Namm's in Brooklyn, Porch & Schlagober's in Dallas, the Boston Store in Cleveland, the Cleveland Store in Boston, and Kerosene Brothers in Denver." As for the legitimate theater, it will probably preserve its usual stiff-necked attitude for a while, but in time it must adapt itself to the external pressure of pictures and radio.

As little more than a trial balloon in this direction, I append the following blueprint for a new department-store dramaturgy. In the event of a production, I suggest a week's tryout in Philadelphia, at some house like Strawbridge & Clothier's, before bringing it into Wanamaker's or Hearns for the New York run:

SCENE: *The music room in the palatial villa of Mrs. Lafcadio Mifflin at Newport. Mrs. Mifflin, a majestic woman in a slim-pin Bemberg corselet well boned over the diaphragm (Stern Brothers, fourth floor), is seated at the console of her Wurlitzer, softly wurlitzing to herself. Mr. Mifflin, in a porous-knit union suit from Franklin Simon's street floor, is stretched out by the fire like a great, tawny cat. Inasmuch as there is a great, tawny cat stretched out alongside him, also wearing a porous-knit union suit, it is not immediately apparent which is Mifflin. Enter Celeste, a maid, in a shadow silhouette girdle and bra (Junior Misses, Lord & Taylor, fifth floor). She carries a note on a salver.*

MRS. MIFFLIN: Hello, Celeste. What's new in the servants' hall?

CELESTE: Divil a bit. It's been sittin' on the lap av Moike, the polisman, Oi've been, bad cess to the murtherin' gossoon.

MRS. MIFFLIN: Have you and Mike had words then?

CELESTE: No, Oi loike the larrikin all roight, but Oi've me doubts as to his sincerity. Oi suspect the craythur av havin' a woife and two childer, alanna.

MRS. MIFFLIN: Then brush him off, lest you become involved in a bigamous action. (*taking the note*) My, what attractive stationery! Eaton, Crane & Pike (Bloomingdale's mezzanine), isn't it?

CELESTE (*coarsely*): It ain't Eaton, Crane & Pike's brother.

MRS. MIFFLIN: That will do, Celeste. I obscenity in the obsenity of your obscenity. (*Celeste goes, Mrs. Mifflin opens note.*) Oh, how provoking!

MIFFLIN: What's the matter, dear?

MRS. MIFFLIN: Our big gray gelding kicked one of the grooms in a fit of temper.

MIFFLIN: Better sell the brute. He hurt two stableboys last week.

MRS. MIFFLIN: No, that was a horse of a different choler. (*thoughtfully*) Martin, I'm worried.

MIFFLIN: What about?

MRS. MIFFLIN: Our daughter Gisèle, yclept Tucky. As you know, she has conceived an unfortunate attachment for a barber. Inquiries I have caused to be made reveal the man to be little better than a fortune-hunter.

MIFFLIN: This is alarming news. As you know, her engagement to Stacy Bonbright IV was a foregone conclusion.

MRS. MIFFLIN: You mean the brilliant young aviator and six-goal man whose athaletic career at Bowdoin and subsequent speculations in Wall Street have made him the catch of the season?

MIFFLIN: The same.

MRS. MIFFLIN: Martin, this tawdry infatuation with a barber must be terminated.

MIFFLIN: How did she first meet this—this person?

MRS. MIFFLIN: It was a typical Tucky Mifflin escapade. Headstrong child that she is, she refused to have her hair washed in any one of several department-store salons where courteous attendants and sympathetic service insure satisfaction. Instead, she visited an establishment upstairs over a poolroom and encountered the coiffeur in question.

MIFFLIN: How to resolve this perplexing state of affairs?

MRS. MIFFLIN: I have a plan. Why not consult our favorite department store? As you know, nationwide credit facilities maintain a close surveillance on the character and reliability of customers. Should this Luigi, as he styles himself, have come under their scrutiny—

MIFFLIN: Capital. (*He picks up a tomato can connected by a length of waxed string with New York.*) Hello, Central, give me the credit bureau of my favorite department store. . . . Hello? This is Martin Mifflin. What information have you on a party named Luigi? . . . Yes? . . . Yes . . . Indeed. Thank you.

MRS. MIFFLIN (*anxiously*): Were our apprehensions justified?

MIFFLIN: Fully. This scalawag who has led Gisèle down the garden path is none other than Mike, the quondam policeman currently laying siege to Celeste. As she feared, the rogue has a wife and two children. But thanks to the watchdog who never sleeps (organized retail credit investigation), our child is safe. (*The door opens and Gisèle bursts in, accompanied by Stacy Bonbright IV.*)

GISÈLE: Oh, Mother, what a little goose you must think me! Fortunately, I discovered my error in time and married Stacy Bonbright IV.

MIFFLIN: Take her, my boy. You've earned her, as well as this sight draft for several million dollars.

STACY (*warmly*): Thanks, sport.

GISÈLE: How do you like my wedding tailleur, Mother?

MRS. MIFFLIN: It's a heller. Altman's, of course?

GISÈLE: Yes, and available in nineteen different shades—among them wine, russet, beige, peach, grackle, stone, liver, lover, blubber, blabber and clabber.

MIFFLIN: And now, children, what are your honeymoon plans? Hot Springs, Placid? Sun Valley?

GISÈLE (*dimpling*): Not on your tintype, Father. Just plain, old-fashioned Saks.

CURTAIN

❧ SWING OUT, SWEET CHARIOT

A FEW DAYS AGO I happened into my newsdealer's for ten cents' worth of licorice whips and the autumn issue of *Spindrift*, a rather advanced quarterly review in which I had been following an exciting serial called "Mysticism in the Rationalist Cosmogony, or John Dewey Rides Again." In the previous number, the cattle rustlers (post-Hegelian dogma) had trapped Professor Dewey in an abandoned mine shaft (Jamesian pragmatism) and had ignited the fuse leading to a keg of dynamite (neo-Newtonian empiricism). Naturally, I was simmering with impatience to learn how the Morningside Kid would escape from this fix, and I lost no time getting back to my rooms in the Middle Temple and stuffing my crusty old briar with shag. The gesture turned out to be singularly appropriate, for I shortly discovered that my newsdealer had made a mistake in his excitement and that I would have to spend the evening with a journal called *The Jitterbug*.

The Jitterbug is a febrile paper published bimonthly by the Lex Publications, Inc., of 381 Fourth Avenue, devoted to the activities of alligators, hepcats and *exaltés* of swing everywhere. These activities, which consist in hurling one another violently about to popular music, riding astride one another, and generally casting out devils, are portrayed in ten or fifteen pages of photographs and cartoons that need no explanation. What will bear a little exegesis, however, is the text of the half-dozen short stories and articles. Were it not for the glossary of swing terms thoughtfully supplied by the management at the very outset, the magazine might as well be couched in Chinook. It may not concern anybody vitally that a "Scobo queen" is a girl jitterbug, that "frisking the whiskers" is warming up, that a "zeal girl" is a hot girl dancer, or that a "wheat bender" is one who plays sweet music instead of swing, but if you expect to translate such stories as "Jazz Beau," "Riffin' on the Range," and "Noodling with Love" without the aid of a trot, you are one hepcat indeed.

The qualifications of a working jitterbug are succinctly set forth in the national organization's membership blank, which appears on page 21. It reads:

> This is to certify that ——— is a jiving, hot-hosing Jitterbug, a member of the Community of Hep-Cats, and as such entitled to beat it out whenever the music swings out high, wide, and gutbucket.

The characters involved in the aforementioned stories are all that and more. For example, Cal Leonard, the protagonist of "Jazz Beau," is described as "a pair of Mack Truck shoulders, a grinning mouth, and wild, flame-blue eyes." I suppose there was a body linking these goodies together, but the pace is so staccato that the author neglects to mention it. Debby Waite, of "Noodling with Love," on the other hand, has body and to spare, judging from the following tender blueprint:

> Her thick, curly red-gold hair was kind of piled up on top and around her head, and it made a shining halo that framed the white oval of her face. Those sultry lips of hers were red and glistening under the lights, and her gray eyes sparkled like hot rhythm. Debby's figure was never anything to be missed, but in the two years since I'd seen her, several delectable curves I remembered had ripened. And the dress she was wearing wasn't calculated to hide that fact. Its full chiffon skirt tantalized by its seeming transparency, and it clung to the soft roundness of her hips with loving closeness. The waist was high and tight, and above that rose two shields that fitted snugly over the proud mounds of her swelling breasts.

In fine, a Schrafft's Luxuro ice-cream sundae come to life; and, as though I were not overheated enough already, the author has to pile Pelion on Ossa by telling me this glorious blob of girlhood was educated at Bennington. Look, dear, I wouldn't care if she had quit school in the sixth grade.

The plots of the short stories in my copy of *Jitterbug* are fairly basic: Scobo queen meets hep-cat, they find mutual release in barrelhouse or gutbucket, and eventually, on the winsome revelation that one or the other is heir to half a million rugs, shag, peck, and paw their way to the altar. "Jazz Beau" may serve as a clinical example. A young lady describing herself as a Taxi-Tessie or wriggle-wren employed at the Roselane Ballroom is lured into a Broadway movie theater by the harmonies of one Biggie Barnett and his band:

> I heard the wail of a wah-wah pump, the staccatoed stutter of skins. . . . My heart began to thump and swell with the fever of rhythm. I giggled out loud. Crazily, I slid to a stop at the aisle, in

the theater proper, scanned the seats. Full. I felt my breasts tremor angrily.

This mysterious physiological reaction, no doubt experienced by every woman at the sight of an S.R.O. sign, yields to a state bordering on epilepsy when the band really starts giving:

> I began to sway in my seat. My lashes fluttered. My head bobbed in time with the red hot ride rhythm. Jittersauce began to burn up my bloodstream.

At this point, as the *cognoscenti* begin stomping and trucking freely about in a delirium of pleasure, the surrealist owner of the Mack Truck shoulders, grinning mouth, and wild flame-blue eyes enters the proceedings:

> "Lookee," the big guy whispered, "I've *got* to get out in that aisle and whip my dogs! Do we team up? A big gazabo like me is gonna look awfully silly getting off a solo!"

Hesitating a split second lest her suppliant turn out to be a geep, or wolf, Miss Prim surrenders to his emotional plea and joins the gavotte:

> While those cats up on the stage clambaked like nobody's business, my partner and I really cut that rug. . . . All I was conscious of was the driving syncopation and lift of agony pipes, the noodling of the brass section, as barrelhouse blasts whipped my slender legs and weaving hips into a rhythmic frenzy. We did the Suzy Q. We shagged and pecked.

His appetite whetted by this preliminary workout, Cal declares his intention of making a night of it. "My sox are hell-hot and I've got to hop till I wear holes in my soles to cool them off," he avers, and his escort, whose disposition is no less elastic than her frame, readily assents. "We strutted and stuffed to burning boogie-woogie, stayed in the groove until we were both beat right down," she whispers shyly to her diary. Thereupon, in a passage as salty as any you will find in the Kamasutra, the gymnasts take leave of each other until the following evening, when Cal "came swaggering into Roselane looking like a color page from *Esquire*." Maybe the engraver's hand slipped, but the last color page from *Esquire* I saw was slightly off register and showed

a junior executive with a flesh-colored suit and a pale-blue herringbone
face. Had Cal worn something of the sort, however, he could hardly
have caused a greater sensation. In a trice the other hostesses cluster
excitedly about his affinity, asking whether she knows Cal's father is a
millionaire motor magnate in Detroit. The little lady loves Cal for his
floy floy alone, and her disillusion and heartbreak are such that she is
almost thirty seconds recovering from the shock. "You don't think of
those things when you're with a guy who's slowly driving you screwball
with love," she observes with icy disdain. Perhaps not, puss, but it
certainly wouldn't do any harm to look the old gent up in Dun &
Bradstreet—now, would it? I mean just for the heck of it.

Follows an interval of courtship in which, fanned by love and jive,
Cal's passion mounts to a crescendo. He becomes a nightly visitor to
Roselane, buying rolls of dance tickets and "paying out a small fortune" (probably upward of three dollars in a single evening) to keep off
poachers. A drunken geep who engages our miss in the Portland
fancy finds himself "bounced off two walls after Cal hit him." But Cal's
importunate proposals of marriage are met with the only answer a
high-grade heroine of fiction can give: "Everyone would think I was
wedding you for your papa's shekels. You'd even think it yourself,
after the romance wore off." The chilling presentiment of a loveless
union between two graying jitterbugs retired to the bench and soaking
their feet in a pail of Tiz nevertheless fails to dissuade Cal: "He begged.
He pleaded. He made love with words [the last desperate throw of
the dice] like Red Norvo swings 'Reverie.' " Yet all to no avail, for in
a scene of renunciation worthy of Tolstoy (not Leo Tolstoy; a man I
know named Charlie Tolstoy), the narrator gives the mitten to "the
one and only guy who had played on my heart strings like a bass-man
picks at a belly fiddle."

And now, in a Garrison finish, Cal calls forth the tenacity and cunning that have made his father a caution in the automotive industry.
He retains two geeps to enter Roselane, trip up his inamorata while
dancing with her, and so humiliate her that she is forced to resign her
post. This incomprehensibly restores the social equation between the
lovers and sends them on a honeymoon wherein they "shagged and
trucked and Suzy Q-ed and hugged and kissed." The narrative concludes, "Anyhow, when two alligators get together and love sets in,
you've got something."

I'll say I have, sister. Did you ever hear tell of migraine?

TOMORROW—FAIRLY CLOUDY

HEAVEN KNOWS I don't want to sound gossipy, but something rather important has been happening to American advertising. In fact, it almost looks as if there might *be* no American advertising one of these days.

Perhaps a few of you in the Older Business Boys' Division will recall an advertisement which appeared in the late twenties. It showed a well-known Russian princess clasping a Knopf book and bore the starry-eyed admission, "Mindful of my duty to the public, I am careful never to be seen without a Borzoi book." At that time I thought I heard the muffled tread of the *Jacquerie* in the streets, and I even went so far as to buy myself a pike suitable for carrying heads. I guess it was merely a case of wishful thinking. Great, fatuous booby that I was, I imagined advertising would be destroyed from the outside. It won't; it's going to bubble and heave and finally expire in the arms of two nuns, like Oscar Wilde.

The opening note of the *marche funèbre* was sounded in an advertisement for Listerine tooth paste in a recent issue of the *American Home*. It was a cartoon strip called "What Put Patty in the Movies?" and its plot was as follows: Patty, a zestful little breastful, crouches on a beach, daydreaming with her two chums. From her mouth issues a balloon with the caption, "I read somewhere there's a great call for photographers' models. Wouldn't I like to be one . . . lots of money and a chance at the movies maybe." "Why not, Patty?" urges Bob. "You'd be sure to succeed. I'll get Dad to call up his photographer friend, Mr. Hess."

In less than two panels, Mr. Hess is breaking the bad news to Patty. "I'm afraid you won't do, Miss Patty. Your teeth are good, but *not good enough*. For camera work they have to be perfect." To Miss Jones, Mr. Hess's secretary, Patty sobs out her chagrin. "I've failed, Miss Jones . . . and we needed the money so badly!" "Failed! Fiddlesticks!" counters Miss Jones briskly. "All you need to do is use a special type of tooth paste that our best models and screen stars use. LISTERINE TOOTH PASTE is its name. Try it two weeks . . . then come back."

Well, sir, you're probably psychic. "Three Weeks Later—at the Studio" introduces the fifth picture, in which Mr. Hess announces, "The job's yours, Miss Patty . . . $50 a week. I can't believe you're the same girl. Your teeth are simply perfect." "I'm so thankful, Mr. Hess," replies Patty, who is a bulldog for tenacity. "It may lead to the movies. And all the credit is due to Miss Jones." The sixth and last panel is headed "One Year Later." On the observation platform of a train, surrounded by the upturned faces of townsfolk, stands Patty, her smart tailleur festooned with orchids. "You're all so wonderful. Goodbye! Goodbye!" she calls. "She'll click in Hollywood," observes Bob stoutly to Patty's girl chum, and it is Patty's nameless girl chum whose answer should go echoing down the corridors of time. "Maybe we'd better start using LISTERINE TOOTH PASTE too," she murmurs drearily. *"Anything to get out of this hick town."*

The italics are mine, but the desperation is that of the whole advertising confraternity. So all the old tactics have finally broken down— wheedling, abuse, snobbery and terror. I look forward to the last great era in advertising, a period packed with gloom, defeatism and frustration, in which spectacles like the following will be a commonplace:

SCENE: *The combination cellar and playroom of the Bradley home in Pelham Manor. Mr. and Mrs. Bradley and their two children, Bobby and Susie, are grouped about their new automatic oil burner. They are all in faultless evening dress, including Rover, the family Airedale.*

BOBBY: Oh, Moms, I'm so glad you and Dads decided to install a Genfeedco automatic oil burner and air conditioner with the new self-ventilating screen flaps plus finger control! It is noiseless, cuts down heating bills, and makes the air we breathe richer in vitaray particles!

SUSIE: Think of it! Actual experiments performed by trained engineers under filtered water prove that certain injurious poisons formerly found in cellars are actually cut down to thirty-four per cent by switching to a Genfeedco!

MR. BRADLEY (*tonelessly*): Well, I suppose anything's better than a heap of slag at this end of the cellar.

MRS. BRADLEY: Yes, and thanks to Buckleboard, the new triple-ply, satin-smooth, dirt-resisting wall plastic, we now have an ugly little playroom where we can sit and loathe each other in the evening.

BOBBY: Hooray for Buckleboard! Since Dads made this feedbin into a playroom, no more hanging around the livery stable with questionable acquaintances!

MR. BRADLEY: Yes, we now have a livery stable right in our own home. The initial expense was brutal, but the money only gathered two and a half per centum in the bank.

BOBBY and SUSIE (*munching candy bars*): Hooray! Hooray for this new taste sensation!

MRS. BRADLEY: Harvey, I'm worried about the children. Don't you think they have too much energy?

SUSIE: Choc-Nugs are just *loaded* with energy, Moms! These crackly nuggets of purest Peruvian cocoa, speckled with full-flavored, rain-washed nutmeats, call forth a chorus of "Yums" from every wide-awake girl and boy!

BOBBY: In Mexico it's "Viva el Choc-Nugo!" but in America it's "Hooray for Choc-Nugs!" Any way you pronounce it, it is pronounced "Goodylicious" by millions of eager candy-lovers!

MR. BRADLEY: I see that I have fathered a couple of Yahoos. . . . Bobby, answer the door.

BOBBY: Had we installed a set of Zings, the new electric chime, it would not be necessary for callers to wait outside in the rain and sleet. . . .

MR. BRADLEY: Answer the door or I will knock your block off, you murdering little saw-toothed ape. (*Bobby goes to door, admits Mr. and Mrs. Fletcher and their three children, attired in long balbriggan underwear. General greetings.*)

MRS. FLETCHER: Don't mind us, Verna, we just dropped in to sneer at your towels. (*unfolding a towel*) My, they're so absorbent and fluffy, aren't they? You know, they're made of selected fibers culled from high-grade flat-tailed Montana sheep subject to rigid inspection by qualified sheep inspectors.

MRS. BRADLEY (*listlessly*): They fall apart in two days, but we got tired of using blotters.

MRS. FLETCHER: Verna, I think it's about time you and I had a heart-to-heart talk about your skin. You're as rough and scaly as an old piece of birch-bark.

MRS. BRADLEY: I know; it's my own fault. I neglected my usual beauty cocktail.

MRS. FLETCHER: Skins, you know, are divided into three types—cameo, butterscotch, and mock nutria. Yours defies classification.

MRS. BRADLEY (*miserably*): Oh, how can I win back my Prince Charming?

MRS. FLETCHER: Why not follow the example of glamorous Mrs. Barney Kessler, socially prominent matron of the Main Line?

MRS. BRADLEY: What does she do?

MRS. FLETCHER: Each morning, on rising, she scrubs her skin with an ordinary sink-brush. Then she gently pats in any good brand of vanishing cream until Kessler disappears to his office.

MRS. BRADLEY: And then?

MRS. FLETCHER: I can't remember, but she's got a complexion like a young girl.

MR. FLETCHER: Say, Harvey, make this test for yourself. Do some brands of pipe tobacco irritate your tongue, cause your eyeballs to revolve in your head? Then pack your old briar with velvety Pocahontas Mixture and know true smoke-ease. After all, you have to put something into your pipe. You can't just sit there like a bump on a log.

MR. BRADLEY: I get along all right smoking old leaves from my lawn.

MR. FLETCHER: Yes, but look at the fancy tin these people give you. Remember that five hundred of these tins and a fifty-word essay on "Early Kentish Brass Rubbings" entitle you to the Pocahontas Mixture vacation offer, whereby you retire at sixty with most of your faculties impaired.

MRS. FLETCHER: Er—Fred, don't you think it's time we . . .

MR. FLETCHER: Now, Harriet, don't interrupt. Can't you see I'm talking to Harvey Bradley?

MRS. FLETCHER (*timidly*): I know, but there seems to be about two feet of water in this cellar and it's rising steadily.

MR. BRADLEY (*sheepishly*): I guess I should have specified Sumwenco Super-Annealed Brass Pipe throughout. My contractor warned me at the time.

MR. FLETCHER (*bailing like mad with his tin*): Well, this is a pretty how-do-you-do.

MRS. BRADLEY (*comfortably*): At least, whatever else happens, under the Central American Mutual Perpetual Amortizational Group Insurance Plan our loved ones need not be reduced to penury.

MRS. FLETCHER: What good is that? Our loved ones are right here with us!

MR. BRADLEY (*mildly*): You don't tell me.

Mrs. Bradley: I always say the added protection is worth the difference, don't you, Harvey? (*She pats her husband's shoulder reassuringly as they all drown like rats in a trap.*)

CURTAIN

❧ THE LOVE DECOY

A Story of Youth in College Today—Awake, Fearless, Unashamed

"PROFESSOR GOMPERS is ill!" The whisper spread like wildfire through the packed classroom. A feeling of emulsion swept over me. Kindly old Professor Gompers, whose grizzled chin and chiseled grin had made his name a byword at Tunafish College for Women! Ivy Nüdnick, sauciest co-ed in the class, she of the unruly locks and the candied gray eyes, leaned over to impart the latest gossip.

"That new instructor, Russell Gipf, is subbing for him!" The color drained slowly from my face, entered the auricle, shot up the escalator, and issued from the ladies' and misses' section into the housewares department. I remembered Russell Gipf as a lean brown giant in tweeds whose resemblance to Warren William had caused his suspension the year before. It had been an ugly scandal but luckily his nose was broken in an accident soon after and the faculty had restored him. Dreamily I recalled an autumn afternoon when I had visited him in his office in ivy-covered Schneider to discuss a theme I had written. Through the half-open windows drifted the mingled smell of wood smoke and freshmen. He confided that he was doing research in dirty limericks for his doctor's thesis and asked if I knew any "Good Ones." In the twinkling of an eye we were in the gutter. At no time, however, did he allow himself the usual indecent proposal, and I returned to my dormitory room raging, determined never to see him again.

An impatient voice summoned me rudely from my daydream. I looked up; Russell Gipf was addressing me crisply from the platform. My feminine eye noted that he was still a spiffy dresser, a regular up-to-the-minute gink.

"Will you please answer the question, Miss Hornbostel?"

"I—I didn't hear it," I quavered.

"Well, Miss 'Lame Brain,' " he retorted sardonically, "maybe you had better stop galvanizing around nights and pay attention!" A cold fury welled up in me and I longed to hang one on his lug for his in-

115

solence. I was seething but he could not see it, for several of my girl chums were seething in front of me. A moment later the bell tolling in ivy-covered Hoffenstein brought the class to a close. Slipping my pencil box and pen wipers into my corsage I approached his desk, a plan fermenting in my brain.

"Yes, Miss Hornbostel?" Russell Gipf's eyes were dancing with fun.

"Oh, Mr. Gipf," I began, "I hardly know how to say this. It—it's so personal." His eyes stopped dancing with fun and began dancing with sex.

"Go on," he urged.

"I—I can't get the cap off my tooth paste," I faltered, a tear trembling on my nose. "If you could only help me . . ." I gazed out of my huge bedroom eyes appealingly.

"Well, now—ahem—this is serious," he said slowly. "No wonder you weren't prepared in class just now. Naturally, you were upset."

"And you were cruel," I said.

"I'm sorry," he added Quigley.

"Why did you add Quigley?" I begged him. He apologized and subtracted Quigley, then divided Hogan. We hastily dipped the slices of Hogan into Karo, poured sugar over them, and ate them with relish.

"Tell me," said Gipf, as he wiped his mouth on the tail of his shirt, "about this tooth paste: if you could bring the tube to my office . . ."

I explained hurriedly that it was too heavy to carry and that he would have to come up to my dormitory room that evening after "lights out." He readily fell in with my wish and promised. As we walked across the campus toward ivy-covered Lapidus, I drew him out craftily. He had been in the north of Scotland that summer shooting bobtail flushes, and he was full of his subject. Although I hated him, I had to confess that his smile made my pulses sing, and I gladly would have leaped through a hoop had he asked me to. He must have been aware of it, for he suddenly reached into his green baize bag and produced a hoop.

"Here, leap through this hoop, you," he ordered. I did so and he flicked me lightly with his whip. I saw his face go dark with passion. "Dolores—I love you!" he whispered, his hand closing over mine. Mine in turn closed over his. In an instant we had chosen up sides, it was my turn at bats, and I knocked a sizzling bunt to Pipgrass in the daisies.

"Ah, *cara mia*, giz a kiz," panted Russell. I tried to resist his overtures, but he plied me with symphonies, quartets, chamber music and cantatas. I felt myself softening, but I was determined to go through with my plan.

"Are you mad, Russell?" I stopped him haughtily. He bit his lip in a manner which immediately awakened my maternal sympathy, and I helped him bite it. Foolish man! In a trice the animal in him rose to the surface again. He caught my arm in a vicelike grip and drew me to him, but with a blow I sent him groveling. In ten minutes he was back with a basket of appetizing fresh-picked grovels. We squeezed them and drank the piquant juice thirstily. Then I blew him an airy kiss.

"Tonight—at ten-thirty, *mon désir!*" I flung at him over my shoulder. Even in my room I could hear him panting four floors below on the campus as I changed to a filmy negligee and began to cold-cream my glowing cheeks.

The dim glow of shaded lamps and the heady intoxication of incense had transformed my room into a veritable Oriental bower when Russell Gipf knocked cautiously on my door at ten-thirty. From the ostermoor where I was stretched out lazily, I murmured an inviting "Come in!"

"Come in!" I murmured invitingly. He entered shaking himself vigorously. There had been a heavy fall of talcum several hours before and as far as the ground could see the eye was white. I offered Russell a dish of soap flakes, but despite my attempts to put him at his ease he seemed nervous.

"The—the tooth paste," he began, looking about suspiciously. I indicated the bathroom with a lazy finger. In a moment he reappeared, his face haggard and his eyes like burning holes in the snow.

"Yes," I shot at him coldly, "I tricked you. No, it's useless to try the door—and it's a four-story drop straight down from those windows, Mr. Russell Gipf. Perhaps you're wondering what I intend to do now." I picked up the telephone, my voice a snarl. "In five minutes the faculty will break in and find you in a co-ed's room. What will your wealthy old father Prosper Gipf, president of the Absconders' and Defaulters' National Bank, say to that?" He backed away from me whimpering piteously. But I was goading him on as only a raging woman can. "You humiliated me in front of all my classmates today. Now—you shall pay." My hand was lifting the receiver when a faint scratching sounded at the door, followed by stertorous breathing. I threw it open. Dean Fothergill, his face that of a man mad with desire, lunged at me.

"Dolores," he implored, "you adorable little witch—I've been following you with my eyes—I . . ."

"You rotter!" I turned in surprise at Russell Gipf's voice as he flashed past me and drove a decisive blow into the aged roué's kidneys. The two men grappled, their teeth bared. Russell's head snapped back as Dean Fothergill, who I forgot to say was once amateur light-heavyweight boxing champion of University of California at Los Angeles, drove a decisive blow to the Gipf kidneys. The noise of fist on kidneys rang out in the still air. I watched the spectacle unmoved. After all, tomorrow I would have to pass my law exam; I opened *Fist on Kidneys* and was deep in it when I heard a groan. I looked up. There, manacled to Russel Gipf, stood Dean Fothergill, a hangdog expression on his face.

"Well, Miss Hornbostel," he admitted shamefacedly, "I guess the jig is up."

"Tell her, you swine!" grunted Russell menacingly, pounding his windward kidney.

"I—I am Jim the Penman," said Fothergill with bowed head. "I forged the notes which sent your father, Harry Trefusis, to the cooler."

"Then you are Donald Fenstermacher, Russell?" I queried, dazed. He put his strong young arms about me and nodded shyly.

"Now may I ask you that question?" he blushed.

"Yes, Donald," I told him, hiding my scarlet face in his shoulder. Outside, the insupportable sweetness of a guitar cleft the warm summer air and bewhiskered, beflanneled, bejasused and bejabered undergraduates strolled under the hoary elms. The Splendid Wayfarer had come home.

❦ HOLD THAT CHRISTMAS TIGER!

ABOUT TEN YEARS AGO there was translated to the screen as a vessel for the talents of Warner Baxter a play called *I Loved You Wednesday*. The result was an amiable little film which undoubtedly recovered its investment, earned a snug profit, and in the normal course of things was retired to be cut into mandolin picks. What makes it still verdant in the memory of connoisseurs, however, is a patch of dialogue that came about the end of the first reel. Mr. Baxter, in beautifully tailored breeches and cordovans, had been established as a construction engineer on a vast, unidentified power project, barking crisp commands at giant cranes and chivying steam shovels. The scene then dissolved to his home, and as the workworn engineer entered, his wife looked up eagerly from her sewing. "What's new, dear?" she inquired. "Well, darling," replied Baxter, inhaling deeply and brushing clouds of alkali from his shoulders, "I just finished Boulder Dam." "Oh, *Jim!*" murmured his wife adoringly.

It may be presumptuous of me to compare myself in any sense with Mr. Baxter (I am twenty pounds lighter, not quite as photogenic, and infinitely less solvent), but if sheer doggedness and fighting heart mean anything, the undertaking I have just completed may yet outclass his. At ten o'clock this morning, fortified with a bottle of Benzedrine and a stoup of black coffee, I kissed my newsdealer goodbye and set out to read through the Christmas-party suggestions in *Mademoiselle*, *Vogue* and *House & Garden*. "It's madness, Derek!" implored the handful of friends who had come down to see me off. "Think it over, old man! You'll never get through!" I smiled grimly, set my jaw as well as a serious case of malocclusion would allow, and plunged into the perfume advertising. Hours later, gray with fatigue and my eyes mere pinpoints in my head, I stumbled out of the back cover of *House & Garden* and fell forward into the waiting arms of my friends.

Perhaps the most soaring imagination displayed in any of the three magazines is that of a Mr. Lester Gaba, whom *Mademoiselle* called in to advise its readers regarding their Christmas décor. It is Mr. Gaba's thesis that, given a little energy and a few everyday materials, Christmas need never be stodgy. His first target is the tree itself. "Dip tips of twisted cotton strips into India ink and trim your tree entirely with 'ermine tails,' " he orders. "Pin a fresh mauve orchid to the treetop." Arresting as the effect might be, the actual execution seems a bit less simple. "Well, what do we do next?" I can hear a Mr. Kapustin asking his wife as he finishes tacking up the last holly wreath. Mrs. Kapustin peers uncertainly at her copy of *Mademoiselle*. " 'Tip dips of twisted crotton sips—' " she begins. "No, wait a minute. 'Sip dips of cristed totton tips—' " Obviously, such an enterprise can only end in disaster. Either Mr. Kapustin, who is extremely short-tempered, snatches the magazine from his wife, provoking a free-for-all, or the dawn discloses two pallid householders on the verge of a breakdown, mumbling "Dip, dip, dip."

Next turning his attention to the lighting, Mr. Gaba says, "Go medieval: get Gothic-lantern effects by shielding ceiling bulbs with pierced, rectangular tin food-graters." It might be well to temper your enthusiasm for this novel hint with a pinch of caution, unless you want a dusky handmaiden mounted on a chair right in the middle of your party, grating carrots over the shoulders of your guests and murmuring bitterly to herself in Gullah. In the event you do, the best plan would be to sprinkle artificial snow around her feet and drape her with silver festoons and candy canes. It is certainly just as feasible as another of Mr. Gaba's suggestions: "Tie blown-up, red penny balloons to your outdoor Christmas trees. The kids in the block will pop them quick like a flash—but who cares?" Who indeed but an old Scrooge? I, for one, can think of no more diverting pastime than beating off stinging pellets from a bean-blower while setting 'em up in the next alley for a little marksman. The same promise of high adventure pervades still another of Mr. Gaba's proposals: "Decorate your mantel with a begged, borrowed, or stolen French horn filled cornucopia-style with holly and mistletoe." No French-horn player around Carnegie Hall will refuse to turn over his instrument to you once the purpose is explained to him. Should he prove reluctant, simply read him Mr. Gaba's article, and if that fails to stun him, sap him just below the left ear with a blackjack. Anybody so deficient in Christmas spirit, and above all a French-horn player, is hardly worth your sympathy.

Conscious of its august tradition, *Vogue* naturally scorns any such pinchpenny devices as the foregoing. Its article on the subject permits the reader to flatten his nose against the windows of several great houses and watch their occupants celebrate. Mrs. Fredrick Frelinghuysen, for instance, occasionally "masques all the curtains in great lengths of red mosquito netting," a mystifying rite, since there are surely no red mosquitoes in Mrs. Frelinghuysen's well-ordered home. (Who the devil Mrs. Frelinghuysen is I have no idea, but it is a cinch from the context that she has a well-ordered home.) Another family brews up an appalling mixture of port, brandy, Burgundy, almonds and raisins, called *glögg*, and then, I presume, proceeds to get quietly glöggy. A deeply religious bachelor, whose name is unfortunately not given, "once set his Christmas table with all sorts of mechanical toys. As the guests entered the dining room, the wound-up dolls, acrobats, animals, merry-go-rounds began performing their mechanical tricks." The effect on the guests, already reeling with *glögg*, must have been a curious one. Somehow, I have the feeling that everybody started turning handsprings, tearing down the smilax, and beating the tar out of the host—a thing he richly deserved.

No such chronicle, of course, would be complete without mention of Hollywood's method of observing the holiday. Mrs. Richard Barthelmess, I discovered, "often trims her trees with Cellophane tassels or opalescent glass bubbles," so refreshing after the opalescent iron bubbles one encounters everywhere. The Charles Boyers "cajole little pickaninnies to sing the Christmas carols." As one who in eight years has yet to see a pickaninny, big or little, within the confines of Beverly Hills, I can only conclude that the Boyers must range all the way to Georgia and Mississippi for their little sable songsters. Mr. Boyer is a very persuasive article, but that threatens to stand as an all-time high in cajolery.

It was left to that ordinarily staid journal of gracious living, *House & Garden*, however, to emerge with the one truly brilliant inspiration of the season—an upside-down evergreen tree swung from the ceiling. To any human flies within the sound of my voice, here is an open invitation: Drop around at my flat whenever you like on Christmas Eve with your suction shoes and have a cup of *glögg* on our ceiling. The Kapustins will be there and so will Mr. Gaba, if he isn't tied up (figuratively speaking, of course). You'll know me right away because my eyes will be so radiant; and, besides, I'll have a fresh mauve orchid in my hair—to say nothing of *Mademoiselle, Vogue* and *House & Garden*.

🌸 SMUGGLERS IN THE DUST

NEW RACKET, consisting of the smuggling of tourists into film studios, is being stamped out by industry execs, working in collaboration with the Better Business Bureau. Gang in downtown Los Angeles had been slipping visitors, at $7.50 per head, into the picture lots through bribery and other subterfuges.—*Variety.*

SCENE: *A rather sordid opium den in downtown Los Angeles. Two tiers of bunks at left and right contain huddled figures, obviously slaves of the poppy. Downstage, at center, an unearthly greenish glow picks out the figure of an Old Man crouched over a kerosene lamp. He is turning an opium pill on a hat pin over the lamp flame and muttering inscrutable wisdom of the East. At left, a sliding panel in the wall, marked "Sliding Panel" and at right a telephone, unfortunately without any wires.*

OLD MAN (*muttering the inscrutable wisdom of the East*): Five thousand years ago the sage hath said, "If a pepper seed takes wings, it will turn into a dragonfly, yet if a dragonfly loses its wings, it will not revert to a pepper seed." That is what the sage hath said five thousand years ago. (*The door at rear opens suddenly and Bob Bundy, a young motion-picture executive, enters. He looks about curiously.*)

BOB BUNDY (*aside*): What a strange place! My chum Tyrone Rukeiser must have been joking when he told me to meet him here. But then, he is the smartest investigator in the Los Angeles Better Business Bureau and as bright as a new penny. With his resourcefulness and cool daring, we should soon see the last of the gang which has been slipping visitors, at $7.50 per head, into the picture lots through bribery and other subterfuges. (*Sees Old Man huddled over lamp.*) Hullo! Perhaps this bit of human flotsam can assist me. . . . Have you seen a young man answering to the name of Tyrone Rukeiser?

OLD MAN (*querulously*): No savvy Tylone Lukeiser. This No. 1 sordid hop joint, catchum plenty first-chop opium.

BOB (*aside*): John Chinaman is a slick customer; I shall have to match wits with him. . . . Have you a telephone, my flend?

OLD MAN: Telephone here but no wires along him.

BOB: Perhaps it will work without them. (*into phone*) Hello, Central? Give me Tyrone Rukeiser, ace investigator of the Better Business Bureau and sworn nemesis of the gang which has been slipping visitors, at $7.50 per head, into the picture lots through bribery and other subterfuges. . . .What, he left hours ago? Oh, beans!

OLD MAN (*chuckling*): Tylon Lukeiser allee samee big fool.

BOB (*hotly*): Easy, mister, easy! Anything you say about that party goes double for Bob Bundy!

OLD MAN: Bob Bundy him likewise a jerk.

BOB (*advancing with doubled fists*): Darn your impertinence, you scum —(*Old Man rises, slips off his disguise, revealing Tyrone Rukeiser.*)

TYRONE (*good-humoredly*): Not so fast, Bob Bundy!

BOB (*gasping*): You had me nonplused for a moment. You could pass muster anywhere, old man!

TYRONE: You bet I could pass muster [mustard]; I hate it. . . . Now look here, Bob, we have no time to lose. Have you a "roscoe" on your person?

BOB (*patting his pocket significantly*): Yes; I brought my Mauser.

TYRONE: Good. We'll need your Mauser [mouser] for these rats.

BOB: But tell me—where are we?

TYRONE: In the stronghold of "Shameful Roger" Esterhazy, guiding genius of the gang.

BOB: Phew!

TYRONE: Exactly. And tonight finds our precious friend on the threshold of what may well be his most audacious exploit. You recall the recent disappearance of a certain Eunice Haverstraw, only daughter of wealthy Judge Haverstraw of Vandalia, Mo.?

BOB: I thought little of it at the time.

TYRONE: Few did. Through sources of information at my disposal, however, I soon found that "Shameful Roger" is keeping her prisoner in this maze of underground tunnels, employing a drug as yet little known to science, which paralyzes the will. (*lowering his voice*) Bob, I have every reason to believe he plans to substitute her for glamorous Irene Dunne in the R.K.O. production *She Married Her Public Relations Counsel!*

Bob: The man must be a devil in human guise!

Tyrone: Furthermore, he intends to smuggle himself into Metro-Goldwyn-Mayer, pass himself off as Louis B. Mayer, and then embark on a veritable orgy of substitution!

Bob: How to circumvent this mad enterprise calculated to strike at the very heart of the flicker industry?

Tyrone: I have been racking my pate for the solution. Luckily, I have wormed my way into the confidence of "Feathers" Blake, Esterhazy's moll, whom I am expecting here at any moment.

Bob (*soberly*): This is playing with fire, old chap. Keep your nose clean; you are treading on dangerous ground.

Tyrone (*pushing him out the door*): Look, you go and reconnoiter. And if you can't find Eunice Haverstraw, for God's sake dig up some new metaphors. (*As Bob exits, the sliding panel opens and "Feathers" Blake enters sinuously. She wears tight black satin and silver foxes, carries a mesh bag containing a wicked little pearl-handled revolver.*)

Feathers (*her eyes smoldering*): Hello, you two-timing bastard.

Tyrone: Why, what's the matter, Feathers?

Feathers: Nothing. I always say that whenever I enter a room. (*lifting her face to his*) Like me a little?

Tyrone: What do you think?

Feathers: What do I think?

Tyrone: Yes, what do you think?

Feathers: About what?

Tyrone: I forget.

Feathers: The trouble with you is you're more in love with love than you are with me.

Tyrone (*parrying*): Love is a sometime thing.

Feathers: Well, get this, brother. You remain true to me or I'll kill you.

Tyrone (*thinking to pass it off lightly*): You'll have to make me a better offer than that—ha-ha-ha!

Feathers: Quiet, you heel. (*She seals his mouth with a kiss.*)

Tyrone: I wonder if we're being quite fair to "Shameful Roger" Esterhazy.

Feathers: Pah! He's busy with that blond milksop, Eunice Haverstraw.

Tyrone (*craftily*): Where do you suppose he keeps her concealed?

Feathers (*off her guard*): In a suite of apartments directly above, furnished in truly Oriental splendor.

TYRONE: Say, let's sneak up there—it might be a lark! (*A gong sounds; they turn, startled, to find "Shameful Roger" Esterhazy in the doorway. He is a sinister, well-groomed individual on the order of Cesar Romero, educated both here and abroad, speaks several languages miserably. The occupants of the bunks slide down and surround the guilty couple.*)

ESTERHAZY (*blandly*): Good evening, my dear. . . . So you're the young man who has been meddling in my affairs. (*His men seize and bind Tyrone and Feathers.*)

TYRONE (*boldly*): Your goose is cooked, Esterhazy. All the facts relative to your dubious operations are in a safe-deposit box at the Cordwainers' and Poulterers' National Bank—and the D.A. has the key!

ESTERHAZY: Yes, my friend, but I have you. Now, Mr. Rukeiser, we shall have a little *divertissement*, so you will please to sit very quietly in that chair. (*His aides produce a gunnysack, place Feathers inside, and open a hidden trap door.*)

TYRONE (*playing for time*): You are a cunning adversary, "Shameful Roger." I confess I hardly expected to see the Los Angeles River here.

ESTERHAZY: Simply a tributary, my dear fellow, but the effect is the same. You're next, so watch closely. Lower away, lads. (*As they pick up the bag, the sharp notes of a bugle ring out off stage and eight comely misses in Girl Scout uniform burst in the door, brandishing swords made of lath. They quickly overpower Esterhazy and his confederates.*)

CORPORAL DORA AMMIDOWN (*to Tyrone*): We got your message in the nick of time.

ESTERHAZY (*with an oath*): Jeekers! Who are you, anyway?

THE GIRLS: The D.A.R.

ESTERHAZY: Who?

THE GIRLS: The Daughters of Albertina Rasch!

BOB BUNDY (*entering with a beautiful heiress*): And here is Eunice Haverstraw, in fairly good condition. (*A portly gentleman in cutaway and silk hat pushes through the throng and embraces her.*)

JUDGE HAVERSTRAW (*to Tyrone*): You've rounded up a dangerous nest of radicals, my boy. Here is my certified check for fifty thousand dollars Mex. (*his eyes twinkling*) And if Eunice still wants you—well, son, there's always a partnership open in Dostoievski, Griscom, Zarathustra & Haverstraw.

TYRONE: Thanks, Judge, but—well, I guess I have a previous commitment.

JUDGE HAVERSTRAW (*loudly*): Why, what do you mean, you insolent guttersnipe?

TYRONE (*softly, to Bob*): Shall we tell them?

BOB (*blushing*): If—if you like, Tyrone. (*Bob hastily removes his disguise of motion-picture executive, revealing himself to be Rosalind Russell. An instant of surprise, and then all join in a long locomotive for the lovers and troop off, leaving Feathers to kick around disconsolately in her gunnysack until the stagehands release her.*)

CURTAIN

PART II

1944–1950

THE ENSUING PIECES *were published, with one exception, in the* Saturday Evening Post, The New Yorker, *and* Holiday. *The very first compendium,* Acres and Pains, *was the by-product of a dozen years of country living. Of it, critics have been gracious enough to say that it is irradiated by a tenderness, a nobility of vision that recall Ella Wheeler Wilcox at her most glutinous. Throughout its pages resound the cheep of the junco, the croak of bullfrogs, and the wail of the oppidan who has been taken to the cleaners. It is not too remarkable, therefore, that after my exposure to rural highbinders, I should have sought solace in early fantasies—specifically, in the novels (and later the movies) of my adolescence appraised under the running head of "Cloudland Revisited." The omnivorous reader, dismayed at the omission of his childhood favorites like Voynich's* The Gadfly, Girl of the Limberlost, *and* The House of Bondage *by Reginald Wright Kauffman, may suppose that I overlooked them. He is mistaken; from Mrs. E.D.E.N. Southworth up to Viña Delmar, from Warwick Deeping right back to Kirk Munro, I reread every glorious bit of bombast. One rhinestoned tidbit only lingers in*

127

*my memory, from an author I can no longer identify. It ran:
"There were sweetheart roses on Yancey Wilmerding's bureau
that morning. Wide-eyed and distraught, she stood with all her
faculties rooted to the floor."*

Included toward the end of this section is Westward Ha!, *the
record of a trip around the world in 1947, and two chapters
from a subsequent journey in 1949,* The Swiss Family Perelman.
*Their appearance in print, it is proper to note, aroused a storm
of protest in several quarters. Certain Venetians contended that
I had plagiarized Marco Polo shamelessly, while some handker-
chief-heads in Muscat asserted that I had glommed whole pages
from the works of the great fifteenth-century Arab geographer,
Ibn Battuta. Rather than defile myself with mudslinging, I deposited the royalties from the books in an escrow account at my
bankers (Messrs. Cox & Baring, Ltd.), with instructions to pay
them to any heirs of these ancients who might materialize. Both
coins are still there, firmly secured by Scotch tape, which effectively demonstrates, I think, the absurdity of the charges. So
much for chiselers, whether Venetians, Arabs, or publishers.*

❦ ACRES AND PAINS

ONE

IF YOU CAN spare the time to drive sixty miles into the backwoods of eastern Pennsylvania, crouch down in a bed of poison ivy, and peer through the sumacs, you will be rewarded by an interesting sight. What you will see is a middle-aged city dweller, as lean and bronzed as a shad's belly (I keep a shad's belly hanging up in the barn for purposes of comparison), gnawing his fingernails and wondering how to abandon a farm. Outside of burning down the buildings, I have tried every known method to dispose of it. I have raffled it off, let the taxes lapse, staked it on the turn of a card, and had it condemned by the board of health. I have cut it up into building lots which proved unsalable, turned it over to picnic parties who promptly turned it back. I have sidled up to strangers and whispered hoarsely, "Psst, brother, want to buy a hot farm?" only to have them call a policeman. One rainy day, in desperation, I even tried desertion. Lowering a dory, I shouted, "Stern all for your lives!" and began sculling away rapidly. Unfortunately, I had forgotten to remove the flowers that grew in the boat, and nightfall found me still on the lawn with a backache and a fearful head cold.

I began my career as a country squire with nothing but a high heart, a flask of citronella, and a fork for toasting marshmallows in case supplies ran low. In a scant fifteen years I have acquired a superb library of mortgages, mostly first editions, and the finest case of sacroiliac known to science. In that period I made several important discoveries. The first was that there are no chiggers in an air-cooled movie and that a corner delicatessen at dusk is more exciting than any rainbow. On a fine night, no matter how fragrant the scent of the nicotiana, I can smell the sharp pungency of a hot corned-beef sandwich all the way from New York. I also learned that to lock horns with Nature, the only equipment you really need is the constitution of Paul Bunyan and the basic training of a commando. Most of the handbooks on country living are written by flabby men at the Waldorf-Astoria, who lie in bed and dictate them to secretaries. The greatest naturalist I know lives in a penthouse overlooking Central Park. He hasn't raised his window shades in twenty years.

Actually I never would have found myself in the middle of eighty-three unimproved acres had I been a bit less courteous. One day back in 1932, I was riding a crosstown trolley in Manhattan when I noticed a little old lady swaying before me, arms laden with bundles. Though almost thirty, she was very well preserved; her hair was ash-blond, her carmine lips wore a mocking pout, and there was such helpless innocence in her eyes that I sprang to her rescue. Dislodging the passenger next to me, I offered her the seat and we fell into conversation. It soon developed that we had both been reared in the country and shared a mutual love for wildflowers and jam. At the next stop, I persuaded her to accompany me to a wildflower-and-jam store where we could continue our chat. It was only after our fifth glass of jam that my new friend confided her desperate plight. Her aged parents were about to be evicted from their farm unless she could raise five hundred dollars immediately. Through sheer coincidence, I happened to have drawn that amount from the bank to buy my wife a fur coat. Knowing she would have done likewise, I pressed it on the fair stranger and signed some sort of document, the exact nature of which escaped me. After a final round of jam, she presented me with her card and left, vowing eternal gratitude. On examining it, I noticed a curious inscription in fine print. It read, "Licensed Real-Estate Agent."

I still have the card in my upper bureau drawer. Right next to it, in a holster, is a Smith & Wesson .38 I'm holding in escrow for the lady the next time we meet. And we will—don't you worry. I've got plenty of patience. That's one thing you develop in the country.

TWO

OUTSIDE of a spring lamb trotting into a slaughterhouse, there is nothing in the animal kingdom as innocent and foredoomed as the new purchaser of a country place. The moment he scratches his signature on the deed, it is open season and no limit to the bag. At once, Nature starts cutting him down to size. Wells that bubbled over for two hundred years mysteriously go dry, stone walls develop huge fissures, and chimneys sag out of plumb. Majestic elms which have withstood the full fury of the hurricane and the Dutch blight begin shedding their leaves; oaks dating from the reign of Charles II fade like cheap calico. Meanwhile, the former owner is busy removing a few personal effects. He rolls up the lawn preparatory to loading it on flatcars, floats the larger trees downstream, and carts off the corncrib, woodshed and toolhouse. When I first viewed my own property, my dewy naïveté was incredible—even Dewey Naïveté, the agent who showed me around, had to suppress a smile. What sealed the choice was a decrepit hen-house occupied by a flock of white Wyandottes. According to my esti-mate, it needed only a vigorous dusting and a small can of enamel to transform it into a snug guest cottage. Shading my eyes, I could see the magnificent wistaria, heavy with blooms, creeping up a lattice any amateur could construct with ten cents' worth of nails. As soon as I took possession, though, I discovered it must have been on casters, for all that greeted me was a yawning pit trimmed with guano and egg-shells.

This baptism, however, was merely a prelude to the keelhauling the natives had in store. Like any greenhorn from the city, I used to choke up freely at the sight of the man with the hoe. Every bumpkin I encountered reminded me of Daniel Webster; his dreariest platitude had the dignity and sweep of Walt Whitman's verse. Selecting one noble old patriarch, who I was sure had served with John Brown at Harpers Ferry, I commissioned him to paint the barn. Several days later, he notified me that forty-seven gallons were exhausted. "No use skimpin'," he warned. "A hickory stump, a widow woman and a barn has to be protected from the weather." I was chuckling over this bit of folk wisdom without quite understanding it when I detected a slight bulge under his coat similar to that caused by a five-gallon drum. He intercepted my glance and informed me fluently that he usually picked a few cranberries during his lunch hour. Apparently he lunched on Cape Cod, five hundred miles to the north, but since he never took more than half an hour, I overlooked it and ordered more paint. A week afterward, his barn burst forth in a shade of red identical with mine.

"Looks like yours, don't it?" He grinned. "Durned if I can tell 'em apart." I knew what he meant.

I have been taken to the cleaners since by some notable brigands, but the most brazen of the lot was the kinsman of Jesse James who re-paired our road. Edward Mittendorf and his merry men spent a fort-night lounging about in well-cut slacks, pitching quoits and reading

Kierkegaard. Occasionally one of the more enterprising workmen
would saunter over and deposit a pinch of gravel daintily in the ruts.
Whenever my wife passed by, the crew appraised her charms, whistling and clucking spiritedly. I entered a mild demurrer and received
the following instructions: "You tell 'em, corset; you've been around
the ladies." The day of settlement dawned on schedule, and with Mittendorf watching me beadily, I began to examine his bill. It was a
closely typewritten document resembling the annual report of the Federal Reserve. Among other items he listed depreciation on shovels,
lemonades for the men, and some bridgework his niece had ordered.

"Who's Ed Mittendorf?" I inquired, indicating a salary in excess of
Cary Grant's.

"My cousin—the little fat feller," he explained.

"Is he the same as Eddie Mittendorf?" I asked.

"No, that's my dad," he returned smoothly, "and Ned Mittendorf
there, he's my uncle. I'm Edward—got that straight?"

"I should," I snapped. "Your name's down here twice."

"It is?" he gasped. "Well, I swan."

I swanned also on reading the total, but I paid through the nose, a
locale which was rapidly taking on the aspect of a teller's window. If
you ever drive up the lane, be careful. Those diamonds raise hell with
your treads.

THREE

I WOULDN'T live in the city if you paid me a million dollars a year—
well, let's say forty-two dollars a year. How people can exist side by
side with utter disregard for each other, never prying into anybody's
business, is beyond me. In the country, folks are more matey; there is
always an extra stiletto for the newcomer and a friendly hand ready to
tighten around his throat. The moving men have hardly kicked the
rungs out of your Chippendale chairs before neighbors spring up like
mushrooms, eager to point out any flaws you may have missed in your
place and gloat over your predicament. My wife and I were still knee-
deep in a puddle outside our front door, exchanging shrill taunts and
questioning each other's legitimacy, when our first visitor drove up.
Shearing off an irreplaceable dogwood, he pulled into a flower bed and

got out. From the expression of mingled condescension, malice and envy, I knew at once he must be another city man turned farmer. As his gaze traveled slowly over the *estancia*, he took on the look of one who has just bitten into an unripe persimmon.

"Finally unloaded it, did they?" he remarked with a ghoulish smirk.

"What do you mean?" I asked, my hackles rising to attention.

"The old pesthouse," he said intimately. "So they found a simp to take it off their hands."

"Oh, I don't know," I said with what started out as dignity but wound up as a girlish toss of the head. He examined my clothes intently. "You the hired man?" he asked at length.

"No, the simp," I snarled. There was a brief interval during which I could hear his watch ticking.

"No hard feelings, brother," he said eventually. "Nice little spot you've got here. My name's Grundy." He held out his hand.

"Mine's Frankenstein," I said, ignoring it, "and this is the Monster," I added, indicating my wife.

"Glad to know you, Mrs. Monster," he acknowledged. "I see you're having trouble with your foundation."

"I *beg* your pardon," she snapped with considerable hauteur, furtively smoothing her hips.

"I mean, of the house," Grundy corrected himself. "I saw your husband creeping around under the porch a while ago."

"Oh, he was just rooting for truffles," she said sweetly. As she stalked off, Grundy smacked his lips. "Some package," he commented. "Where'd a little shrimp like you ever meet her?"

"Listen here, my friend," I began, taking a step toward him.

"Yes," he said thoughtfully, "you've got plenty of things to worry about. You'll never be able to drink the water—it's tainted. And that woodwork of yours is alive with termites. What did you give for this root cellar?"

"Nothing," I lied. "We took it for a bad debt."

"Well, you were stung," said Grundy. "Come here." He approached one of the windows, and whipping out a jackknife, slashed at the casings. Several panes of glass shivered into fragments on the ground. "Putty's rotten," he said triumphantly. "It's the talk of the countryside. And that's not all. See that stream down there? Every spring it rises to the second story. You'll be doubled up with rheumatism, if the mosquitoes don't get you first. You know, I never saw the shack by daylight before; no wonder they say it's haunted. Now, you take my place—"

We took his place. It had thirty-five rooms and ten baths—snug but adequate for his needs. The attic was hand-hewn out of solid cherry, with burled walnut floors. For odd jobs he employed a lineal descendant of Cellini, whom he paid off in green trading stamps; the latter had just remodeled the barn into a game room and servants' quarters at a total cost of $2.76. The soil was none too fertile, he admitted—it took a week for tomatoes to bear and his dahlias were only a foot across. But there were so many trout in his creek that you could walk across without wetting your feet.

"Tell you what I'd do if I were you," he concluded. "I'd pitch a tent outside and use the dwelling for a cow stable. Only watch out where you camp; the grass is full of black widows." He left, whistling the "Dead March" from *Saul*, and I entered the house to find my wife in tears. She cried for six days and on the seventh created apple butter. It was good, but not like the woman's next door.

FOUR

EVERY now and then on a breathless August evening, I like to draw up my easy chair before a glowing fire, puff on a calabash and stare thoughtfully into the flames. The heat is unendurable and the calabash makes me nauseated, but like a bachelor remembering his summer sweethearts, it helps me recall the architects who have almost remodeled my quaint old stone farmhouse. For the money I have spent on blueprints alone, I could have razed the house, erected a replica of the Taj Mahal, and retired to Sun Valley. If I ever adopt a coat of arms, it will show a ravenous draftsman sighting through a transit, over a shield marked "Soft Pickings."

The most recent architect I engaged was as typical as any. He came highly recommended by my attorney, Newmown Hay, of Ashen, Livid & Hay, a profound student of the dollar. From Hay's account, he had just converted a decrepit feed mill into a lordly mansion complete with ballroom and interior squash courts for a little more than $200. The cost would have been half, the architect explained, if Hay had not insisted on marble stairs. The man seemed to have a shrewd eye for values and I crisply outlined my needs—five rooms, three baths, a sun porch, a rumpus room and a tennis court. He made a hasty calculation on the back of my collar and informed me it would cost $1500. I am not one to haggle over pennies and I signed a contract forthwith. He collected fifty clams as a token of good faith—my good faith—and arranged to inspect the premises shortly.

His arrival coincided unhappily with that of an actor named Cagney, who had dropped in to borrow a cup of film and was exclaiming over my freesias—people come from as far as ten feet around to exclaim over my freesias. The architect kept staring suspiciously at him while I was posing my problem. "I've seen that man somewhere before," he said accusingly.

"Yes, yes," I murmured. "Now if we extend this wing to here—" Suddenly I realized I had lost my audience; he had sneaked up the slope and was peering narrowly at Cagney from behind a syringa bush.

"Listen," he whispered excitedly, clutching my arm. "I can't place this bird, but he's wanted by the police! I got a hunch I saw his picture in a post office—I never forget a face." All at once his jaw dropped and he uttered a squeal. "It's Cagney!" he shrilled. "James Cagney!" Before I could intercede, he had pinned his quarry to the fence, and was re-enacting his favorite scenes in the latter's movies. I fought my way in between them, vainly attempting to restore the architect to his senses.

"I want the master bedroom facing north!" I shouted desperately. "Then we can put the kitchen in the cellar—I mean, the cellar in the attic!" The architect tried to shake me off, but I clung, and we rocked about the lawn like three dancing bears. Finally I managed to loosen his grip, and he made a cursory, grumbling survey of the house.

"It's a mess," he said, "but maybe I can save it." When I suggested he look inside, he grew pale with fury. "Are you trying to teach me my own business?" he snapped. In leaving, he asked Cagney for a small loan, implying that I would probably chisel him out of his fee. I eventually persuaded him to accept a check for a hundred on account, though it was plain he would have preferred cash.

The following Monday, at three o'clock in the morning, he phoned me with a frantic appeal for another hundred; his wife was just undergoing a serious operation. In the background I could hear the characteristic tumult of a hospital amphitheater—the strains of a jukebox, the tinkle of ice, and a male quartet singing "Hold That Tiger." The patient subsequently had two relapses, each of which cost me an additional sawbuck. By the time I got the preliminary sketches, Sir Christopher Wren had put the bite on me for four hundred dollars. The first contractor I consulted estimated the job at $21,942. The second was

136 The Most of S. J. Perelman

unable to read the plans. The third, who took the job, had a nervous breakdown a week later.

Six months afterward I met the architect on Fifth Avenue with a friend. He cut me dead, and as I passed him I heard him say, "See that little sneak? If I had the money he owes me, I'd be in clover."

FIVE

THE events of last Saturday afternoon may be summarized briefly as follows: At 2:30 I was dozing on the porch of my rustic retreat, in tune with the infinite and my fellow-man. Above my head, instead of the usual saw biting through a log labeled "Z-z-z," was an acetylene torch cutting a steel girder; there is no room on the up-to-date farm for anti-quated methods. At 2:35, roused from my reverie by my wife's broom, I was toiling up a ninety-degree incline with two king-sized pails of garbage. At 2:37, with a report like a pistol crack, several vertebrae went off duty, and by three o'clock I was back on the porch, reeking of liniment and watching my wife toil up the incline with the pails. Pain-ful as it was to turn my head, I gamely spurred her on, and were it not for my constant inspiration and advice, she might never have com-pleted her mission.

Every time I step off that porch, something disastrous happens. The worst mistake the owner of a country place can make is choosing a role too ambitious for his talents. A recent neighbor of mine, for instance, found a lawn mower left by the previous tenant. He immediately began pushing it around in the hot sun, unaware that grass dies back anyhow after a sharp frost. Today that man is a hopeless wreck in a sanitarium, shattered in mind and body. When I first settled down on a heap of shale in the Delaware Valley, I too had a romantic picture of myself. For about a month I was a spare, sinewy frontiersman in fringed buck-skin, with crinkly little lines about the eyes and a slow laconic drawl. One look told you that my ringing ax and long Kentucky rifle would tame the forest in jigtime. In fact, as I stepped off the train, I overheard a native remark admiringly, "His ringing ax and long Kentucky rifle should tame the forest in jigtime."

After I almost blew off a toe cleaning an air rifle, though, I decided I was more the honest rural type. I started wearing patched blue jeans, mopped my forehead with a red banana (I found out later it should have been a red bandanna), and crumbled bits of earth between my fingers to see whether it was friable enough. Friable enough for what I wasn't quite sure, but I kept at it until my wife screamed like a banshee if I so much as picked up a clod. I never entered our kitchen like a normal individual; I always stamped in roaring, "Well, Mother, got plenty of vittles for the menfolk? Thrashin' sure makes a man hongry!" The upshot was that the hired girl started leaving a couple of sandwiches behind the barn. I even went so far as to buy a good secondhand tractor. It was dirt cheap, as the engine had disappeared; nevertheless, I got some really effective snapshots of myself against the horizon. At sundown, when the day's loafing was done, I generally repaired to the village store with a quid of cut plug in my cheek, and spent the evening sullenly spitting on my bluchers and cursing the Administration. Sometimes I did a little whittling, but just because a few measly shavings fell into the cracker barrel, the postmaster made a neurotic, half-hysterical scene and I took my custom elswhere.

It was nearly two years before I discovered my true identity. One day, while stretched out on the porch, I realized I needed only a mint julep to become a real dyed-in-the-wool, Seagram's V.V.O. Southern planter. I promptly barked a command, which was ignored. Instead, my wife appeared and confronted me, arms akimbo. "Who do you think you are, you lug?" she demanded. "A Southern planter?" I knew at once my instinct was right and, dismissing her with a cut of my riding crop, set to work assembling the necessary gear. I sent to New York for a broad-brimmed hat and string tie, and at enormous expense trained the local idiot to fan me with a palmetto leaf. Procuring a no-account hound-dog was more difficult; every kennel I wrote to stocked thoroughbreds, so I was finally forced to buy one and starve it into submission. It has taken a lack of energy and a shiftlessness few men are capable of, but after eight years you can't tell me from the genuine article—at least, that's what the hookworms say. Up to last Saturday I never once budged off that porch. Well, I've only myself to blame. I guess I'm my own worst enemy.

SIX

THERE is nothing like a farm, a mountain lodge or a seashore bungalow to bring out the latent mechanic in a man. Once the deed is filed
and he stands alone at last with his utilities, he is Cortez on a peak in
Darien. Of course, if your name is Cortez and you live on a peak in
Darien, Connecticut, your problem is simple. You call in a plumber
from Danbury and forget about it. I couldn't; when I returned to the
soil, I had a ten-cent screwdriver and the mechanical skill of a turtle.
Today, thanks to unremitting study, I can change a fuse so deftly that
it plunges the entire county into darkness. The neighbors call me "the
boy Steinmetz" and things like that (the other things are shorter). The
power company has offered me as high as fifteen thousand dollars a
year to stay out of my own cellar.

The other night, for example. I had invited some guests to dinner at
Hysteria Hall and we were grouped around the groaning board (the
board was groaning because one end was supported by a chair until I
could replace the missing leg). Halfway through the meal, a strident
clanking began under our very feet, as though somebody were striking
the furnace with a length of chain. I raised my voice to drown it out,
but I could see my audience was wool-gathering. At first I suspected
my wife, who will resort to the most shameless devices to spoil an
anecdote. Then I realized she was flinching in concert with the company. The noise redoubled. "Sounds like chains, doesn't it?" I stammered desperately. "You know, this house was a station on the Underground Railway, and there's an old legend—"

I was interrupted by a bubbling effect, as of water seeping through a
dining-room floor, and looked down to find an inch or two of moisture
lapping at my oxfords. Before I could explain that we had chosen a
low, marshy situation to remind us of the English lake country, my
wife rose through a jet of live steam like the devil in *Faust* and placed
a monkey wrench beside my plate. I pretended it was part of the meal,
a pantomime which threw my guests into gales of silence, and slunk off
into the cellar.

As one who flunked trigonometry four times, it took me only a moment to detect the source of the trouble. That little square business on
the electric pump—I forget just what they call it—had worked off.
This in turn disengaged the stopcock or the bushing (it was a bit too

dark to tell which) in such a way that the hot water was feeding into the coal bin instead of the storage tank, or flange. The whole thing was clearly the work of a master criminal, perhaps Professor Moriarty himself, who had further anticipated my movements and laid a carpet sweeper athwart the stairs. I sidestepped neatly, but my head encountered a low rafter and I sustained a bruise roughly the size of a robin's egg; I speak of this with certainty as there chanced to be a robin's egg lying on a nearby shelf. Luckily, I am as tough as nails, and picking myself up at the bottom of the steps, I set to work. By exerting a slight leverage, I succeeded in prying off the gasket, or outer jacket of the pump, exactly as you would a baked potato. (I describe this simply so that even the layman can understand.) This gave me room to poke around the innards with a sharp stick. I cleaned the pump thoroughly, laid all the different wheels and cams on a board where the plumber could find them and, as a final precaution, opened the windows to allow the water to drain off down the slope.

On the way upstairs, I found my passage blocked by a jug of peach brandy, and after some difficulty managed to squeeze past it. Either it was stuffy in the basement or I had given too freely of my strength, for when I rejoined the party, I felt dizzy. My wife said later it wasn't so much the bric-a-brac I smashed as the language I used. It cost me a quart of Bellodgia and a star sapphire to square the rap, to say nothing of a new electric pump. However, the old one was nearly played out. Anybody could have seen it with half an eye—and I had that, Jack.

SEVEN

WEBSTER'S Collegiate Dictionary, which has a crew haircut, a class pipe and a yellow oilskin slicker, describes a farm as "a piece of land leased for cultivation, hence any tract devoted to agricultural purposes." I prefer my own definition. A farm is an irregular patch of nettles bounded by short-term notes, containing a fool and his wife who didn't know enough to stay in the city. In addition, it usually contains a curious piece of statuary that comes to life at mealtimes and answers to the name of Lafe. I have had seven handy men named Lafe since I went back to the soil. One of them was really two twelve-year-old boys who stood on each other's shoulders and shirked as a team. I never could determine their names, as I speak only three languages, but I made out the check to Lafe and it managed to get cashed.

I found the master, or original Lafe, in the weeds near the house the morning after we moved in. His mouth was open and a wren had built a nest in it. I started to train a vine over him, thinking he was part of the lattice, when he yawned suddenly. His first words were characteristic. "She's a white elephant," he said with gloomy relish. "She'll bankrupt you. You'll rue the day—" I had already heard the same aria sung by my bride and was in no mood for an encore. Thrusting a hatchet into his nerveless fingers, I indicated I needed firewood more than a forecast. An hour later I heard a sickening crash and ran out to find our most stately maple lying across the henhouse.

"No sense goin' all the way to the wood lot," commented Lafe. "She'd have blown over in the next storm anyway."

His successor was a gnarled old salt on the order of Popeye, with a face the color of teak and a gold earring. He had followed the sea from boyhood, having spent thirty-five years cleaning fish in Camden, New Jersey. His rolling walk quickly became more pronounced when he discovered the key to my liquor closet. At first he confined himself fastidiously to the rarer champagnes, but in time he let down the bars and would drink Scotch if forced to the wall. One morning, rummaging through the cellar, I came across him reclining face down in a puddle of Benedictine.

"Tastes just like candy, don't it?" he cackled. "Say, mate, I was looking over your wife yesterday. Cute little dish, ain't she?" I paid him off in Spanish doubloons and he departed, gaily humming a chantey. With him went a pair of my best cuff links and a dozen spoons.

He was followed by a drooping, melancholy individual who felt it was useless to plant vegetables or flowers, as the cutworm and the aphid were bound to get them eventually. According to advices he had received, the Japanese beetle was due to take over a week from Tuesday and it was flying in the face of Providence to resist. Most of this worthy's day was spent discussing his diseases, by far the most complex assortment ever suffered by mortal man. He was taking radio treatments for diabetes from a hex doctor in Allentown, the blood clot on his brain was the despair of the medical world, and his legs were slowly turning to stone from overexertion in his youth. Despite a touch of arthritis and a few adhesions, however, he ate like a wolf and slept fourteen hours a night. He was still sleepy the second day when I drove him to the junction to catch the evening train. I asked him about his future plans. He figured he might go out to the Mayo Clinic for a while. He hadn't wanted to alarm me, but his milt was enlarged three times its normal size.

My present Lafe is a man of varied talents. He has been successively a comic artist, a scenario writer and a playwright. In appearance he suggests the Apollo Belvedere, though his brain has the same specific gravity as that of Blaise Pascal. To watch him swing a scythe or clean a cistern is an experience to curl your hair. Under his guidance the farm has become a show place, producing blights and fungi unknown to botany. For my part, he's got a lifetime job, whether he likes it or not. It's kind of a nuisance making out checks to myself as "Lafe," but it has one advantage. There's no back talk.

EIGHT

As THOUGH everyone hasn't trouble enough, a little group of research workers—played by Paul Muni—at the Rockefeller Foundation—played by Morris Carnovsky—has recently been inducing nervous breakdowns in dogs. The boys have been feeding Fido mock hamburger, strafing him with squadrons of heavy-duty fleas, and setting him loose on lifelike burglars made of cardboard. A week of this treatment turns the average dog into a hopeless neurotic, and Dame Rumor —played by Dame May Whitty—has it that they mean to extend the experiments to humans. If so, I can save them considerable time and money with a modest home recipe. Just whip an ordinary stolid citizen into a country house, mix well with carpenters, painters and electricians, and in six hours he will be reduced to the consistency of a plate of warm calf's-foot jelly.

I slunk into my badger hole in the Keystone State some years ago with a couch hammock, an apparatus for making carbonated water which exploded, and a theory which exploded even more quickly. The theory was that I would lie in the hammock under the collected works of H. D. Thoreau and breathe gently through my gills until sleep knitted up the raveled sleave of care. For exercise, I planned to raise to my lips at regular intervals a small vase of fruit juice laced with gin and banked by fronds. My blueprints also called for a deep-bosomed mammy in snowy-white kerchief, who would issue from her laboratory every few minutes and revive my flagging strength with delicate little *canapés*, spoon bread and apple turnovers.

I was still fuming over the knots in the hammock when a virago, played by my wife, entered intoning a dirge. The closets were too shallow for her evening gowns; the original Pennsylvania Dutch settlers had neglected to provide a glassed-in conservatory; she needed a special room with running water for washing dishes. Employing the simplest words, I patiently explained I was not Diamond Jim Brady. With silken insolence, this starveling whom I had rescued from a taxi dance hall confided that, on the contrary, I usually reminded her of Uriah Heep or Old Scrooge. An instant later she regretted her tartness and, after applying beefsteak to her eye, I issued a writ for the necessary artisans.

For a month nobody appeared; then, one morning about four, I awoke to find myself in the midst of Donnybrook Fair. A well digger's derrick had sprung up at the foot of my bed and was boring toward China at two dollars a minute. Masons, plumbers and tinsmiths swarmed through the rooms, wrestling and playing leapfrog. One gang of carpenters had peeled off the roof like the skin of an onion and was beating the rafters with mallets; a second was hurriedly erecting a scaffold to afford a better view of the maid in her shower. I had a slight headache caused by exposure to some poisoned bourbon and the tumult made me restless. I arose and, draped in a torn seersucker bathrobe, fell downstairs over a scantling. Two jubilant carpenters awaited me. "We're all out of cotter pins," they giggled, "and you forgot the side anchors for the sash bolting." I stuffed a shirt into a pair of pants and drove in my robe to Bethlehem, thirty miles away. A canvass of five hardware stores proved fruitless, but a few miles farther, at Easton, I succeeded in picking up some cheap sterling-silver bolts answering the purpose. The carpenters interrupted their rubber of bridge to examine my purchase. "You should of bought the bronze ones," they observed critically. "But we don't need 'em anyway. We used an old piece of baling wire."

At the close of business that evening they presented me with two gables of the original dwelling and the second finest collection of pre-Revolutionary rubble, banana peels and waxed paper in North America. I bedded down my flock in the grape arbor and lived on potato chips for the duration. I paid the final bill from an armored car escorted by six burly guards. The varnish was scarcely dry on the floors when a friend dropped in to see me. As I showed him proudly through the house, he nodded appreciatively. "You've got a dandy layout here, old man," he admitted. "Why don't you shell out a few bucks and re-model it?"

NINE

ACCORDING to recent figures compiled by trained statisticians working under filtered oatmeal, the first thing ninety-four per cent of the population does on acquiring a country place is to build some sort of swimming pool. The other six per cent instantly welshes on the deal and stops payment. I tried to, but the previous owner beat me to the bank. My checkbook had hardly ceased thrashing about in its final agony before I was out in honey-colored corduroy leggings, barking orders at a team of mules and a scoop shovel. I didn't want anything showy, just a fiord about the size of Lake Huron deep enough to float a yawl. In my overheated imagination I saw our anemic little creek transformed into a crystal mirror bordered by gay cabañas. I could almost hear the bevy of Powers models sighing with envy as my tanned, muscular form flashed off the springboard in a perfect swan dive. I even wired the Department of the Interior that if Grand Coulee proved insufficient, I could furnish water power to keep the wheels turning for a year or two.

What I had when the gang of workmen departed was a small, shrunken buffalo wallow infested with every variety of poisonous snake known to man, including several found only in the upper reaches of the Orinoco. Its surface was covered with an attractive green film dotted with decaying stumps and half-submerged oilcans. At night a dense mist shrouded the tarn, eerie lights flickered in the rushes, ghostly chuckles were audible, and if you ventured too close, you were liable to encounter a transparent citizen carrying his head under his arm. Thirteen families of ground hogs had set up light housekeeping in the dam itself, a massive affair of earth and logs that looked like the Union breastworks before Vicksburg. Every time it rained, the water boiled up, punching another hole in the structure, and I ran down the valley to pay the neighbors for the chickens it swept away. My children went hungry and unshod while I poured tons of cement into the coffers to make them hold. One morning I caught myself cackling hysterically and ramming an old mattress into the dam, and I knew I was licked. I called in the local dynamiter, indicated the project with a careless wave, and commanded him to erase it from the face of the earth.

The moment word was bruited about that Loch Wampum was doomed, the local savants gathered on the banks for a gleeful death watch. The man who had done the excavating was especially triumphant. "I could have told him it wouldn't work," he crowed. "By rights he should have dug out that gully where they dump the swill. Good stone bottom there." I asked him why he hadn't mentioned it earlier. "It don't pay to poke your nose in other people's business," he replied virtuously.

It took a day and a half for the dynamiter to drill the charges and string red flags across the township. On the appointed morning, the place was busier than New London during the Harvard-Yale regatta. Whole clans of Mennonites and Amish bearing box lunches arrived from the back country in ancient buckboards. Sightseers wandered through the garden poking sly fun at our vegetables, and one bystander mimicked my gait and speech so cleverly that I could not help sharing the general merriment. When everything was ready, I retired to the toolshed with my family and made them lie flat on the floor. With a warning, "Stand clear, all!" the dynamiter threw his switch. The blast which followed tore the roof off the springhouse and broke windows in the county seat sixteen miles away. Its only effect on the dam, however, was to harden the cement in it. My specialist bit his lip in chagrin. "I must have cut her a bit too fine," he confessed; "I'll fix her tomorrow, by cracky."

He kept his word. When the dust finally settled, I had enough firewood for the next fifty years, most of it right inside the house where I could get at it. And when *I* finally settled, the man next door had a new front porch and a glass eye you couldn't tell from the other one. Of course it's a bit unwieldy for five people to take a bath in a washtub, particularly at one time, but at least you don't have to look out for copperheads.

TEN

YEARS before I bought Rising Gorge, my Bucks County chalet, I used to run into some former friend in a railroad terminal, his arms bristling with garden tools, insecticides and poultry leaflets, and a pair of rose-colored bifocals askew on his nose. Invariably the exile would sashay into a sales talk. "You owe it to the kiddies, old man," he would entreat, choking back a lump in his throat. "Never saw such a change in mine. Junior grew fourteen inches the first week. He's only nine, and he can split a cord of wood, milk twenty-one cows and cultivate a field of corn by sunup. Sister's not even three, but you ought to taste her preserves. They're famous for a hundred miles around."

In time the refrain began to worry me. I felt inferior on my son's third birthday that other men his age were operating combines when he could hardly shoe a horse. It humiliated me profoundly that my daughter, a strapping hulk of two, was unable to bake a pie. This process of slow erosion had its effect; one morning I awoke with a dizzy feeling to find that I had acquired a piece of loam about the size of Nepal as a proving ground for their talents.

At first, in the natural bustle of making the house unlivable, the children were forgotten. Everything had to be scraped down to the original knotty pine, good hardware replaced with rusty hinges, wagon wheels substituted for candelabra, and the place generally made to resemble a rathskeller on the verge of bankruptcy. During this period a nurse stood guard over the brood, a sinister gargoyle with the temper of a wasp and a face hewn out of Indiana limestone. Miss Bramble had lived on some of the finest estates at Newport and had certain standards, even if she *was* working for poor white trash. Every afternoon she dressed her charges in Eton jackets, starched muslin, and velvet ribbons, which seemed rather formal wear for the manure pile. By skillful suggestion, she built up the notion of snakes in the greenery to the point where screams rang out when a salad was placed on the table. Her martyrdom reached a climax, however, at the sight of the master carrying ashes out of the cellar. She observed tartly that her late employer at Bailey's Beach had two foreigners to do that type of work, both of whom were better groomed than myself. I stood it until the children started following me around with a chant Nanny had taught them. "Here comes that ole ash man!" they jeered. "Any rags, any bones, any bottles today?" I caught the pair of them hiding in a drain and Nanny caught the 5:15.

For a month afterward, the hardy young pioneers refused to leave the kitchen. The yard, they moaned, was full of great fur-bearing vampires with human faces on the order of Miss Bramble's. Squealing, kicking and gouging, they were flung outside each morning, only to spend the day baying through the screen door. At length I made an eloquent speech painting the joys of a country childhood, embroidered with references to Huck Finn, slingshots, Barlow knives, and fishing for bullheads. In closing, I presented the boy with a bamboo pole and a bent pin. With instinctive gallantry, the little chap promptly presented it to his sister, in the left eye. Giving him a kindly pat with a hairbrush, I changed my approach. I cited young Abe Lincoln, young Tom Edison, and other movie notables distinguished for their self-reliance. I explained how a poor youth named Benjamin Franklin had arrived in a great city munching a roll and had subsequently discovered the secret of electricity. My plea to emulate his example at once bore fruit. An hour later the porch was strewn with several half-eaten rolls and someone had short-circuited the wiring by forcing a key into a floor plug.

By now, of course, their dexterity and knowledge of country lore is fabulous; they have learned to perform a thousand disagreeable chores around the house. If I need a bean bag dropped into the plumbing to tie up the water system or tacks spread in the driveway so the tires take hold, I can count on the services of two experts. No sparrow falls without finding his way to my bedroom, and there is always a freshly killed woodchuck by the breakfast plate to whet Daddy's appetite. And what with the bill for hay fever, poison oak, summer colic, and anti-tetanus, it takes a bit of whetting.

ELEVEN

ALMOST every Monday morning from May through late October, the Delaware Valley is the scene of a lovely old Pennsylvania Dutch ritual, or passion play, centering around my hovel. It is called "the changing of the maid," and, for sheer drama, suspense and production, far surpasses the changing of the guard at Buckingham Palace. It begins just about dawn with a salvo of saucepans and a poignant oratorio by the current cook. In this composition, the singer portrays herself as a sweet, patient foundling held prisoner by a drunken ogre who compels her to wear shoes while serving and sleep in a room with windows. Its climax is a haunting cadenza representing the boss as a tyrant, a miser and a leech. Soon a deeper baritone voice blends in with a ballad entitled "If We Can Do Without Broadway, We Can Do Without You." Following a brisk andante movement of a fountain pen scratching out a reference, a colorful procession winds toward the garage—the squire in his purple pajamas, with face to match, and behind him a grim domestic muttering to her satchels. As the screech of the gears fades into the distance, the brief tinkle of a telephone dialing a New York employment agency rings down the curtain.

No country home is complete without a surly figure seated in the kitchen like Rodin's Thinker, wishing she was back in a hot little room under the Third Avenue Elevated. Any maid who leaves the city is either suffering from a nervous breakdown or hiding from the Feds, which amounts to the same thing. Most of the ones I employed during the last decade wore a hunted look and carried hatboxes containing powerful short-wave radios. The moment the dishes were done, they would race to their rooms to broadcast our menu and other vital defense secrets to the Wilhelmstrasse. The last one always hummed the Horst Wessel song as she passed the mashed potatoes. She left in a fury when I refused to celebrate Hitler's birthday with a lawn party.

Perhaps the sorriest sight on a rural-free-delivery route is the transplanted jitterbug. Early this semester I imported a tense, wild-eyed creature named Rhodesia whose sole baggage was a make-up kit and a pair of dance clogs. Her face fell as we pulled away from the station. "I don't see no Ferris wheel," she whimpered. "The missus tole me you lived right smack on the midway." I explained that our farm was only three miles from a bustling village of fifty souls and that a neighbor's lights were clearly visible on the next ridge. Passing her tongue over her parched lips, she ventured the opinion that the region was full of wild animals. I quickly assured her that apart from an occasional werewolf, days would elapse without her seeing a sign of life. She spent the balance of the trip alternately caressing a rabbit's foot and consulting the *Witch's Dream Book*. On arriving at the hacienda, she mulishly hid under the porch for two hours, just because one of the dogs had romped with her throat. Dinner that night was fried chicken Maryland style, featuring pin feathers and a dash of coffee grounds. My wife offered her a book to take to bed, but she chose a cleaver instead. In the morning she showed her true colors by spitefully alluding to the maid's room as a chicken coop—pure malice, since no chickens had lived in it for more than a year and it had had a heavy coat of whitewash. Her dream book, she added, predicted a calamity unless she left at once. I had obtained the same prediction by simply studying the oatmeal, and in a trice Rhodesia was free, reasonably white, and twenty-one.

A series of local girls ranging from twelve to fifteen in age pitched out the fodder for a while thereafter, but there was always a rawboned suitor guffawing in the kitchen and shrill squeals of "Stop tickling me!" at mealtime. After eating a bran muffin in which the chef had also included scratch feed and oats, I wired New York for a really competent couple. The next morning, while I was processing a load of fertilizer in front of the barn, a long black Mercedes drew up bearing two poised and gracious gentlefolk. They examined the place attentively. "This is the gatekeeper's lodge," the woman said in Italian. "Ask this peasant where the main house is." I touched my cap, indicated the woods, and I haven't seen them since. My wife looks pretty tacky in a Mother Hubbard and you can get tired of turnips, but give me home cooking every time.

TWELVE

Now that spring again weaves a nest of robins in my hair and the first installment of the income tax fades into a discolored bruise, that annual bugbear, the vegetable garden, arises to plague me. As one who achieved the symmetry of a Humphrey Bogart and the grace of a jaguar purely on pastry, I have no truck with lettuce, cabbage and similar chlorophyll. Any dietitian will tell you that a running foot of apple strudel contains four times the vitamins of a bushel of beans. In my own case, at least, greens are synonymous with poison. Every time I crunch a stalk of celery, there is a whirring crash, a shriek of tortured capillaries, and my metabolism goes to the boneyard. Yet come the middle of April, the family invariably gets an urge to see the old man beating his brains out in the garden patch. It's funny, but nobody ever gets an urge to see him snoozing on the lounge. If he isn't staggering under a wheelbarrow of manure or grubbing in the subsoil, he's a leper.

Planning the garden takes place, as all the handbooks advise, long before the frost is out of the ground, preferably on a night recalling Keats's "Eve of St. Agnes," with hail lashing the windows. The dependents reverently produce the latest seed catalogue and succumb to mass hypnosis. "Look at those radishes—two feet long!" everyone marvels. "We could have them, too, if that lazy slug didn't curl up in the hammock all day." A list of staples is speedily drawn up: Brussels sprouts the size of a rugby, eggplant like captive balloons, and yams. Granny loves corn fritters; a half acre is allotted to Golden Bantam. The children need a pumpkin for Halloween, and let's have plenty of beets, we can make our own lump sugar. Then someone discovers the hybrids—the onion crossed with a pepper or a new vanilla-flavored turnip that plays the "St. James Infirmary Blues." When the envelope is finally sealed, the savings account is a whited sepulcher and all we need is a forty-mule team to haul the order from the depot.

The moment the trees are in bud and the soil is ready to be worked, I generally come down with a crippling muscular complaint as yet unclassified by science. Suffering untold agonies, I nonetheless have myself wheeled to the side line and coach a small, gnarled man of seventy in the preparation of the seedbed. The division of labor works out perfectly; he spades, pulverizes and rakes the ground, while I call out encouragement and dock his pay whenever he straightens up to light his pipe. The relationship is an ideal one, and I know he will never leave me as long as the chain remains fastened to his leg.

Within a few weeks the plants are sturdily poking their heads through the lava and broken glass, just in time to be eaten by cutworms, scorched by drought and smothered by weeds. The weeds native to the Pennsylvania countryside surpass in luxuriance anything you would encounter in the jungles of Cochin China or French Equatorial Africa. One variety I raised last summer had the sly hangdog phiz of a bookie and whispered off-color jokes every time I passed. Another, a revolting little fat weed, possessed the power of locomotion; it used to sneak around like Pecksniff, as though butter wouldn't melt in its mouth. I was also successful in developing a curious man-eating snail; but when the news photographer arrived to get a close-up, he and the snail frightened each other off the premises.

By the end of August the residue left by the rabbits and woodchucks is ready for harvest. It is always the same—tomatoes and squash. Tomatoes and squash never fail to reach maturity. You can spray them with acid, beat them with sticks and burn them; they love it. In forty-eight hours the place is knee-deep in rotting pulp and a fearful miasma overhangs the valley. Soon the most casual acquaintances start dropping in with creaking baskets and hypocritical smiles, attempting to fob off their excess tomatoes and squash. The more desperate even abandon tiny bundles on our doorstep like infants at the House of the Good Shepherd. The kitchen becomes an inferno of steam and the wife a frenzied sorceress stirring caldrons of pink slush. Ultimately, with a fanfare comparable to launching a dreadnought, two minute jars filled with an appalling green emulsion are borne to the table. If you don't taste it, you're a cad; if you do, you're a cadaver. The only solution is to plow everything under and live on pie. Reach for the sky, partner; I'm the Crisco Kid.

THIRTEEN

Look, friends, I'm just an ordinary country boy. I'm slow, and sort of quizzical, and as plain as an old board fence. I prize the quiet, homely things—applejack out of a charred keg, a bundle of faded securities, the rustle of old greenbacks. I love the scent of fresh-mown clover and the giggles that escape from it on a warm summer afternoon. But what I value most is solitude. Years ago, before I renounced the topless towers of Manhattan and settled in the bush, I couldn't get my fill of revelry. When the drummer was stowing away his traps and the last couples lingered in Flirtation Row, I was still dancing the camel walk and the balconade. Today I'm a deep-dish hermit. I'd like to see anyone get *me* into a hot, noisy night club filled with people eating synthetic chow mein and leering at young persons in their frillies. Yes, sir, I want to see him try. My telephone number is Buckwheat 489-Ring 3, and I'll be wearing my tuxedo, just in case.

If rural life has done anything, it has taught me to be self-sufficient; I pity a man who can't be alone. There is nothing like a solitary evening in an old house, cooped up with one's dogs and books, to sharpen the senses and shorten the wind. One night recently, for instance, I suddenly felt I had to think things out and packed my family off to the seashore. It was ten above zero and building to a blizzard, but when I have to think things out I have no time for sentimental considerations. Breathing a sigh of relief, I double-locked the doors, barricaded them with bureaus and chairs, and set about preparing supper. I had some difficulty getting the beans out of the can, but I shortly contrived a serviceable bandage for my wrist and snuggled down in front of a crackling fire with the diaries of Wilfrid Scawen Blunt. I had read little more than three pages when I realized I was holding the diaries upside down and listening intently to a noise in the kitchen.

Loosely speaking, the sound combined a creak and a sigh suggestive of a musical saw. Now and again, it was smothered by a soft, mirthless laugh ending in a sharp click. My dogs, quick to guard their master, formed into a hollow square and withdrew under the couch. I dried my palms, which seemed to have accumulated a slight film of oil, and picked up the fire tongs. "Who's there?" I inquired in a crisp falsetto. (After all, I thought, why waste a trip to the kitchen if nobody was there?) There was no answer; whoever it was didn't even have the common decency to reply. Angered, I strode toward the kitchen, whistling to warn of my approach, and flung open the door. Everything was in apple-pie order, including the apple pie, except that the rocking chair was bobbing slowly back and forth.

"That's odd—very odd," I murmured, re-entering the living room and tripping over a chair. "Probably caused by a draft from an open window or something."

"Or something," agreed one of the dogs from under the couch.

"Who said that?" I demanded sharply. The craven cur was frightened back into silence. I yawned casually, an effort that almost resulted in lockjaw, and consulted my watch. "Well, guess I'll turn in," I observed to nobody in particular. Hearing no objection, I started for the stairs, the dogs clustered about my ankles. A brisk, affable voice cut me short.

"The three homicidal maniacs who fled the county home for the insane are still at large tonight," it said chattily. "If you see a burly man of fifty with an ice pick—" I cannot abide petty gossip; switching off the radio, I went up the steps, taking them four at a time. It was a trifle close under the covers, especially as the dogs persisted in huddling in with me, but it made for a warm, *gemütlich* feeling. About 9:30, someone in the attic started dragging a body across the floor by the hair, occasionally belting it with a strap. My blood boiled at the cruelty, and yet it occurred to me it was really none of my affair. I had lived in the house only eleven years; the people upstairs were undoubtedly the pre-Civil War tenants, who had every right to do as they pleased. I took ten or twelve small fruit tablets and straightway fell into a refreshing doze, which would have lasted until morning had my family not returned unexpectedly. They had a little trouble recognizing me with white hair, though otherwise I was the same kindly, indulgent Dads they had always worshiped. In a way, it was fun seeing them, too, but one of these days I've simply got to get away by myself and think things out.

FOURTEEN

IF YOU tossed a cigarette out of a plane thirty minutes west of La-Guardia Airport, it would probably hit the roof of an enormous red barn decorated with hex symbols, and, just between you and me and the compost, that would be okay with me. For the past fifteen years, until a week ago, this hippodrome served superficially as a receptacle for old newspapers and fly screens, but actually as the focus of a dream. Whenever I was pressed to convert it into a studio, playroom or summer theater—one man tried to rent it for a stocking factory—I assumed a crafty, slow-witted, peasant's smile. In my mind's eye I saw the stalls lined with sleek purebreds gorging themselves on alfalfa, the great silo bursting with high-protein hay. To my fevered senses, no imported perfume could rival the bouquet of a heifer placidly chewing her cud. Every moment I wasn't sleeping, I greedily devoured government bulletins detailing the manufacture of smearcase and clabber. I could almost hear the rich golden milk gurgling in the pails; I grew faint with desire picturing myself at eventide in the north forty, surrounded by lowing kine.

I could have gone on dreaming indefinitely, without ever disbursing a kopeck, had it not been for Lowing Klein, the advertising man next door. For some obscure reason, this worthy unexpectedly tired of feeding a hundred and forty pedigreed Jerseys and put them under the hammer. Trumpeting the historic phrase, "I'm just looking for a small family cow," I donned my most evil-smelling tweeds and raced to the auction. It was held under a striped marquee crowded with scores of fellow-poets and playwrights also avid for a small family cow. Interspersed in the throng were members of the best county families leaning on shooting sticks and surveying one another insolently. As I arrived, a cow roughly the size of the frigate *Constitution* was led into the tanbark ring. The two brawny stable hands petting her seemed pygmies.

"Zangwill's Bijou Lass," droned the auctioneer, "the daughter of

Throaty Contralto by that great sire Glittering Generalization, seven times winner over the Isle of Jersey." The bidding soared dizzily to three hundred and ten dollars, languished and died. Suddenly a voice I dimly identified as my own squeaked, "Three hundred and twenty!" I turned pale with terror, knowing full well I didn't own three hundred and twenty of anything, let alone the artistic pale green rugs issued by the Treasury Department. Before I could extricate myself, the auctioneer had brought me to my knees and was administering the *estocada*. In vain I pleaded I had merely been clearing my throat, that I lived in a hotel for business girls where no cattle were permitted, and that I was a small-time grifter currently under indictment for passing bad checks. With a cold nod signifying I was united in holy matrimony to twelve hundred pounds of brisket, the auctioneer swept on to another item. Two awed yokels nearby eyed me respectfully. "That's Bet-a-Million Titus," I overheard them whispering. "They claim his place is bigger than the King Ranch in Texas." The compliment acted on me like adrenalin; in the next ten minutes I snapped up a towering jumbo with an annual record of two thousand pounds of butterfat, and a trim gazelle reputed to yield sixteen quarts of Devonshire clotted cream at a milking.

By the time I returned home, my giddiness had subsided, leaving me weak and trembling with remorse. I was maundering through an incredible fable about having won a calf at a raffle when a van puffed up the incline bearing my moolies. My dream girl turned a dusty vermilion and uttered a choking sound. I offered to explain to her how milking would strengthen her fingers and broaden her psyche, but the poor creature, irrational as only her sex can be, caught up a nest of flowerpots and was trying to get my range. I spent the night doubled up in a feed bin, listening to the mammoths eating me into bankruptcy and endlessly adding up columns of figures. To date, they have tucked away twelve bales of hay, five blocks of salt and three bushels of a mealy substance weighed out on jewelers' scales. With reasonable economy, every glass of milk I throw a lip over next season should cost in the vicinity of forty dollars. I wouldn't mind particularly, except for a disquieting thought dropped by my doctor the last time we conferred.

"Don't quote me," he said, meditatively stroking my purse, "but I believe you're allergic to milk." And, honey, he's not kidding.

FIFTEEN

Is ANYBODY around here looking for a bargain in an Early Pennsylvania washstand in mint condition, circa 1825? It is genuine pumpkin pine, with ball-and-claw feet, the original brasses, and a small smear of blood where I tripped over it last night in the dark. I am holding it at sixteen dollars, but not so tightly that I wouldn't let it go to the right party for circa ten cents. I also have an authentic trestle table which collapses into a small space when you merely rest your elbows on it, and a patchwork quilt I bought from a very old lady who remembered seeing Lincoln. She must have seen P. T. Barnum as well, for I heard her observe under her breath to her husband that there was one born every minute. In fact, I am disposing of my entire collection of antiques to the lowest bidder, and if he doesn't want it, I intend to set fire to it as soon as I can find an Early American match.

When, back in the mid-thirties, I left a cozy New York flat to exile myself in a stone pillbox in a swamp, I broke clean with the twentieth century. I was ready to dip candles and card my own flax if need be, and the thought of profaning our primitive farmhouse with Grand Rapids furniture made me shudder. I promptly installed a spinning wheel in every room, in case anyone should need some quick home-spun, and replaced our luxurious innerspring bed with a period four-poster. My neighbor hesitated to relinquish it at first, as it had been serving as a roost for his chickens, but finally exchanged it for five acres of prime bottom land. Another party graciously consented to trade our priceless Bokhara carpets for a small hooked rug he had won playing ski-ball at the Lancaster Fair. I even discarded the electric stove and returned to cooking in the fireplace, until my wife, with typical feminine squeamishness, ran a temperature because a couple of grilled tomtits turned up in the soup one evening.

In spite of all our efforts, the house still seemed bourgeois and prosaic. The lamps gave off too much light and the bureau drawers worked too easily. We lusted for lamps made out of old seltzer bottles or apothecaries' jars, and Victorian dressers that nobody could open. One day on a back road near Prosaic, New Jersey, we stumbled into a web run by a spider named Jake Meserve. Outwardly Jake was a farmer; he had a long linen duster, steel-bowed spectacles, and a field of papier-mâché corn in front of his place as a blind. In his hayloft, however, he kept a few choice heirlooms you could persuade him to sell by dropping your hat. We immediately fell in love with a rare old cobbler's bench, as fine a piece as you would find outside the Metropolitan—that is, the Metropolitan Shoe Repair Shop. After a brisk tussle, Jake stowed my thirty-nine dollars in a poke next to his skin and hauled out a rickety sofa specked with mildew.

"You folks ever seen a real old-time Victorian courtin' chair?" he inquired, stroking the plush. "I mind my Uncle Zeb proposed to Aunt Mildew in that chair. I wouldn't part with it if I was starvin'." Suddenly he choked back a sob and turned away. "Take it," he muttered brokenly. "Ninety-three dollars. It's like sellin' my own flesh and blood."

I whittled him down to sixty in a trice, and drying his eyes, he disgorged three more family mementoes—a dough tray, a glass bell containing his mother's baby hair, and a little chest of drawers lettered, "Willimantic Spool & Thread Co." He stripped my wallet of everything but the social-security card and we embarked. As I threw the car into gear, he staggered up, bearing a gate-leg table.

"Just ran acrost this in my feed bin," he panted. "My grandpa bought it off Nancy Hanks. You can scrape off the paint with a stiff brush."

I threw him my watch and chain, and we whizzed away. I spent the next week hacking at the table with a blowtorch, steel wool, and sandpaper. It had six coats of paint, including one like porcelain that had been baked on. When I had finished, I overturned it accidentally and discovered a sticker reading, "R. H. Macy & Co. Reduced to $3.98." And that, children, is how Daddy met his first psychiatrist.

SIXTEEN

IF YOU happen to be lolling around Penn Station of a Friday afternoon and see a sullen couple vaguely resembling crocodiles, carrying tennis rackets and boxes of cheap candy, you can make book that they are weekend guests bound for my pleasure dome in Tinicum Township. I don't know what alchemy there is about those railroad stations, but Jekyll and Hyde aren't in it. I have had stanch lifelong friends, the kind of people you swap neckties with, start down the escalator, chortling in anticipation of my hospitality, and reach the train embittered old crabs, loudly beefing about the service, the beds and the liquor, though they were still seventy miles from it. Possibly the railroad maintains some devilish kind of decompression chamber, like that used by sand hogs, to temper my guests. If so, it needs one added operation, in which the candidate is given a hang-over and a case of ptomaine, infested with wood ticks, and shot out into Seventh Avenue, free to spend the weekend his own way. This would also allow me time for my own work, which is to lie doggo until noon and compose jeremiads about country living.

I was a weekend guest, too, before my favorite cat died and willed me eighteen million dollars, but I remember myself as a sweet, patient duck whom hostesses would give their right eye to entertain—and if you don't think so, just look at the scores of one-eyed hostesses you meet nowadays. The moment I left the bread line and opened my own soup kitchen, however, a bunch of parasites invaded the field. It's not the money that bothers me, mind you; it's the principle of the thing.

Whether I meet them at the railroad personally or dispatch my Chinese houseboy with his rickshaw, they are disgruntled from the start. "Some railroad," they snarl. "Can't even get Pojarski cutlets and wild rice in the diner." Judging from the striped blazers, ski trousers, and fur-lined parkas they descend in, they must think they are visiting Lake Placid or the Laurentians. One man arrived in mid-September with a toboggan and a set of racing blades. He was furious because the Delaware & Lackawanna had no accommodations for his malemutes. When he found no ice in the creek, he flew into a paroxysm. "What the hell is this, the bayou country?" he shouted. "I spent a dollar thirty-eight getting to this hothouse!" I offered him the address of an igloo on West Forty-fifth Street that served a good grade of blubber, but he grudgingly consented to stay and cadge a few meals.

En route to the leprosarium, I customarily make a short historical talk, indicating the covered bridge where Simon Flannel deployed his men to counter the Hessian thrust, the local Lover's Leap, and the like. Such details enchant city people, and they always inquire, "What do you do for French vermouth down here?" They generally begin to get drowsy as we ford the creek below the farm, and by dinner time eurythmic breathing has set in. Since the cook invariably quits at the sight of company, my vixen has to don burnt cork and a turban, but they pinch her with the same easy familiarity they display to all domestics. A certain elderly wolf, undismayed by a cuff on the bugle, even offered her fifty cents to rub his back, pleading that his wife was a hopeless invalid who never really understood him in the first place.

Once the victuals are down, the female waddles painfully to the nearest sofa and collapses, while the male points out little errors of construction I have made around the place. At nine, both retire to bed with a bottle and our honeyed entreaties to sleep as long as they like. In less time than it takes to read *Henry Esmond,* the dishes are washed, cigarettes dug out of the veneer, and we are in bed listening to them giggling through the partition over our stinginess.

About the cocktail hour next day, after the house has rung to reverberating snores like the beat of surf at Coronado, two somnambulists appear and waspishly demand farina, plovers' eggs and Canadian bacon. Any attempt to drag them outdoors is futile; they've seen all the grass they care to in Central Park. They are still in pajamas when the local gentry bursts in, crying, like Cynara's lover, for madder music and stronger wine. From then on, the evening is a montage of broken glassware, stolen embraces, and recriminations. At the grim-lipped caucus on the platform Sunday night, the delegates display a copper nimbus around the skull and undying hatred for each other. Well, here we are, boy. Call me up when you get to town, boy. You bet I will, boy. Now take it easy, boy. And don't drop dead before I see you, boy.

SEVENTEEN

SOMEWHERE in the South Atlantic, off the charted ship lanes, there is thought to be a vast turgid eddy known as the Sargasso Sea, in which the derelicts of the seven seas ultimately come to rest. (My authority for the foregoing is a noted oceanographer named Turgid Eddie whom I met in a small West Side laboratory a few days ago and who drank nothing but Scotch and sea water.) Now this theory is all very well for schoolgirls and neurotic women, but the actual Sargasso is nowhere near the South Atlantic. It is situated in half a quarter section of rolling scrub midway between New York and Philadelphia, and embodies the worst features of both. At its core stands the shabby-genteel spokesman of these lines, slowly shedding his sanity as a terrifying vortex of dogs, debts and petty afflictions swirls sluggishly about his knees.

I might have dragged out my days in our gravel pit in peace, a myopic bookworm in sleeve garters and an alpaca jacket content to fuss among his ageratum, but for a remark of my wife's. It ran: "Couldn't we afford a dog, dear? It'd keep me company while you're in town chasing around with those doxies of yours." Quick to humor a woman's whim, I drove the poor little soul to a roadside kennel that was closing out a job lot of pets. I soon found the ideal companion for her, a ten-cent turtle bearing the legend, "Greetings from Savin Rock," but the willful creature must begin haggling over a chow with the proprietor, a shifty freebooter with only one eye. He could see well enough out of the other, however, to distinguish the bulge of my wallet, toward which he swung constantly, like the needle of a compass.

"You don't find them dogs every day," he told us confidentially. "That pup was stolen from one of the finest homes in Germantown." Aware that any show of feeling would increase the price, my wife cunningly betrayed her indifference by cradling the animal in her arms and covering his muzzle with kisses. The ruse worked, and we got him for only ninety dollars, less than the average man spends a month on Gutenberg Bibles.

It took nearly an hour for Wang's initial shyness to wear off. The last of it disappeared at the general store as motherly old Mrs. Sigafoos bent over him to coo an endearment. With a sibilant hiss, he tore the fichu from her blouse and she fell into a display of fig bars. A hearty laugh and a dizzying bribe quickly restored good spirits, and we set off for home. En route, we stopped briefly at the villa of an artist neighbor for a cup of hot milk and grenadine. The door was opened by Mrs. van Gogh, modishly clad in a new hostess gown for the occasion, bearing a Siamese cat in her arms. Wang joyfully blew battle stations, and Grimalkin, employing his mistress as a Jacob's ladder, hastily went topside and lodged in her coiffure. Over the iodine and gauze we all became fast friends, and I even bought a dry point from them which I needed like a hole in the head. My wife still insists I kept referring to it as a blue point, but of course she was somewhat unnerved.

For the next two days you never would have known there was a dog on the place, apart from an occasional stifled cry as Wang's teeth closed on a child. His daily routine was almost Spartan: in the morning a rapid round of the local garbage piles, at noon a casual lunch off two or three stray pullets, and toward sundown a vigorous uprooting of our shrubs. Thanks to this rigid discipline, he was trained to razor edge for his farewell performance. The setting was the porch and his co-star a schnauzer imported by a fair weekend guest. In the heat of the struggle, milady felt it best to thrust her foot between the actors.

Wang, ever a boy with a sweet tooth, started stuffing himself, and it required a spirited massage with a bone-handled umbrella to distract the glutton. The hushed calm that ensued was broken only by the crackle of a crisp bank note and a deep sigh.

I traded Wang for a collie who brought home skunks, and turned Laddie Boy in for a Kerry who ate maids. At last, in desperation, I bought a bloodhound, a timid thing with great gentle eyes like a fawn. The man swore she was barely able to walk, much less attack anybody. A fortnight later, she knocked down a state trooper, stole his pistol, and held up a cigar store in Doylestown. And if you don't believe me, ask her brother. He's working for the Bureau of Internal Revenue.

EIGHTEEN

A FEW days back, while waiting around my doctor's anteroom to have a swelling excised from my checkbook, I ran across an extremely informative article in a medical journal named *Peeping Tom* or *Hot Dickety*—at least, that was the name on the leather binder. A well-known physician, writing under the nom de plume of Chicken Inspector No. 23, had made a comparative study of ten New York women with an equal number of outlanders to determine which group was healthier. As all the subjects examined chanced to be lightly draped showgirls, those who were stunted or undernourished were immediately obvious to the reader. The conclusions were unmistakable: the city girls had glossy pelts and eyes sparkling with fun, whereas their country cousins were torpid and lackluster. So once again the rosy fiction that country living is wholesome has been disproved. If anyone wants to trade a couple of centrally located, well-cushioned showgirls for an eroded slope ninety minutes from Broadway, I'll be on this corner tomorrow at eleven with my tongue hanging out.

There is probably no more striking illustration of the change wrought by life in the canebrake than my own case. When I first took to the hills, I was a sad apology for a man. Reared on goose cracklings, rich sauces, and liqueur Scotch, I was practically on the verge of collapse. My teeth had achieved a dreary uniformity from excessive dental care and my skin was worn parchment-thin from too much bathing. My system cried out for plain, honest country fare—skimmed milk, margarine, and macaroni. After six months in the tall rhubarbs, I was a new man. My cheeks developed the ruddy vitality of a pail of lard and my fingers were permanently knotted with arthritis. I had all the allergies of Marcel Proust without any of the talent. My life-insurance beneficiaries discussed me openly in the past tense. The more charitable held that I had been a mean little skinflint who might surprise everybody when the will was finally probated.

It was not until I fell afoul of two local doctors, however, that I got my comeuppance. The first was a small, sallow practitioner who had been graduated brilliantly from a mail-order institution a week previously and was waiting to recoup his tuition on the next stray patient. He was out in his back yard splitting a fee when I drove up. His face betrayed the stupefaction of a trapper who sees a sable walk into his snare. In a second, however, he recovered his poise, and barking his shins on a sawhorse to conceal his satisfaction, he swept me into the consulting room.

"That's a nasty throat you have there, brother," he jabbered before I could get my coat off. "Yes sirree, you've got tularemia if I ever saw it. And those adenoids'll have to come out along with the appendix. What did you say your bank was—I mean, your name?" I hurriedly explained that a hornet had stung me in the neck while I was pruning the lilacs and that all I required was a powder to relieve the headache. Thrusting a bronchoscope down my gullet, he cut short my case history.

"Your pancreas is full of tacks, mister," he reported. "Besides, there's a chicken bone lodged in your lung. Better let me have twenty dollars on account; you look sort of sneaky." By the time I regained the open air, he had taken a blood count, a hemoglobin sample, and all the loose change in my vest. He clung to the running board clawing at my stickpin, but an overhanging willow branch brushed him off. The last I heard as my car careered out into the highway was his frenzied promise to sue me for the balance of the bill.

The second prospector to tap the lode was a benevolent old healer, a horse-and-buggy doctor in the great tradition of Lionel Barrymore and Jean Hersholt. To furnish the authentic character touch, he parked his custom-built Packard phaeton at the foot of the lane and pulled up before my door in an ancient sleigh. I was lying abed with a dramatic wheeze and a temperature of 109. The thermometer he plunged into my mouth was encrusted with snuff, and I sneezed.

"What's the matter, got a cold or something?" he inquired, wiping a hypodermic on his coattails. "Here, this'll fix you up." I remonstrated timidly that there was a bit of rust on the needle; he grew scarlet with fury. "Germs, germs, germs!" he shouted. "Who feeds you that infernal poppycock? You can't *see* them, can you?" He advised a poultice of bacon rind, corn meal, and flannel, pocketed all the folding money in sight, and stormed out. That night I swelled up like a sunfish and went into acidotic coma. When I finally reached New York in a solid silver ambulance inlaid with rubies, I found I had double pneumonia with complications. Which is a pretty understatement indeed for a house in the country.

NINETEEN

NOT long ago, while waiting around Grand Central to have my pocket picked, I was approached by a rather dashing woman of the world with a request for a light. I am not one of those who kiss and tell, but, frankly, men, she was the bee's knees. Her general appearance suggested a younger Lillian Russell; she was dressed in skunk-dyed sable, had a sable-dyed skunk on a leash, and altogether resembled a yacht of the *Defender* class. Naturally, I was somewhat wary at first and nervously fingered the lunch money that Mummy had pinned inside my jumper. I indicated a newsstand close by at which matches were being offered for sale, but my fair suppliant confessed the headmistress of her boarding school had cautioned her against strange newsstands. My innate chivalry rose to the surface, and I escorted her forthwith to a snug little *boite* where we could discuss her dilemma.

I mention the incident only because my wife boasted to a dinner party the other evening that I probably knew more tramps than any man alive—meaning, of course, that I knew more hobos. Scarcely a day passes on my demesne that some cheerful vagabond does not drop in for a handout and a flop. From Memphis to Mobile, from Natchez to St. Joe, wherever the cold winds blow, the name of "Cotton Ed" Perelman spells hospitality. As a matter of fact, I chose the farm for its proximity to three railroads and the Lincoln Highway; my money was multiplying at such a rate I was paying people to truck it away and burn it. I still have to scuff the greenbacks off my shoes before entering the house, but at least it's tidier than it was.

Though our clientele is usually a jovial, high-spirited lot, we oc-

casionally draw some sourballs. Last Tuesday afternoon the vicomtesse and I were dawdling on the piazza when a couple of bindle stiffs
appeared. The wayfarers had red putty noses, three-day beards, and
bundles slung over their shoulders on peeled-willow wands. Tags attached to their lapels read "Weary Willie" and "Dusty Rhodes"; they
were perspiring profusely and extremely irritable.

"Why, whoever are those dubious characters?" inquired my chatelaine, surveying them fastidiously through her lorgnette.

"Oh, just a couple of hot cross bums," I ventured. "Step in, gentlemen; this is your home away from home."

"Is dis de spot wit' de free grub?" one of them demanded suspiciously. I assured him it was and, reaching for the bellpull, bade
Uncle Cudgo serve up his most savory repast. From the first mouthful,
they proved petty and disagreeable. Brushing aside the cheese soufflé
Aunt Hagar had prepared, they ordered her to place huckleberry pies
to cool in the kitchen window so they might steal them. They turned up
their noses at the coffee in our Sèvres-china cups, and, creating a replica of a hobo jungle in the living room, brewed a malodorous stew and
coffee in an old tin. Their derision reached a peak when I offered them
my downy feather bed.

"What's de matter, cul, ain't youse got a haymow?" they sneered.
I conducted the pair to the barn, pressed a handful of five-cent stogies
and a pail of canned heat on them, and begged them to sleep until the
cows came home—the cows were at a Princeton house party that
weekend. I then secreted myself behind a bag of mash to eavesdrop on
their conversation.

"Dere's somethin' loony about dis joint," I heard one mutter. "Dey
ain't got no bulldog to bite youse in de seat o' yer pants." The other
reassured him and, lighting their cigars, they settled down to ten minutes of rapid-fire tramp comedy.

"Say, Weary," said Dusty, "why is a hobo like a dentist?"

"Dey both live from hand ter mouth," riposted the other. "Say,
Dusty, I went up to a lady dis mornin' and asked her fer some cold
vittles."

"What did youse get?"

"De cold shoulder," returned Weary. "Say, Dusty, I read an ab-
sorbin' article in de paper today. It was about a sponge."

"Well, well, so dey been writin' up yer brudder again," Dusty remarked. "Say, Weary, one time I fell down a hill wit' ten bottles o' beer
and didn't break one."

"Why was dat, kiddo?" his foil queried.

" 'Cuz dey was inside o' me," Dusty chuckled. Thereupon they be-labored each other with rolled-up newspapers, sang a chorus of "Pie in the Sky," and retired. The next morning I discovered to my chagrin that they had decamped without even rifling the henhouse, and, as a final gesture of contempt, had scrawled on the barn in chalk: "Stay away from dese rubes, men; dey're both dead beats." That's what you get for being an easy mark. I tell you, it's enough to shake your faith in humanity.

TWENTY

NEXT to drinking brandy before breakfast, the most fatal mistake a man can commit is to isolate himself in the country. In no time at all, he becomes broody and morose, a crosspatch and a mope. I avoided the pitfall by a simple device. A week before I bought my grange, I had just signed a three-year lease on a New York apartment—a bit of fore-sight still known in the family as "Daddy's First Stroke, or the Deer-field Massacre." Consequently, I now can run in every other week at my own expense to serve eviction papers, excavate the debris, and gen-erally explain to the police why my tenants drop bags of water on passers-by. This stimulating exercise keeps my blood pressure in the upper brackets and results in what doctors call "tissue tone." It also results in what they call "insolvency"—the medical term for great hol-low circles under the bank balance.

By shrewd selection, I have managed to saddle myself with some fairly spectacular saboteurs, male and female alike. One season I rented my flat to a breezy newspaperman who introduced himself as "Scoops" Conlon of the *Daily Planet*. While he was binding the bar-gain with a counterfeit money order, three brawny colleagues ap-peared, laden with cases of soda, lemons and cracked ice. He disclosed that they were his roommates and had been waiting outside until the deal was consummated. As I crossed the sidewalk to enter a cab, I narrowly escaped an empty bottle of rye. The next time I saw the premises, a month later, they looked as though a cavalry patrol headed by Jubal A. Early had bivouacked there for the night. Somebody had built a bonfire in the bedroom and baked hoecakes in the ashes. What remained of the walls was redecorated with a sprightly series of anatomical studies done in indelible lipstick. Except for a semi-paralyzed stranger under the stove clutching a vial of Jamaica ginger, the place was as neat as a pen.

The following year my advertisement attracted the sweetest old lady in the world, with a lovely patrician head and a velvet choker. From the way her fingers caressed my books and symphony records, I could tell at once she was a connoisseur of the finer things. I asked her whether she liked poetry, of which I had a modest collection. "You're cookin' on the front burner, Mac," she returned hoarsely. "I always got my nose in a poem." I accepted a draft on a bank in Buenos Aires, and, in parting, she casually inquired where the nearest pawnshop was. I thought nothing of it at the time, nor did the superintendent when he saw my piano being moved out. "I figured your mother knew what she was doing," he told me. "Say, you've got a telephone bill for two hundred dollars."

The diggings stood vacant for a while, but by baiting the deadfall with a four-month concession, I turned up a pair of extremely gifted girls. They knew what they wanted and set out at once to achieve it with the scant materials at hand. To begin with, they made a trio of stunning low coffee tables by merely sawing down the legs of the end tables. They then papered the bedroom with a busy pattern of satyrs and dryads and re-covered all the upholstery in bed ticking, using a remnant as a skirt for the telephone. Everything in sight was looped back on itself. As a final touch, they pasted stars on all the mirrors. Apparently the experience went to their heads like May wine, for they ultimately glued them to the andirons, the bathtub and a pair of shoes I had left in a closet. As I entered the foyer with the marshal, the first thing I fell over was an iron pickaninny in jockey costume holding a ring toward me. The second thing I fell over was the lessees, sobbing into a chalice of gin.

Last summer two sets of swallows roosted briefly in my nest. One was an oily gentleman who informed me he was a spice merchant. One evening the Spice Squad broke in, took a gander at his wares, and gave him a room rent-free for the next six months. The other was a retired woodcarver who suddenly returned to his trade, employing his wife as a medium. Next spring I intend to be more particular. I'll consider a nice quiet family—that is, a family of bats.

TWENTY-ONE

FOR my money, the most parochial, unwholesome aspect of contemporary civilization is the life led by the average urban dweller. Cooped up in a stuffy, overheated hotel suite with nothing but a bowl of cracked ice, a blonde, and a fleet bellboy poised on his toe like Pavlova waiting to run errands, he misses the rich, multiple savor of country living. He never knows the fierce ecstasy of rising in a sub-zero dawn to find the furnace cold and the pipes frozen, or the exhilaration of changing a tire by flashlight in an icy garage. No wonder his muscles atrophy as he lies abed until noon, nibbling bits of toast over the latest edition. No wonder his horizons shrink and his waistband swells. And no wonder he'll live twice as long as I will.

When I pitched my silken pavilion in the Appalachian foothills and challenged Nature to knock the chip off my shoulder, I had a buoyant vision of the future. In it I was a bull-necked sport in a corduroy vest ordering retrievers to heel and vilifying the Securities Exchange Commission. Peering deep into the crystal ball, I saw myself cantering across my freehold on a fat cob, cheered on by a devoted peasantry. To prepare for the role, I put in an intensive half hour each morning ingesting chutney, rustling the *New York Times,* and snarling apoplectically at the CIO. The results were unique but disappointing. In two weeks I had a superb duodenal ulcer and a wheeze like a noonday factory whistle. Although I doggedly mounted every cob I could find, the kernels merely shriveled up and I never moved an inch.

It was years before I realized my talents were technical rather than executive and I slipped gracefully into the post of janitor and general scavenger of my farm. Humble as the duties are, they entail certain grave responsibilities. To me falls the task of grading and sorting the household refuse, of deciding what shall be retained and what discarded. One tiny slip, one moment's heedlessness, and a vital fruit rind or chop bone might find itself in the wrong category. Secondary to this work, though equally important, is the task of cataloguing waste paper and bottles, which I prefer to shoulder myself rather than assign to subordinates. Wielding a stick tipped with a nail, I patrol the grounds like a park employee (though much worse paid), and spear any trash I deem offensive. Here again I exercise complete authority; if I see a piece of paper I feel like ignoring, I just don't spear it. What I mean is, the final decision rests with me.

This phase complete, I now turn my findings over to another bureau, of which I am head co-ordinator, for disposal. I place the containers in a special rickety wheelbarrow, and surrounding myself with a swarm of flies to render us invisible to enemy aircraft, proceed straight uphill to a pit about a quarter of a mile away. En route, I convoy my burden through two barbed-wire fences, an operation that produces several salty phrases frowned on by the postal authorities. I thereupon hurl the refuse into the pit with a single deft sprain of the back, set fire to the papers, and filling my lungs with pungent, satisfying smoke, repair to my desk, too exhausted to move the rest of the day.

In winter, naturally, the pressure intensifies and I could almost use another pair of hands in addition to the two heads my enemies maintain I have. After lengthy consultation with a heating engineer now in Matteawan, my wife and I installed a pipeless furnace inlaid with emeralds and jade which feeds the warmth directly into an upstairs clothes closet, leaving the rest of the establishment at the freezing point. This ingenious arrangement has two advantages: it scents the house with an acrid, invigorating smell of frying cloth recalling a tailor shop in the Bronx, and it permits me to tend two kerosene burners, a Franklin stove, and a fireplace. The children have grown to accept the sooty-faced character with the icicle depending from his nose and the large drum of oil as some weird kind of minstrel, and it's probably just as well. What with two spectacular explosions to my credit and a reek like a gas-station attendant, I'm lucky they let me eat in the house. How anybody stays penned up in a sweltering hotel with cracked ice and a blonde is beyond me. I guess the human body can take an awful lot of punishment.

❧ HELL IN THE GABARDINES

AN OLD SUBSCRIBER of *The New Republic* am I, prudent, meditative, rigidly impartial. I am the man who reads those six-part exposés of the Southern utilities empire, savoring each dark peculation. Weekly I stroll the *couloirs* of the House and Senate with T.R.B., aghast at legislative folly. Every now and again I take issue in the correspondence pages with Kenneth Burke or Malcolm Cowley over a knotty point of aesthetics; my barbed and graceful letters counsel them to reread their Benedetto Croce. Tanned by two delightful weeks at lovely Camp Narischkeit, I learn twenty-nine languages by Linguaphone, sublet charming three-room apartments with gardens from May to October, send my children to the Ethical Culture School. Of an evening you can find me in a secluded corner of the White Turkey Town House, chuckling at Stark Young's review of the *Medea*. I smoke a pipe more frequently than not, sucking the match flame into the bowl with thoughtful little puffs.

Of all the specialists on that excellent journal of opinion, however, my favorite is Manny Farber, its motion-picture critic. Mr. Farber is a man zealous and incorruptible, a relentless foe of stereotypes, and an extremely subtle scholiast. If sufficiently aroused, he is likely to quote *The Cabinet of Dr. Caligari* four or five times in a single article (Parker Tyler, whose criticism is otherwise quite as profound, can quote it only once). It has been suggested by some that Mr. Farber's prose style is labyrinthine; they fidget as he picks up a complex sentence full of interlocking clauses and sends it rumbling down the alley. I do not share this view. With men who know rococo best, it's Farber two to one. Lulled by his Wagnerian rhythms, I snooze in my armchair, confident that the *mystique* of the talking picture is in capable hands.

It was in his most portentous vein that Mr. Farber recently sat himself down to chart the possibilities of the concealed camera. In transferring *The Lost Weekend* to the screen, you will recall, the producers sought verisimilitude by bringing Ray Milland to Third Avenue (in the past Third Avenue had always been brought to Ray Milland) and photographing the reactions of everyday citizens to Don Birnam's torment. The necessary equipment was hidden in theater marquees, El stations, and vans along the route of the historic trek, and almost nobody knew that the scenes were being registered on film. Mr. Farber heartily approved this technique and called on Hollywood to employ it more generally. To demonstrate its potentialities, he even sketched a wee scenario. "If," said he, "your plot called for some action inside of a department store, the normal activity of the store could be got by sending trained actors into it to carry on a planned business with an actor-clerk. Nobody else in the store need become conscious or self-conscious of this business, since the cameraman has been slyly concealed inside an ingeniously made store dummy and is recording everything from there."

Through a source I am not at liberty to reveal without violating medical confidence, I have come into possession of a diary which affords an interesting comment on Mr. Farber's idea. It was kept by one Leonard Flemister, formerly a clerk in the men's clothing section of Wanamaker's. I was not a customer of Flemister's, as I get my suits at a thrift shop named Sam's on the Bowery, but I had a nodding acquaintance with him; we often occupied adjoining tables at the Jumble Shop, and I remember him as a gentle, introspective man absorbed in *The New Republic* over his pecan waffle. He is at present living in seclusion (the Bonnie Brae is not a booby hatch in the old-fashioned sense) in New Jersey. I append several extracts from his diary:

JANUARY 12—Today rounds out seventeen years since I started in the men's shop at Wanamaker's, and they have been years filled with quiet satisfaction. As our great Founder constantly observed in his maxims, it is the small things that count. How truly this applies to ready-made suits! To the tyro, of course, one suit is very much like another, but to us who know, there is as much distinction between a Kuppenheimer and a Society Brand as there is between a Breughel and a Vermeer. Crusty old Thomas Carlyle knew it when he wrote *Sartor Resartus*. (Good notion, that; might pay me to keep a couple of his quotations on the tip of my tongue for some of our older customers.)

Ran into Frank Portnoy yesterday at lunch; haven't seen him since he left us for Finchley's. Sound enough chap on cheviots, is Frank, but I wouldn't care to entrust him with a saxony or tweeds. He seems to have put on five or six pounds in the seat, and I thought his 22-ounce basketweave a touch on the vulgar side. "Still working in that humdrum old place?" he asked, with a faint sneer. I kept my temper, merely remarking that he had incurred some criticism for leaving his position after only twelve years. (I did not bother to say that Mr. Witherspoon had referred to him as a grasshopper.) "Oh," he said airily, "I guess I learned enough of those lousy maxims." I said pointedly that he apparently had not learned the one about patience, and quoted it. He termed it "hogwash." "Maybe it is," I retorted, "but don't you wish you could wash a hog like that?" He turned as red as a beet and finished his meal in silence.

Read a disturbing article in *The New Republic* last night. A man named Farber advocates secreting cameramen inside clothing dummies in department stores so that the clerks may unwittingly become actors in a movie. Of course it was just a joke, but frankly, I thought it in rather poor taste.

JANUARY 14—Felt a trifle seedy today; I must find some other lunch spot besides the Green Unicorn. Their orange-and-pimento curry appears to have affected my digestion, or possibly I have had a surfeit of banana whip. In any case, during the afternoon I experienced the most extraordinary sensation, one that upset me considerably. At the rear of our sportswear section, next to the seersucker lounging robes, is a perfectly prosaic wax mannequin wearing a powder-blue ski jacket, canary-colored slacks, and synthetic elkskin loafers. About three o'clock I was hurrying past it with an armful of oilskin windbreakers when I heard a resounding sneeze. I turned abruptly, at first supposing it had come from a customer or salesperson, but the only one in sight was Sauerwein, who was absorbed in his booklet of maxims a good thirty feet away. Ridiculous as it may sound, the noise—a very distinct "Harooch!"—seemed to have emanated from the model. A moment's reflection would have told me that my auditory nerve was rebuking me for overindulgence at table, but unfortunately, in the first access of panic, I backed into a fishing-rod display and hooked a sinker in my trousers. Mr. Witherspoon, chancing by, observed (I thought with some coarseness) that I ought to get the lead out of my pants. Sauerwein, who loves to play the toady, laughed uproariously. I shall be on my guard with Sauerwein in future; I do not think he is quite sincere.

Saw a tiptop revival of *The Cabinet of Dr. Caligari* and *Potemkin* last night at the Fifth Avenue Playhouse; they are having their annual film festival. Enjoyed them both, though most of *Caligari* was run upside down and *Potemkin* broke in three places, necessitating a short wait. Next week they are beginning their annual *Potemkin* festival, to be followed by a revival of *The Cabinet of Dr. Caligari*. Always something unusual at the Fifth Avenue.

JANUARY 17—Mr. Witherspoon is a tyrant on occasion, but as the Founder says so pungently, give the devil his due; every so often the quality that made him floorwalker shines through. This morning, for example, a customer I recall seeing at some restaurant (the Jumble Shop, I believe) created a scene. He was a peppery little gnome named, I think, Pevelman or Pedelman, with shaggy eyebrows and the tonsure of a Franciscan father. I noticed him fidgeting around the low-priced shorts for a half hour or more, trying to attract a salesman, but Sauerwein was behind on his maxims and I was busy rearranging the windbreakers. At length he strode over to Mr. Witherspoon, scarlet with rage, and demanded, in an absurd falsetto, whether he might be waited on. Mr. Witherspoon was magnificent. He surveyed Pevelman up and down and snapped, "Don't you know there's a peace on?" The customer's face turned ashen and he withdrew, clawing at his collar. Old Witherspoon was in rare good humor all morning.

Slight dizzy spell this afternoon, nothing of consequence. I wonder if anything could be amiss with my hearing. Curiously enough, it is normal except in the immediate vicinity of the mannequin, where I hear a faint, sustained clicking as though some mechanism were grinding away. Coupled with this is the inescapable conviction that my every move is somehow being observed. Several times I stole up on the dummy, hoping to prove to myself that the clicking came from within, but it ceased instanter. Could I have contracted some mysterious tropical disease from handling too many vicuña coats?

Sauerwein is watching me. He suspects all is not well.

JANUARY 20—Something is definitely wrong with me. It has nothing to do with my stomach. I have gone mad. My stomach has driven me mad.

Whatever happens, I must not lose my head and blame my stomach. A stomach blamed is a stomach spurned, as the Founder says. The only good Founder is a dead Founder. Or Flounder. Now I *know* I am mad, writing that way about the Flounder.

I must marshal my thoughts very carefully, try to remember what happened. Shortly after one, I was alone in the department, Sauerwein and Witherspoon being at lunch. I was folding boys' windbreakers at the folded boys' windbreaker counter when a customer approached me. Never having seen Fredric March in person, I cannot assert dogmatically that it was he, but the resemblance was startling. From the outset, his behavior impressed me as erratic. He first struck a pose about fifteen feet from the mannequin, taking care to keep his profile to it. As he did so, the clicking sound which had harassed me became doubly magnified. Then, in the loud, artificial tone of one who wished to be overheard, he demanded to be shown a suit with two pairs of pants.

"We haven't any," I replied. "Don't you know there's a peace on?" To my surprise, he emitted a hoarse cry of delight and slapped his thigh.

"That'll be a wow!" he chortled. "We'll leave that line in!" Seventeen years of dealing with eccentrics have taught me the wisdom of humoring them; I pretended not to have heard. He gave me an intimate wink, snatched a sharkskin suit from the rack, and vanished into a dressing room. I was on the point of summoning aid when he reappeared feverishly. The effect of the trousers, at least three sizes too large for him, was so ludicrous that I stood speechless.

"Just what I wanted," he grinned, surveying himself in the mirror. Simultaneously, almost as if by prearrangement, a young lady in flamboyant theatrical make-up appeared. To my horror, the customer forgot to hold on to his trousers and they dropped down around his ankles. "Hello, Vivian!" he cried. "Well, I guess you caught me with my pants down!" And then—I am resolved to spare no detail—a voice from within the mannequin boomed, *"Cut!"*

When I recovered consciousness in the dispensary, the nurse and Mr. Witherspoon were chafing my wrists and Sauerwein was whispering to a store detective. I seem to remember striking Sauerwein, though I also have the impression my hands were entangled in my sleeves. The rest I prefer to forget. It can be summed up in the word "nightmare." Nightmare.

FEBRUARY 5—It is very quiet here at Bonnie Brae and the food is excellent, if a little unrelieved. I could do with one of those tasty watercress-and-palmetto salads they know so well how to prepare at the Green Unicorn. The library here is well stocked with current magazines; I keep abreast of the news via *The New Republic*, though I confess Farber does not grip me as he used to.

I have only one objection to this place. In the library is a suit of medieval armor, and very often I could swear that a pair of eyes are watching me through the casque. As soon as the weather becomes warmer, I expect to spend most of my time on the piazza.

GARNISH YOUR FACE WITH
PARSLEY AND SERVE

ON A BALMY SUMMER EVENING in Los Angeles some years ago, heavy with the scent of mimosa and crispy-fried noodles from the Chinese quarter, I happened to be a member of the small, select audience of cocaine peddlers, package thieves, and assorted strays at the Cozy Theater that witnessed the world première of a remarkable motion picture called *The Sex Maniac*. Most of the production, I grieve to say, is little more than a blur in my memory, but one scene still stands out with cameolike clarity. Into the consulting room of a fairly mad physician, whose name I somehow remember as Lucas Membrane, hurtled a haggard middle-aged woman, towing her husband, a psychotic larrikin about seven feet tall. The doctor examined the patient cursorily through a pocket lens, inspected his tongue, and, muttering "Just as I feared—dementia praecox," inoculated him intravenously with an icing gun like those commonly found in French bakeries. The patient slowly expanded, gnashing his teeth, until his head grazed the ceiling. Then he darted into the next room, where a luscious showgirl in a diaphanous shift unaccountably lay asleep on a slab, and, booming like a bittern, hustled her off into the canebrake. His wife and Dr. Membrane stared after him, shaking their heads in mild perplexity. "Well, Doc," observed the former, inflecting her words in the classic manner of Miss Beatrice Lillie, "I've seen some pretty . . . strange . . . experiments in my time, but *this* . . . is tops."

I was tempted to echo these sentiments yesterday when, in the Sunday edition of the Newark *Star-Ledger* which I received as lagniappe with fifteen cents' worth of sour tomatoes on Division Street, I ran across an arresting article on various home beauty treatments evolved by Hollywood personalities. It appears that, far from favoring expensive skin foods and massage creams, our reigning film favorites prefer cosmetics drawn from their own kitchen shelves. Like Dolores Moran, for instance. Any discussion of lovely Hollywood elbows would be incomplete without a reference to hers; I myself recall more than one such discussion that seemed frustrated and sterile because no reference

172

was made to Miss Moran's elbows. To keep them trig and alluring, the blond starlet rests them on two halves of a lemon for twenty minutes while she rehearses her lines, then rubs them satin-smooth with olive oil. Julie Bishop preserves her hands by rolling them in oatmeal (which, of course, she discards before playing her more romantic love scenes), and Ida Lupino safeguards an already creamy complexion with a poultice of powdered milk. Urging her readers to branch out for themselves, the beauty editor of the *Star-Ledger* appends several other recipes of a similar homely nature, notably a hand pack of corn meal and benzoin, an egg whipped up in lemon juice to rejuvenate tired or muddy faces, and a flocculent suspension of cornstarch in boiling water as an emollient for leathery skins.

What with a soaring luxury tax and a shrinking supply of cosmetics, it was inevitable that Elizabeth Arden would be supplanted by the grocery counter, but I am none too sure of the effect on the masculine gender. I foresee almost certain repercussions in the divorce courts and the Sunday-evening radio tribunals, and I offer the following *mise en scène* as a horoscope of what to expect shortly over any major network:

SCENE: *A radio station. John J. Antennae, spiritual father to millions, broods remotely before his microphone, pondering the philosophy of Ralph Waldo Trine and waiting for the announcer to complete his commercial. Fox-nosed, sallow, closely related to God on his mother's side, Antennae has been by turns an insurance technician, reception clerk in a cut-rate mortuary, and used-car salesman. From the side he dimly resembles a spider, an effect he tries to counteract with a ghastly veneer of benevolence.*

ANNOUNCER: . . . So why not back up our boys in the steaming jungles of New Guinea by chewing Respighi's Bubble Gum, that amazing new blend of chicle, old tea leaves and pine shavings? Remember, folks, maladroit tests by wool-gathering scientists have shown that Respighi's contains no single ingredient that could kill a horse, and even if it did, the hydrochloric acid in your system will dissolve anything. And now, Mr. Antennae, the case of Mr. M. W.

ANTENNAE (*nasally*): Step up, please. (*Milton Wefers, a dispirited taxpayer in his mid-thirties, falters to the podium.*) Very well, sir, tell us your story. (*Wefers blubbers wordlessly.*) Come, come, tears aren't going to help. Here, take my hand. Now then.

WEFERS (*brokenly*): Mr. Antennae, I first met my present wife in high school.

ANTENNAE: Just a moment. Am I to understand that you first met your present wife in high school?

WEFERS: That is correct.

ANTENNAE (*sharply*): You mean you had not met this woman—this little lady to whom you have pledged the most sacred vow the human voice can utter—previous to the time you speak of? Answer yes or no.

WEFERS: No. Well, shortly after we were married—seventeen years, five months, and four days, to be exact—I started in noticing that this party, that is, my wife, was covered with cracker meal.

ANTENNAE: Cracker meal? You don't mean Crainquebille, do you?

WEFERS (*lymphatically*): Crainquebille? What's that?

ANTENNAE: It's a story by Anatole France.

WEFERS: How could my wife be covered with a story by Anatole France?

ANTENNAE (*waspishly*): I'm the one who's asking the questions around here, Percy.

ANNOUNCER: Yes, Mr. Antennae—and friends in our listening audience—do *you* ever ask yourself the question: What am I doing to keep myself sweet and wholesome for those boys in the steaming jungles of New Guinea? It's your patriotic duty as an American to protect the home front with Respighi's, that yummy, gummy confection that irradiates the vocal cords and promotes pharyngeal fun!

ANTENNAE: All right now, go head with your problem.

WEFERS: So like I say, Mr. Antennae, it made me nervous my wife always wearing cracker crumbs at the table. I mean it got on my nerves. It was like living in the same house with a breaded veal cutlet.

ANTENNAE (*silkily*): I see. I take it you've had considerable experience sharing your residence with breaded veal cutlets?

WEFERS: Well, no, but I—

ANTENNAE: Tell me, young man, have you ever had any—ah—psychic disturbances? Ever been confined to an institution?

WEFERS: No, sir.

ANTENNAE: Never received a blow on the head, to the best of your recollection?

WEFERS: No, sir. Well, pretty soon I begun to watch her and I saw all kinds of things that made me suspicious. Every time I come home at night, why she would have her nose in a grapefruit.

ANTENNAE: How do you mean?

WEFERS: I mean she would be lying down with this grapefruit on her countenance. She said it took out the wrinkles.

ANNOUNCER: Yes, folks, and speaking of wrinkles, here's a new one! Did you know that every stick of Respighi's Bubble Gum is subjected to six hundred pounds of live steam to bake in the invigorating freshness of the great north woods? The next time you're in a lumber yard, make this test for yourself: whittle off the end of a fresh spruce plank and chew it to a pulp. That same zestful tang of turpentine and resin comes to you in each factory-fresh packet of Respighi's, the Friendlier Gum, chosen all-time favorite by our boys in the steaming jungles of New Guinea!

ANTENNAE: Now, my friend, continue your story. You claim that this behavior on the part of your loved one caused you a feeling of anguish?

WEFERS: It did, Mr. Antennae. (*sobbing*) I was a loving husband at all times; I was always bringing her little bags of fruit and candy and kissing her on the nape of the neck—

ANTENNAE (*hastily*): Yes, yes, no details, please. Go on with your narrative.

WEFERS: One Sunday morning I went in the kitchen and found her making some fried eggs. I thought they were for my breakfast, but instead of putting them on my plate, she placed them on her chin, like a kind of a hot compress.

ANTENNAE: You discussed the incident with her?

WEFERS: She stated that it would give her a firm, well-molded, youthful throat. Then I started to take some farina out of the double boiler, but she said she was saving it for her forehead. She also told me she planned to use my marmalade under her eyes to banish crow's-feet.

ANTENNAE: What was the upshot of these actions?

WEFERS: Well, I couldn't stand it any longer, so I went down to the public library.

ANTENNAE: To think things out, is that it?

WEFERS: No, sir. To reread a story by Melville Davisson Post called "Corpus Delicti."

ANTENNAE: Oh? What was this story about?

WEFERS (*bashfully*): I'd rather not say.

ANTENNAE: What transpired after that between you and your wife?

WEFERS: I'd rather not say.

ANTENNAE: You seem to have gotten pretty close-mouthed all of a sudden.

WEFERS: Yup.

ANTENNAE: Since the Sunday you speak of, has there been any substantial change in your wife?

WEFERS: Oh, boy.

ANTENNAE: Have you noticed anything out of the ordinary in the household?

WEFERS: Well, there was a funny smell of nitric acid in the bathroom, but it went away after a while.

ANTENNAE: And what, precisely, brings you here tonight? What is your problem?

WEFERS: Well, Mr. Antennae, I tell you. A couple of weeks ago I got interested in a certain party, a hostess in a rumba school. She returns my affection and we were wondering if we should get married.

ANTENNAE: You're sure your wife doesn't stand in the way?

WEFERS: Positive.

ANTENNAE: Well, my boy, I'm going to give you youngsters the sort of advice I don't believe I've ever given anyone before. *Go* to this person, look deep into your hearts, I beg of you, and when you've found the answer—*if* you have the courage in yourselves to face the questions that *need* answering, mind you—*make* up your minds, won't you? . . . You will? . . . (*emotionally*) God bless you!

ANNOUNCER: Folks, have you ever stopped to realize how barren the world would be without a sticky blob of glucose adhering to your dentition? Do you know that in the steaming jungles of New Guinea, your boys consider Respighi's Bubble Gum their number-one ration? They're counting on you, Respighi-chewers; don't let them down. It's *so* juicy—*so* tasty—and golly, we've got *so* much of it on hand!

CURTAIN

❧ WHITE BIMBO, OR, THROUGH DULLEST AFRICA WITH THREE SLEEPY PEOPLE

TAKE ONE THING with another, there are few places I know better than the heart of Africa. Set me down in Bechuanaland or the Cameroons and I will find my way home with less difficulty than I would from Rittenhouse Square or Boylston Street. My entire youth, in a sense, was spent on the Dark Continent. By the time I was eleven, I was probably the world's foremost authority on the works of Sir H. Rider Haggard, or at least the foremost eleven-year-old authority in Providence, Rhode Island. My impersonation of Allan Quatermain tracking down a spoor was so exact and so forthright that a popular movement sprang up among my fellow-citizens to send me to Mombasa. I was, however, not quite ready for Mombasa and begged off. At fifteen, I could quote Livingstone and Paul Du Chaillu so glibly that my sponsors revived their project, this time offering to send me to Tanganyika. It became sort of a good-humored tug of war to get me out of New England. I don't want to sound chesty, but I suppose I've done more harm to Africa in my day than Cecil Rhodes.

It came as a pang, therefore, to learn that my achievement had been overshadowed by that of a complete unknown, a person whose name occurs in no encyclopedia or reference work on Africa. Armand Brigaud may well be a familiar figure in the Explorers Club, and he can probably be found any afternoon at the National Geographic Society swapping yarns with William Beebe and Burton Holmes. Frankly, I never heard of him until yesterday, when I picked up a yellowing copy of a pulp magazine called *Jungle Stories* and read his novelette, *Killers on Safari*. Though it costs me an effort, I shall give the man his due. In *Killers on Safari*, Armand Brigaud has written finis to the subject of Africa. After him, the deluge. Me, I'll have a double deluge with very little soda, please.

To be quite candid, the safari the author celebrates in his title is about as exciting as a streetcar journey from Upper Darby to Paoli, and his flora and fauna suggest the lobby display accompanying a Monogram jungle film. What lifts *Killers on Safari* from the ruck is a

cast of characters out of Daisy Ashford by Fenimore Cooper, with
Superman acting as accoucheur. Their adventures are recorded in some
of the most stylish prose to flow out of an inkhorn since Helen Hunt
Jackson's *Ramona*. The people of Mr. Brigaud's piece, beset by hostile
aborigines, snakes, and blackwater fever, converse with almost unbearable elegance, rolling out their periods like Edmund Burke. Here,
for example, Diana Patten and Walter Huntley, a couple of the characters, in a sylvan glade, as their porters take a short breather:

"A coarse forest pig shuffled out of a ravine and began nibbling on
a bamboo root. The shapely hand of Diana Patten made a gesture
which encompassed the whole scene as she said softly: 'These beasts of
the wilderness know when it is safe for them to come near the most
murderous of all mammals: man!' Walter Huntley stared adoringly at
her symmetrical features, which became so girlish and gentle when her
red lips parted in a smile. For the thousandth time he thought that she
was unusually tall, but breathtakingly gorgeous, from her wavy blond
hair down her statuesque body to her shapely feet. The big pig trotted
back into the ravine."

This tropical idyl pauses for approximately twelve hundred words
of exposition to establish Diana's and Walter's identity, and then:

"The forest hog emerged again from the ravine, leading a sow and
four piglets. 'Are they not coarse, rough, and as perfectly alike as
raindrops in every detail excepting size?' Diana chuckled, snuggling
against Walter's shoulder." I cannot recall a more engaging passage
in fiction, and I've been trying for almost eighteen seconds.

The principals of *Killers on Safari* are three: Dr. Hargrave, a goatish
New York physician traveling through Sierra Leone on a scientific
mission vaguely related to rejuvenation; Walter Huntley, his guide, a
former patron of alcoholic beverages, seeking salvation; and Diana
Patten, the doctor's nurse. Judged by ordinary hospital standards,
Diana is the least conventional nurse ever sent out by a registry. The
decorative heading represents her as a toothsome showgirl, clad in a
minute swath of rayon and transfixing a gigantic black warrior with an
assagai. "As a student in a women's college, she had won prizes in
archery and javelin-throwing contests," Mr. Brigaud fluently explains.
Diana, in all justice, has her softer side; somewhat later, when she and
Walter are rushed by a savage, she cries out instinctively, "Don't kill
him, but put a bullet into one of his legs!" Diana's innate sentimental-
ity continually gets in her way; further on, a black chieftain named
Wambogo invites her to share his pallet and she taunts him into dueling
with javelins, with this result: "It would have been easy for her to dis-

embowel Wambogo before the latter could bring his own spear into play. But she preferred to maim him. . . . Therefore she split open Wambogo's breast muscles, and cut his tendons under his armpit. Then, as he howled with pain and rage, she slid out of his grasp, leaped back, and pinked him through a leg." Lucky for Wambogo that Diana was only pettish, or she might really have unsheathed her claws.

The story opens with Diana warning Walter that their employer, Dr. Hargrave, has become jealous of their attachment and means him no good. Her apprehensions are justified, for the Doctor is everlastingly crouched in the shrubbery, tremulous with desire, cooking up schemes for eliminating the guide. At length he eggs on a treacherous native named Itira Nlembi to ambush Walter, but the latter draws first claret and the aggressor slinks off into the potted palms with the equivalent of a broken neck. The party now proceeds sluggishly to the territory of a tribe of fierce hallboys called the Amutu, where Dr. Hargrave divides his time between healing the sick and pinching Diana. She finds his attentions odious and haughtily terms him a boor. Dr. Hargrave smarts under the insult:

" 'So I am called a boor!' he mouthed angrily. 'I begin to have enough of your sponsoring the cause of the former tramp, Miss Patten!' And turning on his heels, he strode furiously toward the central pavilion. . . . When the portly bulk of Hargrave disappeared behind the lap [*sic*] of the pavilion acting as a door, her spirits sank and she moaned: 'From bad to worse! It is bad, very bad, to be under orders of a man on the verge of insanity! I wonder how it will all end!' " It all ends quite spiritedly, with Hargrave putting a slug in the guide's ribs and Walter bringing his revolver butt down on the Doctor's skull. This surprisingly restores good-fellowship all around, and the rivals unite to repulse an attack by the Amutu. Hargrave herewith exits untidily from the plot, struck down by a battle ax, but thanks to a homemade avalanche and some fast spear work by Diana, Walter and the girl get clear. It then transpires how foresighted Diana was to major in archery at college; she keeps the larder well stocked with antelope meat and liquidates a black leopard who waylays her in the greenery. Some index of her pluck on this occasion may be gained from Walter's words following the event:

" 'You acted with amazing spunk and skill. You are a marvelous heroine. But, damn it! For a moment I nearly got a stroke at the thought that that awful lion was about to tear you to shreds!' " He implores Diana not to go hunting unescorted in future, but, womanlike, she disregards him and sallies forth. Thereupon her lover behaves much in the manner of a Keystone two-reeler: "Walter tore his hat from his head, slammed it on the ground, and kicked it." Whether he jumped up and down on it or flung a custard pie after her is not indicated. His blood pressure again starts vaulting when a courier reports that Diana has been taken captive by Itira Nlembi: "Walter saw blood on his face, and on one of his arms, and almost got a stroke." Walter, in fact, constantly appears to be hovering on the edge of a syncope; the next time he sees Diana, in Itira's lair, he reacts characteristically: "Walter nearly became apoplectic at the sight of her disheveled hair, bruised arms, and torn clothes." My knowledge of hypertension is elementary, but it seems to me Walter would be far better off rocking on the porch of a New Jersey milk farm than mousing around Sierra Leone.

The story (for want of a better term) now develops what is unquestionably the teeniest crescendo in the annals of modern typesetting. Itira Nlembi, overcome by Diana's charms, offers to make her his queen. Diana responds in her usual polished forensic style: " 'I have been waiting for some hare-brained proposals ever since your evil-smelling grub-eaters ambushed and overcame me by sheer strength of numbers!' " Nevertheless, playing for time, she pretends to accede on condition that he court her for two months, as befits a lady of rank. Itira, anxious not to breach the rules of etiquette, assents. Then, aided by two ladies of the harem, the lovers vamoose and race to meet a British relief column they have magically notified. Itira's hatchetmen, of course, give pursuit. At the couple's darkest hour, just as Walter's arteries are snapping like pipestems, comes deliverance: "Walter's calm voice was belied by the feverish look of his eyes and his twitching lips. Suddenly he beamed ecstatically and shouted at the top of his lungs: 'Oh, my dear, there will be no reason of hurting that pretty head of yours! Look down there, toward the north! Don't you see gun barrels gleaming under the sun? They are coming, the British!' " A few rounds of grape disperse the blacks, and the British officer in command benignly advises Walter and Diana to get themselves to the nearest chaplain. " 'And,' he adds, with a gruff chuckle, 'could I be best man? I sort of think it would round up my memories of this chapter of adventures spiced by human interest.' "

And so, as apoplexy and archery join lips under the giant clichés and Kipling spins in his grave like a lathe, let us bid adieu to Armand Brigaud, a great kid and a great storyteller. Dig you around Lake Chad, old boy, and don't take any guff from Romain Gary.

❦ DENTAL OR MENTAL, I SAY IT'S SPINACH

A FEW DAYS AGO, under the heading, MAN LEAPS OUT WINDOW AS DENTIST GETS FORCEPS, *The New York Times* reported the unusual case of a man who leaped out a window as the dentist got the forceps. Briefly, the circumstances were these. A citizen in Staten Island tottered into a dental parlor and, indicating an aching molar, moaned, "It's killing me. You've got to pull it out." The dentist grinned like a Cheshire cat—*The New York Times* neglected to say so, but a Cheshire cat who was present at the time grinned like a dentist—and reached for his instruments. "There was a leap and a crash," continues the account. "The astonished dentist saw his patient spring through the closed window and drop ten feet to the sidewalk, where he lay dazed." The casualty was subsequently treated at a nearby hospital for abrasion and shock by Drs. J. G. Abrazian and Walter Shock, and then, like a worm, crept back to the dentist, apologized and offered to pay for the damage. On one point, however, he remained curiously adamant. He still has his tooth.

As a party who recently spent a whole morning with his knees braced against a dentist's chest, whimpering "Don't—don't—I'll do anything, but don't drill!" I am probably the only man in America equipped to sympathize with the poor devil. Ever since Nature presented me at birth with a set of thirty-two flawless little pearls of assorted sizes, I never once relaxed my vigilant stewardship of same. From the age of six onward, I constantly polished the enamel with peanut brittle, massaged the incisors twice daily with lollipops, and chewed taffy and chocolate-covered caramels faithfully to exercise the gums. As for consulting a dentist regularly, my punctuality practically amounted to a fetish. Every twelve years I would drop whatever I was doing and allow wild Caucasian ponies to drag me to a reputable orthodontist. I guess you might say I was hipped on the subject of dental care.

When, therefore, I inadvertently stubbed a tooth on a submerged cherry in an old-fashioned last week and my toupee ricocheted off the ceiling, I felt both dismayed and betrayed. By eleven the next morning, I was seated in the antechamber of one Russell Pipgrass, D.D.S., limply holding a copy of the *National Geographic* upside down and pretending to be absorbed in Magyar folkways. Through the door communicating with the arena throbbed a thin, blood-curdling whine like a circular saw biting into a green plank. Suddenly an ear-splitting shriek rose above it, receding into a choked gurgle. I nonchalantly tapped out my cigarette in my eardrum and leaned over to the nurse, a Medusa type with serpents writhing out from under her prim white coif.

"Ah—er—pardon me," I observed, swallowing a bit of emery paper I had been chewing. "Did you hear anything just then?"

"Why, no," she replied, primly tucking back a snake under her cap. "What do you mean?"

"A—kind of a scratchy sound," I faltered.

"Oh, that," she sniffed carelessly. "Impacted wisdom tooth. We have to go in through the skull for those, you know." Murmuring some inconsequential excuse about lunching with a man in Sandusky, Ohio, I dropped to the floor and was creeping toward the corridor on all fours when Dr. Pipgrass emerged, rubbing his hands. "Well, here's an unexpected windfall!" he cackled, his eyes gleaming with cupidity. "Look out—slam the door on him!" Before I could dodge past, he pinioned me in a hammer lock and bore me, kicking and struggling, into his web. He was trying to wrestle me into the chair when the nurse raced in, brandishing a heavy glass ash tray.

"Here, hit him with this!" she panted.

"No, no, we mustn't bruise him," muttered Pipgrass. "Their relatives always ask a lot of silly questions." They finally made me comfy by strapping me into the chair with a half a dozen towels, tilted my feet up and pried open my teeth with a spoon. "Now then, where are his X-rays?" demanded the doctor.

"We haven't any," returned the nurse. "This is the first time he's been here."

"Well, bring me any X-rays," her employer barked. "What difference does it make? When you've seen one tooth, you've seen them all." He held up the X-rays against the light and examined them critically. "Well, friend, you're in a peck of trouble," he said at length. "You may as well know the worst. These are the teeth of an eighty-year-old man. You got here just in time." Plucking a horrendous nozzle from the rack, he shot compressed air down my gullet that sent me into a strangled paroxysm, and peered curiously at my inlays.

"Who put those in, a steamfitter?" he sneered. "You ought to be arrested for walking around with a job like that." He turned abruptly at the rustle of greenbacks and glared at his nurse. "See here, Miss Smedley, how many times have I told you not to count the patient's money in front of him? Take the wallet outside and go through it there." She nodded shamefacedly and slunk out. "That's the kind of thing that creates a bad impression on the layman," growled Dr. Pipgrass, poking at my tongue with a sharp stick. "Now what seems to be the trouble in there?"

"Ong ong ong," I wheezed.

"H'm'm'm, a cleft palate," he mused. "Just as I feared. And you've got between four and five thousand cavities. While we're at it, I think we'd better tear out those lowers with a jackhammer and put in some nice expensive crowns. Excuse me." He quickly dialed a telephone number. "Is that you, Irene?" he asked. "Russell. Listen, on that white mink coat we were talking about at breakfast—go right ahead, I've changed my mind. . . . No, I'll tell you later. He's filthy with it."

"Look, Doctor," I said with a casual yawn. "It's nothing really—just a funny tickling sensation in that rear tooth. I'll be back Tuesday—a year from Tuesday."

"Yes, yes," he interrupted, patting me reassuringly. "Don't be afraid now; this won't hurt a bit." With a slow, cunning smile, he produced from behind his back a hypodermic of the type used on brewery horses and, distending my lip, plunged it into the gum. The tip of my nose instantly froze, and my tongue took on the proportions of a bolt of flannel. I tried to cry out, but my larynx was out to lunch. Seizing the opportunity, Pipgrass snatched up his drill, took a firm purchase on my hair and teed off. A mixture of sensation roughly comparable to being alternately stilettoed and inflated with a bicycle pump overcame me; two thin wisps of smoke curled upward slowly from my ears. Fortunately, I had been schooled from boyhood to withstand pain without flinching, and beyond an occasional scream that rattled the windows, I bore myself with the stoicism of a red man. Scarcely ninety minutes later, Dr. Pipgrass thrust aside the drill, wiped his streaming forehead and shook the mass of protoplasm before him.

"Well, we're in the home stretch," he announced brightly, extracting a rubber sheet from a drawer. "We'll put this dam on you and fill her in a jiffy. You don't get claustrophobia, do you?"

"Wh-what's that?" I squeaked.

"Fear of being buried alive," he explained smoothly. "Kind of a stifling feeling. Your heart starts racing and you think you're going crazy. Pure imagination, of course." He pinned the rubber sheet over my face, slipped it over the tooth and left me alone with my thoughts. In less time than it takes to relate, I was a graduate member, *summa cum laude*, of the Claustrophobia Club. My face had turned a stunning shade of green, my heart was going like Big Ben, and a set of castanets in my knees was playing the "Malagueña." Summoning my last reserves of strength, I cast off my bonds and catapulted through the anteroom to freedom. I bequeathed Pipgrass a fleece-lined overcoat worth sixty-eight dollars, and he's welcome to it; I'll string along nicely with this big wad of chewing gum over my tooth. On me it looks good.

🌿 TAKE TWO PARTS SAND, ONE PART GIRL, AND STIR

OUTSIDE OF THE THREE R'S—the razor, the rope, and the revolver—I know only one sure-fire method of coping with the simmering heat we may cheerfully expect in this meridian from now to Labor Day. Whenever the mercury starts inching up the column, I take to the horizontal plane with a glass graduate trimmed with ferns, place a pinch of digitalis or any good heart stimulant at my elbow, and flip open the advertising section of *Vogue*. Fifteen minutes of that paradisiacal prose, those dizzying non sequiturs, and my lips are as blue as Lake Louise. If you want a mackerel iced or a sherbet frozen, just bring it up and let me read the advertising section of *Vogue* over it. I can also take care of small picnic parties up to five. The next time you're hot and breathless, remember the name, folks: Little Labrador Chilling & Dismaying Corporation.

It would require precision instruments as yet undreamed of to decide whether *Vogue*'s advertisements contain more moonbeams per linear inch than those of its competitors, but the June issue was certainly a serious contender for the ecstasy sweepstakes. There was, for instance, the vagary which portrayed a Revolutionary heroine setting fire to a field of grain with this caption: *"The Patriotism in Her Heart Burned Wheat Fields.* It took courage that day in October 1777 for Catherine Schuyler to apply the torch to her husband's wheat fields so that food would not fall into the hands of the enemy. The flames that consumed the wheat fields on the Schuyler estate near Saratoga burned with no greater brightness than the patriotism in Catherine Schuyler's heart." Then, with a triple forward somersault that would have done credit to Alfredo Codona, the wizard of the trapeze, the copywriter vaulted giddily into an appeal to American women to augment their loveliness with Avon Cosmetics. Somewhat breathless, I turned the page and beheld a handsome young air woman crouched on a wing of her plane. "Test Pilot—Size 10," read the text. "Nine thousand feet above the flying field, a Hellcat fighter plane screams down in the dark blur of a power dive. Holding the stick of this four-hundred-mile-an-hour ship is a small firm hand." The owner of the small firm hand, I shortly discovered in the verbal power dive that followed, is an enthusiastic patron of DuBarry Beauty Preparations. The transition in logic was so abrupt that it was only by opening my mouth and screaming briefly, a procedure I had observed in the movies, that I was able to keep my eardrums from bursting.

The most singular display of the advertiser's eternal lust for novelty, though, was a bold, full-color photograph of an olive-skinned beauty, buried up to her corsage in sand, in the interests of Marvella Simulated Pearls. A matched string of the foregoing circled her voluptuous throat, and dimly visible in the background were a conch shell and a sponge, identifying the locale as the seaside. The model's face exhibited a resentment verging on ferocity, which was eminently pardonable; anybody mired in a quicksand, with only a string of simulated pearls to show for it, has a justifiable beef. And so have I. The connection between burning wheat field and cosmetic jar, Hellcat fighter and lipstick, is tenuous enough, God knows, but somehow the copywriter managed to link them with his sophistries. Why in Tophet a scowling nude stuck bolt upright in a sand bar should influence the reader to rush to his jeweler for a particular brand of artificial pearl, however, I cannot possibly imagine.

Perhaps if we reconstruct the circumstances under which this baffling campaign was conceived, a clue might be forthcoming. Let us, therefore, don a clean collar and sidle discreetly into the offices of Meeker, Cassavant, Singleton, Doubleday & Tripler, a fairly representative advertising agency.

SCENE: *The Brain Room of the agency, a conference chamber decorated in cerebral gray, Swedish modern furniture, and the inevitable Van Gogh reproductions. As the curtain rises, Duckworth, the copy chief, and four members of his staff—Farish, Munkaczi, DeGroot, and Miss Drehdel—are revealed plunged in thought.*

DUCKWORTH (*impatient*): Well, what do you say, Farish? Got an angle, DeGroot?

FARISH: I still keep going back to my old idea, V. J.

DUCKWORTH: What's that?

FARISH (*thirstily*): A good red-hot picture of a dame in a transparent shimmy, with plenty of thems and those (*suddenly conscious of Miss Drehdel's presence*)—oh, excuse me.

MISS DREHDEL (*wearily*): That's all right. I read Earl Wilson's column, too.

FARISH: And a balloon coming out of her mouth saying, "I've had my Vita-Ray Cheese Straws today—*have you?*"

DUCKWORTH: No-o-o, it doesn't—it doesn't *sing*, if you know what I mean. I feel there's something gay and youthful and alive about these cheese straws. That's the note I want to hear in our copy.

DEGROOT: How about a gay, newborn baby in a crib? That would include the various elements. I'd like to see a line like "No harsh abrasives to upset tender tummies."

DUCKWORTH: No, it's static. To me it lacks dynamism.

MISS DREHDEL: What's wrong with a closeup of the cheese straws and "20 cents a box" underneath?

DUCKWORTH: Oversimplification. They'd never get it.

MUNKACZI (*violently*): I've got it, V. J., *I've got it!*

DUCKWORTH: What?

MUNKACZI: We'll take one of these Conover models and bury her up to her neck in sand! Maybe some driftwood or a couple of clams for drama!

FARISH: How do we tie in the cheese straws?

MUNKACZI: I haven't worked it out yet, but it smells right to me.

DUCKWORTH (*excitedly*): Wait a minute, now—you threw me into something when you said "sand." What we need is grit—punch—conflict. I see a foxhole at Anzio—shells bursting—a doughboy with shining eyes saying, "This is what I'm fighting for, Ma—freedom of purchase the American Way—the right to buy Vita-Ray Cheese Straws on every drug, grocery, and delicatessen counter from coast to coast!"

FARISH: Man, oh man, that's terrific! I'll buy that!

DEGROOT: It's poetic and yet it's timely, too! It's a blockbuster, V. J.!

DUCKWORTH (*radiant*): You really mean it? You're sure you're not telling me this just because I'm the boss? (*indignation in varying degree from all*) O.K. If there's one thing I can't abide, it's a lot of yesmen around me. Now let's get on to the Hush-a-Bye Blanket account. Any hunches?

DEGROOT: We got a darb. (*producing two photographs*) This is what the nap of a Hush-a-Bye looks like under the microscope.

FARISH: And here's the average blanket. See the difference?

DUCKWORTH: Why, yes. It has twice as many woolen fibers as the Hush-a-Bye.

DeGroot (*happily*): Check. There's our campaign.

Duckworth: Hmm. Isn't that sort of defeatist?

Farish: A little, but it shows we don't make extravagant claims.

DeGroot: We could always switch the photographs.

Farish: Sure, nobody ever looks at their blanket through a microscope.

Duckworth (*dubiously*): We-e-ll, I don't know. I like your approach to the challenge, but I don't think you've extracted its—its thematic milk, shall I say. Now, I for one saw a different line of attack.

Farish (*instantly*): Me too, V. J. What I visualize is a showgirl with a real nifty chassis in a peekaboo nightgown. Here, I'll draw you a sketch—

Miss Drehdel: Don't bother. We can read your mind.

Munkaczi: Listen, V. J., do you want a wrinkle that'll revolutionize the business? Answer yes or no.

Duckworth: Does it fit in with the product?

Munkaczi: Fit in? It grows right out of it! You're looking at a beach, see? Voom! Right in front of you is a Powers girl buried up to the bust in sand, with some horseshoe crabs or seaweed as an accent.

Duckworth: Do you see a Hush-a-Bye blanket anywhere in the composition?

Munkaczi: No, that would be hitting it on the nose. Indirection, V. J., that's the whole trend today.

Duckworth: You've realized the problem, Munkaczi, but your synthesis is faulty. I miss a sense of scope. Who are we rooting for?

Munkaczi: Well, of course I was only spitballing. I haven't had time to explore every cranny.

Duckworth: Look, kids, if you don't like what I'm about to suggest, will you tell me?

Farish (*fiercely*): I've never been a stooge for anyone yet.

DeGroot: You said it. There's not enough money in the world to buy *my* vote.

Duckworth: That's the stuff. I want guts in this organization, not a bunch of namby-pambies scared that I'll kick 'em out into the breadline. Now this is hazy, mind you, but it's all there. A beachhead in the Solomons—a plain, ordinary G.I. Joe in a slit trench, grinning at the consumer through the muck and grime on his face, and asking, "Are you backing me up with Hush-a-Bye Blankets at home? Gee, Mom, don't sabotage my birthright with sleazy, inferior brands!"

DeGroot: Holy cow, that'll tear their hearts out!

FARISH (*with a sob*): It brings a lump to your throat. It's a portion of common everyday experience.

DUCKWORTH: Remember, men, it isn't sacred. If you think you can improve the phrasing—

DEGROOT: I wouldn't change a word of it.

FARISH: It's got balance and flow and discipline. Say it again, will you, V. J.?

DUCKWORTH: No, it's pretty near lunch and we still need a slant for the Marvella Pearl people.

MUNKACZI (*exalted*): Your troubles are over, boss. I got something that leaps from the printed page into the hearts of a million women! It's four A.M. in the Aleutians. A haggard, unshaven Marine is kneeling in a shell hole, pointing his rifle at you and whispering, "Start thinking, sister! When Johnny comes marching home are you going to be poised and serene with Marvella Pearls or just another housewife?"

FARISH: Cripes, I had the same notion, V. J. He took the words right out of my mouth!

DEGROOT: I'll go for that! It's as timely as tomorrow's newspaper!

DUCKWORTH: There's only one thing wrong with it. It's *too* timely.

DEGROOT (*eagerly*): That's what I meant. It's depressing.

FARISH: It reminds people of their troubles. Ugh!

DUCKWORTH: Precisely. Now, I've been mulling a concept which is a trifle on the exotic side but fundamentally sound. Mark you, I'm merely talking out loud. A girl on a bathing beach, almost totally buried in the sand, with a Marvella necklace and a brooding, inscrutable expression like the Sphinx. Haunting but inviting—the eternal riddle of womankind.

DEGROOT (*emotionally*): V. J., do you want my candid opinion? I wouldn't tell this to my own mother, but you've just made advertising history!

FARISH: It's provocative, múscular, three-dimensional! It's got a *spiral* quality, the more you think of it.

DUCKWORTH: How does it hit you, Munkaczi?

MUNKACZI (*warmly*): I couldn't like it more if it was my own idea.

DUCKWORTH: I wonder if Miss Drehdel can give us the woman's reaction, in a word.

MISS DREHDEL (*rising*): You bet I can. The word I'm thinking of rhymes with Sphinx. (*sunnily*) Well, goodbye now. If anybody wants me, I'm over at Tim's, up to here in sawdust and Cuba Libres. (*She goes; a pause.*)

FARISH: I always said there was something sneaky about her.

DEGROOT: Women and business don't mix.

MUNKACZI: You can never tell what they're really thinking.

FARISH (*cackling*): Old V. J. smoked her out though, didn't he?

DUCKWORTH (*expansively*): Yes, I may be wrong, but this is one conference she won't forget in a hurry, eh boys? (*The boys chuckle loyally and scuffle to light his cigar.*)

CURTAIN

❧ FAREWELL, MY LOVELY APPETIZER

ADD SMORGASBITS to your ought-to-know department, the newest of the three Betty Lee products. What in the world! Just small mouth-size pieces of herring and of pinkish tones. We crossed our heart and promised not to tell the secret of their tinting.—*Clementine Paddle-ford's food column in the* Herald Tribune.

The "Hush-Hush" Blouse. We're very hush-hush about his name, but the celebrated shirtmaker who did it for us is famous on two continents for blouses with details like those deep yoke folds, the wonderful shoulder pads, the shirtband bow!—*Russeks adv. in the* Times.

I CAME DOWN the sixth-floor corridor of the Arbogast Building, past the World Wide Noodle Corporation, Zwinger & Rumsey, Account-ants, and the Ace Secretarial Service, Mimeographing Our Specialty. The legend on the ground-glass panel next door said, "Atlas Detective Agency, Noonan & Driscoll," but Snapper Driscoll had retired two years before with a .38 slug between the shoulders, donated by a snow-bird in Tacoma, and I owned what good will the firm had. I let myself into the crummy anteroom we kept to impress clients, growled good morning at Birdie Claflin.

"Well, you certainly look like something the cat dragged in," she said. She had a quick tongue. She also had eyes like dusty lapis lazuli, taffy hair, and a figure that did things to me. I kicked open the bottom drawer of her desk, let two inches of rye trickle down my craw, kissed Birdie square on her lush, red mouth, and set fire to a cigarette.

"I could go for you, sugar," I said slowly. Her face was veiled, watchful. I stared at her ears, liking the way they were joined to her head. There was something complete about them; you knew they were there for keeps. When you're a private eye, you want things to stay put.

"Any customers?"

"A woman by the name of Sigrid Bjornsterne said she'd be back. A looker."

"Swede?"

"She'd like you to think so."

I nodded toward the inner office to indicate that I was going in there, and went in there. I lay down on the davenport, took off my shoes, and bought myself a shot from the bottle I kept underneath. Four minutes later, an ash-blonde with eyes the color of unset opals, in a Nettie Rosenstein basic black dress and a baum-marten stole, burst in. Her bosom was heaving and it looked even better that way. With a gasp she circled the desk, hunting for some place to hide, and then, spotting the wardrobe where I keep a change of bourbon, ran into it. I got up and wandered out into the anteroom. Birdie was deep in a crossword puzzle.

"See anyone come in here?"

"Nope." There was a thoughtful line between her brows. "Say, what's a five-letter word meaning 'trouble'?"

"Swede," I told her, and went back inside. I waited the length of time it would take a small, not very bright, boy to recite *Ozymandias*, and, inching carefully along the wall, took a quick gander out the window. A thin galoot with stooping shoulders was being very busy reading a paper outside the Gristede store two blocks away. He hadn't been there an hour ago, but then, of course, neither had I. He wore a size seven dove-colored hat from Browning King, a tan Wilson Brothers shirt with pale-blue stripes, a J. Press foulard with a mixed red-and-white figure, dark-blue Interwoven socks, and an unshined pair of oxblood London Character shoes. I let a cigarette burn down between my fingers until it made a small red mark, and then I opened the wardrobe.

"Hi," the blonde said lazily. "You Mike Noonan?" I made a noise that could have been "Yes," and waited. She yawned. I thought things over, decided to play it safe. I yawned. She yawned back, then, settling into a corner of the wardrobe, went to sleep. I let another cigarette burn down until it made a second red mark beside the first one, and then I woke her up. She sank into a chair, crossing a pair of gams that tightened my throat as I peered under the desk at them.

"Mr. Noonan," she said, "you—you've got to help me."

"My few friends call me Mike," I said pleasantly.

"Mike." She rolled the syllable on her tongue. "I don't believe I've ever heard that name before. Irish?"

"Enough to know the difference between a gossoon and a bassoon."

"What *is* the difference?" she asked. I dummied up; I figured I wasn't giving anything away for free. Her eyes narrowed. I shifted my two hundred pounds slightly, lazily set fire to a finger, and watched it burn down. I could see she was admiring the interplay of muscles in my shoulders. There wasn't any extra fat on Mike Noonan, but I wasn't telling *her* that. I was playing it safe until I knew where we stood.

When she spoke again, it came with a rush. "Mr. Noonan, he thinks I'm trying to poison him. But I swear the herring was pink—I took it out of the jar myself. If I could only find out how they tinted it. I offered them money, but they wouldn't tell."

"Suppose you take it from the beginning," I suggested.

She drew a deep breath. "You've heard of the golden spintria of Hadrian?" I shook my head. "It's a tremendously valuable coin believed to have been given by the Emperor Hadrian to one of his proconsuls, Caius Vitellius. It disappeared about 150 A.D., and eventually passed into the possession of Hucbald the Fat. After the sack of Adrianople by the Turks, it was loaned by a man named Shapiro to the court physician, or hakim, of Abdul Mahmoud. Then it dropped out of sight for nearly five hundred years, until last August, when a dealer in secondhand books named Lloyd Thursday sold it to my husband."

"And now it's gone again," I finished.

"No," she said. "At least, it was lying on the dresser when I left, an hour ago." I leaned back, pretending to fumble a carbon out of the desk, and studied her legs again. This was going to be a lot more intricate than I had thought. Her voice got huskier. "Last night I brought home a jar of Smorgasbits for Walter's dinner. You know them?"

"Small mouth-size pieces of herring and of pinkish tones, aren't they?"

Her eyes darkened, lightened, got darker again. "How did you know?"

"I haven't been a private op nine years for nothing, sister. Go on."

"I—I knew right away something was wrong when Walter screamed and upset his plate. I tried to tell him the herring was supposed to be pink, but he carried on like a madman. He's been suspicious of me since—well, ever since I made him take out that life insurance."

"What was the face amount of the policy?"

"A hundred thousand. But it carried a triple-indemnity clause in case he died by sea food. Mr. Noonan—Mike—" her tone caressed me— "I've got to win back his confidence. You could find out how they tinted that herring."

"What's in it for me?"

"Anything you want." The words were a whisper. I leaned over, poked open her handbag, counted off five grand.

"This'll hold me for a while," I said. "If I need any more, I'll beat my spoon on the high chair." She got up. "Oh, while I think of it, how does this golden spintria of yours tie in with the herring?"

"It doesn't," she said calmly. "I just threw it in for glamour." She trailed past me in a cloud of scent that retailed at ninety rugs the ounce. I caught her wrist, pulled her up to me.

"I go for girls named Sigrid with opal eyes," I said.

"Where'd you learn my name?"

"I haven't been a private snoop twelve years for nothing, sister."

"It was nine last time."

"It seemed like twelve till you came along." I held the clinch until a faint wisp of smoke curled out of her ears, pushed her through the door. Then I slipped a pint of rye into my stomach and a heater into my kick and went looking for a bookdealer named Lloyd Thursday. I knew he had no connection with the herring caper, but in my business you don't overlook anything.

The thin galoot outside Gristede's had taken a powder when I got there; that meant we were no longer playing girls' rules. I hired a hack to Wanamaker's, cut over to Third, walked up toward Fourteenth. At Twelfth a mink-faced jasper made up as a street cleaner tailed me for a block, drifted into a dairy restaurant. At Thirteenth somebody dropped a sour tomato out of a third-story window, missing me by inches. I doubled back to Wanamaker's, hopped a bus up Fifth to Madison Square, and switched to a cab down Fourth, where the secondhand bookshops elbow each other like dirty urchins.

A flabby hombre in a Joe Carbondale rope-knit sweater, whose jowl could have used a shave, quit giggling over *The Heptameron* long enough to tell me he was Lloyd Thursday. His shoebutton eyes became opaque when I asked to see any first editions or incunabula relative to the *Clupea harengus*, or common herring.

"You got the wrong pitch, copper," he snarled. "That stuff is hotter than Pee Wee Russell's clarinet."

"Maybe a sawbuck'll smarten you up," I said. I folded one to the size of a postage stamp, scratched my chin with it. "There's five yards around for anyone who knows why those Smorgasbits of Sigrid Bjornsterne's happened to be pink." His eyes got crafty.

"I might talk for a grand."

"Start dealing." He motioned toward the back. I took a step forward. A second later a Roman candle exploded inside my head and I went away from there. When I came to, I was on the floor with a lump on my sconce the size of a lapwing's egg and big Terry Tremaine of Homicide was bending over me.

"Someone sapped me," I said thickly. "His name was—"

"Webster," grunted Terry. He held up a dog-eared copy of Merriam's Unabridged. "You tripped on a loose board and this fell off a shelf on your think tank."

"Yeah?" I said skeptically. "Then where's Thursday?" He pointed to the fat man lying across a pile of erotica. "He passed out cold when he saw you cave." I covered up, let Terry figure it any way he wanted. I wasn't telling him what cards I held. I was playing it safe until I knew all the angles.

In a seedy pharmacy off Astor Place, a stale Armenian whose name might have been Vulgarian but wasn't dressed my head and started asking questions. I put my knee in his groin and he lost interest. Jerking my head toward the coffee urn, I spent a nickel and the next forty minutes doing some heavy thinking. Then I holed up in a phone booth and dialed a clerk I knew called Little Farvel in a delicatessen store on Amsterdam Avenue. It took a while to get the dope I wanted because the connection was bad and Little Farvel had been dead two years, but we Noonans don't let go easily.

By the time I worked back to the Arbogast Building, via the Weehawken ferry and the George Washington Bridge to cover my tracks, all the pieces were in place. Or so I thought up to the point she came out of the wardrobe holding me between the sights of her ice-blue automatic.

"Reach for the stratosphere, gumshoe." Sigrid Bjornsterne's voice was colder than Horace Greeley and Little Farvel put together, but her clothes were plenty calorific. She wore a forest-green suit of Hockanum woolens, a Knox Wayfarer, and baby crocodile pumps. It was her blouse, though, that made tiny red hairs stand up on my knuckles. Its deep yoke folds, shoulder pads, and shirtband bow could only have been designed by some master craftsman, some Cézanne of the shears.

"Well, Nosy Parker," she sneered, "so you found out how they tinted the herring."

"Sure—grenadine," I said easily. "You knew it all along. And you planned to add a few grains of oxylbutane-cheriphosphate, which turns the same shade of pink in solution, to your husband's portion, knowing it wouldn't show in the post-mortem. Then you'd collect the three hundred *G*'s and join Harry Pestalozzi in Nogales till the heat died down. But you didn't count on me."

"You?" Mockery nicked her full-throated laugh. "What are you going to do about it?"

"This." I snaked the rug out from under her and she went down in a swirl of silken ankles. The bullet whined by me into the ceiling as I vaulted over the desk, pinioned her against the wardrobe.

"Mike." Suddenly all the hatred had drained away and her body yielded to mine. "Don't turn me in. You cared for me—once."

"It's no good, Sigrid. You'd only double-time me again."

"Try me."

"O.K. The shirtmaker who designed your blouse—what's his name?" A shudder of fear went over her; she averted her head. "He's famous on two continents. Come on Sigrid, they're your dice."

"I won't tell you. I can't. It's a secret between this—this department store and me."

"They wouldn't be loyal to you. They'd sell you out fast enough."

"Oh, Mike, you mustn't. You don't know what you're asking."

"For the last time."

"Oh, sweetheart, don't you see?" Her eyes were tragic pools, a cenotaph to lost illusions. "I've got so little. Don't take that away from me. I—I'd never be able to hold up my head in Russeks again."

"Well, if that's the way you want to play it . . ." There was silence in the room, broken only by Sigrid's choked sob. Then, with a strangely empty feeling, I uncradled the phone and dialed Spring 7-3100.

For an hour after they took her away, I sat alone in the taupe-colored dusk, watching lights come on and a woman in the hotel opposite adjusting a garter. Then I treated my tonsils to five fingers of firewater, jammed on my hat, and made for the anteroom. Birdie was still scowling over her crossword puzzle. She looked up crookedly at me.

"Need me any more tonight?"

"No." I dropped a grand or two in her lap. "Here, buy yourself some stardust."

"Thanks, I've got my quota." For the first time I caught a shadow of pain behind her eyes. "Mike, would—would you tell me something?"

"As long as it isn't clean," I flipped to conceal my bitterness.

"What's an eight-letter word meaning 'sentimental'?"

"Flatfoot, darling," I said, and went out into the rain.

❧ CLOUDLAND REVISITED: INTO YOUR TENT I'LL CREEP

I FIRST READ *The Sheik*, by E. M. Hull, during the winter of 1922–23, standing up behind the counter of a curious cigar store of which I was the night clerk, though I preferred the loftier designation of relief manager. I was, at the time, a sophomore at Brown University and had no real need of the job, as I was wealthy beyond the dreams of avarice. I had taken it solely because my rooms were a rallying point for the *jeunesse dorée* and were so full of turmoil and inconsequential babble that I was driven to distraction. Like Stevenson's Prince Florizel of Bohemia, who retired into Soho to conduct his cigar divan under the pseudonym of Theophilus Godall, I wanted anonymity and a quiet nook for study and speculation. I got enough of all these to last a lifetime, and, by discreet pilfering, sufficient cigarettes to impair the wind of the entire student body. Five months after I joined the enterprise, it was stricken with bankruptcy, the medical name for mercantile atrophy. To claim that I was wholly responsible would be immodest. I did what I could, but the lion's share of the credit belonged to Mr. Saidy, who owned the store.

Mr. Saidy was a hyperthyroid Syrian leprechaun, and a man of extraordinarily diversified talents. He was an accomplished portrait painter in the academic tradition, and his bold, flashy canvases, some of which were stored in our stockroom, impressed me as being masterly. John Singer Sargent and Zuloaga, whom he plagiarized freely, might have felt otherwise, but since neither was in the habit of frequenting our stockroom, Mr. Saidy was pretty safe from recrimination. In addition to the painting, playing the zither, and carving peach pits into monkeys to grace his watch chain, he was an inventor. He had patented a pipe for feminine smokers that held cigarettes in a vertical position and a machine for extracting pebbles from gravel roofs. Saidy's entry into the tobacco business had been motivated by a romantic conviction that he could buck the United Cigar Store combine, using its own methods. We issued coupons with all purchases, redeemable, according to their guarantee, for hundreds of valuable pre-

197

miums. I saw only four of them in my tenure—an electric iron, a catcher's mitt, a Scout knife, and one of those mechanical blackamoors of the period that operated on victrola turntables and danced a clog to "Bambalina" or "The Japanese Sandman." At first, I was uneasy lest some patron present a stack of coupons he had hoarded and demand one of the other premiums listed. There was no basis for my anxiety. Mr. Saidy's prices were higher than our competitors', so the customers stayed away by the thousands, and the infrequent few who blundered in spurned the certificates as if they were infected.

At any rate, it was in this pungent milieu that I made the acquaint-ance of the immortal Lady Diana Mayo and the Sheik Ahmed Ben Hassan, and when, after a lapse of twenty-five years, I sat down re-cently to renew it, I was heavy with nostalgia. A goodish amount of water had gone over the dam in the interim and I was not at all sure Miss Hull's febrile tale would pack its original wallop. I found that, contrariwise, the flavor had improved, like that of fine old port. There is nothing dated about the book; the bromides, in fact, have a creami-ness, a velvet texture, I am certain they lacked a quarter of a century ago. Any connoisseur knows that a passage like "She hated him with all the strength of her proud, passionate nature" or "I didn't love you when I took you, I only wanted you to satisfy the beast in me" acquires a matchless bouquet from lying around the cellar of a secondhand bookshop. No slapdash artificial aging process can quite duplicate the tang. It must steep.

The opening paragraph of *The Sheik* is, possibly, the most superb example of direct plot exposition in the language. Instead of fussing over the table decorations and place cards, like so many novelists, the author whisks open the door of the range and serves the soufflé piping hot. In the very first line of the book, a disembodied voice asks some-one named Lady Conway whether she is coming in to watch the danc-ing, and gets a tart reply: "I most decidedly am not. I thoroughly dis-approve of the expedition of which this dance is the inauguration. I consider that even by contemplating such a tour alone into the desert with no chaperon or attendant of her own sex, with only native camel drivers and servants, Diana Mayo is behaving with a recklessness and impropriety that is calculated to cast a slur not only on her own repu-tation, but also on the prestige of her country. . . . It is the maddest piece of unprincipled folly I have ever heard of."

That, I submit, is literary honesty of a high order, to say nothing of a forensic style Cicero would have envied. It does not abuse the reader's patience with a complex psychological probe of Diana's youth, her awakening womanhood, her revolt against narrow social conventions. It tells him with a minimum of flubdub that a madcap miss is going to be loused up by Arabs and that there will be no exchanges or refunds. After making this speech, Lady Conway storms off. It transpires that she has been addressing two gentlemen on the veranda of the Biskra Hotel, an Englishman named Arbuthnot and an unnamed American, who take an equally dim view of Diana's temerity. Though both adore her, they are dismayed by her imprudence and heartlessness. "The coldest little fish in the world, without an idea in her head beyond sport and travel," as Arbuthnot subsequently describes her, has been reared by her brother, Sir Aubrey, a typical Du Maurier baronet, and obeys no bidding but her own whim. When Arbuthnot leaves to beg a dance of the minx, his rival speeds him with characteristic Yankee jocosity: "Run along, foolish moth, and get your poor little wings singed. When the cruel fair has done trampling on you I'll come right along and mop up the remains." I presume he punctuated this metaphoric nosegay with a jet of tobacco juice, slapped his thigh, and blew his nose into a capacious bandanna, but the text delicately makes no mention of it.

The singe, more of a second-degree burn, is administered in the garden, where Arbuthnot offers his hand to Diana, along with two memorable chestnuts to the effect that beauty like hers drives a man mad and that he won't always be a penniless subaltern. His avowals, however, go for nought, as does his plea that she abandon her foolhardy undertaking. She exhibits the same intransigence toward her brother the next evening, at the oasis to which he has escorted her. "I will do what I choose when and how I choose," she declares, turning up an already snub nose at his dark predictions, and, blithely promising to join him in New York, plunges into the trackless Sahara, accompanied only by a guide and several bodyguards. Had you or I written the story, our heroine would have cantered into Oran in due course with her nose peeling and a slight case of saddle gall. But sunburn alone does not create best sellers, as Miss Hull well knew, and she has a bhoyo concealed in the dunes who is destined to put a crimp in Diana's plans, to phrase it very tactfully indeed.

For brevity's sake, we need not linger over the actual abduction of Diana by the Sheik; how her party is waylaid, how she is tempestuously swept onto his steed and spirited to his lair, must be tolerably familiar even to those too youthful to have seen it enacted on the screen by Agnes Ayres and Rudolph Valentino. The description of the desert corsair, though, as he takes inventory of his booty, attains a lyrical pitch current fiction has not surpassed: "It was the handsomest and cruelest face that she had ever seen. Her gaze was drawn instinctively to his. He was looking at her with fierce, burning eyes that swept her until she felt that the boyish clothes that covered her slender limbs were stripped from her, leaving the beautiful white body bare under his passionate stare." Under the circumstances, one cannot help feeling that her question, "Why have you brought me here?" betrays a hint of naïveté. The average man, faced with such a query, might have been taken unawares and replied weakly, "I forget," or "I guess I was overwhelmed by the sight of a pretty foot," but Ahmed's is no milksop answer: *"Bon Dieu!* Are you not woman enough to know?" This riposte so affected one spark I knew back in the early twenties that he used it exclusively thereafter in couch hammocks and canoes, but with what success is immaterial here. In the novel, at all events, the Arab chief, without further ado, works his sweet will of Diana, which explains in some measure why the book went into thirteen printings in eight months. I could be mistaken, of course; maybe it was only the sensuous lilt of the prose.

It may be asked, and reasonably, what the rest of the book deals with if such a ringing climax is reached on page 59. The story, simply, is one of adjustment; Ahmed Ben Hassan goes on working his sweet will of Diana with monotonous regularity, and she, in time, becomes reconciled to the idea. To be sure, she does not accept her martyrdom slavishly. She rages, threatens, implores, all to no purpose. Anguished, she demands why the Sheik has done this to her. "Because I wanted you," he returns coolly. "Because, one day in Biskra, four weeks ago, I saw you for a few moments, long enough to know that I wanted you. And what I want I take." All the scene needs to achieve perfection is a sardonic smile and a thin thread of smoke curling away from a monogrammed Turkish cigarette. These make their appearance in short order. Diana quaveringly asks when he will let her go. When he is tired of her, returns Ahmed with a sardonic smile, watching a thin thread of smoke curl away from a monogrammed Turkish cigarette. Small wonder every fiber of Diana's being cries out in protest.

"He is like a tiger," she murmurs deep into the cushions, with a shiver, "a graceful, cruel, merciless beast." She, in turn, reminds the Sheik of still another quadruped: "The easy swing of her boyish figure and the defiant carriage of her head reminded him of one of his own thoroughbred horses. . . . And as he broke them so would he break her." The connubial relationship between horse and tiger, while a trifle perplexing from the biological point of view, settles into a surprisingly domestic pattern. Yet instead of rolling with the punches, so to speak, Diana willfully upsets the applecart by running away. Ahmed overtakes her, and it is when she is being toted home, slung across his pommel like a sack of oats, that she experiences the great awakening: "Why did she not shrink from the pressure of his arm and the contact of his warm, strong body? . . . Quite suddenly she knew—knew that she loved him, that she had loved him for a long time, even when she thought she hated him and when she had fled from him. . . . He was a brute, but she loved him, loved him for his very brutality and superb animal strength."

Naturally, it would be infra dig for any woman, especially a member of the British peerage, to bluntly confess a *béguin* for an obscure tribesman. Hence, there ensues an interval in which Diana plays cat-and-mouse with the chieftain, instead of horse-and-tiger, and arouses his wrath by her ladylike reserve. *"Bon Dieu!* . . . Has the vile climate of your detestable country frozen you so thoroughly that nothing can melt you?" he mutters thickly, contemning even the weather in his scorn. "I am tired of holding an icicle in my arms." Eventually, though, his dear nearness, scorching kisses, and equally fiery rhetoric produce a thaw, and Diana favors him with a few caresses of signal puissance. Strange to say, their effect is not precisely what one would imagine: " 'You go to my head, Diane,' he said with a laugh that was half anger, and shrugging his shoulders moved across the tent to the chest where the spare arms were kept, and unlocking it took out a revolver and began to clean it." Perhaps I was unduly stimulated, but after that torrid build-up, dilettantism with a pistol seemed no substitute for a volcano.

For all practical purposes, nevertheless, and halfway through her narrative, the author has proved to everyone's ennui that pride crumbles before primitive passion. Given another setting, the boy and girl could now trot around to the license bureau and legalize their union, but here, in addition to the lack of such facilities, there is still the embarrassing racial barrier confronting Diana. Bewitched as she is by her swain, she cannot quite blink at the fact that he is an Arab, a grubby little native by her social standards. To nullify this obstacle, the author puts some fairly ponderous machinery in motion. She introduces a lifelong chum of the Sheik, a novelist named the Vicomte Raoul de Saint Hubert, who also happens to be a crackajack surgeon. Then she causes Diana to be kidnaped by a rival sachem, from whom Ahmed rescues her, sustaining a grievous wound. As he hovers between life and death, watched over by the Vicomte and Diana, the gimmick is unveiled:

" 'His hand is so big for an Arab's,' she said softly, like a thought spoken aloud unconsciously.

" 'He is not an Arab,' replied Saint Hubert with sudden impatient vehemence. 'He is English. Yes,' he continues, stunning Diana, if not the reader, 'his father is the Earl of Glencaryll.' " This news provokes a truly classic reaction from Diana: "Oh, now I know why that awful frown of Ahmed's has always seemed so familiar. Lord Glencaryll always frowns like that. It is the famous Caryll scowl." To soothe the literal-minded, there is a thirteen-page exegesis of the hero's background, complete with such reassuring details as a formal European education and a mother of noble Spanish birth. Diana doesn't really care, for she realizes that her woman's intuition, assisted by a bit of roughhouse from the Sheik, has guided her aright. When, on his recovery, he undergoes the mandatory change of heart and offers her freedom, the horse turns into a phoenix and rises reborn from the ashes: "She slid her arm up and around his neck, drawing his head down. 'I am not afraid,' she murmured slowly. 'I am not afraid of anything with your arms round me, my desert lover. Ahmed! Monseigneur!' "

If my examination of *The Sheik* did nothing else, it confirmed a suspicion I have been harboring for over two decades; namely, that the relief manager of a small cigar store in Providence about 1922 showed the most dubious literary taste of anyone I ever knew. To add to his other defects—he was shiftless, scheming, and transparently dishonest—he was an incorrigible romantic, the type of addlepate that, in later life, is addicted to rereading the books of his youth and whining over their shortcomings. Altogether, an unattractive figure and, I fear, a hopelessly bad lot. But then I suppose there's no point in being too tough on the boy. You can't judge people like him and Diana Mayo by ordinary standards. They're another breed of cat.

❧ PHYSICIAN, STEEL THYSELF

Do you happen to know how many tassels a Restoration coxcomb wore at the knee? Or the kind of chafing dish a bunch of Skidmore girls would have used in a dormitory revel in 1911? Or the exact method of quarrying peat out of a bog at the time of the Irish Corn Laws? In fact, do you know anything at all that nobody else knows or, for that matter, gives a damn about? If you do, then sit tight, because one of these days you're going to Hollywood as a technical supervisor on a million-dollar movie. You may be a bore to your own family, but you're worth your weight in piastres to the picture business.

Yes, Hollywood dearly loves a technical expert, however recondite or esoteric his field. It is a pretty picayune film that cannot afford at least one of them; sometimes they well-nigh outnumber the actors. The Sherlock Holmes series, for instance, employs three servants on a full-time basis—one who has made a lifelong study of the décor at 221-B Baker Street, a second deeply versed in the great detective's psychology and mannerisms, and a third who spots anachronisms in the script which may distress Holmesians, like penicillin and the atomic bomb. An ideal existence, you might think, and yet there have been exceptions. I once knew a French artillery officer at M-G-M, imported at bloodcurdling expense from overseas as adviser on a romance about Indo-China, who languished for two years in an office under the Music Department. Over the noon yoghurt, his voice trembled as he spoke of his yearning to return to Saigon, where they were waiting to shoot him, but the director of *Blistered Bugles* felt him indispensable. At last he departed, with close to forty thousand rutabagas in his money belt, a broken man. His sole contribution was that he had succeeded in having "*pouf*" altered to "*sacré bloo.*" Another expert I met during the same epoch was a jovial, gnarled little party named Settembrini, conceded to be the foremost wrought-iron craftsman in the country. He had been flown three thousand miles to authenticate several flambeaux shown briefly in a night shot of Versailles. We subsequently chanced to be on the same train going East, and except for the fact that he wore a gold derby and was lighting his cigar with a first-mortgage bond, he seemed untouched. "Fine place," he commented, flicking ashes into the corsage of a blonde he had brought along for the purpose. "Sunshine, pretty girls, grapefruit ten for a quarter." I asked him whether the flambeaux had met the test. "One hundred per cent," he replied, "but they threw 'em out. In the scene where Marie Antoinette comes down the steps, a lackey holds a flashlight so she don't trip over her feet."

The latest group of specialists to be smiled upon by the cinema industry, it would appear, are the psychoanalysts. The vogue of psychological films started by *Lady in the Dark* has resulted in flush times for the profession, and anyone who can tell a frazzled id from a father fixation had better be booted and spurred for an impending summons to the Coast. The credit title of *Spellbound*, Alfred Hitchcock's recent thriller, for example, carried the acknowledgment "Psychiatric sequences supervised by Dr. May Romm," and Sidney Skolsky, reporting on a picture called *Obsessed* (formerly *One Man's Secret* and before that *One Woman's Secret*), states, "Joan Crawford is huddling with an eminent psychiatrist who will psych her forthcoming role in *The Secret* for her." A psychiatrist suddenly pitchforked into Hollywood, the ultimate nightmare, must feel rather like a small boy let loose in a toy store, but I wonder how long he can maintain a spirit of strict scientific objectivity. The ensuing vignette, a hasty attempt to adumbrate this new trend, is purely fanciful. There are, naturally, no such places as the Brown Derby, Vine Street, and Hollywood Boulevard, and if there should turn out to be, I couldn't be sorrier.

Sherman Wormser, M.D., Ph.D., came out of the Hollywood Plaza Hotel, somewhat lethargic after a heavy Sunday brunch, and paused indecisively on the sidewalk. The idea of taking a walk, which had seemed so inspired a moment ago in his room, now depressed him immeasurably. To the south, Vine Street stretched away interminably— unending blocks of bankrupt night clubs, used-car lots, open-air markets, and bazaars full of unpainted furniture and garden pottery. To the north, it rose abruptly in a steep hill crowned by a cluster of funeral homes and massage parlors in tan stucco. Over all of it hung a warm miasma vaguely suggestive of a steam laundry. Sherman moved aimlessly toward the Boulevard and paused for a brief self-inventory in the window of the Broadway-Hollywood department store.

Most of Dr. Wormser's patients in New York, accustomed to his neat morning coat and pencil-striped trousers, would have had some difficulty in recognizing their father confessor at the moment. He wore a pea-green playsuit with deep, flaring lapels, tailored of rough, towel-like material, arbitrarily checked and striated in front but mysteriously turned to suède in back. Over a gauzy, salmon-colored polo shirt he had knotted a yellow foulard handkerchief in a bow reminiscent of George Primrose's Minstrels, and on his head was sportily perched an Alpinist's hat modeled after those worn by the tyrant Gessler. Eight weeks before, when he had arrived to check on the dream sequences of R.K.O.'s *Befuddled*, he would not have been caught dead in these vestments, but his sack suits had seemed so conspicuous that, chameleon-like, he soon developed a sense of protective coloration.

He had settled his hat at a jauntier angle and was turning away from the window when he became aware that a passer-by was staring fixedly at him. The man wore an off-white polo coat which hung open, its belt trailing on the pavement. Underneath were visible pleated lavender slacks and a monogrammed yachting jacket trimmed with brass buttons. The face under the scarlet beret was oddly familiar.

"I beg pardon," hesitated the stranger, "I think we—you're not Sherman Wormser, are you?" At the sound of his voice, Sherman's mouth opened in delight. He flung his arm about the man's shoulders.

"Why, Randy Kalbfus, you old son of a gun!" he crowed. "Two years ago! The Mental Hygiene Convention in Cleveland!"

"Bull's-eye," chuckled Kalbfus. "I thought it was you, but—well, you look different, somehow."

"Why—er—I used to have a Vandyke." Wormser felt his cheeks growing pink. "I shaved it off out here. The studio, you know. Say, you had one, too, for that matter. What became of yours?"

"Same thing," Kalbfus admitted sheepishly. "My producer said it was corny. He's got a block about psychiatrists wearing goatees."

"Yes, involuntary goatee rejection," nodded Wormser. "Stekel speaks of it. Well, well. I heard you were in town. Where you working?"

"Over at Twentieth. I'm straightening out a couple of traumas in *Delirious*."

"You don't say!" Despite himself, Sherman's tone was faintly patronizing. "I turned down that assignment, you know. Didn't feel I could justify the symbolism of the scene where Don Ameche disembowels the horse."

"Oh, that's all out now," said Kalbfus amiably. "That was the early version."

"Well," said Sherman quickly, eager to retrieve himself, "it's the early version that catches the Wormser, what?" Kalbfus laughed uproariously, less at the witticism than because this was the first time anyone had addressed him in three days.

"Look," he suggested, linking arms with Sherman, "let's hop over to the Bamboo Room and have a couple of Zombolas." On their way across to the Brown Derby, he explained the nature of the drink to Wormser, who was still a bit staid and Eastern in his choice of beverages. "It's just a tall glass of rum mixed with a jigger of gin, some camphor ice, and a twist of avocado," he said reassuringly.

"Isn't that a little potent?" asked Wormser dubiously.

"You're cooking with grass it's potent," returned his companion pertly, if inaccurately. "That's why they won't serve more than six to a customer." Seated in the cool darkness of the bar, with three Zombolas coursing through their vitals, the colleagues felt drawn to each other. No trace of professional hostility or envy lingered by the time they had finished reviewing the Cleveland convention, the rapacity of their fellow-practitioners, and their own stanch integrity.

"How do you like it out here, Randy?" Wormser inquired. "I get a slight sense of confusion. Perhaps I'm not adjusted yet."

"You're inhibited," said Kalbfus, signaling the waiter to repeat. "You won't let yourself go. Infantile denial of your environment."

"I know," said Wormser plaintively, "but a few weeks ago I saw Jack Benny in a sleigh on Sunset Boulevard—with real reindeer. And last night an old hermit in a pillowcase stopped me and claimed the world was coming to an end. When I objected, he sold me a box of figs."

"You'll get used to it," the other replied. "I've been here five months, and to me it's God's country. I never eat oranges, but hell, can you imagine three dozen for a quarter?"

"I guess you're right," admitted Wormser. "Where are you staying?"

"At the Sunburst Auto Motel on Cahuenga," said Kalbfus, draining his glass. "I'm sharing a room with two extra girls from Paramount."

"Oh, I'm sorry. I—I didn't know you and Mrs. Kalbfus were separated."

"Don't be archaic. She's living there, too." Kalbfus snapped his fingers at the waiter. "Once in a while I fall into the wrong bed, but Beryl's made her emotional adjustment; she's carrying on with a Greek in Malibu. Interesting sublimation of libido under stress, isn't it? I'm doing a paper on it." Wormser raised his hand ineffectually to ward off the fifth Zombola, but Kalbfus would not be overborne.

"None of that," he said sharply. "Come on, drink up. Yes, sir, it's a great town, but I'll tell you something, Sherm. We're in the wrong end of this business. Original stories—that's the caper." He looked around and lowered his voice. "I'll let you in on a secret, if you promise not to blab. I've been collaborating with the head barber over at Fox, and we've got a ten-strike. It's about a simple, unaffected manicurist who inherits fifty million smackers."

"A fantasy, eh?" Wormser pondered. "That's a good idea."

"What the hell do you mean, fantasy?" demanded Kalbfus heatedly. "It happens every day. Wait till you hear the twisteroo, though. This babe, who has everything—houses, yachts, cars, three men in love with her—suddenly turns around and gives back the dough."

"Why?" asked Wormser, sensing that he was expected to.

"Well, we haven't worked that out yet," said Kalbfus confidentially. "Probably a subconscious wealth phobia. Anyway, Zanuck's offered us a hundred and thirty G's for it, and it isn't even on paper."

"Holy cow!" breathed Wormser. "What'll you do with all that money?"

"I've got my eye on a place in Beverly," Kalbfus confessed. "It's only eighteen rooms, but a jewel box—indoor plunge, indoor rifle range, the whole place is indoors. Even the barbecue."

"That can't be," protested Wormser. "The barbecue's always out-doors."

"Not this one," beamed Kalbfus. "That's what makes it so unusual. Then, of course, I'll have to give Beryl her settlement when the divorce comes through."

"You—you just said everything was fine between you," faltered Wormser.

"Oh, sure, but I've really outgrown her," shrugged Kalbfus. "Listen, old man, I wouldn't want this to get into the columns. You see, I'm going to marry Ingrid Bergman."

A strange, tingling numbness, like that induced by novocain, spread downward from the tips of Wormser's ears. "I didn't know you knew her," he murmured.

"I don't," said Kalbfus, "but I saw her the other night at the Mocambo, and she gave me a look that meant only one thing." He laughed and swallowed his sixth Zombola. "It's understandable, in a way. She must have known instinctively."

"Known what?" Wormser's eyes, trained to withstand the unusual, stood out in high relief.

"Oh, just that I happen to be the strongest man in the world," said Kalbfus modestly. He rose, drew a deep breath, and picked up the table. "Watch," he ordered, and flung it crisply across the bar. Two pyramids of bottles dissolved and crashed to the floor, taking with them a Filipino busboy and several hundred cocktail glasses. Before the fixtures had ceased quivering, a task force of bartenders and waiters was spearing down on Kalbfus. There was an obscure interval of scuffling, during which Wormser unaccountably found himself creeping about on all fours and being kicked by a fat lady. Then the shouts and recriminations blurred, and suddenly he felt the harsh impact of the pavement. In a parking lot, eons later, the mist cleared and he was seated on the running board of a sedan, palpating a robin's egg on his jaw. Kalbfus, his face puffier than he last remembered it, was shakily imploring him to forgive and dine at his motel. Wormser slowly shook his head.

"No, thanks." Though his tongue was a bolt of flannel, Sherman strove to give his words dignity. "I like you, Kalbfuth, but you're a little unthtable." Then he got to his feet, bowed formally, and went into the Pig'n Whistle for an atomburger and a frosted mango.

🌿 HOW SHARPER THAN A SERPENT'S TOOTH

THE OTHER EVENING, with nobody leveling a gun at my temple, I deserted a well-sprung armchair and a gripping novel, sloshed forty blocks uptown in a freezing rain, and, together with five hundred other bats, hung from the rafters at Loew's Strabismus to see Joan Crawford's latest vehicle, *Mildred Pierce*. Certain critics, assessing the film, maintained that Miss Crawford rose to heights never before scaled. Whether she did or not, I certainly did; the only person higher than me was the projectionist, who kept flicking ashes down my coat collar and sneezing so convulsively that twice during the performance my head rolled down the balcony steps. Oh, I was kept busy, I can tell you, running downstairs to retrieve it and following the story at the same time. Yet even under these trying conditions, aggravated by the circumstance that someone had liberated a powerful sleep-inducing drug among the audience, I was gripped by a brief passage between the star and her daughter, played by Ann Blyth. It had been established that Joan, eager to give the child every advantage, had worked tirelessly as a waitress, shielding the fact from her, and had eventually built up a chain of restaurants. Ann, though, inevitably discovers her mother's plebeian calling, and at the proper kinetic moment her disdain boils over in a speech approximately as follows: "Faugh, you disgust me. You reek of the kitchen, of blue plates and sizzling platters. You bring with you the smell of grease and short-order frying, you—you restaurateuse, you!" At that juncture, unluckily, the projectionist sneezed again, with such force that I was blown clear into the lobby and out into Times Square, and deciding that it would be tempting fate to return to my perch, I sloshed quickly downtown while the sloshing was good.

Reviewing the scene in my mind (or, more properly, what remained of the scene in what remained of my mind), I realized that however fruity the phrasing, its psychology was eminently sound. The instinct to conceal one's true livelihood from the kiddies, for fear of their possible scorn, is as normal as snoring. A highly solvent gentleman in Forest

209

Hills, a vestryman and the father of three, once told me in wine that for thirty years, under twelve different pseudonyms, he had supplied the gamiest kind of pulp fiction to *Snappy Stories* and *Flynn's*, although his children believed him to be a stockbroker. The plumper the poke, the more painful is any reference to its origin.

The most recent victim of indiscreet babble of this sort is Barbara Hutton Mdivani Reventlow Grant, with whose predicament Charles Ventura lately concerned himself in his society column in the *World-Telegram*. Wrote Mr. Ventura: "Relations between the chain-store heiress and her ex-husband, Kurt, are still strained. Barbara tells friends her most recent annoyance from Kurt came with the discovery he had gone out of his way to tell Lance his mother's money came from the ten-cent store."

The item poses all sorts of interesting questions. What constitutes going out of your way to tell a lad his mother's money came from forty or fifty thousand ten-cent stores? How did Lance take the news? Did he, in the first shock of revelation, force his father to his knees and demand retraction of the slur? Did he fling himself with a choked cry into the Countess' lap, all tears and disillusion, or did he heap coals on her head? Mr. Ventura does not say. Mr. Ventura, it would seem, is an old tease. With the implication that he has other fish to fry, he leaps straightway into the domestic problems of slim, attractive Yvette Helene LeRoux Townsend, leaving me in my ragged shawl out in the snow, nursing Barbara Hutton's predicament. I hope that the dimly analogous situation which follows, served up for convenience in a dramatic fricassee, may shed some light on the matter and bring chaos out of confusion.

SCENE: *The library of the luxurious Park Avenue triplex of Mr. and Mrs. Milo Leotard Allardyce DuPlessis Weatherwax. The furnishings display taste but little ostentation: a couple of dozen Breughels, fifteen or twenty El Grecos, a sprinkling of Goyas, a smidgen of Vermeers. The room has a lived-in air: a fistful of loose emeralds lies undusted in an ash tray, and the few first folios in evidence are palpably dog-eared. The curtain rises on a note of marital discord. Octavia Weatherwax, a chic, poised woman in her mid-forties, has just picked up a bust of Amy Lowell by Epstein and smashed it over her husband's head. Milo, a portly, well-groomed man of fifty, spits out a tooth, catches up a bust of Epstein by Amy Lowell, and returns the compliment.*

OCTAVIA (*brushing plaster from her coiffure*): Listen, Milo, we can't go on this way.

MILO: Why not? I've still got this left. (*He picks up a bust of Amy Epstein by Lowell Thomas.*)

OCTAVIA: No, no, this is the handwriting on the wall. Our marriage is washed up—napoo—*ausgespielt.*

MILO: Maybe you're right. I've felt for some time that things haven't been the same between us.

OCTAVIA: Oh, well, the fat's in the fire. How are we to break the news to Rapier?

MILO: Rapier? What Rapier is that?

OCTAVIA: Why, our nineteen-year-old son, which he's home from Yale on his midyears and don't suspicion that his folks are rifting.

MILO: Oh, yes. Where is our cub at the present writing?

OCTAVIA: In the tack room, furbishing up the accouterments of his polo ponies.

MILO (*acidly*): Far better off to be furbishing up on his Euclid, lest he drag the name of Weatherwax through the scholastic mire.

OCTAVIA: Shhhh, here he comes now. (*The sound of expensive Scotch brogues approaching on a parquet floor is heard, an effect achieved by striking two coconut shells together.*) If you need me, I shall be laying down on my lounge with a vinegar compress. (*She exits as Rapier enters—a rather awkward bit of stagecraft, as they trip over each other, but if the play runs, the property man can always saw another door in the set. Rapier, albeit somewhat spoiled, is a blueblood to his finger tips, carries his head and feet as though to the manner born.*)

RAPIER: Hiya, Jackson. What's buzzin', cousin?

MILO: Humph. Is that some more of your new-fangled college slang?

RAPIER: Don't be a sherbet, Herbert. (*lighting a gold-monogrammed Egyptian Prettiest*) What's cookin', good-lookin'?

MILO (*gravely*): Son, I'm not going to mince words with you.

RAPIER: Don't mince, quince. I'm waitin', Satan.

MILO: My boy, the Weatherwax union has blown a gasket. Our frail matrimonial bark, buffeted by the winds of temperament, has foundered on the shoals of incompatibility.

RAPIER: Get in the groove, fatso. I don't latch onto that long-hair schmaltz.

MILO: To employ the vulgate, your mother and I have pphhht.

RAPIER (*with quick sympathy*): That's rum, chum.

MILO: Yes, it's hard on us oldsters, but it isn't going to be easy for you, either.

RAPIER (*frightened*): You mean I've got to go to work?

MILO: Certainly not. As long as there's a penny of your mother's money left, we'll make out somehow.

RAPIER: Look, guv'nor, I . . . that is, me . . . aw, cripes, can I ask you something man to man?

MILO (*aside*): I was afraid of this.

RAPIER: Well, I've been running with a pretty serious crowd up at New Haven—lots of bull sessions about swing and stuff—and I've been wondering. Where does our money come from?

MILO (*evasively*): Why—er—uh—the doctor brings it. In a little black bag.

RAPIER: Aw, gee, Dad, I'm old enough to know. *Please.*

MILO: There, there. Now run along and play with your ponies.

RAPIER: Wouldn't you rather tell me than have me learn it in the gutter?

MILO: We-e-ell, all right, but my, you children grow up quick nowadays. Have you ever heard of the Weatherwax All-Weather Garbage Disposal Plan?

RAPIER: You—you mean whereby garbage is disposed of in all weathers by having neatly uniformed attendants call for and remove it?

MILO: Yes. That is the genesis of our scratch.

RAPIER (*burying his face in his hands*): Oh, Daddy, I want to die!

MILO: Steady on, lad. After all, think of the millions which their flats would be a welter of chicken bones, fruit peels, and old teabags were it not for our kindly ministrations.

RAPIER (*sobbing*): I'll never be able to hold up my head in Bulldog circles again.

MILO: Nonsense. Why, you wear the keenest threads on the campus and are persona grata to myriad Eli frats.

RAPIER (*his face drawn and a new maturity in his voice*): No, Father, this is the end of halcyon days in the groves of Academe. I'm going away.

MILO: Where?

RAPIER: Somewhere beyond the horizon—to fabled Cathay or Samarkand and Ind, if need be. Anywhere I can find other values than the tinkle of money and the clang of refuse cans.

MILO (*his eyes shining*): There speaks a Weatherwax, my boy. Here, I want you to have this little keepsake.

RAPIER: What is it?

MILO: A letter of credit for seven hundred grand. It won't buy much except dreams, but it belonged to your mother.

RAPIER: Thank you, sir. (*He starts out.*)

MILO: Wait a minute, I can't let you go like this. You'll need money, introductions, shelter—

RAPIER: I'll patch up that old private railroad car of mine—the one underneath the Waldorf-Astoria.

MILO: Take ours, too. It's only using up steam.

RAPIER (*simply*): I'm sorry, Dad. From now on I walk alone. Goodbye. (*He exits, colliding with his mother—there simply* must *be two doors in this set. Octavia looks back at him, puzzled.*)

OCTAVIA: Why, goodness, what ails the child? What's that exalted look on his face?

MILO: That, Octavia, is what a very great Russian named Louis Tolstoy once called "redemption."

OCTAVIA: Milo! You didn't tell—you couldn't—

MILO (*his shoulders bowed*): It just soaked in through his pores. (*Octavia, her eyes tragic, picks up a bronze caryatid, smashes it over his head, and exits. He shrugs, picks up a Greek bacchante loitering in the wings, and consoles himself.*)

CURTAIN

❧ NO DEARTH OF MIRTH—FILL
OUT THE COUPON!

IF, ABOUT CHRISTMAS TIME, you notice me sporting a curious insignia on my vest, a stipple of small white spots as though I had been eating Royal Riviera pears with a spoon, it may interest you to know that you are looking at a full-fledged, bonafide member of the original Fruit-of-the-Month Club. This is not to be confused with the Fruit-of-the-Loom Club, an organization I also belong to, which allows me to sleep an hour later than nonmembers, or the Fruit-of-the-Moola Club, a society that sells me United States currency at ten per cent off the list price. No, the Fruit-of-the-Month Club is a powerful and exclusive sodality originating at the Bear Creek Orchards in Medford, Oregon, consecrated to supplying me and mine with Royal Riviera pears in December, grapefruit in January, apples in February, rare preserves in April, plums in June, summer pears in August, peaches in September, and Lavelle grapes in October. I became a member of this singular brotherhood quite by chance; a trifling favor I did a stranger earned his gratitude.

Late one afternoon several months ago I was seated at a rear table in Sardi's, browsing through *Billboard* over a cup of bohea, when a conversation nearby arrested my attention. Two plausible characters in billycock hats, whose fly manner and diamond-paste stickpins stamped them theatrical promoters, were inveigling a defenseless old cotton converter into backing a costume drama.

"Why, it's as safe as houses," purred one of them. "Tell him the prologue again, Skins."

"Sure," agreed the individual addressed by that unsavory appellation. "We open in an Italian grotto back in the sixteenth century. That's on account of the public's crazy about the sixteenth century."

"Is that so?" inquired the converter. "I didn't know that."

"Just can't get enough of it," Skins assured him. "That's all they ask for in the ticket agencies—a good meaty show about the sixteenth century. Well, anyhow, our leading man is discovered in this grotto, writing on a parchment scroll with a feather. Pretty soon he sprinkles sand over the manuscript, pulls a bell rope, and his apprentice comes in. 'There, Giovanni, it's finished,' he says. 'Rush it to the printer.' 'What are you going to call it, Signor Boccaccio?' says the apprentice. '*The Decameron*,' says Boccaccio. 'It may be just a lot of smutty stories to you, but some day this here vellum will be immortal.' "

"Yes, that's very effective," said the converter thoughtfully. "And you say Charles Laughton's offered to play Boccaccio?"

"We've got him under wraps at the Hotel Edison," the first promoter replied smoothly. "He starts rehearsing the minute your check is dry. Here," he said, unscrewing a fountain pen. "Just make it out to Thimblerig Productions." My ire boiled over at their pettifoggery and, rising, I laid about me with the folded *Billboard* to such effect that the blackguards took to their heels, howling with pain. The victim, once I had exposed their duplicity, was naturally all gratefulness—filled my case with cigars, offered to convert some cotton for me, besought me to share a home-cooked meal he had in his pocket. He finally gave me my liberty in exchange for my address, and a few days later a handsomely engraved certificate informed me that I had been proposed for and elected to the Fruit-of-the-Month Club.

It recently occurred to me while munching the alternate November selection, a rather mealy Winesap, that though there are countless kindred services designed to provide people with books, flowers, records, regional delicacies, and even diapers, no machinery has ever been devised to furnish them old jokes on a seasonal basis. "Would not the discerning," I asked myself, "welcome an association patterned after the Fruit-of-the-Month Club, purveying flavorful, old-fashioned gags —the kind of time-honored nifties Father used to make?" In my mind's eye, I envisioned thousands of subscribers to the Jape-of-the-Month Club receiving at specified intervals their hand-culled jokes packed in dry ice, suitable for use in domestic arguments, encounters with bill collectors, visits to the dentist—in short, in all the trivial, everyday contingencies that recur throughout the year. Simultaneously, it struck me that the only person in America capable of grasping the magnitude of the scheme was Barnaby Chirp. Brilliant young publisher, writer, book reviewer, anthologist, columnist, and flaneur, Chirp had fathered many a compendium of hilarious rib-ticklers. His latest, *Laughing Gasp*, had sold six hundred and fifty thousand copies prior to publication; so well had it sold, in fact, that a first edition was never published. His motto, "Git thar fustest with the mustiest jokes," indubitably made him my man, and I rushed to his office to broach the idea. He jumped at it.

"It's the cat's pajamas—a peachamaroot!" he proclaimed, jumping at it. "Here, let me get this stuff out of the way so we can talk." Turning back to his desk, he delivered two radio broadcasts into a lapel microphone, organized a ten-cent-book cartel, wrote a thirty-five-thousand-word preface to *Higgledy-Piggledy: An Omnibus of Jocose Jugoslav Stories*, and sold the Scandinavian dramatic rights of *Laughing Gasp* to a small Danish producer in the bottom drawer. "Now then," he said, swinging toward me, "we'll fix the annual membership fee of the Jape-of-the-Month Club at twenty-five hundred a year."

"Isn't that a bit steep?" I asked.

"Not for people of discrimination, those who can afford the finer things," said Chirp. "We've got to winnow out the ragtag and bobtail. The next step is to find an impartial board of judges to choose our monthly wheezes. How about a publisher, a writer, a book reviewer, an anthologist, and a columnist?"

"Good notion," I said. "What say to a panel like this: Nelson Doubleday, MacKinlay Kantor, Harry Hansen, Whit Burnett, and Louis Sobol?"

"Too diverse," he said. "They'd never get on. I'll tell you what—why don't we get one man who's *all* those things? Then there wouldn't be any silly squabbling."

"Listen," I said, "anyone who's all those things is a genius."

"Why, thank you," said Chirp, coloring with pleasure. "I like you, too. Of course, I don't know whether I can crowd the job into my schedule, but I'll do my best. Now, exactly how would the Jape-of-the-Month function?"

"Well," I said, "during January and February we'd ship our subscribers good, pre-tested chestnuts about the weather. For example, if someone complains to you of the cold, you advise him to go to Mexico. He naturally asks why. 'Because,' you tell him, 'down there it's chili today and hot tamale.' "

"Fan my brow," giggled Chirp, scribbling a note on a pad. "That's a sockdolager! Mind if I use it in my column?"

"Not at all," I said. "That's where I read it last week. In July and August, applying the same principle, we mail our members warm-weather rejoinders. Suppose you're asked whether it's hot enough for you. 'Hot?' you say. 'It's so hot I feed my chickens cracked ice to keep 'em from laying hard-boiled eggs!' "

"I've heard that one somewhere before," muttered Chirp dubiously. "Ah, what the hell, I can always credit it to Dorothy Parker. What sort of jokes could we guarantee the rest of the year?"

"Whatever the occasion demands," I answered. "In April, when your wife's mother generally pays a visit, we send out our Easter special. 'They ought to call our car a mother-in-law model,' you tell your wife. 'Why is that?' she asks. 'Because it's got a crank in the back seat.' Along about June, after your son's home from college, you'd say to your friends, 'Yes, Willie's got his B.A. and his M.A., but his P.A. still supports him.' See how it works?"

"Aha," said Chirp, "and I'll tell you what's wrong with it. It's too sophisticated for the average person. You've got to hoke it up."

"How do you mean?"

"Well, take that January selection. I'd change it to 'Down in Mexico it's chilly today and hot tomorrow.' "

"But what becomes of the point?" I asked.

"The point, the point!" bawled Chirp. "Everybody's always griping about the point! How do you think I'd fill my column every week if all the stories had to have a point?"

"You win," I yielded. "After all, you've got your finger on the popular pulse."

"Right," he said. "I find that if you leave the nub out of your anecdotes once in a while, it intrigues the reader enormously. Here, look at the response I got on last week's column." He opened a drawer, took out a response, and showed it to me. Then he leaned back and gave me the dazzling smile with which he ushers in any discussion involving money. "O.K., son, how do we set this thing up?"

"Well," I said haltingly, "I suppose that since I thought of it—"

"Precisely," he finished. "You're certainly entitled to a share of the profits." He drew a pie chart on his pad, snipped out a minute wedge with a pair of scissors, and handed it to me. "There's your cut," he explained. "The rest goes into advertising, research, judges' fees, stuff like that. Can you wrap bundles?"

"Gee," I protested, "I saw myself in more of an executive role."

"Oh, a white-collar snob, eh?" sneered Chirp. "What are you afraid of—soiling your hands? I expect you to get out and do some canvassing, too. Ever been a salesman?"

"No," I said, stealthily reaching for my hat, "but I heard a pip of a quip about one yesterday."

"You did?" Chirp caught up his pencil, his eyes gleaming.

"Yes," I said. "It seems that a salesman called Moss Hart stopped at a Bucks County farmhouse one night. The farmer's daughter, who was named Dorothy Parker, asked what his profession was. 'I'm a traveling man,' he said. 'Yes,' she riposted, 'I can see that by the bags under your eyes.' " As Chirp rocked back in his chair, helpless with laughter, I silently stole out the door. I left behind a pair of arctics, a solid gold briefcase, and a little portion of my reason, but I don't really care. Who would, with that kind of money coming in like clock-work every month?

❧ PALE HANDS I LOATHE

To PARAPHRASE Omar the Tentmaker slightly (oh, come on, it can't hurt to paraphrase Omar the Tentmaker just a teeny bit), I often wonder what the editors of the *Woman's Home Companion* buy one half so precious as the thing they sell. The thing they sell me, specifically, is nepenthe; whenever my salt loses its savor, I know I can find heartsease in those shiny, optimistic pages, whether in the latest prize-winning recipe for macaroni-and-cheese timbales or some ingenious method of canning babies for winter use. More than a companion, yet less than a mistress, it is my home away from home, my wife away from my wife, my dream girl of the magazine world. *Woman's Home Companion*, I adore you.

It was, therefore, with a sense of disquietude that I detected in the February issue a certain monotony I had never noticed before. The infants gurgled on as darling and cuddlesome as ever; the meat loaves and veal birds were, if anything, even more economical than they had been in the January number. But instead of the rich pastiche of lingerie and soufflés I expected in the advertising columns, I found only a series of variations on a single theme—the care of Milady's hands. For page after page, the manufacturers of innumerable unguents and lotions endlessly conjugated the tragedy of rough, chapped hands. "My poor hands!" snuffled the housewife in the advertisement for Pacquins Hand Cream. "They made me feel like an OLD TURKEY," and to dramatize the full poignancy of her affliction, the victim was shown in a second phase transmuted into an aged, weather-beaten turkey. "I use HINDS—that HONEY of a lotion," crowed another housewife, hefting a coal scuttle and celebrating you-know-whose Honey and Almond Cream. Jergens Lotion took a rather more romantic approach and portrayed a handsome officer nibbling at his fiancée's fingers, while Campana Cream Balm presented a pair of war sweethearts over the hushed caption: "It was one of those golden, delirious moments . . . impulsively his hands sought mine . . . and together we welcomed the first tender touch of romance." Toushay, the "Beforehand" Lotion, demonstrated its versatility with four mysterious vignettes of a young lady stroking a kitten, washing her undies, simpering at some convalescent soldiers, and finally nuzzling her warrior, home on leave.

It was our humdrum old friend, Ivory Soap, though, that put its competitors to shame and set my ordinarily robust stomach palpitating like a plate of junket. It depicted a personable matron fondly discussing her mate over the telephone with some undisclosed critic, as follows: "Hard-boiled? *Him?* Don't you believe it! What hard-boiled husband would tramp halfway across town to get that special coffee cake I adore so for Sunday breakfast? Would a really tough guy take time out now and then—like in the middle of his favorite pecan pie—just to grab my hands and kiss them? Yes—gruff as he seems to others, in private, he fairly *raves* about my pretty hands!"

I have searched diligently through Freud, Jung, Brill, Menninger, and Zilboorg for a clue to this interesting form of hand worship, but can find no analogous instance, either with or without pecans. I suspect, however, that if we pull on a pair of waders and whip the husband's stream of consciousness, using the kind of tackle Mr. Joyce employed on Leopold Bloom, we may catch a few shiners. Here, then, is the interior monologue of Lester Wagenhals, incisive, hard-bitten office manager of the Puissant Valve & Flange Corporation, as he sits at his desk about five o'clock of a midwinter afternoon:

Funny taste in my mouth. Must be that noodle ring I had for lunch. Urr-r-gh. Good thing I keep extra bag of pecans in desk drawer. Careful now. Secretary might walk in. Nasty little snooper. Lovely hands, though. Wish I could bite them. Better not. Can't afford scandal. Just one quick bite? No. Complications. Lose my head. One bite leads to another. Road to hell paved with soft white hands. Good thought there. Wasting my time in business. Should have been a poet. Plenty of mazuma in poetry if a man went at it efficiently. Snug studio in Greenwich Village. High jinks. Red wine and red-hot mammas. Turn your damper down. Life in the old boy yet. Man is as young as he feels. Lick my weight in wildcats.

Ought to finish this letter to Abernethy about those bushings. *Yours of the 14 inst. to hand.* There I go again. Hands all over the place. Try again. *Cannot see our way clear to take consignment off your hands.* No good. Sleep on it. Best not to rush into these things, anyway. Past five o'clock. Eunice waiting. Comb my hair and wash my. Steady. Lean against filing cabinet a second. Buzzing in the temples. Never should have eaten that noodle ring. Scores die as police blame poisoned noodle ring. FBI uncovers secret noodle ring in Midwest. Wait. Wipe

perspiration off forehead. Reception clerk might blab to J.B. Can hear
them talking right now. Wagenhals slowing up. Nice old duffer but
can't keep abreast of modern methods. Organization full of dead
ducks. Terminating as of the first. One month's salary in recognition
of the service you have ren. Appreciate if you will explain system to
Mr. Samish, the dirty sneak you have been protecting right in your
own office. Law of the jungle, dog eat dog, root or die. Alert, capable
executive desires wide-awake connection. Sorry, position just filled.
Sorry, looking for aggressive younger man. Will call you if anything.
Compelled to foreclose. Beg to advise that insurance has lapsed. Some
bank with facilities for handling smaller accounts like yours. Eunice
taking in washing. Rough laundry hands. No more pecan pies. Bellevue.
Oh, my God.

Buck up now. Walk slowly past their desks. Bunch of clock-
watchers. Lazy, no-good riffraff. Give them the old glare. Snap their
heads off. Carlson at the water-cooler. O.K., Carlson, your goose is
cooked. *Running Horse* sticking out of Bender's pocket. Knock them
off tonight. No, tomorrow will do. Much too kindhearted for my
own good.

There. Lucky my getting this elevator car. Cute brunette, that operator. Pity she wears gloves. Bet she has superb hands. Ask her for a
peek? No, might misunderstand. Invite her out for cocktail sometime.
Pretend I'm big advertising man. Need model with special type of fingers to pose for national account. Strictly business, no monkeyshines.
Careful not to frighten her off. Discuss various types of hands. Purely
scientific spirit. Index of character, they say. Yours, for example. Cold
hands, warm heart. Paternal smile, old enough to be your father.
Casually mention wife. Hopeless invalid. Haven't had anything to do
with her for years. Pile it on. Man needs pair of soft white hands to
come home to. Home is where the hands are. Just the same, better use
pseudonym. Never can tell about these dolls. Lead you on and then
the shakedown. Man in Cleveland who fell for a lady elevator starter.
Turned out to be head of Midwest blackmail ring. Stripped him of his
last noodle. Urr-r-gh. That taste again.

Fresh air feels good. Where did I say meet Eunice? Astor? Plaza?
No, Biltmore lobby. Walk along Sixth. Interesting shops around here.
Secrets of the Polynesian Love Cults. Figure Drawing for Second-Year
Sadists. Nice prints in this art store. French kid wearing porcelain cas-
serole on head. Pretty racy if you could read the text. Plaster-of-Paris
Venus. Ditto foot and hand. Chap who designed that never saw
woman's hand. Do better with my eyes closed. Outrage the way they

mulct unsuspecting public. Law against it. Letter to the *Times*.
Couldn't palm it off on yours truly. Palm off hand. Neat phrase. Work
it in.

Green light. Cross now. Too late, catch it next corner. Automat
coming up. Just time for fast pecan bun before Eunice. No, mustn't.
Sure to smell it on my breath. Use cloves. Only an evasion. Can't hurt
to look in window, though. Row on row of delicious, crackly. Who's to
tell? Never know when some friend of Eunice. Oh, rats. Only live once.
Long time dead. Long time no pecan bun. Look up and down first.
Hurry.

Easy now. People looking at you. Stop trembling. Debonair stroll.
Man of the world dropping in for late-afternoon snack. Nothing out of
the ordinary. Draw hot chocolate first. Enough. Don't bother with
saucer. Now the pastry. More pecans on the twist than the buns.
Count them. Don't be a sheep. Get your money's worth. Look out,
manager watching you. Three nickels, quickly. Something wrong. Door
is stuck. Hit it. Pound it. There, it's opening. So is the panel in back.
Woman's hand reaching through. Exquisite, tapering fingers redolent
of Ivory Soap. One little kiss. Opportunity of a lifetime. Grab them,
you fool! Yum yum yum yum yum. . . . Capital. Now all I have to do
is talk my way out of this.

❦ THE CUSTOMER IS ALWAYS WRONG

I DARE SAY that one of the strangest contradictions to beset contradiction fanciers recently was the situation confronting anybody who was seeking shelter in New York City. Not only were hotel rooms scarcer than the heath hen—after all, you *could* pick up an occasional heath hen before Christmas if you didn't mind going into the black market for it—but the reason for their scarcity was that most of them were occupied by people who had flocked to the National Hotel Exposition to discuss the scarcity of hotel rooms. Sounds paradoxical, doesn't it? I mean, if there aren't any other paradoxes around.

The National Hotel Exposition, it seems, is an annual powwow at which innkeepers forgather to discuss trade secrets: the maintenance of proper standards of insolence among room clerks, improved methods of juggling shower faucets so that guests are alternately frozen and parboiled, artful techniques for making windows stick, and the like. The chief topic of the convention, understandably, was overcrowding. A variety of speakers addressed the gathering, analyzing the congestion and suggesting remedies. The majority plumped for "good public relations" and similar shadowy panaceas, but one delegate from the City of Brotherly Love came out of his corner snarling. "The resident manager of the Warwick Hotel, in Philadelphia," stated the *Times*, "suggested a more selective method of meting out rooms . . . declaring himself in favor of the 'prestige guest who will be a source of revenue to the hotel,' adding that many long-term guests who are 'meaningless people' were cluttering up hotels and preventing them from gaining good prospects." This acid diagnosis was challenged from the floor (I use the term in its parliamentary sense; I would not wish to imply the gentleman was under the table), by an official of Chicago's Palmer House with the hot assertion that "the unimportant guest of today may be the 'big shot of tomorrow.' " The *Times* did not divulge the outcome of the spat, but I presume the principals invoked the code duello and pelted each other with Nesselrode pudding until the weaker cried uncle.

It so happens that several days ago I was privileged to see the Chi-

cagoan's philosophy dramatically vindicated before my very eyes in
the lobby of the San Culotte, a rather dusty family hotel in the West
Forties. I had gone there to meet a friend with whom I was lunching,
Tom Pulsifer. Now Pulsifer is a good fellow (as a matter of fact, he is
nothing of the sort; he is a mealy-mouthed sponger and a sneak), but
he is never less than a half-hour late for appointments, and as I am invariably a half-hour early, I had oodles of time. I consumed a few by
reading the *Sun* in its entirety, including such stop-press items as the
news that Luna moths frequently attain a wing span of four inches and
that the scup, or porgy, feeds on plankton. I don't know what it is
about plankton that fascinates the *Sun*'s make-up editor; he would
rather run a good sparkling dispatch about plankton than the size of
Nita Naldi's superstructure or some matter of genuine civic importance. Anyway, it set me wondering what Pulsifer, whose features are
indistinguishable from those of a scup, would feed on, and borrowing
a menu from a waiter, I worked out a series of light, nutritious salads
and entrées I could gracefully direct to his attention. It was sheer
boondoggling, I knew; he would inevitably start clamoring for canvas-
back and muscat grapes, and I would have to live out the month on
salt cod to foot the bill. I had worked myself up into a very respectable
fury at Pulsifer's gluttony and was about to phone him to cadge a meal
from somebody else when I heard an irate voice behind me.

"Look at this lobby!" it was saying. "Did you ever see such a pack of
crumbs? Of all the inconsequential, meaningless loafers—" I stole a
glance over my shoulder and beheld a pursy, apoplectic gentleman, unmistakably the manager, surveying the lounge with arms akimbo. He
was addressing a lathlike subordinate in mournful black and rimless
bifocals, quite obviously his assistant.

"Shh, Mr. Leftwich," the younger man placated. "They're all steady
guests, except one or two. Been here for years."

"You bet they have," snapped his superior. "That's what's wrong
with the San Culotte. I tell you, Rightwich, I've had enough of these
measly nonentities lousing up my establishment. I want people that
mean something—celebrities, d'ye hear? Diplomats, movie stars, suave
men of letters!"

"We had a suave man of letters last summer," reminded Rightwich,
"but he left on account of the roaches."

"Listen," grated the manager. "I put thirteen thousand dollars'
worth of roaches into this place to give it a homelike atmosphere, and
anybody who doesn't like 'em can start packing!" He moved into my
line of vision and indicated a commonplace citizen sleepily engaged in

paring his nails. "Now, take that chump, for instance," he went on in a lower voice. "Who is he?"

"That's Mr. Detweiler," replied Rightwich. "He's an ideal guest. Never missed a bill. Why, he's so prompt—"

"Never mind that," interrupted Leftwich. "Promptness don't get you into *Who's Who*. What's he *do*?"

"Well," hesitated Rightwich, "he just sort of grooms his nails."

"You see?" snorted the other, triumphantly. "Dead wood. What I want is Yul Brynner sitting there grooming his nails, not a cipher named Detweiler. How about the one with the *Racing Form*, by the potted palm?"

"Mr. Pfannkuchen?" protested Rightwich, aggrieved. "Ah, gee, boss, he's gilt-edged—he pays us a year in advance. And he doesn't even ask for a room. He sleeps in a broom closet."

"He's a bottleneck," grunted Leftwich inexorably. "The place is full of 'em. That old lady knitting the afghan there—"

"She's kind of distinguished, though," appealed the assistant. "She looks like Dame May Whitty if you close your eyes a little."

"I'm closing my ears, too," growled Leftwich. "Get this straight, now. We're combing the small fry out of the register once and for all. I'll have public personalities like Jerome Zerbe and Choo Choo Johnson snoozing around this lobby or, by jiminy, I'll padlock the joint!"

"But gosh, Mr. Leftwich," implored the young man. "You can't tell, one of our guests *might* become famous all of a sudden. Every dog has his day."

"Just a minute," rapped the manager, wheeling on him. "Are you trying to take sides with the clientele?"

"No, no, of course not," stammered Rightwich, overcome with confusion. "All I mean is—"

"We've got an ugly name for that in our business, boy." Leftwich's eyes had narrowed to mere slits. "It's called taking sides with the clientele."

"You know I wouldn't do a thing like that, sir," Rightwich pleaded.

"Well, I'm not so sure," his superior said suspiciously. "You worked at the Palmer House in Chicago, I seem to recall. If I hear any of that vicious Socialist twaddle about treating guests like human beings—"

"That was before I had my nervous breakdown," confessed Rightwich. "Oh, I know they're a lot of numskulls, but perhaps they're lucky, too. That girl sitting near the magazine stand with her mouth open might turn out to be another Jennifer Jones."

"She'd better work fast," retorted the manager, "because I'm going to screen the whole damn bunch right now. March 'em into the banquet room—and better pass out barrel staves to the help. They might turn nasty." Impervious to Rightwich's attempts to pacify him, Leftwich swung about and neatly caromed into a vital, incisive individual who had just entered the lobby. Before Leftwich could kick him, the newcomer whisked a briefcase from under his arm and unbuckled it.

"May I have your very kind attention for a moment, folks?" he asked in a ringing voice. The hum of chatter died away and heads turned inquisitively. Leftwich's dewlaps flushed scarlet.

"See here, Mac," he began. "We don't allow any pitchmen—"

"I beg your pardon," the stranger returned icily. "I'm Victor Robinette of Menafee, Soutache, Heppenstall & Preiselbeere, the advertising agency. Is there a Mr. Aubrey Detweiler here?"

"Why—er—yes," spoke up the dim man with the nail file. "That's me."

"Congrats, Mr. Detweiler!" boomed Robinette. "You've just been awarded first prize by the Invisible Mitten Corporation in their America's Most Expressive Hands Contest. Here is our check for ten thousand dollars." A spontaneous cheer burst from the throats of the assemblage, and well-wishers clustered about Detweiler, stroking his hands curiously and attempting to put the bite on him. Simultaneously, above the excited babble, the shrill pipe of a bellboy arrested the attention of all.

"Mr. Pfannkuchen, call for Mr. Dorian Pfannkuchen!" An overwrought lad in buttons threaded his way to the student of the *Racing Form*. "It's your bookmaker! You've won the daily double at Hialeah Park!"

"But the nags don't start running till three hours from now," objected Pfannkuchen, dumfounded.

"That's mere shilly-shallying," dismissed the boy, tumbling twenty-six thousand dollars in crisp greenbacks into his lap. "The fact remains that you are a veritable Monte Cristo, as sure as God made little green apples."

"Yes, and that's not all!" sang out Mrs. Roraback, the erstwhile anonymous knitter, jubilantly waving a money order in five figures. "A special-delivery screed from the Albright Gallery in Buffalo informs me that they consider my last afghan an outstanding example of American folk art! Commissions are pouring in like herrings," she beamed, displaying sizable advance orders for throws, coverlets, and foot warmers. As flashlight bulbs exploded and newsreel cameramen jostled each other for advantage, Leftwich stood rooted to the spot, boiling with frustration.

"Try and cross me, will they?" he panted. "I'll get the spiteful creatures out of here if I have to burn the building down!" But fresh surprises still lay in store for him; two Hollywood directors, complete with megaphones, white riding breeches, and reversed linen caps, had appeared and were closely scrutinizing the girl near the magazine stand.

"She's dynamite!" the first murmured, awe-struck. "She's another Jennifer Jones!"

"You skimmed the words off my lips," assented the second. "I see her as Eppie in *Silas Marner*, or *The Mill on the Frost*."

"No, I see her more as the scheming quadroon in *Pudd'nhead Wilson*," his companion demurred.

"That's what I say," nodded the first. "She's versatile—she can play anything. Pact her!" In a trice, their discovery was signed to a seven-year contract, had had her hair restyled by Antoine, and, swathed in platina mink and orchids, was announcing her retirement from the screen to return to Broadway. Gloating unashamedly, Rightwich clapped his elder colleague on the back.

"Well, sir," he observed slyly, "this'll teach you not to go off half-cocked in future, ah?"

With a hoarse bellow, Leftwich struck his arm away. "I'll find *somebody* around here who's a no-account stooge!" he roared. His eyes darted about about wildly and fastened on me. He extended an accusatory finger. "Who are you? What are you doing here?"

"Me? Why, nothing," I said automatically, and then caught myself at the indiscretion. "I—I mean, I've got a couple of diamond mines in the Rand, but please, I loathe publicity—"

"I knew it!" crackled Leftwich. "He's the one who's been cluttering up the building. Grab him, men!" In vain to protest that I was no guest of the house; rude hands seized my coat collar and frog-marched me toward the manager's office. Then, at the darkest hour, dawned deliverance. Through the revolving doors swept Tom Pulsifer—a Pulsifer reborn, a new authority in his bearing.

"Stop!" he thundered. "That man is my friend. Year in, year out, he has paid for my lunches, even when it meant denying himself luxuries and subsisting on soup greens. Now, thanks to the untimely demise of a crusty uncle in Australia, I can make belated restitution." And despite my most vigorous protestations, he stuffed my pockets with wad on wad of large-denomination currency. The discomfiture on Leftwich's countenance was comical in the extreme. Deferential to the point of servility, he fawned on us.

"Won't you stay and have lunch in my suite, gents?" he begged silkily. "I've a bottle of mellow Vouvray saved for just such an occasion."

"You have no suite, Leftwich," corrected Pulsifer in level tones. "On my way here, I bought the hotel and appointed Rightwich as manager in your stead. Let us hope that this has proved a salutary lesson to all."

"It has indeed," said the new manager, escorting us to the door as Leftwich was led away to become a dishwasher. "The next time you visit this fleabag, you will be greeted by a lobbyful of *schlemiehls* and nincompoops that will curl your hair." And with a genial wave, he placed his foot in the small of our backs and gave us a comradely shove into the stream of humanity eddying past the San Culotte.

❧ *WHATEVER GOES UP*

WHEN IT WAS ANNOUNCED a few days ago in *Variety* that a new musical comedy named *What's Up?* dealing with the misadventures of some aviators whose plane is grounded near a girls' school, was cooling on top of the oven, Broadway's reaction was not slow in coming. "That's for me," observed one astute old showman with whom I was lunching at Lindy's. "I'll take a piece of that." The moment the waiter had brought him the strudel, however, he seemed less certain. "I don't know," he hesitated, trying to ingest the strudel without removing his toothpick and cigar. "It's a kind of a sophisticated idea. The public don't want to think —they want to laugh. Look at Chekhov." We looked at Chekhov, who had just come in and was having a rolled-beef sandwich and a bottle of Dr. Brown's Celery Tonic in the corner. I got up and went over to his table.

"Hello, Chekhov," I said.

"Hello," he said.

"What happened to *you* last night?" I said.

"Brett and I waited for you at the Dingo," he said. Good old Chekhov. I could see him looking at the *Variety* in my pocket.

"Well, I guess you know," I said.

"Sure," he said. "Sure. I know."

"I suppose it had to happen," I said.

"Not that way it didn't," he said. "Not that way, old man. When I wrote *Uncle Vanya* none of *my* aviators was grounded near a girls' school."

"You didn't have any aviators in *Uncle Vanya*," I said.

"You bet I didn't," he said. "That's the point." He ordered another Celery Tonic.

"Better ease off, Chekhov," I said. "That makes four."

"I'm all right," he said cheerfully. That's one thing about Chekhov. No matter how many Dr. Browns he's had, he never shows it. "Mind if I file some cables?" He drew some cables from his pocket and started filing them. I went back to my table and told my friend what he had said.

"Certainly," he nodded. "It ain't believable, aviators mixed up in a girls' school. Listen," he said confidentially, impaling a sour tomato on his index finger, "do you want to know what an astute old showman like I would do with that plot? I'd make them a bunch of girl aviators which they fall down near a boys' school. Paste that in your hat and smoke it."

I have been smoking it ever since last Tuesday and have arrived at the same conclusion. The basic idea of *What's Up?* is a dilly, but unless it is handled with extreme delicacy it may very well curdle. In the following libretto, I have taken the liberty of indicating one of the directions in which the story might go. There is still another, but I doubt whether the authors could be influenced to accept it at this point.

SCENE 1: *The cockpit of a fast monoplane high above the clouds. At rise, three fair aeronauts are discovered in white sateen uniforms with cute fur-trimmed collars and goggles: Phyllis Brontislaw, a gorgeous blonde; Valuta Imbrie, a gorgeous brunette; and Punkins Janeway, a gorgeous redhead. Valuta has just finished washing her luxuriant tresses and, while Phyllis busies herself steering their frail craft, spreads her crowning glory out to dry in the rays of the late-afternoon sun. Punkins, curled up on a sofa, is gorging herself on Tango Kisses and devouring the latest Donn Byrne novel.*

VALUTA: Well, here we are in the trackless empyrean, where every prospect pleases and only man is vile.
PHYLLIS: Men, men, men—can't you think of anything else?

> PHYLLIS (*solo*):
> *"Men, Men, Men"*
> *Oh, maidens fair, beware,*
> *And likewise have a care,*
> *Lest passion's kiss betrays*
> *And lose you in a maze.*
>
> *Men, men, men,*
> *They're quite outside our ken,*
> *Their ways are very devious,*
> *It's lovey-us and leavey-us,*
> *Men, men, men.*

PUNKINS: Why so pensive, Val?

VALUTA: That's for me to know and you to find out.

PHYLLIS: Stuff and double stuff! All the world is aware that your aunt, Mrs. Morris Fenchurch of Shaker Heights and Piping Rock, made me take you along on my transcontinental dash to nip your budding romance with Señor Ramón Mulcahy, the Argentinian polo flash that has been turning feminine heads this season!

VALUTA (*hotly*): I'll have you know I'm in love with Ramón and propose to marry him!

PHYLLIS: We shall see what we shall see.

PUNKINS: Oh, stop scrapping, you two! Say, Phyl, what time are we due in Bethesda, Maryland?

PHYLLIS: Unless my eyes are playing me false, I believe I descry her environs now. *Oh!*

PUNKINS: What's the matter?

PHYLLIS: The engine's missing!

PUNKINS (*innocently*): Then how did we ever get this far?

PHYLLIS (*impatiently*): Something has gone wrong with the mechanism, silly. (*thoughtfully*) Doubtless one of those little wheels inside is stuck.

VALUTA: Then it behooves us to "bail off" apace, lest we dash out our brains in the ensuing holocaust. Parachutes at the ready! (*Galvanized into action, the three pull their ripcords and float gently to earth. Midway they are joined by the ladies of the ensemble, forming a stunning aerial ballet which should leave the critics breathless in their seats. Note: This may be a bit difficult to stage, as the plane is resting on two sawhorses and the parachutes are bound to create hell's own tangle, but it can all be cut out on the road.*)

SCENE 2: *A dormitory room at Peachpit Military Academy. At rise, Perry Yeast, president of the senior class, is stretched disconsolately on a window seat, staring at the ceiling. His adoring henchman, "Skinny" Beaumarchais, whose bulk belies his sobriquet, surveys him with a look of anxiety on his rubicund physiognomy.*

PERRY: Well, here we are on the eve of the annual Senior Hop and every girl at Miss Breitigam's sequestered with botulism resulting from substandard tinned meats. What to do?

SKINNY (*struck by an inspiration*): I've got it, Chief! Why not charter a speedboat and run down to Montevideo, fabled for its feminine pulchritude?

SKINNY (*comic rumba*):
> *We'll throw a party with the señoritas lively,*
> *There'll be rum and gourds and castanets, so drive me*
> *To that cluster of palmettos and cabañas,*
> *Where the mangoes are so fine, and the bananas. Etc.*

PERRY: That's all very well, but the dance is scheduled to begin in half an hour, and if crusty Dean Vogelsang discovers we have no girls he will call it off, thereby making us a laughing stock.

SKINNY: It looks like we're sunk, unless some girls drop out of the sky. (*A knock at the door; enter Phyllis, Valuta, and Punkins, scantily clad.*)

PHYLLIS: Quick—hide us!

PERRY (*curiously*): What's the matter?

PHYLLIS: Crotchety, nearsighted Dean Vogelsang's suspicions are aroused! There he is on the staircase now!

PERRY: What's your name?

PHYLLIS: Phyllis Brontislaw.

PERRY: That's the most beautiful name I've ever heard.

PERRY *and* PHYLLIS (*duet*):
> *A man and a maid were strolling*
> *In some grass that was covered with dew,*
> *When he took her hand and boldly pledged,*
> *"I'll e'er remember you.*
> *Come place your ruby lips on mine,*
> *And love is all too fleeting,*
> *We're here where journeys always end,*
> *I.e., in lovers' meeting."*

(*Skinny hastily pushes the girls into a closet; enter Dean Vogelsang.*)

DEAN (*sternly*): Did I see three chickens run in here a minute ago?

PERRY: No, and you're a nearsighted old fossil.

DEAN (*adjusting his ear trumpet*): What's that? What's that?

PERRY: I said you sing as sweet as a throstle.

DEAN (*placated*): Well, that's different. Now mind you, Yeast, you have ten minutes to find partners for the Senior Hop or it's off.

PERRY (*deliberately*): I think . . . I may have . . . a surprise for you, Dean Vogelsang.

SCENE 3: *The school auditorium, that evening. Gay lanterns have transformed it into a veritable fairyland, and a three-piece combination consisting of Zinkeiser (piano), Hildebrand (drums), and Suppositorsky (alto sax) is dispensing torrid rhythm. As laughing couples swirl by in the background, Skinny enters to the punchbowl at right, attended by his faithful henchman, "Happy" Telekian, whose mournful visage gainsays his nickname.*

HAPPY: Well, everybody is having loads of fun tonight, thanks to Perry's resourcefulness, but what are you putting in the punchbowl, Skinny?

SKINNY: Don't you catch on, stupid? It's our only chance. If Dean Vogelsang gets tipsy, he may not decide to flunk Perry in his forthcoming histology quiz, thus enabling us to beat Meatcliff and win the track crown at the conference.

HAPPY (*tensely*): We've only minutes to spare! (*The starter's pistol is heard off scene and the Meatcliff relay team flashes by on a treadmill at rear, a lap ahead of Peachpit. The crowd groans. Enter Punkins on Dean Vogelsang's arm.*)

PUNKINS (*flirtatiously*): Why, Vogie, you're a wonderful dancer—a regular Fred Astaire!

DEAN (*suspiciously*): What did you say about a chair?

PUNKINS: I said you were afraid to take a dare.

DEAN: Well, that's different. (*He drains a cup of punch, stifles a hiccough.*) Shay, girlie—hic—lesh you and I dansh.

PUNKINS (*craftily*): Will you let Perry run against Meatcliff? (*The crowd trembles on his decision.*)

DEAN: Yesh. (*He collapses in a drunken coma. As Perry doffs his "tux" and darts after the Meatcliff aggregation, the crowd goes wild with joy.*)

PHYLLIS: He's gaining!

VALUTA: Now he's at the turn! Now he's coming down the stretch! (*With a Herculean effort, Perry breasts the tape and the rooters execute a frenzied snake dance to "Peachpit, Mother of Men."*)

VALUTA (*nestling shyly in Perry's arms*): Well, thank goodness I got shut of that greaser Ramón in time to marry a clean-limbed American boy.

SKINNY (*to Mrs. Vetlugin, the house mother, who is extremely stout*):
Well, I guess that's telling 'em, eh, fat lady? (*As Skinny and Happy pair off with Punkins and Valuta, the ensemble goes into a whirlwind finish, George Abbott goes into a passion, and the producers go into bankruptcy.*)

CURTAIN

❧ SO LITTLE TIME MARCHES ON

> Marquand's principal contact with Hollywood was in 1941, when *H. M. Pulham, Esquire* was produced by King Vidor for M-G-M and Marquand went to the Coast to work on the dialog. On Dec. 4, 1941, the film was released at a dual "world première" in Loew's State and Loew's Tremont Theaters in Boston. . . . Marquand was rushed around from one press conference to another and photographed wearing a sad smile as he presented to a Harvard librarian the original movie script. Marquand got back to New York for the world première with a slight cold and a nervous feeling that something drastic was about to happen. Two days later the Japanese attacked Pearl Harbor.—*From Roger Butterfield's biography of J. P. Marquand in* Life.

OUT OF THESE THINGS, and many more, is woven the warp and woof of my childhood memory: the dappled sunlight on the great lawns of Chowderhead, our summer estate at Newport, the bitter-sweet fragrance of stranded eels at low tide, the alcoholic breath of a clubman wafted on the breeze from Bailey's Beach. That my family was fantastically wealthy I was early aware, although good taste naturally forbade any excessive display. My father occasionally appeared at table in sack suits checkered with dollar signs, and the gardeners used rubies instead of gravel on the paths, but the guest who so far forgot himself as to exclaim "Hot puppies!" and fill his pockets with the baubles was rarely invited again. One of my first distinct recollections is of watching the men burn leaves under the giant elms and my momentary surprise when I found that they were not leaves but old banknotes. I felt then, with the kind of intuition children alone know, that my lot would be different from that of my fellows.

Almost from the moment of birth, it seems to me, I was passionately fond of books; before I was quite five, I devoured in a single afternoon Doughty's *Arabia Deserta*, the Pandects of Justinian (in translation, of course), and the novels of Mrs. Aphra Behn, a piece of gluttony that ultimately involved the services of three stomach specialists from the Massachusetts General Hospital. It was this youthful predilection for belles lettres that first brought me into conflict with my father. He had been reading *The Private Papers of Henry Ryecroft* and had mislaid it. Fearful lest I might have eaten it, he invaded the nursery and demanded, "Have you noticed any Gissing around here?" "No, sir," I replied submissively, "but I saw you pinching Nannie in the linen closet." He frowned thoughtfully and withdrew, leaving me prey to a strange uneasiness. Four days later, Italy declared war on Tripoli.

Though life at Chowderhead was spacious, to say the least, my father did not believe in pampering the young, and constantly strove to imbue in me a sense of frugality. Until I was eight, I received an allowance of five cents a month, for which I was held strictly accountable. Of course, five cents in those days bought a good deal more than it does now; it bought a firkin of gherkins or a ramekin of fescue or a pipkin of halvah, but since I was expected to furnish my own clothes out of this sum, I had little left for luxuries. I well recall my bitterness when I discovered that the small hoard of pennies I had accumulated over the summer was missing from my knickerbockers. There had been a series of minor peculations at home that year and I suspected the housekeeper's son, a rather ferret-faced lad. I wrung a confession from him, and, to teach the pickpocket a lesson, plunged his head repeatedly into the bay. As luck would have it, my father happened along at this juncture. His jaw dropped. "What are you doing there, young man?" he snapped. "Well, guv'nor," I chuckled, "I guess you might say I was taking a little dip in the ocean." Retrieving his jaw, my father continued his constitutional with a glance that boded me no good. Nine days later, Bosnia severed relations with Herzegovina.

If my father prided himself on anything, it was his unconventional theories about education. To him the customary progression from the grammar grades through high school to college was so much poppycock. Consequently, when I was eight, I was apprenticed to the proprietor of a delicatessen store in Portland, Maine, to acquire worldly experience before entering a university. The nine exciting years I spent under the tutelage of genial Ned Harnischfeger did more to mold my character than anything I could possibly imagine. As I wrapped a succulent cut of smoked salmon for a customer, Ned would painstakingly describe the topography of Nova Scotia, the tides in the Bay of Fundy, and the dynamics of spawning; a corned-beef sandwich on rye was a handy pretext for a lecture on domestic cattle, cereal grains, or the general subject of indigestion. My Portland phase terminated in a curious fashion. One noon I was busily filling orders behind the counter. Suddenly, out of the corner of my eye, I saw Grimalkin, our tabby, leap upon a table, seize a customer's lunch, and bolt out into the alley. The customer, thunderstruck, stammered forth some inarticulate comment. "What's the matter, stupid?" I demanded roughly. "Has the cat got your tongue sandwich?" He went scarlet. I saw Harnischfeger's lips tighten and I knew subconsciously that a turning point in my life was at hand. Two days later, Georges Carpentier climbed into the ring at Boyle's Thirty Acres and I entered Harvard.

From the beginning I was recognized as a leader in my class, one of the few whose destiny it is to inspire and guide their less gifted mates. (I often say that college is a microcosm, a tiny world in which is foreshadowed the turbulence of actual life. That is what I often say.) My freshman year, unluckily, was marred by family dissension. Unbeknownst to me, violent quarrels were raging at home, my mother accusing my father of pettiness and cupidity. At last she could abide his stinginess no longer and departed for Reno. The news reached me, oddly enough, during a French class, as we were translating an absorbing passage of Erckmann-Chatrian. His face grave, the instructor halted the lesson and read aloud a curt message stating that my mother had left home because of my father's avarice. "I hope this isn't too much of a shock, old man," he said sympathetically. "No, that's the way of the world," I replied. "Money makes the *mère* go." An expression I could not fathom clouded the instructor's face and I was oppressed by a vague sense of disaster. Three days later a society bridge expert named Joseph B. Elwell padded downstairs with a sleepy yawn, bringing an era to a close.

It would be both immodest and redundant to detail the triumphs I scored in the balance of my stay at Cambridge. Suffice it to say that I won what paltry distinctions the gridiron, the diamond, and the debating platform could afford, not to mention completing the usual academic course in two and a half years. In one single instance did I come off second best, and then because I disdained to take unfair advantage of a rival in love. The latter was an immensely rich young Corsican upperclassman whose successes with the opposite sex were well-nigh as spectacular as my own. On the surface my relations with César Sporchini were friendly. We often sent each other a dancing girl or a dozen of Imperial Tokay, but we both knew who would be a victor if our blades crossed. One evening, at the Old Howard Burlesque, we were both smitten with the same pair of captivating blue eyes. I subsequently persuaded their owner to share a cozy lobster-and-champagne supper in a private dining room at Locke Ober's. Despite the fabulous string of pearls I slyly insinuated under her plate, the silly creature remained obdurate. Again and again, in the weeks that followed, I plied her with gifts, only to discover that Sporchini was outbidding me for her favor. The Homeric struggle that ensued is still a legend in the chop houses along Scollay Square. At length, sacrificing heaven knows what vineyards and olive groves, Sporchini presented the fair tyrant with a solid-gold Stutz Bearcat and she yielded up her tawdry charms. I received word that I had been worsted with a philosophical shrug. "Oh, well," I observed, brushing a nascent mustache with my pinkie in the manner of the late Lew Cody, "money makes the Margot." My roommate stiffened and emitted a cryptic grunt that somehow filled me with anxiety. Five days later, Harry C. Klemfuss, the press agent for Campbell's Funeral Home, formally announced the passing of Rodolpho Alfonzo Raffaelo Pierre Filibert Guglielmi di Valentina d'Antonguolla, better known as "Rudy" Valentino.

The strident note of a distant banjo was stilled, the echo of undergraduate voices in the corridors hushed at last. It was time for me to face stern realities, to take over the reins of my father's vast industrial empire. Yet somehow I hungered for a creative outlet instead of the sordid money grubbing that awaited me. Acting on impulse at the eleventh hour, I joined a strolling Shakespearean troupe. For a time I was a mere supernumerary and fourth assistant stage manager. Then a dazzling stroke of fortune presented a chance to play a really important role. On the afternoon we were to give *Othello*, the leading man demanded an increase in salary. Denied it, he resigned in a temper. Shortly afterward, I encountered our impresario seated in the darkened auditorium, head buried in his hands. "I picked him up from the gutter!" he wailed. "I don't understand it!" "It's simple enough," I comforted him. "Money makes the Moor go." He looked up sharply and there was a challenge in his eyes that set my heart racing. One day later, Frances "Peaches" Browning sued for divorce and my theatrical career was a thing of the past.

And there, on the very threshold of life, face to face with the rich, dark promise of the years that lay ahead, let us leave me. Except for the beauty of Apollo and the mind of a Jesuit, I had scant equipment for the struggle: a trifling million or two in tax-free bonds, a leaky old yacht, a great, drafty mansion on Fifth Avenue peopled by ghosts. The Turgid Thirties were dawning, bringing with them the depression, Henry Luce, and, above all, the outsize picture magazine. A sense of prophecy was not enough. From now on I must learn how to duck.

❧ CLOUDLAND REVISITED: SODOM IN THE SUBURBS

THE CLOSEST I ever came to an orgy, aside from the occasion in Montparnasse twenty years ago when I smoked a cigarette purported to contain hashish and fainted dead away after two puffs, was at a student dance at Brown around 1922. I did not suspect it was an orgy until three days later; in fact, at the time it semed to me decorous to the point of torpor and fully consonant with the high principles of the Brown Christian Association, under whose auspices it was held. Attired in a greenish Norfolk jacket and scuffing the massive bluchers with perforated toe caps and brass eyelets considered *de rigueur* in that period, I spent the evening buffeting about in the stag line, prayerfully beseeching the underclassmen I knew for permission to cut in on their women and tread a few measures of the Camel Walk. At frequent intervals, noisily advertising an overpowering thirst, I retired to a cloakroom with several other blades and choked down a minute quantity of gin, warmed to body heat, from a pocket flask. Altogether, it was a strikingly commonplace experience, and I got to bed without contusions and stayed there peaceably riffling through *Jurgen* and humming snatches of "Avalon."

The following Sunday, I learned, to my astonishment, that I had been involved in a momentous debauch; the campus reeked of a scandal so sulphurous that it hung over our beanies like a nimbus for the rest of the academic year. In blazing scareheads, the Hearst Boston *American* tore the veil from the excesses tolerated at Brown University dances. At these hops, it thundered, were displayed a depravity and libertinism that would have sickened Petronius, made Messalina hang her head in shame. It portrayed girls educated at the best finishing schools, crazed with alcohol and inflamed by ragtime, oscillating cheek to cheek with young ne'er-do-wells in raccoon coats and derbies. Keyed up by savage jungle rhythms, the *abandonnés* would then reel out to roadsters parked on Waterman Street, where frat pins were traded for kisses under cover of darkness. Worst of all, and indicative of the depths to which the Jazz Age had reduced American woman-

hood, was the unwritten law that each girl must check her corset before
the saturnalia. Painting a picture that combined the more succulent aspects of the Quatz' Arts Ball and a German officers' revel in occupied
Belgium—two types of wassail long cherished by Hearst feature writers
—the writer put all his metaphors in one basket and called upon outraged society to apply the brakes, hold its horses, and retrieve errant
youth from under the wheels of the juggernaut. It was a daisy, and
whoever did the pen drawings that enhanced it had given a lot of
thought to the female bust.

I was poignantly reminded of that epoch and its turbulent escapades
the other afternoon as I sat puffing a meerschaum and turning the
leaves of a novel called *Flaming Youth*, which attained an immense
vogue about that time not only with the general public but with the
owner of the meerschaum. The book was hailed by press and pulpit as
a blistering, veracious study of the moral chaos prevalent in the upper
brackets, and it was popularly believed that its author, ostensibly a
physician writing under the pseudonym of Warner Fabian, was, in
reality, a top-drawer novelist. If he was, he successfully managed to
conceal it; his style, at once flamboyant, euphuistic, and turgid, suggested nothing quite so much as melted marzipan. Fabian was plainly
determined to leave no scintilla of doubt that he was a neophyte, for
he wrote a windy foreword affirming it, the final segment of which
seems to me to prove his claim incontestably: "To the woman of the
period thus set forth, restless, seductive, greedy, discontented, craving
sensation, unrestrained, a little morbid, uneducated, sybaritic, following blind instincts and perverse fancies, slack of mind as she is trim of
body, neurotic and vigorous, a worshiper of tinseled gods at perfumed
altars, fit mate for the hurried, reckless, and cynical man of the age,
predestined mother of—what manner of being?: To Her I dedicate
this study of herself." I don't know why, but I got the feeling from the
foregoing that the doctor was a precise and bloodless little creep with
a goatee I would dearly love to tweak. I could just see him whipping
to his feet at a panel of nose specialists, removing his pince-nez with
maddening deliberation, and beginning, "With the permission of the
chair, I should like to amplify Dr. Westerphal's masterly orientation of
the Eustachian tubes."

The fictional family chosen by the author to typify the decadence
of the twenties is named Fentriss, resident in a well-to-do Westchester
or Long Island suburb called Dorrisdale. Stripped of its gingerbread,
the story concerns itself with the amours of the three Fentriss daughters, Constance, Dee, and Pat, whose adolescence has been colored by

their mother's reckless hedonism. She, while delectable, sounds from Fabian's thumbnail description very much like an early Cubist portrait by Picasso: "She was a golden-brown, strong, delicately rounded woman, glowing with an effect of triumphant and imperishable youth. Not one of her features but was faulty by strict artistic tenets; even the lustrous eyes were set at slightly different levels." Mona Fentriss' life of self-indulgence has done more than throw her features out of whack; in the opening stanza, we see her being told by her physician and devoted admirer, Dr. Robert Osterhout, that there are fairies at the bottom of her aorta and that her days are numbered. Osterhout is a gruff, lovable character in the best medico-literary tradition: "Like a bear's, his exterior was rough, shaggy, and seemed not to fit him well. His face was irregularly square, homely, thoughtful, and humorous." Ever the heedless pagan, Mona turns a deaf ear to the voice of doom and, over the single shakerful of cocktails the doctor has restricted her to daily, confesses no remorse for her numerous extramarital affairs. Her husband, she confides, is equally unconcerned at her peccadilloes ("They say he's got a floozie now, tucked away in a cozy corner somewhere"), and it is a lead-pipe cinch that, given this profligate environment and dubious heredity, the Fentriss girls are going to cut some pretty spectacular didos once the saxophones start sobbing.

We get our first peep at the dissipation extant in the household at a party thrown by Mona shortly afterward and characterized as follows: "The party was a Bingo. . . . Lovely, flushed, youthful, regnant in her own special queendom, Mona Fentriss sat in the midst of a circle of the older men, bandying stories with them in voices which were discreetly lowered when any of the youngsters drew near. It was the top of the time." Pat, the youngest daughter, has been considered too young to attend, but she abstracts a dinner dress from one of her sisters and eavesdrops in the shrubbery. A furious crap game rages in the breakfast nook, furtive giggles emanate from parked cars, and, in the conservatory, Pat overhears her mother holding an equivocal duologue with Sidney Rathbone, an elderly but distinguished Baltimorean of nearly forty. A moment later, a glass of home brew is rudely forced to Pat's lips; as she recoils from the searing liquid, she is kissed violently and an insinuating voice pleads in her ear, "Come on, sweetie! We'll take a fifty-mile-an-hour dip into the landscape. The little boat [hotrod, in the argot of '22] can go some." Much to Pat's discomfiture, however, her mother intercedes, routs the befuddled Princetonian besieging her daughter, and packs her off to bed. But the damage has been done, and, as Fabian darkly observes, tucking back his sleeves and preparing to fold a spoonful of cantharides into his already piquant meringue, that first smacker is the one a girl never forgets.

The narrative jogs along uneventfully for a spell, enlivened by a couple of minor scandals: Mrs. Fentriss shacks up briefly at a hotel called the Marcus Groot, in Trenton, with the aforesaid Sidney Rathbone, and Constance, the eldest daughter, underestimates her resistance to Bacardi, passes out in her cavalier's room, and is forced to still gossiping tongues by marrying him. A quick time lapse now enables the author to dispose of the exuberant Mrs. Fentriss and dress the stage for the entrance of the hero, Cary Scott, a former flame of hers encountered on a trip abroad. The description of Scott, clad in a sealskin coat and astrakhan cap, sufficiently explains why he sets the Fentriss girls by the ears: "No woman would have called him handsome. His features were too irregular, and the finely modeled forehead was scarred vertically with a savagely deep V which mercifully lost itself in the clustering hair, a testimony to active war service. There was confident distinction in his bearing, and an atmosphere of quiet and somewhat ironic worldliness in voice and manner. He looked to be a man who had experimented much with life in its larger meaning and found it amusing but perhaps not fulfilling." Nor does he become less glamorous when he admits, in the cultivated accents of one more at home in French than in his native tongue, that he has lived much out of the world: "The East; wild parts of Hindustan and northern China; and then the South Seas. I have a boy's passion for travel." This suave customer, undertandably, makes the youths at the Dorrisdale country club seem pretty loutish to radiant, eighteen-year-old Pat, and she falls headlong. He reciprocates in flippant, half-serious fashion, regarding her as merely another spoiled flapper; besides, like all distinguished men of the world with deep Vs, he is chained to an impossible wife in Europe, and even the most beef-witted reader must appreciate what plot convulsions are required to reconcile such opposites.

An episode of mixed nude bathing next ensues to blueprint the élan of the younger set, in the course of which the guests, emboldened by draughts of a potation called a "submarine cocktail," cavort about a pool in a thunderstorm pinching each other. In consequence, Dee, the second Fentriss girl, weds a rotter; Cary Scott goes back to Paris; and Pat is sent away to school. When Cary sees her on his return, she has burgeoned into what he terms a "*petite gamine*," a phrase she does not understand; evidently she has been attending some technical school, like the Delehanty Institute. "You know what a gamin is?" he inquires.

"*Gamine* is the feminine. But there's a suggestion in it of something more delicate and fetching; of verve, of—of *diablerie*." Leave it to those expatriates to explain one French word with another; he might at least have gone on to tell her that *diablerie* was derived from the game of diavolo, just making its appearance in the smarter salons of the Faubourg St. Honoré. Anyhow, he takes her to a concert, where Tchaikovsky's Fifth Symphony makes them kinsprits, and, swept away by the bassoons, kisses her. Almost instantly, though, he feels the lash of conscience and excoriates himself in a noteworthy solilo- quy: "It was incredible; it was shameful; it was damnable; but this child, this *petite gamine*, this reckless, careless, ignorant, swift-witted, unprincipled, selfish, vain, lovable, impetuous, bewildering, seductive, half-formed girl had taken his heart in her two strong, shapely woman- hands, and claimed it away from him—for what? A toy? A keepsake? A treasure? What future was there for this abrupt and blind encounter of his manhood and her womanhood?" Follows a thirty-one-page re- nunciation jam-packed with rough tenderness, eyes shadowed with pain, and germane claptrap, and Cary vamooses to California. There was one thing you could be reasonably sure of in any novel published between 1915 and 1925: the minute the protagonists got within biting distance of each other, one of them was fated to board a boat or choo- choo within seventy-two hours.

As might be anticipated, Pat thereupon reacts in accordance with the protocol governing the brokenhearted and plunges into a mad round of pleasure, careering around the countryside at 40 mph in sleek Marmon runabouts, ingesting oceans of hooch, and inhaling straw-tipped Melachrinos. When Cary, despite himself, is drawn back to her, he finds her more provocative than ever, a disturbing amalgam of elf, kitten, and bacchante: "She shook the gleamy mist of her hair about her face, gave a gnomish twist to body and neck, and peered sidelong at him from out the tangle." His punctilio holds fast until someone next door idly starts plucking a fiddle, and then hell breaks loose again: "The long, thrilling, haunted wind-borne· prayer of the violin penetrated the innermost fiber of her, mingling there with the passionate sense of his nearness, swaying her to undefined and flashing languors, to unthinkable urgencies. . . . With a cry he leapt to her, clasped her, felt her young strength and lissome grace yield to his en- foldment. . . . Outside the great wind possessed the world, full of the turbulence, the fever, the unassuaged desire of spring, the *allegro furi- oso* of the elements, and through it pierced the unbearable sweetness of the stringed melody."

Well, sir, that would seem to be it. By all the ordinary rules of physiology and pulp fiction, Pat and Cary should have been allowed at this juncture to retire tranquilly to the Fruit of the Loom without let or hindrance and frisk as they pleased. But Fabian, in inverse ratio to the reader, is just getting interested in his characters and figuring out new ways to frustrate them. They keep everlastingly melting into scorching embraces and springing apart the moment a rapprochement impends between them. She wants, he don't want; he wants, she don't want—your exasperation eventually reaches such a pitch that you would like to knock their heads together and lock them up in a motel with a copy of van der Velde's *Ideal Marriage*. The subplot bumbles in at intervals, adding to the general obfuscation a thwarted intrigue involving Dee Fentriss and a British electrician stylishly named Stanley Wollaston. At last, with the rueful conclusion: "We're terrible boobs, Cary. . . . Let's stop it"—a suggestion hardly calculated to provoke a quarrel with me—Pat sends her lover away to think things out and pins her affections on Leo Stenak, a brilliant violinist. This peters out when she discovers that he washes infrequently ("She forgot the genius, the inner fire; beheld only the outer shell, uncouth, pulpy, nauseous to her senses"), and she becomes affianced to Monty Standish, a Princeton football idol whose personal daintiness is beyond reproach. And then, in a smashing climax, so suspenseful that the least snore is liable to disrupt the delicate balance of his yarn, Fabian deftly turns the tables. Cary appears with the providential news that his wife has freed him, lips settle down to an uninterrupted feast, and, oblivious of the dead and dying syntax about them, the lovers go forth in search of Ben Lindsey and a companionate marriage.

It may be only a coincidence, but for a whole day after rereading *Flaming Youth*, my pupils were so dilated that you would have sworn I had been using belladonna. My complexion, though somewhat ruddier, recalled Bartholomew Sholto's in *The Sign of Four* as he lay transfixed by an aboriginal dart that fateful night at Pondicherry Lodge. Luckily, I managed to work out a simple, effective treatment I can pass on to anyone afflicted with star-dust poisoning. All you need is an eyedropper, enough kerosene to saturate an average three-hundred-and-thirty-six-page romance, and a match. A darkened room, for lying down in afterward, is nice but not absolutely essential. Just keep your eyes peeled, your nose clean, and avoid doctors and novels written by doctors. When you're over forty, one extra bumper of overripe beauty can do you in.

🌸 *AMO, AMAS, AMAT, AMAMUS, AMATIS, ENOUGH*

THE OTHER DAY I surfaced in a pool of glorious golden sunshine laced with cracker crumbs to discover that spring had returned to Washington Square. A pair of pigeons were cooing gently directly beneath my window; two squirrels plighted their troth in a branch overhead; at the corner a handsome member of New York's finest twirled his night stick and cast roguish glances at the saucy-eyed flower vendor. The scene could have been staged only by a Lubitsch; in fact, Lubitsch himself was seated on a bench across the street, smoking a cucumber and looking as cool as a cigar. It lacked only Nelson Eddy to appear on a penthouse terrace and loose a chorus of deep-throated song, and, as if by magic, Nelson Eddy suddenly appeared on a penthouse terrace and, with the artistry that has made his name a word, launched into an aria. A moment later, Jeanette MacDonald, in creamy negligee, joined the dashing rascal, making sixty-four teeth, and the lovers began a lilting duet. The passers-by immediately took up the refrain; windows flew up at the Brevoort, flew down again; the melody spread rapidly up Fifth Avenue, debouched into Broadway, detoured into Park, and soon the entire city was humming the infectious strain in joyous tribute to Jeanette's and Nelson's happiness.

Caught up in the mood of the moment, I donned a jaunty foulard bow, stuck a feather in my hatband and one in my throat, and set out to look over spring fashions in love. That I ultimately wound up with a slight puff under one eye and a warning from a policewoman is not intrinsic to the discussion. Truth is a wood violet that blooms in the least likely corner, and I found it in a couple of obscure pulp magazines called *Gay Love Stories* and *Ideal Love*, which retail at a dime apiece. Twenty cents for a postgraduate course in passion—*entre nous*, kids, I think I've got the only game in town.

Biologically, it was reassuring to find that the war had wrought no intrinsic change in the characters who people cut-rate romantic fiction; the smooth and deadly function of the glands continues undisturbed by the roar of high explosives. The ladies are as cuddly and adorable as they were before Pearl Harbor, the cavaliers as manly and chivalrous as any immortalized by Nell Brinkley and Leyendecker. Consider, for instance, Linda Marshall, the colleen of "Little Ball of Catnip," in the May *Ideal Love*, as she stands lost in dreams in her garden at Santa Monica, "slender and poised in a brown and white seersucker dress, the tight bodice cunningly trimmed in rickrack braid. She had a clear skin, nicely accented by dark eyebrows, lively hazel eyes, and beautifully fashioned cherry-red lips. The general impression was that of youth on the wing." Incidentally, there seems to be a strange, almost Freudian compulsion in both magazines to describe the heroine in avian terms—*vide* Kitty Malcolm in "Barefoot Blonde" (*Gay Love*): "That evening, after finishing a careful toilette, Kitty glanced at herself in the mirror, and knew that she had never looked lovelier. The black velvet gown molded her slim figure to perfection. In the gleaming nest of curls which she had scooped atop her head, Steve's gardenias, which had arrived via messenger, provided the last, elegant touch." It seems almost picayune of Steve not to have included a clutch of cold-storage eggs in the nest atop his inamorata's head as an earnest of eventual domesticity.

An even more tempting *bonne bouche* than Kitty is Bonita Kellsinger, grooming her lovely frame for the evening in "Shadow of Her Past" (*Gay Love*, June): "The very thought of such a triumph [winning the richest boy in Barnesville] brought roses to her richly tanned cheeks, brought a fiery sparkle into her wide, greenish-blue eyes. She brushed her thick, ripe-wheat-colored hair until it hung on her straight slender shoulders in rich gleaming waves. A pair of small jeweled clips held back one wave of hair on either side of the girl's high, intelligent forehead. She made an enticing red rosebud of her mouth, and wound ropes of scarlet wooden beads around her neck and arms." Small wonder indeed that her gallant fidgets impatiently off scene at the wheel of his station wagon, which the author introduces parenthetically in one of the most syncopated bits of whitewash on record: "Cary had explained that he couldn't get adequate rations of gas for any of his cars but the wagon, which he used in working hours to haul people to and from his canning factory that was so busy putting up dehydrated foods for the Army and Navy." For sheer pith, the passage deserves a niche in the Hall of Ungainly Exposition beside my all-time favorite, which graced one of the early Fu Manchu films. Briefly, the artful Doctor had eluded Nayland Smith by swarming down a rope ladder into the Thames. The ensuing scene revealed a vast underground cavern, in the foreground a rough deal table piled high with crucibles, alembics, and retorts bubbling with sinister compounds. After a pause, the table swung away, a trap door opened, and Dr. Fu crept up, followed by a henchman (Tully Marshall). "Well, Wing Chang," remarked the Doctor with a fiendish chuckle, "these old dye works certainly make an admirable laboratory of crime, do they not?"

Since every one of the nineteen novelettes and short stories I dipped into was written by a woman, the result is a gallery of fairly glamorous males, nearly all of them named Michael. It is practically six, two, and even that at some point in the action tiny muscles are going to flicker in lean jaws, eyes crinkle up quizzically at the corners, and six feet of lanky, bronzed strength strain a reluctant miss against a rough khaki shoulder (apparently the supply of smooth khaki shoulders has been exhausted, for whatever reason). There must have been a singularly dreamy look in the eye of Betty Webb Lucas, the author of "Blue Angel" (*Gay Love*), when she hatched Dr. Michael Halliday, chief surgeon of the City Hospital: "He was more like a Greek god, in spite of the flaming hair that threatened to break into rebellious curls at any moment, and the sterile white jacket straining over broad shoulders. His eyes were incredibly blue, and his sun-bronzed skin made them seem bluer still." Much as I respect honest emotion, I am afraid Miss Lucas became a trifle too dreamy in her medical dialogue: "Judy could only stare until he said impatiently: 'Haven't you anything else to do but stand there peering at me like a—a biological specie?' " The most charitable assumption in defense of Miss Lucas must be that the dear nearness of Judy in her crisp white nurse's uniform unnerved the eminent man.

It is hardly surprising that when these golden lads and lasses finally have at one another, they produce an effect akin to the interior of a blast furnace. Observe the Wagnerian encounter between the aforementioned Bonita Kellsinger and her beau ideal: "He caught her close to him, pinned her cheek against the rough khaki shoulder of his uniform, and slowly, deliberately covered her mouth with his, in a kiss that made her forget everything for the moment in the heady rapture of it. . . . They seemed to ascend to the top of a very high mountain, where there hung a white disc of moon in a sparkling bed of stars, and a soft breeze scented with jasmine swept over them. But when his lips lifted from hers, it was as though the cables had been cut from an elevator. She hit earth with a bump that shocked her awake." While Bonita brushes the meteorites from her hair and recovers her land legs, take a hinge at Lieutenant Lex McClure flinging a bit of woo in "Glass Walls Are Cold" (*Ideal*): "Sally fought against it, but she felt as though she would die of the ecstasy that poured through her body. All of her senses quickened and became alert. She smelled the piney fragrance of his tobacco [that mixture of sun-dried burley and evergreen cones so popular of late with the armed forces] and the light scent of her own perfume. Her lips softened under his pressure, then she drew away softly, drawing her cheek across his chin, feeling the roughness of his day-old beard." Luckily, as one weaned on *The Perfumed Garden* and the Mardrus translation of *The Arabian Nights*, I was able to withstand this erotic play. Even so, I must confess that a bestial flush invaded my cheek and I had to fight off an overmastering impulse to pinch the hired girl.

At the risk of slighting any individual author, I must say the brightest star in the galaxy is unquestionably Leonora McPheeters, whose "Perfumed Slacker" (*Ideal*, May) is subheaded "How could you love a man who always smelled like a boudoir?" For timeliness, melodrama, and a good old-fashioned concupiscence like Mother used to make, I haven't met its equal since the *Decameron*. The principals in this droll tale are two: John Craig, "tall, masculine, tweedy . . . a big overgrown Newfoundland pup, with his rough tawny hair and steady brown eyes," and Judy, a *zäftick* little proposition bent on bringing him to heel. Ostensibly the pair are engaged in running a cosmetic laboratory; actually, they seem to spend the business day rubbing around each other, trading molten kisses, and generally overheating themselves. Occasionally Judy varies the routine by kissing Bob, a shadowy member in a soldier suit who drifts in from an unspecified reservation, but these ersatz embraces only sharpen her appetite for the brand of judo dispensed by Craig. Unfortunately, the intra-office romance withers when Judy detects her employer's lack of enthusiasm for military service, and excoriating him for a coward and a caitiff, gives him his quittance. Then, in a whirlwind denouement, she captures two enemy agents by upsetting a carboy of wave-set over their heads and learns to her stupefaction that Craig has really been evolving explosives for the government. As the curtain descends, Philemon seizes Baucis in a sizzling hammer lock, superbly indifferent to the fact that they are standing ankle-deep in thermite and TNT, and rains kisses on her upturned face.

By one of those coincidences that are positively spooky, the hired girl opened my door at this juncture and found the boss-man ankle-deep in a roomful of shredded pulp fiction, baying like a timber wolf. Before she could turn to flee, five feet seven of lanky, bronzed strength reached out and strained her against a rough pajama shoulder. I'm still trying to explain things to the employment agency, but they keep hanging up on me. You don't know anybody with full-fashioned cherry-red lips and a high, intelligent forehead who could help me with the housework, do you? She needn't bother about a uniform; just tell her to meet me in the Lombardy Bar at five tomorrow. They've got the best Dutch Cleanser in town.

✤ INSERT FLAP "A" AND THROW AWAY

ONE STIFLING summer afternoon last August, in the attic of a tiny stone house in Pennsylvania, I made a most interesting discovery: the shortest, cheapest method of inducing a nervous breakdown ever perfected. In this technique (eventually adopted by the psychology department of Duke University, which will adopt anything), the subject is placed in a sharply sloping attic heated to 340°F. and given a mothproof closet known as the Jiffy-Cloz to assemble. The Jiffy-Cloz, procurable at any department store or neighborhood insane asylum, consists of half a dozen gigantic sheets of red cardboard, two plywood doors, a clothes rack, and a packet of staples. With these is included a set of instructions mimeographed in pale-violet ink, fruity with phrases like "Pass Section F through Slot AA, taking care not to fold tabs behind washers (see Fig. 9)." The cardboard is so processed that as the subject struggles convulsively to force the staple through, it suddenly buckles, plunging the staple deep into his thumb. He thereupon springs up with a dolorous cry and smites his knob (Section K) on the rafters (RR). As a final demonic touch, the Jiffy-Cloz people cunningly omit four of the staples necessary to finish the job, so that after indescribable purgatory, the best the subject can possibly achieve is a sleazy, capricious structure which would reduce any self-respecting moth to helpless laughter. The cumulative frustration, the tropical heat, and the soft, ghostly chuckling of the moths are calculated to unseat the strongest mentality.

In a period of rapid technological change, however, it was inevitable that a method as cumbersome as the Jiffy-Cloz would be superseded. It was superseded at exactly nine-thirty Christmas morning by a device called the Self-Running 10-Inch Scale-Model Delivery-Truck Kit Powered by Magic Motor, costing twenty-nine cents. About nine on that particular morning, I was spread-eagled on my bed, indulging in my favorite sport of mouth-breathing, when a cork fired from a child's air gun mysteriously lodged in my throat. The pellet proved awkward for a while, but I finally ejected it by flailing the little marksman (and his sister, for good measure) until their welkins rang, and sauntered

250

in to breakfast. Before I could choke down a healing fruit juice, my consort, a tall, regal creature indistinguishable from Cornelia, the Mother of the Gracchi, except that her foot was entangled in a roller skate, swept in. She extended a large, unmistakable box covered with diagrams.

"Now don't start making excuses," she whined. "It's just a simple cardboard toy. The directions are on the back—"

"Look, dear," I interrupted, rising hurriedly and pulling on my overcoat, "it clean slipped my mind. I'm supposed to take a lesson in crosshatching at Zim's School of Cartooning today."

"On Christmas?" she asked suspiciously.

"Yes, it's the only time they could fit me in," I countered glibly. "This is the big week for crosshatching, you know, between Christmas and New Year's."

"Do you think you ought to go in your pajamas?" she asked.

"Oh, that's O.K.," I smiled. "We often work in our pajamas up at Zim's. Well, goodbye now. If I'm not home by Thursday, you'll find a cold snack in the safe-deposit box." My subterfuge, unluckily, went for naught, and in a trice I was sprawled on the nursery floor, surrounded by two lambkins and ninety-eight segments of the Self-Running 10-Inch Scale-Model Delivery-Truck Construction Kit.

The theory of the kit was simplicity itself, easily intelligible to Kettering of General Motors, Professor Millikan, or any first-rate physicist. Taking as my starting point the only sentence I could comprehend, "Fold down on all lines marked 'fold down'; fold up on all lines marked 'fold up,' " I set the children to work and myself folded up with an album of views of Chili Williams. In a few moments, my skin was suffused with a delightful tingling sensation and I was ready for the second phase, lightly referred to in the directions as "Preparing the Spring Motor Unit." As nearly as I could determine after twenty minutes of mumbling, the Magic Motor ("No Electricity—No Batteries—Nothing to Wind—Motor Never Wears Out") was an accordion-pleated affair operating by torsion, attached to the axles. "It is necessary," said the text, "to cut a slight notch in each of the axles with a knife (see Fig. C). To find the exact place to cut this notch, lay one of the axles over diagram at bottom of page."

"Well, *now* we're getting someplace!" I boomed, with a false gusto that deceived nobody. "Here, Buster, run in and get Daddy a knife."

"I dowanna," quavered the boy, backing away. "You always cut yourself at this stage." I gave the wee fellow an indulgent pat on the head that flattened it slightly, to teach him civility, and commandeered a long, serrated bread knife from the kitchen. "Now watch me closely, children," I ordered. "We place the axle on the diagram as in Fig. C, applying a strong downward pressure on the knife handle at all times." The axle must have been a factory second, because an instant later I was in the bathroom grinding my teeth in agony and attempting to stanch the flow of blood. Ultimately, I succeeded in contriving a rough bandage and slipped back into the nursery without awaking the children's suspicions. An agreeable surprise awaited me. Displaying a mechanical aptitude clearly inherited from their sire, the rascals had put together the chassis of the delivery truck.

"Very good indeed," I complimented (naturally, one has to exaggerate praise to develop a child's self-confidence). "Let's see—what's the next step? Ah, yes. 'Lock into box shape by inserting tabs C, D, E, F, G, H, J, K, and L into slots C, D, E, F, G, H, J, K, and L. Ends of front axle should be pushed through holes A and B.' " While marshaling the indicated parts in their proper order, I emphasized to my rapt listeners the necessity of patience and perseverance. "Haste makes waste, you know," I reminded them. "Rome wasn't built in a day. Remember, your daddy isn't always going to be here to show you."

"Where *are* you going to be?" they demanded.

"In the movies, if I can arrange it," I snarled. Poising tabs C, D, E, F, G, H, J, K, and L in one hand and the corresponding slots in the other, I essayed a union of the two, but in vain. The moment I made one set fast and tackled another, tab and slot would part company, thumbing their noses at me. Although the children were too immature to understand, I saw in a flash where the trouble lay. Some idiotic employee at the factory had punched out the wrong design, probably out of sheer spite. So that was his game, eh? I set my lips in a grim line and, throwing one hundred and fifty-seven pounds of fighting fat into the effort, pounded the component parts into a homogeneous mass.

"There," I said with a gasp, "that's close enough. Now then, who wants candy? One, two, three—everybody off to the candy store!"

"We wanna finish the delivery truck!" they wailed. "Mummy, he won't let us finish the delivery truck!" Threats, cajolery, bribes were of no avail. In their jungle code, a twenty-nine-cent gewgaw bulked larger than a parent's love. Realizing that I was dealing with a pair of monomaniacs, I determined to show them who was master and wildly began locking the cardboard units helter-skelter, without any regard for the directions. When sections refused to fit, I gouged them with my nails and forced them together, cackling shrilly. The side panels collapsed; with a bestial oath, I drove a safety pin through them and lashed them to the roof. I used paper clips, bobby pins, anything I could lay my hands on. My fingers fairly flew and my breath whistled in my throat. "You want a delivery truck, do you?" I panted. "All right, I'll show you!" As merciful blackness closed in, I was on my hands and knees, bunting the infernal thing along with my nose and whinnying, "Roll, confound you, roll!"

"Absolute quiet," a carefully modulated voice was saying, "and fifteen of the white tablets every four hours." I opened my eyes carefully in the darkened room. Dimly I picked out a knifelike character actor in pince-nez lenses and a morning coat folding a stethoscope into his bag. "Yes," he added thoughtfully, "if we play our cards right, this ought to be a long, expensive recovery." From far away, I could hear my wife's voice bravely trying to control her anxiety.

"What if he becomes restless, Doctor?"

"Get him a detective story," returned the leech. "Or better still, a nice, soothing picture puzzle—something he can do with his hands."

❧ SEND NO MONEY, HONEY

I HAVE A WELL-DEFINED SUSPICION, bounded on the south by Fortieth Street and the north by Fifty-seventh, that anybody venturing into the Times Square area who was not already sick of phosphorescent carnations is, by now, sick of phosphorescent carnations. Exactly when the craze for these luminous hybrids captured the popular imagination is uncertain—possibly during the dimout. At any rate, since then every midtown cranny too small for a watchmaker, a popcorn machine, or a publisher's remainders boasts its own little altar of black velvet from which carnations and brooches of debatable value give off a spectral greenish glow. It is not altogether clear, incidentally, whether people buy them to wear or to worship in private. The only time I believe I ever saw one off the leash was at the Rialto Theater, when a woman's head, radiating a distinct nimbus, rose in a grisly, disembodied fashion and floated past me up the aisle. I assume it was illuminated from below by a phosphorescent corsage, but it may merely have been an ordinary disembodied head viewing the feature at a reduced rate of admission.

The vogue could be discounted as a sheerly local phenomenon except that a short time ago a prominent jobber of glowing novelties decided to invade the mail-order field. Hiring the back cover of a breezy magazine called *Laff*, the Glow-in-the-Dark Necktie Company of Chicago exhibited a twinkling four-in-hand flashing the words "WILL YOU KISS ME IN THE DARK, BABY?" accompanied by this text:

> Girls Can't Resist this KISS ME NECKTIE as it GLOWS in the Dark! By Day a Lovely Swank Tie . . . By Night a Call to Love in Glowing Words! . . . Here's the most amazing spectacular necktie that you ever wore, a smart, wrinkleproof, tailored cravat, which at night is a thrilling sensation! It's smart, superb class by day, and just imagine in the dark it seems like a necktie of compelling allure, sheer magic! Like a miracle of light there comes a pulsing, glowing question—WILL YOU KISS ME IN THE DARK, BABY? Think

of the surprise, the awe you will cause! There's no trick, no hidden batteries, no switches or foolish horseplay, but a thing of beauty as the question emerges gradually to life, touched by the wand of darkness, and your girl will gasp with wonder as it takes form so amazingly. . . . Send no money, here's all you do . . .

However unpredictable its reception by the beau monde, there is no gainsaying the romantic appeal of the glowing necktie in terms of theater. Before some energetic dramatist weaves the idea into a smash operetta or Leon Leonidoff pre-empts it for one of his opulent Music Hall presentations, I hasten to stake out my claim with the following playlet. If Metro-Goldwyn-Mayer would like it as a vehicle for Greer Garson (and I'm ready to throw in a whiffletree and two wheels), I shall be wearing a corned-beef sandwich this evening in the third booth at the Brass Rail. Just walk by rapidly ånd drop the three dollars on the floor.

SCENE: *The conservatory of the country club at Heublein's Fens, Ohio. Fern Replevin, an utterly lovely creature of twenty-four whose mouth wanders at will over her features in the manner of Greer Garson's, sits lost in dreams, watching a cirrus formation in the moonlit sky. Offstage the usual Saturday-night dance is in progress, and as mingled laughter and music drift in to Fern, she softly hums the air the orchestra is playing, "If Love Should Call."*

FERN:
If love should call, and you were I,
And I were you, and love should call,
How happy I could be with I,
And you with you, if love should call.
Your shoulders broad, your instep arched,
Without your kiss my lips are parched.
For love comes late, and now, and soon,
At midnight's crack and blazing noon.
My arms are ready, the wine is heady,
If love should call.

(*Lafcadio Replevin, Fern's father, enters. He belongs to the Vigorous and Tweedy school—is headmaster, in fact—is leader in his community and a man who knows his way around the block, if no further. He has, as the saying goes, a groatsworth of wit in a guinea-sized noddle. Maybe the saying doesn't go just this way, but it certainly describes Lafcadio.*)

LAFCADIO: Oh, there you are, daughter; I've been looking all over for you. Why aren't you inside dancing with your fiancé, Fleetwood Rumsey, that is by far the richest man in town and owner of feed mills galore throughout the vicinity? There hasn't been any tiffin' between you, has there?

FERN (*indicating some scones and tea on the table*): Only what you see on this tray.

LAFCADIO: Then why are you staring at those clouds so pensively?

FERN: Perhaps I'm more cirrus-minded than the other girls.

LAFCADIO: Well, I don't like to see you moon around. As for me, I'm going in and have a drink with that new librarian. She's as thin as a *lath* and pretty *stucco* on herself, but I guess we can get *plastered*. (*He exits chuckling. Sunk in reverie, Fern is unaware that a man has emerged from behind a rubber plant and is regarding her narrowly. Rex Beeswanger is thirty-odd, a thoroughbred from his saturnine eyebrow to the tip of his well-polished shoe. His clothes, which he wears with casual elegance, bear an unmistakable metropolitan stamp. He is shod by Thom McAn, gloved by Fownes, belted by Hickok, and cravatted by Glow-in-Dark.*)

REX (*softly*): If you don't love him, why go through with it?

FERN (*whirling*): Oh! You startled me.

REX: Did I?

FERN: Did you what?

REX: Startle you.

FERN: Yes. I mean I was sunk in a reverie, and you spoke to me suddenly, and that startled me.

REX: You see things clearly, don't you? You're a very direct person.

FERN: Am I?

REX: Are you what?

FERN: A very direct person.

REX: Yes. When I startled you out of the reverie in which you were sunk, you didn't pretend I hadn't. That would have been cheap. And you're not cheap.

FERN: What are we talking about?

REX: Does it matter? Does anything matter but silver slanting rain on the cruel lilacs and compassion in the heart's deep core?

FERN: Who are you? You haven't even told me your name.

REX: Just a bird of passage. Call me Rex Beeswanger if you like.

FERN (*savoring it*): Rex Beeswanger. I've always wanted to know someone named Rex Beeswanger. It's—it's instinct with springtime and the song of larks.

REX: May I kiss you?

FERN: Oh, Rex, you've got to give me time to think. We've known each other less than forty-eight hours.

REX (*fiercely*): Is that all love means to you—narrow little conventions, smug barriers holding two kinsprits apart? I thought you finer than that.

FERN: Yes, but there's so much light in here. It's like a cafeteria or something. (*For answer, Rex extinguishes the lamp. Instantly the legend "WILL YOU KISS ME IN THE DARK, BABY?" springs into relief on his tie. The music inside swells and, silhouetted against the window, Fern lifts her voice in vibrant melody.*)

> FERN:
> *You glowed in the dark, I saw your spark,*
> *You left your mark on me.*
> *You're wrinkleproof, and so aloof,*
> *You made a goof of me.*
> *I might have been coy with another boy,* °
> *But not when you said "Ahoy" to me.*
> *I'm a pearl of a girl, so give me a whirl.*
> *Ah, don't be a perfect churl to me.*

(*As Fern and Rex lock lips, harsh light floods the room, and Fleetwood Rumsey, his bull neck distended with rage, stands glaring balefully at the pair.*)

FLEETWOOD: So this is what gives out behind my back.

FERN (*returning his ring*): Fleetwood, I think there is something you ought to know.

FLEETWOOD: In due time. First, I mean to show this meddling upstart how we deal with kiss thieves in Heublein's Fens. (*Sidestepping nimbly, Rex pins him in a grip of steel and slowly forces him to his knees.*)

REX: *Les jeux sont faits*, "Short Weight" Rumsey!

FLEETWOOD (*paling*): You—you know me then?

REX: Your leering visage adorns every rogue's gallery in the country. (*encircling his captive's wrists with a set of shiny handcuffs*)

Thanks to you, Miss Replevin, a notorious malefactor has received his just lumps. He had been adulterating his poultry mash with sawdust and subspecification brans, causing a serious crimp in egg production.

FERN: My woman's intuition warned me. I wouldn't wipe my feet on the best part of him.

REX: Governmental appreciation will follow in due course. We have every reason to believe him the agent of a foreign power.

FLEETWOOD (*gutturally*): I get efen wiz you for zis zome time, Mr. Rex Beeswanger!

REX: Take him away, boys. (*Fleetwood is removed by two burly operatives as a corps de ballet of forty trained dancers swirls about Fern and Rex, symbolizing the gratitude of local poultrymen and 4-H Clubs alike. As the spectacle reaches a climax, the ushers, equipped with phosphorescent truncheons, flit through the darkened theater like myriad fireflies and awaken the audience. On second thought, I don't believe I'll be in the Brass Rail tonight after all. There's no sense sticking my chin out.*)

CURTAIN

❧ NOTHIN' COULD BE FINER THAN TO DINE FROM MANNY'S CHINA IN THE MORNIN'

(A POWER DIVE INTO THE NEW JOURNALISM)

ONCE in every newspaper's life comes a time when it feels it should interview Tommy Manville. PM's time came when it was announced that Thomas Franklin, Jr., was going to take Darlene Marlowe as his eighth wife. We called one of our girls over, told her we couldn't recall that any paper had ever tried to explain why Tommy was that way or what he seriously sought in life. Would she see what could be done along those lines?

Starting with a clipping that said Tommy sometimes stayed at the Savoy-Plaza, our girl called there.

"No, dear," said the Savoy-Plaza operator, "he's not here. He hasn't been here in over a year."

Our girl sent out some telegrams, made a lot of phone calls to hotels and night clubs. The net result was a lot of reports the Manville-Marlowe romance was off.

Then our girl's phone rang. She answered it and heard: "This is good old Tommy Manville," in a man's voice that ended in a little low giggle.—*From a recent Sunday* PM.

[*Every once in a while a little fifteen-cent magazine like* The New Yorker *hears that some out-of-town person or other has arrived in New York. Being a little fifteen-cent magazine, we naturally have sources of information, or "pipe lines," that other folks don't. So when we heard that Manuel Dexterides, who is supposed to know more about Tommy Manville than Tommy Manville knows about himself, was in town from the Coast, we thought you'd like to know what Dexterides was thinking these days. We called in one of our girls and asked her to see what she could find out. She said she would have loved doing it, but she was having her nails done that day at*

259

Elizabeth Arden's (The New Yorker *carries no advertising it cannot get), and she hoped we would ask her again soon. Her roommate happened to walk in just then, so we asked her to take over, and this is what she learned. We'll let her tell it in her own words, because we believe they are pretty good words for a Sarah Lawrence alumna, and because they reflect what people are thinking and feeling down here at* The New Yorker *office.*]

THE PHOTOGRAPHER and I started out one cold morning last week from the corner of Forty-fifth and Forty-sixth to find Mr. Dexterides. (The copy desk says Forty-fifth and Forty-sixth don't intersect, but ordinary people, the kind who bear their own children and rarely go to the Persian Room, don't look at things through the eyes of a copy desk.) We had some trouble figuring out how to get uptown, as that part of Manhattan is full of short streets running at different angles, so we decided not to look for Mr. Dexterides until the following day and went instead to Café Society Downtown to interview genial Barney Josephson, but he was out of town. The next morning I met the photographer at the Kiss Room of El Borracho, and we called the Sherry-Netherland to see if Mr. Dexterides was staying there. The operator sounded pretty suspicious, though she finally put us through. A woman's voice with a faint foreign accent answered. She got excited when we explained what we wanted.

"Use the towels in the hamper!" she cried. "You think I'm made of towels?" I jiggled the hook and asked the operator whether she had given me the right connection. She rang off. I didn't need to be told twice what the policy of the Sherry-Netherland's management was toward *New Yorker* employees. We went round the corner to the Hamburger Hearth, had a cup of coffee you would have paid fifteen cents for at any de-luxe hotel, and talked it over. The photographer suggested we call up Celebrities Service, which tells you where prominent people are staying, but that seemed too uncomplicated. Eventually, after checking half a dozen columnists and Broadway tipsters, we picked up a rumor that Dexterides was registered under the name of Barney Zweifel at the Hotel Whitebait on Forty-fifth Street. A cold, tight voice told us to come over whenever we liked. We killed a little time to show we weren't too anxious, had a nickel cup of coffee in a drugstore that would have cost a dime in any hamburger joint, and headed for the Whitebait.

There were four men playing poker in Room 602, and the air was thick with some sort of tobacco smoke I couldn't identify. Then I noticed that all of them had curious brown cylinders clamped in their teeth. I asked if these were cigars.

"You said it, dearie," one man told me. (I discovered later that terms of endearment like "darling" and "honey" are frequent in the colorful horse-racing patois of Times Square.) I said I'd been sent by *The New Yorker* to sound out Dexterides. A heavy-set man, kind of benevolent, yet sneaky in the way you remember your uncle, looked up quickly. His cigar fell out of his mouth. I could tell he was startled.

"You're Zweifel, aren't you?" He nodded. "The grapevine says Zweifel is Dexterides. That means you're Dexterides."

"It does, hey?" he asked cautiously, hugging his hand closer to him.

"You play your cards pretty close to your chest, don't you, Mr. Dexterides?" I said.

"It's the only way I can see them," he apologized. "I'm a very near-sighted man."

"Look," I said, taking the bull by the horns, "our readers want to get behind your façade. To them Dexterides is an enigma. What are you really like, underneath?"

"Scram, boys," said Dexterides briefly. Two of his friends rose and went out. The other went out without rising. Dexterides gave me a shy, pleasant smile that reminded me of a little boy, and indicated the photographer. "Do we need him too? It could be real clubby in here." I saw that the presence of a third person embarrassed him, and asked the photographer to wait in the corridor. Dexterides explained that the hotel had a rule prohibiting visitors from waiting in the corridor, and suggested that he wait in the lobby, or, better still, the *New Yorker* office. As soon as we were alone, Dexterides' air of reserve vanished. He mixed two ginger-ale highballs, adjusted the Venetian blind so the sun wouldn't shine in my eyes while I was writing, and seated himself on the davenport by me. I told him our readers wanted to know what he was thinking about Tommy Manville these days. He frowned.

"Hats off to that question," he said seriously. "It's a good one. I'd say Tommy is a man that is in the prime of life at the present time." His eyes twinkled. "Funny thing about age. Now, I place you about eighteen or a little younger."

"I'll be twenty-three in March."

"Then I'm in the clear," he said, with a deep, full-throated chuckle that was thoroughly infectious. You knew instinctively that this warm, friendly man enjoyed simple things and people, and still there was a wholesome faith, almost akin to idealism, about him. Somehow I saw him standing at the right hand of King John on the Field of the Cloth of Gold as the Magna Carta was being signed. I asked him to outline his personal philosophy.

"I believe the day is coming when it will be possible to tell a person's age from their hands," he said. "I've made a study of the subject over the last few years. Take yours, for instance." To illustrate his theory, he gently manipulated my fingers, showing how excessive writing causes fatigue and how the soft cup of the palm acts as a cushion.

"As a matter of fact," he went on, "a girl with your type hands shouldn't be engaged in your particular type work. You ought to have a little spot of your own, which you could stick around all afternoon there in merely a kimono and play with a little poodle or so."

"But, Manny," I said (he had insisted we conduct the interview as informally as possible), "don't you think the American woman of today must take her place shoulder to shoulder with men?"

"Hats off to that spirit," endorsed Dexterides emphatically. "Shoulder to shoulder is my motto one hundred per cent. Here, babe, leave me throw that pillow out of the way so it don't distress your back." It was impossible, I said to myself, that I had met this kindly, considerate man only today; I felt we had known each other for years. His voice had a husky quality that was oddly appealing. "At the same time," he continued, "it behooves each and every one of you to make the most of theirself, so as to keep faith with the boys in the forward areas. Take your hair, now," he said thoughtfully. "Why do you wear it in a flat bun like that? Allow me." He took it down and draped it loosely over my shoulders. "And those moccasins," he went on, "they're stifling your feet. You never saw a wild animal wearing moccasins, did you? It's flying in the face of Nature." I removed them and was amazed at the sense of liberation it gave me.

"If I may turn personal for a moment," I asked, "what reactions do you, as a public figure, have regarding women's clothes?"

"There you will think me a bit unconventional," laughed Dexterides. "I think they wear too many—that is, too many of the wrong kind," he added hastily. "You got to let your body breathe. It is my belief that young women today are deliberately strangling their form under layers of rayon and acetate, thus doing untold harm to future generations. Of course, I do not include garments with a bit of spice to them, such as those lacy black doodads, which I am personally very partial to them. I forget exactly what you call them." He poured a fourth highball and we tried to think of the word he meant. "I'll show you later," he offered. "I know a little specialty shop nearby that stays

open till nine." The mention of time recalled me to a sense of my responsibilities. I looked quickly at my wrist watch, but it was gone. So
was my pad and pencil, and to make matters worse, I had completely
forgotten to bring along my press pass. For all Mr. Dexterides knew,
I might have been any little tramp from across the hall, but it never
made a particle of difference in his attitude.

Sitting here in the office and looking back over the rest of our interview, I don't recall much of general interest that happened after this
point. Broadly speaking, I got the impression of a masterful, com-
pelling personality governed by the maxim "If you don't see what you
want, ask for it." Hats, shoes, and clothes off to Manuel Dexterides, a
rugged, unaffected American and a generous host, a man whose single-
mindedness of purpose takes your breath away and points toward
the dawn of a new tomorrow.

🌷 *THE SWEETER THE TOOTH, THE NEARER THE COUCH*

IT MUST HAVE BEEN about ten days after my arrival on the island of Penang, in British Malaya, that I first became positive I was talking to myself. The realization dawned on me at four-thirty one afternoon as I was seated in a room at the Western & Occidental Hotel examining the tea tray the native boy had just left. On it was the same everlasting finger banana and potted-meat sandwich he had been bringing me every morning and afternoon for the past week. "Finger bananas and potted-meat sandwiches," I suddenly heard myself say in a strained, furious voice. "Potted-meat sandwiches and finger bananas. So that's what you came all the way to the storied East for—to sit in this benighted, pestilential hole reading Penguin reprints and eating potted-meat sandwiches. And now," I went on bitterly, "you're talking to yourself to boot. Nice going. Keep on this way, lover, and the next thing you know, you'll be running amok with a kris in your teeth."

The conviction that I was batting a very sticky wicket had, as a matter of fact, been growing steadily in me almost from the moment I had set foot on the island. Penang (unless it has since sunk into the sea without leaving a trace, a thought that fills me with equanimity) lies off the Malayan coastline twenty-four hours northwest of Singapore. In a moment of aberration, I had proceeded from Siam to Penang, assured by everyone that I could expect an idyllic interlude there before going on to Ceylon on the steamer due within the fortnight. I found that at least two of the claims my informants had made for Penang were accurate. Its beaches *were* the equal of any in the South Seas, and, they should have added, equally accessible. The food at the Western & Occidental was indeed as good as that of the Raffles in Singapore, and a more ambiguous compliment is hardly conceivable. Both establishments served a variety of fried bread that melted in the mouth, fusing your inlays with it. In the hands of their chefs, the mango lost none of its unique aromatic flavor, and to anyone who loves kerosene there can be no warmer tribute.

After a trip—freely punctuated with nosebleeds—up the funicular

264

railway, a visit to a couple of sleazy dance halls full of overwrought fifteen-year-old Malay jitterbugs, and a hike through the botanical gardens culminating in a painful bite from a parakeet, I decided I had had a plethora of sightseeing and badly needed the society of Europeans. The only ones in evidence were the British civil servants in the hotel lobby glowering into their gin pahits and gimlets and explaining to each other that the Nips had captured Singapore by trickery. My tentative efforts to fraternize with them quickly defined the status of the American tourist in Penang. "The cheek of that beggar!" I overheard a scarlet-faced bureaucrat exploding when he thought I was out of earshot. "Did you see him cotton up to me with that smarmy smile?" His companion shook his head commiseratingly. It always happened when you let these Yankees in, he said. Nothing but a pack of cardsharps and blacklegs. The whole tone of the place went to the demnition bow-wows.

It was on the twenty-third of May, however, that the real nightmare began—the chain of afflictions that determined me to restrict my future tropical travel to a tufted ottoman and the pages of Somerset Maugham. I remember the date because it was my wife's birthday, and, having sent off a congratulatory cable collect, I threw down an extra peg in her honor before dinner. It was just as well I did, for it helped anesthetize me to a meal that would have touched off a mutiny in the hulks at Portsmouth. I struggled inadequately with a viscous chlorinated soup, filet of squid basted with lard, and a dollop of tapioca awash in sorghum, and then, sore in spirit, plodded out into the town, desperate for some way to occupy the hours until bedtime. The prospect of seeing either of the two Tarzan films was insupportable, especially as I had seen them twice already—on the two previous evenings—and my knowledge of the Hokkien dialect was too rudimentary to enable me to appreciate the Chinese ritual play at the New World amusement park.

I had been drifting about aimlessly for over an hour, gaping at the fighting fish in the pet shops and watching the rattan weavers plait their baskets, when an overwhelming urge for candy gripped me. Now, I am perfectly aware what scorn a confession of this sort may arouse; a passion for sweets has subjected me for years to the derision of friends and family alike. Notwithstanding, at the risk of being classed as a leper, I can envisage circumstances under which one might prefer a peanut cluster to a pony of armagnac, when the craving for a caramel can become so keen as to amount to an obsession. That evening in the Penang Road was one of those occasions. I knew that unless I came by a gumdrop or a bit of licorice forthwith, it was goodbye Charlie. Short of murder, there were no lengths I was unprepared to go for a piece of candy, and if murder was unavoidable, I was not going to let mere squeamishness stand in my way.

Luckily, nothing quite so drastic was necessary; scarcely fifty yards away was a fine confectionery store, loaded with all manner of goodies and run by an extremely obliging Chinese. Through whatever devious black-market channels, he had procured a supply of Swiss bitter chocolate, a delicacy esteemed by connoisseurs above white jade, and ten times as rare in the Orient. Purely as a stopgap, I purchased two economy-size bars, half a pound each of peanut brittle and crystallized ginger, and a dozen caraway cookies, and, assuring the proprietor that I would return the next day to lay in a real stock if they proved satisfactory, sprinted back to my room. I would have preferred to hold my debauch elsewhere than under a mosquito netting that kept entangling itself in the peanut brittle, but except for the light by the bed the room was bathed in dense shadow, and a man is entitled to see what he is eating. Nevertheless, and despite an uncomfortable suspicion that the affair was akin to a dormitory revel, it was a deeply satisfying experience, and conscious for the first time since landing on Penang of a measure of contentment, I fell asleep.

My serenity was short-lived. The next morning at seven-thirty, as I sat up in bed gulping down the perpetual tea, potted-meat sandwich, and banana, I noticed a fuzzy, darkish line vibrating across the floor from the windows to the dresser. I dismissed it as some trifling myopia caused by my gluttony of the night before, but when it was still there an hour later, an obscure disquietude stole over me. It turned to horror when I investigated the bag of sweets I had left lying open on the dresser top. Swarms of tiny red ants were churning through the candy, purloining huge fragments of ginger and chocolate. Leaning perilously over the window sill, I could see their caravan extending three stories up the façade of the building, right to my quarters. In the first access of panic, I went numb. It seemed futile to join battle with an enemy numbering into the millions, whose patience was proverbial and who knew the local terrain so much better than I. Then a cold fury possessed me. Nobody was going to deprive *me* of the one consolation I had found in this miserable backwater; I'd show the little red devils what American know-how is capable of under pressure. "Think you can bulldoze me, do you?" I cried. "Well, you wait, my friends. I've got a couple of tricks up my sleeve you never heard of, and, what's more, I have not yet begun to fight!"

By dint of searching over half of Penang that afternoon, I finally located a tinsmith's shop, where I bought a metal box about six inches long and four deep. It had a tight-fitting cover I was sure would exclude any marauders, but to make doubly certain I also provided myself with a roll of rubber bicycle tape. The Chinese candy merchant started making obeisances a full block away as I approached his bazaar. Though he exerted every possible blandishment, I waved aside the assortment of lozenges, lollipops, and peppermints he had prepared and bade him fill the box with a duplicate of my previous purchase.

If a single ant remained in my bedchamber when I got back to it, the sharp eye of the room boy had overlooked it. A penetrating odor of disinfectant hung over everything, including, to my particular chagrin, the mosquito netting, so that my bedtime snack lost some of its savor. This was compensated for, however, by the triumph I felt as I sealed the box with the rubber tape and concealed it in a dresser drawer before turning in. Maybe I wasn't pukka enough for those stuffed shirts in the lobby, I chuckled, but I could teach them a thing or two about ants.

My house of cards tumbled abruptly when I got up the following morning. Not only were the poachers back but they had insinuated themselves into the drawer and were rifling the box with complete contempt for the lid and the rubber tape. Their persistence might have moved me to admiration had I not been so thoroughly enraged. Apart from the shock to my vanity, it was clear a way must be found to circumvent them before they bankrupted me. At length, I hit on a solution that should have occurred to me earlier. There was one barrier they could never breach—a good, lethal insect powder. That night, equipped with a totally fresh batch of candy and a can of ten-per-cent DDT, I took special pains to render the box impregnable. I crisscrossed it with tape, sprinkled a moat of DDT around it, sealed the drawer itself with tape, and dusted the powder along the route the ants had followed. My slumber was chaotic and intermittent; twice I got up to reconnoiter, the second time just prior to dawn, but there was no sign of them. I sank back into bed suffused with an overpowering sense of relief. However costly the contest had been in self-esteem and nervous strength, victory was mine at last.

I pray I shall never again suffer the anguish I experienced when I opened my eyes and beheld the blurred, wavering column pulsating across the floor and up the front of the dresser. None of my obstacles had retarded the creatures in the slightest; on the contrary, to judge from their vigor and increased number, the DDT had stimulated them and whetted their appetite. They scurried in and out of the drawer, singing chanteys as they worked, pausing only to thumb their noses jeeringly in my direction. By the time the boy padded in with the tea, the sandwich, and the banana, I had recovered sufficient aplomb to consider the situation with some degree of detachment. I hesitated to employ the one remaining arrow in my quiver, and yet to quit Penang knowing I had been worsted by both man and beast would throw a pall over the rest of my journey. Using bribery and every scrap of pidgin I could muster, I explained to the boy that I wished a set of glass casters filled with gasoline placed under the legs of the dresser. The smirk that invaded his face clearly betrayed his opinion of white eccentricity and I could tell there would be high hilarity belowstairs, but I was hardly in a position to take umbrage. At the candy shop, buying the same merchandise the fourth day in a row, I cloaked my humiliation with an unnecessary display of brusqueness. Significantly enough, the sweet-meats no longer inflamed me as they had; in fact, I had difficulty in repressing a shudder when the storekeeper invited me to try a coconut bar on the house, an offer that formerly would have brought the roses to my cheeks. On the way back to the hotel I filled in the keystone of the arch; I stopped in at the chemist's and bought a quart jar of ant paste.

What the final outcome was, unfortunately, will have to remain a secret until I revisit Penang, which I plan to do the week of the millennium. Just before dinner that evening, as I was smearing ant paste on the candy and taping the entire front of the dresser, talking away to myself thirteen to the dozen, the desk clerk telephoned. My ship was in the harbor and was due to sail in two hours. He was afraid, he said anxiously, that I might have trouble getting aboard on such short notice. No fears were ever less well founded. Fifteen minutes later, a jagged flash, described by some as Halley's comet and by others as an ecstatic American bearing satchels, momentarily lit up the portico of the Western & Occidental Hotel and disappeared in the direction of the waterfront. I gave the room boy five Straits dollars and a Bombay mail address to let me know what he found in 318 the next morning, but I never heard from him. Beggar probably ate the candy, ant paste and all. That's the trouble with those natives—you can't depend on them. Pack of lazy, good-for-nothing loafers; if it weren't for our chaps out there, the whole lot'd go to the demnition bow-wows. And this isn't hearsay, mind you. I've seen the thing with my own eyes.

❦ DON'T BRING ME OSCARS

(*When It's Shoesies That I Need*)

IS THERE ANYDODY hereabouts who would like to pick up, absolutely free, the exclusive American rights to one of the most thrilling documentary films ever left unfinished? I know where such a property can be acquired, together with the exclusive world-wide rights, a brand-new Bell & Howell camera, a director's whistle, a folding canvas chair (my name can always be painted out and your own substituted), a pair of white riding breeches, and a megaphone for barking orders at actors. In fact, I am even prepared to slip a deuce to anyone who removes a bundle containing the foregoing from my flat, and, what's more, I'll throw in the issue of the *Times* that inspired the whole business.

The impulse to capture on film a small but significant segment of the life around me was awakened by a feature article, in the Sunday screen section of that paper, on Roberto Rossellini. "Armed only with a movie camera and an idea," reported a Berlin correspondent, "the gifted director of *Open City* and *Paisan* has been shooting a picture called *Berlin, Year Zero*, with a nonprofessional cast headed by an eleven-year-old street urchin." It was the account of Rossellini's iconoclastic production technique that particularly riveted my attention:

> The script is literally being written as the shooting progresses in an effort to keep it as realistic as possible. When young Edmund, the star, is in a dramatic situation, Rossellini asks, "What would you say if this really happened to you?" The boy comes back with some vivid remark which probably would not get by the Eric Johnston office and if it isn't too obscene it goes into the script. Once during a street scene a truckload of bread went by. Forgetting everything, Edmund piped, "My goodness, I could eat all that bread!" "Don't cut, don't cut!" shouted Rosellini. "Leave it in!"

The unabashed, Rabelaisian coarseness of Edmund's remark understandably made me blush like a scarlet peony, but when the shock

269

had subsided, it presented a challenge. If Edmund's exclamation was dramatic, the casual dialogue around my own household was pure Ibsen. For all I knew, the prattle I brushed aside as humdrum or picayune had a truly Shakespearean majesty and sweep; collected on celluloid, it might wring the withers of moviegoers across the nation, send them alternately sobbing and chuckling into a thousand lobbies to extol my genius. I saw myself feted as the poet of the mundane, the man who had probed beneath the banality and commonplaceness of the American home and laid bare its essential nobility. The thought of the prestige and money about to accrue made me so giddy that I felt a need to lie down, but as I was already lying down I merely removed the *Times* from my face and consolidated my plans. Using the family as actors, and the Rossellini method of improvisation, I would make a documentary of an afternoon in the life of some average New York apartment dwellers. I summoned my kin and excitedly outlined the project. My wife's enthusiasm was immediate, though she cloaked it under a show of apathy; it was evident she was livid at not having conceived the idea herself.

"A really crackpot notion," she admitted, confusing the word with "crackerjack" with typical feminine disregard for the niceties of slang. "You've outdone yourself this time."

"I ought to be the star," whined my son, an eleven-year-old house urchin. "I was in our school play last year."

"No, me, me!" shrilled his sister. "I want to wear Mummy's mascara!"

"Get this, Mr. Burbage," I snapped, "and you too, Dame Terry. This is one picture without stars, or make-up, or any of that Hollywood muck. I want authenticity, see? Don't try to act; just be natural. Behave as if there were no camera there at all."

"If you want *complete* realism," began my wife, her face brightening hopefully, "why not do away with the cam—"

"That'll do," I interposed. "Now put on your *rebozos* and slope out of here, the lot of you. I've got a pretty heavy production schedule, and I haven't time to *schmoos* with actors. Remember, everybody on the set tomorrow at three sharp—we start grinding whether you're here or not." I spent the remainder of the day as a seasoned old showman would, gulping bicarbonate of soda, reading *Variety*, and evolving a trademark for my stationery. The trademark offered something of a problem. After toying with the idea of combining the emblems of J. Arthur Rank and M-G-M, to show a slave striking a lion, I rejected it as socialistic and devised one that portrayed a three-toed sloth pendant from a branch, over the motto *"Multum in Parvo."* The exhibitors might not understand it too well, and, frankly, I didn't either, but it had dignity and a nice swing to it.

The first player to report at the appointed hour next day was my son; he entered the foyer wearing an Indian war bonnet and a bathrobe, an outfit that did not seem characteristic of a lad fresh from school, especially in the dead of winter. He assured me, though, that he and his mates occasionally liked to vary their standard costume of snow jackets and arctics, and I got a trucking shot of a small Indian in a pitch-black hallway that I will match against anything of the sort Hollywood has to offer. Renewing my strictures that my son was to behave spontaneously and follow his normal routine, I dissolved to the living room, crouched down between the andirons, and prepared to take an arresting camera angle of his movements, shooting through the fire screen. In a rather self-conscious, stagy manner, the boy deposited his briefcase on a table, lit a pipe, and, settling into an armchair, buried himself in an article on holystoning in the *Antioch Review*.

"Hold on a second, Buster," I said, puzzled. "There's something wrong here. I don't know what it is, but an artificial note's crept in. Somehow I get the feeling you're acting. Think hard—is this what you actually do every afternoon?"

"Sure." He nodded. "Sometimes I add up the checkbook and then kick the dog, the way you do. Shall I do that?" Eventually, I managed to impress on him the difference between reality and make-believe, a distinction philosophers have been struggling to clarify for the last twelve hundred years, and he consented to re-enact his habitual procedure, warning me, in all fairness, that it might entail a certain amount of damage.

"Smash anything you like," I ordered impatiently. "Let's have the truth, the more gusto the better. The rest is mere bookkeeping." He shrugged and, retrieving his briefcase, scaled it across the room to indicate how he generally discarded it. An exquisite porcelain Buddha that had cost me thirty dollars and two days of haggling in Hong Kong crashed to the floor. It made such a superb closeup that I could not repress a cry of elation.

"Bravo! Tiptop!" I encouraged. "Whatever you do, keep rolling—don't break the rhythm! I'm getting it all!" Humming a gay little air, the actor turned into the kitchen and helped himself to a bowl of rice pudding, half a cream cheese, an orange, a stalk of celery, and a glass of charged water, leaving the cap off the bottle and the door of the refrigerator open. I then panned with him to the breadbox, where he surreptitiously trailed his finger through the icing on a chocolate cake and nibbled the corner of a napoleon. In the ensuing shot, another transition, we milked the hall closet for some surefire footage. He made a routine check of my overcoat, observing that he frequently found change in the pockets and that it tended to gather rust if left there indefinitely. On the threshold of his room, a strange hesitancy overcame him. He paused, obviously loath to reveal the next phase for fear of parental censure.

"I—I just turn on Jack Armstrong and do my homework till it's time to black Sister's eye," he said evasively.

"Come, come," I prodded. "We're not in the cutting room yet. You left something out."

"Well-l-l," he said, "once in a while I blow up the toilet."

"What for?" I demanded, aghast.

"Nothing," he replied. "It makes a nice sound." All the fellas, it appeared on cross-examination, diverted themselves with this scholarly pastime, and since I realized that my canvas must stand or fall on its fidelity to nature, I set myself to film it. Preparations were soon complete; with smooth efficiency, the boy emptied a can of lye into the bowl, attached a long cord to the handle, and, flinging a lighted match into the lye, yanked the cord. There was a moment's ominous silence. Then a roar like the bombardment of Port Arthur shook the plumbing, and a nine-foot geyser of water reared skyward, subsiding in a curtain of mist. The effect, photographically speaking, was similar to what one sees when standing under Niagara Falls (except for the towels and the toothbrushes in the background, of course); actuarially speaking, it shortened my life ten years. The end result, nevertheless, was worth while, for in his exultation the child uttered a line immeasurably more graphic than that of Rossellini's young hero.

"My goodness!" he exclaimed. "I'd certainly hate to have to mop up all that water!"

"Don't cut, don't cut!" I shouted. "Leave it in!" The fact that we had no sound equipment and that Junior's *mot* had not been recorded in the first place weakened my position somewhat, but then, you can't have everything.

With the poor sense of timing you might expect of amateurs, my wife and daughter chose this, of all moments, to arrange their entrance, arms heaped with groceries, and in the restricted area of the foyer I was unable to jockey the camera to obtain a first-rate composition. The

good woman instantly raised a hue and cry over the state of the bathroom, forgetful of the fundamental movie axiom that omelets are never
made without breaking eggs. My brief statement that we had simply
blown up the toilet reassured her, however, and, pointing out how the
overhead was piling up, I urged her to go about her customary activities. A sequence chock-full of human interest resulted, in which she
deliberately mislaid or hid all my important papers and shirt studs, sent
out the wrong ties to the cleaners, and made a series of dinner dates on
the telephone with people she knew I could not abide. To quicken the
tempo and ensure flexibility of mood, I intercut several shots of my
daughter daubing water colors on the rug and writhing in a tantrum
before her music stand.

"Capital," I applauded my troupe. (Performers, and very young
ones in particular, are like children—you have to play upon their
vanity.) "Now, Son," I said, "you'll have to handle the camera, because here's where I usually come home." To a man, they all cringed
involuntarily, but my directorial eye was quick to detect and rectify
the fallacy. "Get those two shakers of Martinis ready, and remember,
everyone, shouts of glee when Daddy walks in." In a trice, I had slipped
into the part—merely a matter of sagging a shoulder or two and assuming a murderous scowl. Just as I was shuffling toward the outside
door to build up suspense for my arrival, it burst open violently, and
three characters I had not foreseen in my budget catapulted in. In the
order of their ascending hysteria, they were the furnaceman, the elevator boy, and the superintendent. The last carried what we theatrical
folk call a prop—a fire ax—and, in the parlance of the greenroom, he
was winging.

The scene that followed, though noisy and fraught with tension, was
of little cinematic consequence. It dealt with some argle-bargle about
a flood in the apartment below, and its audience appeal, except to
plumbers and, possibly, a lawyer or two, would be slight. I understand
that additional scenes, or "retakes," are to be made on it very shortly
in Essex Market Court. I may drop down there just out of sheer curiosity. My schedule isn't nearly as heavy as it was, now that I've shut
down active production at the studio.

❧ *DANGER IN THE DRAIN*

CASE HISTORIES from Macy's Bureau of Standards' files. THE CASE OF THE INDELIBLE BATH. *Offered to Macy's:* a preparation purported to reduce obese persons while bathing. *Rejected* for its dubious merits, with the side comment that should a few drops of iodine chance to fall into the tub while this preparation was being used, the bather would turn a bright and unforeseen blue. In drugs, you are protected by city, state, and federal authorities. In Macy's, you are further protected by our own tests, run off on the spot, when we consider stocking anything.—*Macy adv. in the* Times.

INSPECTOR GREGORY STAINES, second in command of the Central Confidential Division of Macy's Bureau of Standards (frivolously referred to as C.C.D.M.B.S. by those "in the know" if they deem one trustworthy and unlikely to tattle), leaned his elbows on the checked tablecloth of our booth in the Blue Ribbon and regarded me quizzically out of a mild blue eye. It was the only one he could regard me out of, the other having atrophied permanently over the years from excessive waggishness. A large, shaggy sheep dog of a man, Gregory affects a deliberate untidiness in his dress and constantly pulls on a foul-smelling pipe, in accord with the prevailing convention in detectives. Though the pipe causes him acute nausea and he is constitutionally thin and meticulous, an unremitting study of English crime films and the novels of Georges Simenon has helped make him authentic. It has required a perseverance and gluttony few men are capable of to transform himself into a picturesque slob, but Staines has done it. As for his ability, that is unquestioned. There is no eye quicker to spy a defective bit of kapok in a mattress, nobody who can sniff out with such celerity the single mildewed olive in the jar. Not for nothing—in other words, for something—do his admiring co-workers call him the Bulldog of the Bureau.

"I say, old man," he observed tolerantly. "Of course, it's none of my business, but aren't you playing rather fast and loose with your dry cleaner?"

"Why, how do you mean?" I asked, nonplused. Gregory has a way of pouncing when one is sodden with cheesecake that makes it easy to understand why his colleagues also call him the Jaguar of the Bureau.

"Your sleeve," he pointed out. "It's resting in a pool of ketchup." I looked down with a surprised start. It was true; his uncanny orb, swift to note minutiae the layman overlooks, had unerringly spotted the deviation from the norm. As I hastened, somewhat flustered, to sponge it off, Gregory revealed how he had arrived at his conclusion. "I thought at first it was blood," he disclosed, "but then I saw an upset condiment bottle next to it, and ruled out all possibilities until I hit on the right one."

"It sounds easy enough when you explain it," I said ruefully.

"Just routine." He shrugged. "By the way, better brush those caraway seeds off your vest while you're at it. We've found down at the Bureau that the spores work their way into tweed and produce a condition in the wearer known as 'dismay.' " He went on to relate an instance where poppy seeds that had become embedded in a customer's suit in a West Side delicatessen had led to a bothersome action for damages against Macy. The customer, alleging that he was continually being beset by flocks of English sparrows, charged that the seeds had originally been woven into the fabric. Weeks of patient investigation, costly chemical analyses, and the testimony of scores of witnesses had been needed to refute his claim.

"Extraordinary life you chaps lead," I commented. "Take that case of yours I read about in the *Times*—the reducing preparation that turned its users bright blue."

"The *Times*?" He frowned. "What's that?" For a man whose knowledge is practically encyclopedic, Staines at times betrays a surprising ignorance of his environment. I told him it was a daily newspaper serving the New York area.

"I don't believe I know it," he ruminated. "At any rate, that *was* a puzzler, the affair of the indelible bath. Care to hear the story?"

"No," I replied. Gregory knocked the ashes from his pipe into the sugar bowl, stirred the mixture reflectively, and began. It was as strange a tale, God wot, as those hoary walls had heard in many a moon, and when he got through telling it, they were no younger.

The first inkling Staines had that anything was amiss was the arrival, on a raw March morning, as he was finishing a kipper in his office, of a messenger with a chit from Grimsditch, his superior. Not to put too fine a point on it, Gregory was feeling a bit peckish. To begin with, he

abhors kippers and forces himself to eat them only because it is unthinkable for an inspector to start the day otherwise. For another thing,
Grimsditch's chits—or the chits of Grimsditch, to employ a more felicitous phrase—are totally unnecessary. His office is right next door,
and he could as easily have summoned Gregory over the ground-glass
partition. But his colonial love of ceremony (he trained in various remote outposts like Neiman-Marcus in Dallas and Gump's in San Francisco) finds its outlet in these irritating formalities. With a sigh, Gregory detached the gas ring he had used to broil the fish and stowed it in
his desk. Under his breath, he cursed the regulations that forbade
Macy employees to cook during store hours, forcing them into a hundred ignoble stratagems. For, you see, Gregory is something of an
idealist *manqué*.

"Humph," growled Grimsditch when his subordinate entered.
"Morning, Staines. I'd appreciate a moment or two of your valuable
time, if I'm not interrupting an after-breakfast nap." Gregory was not
sure, but he thought he detected an undercurrent of sarcasm in the Old
Man's greeting. More than likely, he had got the wind up over some
customer's complaint, and so it proved.

"Look at that!" he snapped, extending a half-eaten baby rattle.
"Woman from Sunnyside brought it in this morning. Our guarantee
says it's inedible."

"Our guarantee *is* inedible," retorted Staines. "I defy anybody—"

"No, no, man, the *rattle*," Grimsditch broke in, exasperated. "I
thought our laboratory had tested it."

"They did," said Gregory. "I had two of the junior operatives teeth-
ing on it for donkey's years." He scrutinized the toy closely and
straightened up in triumph. "No baby chewed that," he declared positively. "Those are the tooth marks of a three-year-old schnauzer."

"The deuce you say!" exclaimed Grimsditch.

"Unmistakable," Gregory said. "Note the aggressive upward sweep
of the canines, the powerful, even crunch of the molars. You are familiar with my monograph on the tooth marks of the three-year-old
schnauzer?"

"No, but I certainly plan to be," said Grimsditch, impressed. "By
gad, my boy, I shan't forget the way you handled this."

"Nothing at all, sir." Gregory dismissed it. "I merely used the old
think-box, is all. What's new in that matter of the reducing preparation?"

"Blowed if I know," confessed the chief peevishly. "We can't break
down the manufacturer's claim that it melts away the fat—three of our

researchers disappeared completely yesterday—but it also seems to affect the pigmentation. Here's the chart." Gregory's forehead puckered as his eye skimmed over the findings; something was definitely out of whack. Latrobe and Shenstone had turned forest green as a result of bathing in the solution, Kugler had emerged streaked with vermilion, and Dismukes was a rich cocoa-brown plaid. Furthermore, the colors were fast; pumice, paint remover, and even emery wheels had been tried without success on the subjects' skins.

"Mind if I take a dekko at the experiment?" proposed Staines. Deep in his subconscious, a hypothesis, as yet little more than intuitive, was forming that some unknown element in the bath must be responsible for the change. Grimsditch, helpless in the face of an enigma that had baffled the keenest minds in the deparment, embraced the offer eagerly. Placing his entire resources at Gregory's disposal, he escorted him to the door and slipped a compact blue-nickeled charge account into his palm.

"I don't think you'll need it," he counseled, "but if any agents from Saks-Thirty-fourth Street or Altman's are mixed up in this, it's just as well to be prepared." Gregory thanked him and, descending to the kitchenwares, in the basement, took an elevator to the testing laboratory on the roof. To anyone watching him, the maneuver might have appeared purposeless; years of experience, however, had taught him the value of extreme caution. He made his way through a sunny workroom in which besmocked technicians were engaged in tasting oilcloth, setting fire to girdles, jumping up and down on bedsprings, and generally submitting merchandise to normal wear. One of the more unusual probes going forward involved a wheel to each of whose spokes was affixed a metal foot; in the five years the wheel had been revolving, the feet were estimated to have covered a distance of six hundred thousand miles. Inasmuch as Macy's did not sell metal feet, the object of the inquiry was not too clear, but, thought Gregory, it made a whizbang display.

Crabtree, the head supervisory engineer, was awaiting him when he reached the drug section; Grimsditch had sent ahead a chit to herald Gregory's advent. Crabtree was answerable only to Grimsditch, and Grimsditch, in turn, was answerable only to Crabtree—an arrangement that ensured a maximum of harmony and prevented leaks. The strain of the past couple of days had begun to tell on the engineer. His usually rubicund physiognomy was ashen and his face had paled perceptibly.

"Frankly, we're up a tree," Crabtree admitted, conducting Staines into an improvised bathroom where a fat man was disrobing. "We're convinced some foreign substance is tinting our guinea pigs, but hanged if we can isolate the blamed thing. Are you ready, Wagenhals?" The fat man returned a melancholy nod and lowered himself gingerly into the steaming bath. Crabtree, about to add the obesity fluid, suddenly checked his hand.

"What's the matter?" he inquired of the man. "Don't you feel well?"

"I'm O.K.," croaked Wagenhals, his expression belying his words. "It's only—well, I—I heard a rumor that folks looked different after bathing in here."

"Different in what way?"

"That—that they turned various colors, like purple, and orange—"

"Now, hold on, Wagenhals," said Crabtree impatiently. "Have you ever seen any orange people?"

"Just in *Lassie*," faltered the man, "and one time I saw a whaling picture with Don Ameche—"

"Exactly," interposed Crabtree. "Well, forget that cafeteria gossip. You know how people love to talk." He emptied the solvent into the water; instantaneously its surface boiled into an agitated froth, lashing the sides of the tub with extraordinary violence. Had Gregory been watching the bather, he might have seen a hint of clavicle appear below the fleshy throat, the double chin grow taut, but his eyes were pinned on the medicine chest in the wall above Wagenhal's head. Its door was ajar, and from an overturned bottle inside, bluish drops splashed into the bath below.

"Look, look!" cried Crabtree. "He's turning indigo!"

Staines paid him no heed. With the peculiar, catlike spring that earned him the sobriquet of the Polecat of the Bureau, he crossed the floor in a single bound, caught up the bottle, and slammed shut the door of the cabinet. "Get this man into a tubful of fresh water at once!" he barked at the amazed Crabtree. "Another sixty seconds in that witch's broth and I won't answer for the consequences."

"But I don't understand," quavered Crabtree. "What was in the bottle?"

"Eyewash," said Gregory sternly. "An ordinarily innocuous liquid that, as we have learned to our considerable chagrin, can play strange chemical pranks on the unwary, and that, along with iodine, hair tonic, after-shave lotion, and a host of other brews, you have thoughtlessly allowed to fall into the testing medium." And, leaving an openmouthed Crabtree to fold a considerably diminished Wagenhals into a pretested towel, he went downstairs to file his report.

"Well, there you have it," concluded Staines, refilling the bowl of his pipe with ashes and sugar. "The clue was right under their noses, but, of course, they hadn't the sense to see it. Pure, unadulterated eye-wash, found in every bathroom."

"Not to mention one other place," I suggested diffidently.

"What's that?"

"Advertising copy," I said.

Staines rose majestically. "I consider that remark in very poor taste," he announced, "and I intend to convey it to Grimsditch at once." Before I could temporize, he had jammed on his hat and stalked from the restaurant. Not until three seconds after he had gone did I realize that he had forgotten to pay the check. For a man whose love of detail has made his name a watchword at the Blue Ribbon, Staines is at times surprisingly lax.

❦ CLOUDLAND REVISITED: TUBEROSES AND TIGERS

BACK IN THE SUMMER of 1919, a fifteen-year-old youth at Riverside, Rhode Island, a watering place on the shores of upper Narragansett Bay, was a victim of a temporary but none the less powerful hallucination still referred to in southern New England as the "Riverside hallucination." For a space of three or four days, or until the effects of a novel called *Three Weeks*, by Elinor Glyn, had worn off, the boy believed himself to be a wealthy young Englishman named Paul Verdayne, who had been blasted by a searing love affair with a mysterious Russian noblewoman. His behavior during that period, while courteous and irreproachable to family and friends alike, was marked by fits of abstraction and a tendency to emit tragic, heartbroken sighs. When asked to sweep up the piazza, for instance, or bike over to the hardware store for a sheet of Tanglefoot, a shadow of pain would flit across his sensitive features and he would assent with a weary shrug. "Why not?" he would murmur, his lips curling in a bitter, mocking smile. "What else can life hold for me now?" Fortunately, his parents, who had seen him through a previous seizure in which he had identified himself with William S. Hart, were equipped to deal with his vagaries. They toned up his system with syrup of figs, burned his library card, and bought a secondhand accordion to distract him. Within a week, his distraction and that of the neighbors were so complete that the library card was hastily restored and the instrument disposed of—the latter no minor feat, as anyone knows who has ever tried to burn an accordion.

Not long ago, in a moment of nostalgia laced with masochism, it occurred to me to expose myself again to Miss Glyn's classic and see whether the years had diluted its potency. The only vivid recollection I preserved of the story was one of a sultry enchantress lolling on a tiger skin. I realized why the image had persisted when I ultimately tracked down a copy of the book. It was illustrated with scenes from the photoplay production Samuel Goldwyn gave it in 1924, and on the dust jacket, peering seductively at me across a snarling Indian man-eater, lay Aileen Pringle, mascaraed, braided, and palpitant with sex appeal. The very first page I sampled, before settling down to a leisurely feast, yielded a sweetmeat that corroborated my boyhood memory:

"A bright fire burnt in the grate, and some palest orchid-mauve silk curtains were drawn in the lady's room when Paul entered from the terrace. And loveliest sight of all, in front of the fire, stretched at full length was his tiger—and on him—also at full length—reclined the lady, garbed in some strange clinging garment of heavy purple *crêpe*, its hem embroidered with gold, one white arm resting on the beast's head, her back supported by a pile of the velvet cushions, and a heap of rarely bound books at her side, while between her lips was a rose not redder than they—an almost scarlet rose." It was very small wonder that when I originally read this passage, my breathing became shallow and I felt as if the Berea College choir were grouped in the base of my skull singing gems from Amy Woodford-Finden. Even the author seems to have had some fleeting compunction after writing it, for she went on hastily, "It was not what one would expect to find in a sedate Swiss hotel." If it thus affected Paul, you can guess what the impact was on Riverside, where our notion of barbaric splendor was a dish of fried eels.

Three Weeks touched off such a hullabaloo in England that, on its publication here, Miss Glyn wrote an exasperated preface for American readers, enjoining them to consider the spiritual rather than the fleshly aspects of her romance. "The minds of some human beings," she declared scornfully, "are as moles, grubbing in the earth for worms. . . . To such *Three Weeks* will be but a sensual record of passion." The real story, however, she explained, was the purifying effect upon a callow young Englishman of his gambol with a heroine whom Miss Glyn likened to a tiger (a simile she milked pretty exhaustively before the whistle blew) and described as "a great splendid nature, full of the passionate realization of primitive instincts, immensely cultivated, polished, blasé." She concluded her message with a request I am sure every novelist has longed to make at one time or another, and would if he had the courage: "And to all who read, I say—at least be just! and do not skip. No line is written without its having a bearing on the next, and in its small scope helping to make the presentment of these two human beings vivid and clear." I took the entreaty so much to heart that every last asterisk of *Three Weeks* was literally engraved on my brain, which, after two hundred and ninety pulsating pages, must have borne a striking resemblance to an old bath sponge peppered with buckshot.

The situation that obtains at the opening of Miss Glyn's fable, in all honesty, does not rank among the dizzier flights of the human imagination, but, in the vulgate of Vine Street, it's a springboard and what the hell. Paul Verdayne, twenty-two years old, devastatingly handsome, and filthy with the stuff, has been dispatched by his elders on a tour of the Continent to cure his infatuation for a vicar's daughter. Nature, it appears, has been rather more bountiful to Paul's body and purse than to his intellect; above the ears, speaking bluntly, the boy is strictly tapioca. As the curtain rises on what is to be the most electrifying episode of his life, he is discovered moodily dining at a hotel in Lucerne and cursing his destiny. Suddenly, there comes to his nostrils the scent of tuberoses, and a lady materializes at the next table. At first, her exquisite beauty and sensuous elegance are lost on him; then, as she proceeds to sup on caviar, a blue trout, *selle d'agneau au lait*, a nectarine, and Imperial Tokay, he perceives he is face to face with a thoroughbred, and the old familiar mixture of fire and ice begins stirring in his veins. Without any sign that she has noticed his presence, she glides out, overwhelming the young man with her figure: " 'She must have the smallest possible bones,' Paul said to himself, 'because it looks all curvy and soft, and yet she is as slender as a gazelle.' " On a diet like the foregoing, I wouldn't give odds the lady would stay gazelle-slender perpetually, but perhaps her metabolism was as unusual as her charm. In any case, there is, as everyone is aware, a standard procedure for those smitten by mysterious sirens smelling of tuberoses; namely, to smoke a cigar pensively on the terrace, soothe one's fevered senses, and await developments. Paul faithfully adheres to the convention, and at length the lady, presumably having nullified gastritis with a fast Pepto-Bismol, slithers out onto her balcony and casts him a languishing glance. From that point on, it is *sauve-qui-peut* and prudent readers will do well to hold *Three Weeks* at arm's length, unless they want to be cut by flying adjectives.

In the ensuing forty-eight hours, Mme. Zalenska, as Paul ascertains her name to be from the register, plays a hole-and-corner game with her caballero, ogling him from behind beech trees, undulating past him in hotel corridors, and generally raising the deuce with his aplomb. Finally, when she has reduced him to the consistency of jellied consommé, she summons him to her suite for a short midnight powwow. The décor is properly titillating and, inevitably, includes Miss Glyn's favorite carnivore: "The lights were low and shaded, and a great couch filled one side of the room beyond the fireplace. Such a couch! covered with a tiger skin and piled with pillows, all shades of rich purple velvet and silk, embroidered with silver and gold—unlike any pillows he had ever seen before, even to their shapes." Paul, in his pitiable innocence, assumes he has been called to render some neighborly service, like installing a new Welsbach mantle or cobbling Zalenska's shoes. Actually, she wishes to warn him how lethal she is:

" 'Look at me,' she said, and she bent forward over him—a gliding feline movement infinitely sinuous and attractive. . . . Her eyes in their narrowed lids gleamed at him, seeming to penetrate into his very soul. . . . Suddenly she sprang up, one of those fine movements of hers, full of catlike grace. 'Paul,' she said . . . and she spoke rather fast. 'You are so young, so young—and I shall hurt you—probably. Won't you go now—while there is yet time? Away from Lucerne, back to Paris— even back to England. Anywhere away from me.' " Had Paul, at this juncture, slipped into his reefer and whistled for a fiacre, it might have saved both him and me considerable anguish, but Miss Glyn's royalties certainly would have been stricken with anemia. He therefore gallantly confides his heart into the lady's custody, snatches up an armful of tuberoses, and retires to the terrace to stride up and down until dawn, soothing his fevered senses. This is technically known in Publishers' Row as a tease play or the punch retarded, a stratagem designed to keep the savages guessing.

In a brief pastoral interlude next day, idling about the lake in a luxurious motor launch heaped with even stranger pillows and dialogue, Mme. Zalenska's mood is alternately maternal and bombastic. "I wish to be foolish today, Paul," she says (a program she achieves with notable success), "and see your eyes dance, and watch the light on your curls." His ardor becomes well-nigh unendurable when, before teatime, she bends over him with the tantalizing comment "Great blue eyes! So pretty, so pretty!" and he hoarsely begs her for instruction in the art of love. Her orotund answer sets the placid bosom of the lake rippling: "Yes, I will teach you! Teach you a number of things. Together we will put on the hat of darkness and go down into Hades. We shall taste the apples of the Hesperides—we will rob Mercure of his sandals—and Gyges of his ring." Just as the steam is bubbling in Paul's gauges, however, Mme. Zalenska laughingly twists out of his grasp, and another sequence ends with the poor *schlemiel* patrolling his beat on the terrace. Whatever deficiencies of logic the author may display on occasion, she surely cannot be accused of hurrying her climax.

The spark that ignites the tinder, oddly enough, is a gift Paul purchases for his affinity—one of those characteristic souvenirs that litter sedate Swiss hotels, a tiger skin. "It was not even dear as tigers go, and his parents had given him ample money for any follies." Sprawled out on it, strange greenish flames radiating from her pupils, Mme. Zalenska goads the boy to the brink of neurasthenia by withholding the tuition she promised and proposing in its stead a literary debauch. " 'Paul,' she cooed plaintively, 'tomorrow I shall be reasonable again, perhaps, and human, but today I am capricious and wayward, and mustn't be teased. I want to read about Cupid and Psyche from this wonderful *Golden Ass* of Apuleius—just a simple tale for a wet day—and you and—me!' " By then, though, the lad in his own stumble-foot fashion has evolved a more piquant formula for passing a rainy day, and, with a prodigious amount of whinnying, purring, gurgling, and squealing, the education of Paul Verdayne swings into its initial phase.

How high a voltage the protagonists generate in the two remaining weeks of their affair, I cannot state with precision; the dial on my gal-vanometer burst shortly afterward, during a scene where they are shown cradled in a hotel on the Bürgenstock, exchanging baby talk and feeding each other great, luscious red strawberries. At Venice, to which they migrate for no stringent reason except that the author wanted to ring in a vignette of Mme. Zalenska biting Paul's ear lobes in a gondola, there is an account of their pleasure dome that deserves attention:

"The whole place had been converted into a bower of roses. The walls were entirely covered with them. A great couch of deepest red ones was at one side, fixed in such masses as to be quite resisting and firm. From the roof chains of roses hung, concealing small lights— while from above the screen of lilac-bushes in full bloom the moon in all her glory mingled with the rose-shaded lamps and cast a glamour and unreality over the whole. . . . The dinner was laid on a table in the center, and the table was covered with tuberoses and stephanotis, sur-rounding the cupid fountain of perfume."

And now the plot, hitherto snowed under by suchlike verdant *Katz-enjammer*, refuses any longer to be denied. Awakening one noonday from his finals, which he has evidently passed *summa cum laude*, Paul finds a farewell note from his coach, setting forth that they must part forever, inasmuch as sinister forces in her background endanger both their lives. There have been sketchy intimations earlier that Mme. Zalenska is some sort of empress on a toot, or at least a margravine, and Paul has observed several dubious Muscovites tailing them around St. Mark's but, in his exaltation, has dismissed them as phantoms in-duced by overwork. The realization that he is henceforth cut off from postgraduate study exerts its traditional effect, and he goes down like a poled ox. By the time Sir Charles, his father, has arrived bearing cold compresses and beef tea, Paul lies between life and death, madly raving with brain fever. His convalescence, of course, follows the mandatory pattern—the Adriatic cruise aboard a convenient yacht, the Byronic soliloquies in the moonlight, and, back in England, the solitary rambles on the moors with the devoted rough-coated terrier. As time assuages his grief, a new Paul re-enters British society, older, fluent, worldly-wise. He prepares to stand for Parliament, scores a brilliant social success: "He began to be known as someone worth listening to by men, and women hung on his words. . . . And then his complete indifference to them piqued and allured them still more. Always polite and chivalrous, but as aloof as a mountain top." I don't want to sound vindictive, but can you imagine asking a man like that to scoot over to the hardware store for ten cents' worth of fly rolls? That's the kind of thing I was up against on Narragansett Bay thirty years ago.

The rest of *Three Weeks* is soon told, although not soon enough, frankly, by Miss Glyn, who consumes fifty marshmallow-filled pages to accomplish what she might have in two. After an endless amount of palaver, she discloses that Paul's and Zalenska's seminar has resulted in a bonny little cub and that, for all their pledges of devotion, the lovers are never reunited. The latter oversight is excused by as nimble a washup as you will find anywhere in the post-Victorian novel: "Everyone knows the story which at the time convulsed Europe. How a certain evil-living King, after a wild orgie of mad drunkenness, rode out with two boon companions to the villa of his Queen, and there, forcing an entrance, ran a dagger through her heart before her faithful servants could protect her. And most people were glad, too, that this brute paid the penalty of his crime by his own death—his worthless life choked out of him by the Queen's devoted Kalmuck groom." This salubrious housecleaning elevates the tot to the throne, and as the book ends, Paul kneels in the royal chapel before the boy, quivering with paternal pride and chauvinism: "The tiny upright figure in its blue velvet suit, heavily trimmed with sable, standing there proudly. A fair, rosy-cheeked, golden-haired English child . . . And as he gazed at his little son, while the organ pealed out a Te Deum and the sweet choir sang, a great rush of tenderness filled Paul's heart, and melted forever the icebergs of grief and pain."

A few hours after finishing *Three Weeks*, there came to me out of the blue a superb concept for a romantic novel, upon which I have been laboring like a demon ever since. In essence, it is the story of an incredibly handsome and wealthy youth of forty-four whose wife and children, dismayed by his infatuation for servant-girl literature, pack him off to Switzerland. There he meets and falls in love with a ravishing twenty-three-year-old girl, half tigress and half publisher. The tigress in her fascinates him at the same time that the publisher revolts him, and out of this ambivalence, so to speak, grows the conflict. . . . But why am I telling you all this? I can see you're really not listening.

❦ MORTAR AND PESTLE

SCENE: *The office of Bruce Hyssop, general manager of the Condor Pharmacies, a chain of Los Angeles drugstores. This is a handsome oval room sixty feet long with spun-glass fiber walls, carpeted in Turkey-red vicuña; from the production standpoint, a ruinously expensive set which would tax the facilities of the Radio City Music Hall or La Scala in Milan, but don't let's start by pinching pennies. At center, strung from the ceiling by two wires of unequal length, is the executive's nonobjective desk, a vast slab of Philippine mahogany that vibrates capriciously at the slightest touch. Since it contains no drawers and its surface is so tilted that pencils and mail promptly slide off, its value is debatable, but not with Hyssop, who conceived it and whose arrival is momentarily expected as the curtain rises. Facing the desk, and exquisitely uncomfortable in their nonrepresentational chairs, are three of his lieutenants—Swickard, Thimig, and Miss Fackenthal.*

MISS FACKENTHAL: You really ought to try their food, Cyprian. That is, if you like something on the unusual side.

SWICKARD: What's the name of it again?

MISS F.: Frenzi's Fish Grotto. It's out in North Hollywood, just this side of that big musical hypodermic that advertises the hospital plan.

THIMIG: Oh, yes, I've seen it. It's shaped like a casserole.

MISS F.: No, it's shaped like a restaurant. It's a kind of novel idea.

SWICKARD: Say, that's a new twist. Food's good, eh?

MISS F.: Yummy. They take these big Idaho potatoes—honestly, they're almost two feet long—scoop out the inside, and fill them with macaroni. You'd swear you were eating potatoes.

THIMIG: What do they do with the part they scoop out?

MISS F.: They serve it in an eggnog with sour cream, and it's simply heavenly. Ricky and I were so full by the time we got to the Friendly Fevers we could hardly climb up into our trays.

SWICKARD: I've always meant to drop into that fever spot. A lot of picture people go there, I understand.

MISS F.: It's packed. Lauren Bacall's cousin was right in the next oven to me, and she was so gracious and democratic, she couldn't be sweeter. Believe me, when they finish baking out the fatigue, you haven't got a nerve left in your body. And *hungry*! On the way home, we stopped at a Chinese drive-in and had two whole dishes of pork fooyoung.

SWICKARD: Sounds first-rate, Thimig. Let's make up a party some night.

THIMIG: Well, Bedraglia and I haven't stepped out much since we bought our ranch in the Valley. She likes to stick pretty close to her ouija board, you know, and after I rake up the grounds, it's practically bedtime.

SWICKARD: Seems to me you spend half your life raking that place.

THIMIG: I have to. There's an apricot ranch alongside us, and the fruit keeps piling up in our patio and attracting flies.

MISS F.: That's the trouble with those small ranches. You don't have any privacy.

THIMIG: No, ours is good-sized. We've got a forty-foot frontage. But it's the incinerator that makes the property. You'll have to come out some Sunday and taste our ribs.

SWICKARD: How do you fix them?

THIMIG: It's very simple. All you do is mix the barbecue sauce, paint it on, and then, when it's almost dry, lick it off. We got the recipe from an old Spanish hidalgo in Santa Monica.

MISS F.: Gee, I wonder what's holding up Mr. Hyssop. He's usually on the dot.

THIMIG: He went over to inspect the new store in Pasadena. Probably delayed in traffic.

SWICKARD: I wish he'd get a move on. I was planning to have my blood pressure tested before lunch.

THIMIG: Where do you go? Over on South Hill Street?

SWICKARD: Yes, the open-air stand across from where they sell the goat glands. They charge a quarter, but they validate your parking check.

THIMIG: A *quarter*? Most of them do it for fifteen cents.

SWICKARD: Listen, brother, it doesn't pay to skimp on your health. So it costs a little extra; at least you know where you stand. (*Hyssop enters, petulance visible on his plump, sallow face. His aides greet him deferentially.*)

OMNES: How did the sneak preview go last night, B. H.? Did we get a hand on the citrate of magnesia? How many bolts of linoleum did we sell?

HYSSOP (*frowning*): It needs work. From the reaction cards, it looks as if my hunch were right. The average public isn't ready for phone booths in the front of the store.

SWICKARD: Remember my prediction, Bruce? I said it would confuse them!

THIMIG: I experienced dubiety anent it, too. You've got to hide telephones in the back, among the cigarette cartons.

MISS F.: Or down a good, dark stairway, so you can use a neon arrow. Dramatize it—appeal to their sense of adventure, of the unknown.

HYSSOP (*nodding*): Correct. Now, myself, I like the front of our stores kept severe, even a shade Spartan. Just a few airplane tires on a counter, some electric pads, money belts, facial tissues, or so. That whets people's interest and tempts them to browse. (*They all vigorously echo his sentiments. Meanwhile, the desk before him sways erratically, dumping the papers and fountain pen he has placed on it on the floor. As Swickard and Thimig scramble to retrieve them, Hyssop's brow darkens.*) Have any of you been fiddling with these wires?

THIMIG: Gosh, no, Bruce! (*unthinking*) You see, the damp weather causes them to expand and contract, and consequently—

HYSSOP (*instantly*): What's that? Aren't you satisfied with our Southern California climate?

THIMIG (*anguished*): Me? I'm wild about it! I'd rather be dead here than alive in Cedar Rapids—you know that, Bruce!

HYSSOP: You're an Easterner, Thimig. Sooner or later, they always sell you out. (*Thimig demonstrates his loyalty by producing an aerial view of Cedar Rapids, tearing it to shreds, and grinding them under his heel. Hyssop relents.*) All right, but better watch your step hereafter. Well, let's hear the weekly suggestions. Anything promising come in?

MISS F.: There's one from the manager of the Beverly Hills branch. They get a studio-type clientele, mostly, in their fountain, individuals with an acid condition and nervous indigestion.

HYSSOP (*impatiently*): We went into all that last fall. It isn't feasible to spray the customers with cocaine.

MISS F.: No, this is another approach. He says why not add pepsin to some of the ready dishes and feature a line of heartburn specials.

HYSSOP: There's no royal road to stomach relief. Seymour Erstweil is a real go-getter, but he doesn't grasp the basic psychology. The patron *wants* to feel distress coming on, so he can counteract it with the proper medication. Take that away and half the pleasure of eating is gone. You follow?

SWICKARD: I never thought it through before, but you've put your finger on the crux of the matter.

THIMIG (*sotto voce*): Has that man got a gift for congealing the whole thing in a nutshell! It's spooky.

HYSSOP (*modestly*): My mind runs that way. Ever since I'm a tad, why, I've had a restless impulse to probe beneath the surface, to constantly analyze, analyze, analyze.

SWICKARD: Which it's the hallmark of every industrial wizard worth a hoot.

THIMIG: You can say *that* again. (*Swickard starts to say it again, trails off as Hyssop rises and stands plunged in thought.*)

HYSSOP: For instance, the lighting in our stores. I don't know what's wrong, but the clerks still look too normal. They're not waxy enough.

MISS F.: We installed the pistachio-tinted bulbs you wanted.

HYSSOP: Uh-uh, it's a sort of a phosphorescent glow in their skins that I'm after. Unearthly, so to speak.

THIMIG: Would it help any to pipe in organ recitals? Maybe if we slowed down the tempo, we'd get a more trancelike effect.

HYSSOP: No, I guess I'm just reaching for the moon. I only cite this as an example of how the over-all organization could be improved. You can't be petty. You've got to set new horizons on your thinking. I believe Swickard made the point a moment ago that my attack was global. That pleased me.

SWICKARD (*blushing with pleasure*): Thanks, Bruce. In line with that, I've been cuddling my wits for some solution as regards our triple-decker sandwiches. Why can't we make the doily an essential part of the whole, thus luring the diner to consume it along with his repast?

HYSSOP: By George, I think you're on the right track. An edible doily.

SWICKARD: Made out of the same brake lining we use for the toast and the filling. That way, we wouldn't sacrifice the ungainliness we have to retain and there wouldn't be any disgusting leftovers on the dish.

HYSSOP: You've got an exciting notion there, Swickard, but it's earthbound. The plate should be edible too.

THIMIG: And the forks, and the spoons! Why not the whole fountain?

HYSSOP: No, no. One thing at a time. It's vital to keep a line of demarcation between the food and the fixtures.

THIMIG: I was just trying to think globally, Bruce.

HYSSOP: I'll take up the plate idea with the lab. It mustn't be too tasty; it should duplicate the cardboard flavor of the plates we're using at present. Now, was there anything else?

MISS F.: Well, B. H., I've had my ear to the ground lately and I hear a lot of criticism of our soda dispensers. Everyone says they look drab.

HYSSOP: I thought I gave orders to put epaulets and frogs on their tunics.

MISS F.: We did. We even changed their forage caps to bearskins like the Coldstream Guards wear, but the novelty wore off and the patrons are muttering again.

SWICKARD: Boss, can I voice a proposal that it might floor you with its boldness, albeit it's freighted with the germ of an arresting idea?

HYSSOP (*joining his fingertips*): Sketch in the outlines, however nebulous.

SWICKARD: Why not caparison our dispensers in a different costume each week, so as to typify various current fiestas and sports events in the public eye?

HYSSOP: Hm-m. It's a meaty concept. You mean like during the Rose Bowl tourney they would be accoutered in nose guards and moleskins, during the Santa Ana baby parade in rompers and bibs, and so forth?

SWICKARD: Yes, only made out of crepe paper in attractive pastel shades; viz., orange, lilac, and puce. Can you visualize how that would pep up the personnel if bathed in a pink spotlight to boot?

HYSSOP: I like it, Swickard. There's a nice lilt to it. Naturally, it's a speck humdrum as it stands—we've got to put wings on it—but it's a beginning. You agree, Miss Fackenthal?

MISS F.: Bruce, I'm crazy for it. Speaking as a woman, it slakes my feminine thirst for color.

THIMIG: Personally, I'd like to see it carried over into the drug department, too. Couldn't our pharmacists wear a conical hat like Nostradamus—you know, embroidered with planets and signs of the zodiac?

HYSSOP (*dangerously*): Why don't you go the whole hog, Thimig? Maybe you'd like us to fill our prescriptions with newts and salamanders.

THIMIG (*involuntarily*): They'd probably do the trick as well as those pills and powders we stock. (*He turns deadly pale as Hyssop's eyes bore into him.*) That is, I mean—

HYSSOP: Yes? Was there something you wished to add?

THIMIG: No, I—er—I was just thinking of the spirit message my wife got the other night. It said a change was impending. I—guess she meant a change of garb.

HYSSOP: That depends on how you interpret it. (*Swickard and Miss Fackenthal fade swiftly out. Hyssop's smile gleams like a scimitar and his voice sinks to a coo; his morning is made.*) You know, Thimig, for some time now I've had the feeling you were homesick for Cedar Rapids.

CURTAIN

❧ METHINKS HE DOTH PROTEIN
TOO MUCH

SHE HAS given beauty a new category, he thought, for she appears to be edible. She is the word made fruit, rather than flesh, and with sugar and cream she would be delicious. Her neck would taste like an English apple, a pippin or nonpareil; and her arms, still faintly sunburned from the mountain snow, like greengages.—*From a short story by Eric Linklater in* Harper's Bazaar.

IN THE PRECISE, methodical manner that characterized everything he did, Monroe Fruehauf unhurriedly read his way through the weather summary and the maritime intelligence in his morning newspaper. A low-pressure area obtained over the Laurentian Plateau, and scattered showers impended in the Carolinas. According to the list of outgoing freighters carrying mail, the *Zulu Queen* was accepting parcel post and printed matter for Lourenço Marques, Nyasaland Protectorate, Kenya, and Uganda. None of these advices occasioned Monroe surprise, or, indeed, any overwhelming concern. For all he cared, it could rain frogs over the Carolinas, and the *Zulu Queen* could carry marijuana if she were so disposed; he was merely pursuing an ingrained custom of thoroughly digesting the paper before he left for work. Not that there was any particular urgency in that respect. Nobody cared what time he opened his secondhand bookshop on West Fourth Street, and it would be hours before the first furtive schoolboy appeared in quest of the *Heptameron* or the works of Sacher-Masoch. Monroe leafed back through the paper for a final, encompassing glance and discovered that he had neglected the food column. With the same tranquillity he had shown the weather and the shipping news, he learned that a new water-ground corn meal was being milled in Vermont, that an even more expensive turkey had been deviled for the millionaire palate, and that anchovies could be blended with mucilage to form an effective centerpiece for the *smörgåsbord* tray.

The last item in the column, however, definitely pricked Monroe's interest. An alert organization known as Yale Lox Associates had instituted a service to deliver a tasty assortment of smoked salmon, pot cheese, and bagels suitable for Sunday breakfast to one's door by fleet-footed, courteous messenger. A piquant notion, thought Monroe. The cooking facilities in his one-room apartment were limited, and he liked to linger abed of a Sabbath morning. The idea of having so baronial a tidbit brought to his couch was seductive. Acting on impulse, a thing he rarely did, he rang up the service forthwith. The brisk, executive voice that answered assured him that, barring a cataclysm, the lox would go through on time.

"Better throw in an extra order of rolls," said Monroe in a burst of recklessness. After all, once he had made the gesture, there was no sense stinting himself.

"Double bagels it is, sir," confirmed the voice, and Monroe almost fancied he heard heels clicked smartly. Before the day's trivia crowded the matter from his mind, he reflected pleasantly on the sybaritic experience in store. The step he had taken was hardly significant, and yet he had the inescapable feeling that he was standing on the threshold of a new life.

At eleven o'clock Sunday morning Monroe rolled over with a groan and groped about blindly for his slippers. The repeated buzz of the doorbell had settled into a long, maddening whine. Struggling into a robe, he reeled across the room, fumbled with the chain latch, and wrenched open the door. In the hallway stood a pert young woman clad in the parade uniform of a horse dragoon—giant black shako, befrogged tunic, jackboots, and sabretache depending from her belt. As Monroe goggled at her, she raised a bugle to her lips and executed a brassy flourish that sent echoes vibrating through the stair well.

"Hey, for Pete's sake!" protested Monroe, recoiling. "You'll wake up the whole block!"

Ignoring his protest, the young woman saluted crisply and addressed him in a ringing, declamatory tone: "The Yale Lox Associates bid you good appetite. From the ice-blue waters of Newfoundland, we bring you the pink perfection of Nova Scotia salmon smoked over hickory fires; from lush upstate New York farms, loud with the hum of bees, the crumbly goodness of snowy pot cheese made of richest Jersey milk; and from the aromatic ovens of Hester Street, the lordly, succulent bagel, agleam with flavorful spar varnish. Allow me." She picked up the field kitchen at her side and brushed past Monroe into his cubicle. Dazed and unnerved by her masterful manner, he followed, feebly muttering excuses for the disordered state of the room.

"Perfectly all right. We're used to it in our work," she assured him, deftly producing a number of wax-paper packages from the container. "That the kitchenette there? Now, you just laze around. I'll have everything ready in a jiffy." She was as good as her word; by the time he emerged from the bathroom, feeling a bit less thorny, the breakfast was invitingly spread on the table, and coffee was brewing in the percolator. Impressed, Monroe inquired if these ministrations were routine.

"All part of the service." She smiled, extracted a pencil from her shako, and scribbled a bill. "Natch, if you want the comics read to you, that's a quarter extra." Not ordinarily susceptible to feminine charm, Monroe had to admit that the girl was deucedly pretty. Her cheeks had the delicate flush of a ripe peach, her ears glowed like tiny shrimps below her taffy-colored hair, and the curve of her firm, gracile hips, encased in skin-tight breeches, called to mind the rounded outlines of a prize Bartlett pear.

"Look, miss," Monroe began lamely. "Please don't misunderstand me, but I was wondering if—that is, would you share this with me, maybe?"

"Oh, I couldn't do that, sir," she said quickly. "Mr. Fabricant's rules are very strict." One of the dragoons, it seemed, had been court-martialed for just such a breach of discipline and sentenced to slice sturgeon for thirty days. So free of guile was Monroe's entreaty, though, so candid his demeanor, that at length she consented to accept a cup of coffee. Under skillful cross-questioning, she revealed that her name was Norma Ganz, that her hobbies were cooking, baking, and cleaning, that she made her own clothes (except, to be sure, those she was wearing), that she preferred symphony concerts to night clubs, and a good book to either, and that she thought most girls nowadays were extravagant, selfish, and shallow. Confronted with this paragon, Monroe's eyes glistened. Her husband, he suggested, excusing himself for the personal nature of the remark, must be a happy man indeed. Not only was she unmarried, Norma replied forlornly, but she was practically an orphan, unless one counted her father, a wealthy oil operator in Oklahoma, to whose estate she was sole legatee.

It cost Monroe a series of expensive dinners, numerous theater tickets, and over sixty dollars' worth of flowers and baubles to test the validity of Norma's story, but he eventually satisfied himself. Not one word of it was true. In addition to being an inveterate liar, Norma led a complicated dream life in which she steadfastly identified herself with the heroine of whatever movie or confession romance impressed her at the moment. She was slovenly, vain, illiterate, and altogether a source of increasing anguish to her admirer. And yet to Monroe, fully aware of her defections, she was the most toothsome morsel imaginable. His taste buds yearned for her; he could not look upon her plump white shoulders, the creamy expanse of her throat, without wanting to gobble them up as greedily as a schoolgirl might a charlotte russe. In his amorous fancy, her charms acquired a lusciousness, a dietary significance, unlike those of any other woman he had ever known. As his craving for Norma intensified, he was alarmed to find that she daily grew more disembodied; repeatedly he caught himself regarding her less as a person than a snack, a delectable hors-d'œuvre that dominated his dreams. Sometimes, standing in his shop staring emptily at a first edition of *Jurgen* that in the past would have moved him to rapture, the thought of her succulence set his heart hammering and he groaned. Conversely, his desire for food slackened. Appreciably thinner, his eyes sunk in their sockets, he paced the streets for hours struggling to throw off his obsession, although deep down he knew the struggle to be futile. It was only a question of time, an obscure voice whispered, before the demon that bestrode him would assert itself. With a conviction of utter fatality, Monroe drearily awaited the climax of the nightmare.

The first hint of it came several evenings later as he sat in a booth at a Brass Rail, a fork idle in his nerveless fingers and his gaze ravenously fixed on Norma. She had never looked lovelier or more esculent; it required every ounce of Monroe's self-control to prevent his hurdling the table and sinking his teeth into her rosy rind. She ate with the slow, ponderous concentration of a heifer, incapable of speech while her energies were devoted to masticating. Sated at last, she suddenly took cognizance of her escort's reverie.

"What's the matter?" she asked. "Aren't you hungry?"

"Hungry?" repeated Monroe. He uttered a harsh, melodramatic snort. "I'll say I am. I'm starving."

"Then why don't you eat your London broil?" asked Norma reasonably. "Go on, try it."

"Listen, Norma," said Monroe with low, fierce intensity, leaning forward and clasping her hand in both of his. "I've never felt this way toward any girl before."

"I *beg* your pardon," said Norma haughtily, endeavoring to disentangle herself and upsetting horseradish in the process. "I hardly think this the time or place—"

"There couldn't be a better," Monroe interrupted. "Norma—please —hear me out. I need you, I want you."

"Have you gone crazy?" Norma asked. "In a public restaurant. I ought to slap your face."

"You don't know what you do to me," pleaded Monroe, salivating as his words tumbled impetuously over one another. "You have eyes like black olives, your teeth are like pearl onions, your lips like strawberry cheesecake! I could swallow you in one big gulp."

A sudden gleam of comprehension, mingled with relief, flashed over Norma's face. "Oh, is *that* all?" she said indifferently. "You mean I make you hungry."

"Has—has anyone else told you that?" asked Monroe, thunderstruck.

"*Have* they?" Norma snickered. "Practically every wolf that subscribes to the Yale Lox Associates, not to mention Mr. Fabricant."

"I thought it was just my own imagination," her swain faltered.

"Be your age," she advised maternally, squinting into her compact. "Why do you suppose I wear those cowboy gauntlets with the fringe? Some *shmendrick*'s always trying to nibble on my wrists. Brother, you should see what I go through on a Sunday morning."

"But it's dangerous," objected Monroe. "You might run into a party you couldn't handle. Someone who's really—well, anthropophagous." As delicately as he could, and with guarded allusions to the Ituri Forest and the remoter tribes of Micronesia, he explained that long pig is still esteemed by primitive connoisseurs and that the likelihood of Norma's encountering similar eccentrics in her hazardous profession must not be discounted. Norma was inclined to treat his qualms airily. The most difficult situations could be resolved with a well-placed kick in the groin, she asserted, and Monroe would be the first to get one if he stepped out of line.

Looking back at this occasion afterward, in the light of the ultimate tragedy, Monroe was wont to chide himself bitterly. He should have forced the issue, compelled Norma to quit her job, had her shadowed or even kidnaped to protect her from harm. But then, he would tell himself with numb despair, how bootless to attempt to circumvent destiny; it was kismet, it had all been ordained from their very germ plasm.

What little remained of the gruesome masque was played out with grim inevitability. When Monroe awoke to the strident clangor of the bugle the following Sunday, he found in Norma's stead a gruff Levantine with a blue jowl, whose busby and scarlet regimentals contrasted oddly with the cigar stump he was chewing. In a perfunctory mumble utterly devoid of esprit de corps, he rattled off the standard salutation of Yale Lox Associates and with uncouth bad grace brought forth some dismal marinated herring and salt-stengels.

Monroe blinked at him apprehensively. "Where's Norma?" he croaked in a peevish, tremulous voice he scarcely recognized as his own. A vague foreboding gripped him. "What happened to Miss Ganz?"

"Search me, Percy," returned the messenger. "We ain't responsible for your love life. Maybe she sneaked off before dawn." He gave a coarse chuckle.

"No, no," said Monroe, conscious of a sudden constriction in his windpipe. "Norma Ganz, the girl that usually delivers my breakfast."

"Never heard of her," said the other flatly. Pressure and appeals to his magnanimity went for naught; he was simply a cog in a vast mechanism, he indicated, whose hub was the potent and unapproachable Mr. Fabricant.

Momentarily expecting a phone call or other word from Norma, Monroe allowed the day to dissipate in an agony of indecision and fear. By the next afternoon, his inquietude had reached an almost unbearable pitch. In an interview with the girl's landlady, he ascertained that she had not been home for five days. It was possible she might have gone to Rochester to visit her folks, the landlady admitted, but she personally suspected foul play. Monroe at once telephoned Mr. Fabricant. The director of Yale Lox Associates proved remarkably elusive. When, after interminable evasion and subterfuge, he consented to answer, his reticence hinted that he knew more than he cared to disclose. Perhaps there was an overtone of special exigency in Monroe's appeal, for after a careful pause Mr. Fabricant grudgingly invited him to come in for a talk.

Seated in an office that would have made any Park Avenue kidney specialist sick with envy, Mr. Fabricant rested a basilisk stare on Monroe and listened to his chronicle. When his caller had concluded, he shook his head pityingly. "My boy," he said, "you don't have to be ashamed of the love you bore that Norma Ganz. She had the same effect on me."

"What the hell are you using the past tense for?" Monroe asked hoarsely. "For heaven's sake, tell me the worst!"

"Hold your horses." Fabricant quieted him. "I'm in the personal-catering game nine years and it's things like this that's made an old man of me."

"Things like what?" cried Monroe. "Get the marbles out of your mouth!"

"This," said Mr. Fabricant, wearily opening a drawer and extending a newspaper cutting. Under a photograph of a gigantic Masai warrior posed with shield and spear, a silk hat on his head, and his neck encircled with lion's teeth, was the curt report that Prince Balegula had embarked for Dar es Salaam after a good-will tour of Hollywood, Washington, and New York. "The African potentate," concluded the account, "expressed himself as overwhelmed by the hospitality shown him during his Manhattan visit. Even his favorite delicacy, he said, had been forthcoming while here, and, in fact, he had not been compelled to leave his suite to enjoy it."

"It can't be," sobbed Monroe, cradling his face in his arms. "Maybe she eloped with him. I'll get the inside story."

"You got it in front of your nose, son," said Mr. Fabricant. He laid before the other a gold epaulet Monroe remembered only too well. "They found this in his kitchenette at the Waldorf after he checked out." A tear coursed down his cheek as he leaned over and patted Monroe's heaving shoulders. "Life goes on," he sighed. "We all arrive at the city of God, but some by different gates. *Lox vobiscum.*"

🌿 STRINGING UP FATHER

PARDON ME, friend, would you happen to know the technical term for a man who walks around for three days with a letter in his pocket he's afraid to mail? Not a blackmail note, a billet-doux, or a plea for a small loan—nothing like that; a perfectly straightforward letter to a publisher containing a coupon and my check for five dollars. Ever since Sunday, I've been screwing up courage to drop it into a postbox, but I just can't bring it off. The thing is, if I temporize any longer, my son isn't going to have a copy of *The Life Stories of America's 50 Foremost Business Leaders* for his birthday, and that would be calamitous. Or would it? God, I wish I knew.

What pitchforked me into this imbroglio was a full-page advertisement for the work in *The New York Times Book Review*, bordered with photographs of the fifty industrialists reputed to control our destiny. At first glance, I mistook them for trophies used to illustrate some book like Jim Corbett's *Man-Eaters of Kumaon*, but on closer examination I saw that their heads were much smaller than the average Bengal tiger's, and that a few of them, including Henry Luce and David Sarnoff, looked surprisingly benign. "What intriguing quirks of fate swayed the early careers of these men?" the text asked, buttonholing me and exuding an opulent aroma of Drambuie and Corona Coronas. "You'll be amazed by these revealing life stories, telling how the 50 foremost business leaders in the country sensed their opportunities and made the most of them! . . . An ideal book for distribution to executives. Or the perfect gift from father to son." The final sentence brought me into camp. I had been casting about for some useful remembrance for a twelve-year-old who already has more chemistry kits, cyclotrons, and disintegrators than you can shake a fist at, and it struck me that here was the ideal present—romantic but factual, pragmatic, shrewdly designed to stimulate youthful incentive. Crowing with self-satisfaction at my acumen, I filled out the necessary details and, sealing them in an envelope, leisurely resumed reading the advertisement.

My *amour-propre* deserted me abruptly when I reached a paragraph indicating how one of our most noted tycoons got his start. It was the account of his preternatural initiative that pinned back my ears and begot an odd, gnawing squeamishness about putting *The Life Stories of America's 50 Foremost Business Leaders* into Junior's hands. "James H. Rand," blandly read the blurb, "working under his father, suddenly hit upon the invention of a visible index. With full confidence in his abilities, he immediately launched his own business in direct competition with his father. Several years of intense and heated rivalry followed. The outcome saw the father completely bought out . . . the son well on his way to forming the giant Remington Rand of today."

It may be psychologically wholesome to prime the young with examples like the preceding, but, indulgent father though I am, I'm beginning to think that I would sooner present mine with a can of smokeless powder and a stiletto. I submit that the latent desire to make a monkey out of Daddy will flourish of its own accord, and I do not propose to lug pails of water to insure its growth. I do, nevertheless, feel it incumbent on me to elucidate the tensions implicit in such a father-and-son relationship, and, with that object, I offer in easily digestible dramatic form the case of John Prester, of the Prester John Pistol Company. Overture and incidental music, *Kapellmeister*.

SCENE: *The office of John Prester, head of the Prester John Pistol Company, manufacturers of the celebrated Presjo Water Pistol. The roll-top desk, wall telephone, and Oliver typewriter invest the premises with an air of fusty conservatism, accentuated by the presence onstage of Millspaugh, an elderly Dickensian bookkeeper in sleeve guards and green eyeshade. As the curtain rises, he is staring glumly at a faded oleo that portrays a Victorian schoolboy spraying a pompous banker in silk hat and Prince Albert with a water pistol, surmounted by the legend "Presjo— Best by Test." He has turned away with a lugubrious sigh when Prester, a vigorous, hearty soul in his mid-forties, bustles in. His plump, freshly shaven face and his eyes, twinkling behind octagonal lenses, bespeak a buoyant optimism. Scaling his Homburg at a coat tree, he claps Millspaugh ebulliently on the back.*

PRESTER: Morning, Millspaugh! Glorious day, what? (*inhaling noisily*) Gad, it's great to be alive.
MILLSPAUGH: Is it?
PRESTER: Crest of the wave, dear boy—treading on air. (*humorously*) How's your corporosity sagaciating?
MILLSPAUGH: It isn't.

PRESTER: Little touch of liver, eh? Thought you looked a shade re-gusted. Well, bear up—rise above it. We're only dead once. Ha, ha, ha.

MILLSPAUGH: Full of ginger today, aren't you?

PRESTER: Who wouldn't be? Fine fall weather, orders pouring in—

MILLSPAUGH: What makes you think so?

PRESTER (*waving toward window*): Why, all our vans rolling by, loaded with merchandise.

MILLSPAUGH: Don't you notice anything strange about them?

PRESTER (*perplexed*): No-o-o. Well, now you speak of it, they seem to be rolling in the wrong direction.

MILLSPAUGH: Precisely—right back to the warehouse.

PRESTER: You—you mean those are cancellations?

MILLSPAUGH: Chief, I don't like to upset you, but we've got the largest inventory of water pistols in the Western Hemisphere, and fresh carloads are arriving by every freight.

PRESTER: But, confound it, it's impossible—it can't be! Prester John's pioneered in squirt guns since 1889! Every red-blooded Ameri-can boy—

MILLSPAUGH: Yes, yes, I've read the promotion, too. John, don't fight your custard. The public taste has changed.

PRESTER: Stuff and nonsense! Nothing'll ever replace the old-fashioned water pistol.

MILLSPAUGH (*gloomily*): Nothing but bankruptcy.

PRESTER: Damn it all, we're tops in the nuisance field! For silent, deadly accuracy, for sheer aggravation power, what other mis-chief-maker can touch the Presjo?

MILLSPAUGH: Well, if you must know, the Griller-Diller.

PRESTER: Pah! That toy!

MILLSPAUGH: All right, but whoever got the hunch to use muriatic acid to administer a superficial burn was a genius. It's sweeping the nation.

PRESTER: So did the exploding cigar, the dribble glass, and the hotfoot. I've seen these fads mushroom before.

MILLSPAUGH: Look, boss, just to meet the threat, couldn't we use a mild acid solution, too? Not enough to blind the victim—just give him a bad fright.

PRESTER: Now, see here, Millspaugh. Water was good enough for my father and it's good enough for me.

MILLSPAUGH: Well, then, you'd better face facts. We've got nineteen dollars in the bank. We're stony—*nettoyé*—snafu. The next voice you hear will be that of the bailiff.

PRESTER (*aghast*): What are you saying?

MILLSPAUGH: Furthermore, the president of Griller-Diller's due here any minute to buy you out, and if you want to save your skin, you'll knock under.

PRESTER: I'm not licked yet! They want a scrap, eh? I'll mortgage every penny—Thisbe can take in washing—

MILLSPAUGH: It's no good, John. He's got the whip hand.

PRESTER (*shoulders bowed*): Who is this—this upstart?

MILLSPAUGH: Nobody knows. He's sort of a mystery man, a younger Howard Hughes. He may even be the man *behind* Howard Hughes. (*There is a peremptory knock at the door, and Millspaugh exits through the window—a pretty maladroit* jeu de théâtre, *but better than having two characters carom off each other in the doorway. Lester Prester enters. Though scarcely thirteen, his suavity and poise are immediately manifest. He wears a morning coat, bowler, and boutonnière, and rotates between his clenched teeth an unlit Havana—clearly a man accustomed to give orders and have them obeyed on the double.*)

PRESTER: Oh, hello, son. Er—listen, I'm tied up—I expect a party—

LESTER: I know you do. He's here.

PRESTER (*jumping up agitatedly*): Where? Outside?

LESTER (*with a wintry smile*): No, inside. You're face to face with him. (*Prester's lips go ashen and he clutches the desk for support.*) Now, look, old-timer, let's have no blubbering or histrionics. You're on a lee shore and you're breaking up fast. Do you want me to throw you a line or don't you?

PRESTER (*smiting his breast*): That my own flesh and blood should spawn the Griller-Diller—no, no, I can't stand it!

LESTER (*crisply*): Yup, we live in a changing world. Well, suppose we drop the Old Testament delivery and get down to brass tacks. I'll give you two hundred frogskins for the good will and fixtures, and I'll try to make a job for you in my shipping room. I know it's a silly, sentimental gesture and I'll live to regret it, but there it is.

PRESTER: You loathsome little scorpion. To think I dandled you on my knee.

LESTER: Relax, governor, or you'll blow a fuse. What the hell, it happens to everyone. You just got caught in the technological buzz saw, that's all.

PRESTER (*trembling*): Where'd you get the money to float that rotten contraption? Out of my cashbox?

LESTER: No, I sold the old lady's solitaire. After all, I had to hire a public-relations counsel, didn't I?

PRESTER: What for?

LESTER (*pityingly*): Cripes, you certainly are living in the Ice Age. Why, to start a whispering campaign about your product—to poison kids' minds against it.

PRESTER: How—how did you do that?

LESTER: Oh, by saying it was sissy, and full of germs, and a mosquito breeder—elementary stuff. Then we got an unfrocked psychiatrist to write a paper proving it was harmful to the libido.

PRESTER: But *you* couldn't manufacture the Griller-Diller and distribute it, you little snake.

LESTER (*coolly*): Your competitor could. I just gave Twinkletoy a list of your customers in return for fifty-one per cent of the stock, we undercut your prices, and the rest was lagniappe.

PRESTER (*foundering in a bog of metaphor*): Even a roach wouldn't stab his sire in the back the way you have.

LESTER: It's business, Fatso. Dog eat dog, law of the jungle. Well, can't stand here jawing with you all day. (*He opens door, beckons in a pair of burly workmen laden with dictaphones and fluorescent lamps.*) O.K., boys, make with the brawn. Better strike that desk. I won't need it.

WORKMAN: What'll we do with the old gink?

LESTER: Tuck him in a storeroom somewhere, he's strictly non compos. (*As the workman slings Prester's inert body over his back and goes off, Lester crosses to the telephone, whips off the receiver.*) Get me Raymond Loewy. . . . Hello, Ray? Lester Prester. Now, look, I want a desk a helicopter can land on.

CURTAIN

✵ SLEEPY-TIME EXTRA

WHEN IT WAS FIRST NOISED along Publishers' Row that the John B. Pierce Foundation, a nonprofit research organization, had instituted a survey dealing with American family behavior, attitudes, and possessions, public opinion was instantly split into two camps—into the larger and drowsier of which I fell. There is nothing like a good, painstaking survey full of decimal points and guarded generalizations to put a glaze like a Sung vase on your eyeball. Even the fact that the results of the poll were to be printed in that most exciting of current periodicals, *Business Week*, did little to allay my fatigue. Then, one morning in early April, hell started popping at my corner stationery store. "What's good today, Clinton?" I asked, browsing over the magazine rack. "Well, I tell you," replied Clinton, thoughtfully scratching the stubble on his chin (he raised corn there last year but is letting it lie fallow this season), "we just got the new number of *Business Week* containing the John B. Pierce Foundation survey on American family behavior, attitude, and possessions." "Well, dog my cats!" I exclaimed, struck all of a heap. "Let's have a nickel's worth of those licorice gumdrops, will you, Clinton?" "Sure," said Clinton reluctantly, "but how about this new number of *Business Week* containing the John B. Pierce Foundation—" "Listen, Clinton," I said suddenly, "did you hear a funny little click just then?" "Aha," breathed Clinton, round-eyed. "What was it?" "A customer closing his account," I snapped, closing my account and taking my custom elsewhere.

It took a stray copy of the Buffalo *Evening News*, abandoned late yesterday afternoon on my bus seat by some upstate transient, to reveal the true nature of the survey and dispel my apathy. "Married Couples Favor Double Beds," trumpeted the dispatch. "Eighty-seven per cent of husbands and wives sleep together in double beds but 5% of the wives are dissatisfied with this and 40% think maybe twin beds would be ideal, *Business Week* magazine reported today on the basis of a survey by the John B. Pierce Foundation, nonprofit research organization. Other conclusions of the survey . . . included: In summer, 70.3% of the wives sleep in nightgowns, 24% in pajamas, 5% in the

nude, and seven-tenths of 1% in shorts. Sixteen per cent of the women
reported they would like to sleep in the nude, causing the Pierce Foundation to comment: 'Here we have clear-cut evidence of an inhibi-
tion.'. . . Fifty per cent of the husbands report no activity after getting
into bed, 22% read, 12% talk, 7% listen to the radio, 3% say their
prayers, 4% smoke, 2% eat. Comparable percentages for wives were
40% no activity, 29% read, 11% talk, 8% listen to the radio, 5%
say their prayers, 3% think, 2% smoke, 2% eat."

Though one could speculate on the foregoing until the cows came
home and distill all manner of savory psychological inferences, I cannot help wondering what machinery the Foundation used to obtain its
statistics. Even the most incurious student of the report, I think, must
ask himself eventually whether these delicious confidences were stammered into a telephone mouthpiece, or haltingly penned in a questionnaire, or whispered to a clear-eyed, bedirndled Bennington girl at
the kitchen door. Somehow there is a grim, authoritative quality
about the project which convinces me that the researchers went right
to the source for their data, and I venture to think that more than one
must have found himself embroiled in a situation like the following:

SCENE: *The bedroom of the Stringfellows, a standard middle-aged
couple. Monty Stringfellow is a large, noisy extrovert who conceals his insecurity under a boisterous good humor. He affects
heavy, hobnailed Scotch brogues and leather patches at the elbows of his sports jackets, is constantly roaring out songs com-
manding you to quaff the nut-brown ale, and interlards his speech
with salty imprecations like "Gadzooks" and "By my halidom."
Tanagra, his wife, is a sultry, discontented creature on whom
fifteen years of life with a jolly good fellow have left their mark.
As the curtain rises, Monty, in a tweed nightgown, is seated upright in their double bed singing a rollicking tune, to which he
beats time with a pewter tankard and a churchwarden pipe. Tanagra, a sleep mask over her eyes, is trying to catch a little shut-
eye and getting nowhere.*

MONTY (*con brio*):

> *Come quaff the nut-brown ale, lads,*
> *For youth is all too fleeting,*
> *We're holding high wassail, lads,*
> *And life's dull care unheeding,*
> *So quaff the nut-brown ale, lads—*

TANAGRA: Oh, shut up, for God's sake! You and your nut-brown ale.

MONTY: What's wrong?

TANAGRA: Nothing. Nothing at all. What makes you think anything's wrong?

MONTY: I don't know—you seem to be on edge lately. Every time I open my mouth, you snap my head off.

TANAGRA: Every time you open your mouth, that blasted tune comes out. Haven't you anything else in your song bag?

MONTY: Gee, Tanagra, I always looked on it as our theme song, you might say. (*sentimentally*) Don't you remember that first night at the Union Oyster House in Boston, when you made me sing it over and over?

TANAGRA: You swept me off my feet. I was just a silly little junior at Radcliffe.

MONTY: You—you mean our moment of enchantment has passed?

TANAGRA: I'll go further. Many's the night I've lain here awake studying your fat neck and praying for a bow string to tighten around it.

MONTY (*resentfully*): That's a heck of a thing to say. You keep up that kind of talk and pretty soon we'll be sleeping in twin beds.

TANAGRA: O.K. by me, chum.

VOICE (*under bed*): Aha!

MONTY: What's that? Who said that?

TANAGRA: I'm sure I don't know.

MONTY: There's somebody under this bed!

VOICE: There's nobody here except just us researchers from the John B. Pierce Foundation.

MONTY: W-what are you doing down there?

VOICE: Conducting a survey. (*Otis "Speedball" Ismay, ace statistician of the Foundation, a personable young executive, crawls into view from under the Stringfellow four-poster, flips open his notebook.*) Evening, friends. Close, isn't it?

TANAGRA (*archly*): I never realized how close.

ISMAY: You the lady of the house? I'd like to ask a few questions.

MONTY: Now just a minute. I don't know whether I approve—

TANAGRA: Batten down, stupid, he's not talking to you. (*brightly*) Yes?

ISMAY: Let me see. You prefer sleeping in a nightgown rather than pajamas?

TANAGRA: Well, that depends. With this clod, a girl might as well wear a burlap bag.

ISMAY (*with a disparaging glance*): Yeah, strictly from Dixie. You know, that's a darned attractive nightie you've got on right now.

TANAGRA: What, *this* old thing?

ISMAY: It sends *me,* and I'm a tough customer. What do they call these doodads along the top?

TANAGRA: Alençon lace.

ISMAY: Cunning, aren't they?

TANAGRA (*provocatively*): Think so?

ISMAY (*tickling her*): Ootsie-kootsie!

TANAGRA: Now you stop, you bad boy.

MONTY: Hey, this is a pretty peculiar survey, if you ask me.

TANAGRA: Nobody asked you.

ISMAY: Wait a second. You *could* tell me one thing, Mister—Mister—

MONTY: Stringfellow. Monty Stringfellow.

ISMAY: Do you belong to any lodges, fraternal associations, or secret societies?

MONTY: What kind do you mean?

ISMAY (*impatiently*). It doesn't matter. Any kind that keeps you busy evenings.

MONTY: Why, yes. I'm Past Grand Chalice of the Golden Cupbearers of the World, field secretary of the Rice Institute Alumni—

ISMAY: Fine, fine. Don't bother to list them. We merely wish to know what evenings you spend away from home.

MONTY: Every Tuesday and every other Friday. Is this all part of the survey?

ISMAY: Part? It's practically the lifeblood. Well, I think you've given me all the information I need. Oh, just one more detail, Mrs. Stringfellow. You understand there's a high percentage of error in an informal cross-section of this type and naturally we like to check our findings.

TANAGRA: Naturally.

ISMAY: I'd ask you to drop in at my office, but it's being redecorated.

TANAGRA: Yes, I read something in the paper to that effect. Is it serious?

ISMAY: No, no, it'll be all right in a day or two. For the time being, I've moved my charts and figures to the Weylin Bar, third table on the left as you come in at four-fifteen tomorrow afternoon.

TANAGRA: I'll be there half an hour early.

ISMAY: Splendid. (*to Stringfellow*) Thanks, old man, don't bother to show me to the door; I'll use the fire escape. Couple more calls to make in the building. Good night, all! (*He goes.*)

MONTY (*chortling*): Ho ho, that bird certainly pulled the wool over

your eyes! He's no statistician. He didn't even have a fountain
pen!

TANAGRA (*placidly*): Well, I swan. He sure took me in.

MONTY: Yes sirree bob, you've got to get up pretty early in the morning to fool old Monty Stringfellow! (*He slaps her thigh familiarly
and Tanagra sets her alarm for six-forty-five.*)

CURTAIN

❧ WESTWARD HA!

GOODBYE BROADWAY, HELLO MAL-DE-MER

THE WHOLE SORDID BUSINESS began on a bleak November afternoon a couple of years ago in Philadelphia, a metropolis sometimes known as the City of Brotherly Love but more accurately as the City of Bleak November Afternoons. Actually, the whole business began sixteen years ago, as do so many complex ventures, with an unfavorable astrological conjunction, Virgo being in the house of Alcohol. Late one August day in 1932, I was seated at the Closerie des Lilas in Paris with my wife, a broth of a girl with a skin like damask and a waist you could span with an embroidery hoop. I had had three mild transfusions of a life-giving fluid called Chambéry Fraise and felt a reasonable degree of self-satisfaction. Halfway through my imitation of Rudolph Valentino in *Blood and Sand*, my wife wiped the tears of laughter from her eyes and arose.

"Look, Julian Eltinge," she smiled, naming an actor who had achieved some transitory fame for his powers of mimicry, "*descendez de cette table, salop, et dinons* (come down off that there table, sweetheart, and let us feed the inner man)."

Ever the thrall of a pair of saucy blue eyes, I good-naturedly complied and sprang down with a graceful bound, sustaining a trifling fracture of the spleen. There then ensued a long, absurd debate as to which of us would pay the tab. An innate sense of gallantry prevented me from taking money from a woman, but I stifled it and soon we were bowling along the Boulevard St. Michel in a fiacre. In less time than it takes to build a fourteen-room house, we had crossed the Seine, got lost in Passy, and arrived at a quaint Javanese restaurant in the Rue Pigalle. Lighting my cigarette with a hundred-franc note to show the maître d'hôtel I was a real Parisian boulevardier, I chose an inconspicuous table and ordered *rijstaffel* and a thimbleful of Holland gin for myself and a glass of water for my lady. Presently a young woman I knew, who reported the *haute couture* for several American magazines, approached, followed by a gentleman. My years in the Ochrana had so trained me to absorb vital details that I saw at once he had a beard.

"This is Hirschfeld," said the fashion writer, "the theatrical cari-
caturist of *The New York Times*." I instantly scented a touch and, furtively secreting my wallet in my wife's stocking, pretended to be stone-
deaf. The young woman's tongue, ordinarily a quiet, reserved sort of
chap, was wagging more than its usual wont.

"Hirschfeld wants to do a caricature of you," she said brightly.

"*Je comprends pas*," I shrugged, "me stony, you savvy? Plenty bankruptcy along me."

"It's free," explained Hirschfeld, who up to that time had been mute.
My deafness vanished forthwith, and turning my good profile to him,
I waited patiently whilst his pencil flew. In no time at all—five minutes,
to be exact—we were laughing and chatting away as though we had
known each other five minutes.

Hirschfeld left for the States that night, just before the check arrived, and I did not see him for a spell. One day in New York, I ran
into him outside a little specialty shop in the Forties where I had just
bought a black girdle with rose panels and a bias-cup brassière for my
mother. We had a stoup of kumiss together and renewed our friendship.
Whether he stole the cufflinks I missed subsequently, I would prefer
not to say, but it seemed more than coincidence. Nevertheless, I am one
who forgives easily, and it was hardly more than eleven years before I
found myself one morning excitedly telephoning him.

"I've got an idea for a musical comedy, old man," I said directly (I
rarely beat about the bush). "Meet me at the Lafayette Coffee Rooms
at one o'clock." Had Hirschfeld not met me at the Lafayette Coffee
Rooms at one o'clock, this might never have been written. Another
thing that might never have been written, if it gives twenty-three de-
spondent investors any comfort, was a musical comedy named *Sweet
Bye and Bye*, which closed in Philadelphia like a ten-cent mousetrap
the day this story opens.

Ogden Nash, who wrote the lyrics of *Sweet Bye and Bye*, Vernon
Duke, the tunesmith responsible for its airs, and Hirschfeld and I, who
spawned the libretto, had been sequestered in a room in the Warwick
Hotel there for nineteen hours administering extreme unction to the
show. At length our efforts were unavailing; as the turkey lay cold and
lifeless on the operating table before us, Nash retired to his room to
hang himself with a dangling participle, Duke returned to writing singing commercials, and we groped our way to the Anguish Room of the
Warwick for a final cup of coffee. We were both sobbing brokenly into
a wisp of cambric when the editor of a journal named *Holiday*, a fur-

tive personality in a hand-me-down suit and linen of dubious cleanliness, shambled up to us. In an effort to shatter his torpor, I informed him that the show had just breathed its last. Our plight would have moved a heart of stone, and he certainly had it.

"What are you going to do now?" he inquired, stroking Hirschfeld's beard thoughtfully.

"Oh, I don't know," I replied carelessly, "I may join the Foreign Legion, or, on the other hand, I may take a hot bath." My companions looked around startled, under the impression that Noel Coward had spoken, but of course Coward was nowhere to be seen, as it was I who had spoken. Suddenly I became conscious of the editor's close scrutiny.

"Why don't you take a trip around the world for us?" he proposed. There was a moment of portentous silence. When a man you scarcely know suggests a trip lasting nine months and covering twenty-seven countries, you are justified in leaping to one of four assumptions: first, that he is an impostor; second, that he is hopelessly in love with your wife and will go to any lengths to get you out of the country; third, that you have blundered by mistake into an Alfred Hitchcock film; and fourth, that you have succumbed to a combination of *ennui de moyen âge*, wanderlust, paranoia, and brandy. Almost immediately, however —in fact, just as soon as the waiters had finished applying cold towels to my forehead—I regained my aplomb.

"All right, if you insist," I consented, stifling a yawn. "I suppose it's weak of me, but I just can't refuse you anything. Silly, isn't it?"

And before you could say "bo" to a goose, the whole matter had been arranged. Hirschfeld, who had done the Giant Swing once before, was unquestionably the ideal person to share my stateroom and illustrate our experiences; besides, I needed someone to protect me from whatever sultry womanhood, bloodthirsty brigands, and carnivorous fauna lay in wait. His qualifications were obvious: a pair of liquid brown eyes, delicately rimmed in red, of an innocence to charm the heart of the fiercest aborigine, and a beard which would engulf anything from a tsetse fly to a Sumatra tiger. In short, a remarkable combination of Walt Whitman, Lawrence of Arabia, and Moe, my favorite waiter at Lindy's.

Our itinerary was soon settled; commandeering an airmail envelope from the desk clerk, we drew a line west from Hollywood, hemstitching all the areas celebrated by Kipling, Conrad, and Maugham. For one delicious moment I toyed with the possibility of a side trip up to Tibet. My pulses throbbed as I envisioned us entering Shangri-La, our ears loud with the buzz of prayer-wheels, fawned on by the Grand Dalai

Lama (played by Sam Jaffe). When Hirschfeld pointed out, however, that a couple of middle-aged aesthetes trained on corned beef and Dr. Brown's Celery Tonic were ill equipped to ascend the slopes of Kanchenjunga, I reluctantly gave way. Finally our route was complete— Samoa, the Fijis, New Zealand, Australia, the Netherlands East Indies, the Federated Malay States, Siam, Indo-China, India, Iraq, Syria, Palestine, Turkey, Egypt, the Anglo-Egyptian Sudan, British East Africa, the Belgian Congo, North Africa, France, Switzerland, England, and Ireland. We would have included South America, Russia, and China, but my fountain pen, which writes even under hysteria, unexpectedly ran dry.

The financial arrangements, of course, were left to subordinates and bookkeepers, outside of a brief, spirited wrestle in which we kicked, bit, and gouged each other until our skins glowed. Eventually, the magazine grudgingly agreed to settle upon us as expense money a sum sufficient to feed a family of starlings through a Labrador winter. In vain I protested that my dependents would be reduced to beggary; the editor's face remained flinty. "About time those *schleppers* went to work," he grunted. "That brother-in-law of yours hasn't pulled his weight in the boat since you sprung him from Dannemora."

My heart was beating an irregular tattoo the following evening as I entered my apartment in New York, primed to make a dramatic announcement of the trip. I pictured the family's stunned surprise, the entreaties of my wife, the children whimpering at my knee and imploring me not to desert them. Poor little chaps, deprived of a father's wise counsel and love through a cruel caprice of Fate! I resolved at all costs not to yield to my emotions. From the living room, as I tiptoed toward it, came childish merriment, voices uplifted in song. Setting my shoulders squarely, I strode in.

"Well, folks," I said casually, "Daddy's off to the Seven Seas." Unfortunately, at this precise moment my foot encountered a roller skate lying athwart the threshold. As my wife and the dwarfs looked up in astonishment, I ricocheted across the room, clawed ineffectually at the *toile de Jouy* drapes, and stemming myself with a Christiania turn, crashed to the floor, taking a cloisonné vase with me. The memsahib sighed heavily.

"It's no use trying to conceal it any longer, children," she told them. "He drinks."

"Does he beat you, too, Mummy?" demanded the boy, a manly little fellow of ten, as he took a step forward and doubled his fists. "Because if he does, I—I'll—" So fierce was his ire I dare say he would have thrashed me soundly had not his mother interfered; but the good woman soon restored harmony, and, applying a raw beefsteak to my eye to reduce the swelling, I poured out a breathless account of my project. The effect was somewhat lessened by the fact that I was alone in the room, the others having gone to the movies in the interval, but upon their return I broke the great news and apathy was the order of the day. Soon the gentle snores of the household were the only sounds to be heard, and rolling myself in my blanket, I lay awake excitedly anticipating the morrow.

How to describe the days that followed? There was Hirschfeld to be put on the train to Hollywood (and Hirschfeld to be taken off again, when it turned out to be the wrong train); there was Hirschfeld's thirteen-months-old baby to be shipped west to be present at our sailing, though the poor thing was so backward it could not even speak English; it was Hirschfeld this and Hirschfeld that until sometimes I thought I must go mad. I lived in a whirlwind of activity, haunting cut-rate luggage shops for bargains in paper satchels, falsifying declarations for my passport, issuing ukases to my tailors for cummerbunds and stengah shifters. Hardly a day passed that I did not issue at least three ukases, and hardly a day that I did not receive three back informing me that my credit was exhausted. Nevertheless, by judicious shopping I managed to gather a splendid kit for my journey—a machete, a sola topee, a poncho, an apparatus for distilling sea water, and deuce knows what-all. The Army-and-Navy stores I bought them at will be paid just as soon as the lawyers probate the will of my uncle in Australia, a very wealthy man.

Even the veriest tyro knows that the first consideration of the experienced world traveler is a good set of maps. The air was like wine and my step was springy one fall morning as I pushed open the door of the Aardvark map shop in Radio City. A listless citizen in an alpaca jacket ceased scratching his fundament long enough to survey me vacuously. I outlined my simple needs—a detail map of Melanesia, one of India, and still another of Africa. With an air that clearly implied he found the role of salesman demeaning, he nodded toward a rack. I dug out what I needed and reached for my wallet. To my chagrin, I discovered I had only thirty-seven cents in change. Producing a blank check on the Vulturine and Serpentine National Bank, in which I am an important depositor, I scribbled out a draft for two dollars and fifty-five cents. The salesman picked it up as though it were infected, vanished into the stockroom, and returned with another incompetent.

"This is our manager, Mr. Register," he said.

"Cass Register," his superior added with an important cough, "at your service. Is this your check?"

"No," I replied sweetly, "it's an old sampler woven shortly after the Deerfield Massacre by Charity Sumpstone, my great-grandmother fifth removed."

"How's that again?" he frowned, a puzzled expression invading his fat face. I instantly regretted the frivolous line I had taken, and, with extreme civility, requested him to okay the check. He asked for some identification; I drew out various letters of accreditation for the trip, a note from Admiral Halsey asking me to have a collar starched for him in Shanghai, and other trivia of the sort.

"Hm-m-m," he murmured skeptically, "got any other identification? Social Security card?" My wattles flushing a dusty pink, I extended my Pennsylvania driving license. He examined it closely under an infra-red ray, shook his head majestically. "No good—this comes from Pennsylvania."

"Look," I said patiently, "the leather in these shoes I'm wearing comes from the Argentine. But *I* come from New York."

"So do a lot of other dead beats, brother," he remarked with an intimate smile. I disemboweled him with a glance.

"You know, of course," I reminded him, "that it happens to be a state and federal offense to pass a bad check. Do you think I'd put my neck in the noose for a measly two dollars and fifty-five cents?"

"Well, we get some pretty shifty specimens in here," he replied steadily. Ultimately, by leaving behind a platinum watch and a 25 cc. test tube of arterial fluid, I won my freedom. I spent the balance of the forenoon in a dark booth at Tim Costello's, reducing my blood pressure with Golden Wedding laced with paraldehyde and weaving dirty limericks around the name of a certain map company.

Purely out of deference to my life insurance company, I underwent the customary routine of inoculations for typhoid, paratyphoid, typhus, smallpox, tetanus, yellow fever, plague, and cholera. A physique hardened in every bodega in Manhattan withstood the shock admirably, except that now and again, without any warning, I abruptly ran a fever of 108 and pitched forward in a dead faint. An infinitely more grueling complication, though, came about quite by accident. One evening, at a musical soirée, I found myself vis-à-vis a young person of the most extravagant charms, whose manner left no doubt that she wished to trifle in the conservatory. I allowed myself to be beguiled out behind a potted palm, but just as I was slipping my arm around her yielding waist she sharply brought me back to earth. It transpired that she was a contact lens technician and that her interest in my eyes was entirely professional.

"We're going to throw away those glasses of yours, Charlie," she announced forcefully. "I wouldn't let you go on a trip like that with those crutches. Report to my web tomorrow morning at ten-fifteen."

Sheep that I am, I found myself stretched out at the appointed hour on a surgical table in her office. A sinister Torquemada with a Brooklyn accent was bending over me with what he conceived to be a reassuring manner.

"Now hold still a second, sonny," he said silkily, "we'll just make a little mold of your eyeball—hey presto!" A hoarse cry died stillborn in my larynx; simultaneously I felt the impact of hot cobbler's sealing wax on my retina. I reared up like Levi Jackson bucking the Harvard backfield, at the same time kicking outward as in the French *savate*. When the technician had finished probing bits of Erlenmeyer flask and optical glass out of my face, the hands of the clock pointed to four and I was compelled to leave, as it was time for my Malay lesson at the Berlitz School. Promising to return the next afternoon for my try-on—a pledge I had no intention of fulfilling—I tottered out.

My reasons for taking Malay were fivefold, the other four of which I seem to have forgotten. The chief object was to get rid of eighty dollars which was burning a hole in my pocket, though I pretended to myself that the language would be indispensable from Australia to Singapore. I also wanted to be able to salt my speech with an occasional picturesque phrase like "Boy, tell Missy's amah to take this chit to the Residency chop-chop."

The first fifteen minutes of the session with Dr. van Oost, my Malay teacher, went off swimmingly. I was compelled to bellow slightly to make myself audible, since the doctor wore a formidable hearing aid, but in a few seconds my accent was indistinguishable from that of a native of Batavia (Batavia, New York, that is). Midway through a typical colloquialism, "Boy, beli besok ayam di atas papan tulis" (Boy, buy me tomorrow a chicken in the blackboard), I experienced the distinct sensation of being alternately smothered and roasted. The classroom could not have been at fault; it was over five feet square and had a nice large transom to admit the air. Dr. van Oost's voice gradually began to fade in volume and a rivulet of perspiration coursed down my nose; I realized with a sinking sensation that the typhoid inoculation was taking hold by the moment. I half rose, plucked ineffectually at my collar, and sank limply into the doctor's arms. Aeons later, I came to in the principal's office, revived by a flabby Mittel-Europan who kept blowing cigar smoke into my face and making pointed references to my manhood.

I acquired my contact lenses a day or two later and they worked superbly. To insert them was but the work of a moment; all I had to do was pry open my eyes with a buttonhook, force the lenses in, and gulp as though swallowing a Chincoteague oyster. The resulting vision was practically 20-20. Everything looked milky and I could drill a photo of Nelson Eddy between the eyes at point-blank range. The lenses also materially enhanced my comeliness; in profile I had the melancholy grandeur of a carp at Fontainebleau. The effect on family and friends was equally gratifying. My children turned to stone at the first glimpse of their sire, and then broke wildly for cover. It took a fabulous bribe to tempt them out from underneath the bed. The mem, more articulate, put her opinion in a single succinct sentence.

"Stunning," she observed. "You certainly ought to set Singapore aflame with those immies in your head." Perhaps the most practical suggestion came from an old college classmate I met on the street.

"Why don't you have another one made up?" he proposed.

"Why? They're unbreakable—they're made of plastic."

"Sure," he agreed, "but it's a great chance for a shell game. If you meet an easy mark on your travels, you can always whip 'em out of your eyes, shuffle 'em, and say, 'Now, under which one of these is my cornea?' "

In the cold gray light of a winter dawn they gathered at the airport to bid me Godspeed, the gallant band of relatives who had stuck by me through thick and thin like leeches. Tears streamed down the cheeks of cousins and nephews who now would have to go back to work. One crapulous uncle, last employed shortly before the battle of Cerro Gordo, was especially eloquent. "Won't seem like the same place any more without you," he snuffled. He was dead right; his days of freeloading were over.

Only my immediate family betrayed its sincere feelings. My wife looked ten years younger already; the sudden release from years of tyranny acted on her like vintage champagne. The children's eyes danced at the prospect of the destruction they could now cause with impunity. They signaled their freedom by firing off cap pistols in my ear, sprinkling sneeze powder over the luggage, and generally behaving with such winsomeness that I promptly made a note to cut them off without a farthing.

The motors roared, a final embrace, and we were aloft. The airstrip receded; I was alone in the empyrean except for two dozen other escapists speeding toward Cathay. Seventy minutes later, my wife heard the shrill repeated ring of the telephone. She laid down her glass, picked up the receiver. The voice of the man she loved drifted faintly over the wire.

"What?" she demanded mystified. "Are you in Bali already?"

"Well—er—not exactly," I hesitated. "The plane was grounded in Camden. I'm calling you from Joe's Coffee Pot."

"That's nice," she replied. "Give my regards to the other loafers." And she hung up. I drew my balmacaan a bit tighter about me, kicked over a spittoon, and went slowly up the tarmac. From now on I would have to play it solo, a high heart set resolute and unafraid against the unknown.

PLEASE DON'T GIVE ME NOTHING TO REMEMBER YOU BY

WEIGHTLESS, IMPONDERABLE, as idle as a painted ship upon a painted ocean, the great airliner hung high in the thin air above the Sierra Nevadas, its wolfish snout strained toward the paling horizon. Two hundred miles away, in the broad plain washed by the Pacific, lay its goal, the Athens of the West, the mighty citadel which had given the world the double feature, the duplexburger, the motel, the hamfurter, and the shirt worn outside the pants—the Great Pueblo, the City of Our Lady the Queen of the Angels—Los Angeles. Thirty-five hundred feet below the plane, two turkey vultures clung to a snowy crag and picked idly at some bones.

"This sure was a delicious scenario writer," ruminated the elder, stifling a belch. "You'd have to go all the way to Beverly Hills for one like him."

"Listen," said his companion, "that bad I don't need *anything*." He turned, peering up at the receding roar of motors. "Well," he observed sourly, "there goes the morning flight to L.A. Same old cargo of hopheads, hustlers, and movie satraps."

"Ah, what the hell," said the first indulgently. "They're just people."

"So was Dillinger people," snapped the other. "So was Charlie

Ponzi. I tell you, it's to chill the marrow. I wouldn't eat one of those creeps up there if I was starving. Jeez, I'm not fastidious, but you've got to draw the line *somewhere*."

And yet, shrewd though his estimate of the flagship's passengers was, the bird was not wholly right. For among that raffish, dissolute crew speeding toward the sea was one who by his very goodness retrieved them all. A simple, unpretentious man of a grave but kindly mien, his gaunt profile blended the best features of Robinson Jeffers, Lou Tellegen, Pericles, and Voltaire. A keen, humorous eye sparkled above a seamed cheek which had been tanned a rich oleomargarine at the Copacabana and the Stork Club. His loosely woven tweeds were worn with all the easy authority of a man accustomed to go into a pawnshop, lay down his watch, and take his four dollars home with him. As he sat there, relaxed and skyborne, it was the type of subject that would have inspired Monet or Whistler to reach for his palette—the humble dignity of the wayfarer, the pearly effulgence of the clouds, the sense of perfect equilibrium between man and nature.

Nonetheless, under my seemingly placid exterior—for let us not dissemble longer, dear reader, it was indeed myself I have taken the liberty to describe—behind my outwardly cool mask, I say, I was prey to a hundred conflicting sensations. Hypertension, nausea, anticipation of the events in store for me, the dull ache of parting with my creditors—a host of emotions strove for mastery within my breast. In less than an hour. I would be in the fabulous film colony of Hollywood, on the first leg of my journey around the world. Soon I would be clasping the flabby hands of erstwhile colleagues in the movie industry, listening to the purr of their ulcers, and noting with satisfaction their paunches and the crow's-feet around their eyes. A wave of nostalgia engulfed me as I remembered the decade I had spent writing motion pictures; a suspicious moisture glittered in my orb. What a splendid, devil-may-care band we had been in the thirties, brave lads and lasses all—ever ready to cut a competitor's throat or lick a producer's boot, ever eager to conform our opinions to those in authority, ever alert to sell out wife, child, and principle to attain the higher bracket, the fleecier polo coat, the more amorous concubine. Wave a paycheck at us and we could turn in our own wheelbase, strip ourselves inside out like a glove; the most agile, biddable, unblushing set of mercenaries since the Hessians. Five years ago, standing with one foot on the eastbound *Chief*, I had addressed the small party of sycophants come to wish me farewell. "Wild horses," I had announced with slow emphasis, "wild horses tied tail to tail, mark you, will never drag me back to this leprous, misbegotten

kraal. May a trolley car grow in my stomach if ever again I put foot
west of the Great Continental Divide." But here I was, a little older, a
little grayer, and a little poorer; and as the first straggling vineyards of
San Bernardino appeared in the distance, my impatience grew so acute
as to resemble the effects of Nembutal.

The plane slid smoothly down the asphalt, wheeled, and shuddered
to a stop. Tom Swift (for it was indeed he who had piloted the craft on
our perilous transcontinental dash) emerged from the cockpit, pulling
off his helmet and goggles. "Well, fellows, we made it," he said quietly.
"Thanks, Tom," I said, "Roger and over." I descended and stretched,
drinking in great deep draughts of the characteristic Los Angeles morning effluvia. Outside the terminal, I found that influential friends had
provided me with a taxi which, for a trifling sawbuck, bore me to the
house in suburban Bel-Air I would inhabit during my stay. En route,
I chatted with the *izvozchik*, a strange pinhead with a face like a scul-
pin and a chauffeur's linen duster, who drove at breakneck pace; not
once did the needle on the speedometer fall below ten miles an hour.
I asked if he had ever driven a car before. He shook his head.

"I'm learning, though," he assured me. "I can go around corners
now. Tomorrow I'm going to take a lesson in backing up." There was
a short silence while I fingered my beads.

"How long before you get a driver's license?" I asked.

"Oh, I've got plenty of *them*," he said easily. "They give 'em to you
here when you buy a car. They do that everywhere."

"Not in New York they don't, Buster," I rejoined.

"New York?" he repeated, puzzled. "Where's that?" I let the conversation languish; I realized with overpowering finality that from here
in, I was in *partibus infidelium*. Somehow it recalled the remark once
made to me by the wife of a picture producer. A native Angeleno and
graduate of the Hollywood High School, she had never been anywhere
but Palm Springs, Lake Arrowhead, Tia Juana, and similar local fly-
traps. One rainy day, on a bearskin rug before a glowing fire, she confessed her profound discontent, her overwhelming *Weltschmerz*. I suggested that she take a trip around the world.

"Oh, I know," returned the lady, yawning with ennui, "but there's
so many other places I want to see first."

Safely installed in my Mediterranean palazzo in Bel-Air, I hastily
boarded the windows to exclude the blasted sunshine and telephoned
Hirschfeld, my traveling companion, who had reined into town the

day before. He had just spent three weeks in San Francisco trying to book passage to Samoa and was inclined to be gloomy.

"It's no dice," he said dejectedly. "The next boat doesn't leave for five months. Even if we could get there, the only transportation between Samoa and the Fijis is outrigger canoe."

"Then let's go to Tahiti," I proposed. "They say that's an island paradise."

"Who says so?" rasped Hirschfeld.

"Er—the washroom attendant at '21,' " I confessed. "But I know it's true. Did you see *The Moon and Sixpence?*"

"No, but I saw Tahiti," he said, "and it's just like Washington Heights. It's full of beat-up ukulele players and cheap grifters; they've got a Whelan drugstore on every block."

"Well," I said, "we've got to get to New Zealand somehow."

"What for?" he demanded. "If you've ever been in Nutley, New Jersey, you know what it's like."

"Now wait," I said impatiently, "I don't know about Tahiti and New Zealand, but you can't shrug off Australia. Kangaroos—boomerangs— superbly formed young women riding surfboards down under—"

"Bah," said Hirschfeld contemptuously. "Another Far Rockaway. Listen, brother, get yourself organized. The place we want to head for is Bali. I lived there eight months and it's heaven." In a few badly chosen words, he sketched a picture of a veritable Garden of Eden inhabited by innocent, droll folk who asked nothing but the privilege of barbecuing suckling pigs for us, twining hibiscus in our hair, and entertaining us with superb ritual dances. Such was his eloquence that I could almost hear the beat of the surf on the beaches, smell the dizzying scent of nutmeg borne on a zephyr from the Moluccas. By the time we met at the travel agency that afternoon, I was moving with the languorous feline grace of the true Balinese; passers-by in the lobby paused to exchange admiring whispers at my sinuous slant-eyed charm. So complete was the illusion, indeed, that one young woman in the elevator threw discretion to the winds and flirted boldly with me. Naturally, I avoided her eyes, since her escort was staring suspiciously at me, and merely returned a discreet pinch and my telephone number. She must have been an illiterate, however, as I failed to hear from her subsequently. It may be, on the other hand, that her escort poisoned her mind against me in some way that I cannot comprehend. In any case, she was not very good-looking, and I probably escaped a dangerous entanglement by a hair's breadth.

It took only nine days of tramping the steamship offices to convince us how romantic we were and how elastic our itinerary would have to be. Not only were the Netherlands East Indies aflame, but thousands of *évacués* were piled up in San Francisco seeking passage back to their homes. On Fisherman's Wharf alone, we learned, were eight hundred missionaries drinking themselves blind while they awaited transshipment to their posts. What made it a particularly neat mathematical problem was the fact that only seven freighters were scheduled to sail for the East within the next five weeks, each carrying twelve passengers. Eventually, through a display of guile that would have done credit to Talleyrand, we wheedled the last two berths aboard a vessel named the *Marine Flier*, bound for Chinwangtao, Shanghai, Hong Kong, and Singapore. Then, with tickets snugly stowed in our shiny new passport cases and malodorous five-cent cigars sputtering in our faces, we set about preparing in earnest for the grand tour.

Obviously our first and most vital requisite for such widely disparate locales as Cambodia, Northern India, and French Equatorial Africa was a proper medical kit. Hirschfeld, whether through ignorance or bravado, laid in nothing but a package of Band-Aids and a box of Cow Brand bicarbonate of soda. Luckily for him, I had had two years of premedical training before switching over to the commercial course, and I was able to give him the benefit of expert scientific knowledge. At an army surplus store on South Broadway, I picked up an excellent secondhand first-aid unit. Some of the bandages had been used and would have to be rinsed out, but the forceps, tourniquet, and iodine applicators were in mint condition. I also purchased a pair of surgical gloves and a can of ether in case my confrere was stricken in the veldt and I had to operate on him by candlelight. Oddly enough, instead of being grateful for my vigilance, Hirschfeld turned sullen. From several rather coarse comments he made, I got the impression he doubted my dexterity. "If I have my choice, pal," he sneered, "I'll take tetanus." I realized, of course, that his attitude was characteristic of the typically superstitious and uninformed layman, and secreted the kit in my baggage against a future emergency.

It then occurred to us that, like sandhogs entering a decompression chamber, we ought to accustom ourselves beforehand to the geographical extremes we would encounter—the steaming jungles of Cochin China, the sun-baked wastes of the Sahara, the crocodile-infested waters of Lake Chad, and the woman-infested cafés of Port Said. What more ideal test laboratory than Hollywood, which in a hundred films had re-created every possible latitude, every conceivable hazard? I forthwith approached a number of prominent Hollywood directors and, posing our problem, begged their assistance. To a man, those of them who could understand English responded to our plea. Theirs were names to conjure with—Leon Gordon, who had made the great socio-logical South Seas study, *White Cargo*; John Farrow, whose *China* had done so much to widen the gulf between that country and ours; James Whale, director of *Green Hell*, which had won the Spyros Oblivion prize for the most torpid picture of 1938; Zoltan Korda, creator of *Sahara*, one of the most sought-after personalities in Hollywood, to say nothing of the Sahara; and Henry King, director of *Stanley and Living-stone*, which, by an almost unbelievable coincidence, was released the very same day luminal was first synthesized. A few telephone calls, a crisp word or two spoken into a subordinate's ear, and instantly the complex machinery of the studios was in motion.

In the three ensuing days, Hirschfeld and I underwent every possible vicissitude the globe-trotter can experience short of complete annihila-tion. We were stood up in wind tunnels and subjected to fearful man-made simoons, flung into fetid marshes and pelted with coconuts. We were shipwrecked, marooned, waylaid by banditti, captured by head-hunters, charged by rhinos, and overcharged by hotelkeepers. We were drenched, fried, parboiled, roasted, steamed, and sautéed. In one ap-palling morning, I was made to ride every form of conveyance from a camel to a Swiss funicular; though I pleaded for mercy, I was even carried piggy-back through some artificial saw-grass by a certified Swahili. We spent a night in a malaria-infested tent on the Metro back lot, shivered through another in a ruined temple at Paramount, slap-ping away at bats. Errol Flynn taught us how to woo a brown-skinned Burmese lass, Rex Harrison instructed us in Siamese court etiquette, Johnny Weismuller coached us in the technique of swinging from tree to tree. The final test of our hardihood came when we were permitted to witness a combat virtually never seen: a fight between a mongoose and a cobra, with the victor engaging a motion-picture executive, or jackal. As the vanquished mongoose crept away to die, we knew that after this whatever terrors the future held would fade into insignifi-cance.

Our embarkation date was almost upon us when we suddenly real-ized we had been neglecting the social life of Hollywood. Out came our dinner coats, green with age, their lapels still flecked with soup stains from some forgotten banquet. We let it be bruited about that we were available for cotillions, drags, routs, buffets, and balls. The news had an electric effect; within three days, our mail was filled with sample swatches of cloth from Beverly Hills tailors, pamphlets offering to charter hundred-foot Diesel twin-screw yachts sleeping twelve, and solicitations from relief committees. Ultimately, several more courageous hostesses decided to risk social obloquy and invited us to dine, and from then on we lived at fever pitch.

The most marked change wrought during my five years' absence from Hollywood was the constant preoccupation, everywhere we went, with art. Dinner conversation, formerly compounded of blistering speculations about the love life of one's friends, now consisted of squabbles over the Post-Impressionists and brisk trading in gouaches. Onetime vaudeville bookers who would have considered Frederic Remington's "The Last Water-hole" a bit highbrow were collecting Picasso and Braque by the carload; a new anecdote about Renoir was esteemed far more than one about Ava Gardner. Every time we entered a home in Beverly Hills, we were met with a stench of turpentine and prussic blue that well-nigh swept us off our pins.

The evening with Midge and Dorian Schlagober was typical from the moment we rang the doorbell. A set of chimes within promptly went into "Frère Jacques"; some salesman for "Frère Jacques" door-chimes must have covered Beverly Hills on a bicycle, because they seemed to be standard equipment in no less than nine houses we visited. Midge Schlagober, an ash-blonde with a plunging neckline, swept toward us across the parquet, enveloping us in her fatal charm.

"Too too divine having you," she fluted. "I can't wait for you to see our new Rasmussen." Presuming that she referred to a new kind of deep-freeze mechanism, we started toward the kitchen, but she shepherded us into the living room. Four or five guests, carefully selected with an eye to the length of their studio contracts, were gathered about a finger-painting which could have been executed by any backward boy of nine. They were exclaiming vigorously over its tonality and impasto.

"Yes, it's so—so uninhibited," Midge beamed. "That's what I like about Rasmussen—his freedom. Don't you, Mr. Hirschfeld?"

"Personally," said Hirschfeld, "I think they ought to take it away from him."

"Take what away?" asked Midge with a pained smile.

"His freedom," said Hirschfeld bluntly. There was a short dynamic silence, shattered at last by the entrance of our host, Dorian, his arms piled high with Toulouse-Lautrecs. He bore them with athletic ease, possibly because only six years ago he had similarly borne shoulders of mutton in a Chicago slaughterhouse. But that was before he had

written *Dark Abattoir*, the plagiarism of Upton Sinclair's novel which
had landed him a $1500-a-week job in pictures.

"I was cleaning out a drawer and found these little things," he sim-
pered. "They're not Lautrec's best period, but they may amuse you."
We examined the drawings, which, incidentally, happened to be the
most palpable forgeries, and clucked dutifully. When dinner was announced at last, I fatuously supposed we would have done with aesthetics and descend to a more animal plane. I was mistaken. All the
way from the hot baked grapefruit to the chocolate soufflé, the company was treated to an exhaustive account by the Schlagobers of the
bargain Utrillos they had gleaned on their last visit to New York. The
pressure finally became too much for Hirschfeld.

"Say, men," he remarked, clearing his throat, "I saw a dame with
a honey of a shape on Sunset Boulevard today." Midge rose from her
chair as if someone had given her a hotfoot.

"Dorian, darling, why don't you show everybody *your* paintings?"
she cooed.

"What, does *he* paint too?" I inquired, concealing my agitation.

"Of course," she said haughtily. "All the dealers say he's the most
significant primitive since the Douanier Rousseau." As the guests
trooped toward Dorian's study uttering broken little cries of expecta-
tion, Hirschfeld and I ducked into the powder room and effected an
egress, like Tom Sawyer, down a rainspout. Forty minutes later, we
were seated in the most ribald burlesque theater in Los Angeles, digging each other in the ribs and roaring with laughter at the *double-
entendres* of the comic. He didn't look in the least like one of Rou-
ault's clowns, but that night I could have sworn he was a greater artist
than W. C. Fields.

A fine mist hovered over the City of the Walking Dead as we swung
up over the Cahuenga Pass and pointed our radiator emblem toward
San Francisco. Hirschfeld leaned out and stared pensively at the myriad
twinkling lights of Los Angeles.

"You know," he said at length, "somebody once called this town
Bridgeport with palms. But I'll tell you something about it just the
same."

"What's that?" I asked, never taking my foot off the throttle.

"I'd rather be embalmed here than any place I know," he said slowly.
He turned up the collar of his trench coat and lit a cigarette, and in the
flare of the match I saw that his tiny pig eyes were bright with tears.

BOY MEETS GULL

AT ELEVEN O'CLOCK of a foggy February morning in the year 17——,
waterfront loungers in the quaint old seaport town of Bristol, England,
might have observed a candid, freckle-faced lad of thirteen, accompanied by a freckle-faced pirate with a freckle-faced parrot on his
shoulder, boarding the brig *Hispaniola*, the beginning of a journey
which would take its place one day among the major classics of all
time. History, once called "that inconstant jade" by Carlyle (not
Thomas Carlyle—Gus Carlyle, who used to run the poolroom in
Perkasie, Pennsylvania), has a way of repeating herself. Exactly two
hundred years later and five thousand miles across the world, waterfront loungers on San Francisco's Embarcadero might have observed
a candid lad of forty-three named Perelman, with a portable typewriter
and an elastic conscience, accompanied by a bearded pirate named
Hirschfeld with a freckled portfolio on his shoulder, boarding the
freighter *Marine Flier*, the beginning of a journey which would take
its place one day among the major soporifics of all time. Though neither
of them resembled Stevenson's immortal characters in any way—in
fact, they looked a good deal more like a couple of indigent process
servers or heroin peddlers—the parallel could not be denied. For they
too were freckled and they too were undertaking a voyage fraught with
high adventure and peril to their expense account. Small wonder that
the little knot of bronzed mariners clustered around the stringpiece
should have stared after them with the respect men who have wandered
into far places accord their own kind, and then have paid them the highest tribute they knew, that of silently spitting on the sidewalk. It was
a picture no artist could paint—least of all, Hirschfeld.

    Inside the great echoing shed all was noise and confusion; gangs of
stevedores frantically unloaded last-minute cargo from trailers, trucks
piled with barrels and cartons scuttled about, perspiring cab-drivers
transferred trunks, corded boxes, and bicycles to conveyors. Alongside
the pier, her decks swarming with riggers and carpenters, the *Marine
Flier* lay low in the water, her seven hatches still receiving goods consigned to China, the Straits Settlements, and India. A dozen huge Sam-
son booms, ten of them amidships, one each at bow and stern, ceaselessly swung bales and packing cases inboard. On the port side of the
well deck, a crew of riggers was making fast a giant UNRRA crate of

generators destined for Shanghai; on the starboard, carpenters were busily securing innumerable carboys of nitric, hydrochloric, and sulphuric acid for Colombo. Every available foot of deck space was stacked with oil drums, machinery, and galvanized pipe; immediately behind the after house, several longshoremen deftly lashed down an automobile, swathing it in tarpaulins and bracing its wheels with chocks.

It was a scene of activity calculated to inspire even the most torpid, and, eager to swell the total effort, I moved buoyantly from group to group, lightening the burden of one with a rousing sea chantey, regaling a second with a side-splitting anecdote, executing a nimble hornpipe or jig to revive the flagging spirits of a third. In a few moments, scowls had turned to smiles, men who had been at daggers drawn were exchanging 'baccy and teaching each other how to do scrimshaw work, and the feeling was general that my quick-witted tact had forestalled a serious disaffection which might have spread to the entire dockside. Indeed, company officials, who had rushed to the harbor at the first threat of tension, assured me that my trifling intervention had done more to promote harmony in the merchant marine than fifty years of arbitration, and that henceforward capital and labor, their hatchets buried, would march shoulder to shoulder and hand in hand into a new era of mutual understanding, amity, and prosperity. No doubt this was an exaggeration engendered by their profound gratitude, but it was nonetheless gratifying; and rejoining Hirschfeld, who had been standing by tapping his foot impatiently, we set off to install ourselves in our cabin.

By a stroke of good fortune, the passenger scheduled to bunk with us had dropped dead the day before, leaving us in comparative comfort. Most of the other passengers were lodged three in a cabin with splendid disregard for their background and personalities. The room next to ours, for example, was shared by a sluggish cotton converter from Philadelphia, a gaunt Jesuit missionary, and a small, fibrous mining engineer. The cotton man turned a beautiful shade of hunters' green directly he boarded the boat and retired groaning to his pillow. The missionary and the engineer, fellow-alumni of the Chapei prison camp, engaged from the outset in a heated and interminable argument about their experiences, each plainly inferring the other was a liar. The trio in the other cabin was no less diverse. Tooker, a toothless leprechaun who represented an American canned-goods firm in Shanghai, devoted himself largely to special research involving bourbon, rarely emerging even for meals. Linklater and Cropsey, his cabin mates, were also collector's items. The former, a fattish, corpselike citizen with the benign twinkle of a water moccasin, quickly put every man's hand against him by revealing that he was the ranking mortician of Hong Kong. Cropsey, whose protuberant frog eyes hinted at an obscure thyroid maladjustment deep in his blubber, was a minor insurance official somewhere east of Suez. He spoke with the measured profundity of the true bureaucrat; his most casual opinion was deeply pondered and deliberate, a weighty pronouncement handed down from Sinai. These, together with a Madame Chai, wife of an official in the Chinese Nationalist Government, and her eleven-year-old son, comprised our brave little company outward bound for Chinwangtao, Shanghai, Hong Kong, and Singapore.

The first couple of days out of the Golden Gate were uneventful. I spent them stretched out in the lower tier of my double berth, gritting my teeth to prevent my tongue from escaping and making a minute study of the plywood ceiling above me. Approximately every fifteen seconds, the *Marine Flier* rose with the speed of an express elevator, shivered deliciously, and lurched steeply forward into the trough. As it reached the bottom of the curve, all the bureau drawers flew out, the locker doors opened, suitcases slid halfway out of the top bunk, and our toilet articles teetered toward the washbowl. The moment the ship began its ascent, the process reversed; with a salvo like the bombardment of Port Arthur, drawers and doors banged shut, suitcases smashed into the wall, and bottles splintered the shaving mirror. It was pikestaff-plain and Doomsday-certain to me, a deep-water sailor since boyhood, that the *Marine Flier* was little more than a cheesebox on a raft and would momentarily founder with all hands. Even the veriest land lubber could perceive that the man whose duty it was to drive the ship—the chauffeur or the motorman or whatever you call him—was behaving with the grossest sort of negligence; more than likely he was asleep at the tiller or tickling the waitress, abandoning the craft to any caprice of wind or wave. But Hirschfeld, who had an answer to everything, irritatingly persisted in minimizing the gravity of our plight.

"It's only the Japan Current," he said perfunctorily. "Every ship to the Orient has to pass through the Japan Current." Japan Current indeed; as if dereliction of duty deserving of a court-martial, aboard a mere cockleshell with one measly funnel, in the worst typhoon in the history of navigation, could be fobbed off with a few glib words about a current. The man's fatuity made my blood boil.

During this trying period, when my every faculty was needed to worry about the proper conduct of the ship, I ate frugally if at all, contenting myself with a cup of thin broth or soda cracker taken be-times; whereas Hirschfeld, with the stolidity of the true peasant, outdid himself in gluttony. Bread by the bushel basket, whole beeves, firkins of butter, and hogsheads of jam vanished down his maw; his arrival at table spread consternation in the galley. He lived only for the ship's bell summoning us to meals; twice he deliberately tripped up Jeffrey Chai, the little Chinese boy, to get the first helping. At last a deputation of our fellow-passengers, hardly more than skin and bones, waited on me and begged my intercession. They pointed out what was long since apparent, that if Hirschfeld prolonged his outrageous behavior, the larder would be clean long before we crossed the International Date Line. The crisis was partially solved by chaining Hirschfeld's leg to his bunk every other meal. The resulting howls and execrations penetrated to the bowels of the vessel: so much so that a deputation of sailors waited on me and begged me to use any means, short of slitting my friend's gullet, to still his dreadful clamor. In the end, I drew on my fairly extensive premedical experience and introduced 2.75 gr. of cyclopropane into his matutinal oatmeal, an expedient which kept him in a drowsy, half-animal state most of the day and allowed the rest of us to latch on to a few groceries.

As soon as the advent of a calm sea and favoring winds removed the crushing weight of responsibility from my shoulders and I could again delegate authority to subordinates, I hastened to acquaint myself with the ship's officers and cargo. My knowledge of life on the bridge had been derived from the pages of William McFee and Guy Gilpatric, and I was prepared for weather-beaten, blustering old salts and thorny, iconoclastic Scotch engineers. I looked in vain for them aboard the *Marine Flier*. The relative youth of her officers—her skipper was thirty-two, the first mate thirty-four, and the chief engineer a decrepit thirty—concealed a surprising amount of efficiency and good sense. They were men of taste and a high order of technical skill, refreshingly devoid of heroics or bombast, considerate and socially attractive. The men they commanded were also as far removed from the stock conception of merchant seamen as one could imagine; they had little in common with the alcoholic, improvident sailor of popular fiction and the movies. Many of them were well-schooled and the majority had served with distinction in the war. Through their specialized unions, which sought constantly to improve their status, they had achieved decent living conditions and wages, and, equally important, a sense of self-respect. I could not help feeling that if this ship was any index, there must be a very healthy spirit abroad in the American steamboat business.

The handful of passengers in the after house, of course, was purely incidental to the cargo, worth by rough estimate about a million and a half dollars. It embraced everything imaginable, from shoe polish to bank notes, from steel girders to malted milk. There were, to list only a few items, phonograph records, sardines, jeeps, canned abalone, steam hammers, pencils, bulldozers, haberdashery, beer, railroad ties, telephones, clothespins, aircraft tires, after-shave lotion, quicklime, truck bodies, powdered milk, steel safes, quicksilver, electric ranges, newsprint, resin, plate glass, and depilatories. One of the more curious bits of miscellany was the eleven barrels of ginger which had been spurned by the American palate and was now returning in a crestfallen mood to Hong Kong. In the specie tank on the boat deck aft reposed a hundred and sixty cases of Portuguese brandy speeding to the United States consulates in Tientsin and Shanghai; in Number 3 hatch amidships lay two Chinese cadavers, snugly flanked by mouthwash, desk calendars, insect bombs, and movie film. Day by day, at an average speed of fifteen knots, this vast and terrifying hash stored up by some insane magpie crept steadily along the thirty-first parallel to further aggravate the problems of an already chaotic continent.

And now there befell me an incident so grievous that it requires every bit of fortitude I can muster to set it down: the loss of a friend grown dear to me through myriad trials and tribulations, a mainstay in joy and sorrow, the very breath of life itself—my bank roll. The tragedy took place the evening of our seventeenth day, a scant twelve hours before reaching Chinwangtao. Shortly after dinner, I was seated in the smoking room, drawing on an excellent Larranaga and immersed in a fascinating article on Norwegian rainfall in the *National Geographic*. The saloon was a blaze of lights and gaiety; a single forty-watt electric bulb shed its rays over a cutthroat bridge game involving Linklater, Cropsey, Hirschfeld, and the purser, while at a nearby table the missionary bent his head attentively over a photographic reportage in *Pic* by Marie (The Body) MacDonald on the future of the female bust. The card-players had solicited me to join their party, but I remembered my mother's injunction never to fall in with plausible strangers on ocean greyhounds and declined. Just as I was contemplating a bit of shuteye, the Chinese boy approached. He bore in his palm two unusual amulets of ivory, cube-shaped and speckled with precious stones.

"Why, what are those, Jeffrey?" I inquired, patting the little fellow's head. He explained that they were *su dzai*, an ancient Chinese game of ritualistic origin played on a blanket, in which the contestants wagered on various numerical combinations formed by the amulets.

More to divert him than through any vital interest in the game, I consented to play, and we withdrew to a secluded spot behind the ventilators. Extracting from his pinafore an ancient Chinese wad which would have choked a horse of the Ming dynasty, Jeffrey bade me fade him. I complied, and cupping the amulets in his chubby fist, he spun them out smartly.

"Shau hai dze yau yi saung hai dze!" he entreated hoarsely.

"How would you translate that, Jeffrey?" I inquired.

"It's an old Shintoist prayer," he replied. "It means 'Baby needs a new pair of shoes.' " The invocation evidently exerted a certain amount of influence over the cubes, because they came up seven a dozen times in a row. The odd thing was that whenever I rolled them, the devilish things behaved in the most perverse fashion. Again and again I tried to breathe fire into them, whispered cunning endearments to them, but it was useless; in the hands of the infidel they produced nothing but deuces and boxcars. The ship's bell was striking midnight as I tore the last American Express check out of my entrails and handed it to Jeffrey.

"There you are, you little swindler," I said bitterly, "and the next time you use loaded dice on a man four times your age, wipe that ugly smirk off your face."

"Thanks, sucker," he said, stowing the check in a money-belt the size of an inner tube. "You know, we Chinese have an old proverb—"

"So do we Yankees," I cut him short. "It runs, 'A fool and his money are soon parted.' Well, *geh in d'rerd*, old man."

"How would you translate that, Mr. Perelman?" he asked.

"I wouldn't," I snapped, turning on my heel. At least, I had one consolation. He may have had my last dollar, but I had had the last word. I mounted the companionway and, picking my way across the cluttered deck, leaned on the rail and stared off through the darkness. A hundred miles distant, across the gently undulating Yellow Sea, waited Asia, inscrutable, brooding. I was starting with a clean slate; could China say the same? That was the question. What would be the answer?

THE FLOWERY KINGDOM

AN EARLY morning mist, periodically illuminated by the feeble rays of a wintry sun, shrouded the harbor of Chinwangtao as I thrust my head through our porthole on the *Marine Flier* and stared drowsily about me. All I could discern of fabled Cathay was a sullen range of hills disturbingly similar to those we had left behind in Southern California. Into a mind befogged with sleep there gradually crept a dark, hobgoblin suspicion. Suppose that through some error of navigation, some ghastly official blunder, we had overshot Asia and for the past three weeks had been floundering in a vast, idiotic circle around the Pacific. After all, stranger things had happened in the annals of the sea—the celebrated riddle of the *Mary Celeste*, the mysterious disappearance of the Danish training-ship *Kobenhavn*, the enigma of the *Waratah*. I sank down on the edge of the bunk and, head in hands, weighed the evidence. Yes, there was no doubt of it: the captain had made a serious miscalculation in his charts. Instead of pocketing his pride and availing himself of my superior seamanship to get him out of his pickle, he had manifestly preferred to brazen it out. His manner the past few days, now that I reconsidered it, had been extremely evasive; he had slunk past me deliberately avoiding my eye, fearful lest an unguarded word or gesture betray him. If this were indeed Southern California, the captain's intent became only too clear: he was planning to steam straight for Hollywood and drop anchor at Grauman's Chinese, hoping to fob it off on us as the Temple of the Thousand Sleeping Buddhas. There was not a moment to be lost; unless the man's duplicity was unmasked within the hour, our global junket stood in danger of being knocked into a cocked hat. Crossing with a bound to Hirschfeld, my *fidus Achates*, who lay snoring bestially in his bunk, I shook him into consciousness.

"What is it? What's the matter?" the poor fellow cried out, leaping up with his usual faulty co-ordination and inflicting a small gash on his noggin as it struck the upper bunk. I explained our predicament, but his ignorance of matters maritime was abysmal and I could see he only half understood. Wearying of his dramatic groans and fumbling attempts to stanch the blood with a towel (the injury was petty and ceased bleeding long before nightfall), I went forward to reconnoiter and evolve a plan of action.

My fears, luckily, were unfounded; the first thing I beheld was a couple of junks leisurely standing into the harbor and a pilot tug flying the Chinese flag. Just ahead of us was the silvery line of a breakwater and beyond it the cluster of buildings which marked the Kai Lan Mining Administration, the British coal concession controlling the port. By midmorning, our customs and quarantine inspection completed, the ship edged cautiously into her berth beside a dingy, soot-blackened pier striped with railroad tracks. The coolies awaiting us on the dock were decked out in what was unquestionably the most fantastic collection of rags ever assembled anywhere to ward off the weather. A good half possessed no single garment worthy of the name (that is, worthy of the name of garment); the rest wore mangy fur-lined hats or beanies and long, shapeless coats that trailed handfuls of cotton wadding, looped about with odds and ends of canvas and burlap. Their faces were markedly Mongol, and our first impression of them, *en masse* under a gray, lowering sky, was hardly reassuring. I for one would not have been excessively surprised to see Genghis Khan himself appear, flourishing a yataghan, and begin carving a new empire out of the *Marine Flier*. This judgment, however, shortly proved premature. The stevedores were amicable, even jolly; they greeted us warmly, indulged in a good deal of lighthearted banter, and altogether behaved with much more gusto and spirit than hungry people have any right to display. They were particularly awed by Hirschfeld's beard, and expressed their belief to our Jesuit fellow-passenger, who spoke Chinese, that he must be a renowned sage. It would have been shattering to the illusions of these simple folk, not to say disloyal to my friend, to reveal that he could barely read or write, and I prudently kept silence. Hirschfeld, of course, made the most of their homage; he strutted about, stroked his beard portentously, puckered his brow into a frown, moved his lips as though framing some momentous apothegm, and generally managed to create a pitiable travesty of a man deep in thought.

The only Occidental visible in the shifting crowd was a vinegary, tight-lipped Englishman in flannels and elegant brown suède shoes, who eyed the ship and everyone aboard her with ill-concealed disfavor. It was obvious that to our British cousin the arrival of the *Marine Flier* was no signal to fling his beret into the air. The junior mate, leaning beside us on the docking bridge, watched him with foreboding. "Trouble," he predicted gloomily. It appeared that we had called at Chinwangtao, a port rarely included in the freight schedule, to discharge twenty-five hundred tons of girdles (at least, it sounded like that; the engine-room bell was clanging and he may have said girders). Whatever they were, they lay well down in the hatches, and piled on top of them were quantities of miscellaneous cargo destined for Shanghai. This overstow would have to be removed, stored in godowns, or warehouses, while the girdles were being unloaded, and subsequently replaced. It was an expensive and tedious process, and if, he observed darkly, the port had no godown facilities, we would be in a pretty fix.

"What would we do then?"

"Search me, lover," he shrugged. "The inside of this here vessel is just one big grab-bag." I left him staring balefully at the wharf, and rounding up Hirschfeld, the Jesuit father, and the Philadelphia cotton converter, I proposed a stroll into the town. At the foot of the gangplank, the Englishman accosted us.

"I shouldn't go up there if I were you."

"We were just going to stretch our legs."

"You may get your necks stretched." He uttered a short, mirthless laugh. "There's the very devil to pay. The whole town's under martial law. The Communists are only five miles away. They've been blowing up the tracks between here and Tientsin every other night." Assuming a formidable Russian accent, Hirschfeld informed him that we were American Communist agents sent to bolster the morale of our Red comrades and that we would stick at nothing to help drive the parasites out of China, leaving no question in his voice whom he meant. The Englishman's lip curled. Our political sympathies were our own affair, he said, but he could tell us that if we ventured into Chinwangtao, he could not personally be responsible for our safety. We exchanged smiles tipped with the most malignant hatred and set off.

Our route into town lay across a tangle of railroad tracks skirting the bay; the wind was bitter and the scenery reminiscent of the less attractive suburbs of Carteret, New Jersey. Presently we came out upon a cement highway bordered by dusty, leafless saplings, along which hurried hordes of rather tense Chinese. Dispersed along the road at intervals were brick pillboxes manned by fifteen-year-old soldiers in heavily padded blue uniforms, exhibiting fixed bayonets with some ostentation. Before very long, a party of rickshaw men waylaid us. One of them, not to be put off by our repeated plea that we wanted to walk, scampered beside me. He offered to lead me to a house of tolerance, where, he implied, delights never imagined by Havelock Ellis and Krafft-Ebing might be viewed at moderate cost. I regretfully declined. He pondered a second, then withdrew from his singlet a packet of photographs which I gathered to be sporting scenes. I rarely hunt or fish, and I told him so. Undeterred, he inquired whether I wished to dally with his sister. I assured him I had every regard for her, but I had sworn to remain celibate until Ireland assumes its rightful place in the comity of nations. I was sorry when he finally fell astern and vanished up an alley. He was an engaging rogue, and though he would have cheerfully slit my windpipe for a shiny red apple, it had been fun knowing him.

A veritable fusillade of smells, compounded of the pungent odors of deep fat, shark's fin, sandalwood, and open drains, now bombarded our nostrils and we found ourselves in the thriving hamlet of Chinwangtao. Every sort of object imaginable was being offered by street hawkers—basketwork, noodles, poodles, hardware, leeches, breeches, peaches, watermelon seeds, roots, boots, flutes, coats, shoats, stoats, even early vintage phonograph records. In a pile of the latter, I discovered a fairly well-preserved copy of that classical minstrelsy, "Cohen on the Telephone," but the moment the merchant sensed he was dealing with an American, the price shot up to three cents and I thought better of it. A band of ten or fifteen urchins trooped at our heels constantly, wiping their noses freely on our sleeves and demanding cumshaw. Children, I may as well confess it, are my weakness; I distributed a few worn gold pieces which were of no further use to me and earned their undying gratitude. It is pathetic that trinkets like these, utterly without value in the States, should be sought after so eagerly throughout the rest of the world. The prospective traveler who seeks an advantageous rate of exchange will do far better to fill his trunks with gold pieces than the oft-heralded nylons, chewing gum, and cigarettes.*

It was almost lunchtime when we started back toward the ship, each in his individual rickshaw. I experienced what I am told is the customary sense of embarrassment at having a fellow-creature act as one's beast of burden, but mine was such a wiry specimen, weighing as he did well over eighty pounds and amazingly fleet for a man of sixty with tuberculosis, that I quickly overcame my compunctions. Besides, as your old China hand loves to observe, if everybody stopped riding in rickshaws through humanitarian scruples, their pullers would soon starve. It was, therefore, with the fairly cocky feeling I had done my bit to avert a possible famine that I dismounted and gave my boy his eleven cents. He must have appreciated my altruistic motives, for the instant he ceased coughing and sponged the perspiration from his face, he was profuse in his thanks.

* This was written in the early spring of 1947. The situation may have altered since, of course.—*Author's note.*

We were treading gingerly through the maze of the freight yards
when the faint blast of a steamer whistle echoed from the direction of
the port. We stood momentarily rooted to the spot, and then, like a cork
blown out of a bottle, the Jesuit father took off. I will stake my wig
that, paced by Father Houlihan, the four of us broke every hurdle
record in the last fifty years. It was a gallant try but foredoomed to
failure. By the time we reached the pierhead, tongues lolling out of our
mouths, the *Marine Flier* was beyond the breakwater and fading fast.
The sole person in sight was our English milord, teetering on his heels
and richly enjoying our dismay. "I warned you," he chuckled. Slowly,
and savoring each word, he revealed that since there was no storage
space for the overstow, our ship had left for Shanghai without unloading. It was a bleak prospect: all our passports, luggage, and funds
slipping over the horizon, a civil war five miles away, and no American
consul this side of Peiping. Ultimately, the Englishman finished draining his cup of triumph and relented. A tug was summoned and we were
taken aboard ingloriously, in a heaving sea, amid the jeers and catcalls
of the other passengers. One of them was so unsporting as to snap a
photograph of me creeping on my hands and knees across the gangplank, which he later showed around to much raucous laughter. To
tell the truth, I found the levity a trifle mechanical, but I joined in good-
naturedly, ever ready to guffaw over the discomfiture of another human
being.

Two mornings later, we steamed slowly up the muddy mouth of the
Yangtze past the Woosung Forts and began threading our way through
the sixteen miles of river traffic that separated us from our anchorage.
How the pilot ever managed to maneuver the ship to her berth without running down a single sampan I do not profess to know; a dozen
times it looked like Judgment Day for entire families of Chinese, but
grandmother and three-year-old alike would throw themselves on the
sweep and pump hysterically until the craft veered out of our path.
Freighters from every conceivable port in the world—Oslo, Honduras,
Liverpool, Veracruz, Amsterdam—were being lightered in midstream,
further adding to the hazard. At last, around a bend of the Whangpoo,
Shanghai came into sight and we slid along the Bund, fronted by hotels
and office buildings, up to the Dollar docks on the Pootung side.
    A charming bit of intelligence greeted us. The bowlines were scarcely
secured before word arrived that in three days we were to head back
to Chinwangtao and discharge the girdles after all. A pall descended
on the ship; Hirschfeld and I sat drearily in the deserted smoking room,

wondering whether to transfer to another ship, or stay ashore until the *Flier* returned, or just hang ourselves from the nearest yardarm. We probably would have done the last had not the captain anticipated us and hid it in a locker. Eventually we decided to spend a night or two in Shanghai and see what diversions it offered. All the way across the Pacific there had been rumors of exquisitely complaisant White Russian countesses and unimaginable sins. Neither of us smoked opium, but we had no objection to learning. We thought we might even pick up a priceless bit of jade. We were in a mood for adventure. We got it.

We received the first installment before we even set foot on the levee. The tender which bore us to the Bund had no allotted slip or jetty; it merely tied up in slapdash fashion against five other boats, each moored to the one adjoining it, and the passengers swarmed over the lot like ants over a sugar bowl. In effect, what you had was a Bronx subway rush with water jumps. One moment I was braced against a stanchion gaping at the skyline; the next, I was caught up in a swirl of coolies and shot forward down into a barge full of stones. I clawed my way across it, sprang down a dark companionway, stumbled over three citizens stuffing themselves with bean curd, and landed in a perilously tossing sampan. As I straightened up to catch my breath, the second wave hit me. I saw Hirschfeld go past, flailing and kicking, his beard high in the air. "Hirschfeld!" I screamed piteously, *"Tovarisch!"* He paid me no attention; he had other fish to fry. I lowered my head like a bull and, with two Cantonese encircling me, did a line plunge. I reached terra firma a broken man, my collar in shreds, eyeglasses twisted, streaming with perspiration. Hirschfeld was nursing a wrenched knee, having slipped and fallen between two boats in the melee. He had a bloody nose and had lost a shoe, but otherwise he was as fit as a fiddle.

To regain some measure of poise, we proceeded to the Cathay Hotel, reputedly Shanghai's finest, and had a drink apiece. The bill came to $39,000 Chinese National Currency—about $3.36—and we left a tip of $5000, or 41 cents. The exchange rate at the moment was twelve thousand Chinese dollars to the American one, and prices had more or less kept abreast. Our room, for instance, was $120,000 a day— slightly over ten dollars—and our breakfast $14,000. The real drawback, though, was the complete lack of any form of heat. A ton of coal cost three hundred U. S. dollars—in any case, a purely academic consideration at the Cathay, as the Japanese had stripped it of radiators and boilers. That night will linger in my memory as one of the most agonizing I have ever endured. Our teeth chattered so loudly that several Americans resident there phoned the Embassy to report gunfire.

Just to indicate how cold it was, I left a tumbler of water at my bedside and when I woke up, it was gone. Hirschfeld had drunk it and also had eaten the glass. That was one cold night.

The following day we embarked on a shopping tour of the antique bazaars in the Kwantung Road, charmed at every turn by the indescribable wealth of imagination the Chinese lavish on their art. Surrounded by so much beauty, it was difficult to determine what to choose; Hirschfeld finally settled on an imitation cloisonné cigarette stand complete with match receptacle and ashtrays, and I bought three ivory back-scratchers you could not duplicate in San Francisco for less than a quarter. About midafternoon we traced our steps to the American Club, a pleasant establishment in Foochow Road made doubly delightful by the circumstance that it had the only heated bar in town. Five whisky sours drove the chill from our bones, and we decided to have a drink. There then ensued a hazy interval during which I seem to recall the sound of a cupful of poker dice being thrown repeatedly against a board and a playful attempt on my part to comb Hirschfeld's beard with a back-scratcher. From time to time strange faces swam into my field of vision; I remember a laborious, protracted recital by an UNRRA official of his difficulties in persuading the Chinese to eat canned peaches, but part of it was being given in Russian and some men were accompanying him on balalaikas. It suddenly grew much colder and I found myself in a very dim night club, teaching an exophthalmic Hungarian girl the Cubanola glide. The next morning I felt remarkably listless and there was an outbreak of beef Stroganoff on my tie as though I were coming down with a fever, but these symptoms soon passed, and by noon I was able to keep down a little clear broth made of Angostura, lemon peel, and bourbon.

What with the penetrating cold and the cost of living in Shanghai, it seemed on the whole inadvisable to tarry, and folding our hands submissively we journeyed north once more to Chinwangtao on the *Flier*. It took four interminable days to get rid of our cargo; my companion mooned in the cabin buffing his nails and I made a short excursion to Shanhaikwan to see the Great Wall. The Great Wall can also be seen facing page 556 of the Encyclopaedia Britannica by simply stretching your hand toward the bookcase, though the chances of picking up a flea are very much smaller. Shanhaikwan, it is interesting to note, has the smallest fleas in China; they are much prized by collectors, but I was fortunate enough to secure three or four fine specimens. As the Chinese government strictly forbids their export, I had to smuggle them out in my clothing, but I managed to get them through to Singapore safe and sound.

Shanghai once more, and this time it was the twenty-eighth of March, the end of the first week of spring. All through it we had lain alongside the wharf, the Plimsoll line rising hourly higher as ton after ton of goods went over the side. Across the river, in the barren fields, the trees had begun to show a cloudy green nimbus; the sun was hot, and in the sampans drifting downstream groups of children were playing jacks. I lounged on the boat deck and thought of the Pennsylvania countryside, of the forsythia primrose-yellow against the barn, the Judas tree bursting into bloom, the swollen creek tumbling through the pasture. I asked myself what I was doing ten thousand miles from home, on what obscure quest I had come, and I could find no answer. Perhaps Thoreau knew; he knew everything. I went into my cabin and got out *Walden*. There it was, in that always concise and astringent prose, the *vade mecum* for every wanderer:

"It is not worth the while to go round the world to count the cats in Zanzibar. Yet do this even till you can do better, and you may perhaps find some 'Symmes' Hole' by which to get at the inside at last. England and France, Spain and Portugal, Gold Coast and Slave Coast, all front on this private sea; but no bark from them has ventured out of sight of land, though it is without doubt the direct way to India. If you would learn to speak all tongues and conform to the customs of all nations, if you would travel farther than all travellers, be naturalized in all climes, and cause the Sphinx to dash her head against a stone, even obey the precept of the old philosopher, and Explore thyself. Herein are demanded the eye and the nerve. Only the defeated and deserters go to the wars, cowards that run away and enlist. Start now on that farthest western way, which does not pause at the Mississippi or the Pacific, nor conduct toward a worn-out China or Japan, but leads on direct, a tangent to this sphere, summer and winter, day and night, sun down, moon down, and at last earth down too."

CARRY ME BACK TO OLD PASTRAMI

PRECISELY SIX WEEKS from the raw midwinter evening on which the
S.S. Marine Flier had cleared the Golden Gate for the Chinese ports
and Singapore, a pair of passengers in rumpled seersucker and shirts
that gave every evidence of having laundered themselves teetered
down the accommodation ladder and landed unsteadily on the dockside at Kowloon. Across the bay, at the base of a volcanic peak studded
with opulent villas, lay huddled the historic crown colony of Hong
Kong, Far Eastern bastion of Britain's thin red line of empire. The
two American *Wandervogels* contemplating the panorama before them
were a striking sight—the prognathous jaw of Perelman smoothly
flowing into a skull resembling that of Cro-Magnon Man, Hirschfeld's
cunning ferret eyes gleaming above his unkempt tangle of beard, and
beyond, in the quickening dusk, the mighty colonial outpost immortalized by Hoagy Carmichael in his rondeau of the very unfortunate
Chinaman. For a full minute they paused lost in admiration of this city
hewn from the living rock, so much a symbol of the indomitable British
character, and then Hirschfeld gave vent to a long-drawn sigh.

"You know what I'd do if that were mine?" he asked. I turned toward him impulsively, knowing that in the wellsprings of his heart there
dwelt a true libertarian, a man flash-quick and whippet-fast to sympathize with the oppressed and downtrodden. I was not disappointed;
when he spoke again, it was in a voice vibrant with feeling: "I'd trade
it all for a hot pastrami sandwich." The homely phrase, freighted with
nostalgia, found my Achilles' heel; on the instant all the secret pent-up
longing of weeks burst forth and we wept uncontrollably on each
other's shoulders, shedding hot salt pastrami tears. I believe that had
there been a branch of Lindy's within forty miles of Hong Kong that
night, we would have cheerfully crept there on our hands and knees.
It was the beginning of a homesickness which, as the trip progressed,
took on the proportions of an obsession; time and again, in such unlikely places as the Temple of the Emerald Buddha and the ruins of
Fatehpur Sikri, a vision of strawberry cheesecake would swim before
us, taunting us almost to the brink of madness.

To the naked eye, and ours were reasonably nude as we ventured
up the central avenue of Kowloon, Hong Kong's principal suburb was
indistinguishable from Asbury Park out of season. There were the

same depressingly uniform rows of yellow stucco apartments, the same flyblown stationery stores featuring outdated copies of *Peek* and *Leer,* the same curio shops full of sleazy kimonos, brass daggers, incense burners, and souvenir pillows engraved with the Chinese equivalent of "Fir Yew I Pine and Balsam Too." At the Kowloon Hotel we drank warm Danish beer under the whirling overhead fans and eavesdropped on a quartet of Royal Marine Commandos boasting about their amatory exploits. For a while we sat enthralled at the lushness of their profanity and their dauntless ability to interthread every third word with one of the breezier copulative verbs, but soon ennui supervened and we set off listlessly for the ship. Suddenly, without any warning, adventure appeared in the person of a brisk young American naval intelligence officer. Lieutenant Wilson, it developed, had heard on the grapevine that Hirschfeld and I were footloose in Asia; he was on his way to an audience with Bao Dai, the deposed Emperor of Annam in Indo-China, and wondered if we cared to accompany him. The invitation could not have been more beautifully timed, for, curiously enough, I had just finished observing to Hirschfeld that I could not imagine balmier weather for meeting deposed Annamite emperors. It was one of those creepy coincidences which occur in actual life, but which, when the novelist employs them, sound so implausible.

Riding over to Hong Kong on the ferry, we gleaned a few vital statistics about Bao Dai. He had belonged to possibly the oldest ruling family in the world, was thirty-three years old, was rumored to have thirty-three children, and was regarded as semi-divine by his people. His palace at Hué, before its destruction by the Vietnamese, was reported to have been of a magnificence unparalleled even in the imagination of Darryl Zanuck. For the past sixteen months of his exile, while waiting hopefully for the French to restore him to his throne, he had been living in Hong Kong, attending at least one movie daily and spending his evenings at a taxi dance hall. Other than that, Wilson knew nothing. He had never met the former monarch personally, but poolroom gossip had it that he was a sweet, wholesome kid.

The pleasure dome where His Majesty frolicked nightly turned out to be a somewhat sedater version of Broadway's Roseland; ten or twelve British and Eurasian couples were foxtrotting grimly to "I Found a Roach in the Devil's Garden," played with deafening incompetence by sixteen impassive Chinese. Bao Dai was seated in a snug alcove surrounded by several hostesses whose skinny necks and high-pitched avian cackle lent them more than a passing resemblance to a flock of spring fryers. The royal exile, a short, slippery-looking customer rather on the pudgy side and freshly dipped in Crisco, wore a fixed, oily grin that was vaguely reptilian. Since he spoke almost no English, the interview was necessarily limited to pidgin and whatever pathetic scraps of French we could remember from Frazier and Square. To put him at his ease, I inquired sociably whether the pen of his uncle was in the garden. Apparently the query was fraught with delicate political implications involving the conflict in Indo-China, for he shrugged evasively and buried his nose in his whisky-and-soda.

"Why don't you try him on the movies?" suggested Lieutenant Wilson, gently disentangling the fingers of a hostess from the wallet in his hip pocket. The notion seemed a fertile one; a little adroit questioning revealed that His Highness' favorite screen actress was Jeanette Mac-Donald. Here indeed was a common bond; I disclosed that at a distant epoch of my life, under the lash of hunger, I had helped contrive the *mise en scène* for one of her films, a pestilence called *Sweethearts*. Bao Dai was immediately enchanted. Could I divulge any little personality secrets, any charming traits or whimsies to aid him toward a fuller understanding of the noted *vedette*? I told him regretfully that I could not, apart from the fact that she was known colloquially in Hollywood as "The Iron Butterfly" and her co-star as "The Singing Capon"; I had never wittingly exposed myself to her glamour. A thoughtful five-minute silence followed this cultural exchange, ended by the entrance of a small, silky party who was evidently a combination of finger man, public relations counsel, and court chamberlain. He drew me aside and, to the strains of "Milenberg Joys," cleared up what he termed to be several popular misconceptions about the boss. For example, he said, certain elements had been circulating tales that His Highness liked to smoke a little pipe or two. He could brand this as a calumny; His Highness was a serious student of international affairs who kept abreast of all the latest political developments and was deeply interested in economics, sociology, archaeology, paleontology, epistemology, hagiology, and dendrology. Backbiters were also saying that His Highness was frivolous because he went to the movies every afternoon. If he did, it was only in an effort to improve his English. (I tried to ascertain just what His Highness was improving at the Paramount Ballrooms, but all I got was a grunt.) At this juncture, a bone-cracking yawn contorted the regal lineaments, clearly signifying that the audience was over. We shook hands formally all around, paid through the nose for the refreshments and the society of the ladies, and took off, grateful that we had had this rare chance to cement international good-fellowship.

In the two or three days the *Marine Flier* lingered at Hong Kong, we naturally had only the most fleeting opportunity to look around, but what we saw was a welcome contrast to the confusion and grinding poverty of Shanghai. British authority, if unable to house and feed all the homeless, had nevertheless succeeded in establishing a sense of cleanliness and order. Scattered houses still showed where Japanese bombs had fallen, but they were fast being rebuilt and it was obvious the war had receded in people's minds. The island is a lovely one; the scenery in the vicinity of Repulse Bay and Stanley Village, with its many coves and headlands, is certainly as delightful as any I know. It would have been pleasant to vegetate awhile in the sun and contemplate each other's navels. Hirschfeld, however, was not only self-conscious but had no navel. Perhaps, though, I could get him one; I'd heard you could get almost anything where I was going next—namely, Macao.

It was unthinkable for anyone who had consumed as much pulp fiction as myself to put into Hong Kong without visiting Macao, widely acclaimed as the wickedest city in the East, and I lost no time in making the pilgrimage. Macao, the last remnant of Portuguese glory in China, lies four and a half hours from the crown colony by coastal ferry and is usually mentioned in a furtive whisper after the ladies have left the table. According to Hendrik de Leeuw's *Cities of Sin* and "Rainbow in Blood Alley," a story in a recent issue of *Esquire*, this tiny community is one of the most sinister places on earth; the Casbah in Algiers and the Cannebière in Marseilles are as meetings of the Dorcas Society by comparison. To it, the legend goes, gravitate the cutthroat, gambler, Jezebel, and drug addict when the underworld finally closes its doors; whatever your whim, whether opium, fan-tan, or the sing-song girls, Macao waits to gratify it.

On the basis of an overnight sojourn, I can report that I found the Pearl of the Orient slightly less exciting than a rainy Sunday evening in Rochester. I checked into the Grand Hotel on the Avenida Almeira Ribeiro about nine-thirty in the evening with my pulses playing the *Bolero*, a sheaf of bank notes pinned inside my shirt, and a fever of 102. I was loaded for bear and equipped to cut a wide swath through the night life. Although my enthusiasm had been dampened momentarily by a Portuguese *senhor* on the boat, who informed me that the principal industries were the salting of fish and the manufacture of firecrackers, I figured he was concealing something. After all, a public librarian and licensee in economic and financial law, as his card proclaimed him to be, could not be expected to know the hot spots.

At the Central Hotel, a ramshackle structure advertised as the ultimate in gaiety and chic, I managed to procure at considerable expense one of the worst meals I have ever eaten in my life. It was constructed around a chicken that had accompanied Vasco da Gama on his earliest voyage of exploration; the flesh was in an almost perfect state of petrifaction and the chef, in a palpable effort to tickle my palate, had cunningly skewered it with a hairpin. It was served by three lethargic youths and a couple of equally apathetic teen-age misses in middy blouses, all five of whom moved with the fixed, trancelike rigidity of somnambulists. Fighting off a growing sense of depression, I made my way to the combination gambling casino and cabaret on the roof. My dinner may have been a washout, I conceded, but from here in things were going to be strictly E. Phillips Oppenheim—lovely haggard women staking their last franc on the turn of a card, lean satanic operatives with black monocles and impeccable evening clothes, the mingled scent of Nuit d'Amour, Sobranies, and hashish.

The gambling hell, I was a bit taken aback to discover, was a bleak, echoing auditorium of the type favored by Lithuanian glee clubs for their monthly singfests. The half dozen sleepy Chinese girls presiding over the fan-tan tables eyed me with a pronounced lack of interest and returned to their dog-eared movie magazines. Word must have spread, nevertheless, that a red-hot Yankee spendthrift had entered the premises, because the orchestra in the next room forthwith struck up one of our characteristic popular airs, "Pony Boy." Squaring my shoulders, I entered a murky grillroom such as you might discover in the second-best hotel in Columbia, South Carolina. Here fun was at its maddest; two pairs of Chinese hostesses sporting spectacular gold teeth were dancing torpidly with each other while a few pimply Portuguese sports lay around glassily, fanning themselves and waiting for a coronary thrombosis to put them out of their misery. I had consumed the major portion of a bottle of abominable red wine when the headwaiter came up, chaperoning a fat girl with frizzed hair and a mottled complexion.

"Allow me to present a most beautiful person, Miss Linda Andrada," he fluted. "She has consented to share your company for a small fee." The beautiful person thereupon ordered a lime smash and we conversed haltingly for an hour about life and letters in Macao. By another of those strange literary coincidences, Miss Andrada's favorite actress also turned out to be Jeanette MacDonald, for whom, she confessed archly, she had often been mistaken. I assured her that the resemblance was uncanny and confided that I too had been frequently mistaken for Richard Burbage. Unfortunately, just as our friendship was burgeoning into something that might today be a bitter-sweet memory, the orchestra played a farewell flourish. My vis-à-vis coyly

intimated that if I were masterful enough, she might be prevailed upon
to show me some rare old Portuguese mezzotints at her flat, but as I
could not conceivably have gone there without my duenna, I was
forced to decline. We parted with fervent promises to write each other
daily and I made off for my hotel through a network of dark alleys. It
must have been an off night in Macao, for when I reached my room
and undressed, there was not a single haft of a knife protruding from
the small of my back. True, the springless Chinese bed I slept on could
not compare with my Beautyrest, and I can still taste the toast spread
with yak fat I breakfasted on the next morning, but for sheer profligacy,
for debauchery like Mother used to make, that evening at the Central
will long live in my memory. When I regained the *Marine Flier*, Hirschfeld and the other passengers inevitably insisted on hearing about my
experiences, but I merely laid my finger slyly alongside my nose and
gave them a knowing wink. If the exploit accomplished nothing else, it
raised my prestige in the fo'c'sle. The next morning, as I passed a couple of old sea-dogs splicing rope amidships, I heard one whisper respectfully, "That's the man who spent the night in Macao."

Two days south of Hong Kong, the heat began; awnings appeared
on the afterdeck and the fantail, the cabins were loud with the whine
of electric fans, and life moved in a slower, lazier rhythm. During the
day the metal decks blazed underfoot; there were violent tropical
downpours, sunsets that made the reason totter, nights filled with a
million stars. The young American matron at our table, returning
home to face a difficult divorce, unexpectedly found herself the object
of furious adoration by the third mate; the deck and engineer cadets
dawdled endlessly about her daughter, flexing their muscles and holding long philosophical symposiums about love.

"I think that if a man gives a girl his class ring, why then she
oughtn't to date anybody else."

"Yes, but it's not like an *engagement* ring, dope."

"It could be, if he wants it that way. I heard of a girl that was secretly engaged to a man for four years and everybody thought she was
just wearing his class ring."

"Did they get married?"

"No, he went back to prep school."

"There you are. If this man was really serious about this girl, he'd
have given her a real ring, not a little old *class* ring."

Then, one hot sultry morning, we awoke to the rattle of the anchor
chains in the Singapore roadstead and the realization, at once gratify-

ing and oppressive, that we had reached the midway mark of our journey. Seated in the tender pulling away from the *Marine Flier*, our luggage heaped about us, we waved goodbye to officers and crew with a sense of unreality; already they were strangers, phantoms whose identity we would puzzle over in a drawerful of blackened snapshots. The sun was high overhead and merciless by the time we arrived at the Raffles Hotel, and it was good to relax over a gimlet in the cool darkness, even if the celebrated bar did fall short of my preconceptions. I had expected something straight out of Somerset Maugham, paneled in mahogany and full of aquiline-featured cads involved in desperate intrigues with the wives of neighboring planters. What I saw instead was a double row of tables strongly suggestive of a Childs restaurant, flanking a dance floor that cried out for a mother-of-pearl jukebox to complete its utter commonplaceness. The people about us may have been cads, but their skins had been tanned by gin and bitters rather than fierce tropical suns. At noon the room began taking on the aspect of a New Jersey beach hotel; comfortable bourgeois families exchanged condolences about the servant problem and their children slid up and down the dance floor, whooping and pinching each other. It was very disillusioning, and whether it was due to travel fatigue, or the four gimlets I had taken, or the end of my boyhood dream, it made me want to cry.

That night Hirschfeld and I lay in our mosquito-netted trundle beds in the room we shared with two other birds of passage and listened reverently to the muted pulsebeat of the East. Down the gallery an asthmatic phonograph was scratching out Count Basie's "One O'Clock Jump" and next door an Australian woman whimpered for clemency as her liege lord methodically beat the living kapok out of her. Ever and again the snores of our fellow-lodgers rose antiphonally, interspersed with melancholy groans and paraphrases of *Finnegans Wake*. I heard a vicious slap and Hirschfeld's stifled malediction.

"You know," I murmured thoughtfully, "we could have had all this in the Bronx for a five-cent subway ride."

"Sure," agreed Hirschfeld, "but who the hell would believe it?"

THE ROAD TO MANDALAY

THE OLD Vauxhall saloon swung off the macadam road, emitted a tragic, lingering cough evocative of Camille, and, pistons hammering, panted up the long graveled driveway. Ahead of us, through the casuarinas and banana palms, appeared the outlines of a rambling, cream-colored villa—the residence of the Tungku Makhota. His Highness Ismail, Grandfather of the Shrine, Commander of the Most Noble and Exalted Order of St. Michael and St. George, Prince Regent and Heir Apparent of the throne of the Malay state of Johore. Wedged in the rear seat beside me, Hirschfeld cleared his throat nervously, produced a pocket comb for at least the tenth time that morning, and curried his beard, fluffing it out until it frothed like a zabaglione around his chin.

"Do you think I look all right?" he whispered anxiously. It was evident that the strain of our impending visit to the home of the Malay potentate was telling on him; his hand shook and a drop of perspiration glinted on his forehead, almost obscuring it. By contrast, though I say it in no spirit of braggadocio, I was as glacial and reserved as Sumner Welles at a B'nai B'rith picnic. Despite the fact that I had donned two left shoes and an ambassadorial sash that clashed slightly with my khaki shorts, I bore myself with icy *sang-froid* and a determination not to let myself be overawed. From the moment the Regent had signified through a go-between in Singapore that he would be pleased to receive us at luncheon, I had known exactly what attitude I should adopt toward him. Not for me to play the servile toady, the cringing lickspittle; no hangdog caitiff I. I would slap him on the back with easy backwoods familiarity, offer him a chaw of Mail Pouch, and drawl, "Wa'al, pardner, I reckon we folks over yonder don't sot much store by this king stuff, but by vum, I ain't minded to hold it agin ye. I like my vittles plain, my likker straight, and my women purty. I don't rile easy, but when I'm mean, I'm ornery as pizen, an' I kin whup my weight in bobcats. I aim to shoot squar', but if'n you're a wrong Injun—watch out!"

The car screeched to a stop beneath a cement porte-cochere; a pair of Malay guards in smart gray-green uniforms and bare feet sprang to attention, stiffly presenting their carbines. Simultaneously, a plump, dark-skinned gentleman in a purple sports shirt appeared dynamically at the stairhead, surrounded by half a dozen huge Belgian shepherd dogs gamboling in a frenzy about him. "There you are, there you are!"

he exclaimed, his manner clearly betraying he had not the foggiest notion of our identity. "Come along now, both of you, come along!" I was just preparing to deliver my homespun salutation when one of the dogs darted between my legs from behind and I was catapulted indoors, straddling the brute in a highly undignified and, indeed, perilous fashion. Had I not had the quick-wittedness to wrap my arms tightly about the dog's neck and gallop until he sank under me, I might easily have dashed out my brains on the terrazzo floor. The hazard I stood in must have escaped the spectators, for the Regent, obviously a man with a primitive sense of humor, burst into howls of mirth, in which Hirschfeld, ever eager to scrape favor with persons of consequence, hastily joined. I pride myself that my sense of the absurd is as keen as the next man's, and goodness knows I relish a joke even at my own expense; but what there was in my plight to provoke screams of laughter, I do not know. Possibly they had never seen a man on a dog before.

Administering a surreptitious kick to the mongrel who had almost cooked my goose, I followed our host through a series of vast bilious chambers crowded with modernique skyscraper furniture and presently fetched up in a room that put the Roxy lounge to shame. Scattered about it in frozen groups suggestive of the waxworks at the Eden Musée sat twelve or fourteen British colonials and their ladies, staring frigidly at each other and murmuring "Quaite." Every so often, one of the more mettlesome would lean forward, suck his false dentures into position, and whinny, "I say, I do love a bit of Stilton now and then. It never lets you down." I drained off a cocktail compounded of saddle soap and *crème de cacao* and proceeded to inspect the objects of virtu housed in glass cases around the walls. The jade, rose quartz, and ivories would certainly have made any museum curator swoon with desire; there were porcelains, enamels, and gold ornaments beyond all value; but what made the collection particularly noteworthy was the owner's utter catholicity of taste. Side by side with his most priceless bijoux were gewgaws straight out of a Sixth Avenue schlock store— worry-birds, lynchee dolls, and all manner of related bric-a-brac. A plaster cast of an Italian fisherboy nibbling a bunch of cherries stood cheek by jowl with a jade Buddha that must have cost an entire Chinese province; two fabulous Ming vases shared honors with a Mickey Mouse ash tray from some Coney Island ski-ball concession. Just as Hirschfeld and I were examining, with a certain degree of repulsion, a tinted photograph of the Regent posed before his Mercedes-Benz, which he had caused to be snipped out and mounted on cardboard like an icon, he buzzed over to us.

"Well?" he inquired, preening himself with a small jade preening fork. "What do you think of my collection?"

"So-so, bub," I rejoined carelessly. "I like a couple of those doodads you've got there."

"In other words," purred the Regent, a sinister gleam invading his eye, "you think the rest of it is junk, eh?" Hirschfeld's blood froze; he immediately saw visions of us being garrotted in the courtyard, flung into moats boiling with crocodiles. He trod heavily on my toe to warn me of our danger, but I refused to be deflected.

"Yes, wise guy," I snapped, "a lot of it *is* junk." The prince chuckled.

"I agree with you," he said mildly, "but I like junk. Wait till you see what you get for lunch."

He was as good as his word. Never have I eaten tapioca in so many forms. There was tapioca soup, filet of tapioca, roast vest of tapioca, tapioca cookies, and a special dessert made of tapioca, bamboo, and shad roe that had been run through a carburetor, dried, and buried under a banyan tree for two years. To further add to my tribulations, I was placed opposite the wife of the Regent, who wore in her corsage a diamond of such matchless water that every time I looked up, its brilliance well-nigh blinded me. Hirschfeld, seated next to her, kept eying it with ill-concealed cupidity. At length, having screwed up his courage, he launched into an elaborate paroxysm of coughing, and using his napkin as a shield, tried to wrench the bauble off the royal balcony, but all he got for his pains was a stinging blow across the knuckles with a nut-pick. Conversation between my luncheon partner, a desiccated British gentlewoman in flowered chiffon, and myself was somewhat on the desultory side; she seemed astonished that I was not wearing my tomahawk and declared that she had no desire to visit New York as a friend of hers had been gored by a charging bison in Wall Street. Putting her at ease with a few jocose references to the Boston Tea Party, the War of 1812, and one or two similar highlights in Anglo-American relations, I transferred my attention to the Regent on my left. I found him a keen observer of our domestic scene, notably that portion of it centering about Hollywood.

"Based upon your personal experience," he asked with a thoughtful frown, "would you say that Greer Garson wears falsies?" I assured him that my knowledge of the queenly redhead was purely limited to abhorring her from afar, and, to assuage his disappointment, quoted the opinions of eminent workers in the field like Earl Wilson, Sidney Skolsky, et al. From this we progressed to a consideration of the comparative merits of Ann Sheridan, Esther Williams, Mae West, and, inescapably, Jane Russell. I suggested that His Highness toy with the possibility of buying up the latter and moving her piecemeal to Malaya as a curiosity, much in the way William Randolph Hearst used to with Scotch castles, but I gathered he was appalled by the magnitude of the undertaking.

"Well," he said at length, casting a quick glance about the table to make sure everyone was thoroughly tapioca-happy, "now for the *pièce de résistance*—my zoo." We followed with alacrity, remembering wondrous tales told in the bars of Singapore of his prowess as a big-game hunter. And indeed one would have to go a long way to equal the specimens we saw that day in his compound—all the way to a New Jersey chicken farm, in fact. With the exception of three disgruntled parrots who must have slipped in by mistake, the palace zoo consisted of two hundred of the most beat-out fowls conceivable—Plymouth Rocks, White Wyandottes, and Rhode Island Reds. Their master surveyed them tenderly, yet along with his pride I thought I detected a hint of fear in his face. I was right. Suddenly before my eyes all the pomp and circumstance of the monarch fell away and the Tungku Makhota became just a little harassed citizen caught in the economic deadfall. "You know," he said helplessly, in almost the words my father had used twenty-five years before when our poultry farm went down the drain, "those God-damn things'll eat me out of house and home."

There are other vignettes of Johore sharply etched on the memory—our afternoon with the elderly sister of the Sultan, the Tengku Ampuan, a woman of surpassing grace and distinction; the colorful tattoo put on by the Welsh Fusiliers, quite patently to remind the natives that the British lion still had claws; the reckless profusion of orchids on everyone's dinner table, worth hundreds of dollars by New York midwinter standards; and most unforgettable of all, our visit to a rubber estate. There ought to be some kind of insurance policy available whereby the traveler could protect himself against visiting a rubber estate. Unless your name is Harvey Firestone, it is doubtful whether the sight of twelve thousand acres of future hot-water bottles will affect you as the Grecian urn did Keats. For five agonizing hours under the aegis of a methodical Dane who knew all there was to know about rubber, we were dragged over the largest plantation in Johore and shown it tree by tree. Perhaps I am deficient in what the advertising priesthood refers to as the poetry of big business, but as I stood under a corrugated iron shed, coughing back ammonia fumes and watching the liquid latex dribble out of the centrifuges, it seemed an awful lot of trouble to go to for a simple two-way stretch. But then, knock wood, I don't suffer from middle-aged spread.

Beguiling as was Malaya, it was long since time for us to wend our way toward Siam, our next destination. Hirschfeld, less impatient than myself, preferred to make the journey by ship, so, presenting him with a pair of Ayvad's water wings and my blessing, I took off one sweltering morning for Bangkok in a BOAC flying boat. The five-hour trip was comfortable and uneventful, and as we skimmed effortlessly over the hundreds of tiny islands studding the azure waters of the Gulf of Siam, they seemed to sparkle like hundreds of tiny islands studding the Gulf of Siam. Five other passengers shared the cabin—three extremely wretched-looking Chinese, whose gums cantilevered every time we hit an air pocket, a studious Indian gentleman in massive horn-rimmed spectacles traveling for the Y.M.C.A., and the corpulent, florid-faced representative of an American machinery firm. The latter treated me to the usual diatribe about the alarming inroads of Communism among his servants, the imminent collapse of the democratic ideal due to the fulminations of Henry Wallace, *und so weiter*. When he had concluded and lay back steaming with indignation, the Indian gentleman took over. Producing a stack of back issues of *Reader's Digest*, he read aloud to me in a nasal singsong five or eight dozen of those exhilarating fillers its pages are speckled with—The Cutest Thing My Dog Ever Said, Is Heart-Disease Killing One in Three?, Palo Alto Solves Its Sewage Problem, and You Are Never Too Old to Take Up Fencing. He was just graduating into excerpts from Liebman's *Peace of Mind* and Fink's *Release from Nervous Tension*, both of which my system could have used to advantage, when the aircraft providentially glided down to its anchorage in the Klong Toi outside the Siamese capital.

In my innocence I had supposed that hotel accommodations in a city as remote as Bangkok could be had for the asking, but the one European hostelry I managed to discover, the Ratanakosindr, was full up and no amount of cajolery, bribery, or sign language could induce the staff to part with a shakedown. At last, a kindly American film exhibitor saw me seated on a mound of satchels softly sobbing to myself. He blew my nose, stirred up a jeep, and drove me to the home of our military attaché, who, by some telepathy I still cannot fathom, was expecting me. Colonel Randolph, a lanky, affable Texan, had flown with distinction in the Pacific and European theaters, a service for which his country had rather ambiguously rewarded him by thrusting him into the thick of Siamese political intrigue. He put his extensive, airy house and his twelve servants at my disposal, gave me a fatherly talk about the rate of exchange, and, with consummate tact, left me to my own devices.

From the very beginning I was charmed by Bangkok, and I propose to be aggressively syrupy about it in the most buckeye travelogue manner. I liked its polite, gentle, handsome people, its temples, flowers, and canals, the relaxed and peaceful rhythm of life there. Apart from its shrill and tumultuous central thoroughfare swarming with Chinese and Indian bazaars, it struck me as the most soothing metropolis I had thus far seen in the East. Its character is complex and inconsistent; it seems at once to combine the Hannibal, Missouri, of Mark Twain's boyhood with Beverly Hills, the Low Countries, and Chinatown. You pass from populous, glaring streets laden with traffic into quiet country lanes paralleled by canals out of a Dutch painting; a tree-shaded avenue of pretentious mansions set in wide lawns abruptly becomes a bustling row of shops and stalls, then melts into a sunny village of thatched huts among which water buffalo graze. The effect is indescribably pleasing; your eye constantly discovers new vistas, isolated little communities around every corner tempting you to explore them.

Unfortunately it is hot; it was most damnably hot in April, the very peak of Siamese summer, and sightseeing at ninety-six degrees requires stamina. Most of mine evaporated after trudging through the National Museum and a couple of the Siamese wats, or temples, but it was nevertheless a completely rewarding experience. The Temple of the Emerald Buddha, in the monastery adjoining the palace, is mandatory sightseeing. Its flaunting, sportive improvisations of gilt and lacquer, the glass-and-tile mosaics, the bronze Garudas, and the rows of colossal, multi-colored divinities guarding its approaches dazzle an Occidental accustomed to the severity of Greek and Roman architecture. Surrounding the temple, under an arcade extending for blocks, is an extraordinary mural of the Ramayana; one may be forgiven for gushing shamelessly over the taste and technical skill of the artists who wrought it. The National Museum (ignored in all the guidebooks I encountered) contains a superb collection of Buddhas from every part of Southeast Asia, as well as remarkable exhibits of costumes, musical instruments, theater puppets, and artifacts. One of the more touching items is a full-size wheelbarrow and spade of ivory, mother-of-pearl, and ebony made for some vanished princeling; also on view, in a murky corner, is a quaint model engine and tender, the "Victoria," presented by the eminent Queen to King Mongkut, the sovereign of *Anna and the King of Siam.*

With the arrival of Hirschfeld, wan and greenish after five days of smörgåsbord on a Scandinavian tramp (he had not taken a steamer after all but had ridden up on the shoulders of a Scandinavian tramp), my activities became somewhat less cerebral. We squandered a good three dollars on the midget horse races at the Royal Bangkok Sports Club, flirted outrageously with the cabaret girls at the Cathay, and wandered about the Chinese jewelers' shops in the Ban Moh. Aided by Hirschfeld's expert knowledge of gems and my own shrewd bargaining sense, I was enabled to pick up—at a fraction more than twice what I would have paid for them in America—three emeralds. I had them appraised later in Bombay and was told that they had been cut down from a very rare Coca-Cola bottle. Of course, I had known this at the time I bought them, but preferred not to damage Hirschfeld's self-esteem by mentioning it. Three or four hundred dollars is a small enough price to preserve a friendship, and in any case, I had paid for them in express checks filched from my friend's pants while he lay asleep.

I had but one fault to find with Hirschfeld during these halcyon days: a strange and stubborn fixation, amounting at times to a psychosis, that I might burden our expedition with a little pet or two. It happened that John Royola, who collects wild animals for the Rockefeller Foundation and many American zoological parks, was in Bangkok at the time, preparing to embark a shipment of specimens gathered in Burma, French Indo-China, and Siam. His depot in Bankopi was a fascinating storehouse of elephants, monkeys, and snakes, and we frequently used to drop in to watch him milk the cobras and Russell's vipers, whose crystallized venom is of considerable medical value. One morning I spotted a five-months-old baby elephant, less than a yard high and as cunning as the proverbial bug's ear, wandering around the grounds uprooting the bushes. He seemed to be about the right size for my apartment in New York; I figured I could tether him in the bathroom, and, when he became more robust, the children could ride him to school and economize on bus fares. As Royola, waving my check to dry it, vanished into the house to procure a blue satin bow to tie around the creature's neck, Hirschfeld blew his top.

"I'm through!" he spluttered, his face purple. "I refuse to travel in the same stateroom with that—that pachyderm!"

"Just a second there, Percy," I interrupted, biting the words out between my teeth, "you're talking about a member of my family. I don't interfere in your private life and I'll thank you to keep out of mine." The man's ferocity was startling to behold; he flung himself down in a temper, beat his fists on the earth, and foamed at the chops. It was so alarming, in sooth, that I had to call off the deal to forestall a most certain case of apoplexy. I could see Royola thought my crony's conduct extravagant; he offered to sell me something more compact, like a half-grown leopard or a banded krait, but Hirschfeld was inflexible. No doubt his years of urban living had atrophied that love of animals, that kinship toward things that creep and crawl, which Mother Nature endows us with at birth.

It is one of the profound limitations of the human spirit that even when we are at our most content, some obscure demon goads us on our way. We might have remained forever at Colonel Randolph's, gobbling his food, swilling his whisky, and tyrannizing his servants; indeed, so amiable was he I think we might almost have forced him out of his house altogether; but in less than a month the itch for new horizons was on us. There came a morning, inevitably, when we stood again at the airport, wringing his hand in farewell, bound back to Singapore and the steamer that would take us on to India.

"Goodbye, goodbye!" he called as the powerful motors rose in volume, "I'll never forget you, boys!" And well might he say so, for in our luggage, unbeknownst to him, reposed his best spoons, his wife's diamond clips, and three of his dress shirts. There he stood, erect and soldierly, a symbol of all that was best and most generous in the American way of life. Was it any wonder a lump formed in our throats as we waved adieu to Siam? Was it any wonder a second lump formed on top of the first one at the prospect of paying room rent and board again? Was it any wonder? Now I ask you.

THE BACK OF BEYOND

IF YOU had chanced to stray into the Western & Occidental Hotel in Penang, Malaya, during the ensuing fortnight (and if you did, you ought to have your head examined), you might have observed a curious derelict brooding over a lemon squash in the lobby. The four-day growth of beard, the feverish deep-sunk eyes, the nicotine-stained fingers, and the grimy singlet all told their pitiful but familiar tale of the beachcomber, yet another white man doomed to disintegration under the remorseless tropical sun. Could this brutish mass of protoplasm, one asked himself, really be a thinking, sentient human organism? Could this seedy castaway, mottled with heat rash and bereft of illusions, be the same buoyant pilgrim who had left New York just five months before, his head stuffed with romantic visions and his satchels with nylon hose? Could this bit of flotsam cast up on a lee shore, spurned by civilization and totally dormant above the neckband, conceivably be the author of these present lines? Brother, I hope to kiss a pig he could.

What made my imbroglio especially grievous, of course, was the fact that I had nobody to blame for it but myself. I had flown down from Siam to Singapore with Hirschfeld, only to discover that the *President Monroe*, which was to convey us to India, was lallygagging around somewhere in the South China Sea and would not arrive for at least twelve days. After two memorable nights at the Raffles Hotel, where we shared a mildewed lazaret with three other dupes and choked down what impressed me as the most odious cuisine in Asia, I threw in the towel. Why crucify ourselves in the heat and tedium of Singapore, I argued, when colorful Penang, with its superb beaches, horticultural gardens, and luxury hotels lay a day's journey distant up the peninsula? Since the ship was calling there anyway, the trip would be pure lagniappe, an extra dash of stardust unforeseen in our program. My logic was unassailable and my presentation masterly; but whether through inertia or some mysterious instinct that protects the feeble-minded, Hirschfeld refused to budge. Assuring him he was missing the experience of a lifetime, I engaged a compartment on the Malayan Railway, bid adieu to the Raffles in a philippic that shriveled the manager to a heap of volcanic ash, and squared away.

The first part of the journey, though boring, was supportable; the train wheezed along through endless miles of rubber estates, swampy jungle, and rather squalid villages, pausing at intervals to take on cordwood for the locomotive and permit buffalo gnats to batten on my blood. At Kuala Lumpur, the government seat, a dandy little surprise awaited me—all the first-class sleeping carriages were full up. I threatened, pleaded, ranted to no avail. Eventually I was bedded down in the second-class car, a weird affair of fourteen open bunks set in double tiers, stifling hot and crammed with Chinese, Malays, and Tamils. Every fifteen minutes during the night, a drenching tropical downpour swept in through the open windows, sluicing us out of our berths. About four o'clock, as we were dawdling in a station, someone outside flung in a banana peel which settled on my chest. My visit to the Pasteur Institute in Bangkok had made me a wee bit snake-conscious, and when I felt the clammy embrace, I naturally assumed a fer-de-lance was pitching woo at me. Fortunately, I had enough presence of mind to open my mouth and discharge a piercing scream. The signal penetrated to the caboose, and hastening forward, the conductor extricated me from the washroom where I had barricaded myself. In a few moments, under his calming influence, hysteria was restored, and with many a lighthearted chuckle we proceeded on our way.

All together I spent three and a half weeks in Penang before the *President Monroe* nosed over the horizon, and this much I will say for it: if you ever want a perfect honeymoon spot, a place where scenery and climate fuse to produce unadulterated witchery, where life has the tremulous sweetness of a plucked lute string and darkness falls all too soon, go to the Hotel Plaza in New York. Of all the lethargic, benighted, somnolent fleabags this side of Hollywood, the port of Georgetown on the island of Penang is the most abysmal. At the time I was there, its recreational facilities consisted of four Tarzan films, a dance hall housing eighty-five pock-marked Malay delinquents, a funicular railway, and a third-rate beach situated five miles from nowhere. If, after exhausting the potentialities of these, you retained any appetite for sightseeing, you could visit the Ayer Itam temple and the botanical gardens. The former is possibly the largest, and unquestionably the dullest, Buddhist temple in Malaya, and no wastebasket is complete without a snapshot of this historic shrine. The botanical gardens boast many varieties of cactus not found anywhere, not even in the botanical gardens. The day I was there, I waited almost three minutes for them to show up, but never caught so much as a glimpse of anything resembling a cactus. I related the incident subsequently to a group of passengers aboard ship who were discussing occasions on which they had failed to find cacti, and it was unanimously agreed that my experience was by far the most unusual.

I doubt if anyone short of Dante could describe the cookery at the Western & Occidental Hotel; I have heard it defended on the ground that it is no worse than the fare in any British colonial hotel, which is like saying that measles is no worse than virus pneumonia. The meal usually led off with an eerie gumbo identified as pumpkin soup, puce in color and dysenteric in effect. This was followed by a crisp morsel of the fish called *selangor* for want of a more scathing term, reminiscent in texture of a Daniel Green comfy slipper fried in deep fat. The roast was a pale, resilient scintilla of mutton that turned the tines of the fork, garnished with a spoonful of greenish boiled string and a dab of penicillin posing as a potato. For dessert there was *gula Malacca*, a glutinous blob of sago swimming in skimmed milk and caramel syrup, so indescribably saccharine that it produced a singing in the ears and screams of anguish from the bridgework. As the diner stiffened slowly in his chair, his features settling into the ghastly smile known as the *risus sardonicus,* the waiter administered the *coup de grâce,* a savory contrived of a moldy sardine spread-eagled on a bit of blackened toast. The exact nature of the thimbleful of rusty brown fluid that concluded the repast was uncertain. The only other time I saw it, awash in the scuppers of the *President Monroe,* the sailors called it bilge.

Between the food, the night life, and the uncompromisingly stiff-necked British vacationists guffawing over their pahits and sundowners, it was not very long before I was gibbering with loneliness. My two or three attempts to scrape acquaintance were greeted with the welcome commonly accorded a typhoid carrier. At length, by assiduously cultivating the Chinese night clerk and consenting to smuggle him into the States so that he could marry Barbara Stanwyck, I cadged an invitation to accompany him to his swimming club. We bathed in a tepid, oily swell dotted with fruit rinds and then adjourned to the clubhouse, where we sat in exquisite discomfort on broken rattan chairs, sipping orange crush and masochistically allowing chickens to peck at our bare tootsies. My companion's conversation, though voluble, was somewhat ambiguous; I listened brightly for a full hour to a panegyric on Dale Carnegie under the impression that he referred to the late-lamented Scotch philanthropist. The afternoon, nevertheless, was not wholly unproductive. Within forty-eight hours, I developed a dramatic fungus growth in the left ear indistinguishable from the mushroom the botanists call the Destroying Angel and ascribed by the doctor to bathing in contaminated water. Thanks to sulfanilamide, I was at least spared the final indignity of hobbling into old age brandishing an ear trumpet, but when kind hands assisted me up the Jacob's ladder of the *Monroe,* I was Lazarus risen from the dead.

Over the first decent coffee I had drunk in months, I poured out my doleful tale to Hirschfeld, but his malemute code contained no such word as compassion. Immediately upon my departure, he had fallen in with the wastrel set in Singapore and thereafter had lived like a debutante, guzzling Bollinger '23 and fresh Beluga caviar and roistering till the cows came home; indeed, on one occasion the cows were home three hours, milked, scrubbed, and chewing their cud in their stalls and Hirschfeld was still roistering. If I had any consolation, it was in the thought that Penang was now merely a memory. The moment I evolved that profound bit of philosophy, Fate drew back and gave me another boot in the derrière. For five livelong days, the *Monroe* lay alongside the wharf in the unspeakable heat while a gang of rachitic coolies listlessly transferred seventeen hundred tons of tin and rubber into her hold. As if our cup were not already full to overflowing, a fresh affliction arose; swarms of tiny man-eating midges from the freighter next to us invaded our cabins, brocading our milk-white skins with revolting scarlet weals. When the shoreline of Penang finally receded into the haze, I knelt down on the deck and spontaneously yielded up thanks for my deliverance. I arose with twin splotches of tar disfiguring my only pair of slacks, but I was in no mood to split hairs.

We made the run across the Indian Ocean to Ceylon in four days; it was the season of the southwest monsoon, marked by leaden, overcast skies and frequent squalls. Most of the ship's ninety-odd passengers were branch managers and representatives of American firms like International Harvester, Standard Oil, and Goodyear Rubber, bound home on leave or en route to other stations. They were a glum, abstracted lot who laughed little and spent the day discussing freight rates and tariffs. The only thing distinguishing us from the Sedalia Chamber of Commerce was the small contingent of Spaniards, Italians, and specious Central Europeans with cropped bullet heads and saber-cuts on their cheeks. The latter fervidly assured you that they were Swiss, but they showed a suspicious tendency to prick up their ears and whinny whenever a Strauss waltz was played. Far and away the most spectacular character on the ship, and a little whiff of gelignite that at times bade fair to explode the whole male passenger complement, was Mrs. Fuscher.

Mr. Fuscher, a tall, mealy German said to have been a very eminent Nazi in the employ of I. G. Farbenindustrie in Shanghai, was espoused to a lady who, to put it mildly, had been richly endowed. Every time she strode on deck in the pitifully brief halter and shorts she affected, eyes popped like champagne corks and strong men sobbed aloud. It did not seem possible that mere wisps of silk could confine such voluptuous charms; in fact, there were those who lived in the hope that a truant gust of wind might create a sensational diversion. On one occasion, I lashed myself to the brink of nervous collapse reading the same sentence over and over in Motley's *Rise of the Dutch Republic*, desperately trying to ignore Mrs. Fuscher as she stood silhouetted against the sun in a diaphanous sports dress. I thought it rather poor sportsmanship of Hirschfeld, incidentally, to show her a sketch of his representing me as a wolf baying against the moon, when he himself was so patently on the prowl.

Fuscher, needless to say, was fully aware of the electricity his wife generated and took care to guard her like the Jonker diamond. Then, by a stroke of luck, he was suddenly taken seasick, and it was every man for himself. I saw my chance during boat drill when I encountered the lovely creature hopelessly ensnared in her lifejacket, fluttering like a wounded bird. I quickly drew her into a dark companionway and managed to squeeze her into it properly, though it naturally required a certain amount of fussing with the straps. Just as she was giggling, "What are you doing, you foolish boy?" Hirschfeld slithered around the corner in his typically sneaky fashion.

"Hey, that's no way to put on a lifejacket," he snapped, shouldering me aside. "The tapes go over the front, like this." I let him demonstrate his method for what it was worth (and it was worth plenty, judging from the hammerlock he took on Mrs. Fuscher). We had almost reached the tickling stage when I glanced up accidentally and beheld Mr. Fuscher, arms akimbo, glowering down at us.

"What is the meaning of this—this *Schweinerei*?" he grunted. His wife blubbered out a breathless account of how helpful the American cavaliers had been, but he cut it short midway and marched her off. It was just as well, for the man was patently a dangerous lunatic of some sort and might easily have misconstrued our kindness to his wife. Traveling about the world in these disturbed times, one cannot be too careful to avoid situations like the foregoing, where perfectly laudable motives may lead to the gravest consequences.

As the days wore on, one other personality on board came into bold relief, that of Armand Brissac, the quartermaster. Monsieur Brissac was a grizzled, dapper individual of indeterminate age who confided to the unwary that he had circumnavigated the earth thirty-seven times, exclusive of having made myriad side trips into outlying parishes like the Gran Chaco, Nyassaland, the Gobi Desert, Baffin Bay, and Easter Island. The results of all this gypsying, he added, were codified in nineteen massive scrapbooks he planned to bequeath to the Smithsonian, and if the two I examined were any criterion, the collection may one day emerge as the largest gallery of pin-up girls in the world. Outside of a few faded postcards of the Canal Zone and Starlight Park, the albums contained nothing but thousands of snapshots of simpering young ladies in various stages of dishabille—all taken at his beach house in Venice, California, he solemnly assured me, in a spirit of the strictest scientific inquiry. It was obvious to anyone that Brissac's hobby had cost him an immense outlay of energy and money, and he made no secret of the fact that his lifework was far from complete.

"These are just American types," he explained offhandedly. "Before I'm finished, the record will embrace babes from every race on earth." The precise anthropological value of Brissac's library of cheesecake was, I must admit, a trifle dubious, but even if posterity denies him a place in the pantheon of science, his name will rank for single-mindedness of purpose with those of Casanova and Daddy Browning.

A general strike was in process at the city of Colombo when we reached it, and our anticipated two-day stay there was shortened to a matter of twelve hours. It was a keen disappointment, alleviated in part by a pleasant and quite unexpected compliment I received from the passport control officer. Following the usual inspection of visas and landing permits, he came up to me rather hesitantly.

"Do you mind if I tell you something?" he asked with a shy smile. "I've been stamping passports for years, but I'd just like to say that yours is one of the prettiest I've ever seen. It's done with real taste— not like *some* I could mention. May I ask who did it?" I revealed that I had most of my things done by a little old man in a side street who could copy anything and whose prices, consequently, were cheaper because he was out of the high rent district. "I knew it!" he said triumphantly. "That chap's an artist—he's going places." I told him about several places the old man had already been, and we parted with a warm exchange of handclasps, one of which I later brought back to my wife as a gift.

There is a widespread popular belief, no doubt fostered by obsolete geography books, that Ceylon's fame derives from her production of much of the world's tea crop. The notion is a completely erroneous one. The principal industry of the island is the manufacture of souvenir ebony elephants, cunningly constructed in such a way that the tusks and ears break off the moment one's ship is out of sight of land. This leaves the tourist with a misshapen chunk of wood that can be used effectively as either paperweight or missile, depending on his ability to adjust himself to local conditions. Luckily, Hirschfeld and I had been warned that unscrupulous curio dealers might try to palm off indestructible elephants on us and were very much on our guard. After trudging ceaselessly from shop to shop and deliberating over thousands of carvings, we managed to stumble on a truly gruesome pair which fulfilled every qualification and fell apart before we even reached the gangplank. We also acquired an impressive harvest of tortoise-shell combs, brass slopjars suitable for transplanting ferns, bamboo fans imported from South Attleboro, Massachusetts, and a pair of ingenious fly-whisks made of aigrettes and carabao horn. Apparently someone from the ship must have pointed us out as tourists (certainly nobody could have deduced it from seeing us stroll up the street toting our gimcracks), for a citizen with a knapsack and flute materialized shortly and conned us into angeling a fight between a mongoose and a cobra. For sheer, unalloyed excitement, the spectacle was easily as thrilling as any ballet Martha Graham ever devised; the varmints, so heavily doped that you could smell the barbital a block away, persistently got into a clinch worthy of Ingrid Bergman and Cary Grant and slobbered each other with kisses. The serpent finally vanished down a sewer, and disgorging a sizable slug of valuta to cover the loss, we slunk off to the vessel, bitterly denouncing ourselves for our imbecility.

Two days later, the *Monroe* slowly edged her way into the Alexandra Docks at Bombay and we stood on the threshold of India at last, salt-caked and battered by tempests but dauntless, our pillowcases bursting with soiled laundry, our pocketbooks tenanted only by bats, but hungry withal for the enchantments that lay ahead. To the politicians and religious leaders, the industrialists, lawyers, doctors, and members of the press who crowded about us piteously pleading for the one word that might resolve the difficulties besetting their land, our answer was always the same, "Not yet, fellows—see us at the end of the week." We might have put them off with some all-too-facile phrase, but custodians of the American Way that we were, true uptown Yankee Doodle boys, we knew the obligation that lay heavy on us: to walk softly and carry a big suitcase. It was a pretty important assignment a couple of middle-aged kids had chosen, to straighten out India's four hundred teeming millions by the time the *President Polk* came through a fortnight later, but we had two things on our side—plain old-fashioned gumption and lots of American know-how. We didn't know where we were going or how we'd get there, but we knew one thing—when we got there, we'd be there. And that's something, even if it's nothing.

IT'S NOT THE HEAT, IT'S THE CUPIDITY

THE CUBICLE was tiny, dark, and breathlessly hot, but the lackluster Indian official who occupied it and who was engaged in passing a couple of American camels through the needle's eye of the Bombay police was

even tinier, darker, and hotter. Spread out on the rickety table before
him, the welter of affidavits, permits, cards of identity, and mimeographed applications kept sifting to the floor like snowflakes as he
scratched away painstakingly, recording in quadruplicate such momentous information as the birthplace of our great-grandparents, our Social
Security numbers, the precise quantity of freckles on our buttocks. The
morning sun rose higher in the heavens and the room became suffocat-
ing. Bathed in perspiration, panting like draft animals, Hirschfeld and
I numbly watched our dossiers being woven into the vast crazy quilt
of the Alien Registration Section. From time to time, as if to reassure
himself that our photographs had not undergone some subtle transformation like the portrait of Dorian Gray, the clerk would whip open
our passports and narrowly scan our faces.

"You are S. J. Hirschfeld, you say?"

"Well, that's my name, but not my initials. They're his."

"But his name is Albert Perelman. I have it written down here."

"It's a mistake. The initials belong to the opposite names." The
official's face brightened; he knew there was something shady about us.

"Ah, so," he said hopefully. "Then the initials are made out wrong."

"No, no—they're the right initials, but the wrong *man*."

"Exactly. The passports are clearly not in order." He rose triumphantly and shoveled up a random armful of papers. "Follow me." By
sheer noise, gesticulation, and, inevitably, a folded ten-rupee note
circumspectly shoved under the blotter, we browbeat the man into per-
ceiving his error. Grumbling sourly, he resumed his minute scrutiny
of our credentials. Weeks, years, epochs passed; dynasties rose and fell,
and still the idiot bureaucrat chewed his penholder and deliberated
whether our presence in India ran counter to regulation. The other
visas, though they were completely outside his jurisdiction, fascinated
him unbearably; he continually held them up to the light, grumbled
over the stamps, and clucked appreciation of their terminology. At
length, his last flimsy pretext gone, he affixed his chop with infinite bad
grace and the maximum amount of fussing with rubber stamps. Three
hours after the portals of the Criminal Investigation Division had swallowed us up, we reeled into the street with the grudging permission of
the authorities freely to pass—provided, of course, that we signified
our intention to leave, reported to the police promptly on arrival, and
informed the Bombay Residency immediately of our return. We were
in India, the newest jewel in the diadem of freedom.

Like the half-dozen other passengers debarking from the *President
Monroe*, Hirschfeld and I had made a beeline at once for the Taj Hotel,

a huge Mauro-Gothic edifice of gray stone whose crenelated towers, battlements, and drawbridges more accurately suggested a college dormitory. Much of Bombay's Victorian architecture, in fact, was singularly reminiscent of the campus of a third-rate Ohio university; more than once I could have sworn I heard the ghostly plunk of banjos and the faint despairing bleat of freshmen being paddled. Whatever European and Indian social life had emerged since the war was centered about the Taj, but it was still a rather sickly plant. The tense political feeling between Hindu and Moslem, the riots at Amritsar, Lahore, Calcutta, and the North-West Frontier, and widespread public apprehension about India's future after the British withdrawal dampened the few visible attempts at gaiety. To add to the universal gloom, all alcoholic beverages had been banned in the area two days a week, with the promise that before long the city would be completely dry. Neither of us was particularly intuitive, but we had not been exposed to the sweltering heat and dullness of Bombay very long before we realized that we had bought a pig in a poke.

Our hotel room did nothing to help matters. It was a long, monastic cell facing a courtyard, extremely hot, and so narrow that two persons could not pass without scarifying each other's skins. Someone had made a halfhearted gesture in the direction of cooling it by installing an overhead fan capable of two full revolutions a minute; most of the time it served as a trysting place for flies. The bathroom was a masterpiece of irony. Without either window or toilet—two European fripperies scorned by the management—it was equipped with a set of double doors which, if closed, sealed you in hermetically until you fainted; if left open, exposed your questionable charms to the approval of the entire courtyard. In this unwholesome burrow, flanked by eleven pieces of luggage and grilled by temperatures that hovered in the upper nineties, we dwelt through the first week of our sojourn in India. It might be supposed that the effect of such propinquity in record heat would be to lacerate our tempers, to make us impatient of one another's shortcomings. Far from it; never once did Hirschfeld try to brain me with the commode or I to sever his jugular vein, dearly as we would have loved to. If a point of difference rose between us, we settled it calmly, like gentlemen; we merely fell shrieking on the bed, beat the bolster with doubled fists until our tantrums subsided, and then sulked for two days. I think it will always stand as a tribute to my geniality and unruffled calm that Hirschfeld was finally able to issue from that room under his own power rather than on an undertaker's trestle. In the hands of anyone less tranquil, he might today be wearing a dainty aluminum cloche on his noggin.

In the unending steamy heat, when the smallest physical gesture sent a cascade of sweat coursing down the spine, the days took on the remote, insubstantial quality of a dream. In the mornings we dutifully went sightseeing, toiling up Malabar Hill to the Parsee towers of silence or out to the Elephanta Caves; in the afternoons, having clubbed ourselves with an inferior curry washed down with countless chota pegs, we drifted spiritlessly through the shops in Hornby Road, acquiring those curious knickknacks—the bangles, the brocades, and the Buddhas—which arouse such cries of admiration from the family circle and are forthwith relegated to the attic. We began to sort out familiar faces at the hotel—import-exporters we had run into at Shanghai, Singapore, and Bangkok, strange faceless men who moved energetically between the great Eastern cities manipulating mysterious deals and glibly discussing the complexities of foreign exchange. They are a baffling tribe, these import-exporters. They are dapper, knowledgeable, worldly, and altogether elusive. I met scores of them, became convivial on their expense accounts, shared quarters with them, and cooed over snapshots of their babies; but no amount of devious, cunning questioning could elicit just what they were importing or exporting. Once in a while, one would drop a seemingly careless hint that twelve thousand gross of needles or saccharine laid down in Teheran or Djokjakarta would double a man's money, yet if you asked him point-blank if he was in the needle or saccharine business, he would give you a crafty, inscrutable wink and change the subject. It struck me as an ideal occupation—you traveled in romantic lands, lived in luxury hotels, answered no man's bidding, incurred none of the hazards of the secret agent. Had I been able to crash my way into their confidence, I would have cheerfully forsworn belles-lettres without a backward glance.

The morning came when, by a superhuman effort of the will, we shook off our torpor and struck out for New Delhi, determined to see at least a portion of the country before we gave it back to the Indians. Flying north at nine thousand feet, it was possible to breathe again and pity Hirschfeld, who, with a lively concern for Hirschfeld, was creeping along the burning, barren waste in a railway carriage. At Ahmedabad, where we stopped to refuel, the airdrome restaurant showed splendid contempt for the 102-degree heat by serving cornflakes and scalding hot milk; the stewards presented it with an elaborate flourish, plainly bent on demonstrating that the airline was run with Amerikanski tempo. I came up the ramp at New Delhi with the inexplicable sensation of having seen it all before—the intolerably bright, dry heat, the artificial sky, the trim airport buildings. Then I remembered why. Except for the turbaned porters eying me with hangdog avarice, it might have been Barstow, Phoenix, any one of a dozen Western desert towns. My heart, avid for romance, leaped up at the stately row of camels near the newsstand, but when I drew nigh I saw they were only an advertisement for some obscure Yankee cigarette.

Driving through the tremendous hexagonal parks and plazas that crisscross New Delhi, one has to admit that New Delhi is certainly crisscrossed with tremendous hexagonal parks and plazas. The perspectives are overpowering—endless tree-lined boulevards sweeping up to gigantic official buildings, grandiose monuments that dominate mile-long vistas, everywhere a sense of organized planning that offers a sardonic contrast to the confusion of the politicians behind the façade. The same disparity was obvious at the Imperial, the spacious, ultra-modern hotel where my taxi deposited me. Though I was the only prospective guest in sight, the three Indian clerks instantly gave way to mass hysteria. No, my telegram requesting a reservation had not arrived; the house was full to overflowing, people were sleeping in the corridors; they were expecting a congress of rajahs and could not possibly book a room for at least five months. Eventually the clamor subsided—it was manifestly the normal routine—and I was assigned a suite already tenanted by a corpulent young British officer in the Royal Engineers. Major Fishguard was seated in the living room in his birthday suit, sipping whisky and water and studying a flyblown copy of *Screen Secrets*. He insisted on pouring a small libation on the altar of friendship, which I accepted, of course, on purely medicinal grounds. He then proceeded to expound the highly original philosophy that a bird cannot fly with only one wing and followed it up with a number of dividends. For an Englishman, the major was fairly garrulous; I learned he had been in the Indian Army twenty of his thirty-seven years, was stationed at Rawalpindi in the Punjab, and felt that, all things considered, Betty Grable was the girl he would most like to shack up with. We were still discussing variations on this latter theme five hours afterward when Hirschfeld straggled in, spent and cavernous-eyed from his journey. Any thought of dinner, naturally, was sacrilegious until he could catch up with us, and though he tried manfully, he went down with colors flying. The last thing I recall that evening was the major and myself, heads swathed in improvised turbans made of towels, solemnly beating time on empty bottles with a swagger stick and harmonizing "Pale Hands I Love."

By a happy circumstance, I had encountered in Bombay the American air attaché from New Delhi, who had amiably offered us his quarters for our stay, and we lost no time taking possession next morning. It was a gift verging on the princely, for along with the five-room apartment went a head bearer, two room bearers, a sweeper, a chauffeur, and a sedan, not to mention the privilege of eating in the American mess. One look at the tempting shops in Connaught Circle told us that if we were ever going to see any landmarks, we had better get it over with quickly, so out came the guidebooks and off we went. Our eyes bulged appropriately at the 234-foot Qutb Minar, the tallest single tower in the world and an eminence favored by suicides; a beautiful lovelorn maharanee is reported to have cast herself from it several years ago, but she was probably the same old Indian chieftain's daughter whose legend sanctifies so many Lover's Leaps in our own country. At the burning ghats, where the Hindus cremate their dead, we stood about morbidly staring at three or four mounds of ashes that had no real significance; in the fierce glare of midday, on this eroded riverbank, the impact of the dissolution of the flesh was as paltry as a Boy Scout wienie roast. In the Red Fort at Old Delhi, we trudged miles on swollen feet to see the Peacock Throne, a rather ordinary morris chair made of marble around which skulked a crew of pustular beggars ululating for baksheesh. The Chandni Chauk, or Silver Street, of the old town, nevertheless, was all that had been predicted, even if it was 110 in the shade the afternoon we explored it. It was something out of the Arabian Nights—the incredible, fantastic turmoil, the swarming crowds, the gargantuan bullocks asleep in the roadway, the bazaars with their Benares silks and Kashmir woolens, glass and silver jewelry, and Punjabi shoes. You wanted to buy everything in sight, including a few of those sloe-eyed gazelles in saris, and they were prepared to sell it. Only a humane regard for our chauffeur, who was quietly melting away in the sun like a dish of butter, finally recalled us to our senses.

The ivory shops in Connaught Circle, though, proved to be our real financial Waterloo. By the time the chaffering died down, we had bought enough gold-embroidered evening bags, antique necklaces, powder jars, paper cutters, cocktail forks, Mogul miniatures, and book ends to supply the population of a small Midwestern city (Fort Wayne). The proprietors of the Ivory Palace and the Ivory Mart are unquestionably the world's most consummate salesmen. You are lured into the rear of the shop with nods and becks and wreathed smiles, plied with cooling drinks, and given a thorough coating of Mohammedan schmaltz that lowers your sales resistance to the vanishing point. Then, very casually, there is introduced some exquisite trifle, a four-hundred-year-old bit of Jaipur enamel or a filigreed ivory box—merely as a curiosity, you understand, the shopkeeper beseeches you not to sully his friendship by any thought of purchase. As the victim's blood slowly comes to the boil, more curiosities appear: ivory tusks whose roses or hunting scenes in low relief were three years in the carving, superb bracelets and rings encrusted with gems, chessmen of unbelievable artistry and astronomical cost. I knew that we had definitely broken with reality when I suddenly discovered Hirschfeld haggling for a six-piece bedroom suite of carved ivory, priced at seven hundred thousand rupees, which had taken two men twenty-five years to complete. Why he wanted to possess all this dead tooth structure is beyond me, but he refused to yield to my entreaties and I ultimately had to hit him from behind with a knotted towel and drag him outside before his judgment returned.

We made the 122-mile trip to the Taj Mahal at Agra with a certain amount of trepidation; the famous tomb has inspired so much ecstatic nonsense, so many bad water colors, statuettes, ceramics, paperweights, and postcards, that we were convinced we must be disappointed. Our fears were groundless, for it turned out to be one of the major emotional experiences of the entire journey, despite the insupportable heat, the abysmal food, and the banalities of the guides. Seen in the first pale flush of sunrise, with a cool wind stirring the treetops in the adjacent gardens, it has the fragile delicacy of a soap bubble; no other building I have ever seen has conveyed to me quite that degree of airy grace, of absolute purity. It demands a strenuous effort on the visitor's part, however, to enjoy it privately. At every turn he is beset by a horde of cringing, smarmy mendicants chanting facts and figures and whining for alms. Historians assert that Shah Jehan built the Taj to commemorate his wife Mumtaz Mahal, called the Ornament of the Palace, but if you believe the ceaseless patter of the guides, Lord Curzon, onetime Viceroy of India, deserves the lion's share of the credit. "Lord Curzon's lamp, sahib—presented by Lord Curzon at a cost of five thousand rupees," they jabber. "All these fountains donated by Lord Curzon . . . ninety thousand rupees. . . . Lord Curzon gave these steps out of his own pocket—twelve thousand rupees, sahib . . . this pool gift of noble Lord Curzon . . . rupees . . . Curzon . . . rupees." We backed out through the beautiful red sandstone gate bestowing a pox on the noble lord, grateful nonetheless for at least that first moment of revelation.

Sleep was impossible that night in the hotel at Agra; we sat in the lobby drinking quarts of gin-and-tonic and staring limply at the angry red 104 on the thermometer. The people in the wing opposite ours had dragged their white iron bedsteads out on the lawn and lay gasping in the orbit of an electric fan. By noon the temperature had risen to 115; roaring back to New Delhi, the air that swept in through the car windows was as searing as a blast furnace. There were wild peacocks and baboons under the trees edging the road; villages newly burned out by Moslems and Hindus flicked by every few miles; but every ounce of interest and initiative evaporated under the single fact of the in-human, punishing sun. In spirit, if not in actuality, we were already aboard the *President Polk*; the vision of her air-conditioned dining room, I am sure, was the only thing that sustained us through that in-ferno. Ahead of us, if we only knew it, were further ordeals: the ship delayed interminably, weeks of waiting in Bombay, undreamed-of ennui. The Moving Finger had writ, all right, nor all our calamine lotion could wipe out a word of it. Yet somewhere, at the rainbow's end, was an ice-cold shower, a tall glass beaded with moisture, letters from home. *Per aspera ad astra*, ran the motto on my life insurance policy; come prickly heat, come sunstroke, those chaps at Prudential were betting on me to win through. In that sign, God willing, I would conquer.

BILE ON THE NILE

FITFUL GUSTS of rain drove against the windows of the promenade deck; the ship hung suspended for an eternity, quivered as if mortally stricken, and dipped sickeningly forward into the Arabian Sea. The plump Midwestern clubwoman in the deck chair adjoining mine ex-haled a lugubrious groan that culminated in a graveyard knell and plucked weakly at my sleeve. The tortured, queasy face she turned to-ward me was Lovat green.

"I'm going to die," she whimpered. "I want to die in my stateroom. Help me up."

"Help yourself up, you old bag," I returned chivalrously, closing my eyes to blot out the avalanche of water rearing over us to starboard. Telegraphing my innards to stand at the ready for another plunge into the abyss, I hunched myself into a prenatal ball. Speedier than any toboggan descending the Mount Hovenberg run, the ship plummeted down the hundred-foot slope, rolling over joyously like a sheepdog.

Liver and colon, lung and lights, all the shiny interior plumbing I had amassed so painstakingly in dribs and drabs over the years, fused into a single hard knot and wedged in my epiglottis. I had just drawn a long shuddering gasp and girded myself for the next glissando when a familiar hearty voice addressed me.

"What cheer, Netop?" it inquired. "Feeling a bit peckish?" I opened a tentative eye and beheld Hirschfeld bending over me solicitously. His cheeks glowed with rude health and he exuded an aura of limitless animal energy. In his suit of snowy drill, a linen cap rakishly tilted back on his head in the fashion of the great racing driver, Ralph di Palma, he might have stepped straight out of a four-color laxative advertisement. He was vibrant, sprightly, diligent, the epitome of vigorous optimism and dash, and had I had the strength I would have unhesitatingly cut his throat from ear to ear.

"Go away," I croaked miserably. "Go back to the Breakfast Club in Los Angeles where you belong." My voice cracked into a sob. "You cheerleader you." With a heartless snigger, Hirschfeld straightened up, relit the noisome cigar stub in his teeth, and skipped off to the sports deck to resume his game of shuffleboard. Wheezing painfully, I lay back in the chair and, as the *President Polk* wallowed on toward Aden buffeted by the southwest monsoon, somberly reviewed the events of the past fortnight.

We had crawled back to Bombay from New Delhi in a state of bleary disrepair, thoroughly dehydrated by the savage midsummer heat but starry-eyed at the prospect of quitting India, when kismet, working hand in glove with the steamship company, had again put her knee into our groin. Our next carrier, the *President Polk*, already a week overdue, was delayed another four days; flouting the schedule, not to speak of the common laws of decency, she had put into a whistle stop on the Malabar Coast called Cochin to pick up a cargo of cashew nuts. There was no recourse but to move back into the Taj Hotel and somehow bridge the interval until she appeared. The ensuing week was in many respects the most harrowing I have ever lived through. The reader may get some approximate notion of the discomfort we underwent if he dons a cable-stitch sweater, swallows three gallons of hot lemonade, and locks himself in his shoe-closet on an August afternoon. Sicklied o'er with the pale cast of heat lotion, we sat morosely in the lounge, biting our cuticle and drinking endless Collinses that only intensified our depression. The night life of Bombay is roughly on a par with that of Schwenksville, Pennsylvania; if a natural sense of discretion prevents you from visiting the notorious cages, you are thrown back on a

half-dozen cinemas exhibiting third-run American movies or slum-
brous Hindustani films too recherché for the Western patron. We
viewed one of the latter, a historical epic named *Shahjehan* inspired by
the great Mogul emperor, for four hours without the faintest idea of
what was taking place, other than that it seemed to be full of old silent-
picture emblems like roses with falling petals, candles guttering out,
and bleeding hearts transfixed by daggers. Two nights later an unidentified hothead flung a grenade into this very theater, expunging
eleven taxpayers. The newspapers stated that the outrage was caused
by religious bitterness, but obviously some enraged customer, with
more gumption than myself, was merely venting his opinion of the
feature.

The arrival of the *President Polk*, instead of providing a merciful release from bondage, only brought fresh exasperations. For a full week
she lay out in the roads unable to berth, owing to overcrowded docking
facilities. Hirschfeld and I prowled the waterside like panthers, eying
her yearningly and dreaming of the steaks and blueberry pie just out of
reach. In our overwrought imagination, she began to take on an un-
real luster; we pictured her bar crowded with dazzling, lonely beauties
sipping champagne cocktails, we fancied we heard the unbearable anguish of Louis Armstrong's trumpet echoing across the water, we
reached such a degree of self-hypnosis that we could almost smell the
pungency of the alcohol flame under the crêpes Suzette. When she finally came alongside, her passengers were stunned to behold two creatures that once were men, half-hysterical and babbling incoherently,
blowing kisses to them and behaving for all the world like March hares:
so much so, in fact, that a March hare which had come down to the
steamer to meet a friend was observed to avert its face contemptuously
and extrude its lip in what could only have been a smile of disdain.

Once the first giddy exultation of being aboard had worn off, disillusion came soon enough. For six days during which the temperature
hovered in the high nineties, the *President Polk* clove to the dock receiving goatskins and cinnamon. I am seldom capable of sustained rapture;
I can thrill to Benny Goodman playing "Stealin' Apples" or a seascape
by Marsden Hartley, but I may as well confess freely that goatskins
and cinnamon leave me cold. Speaking practically, when you have seen
one bale of either, you have seen them all. After the five hundredth,
the unending whir and crash of the slings became an abomination. Not
the smallest breeze penetrated to the basin where we were tied up; day
and night the metal hull of the ship gave off a sullen burning glow like
a kitchen range. The few passengers visible at mealtime—the majority

had wearily dragged themselves ashore to explore the dubious pleasures of Bombay—took on the pallor of blanched peanuts. By sailing day, the pair of us were so comatose with ennui, so completely frustrated, exacerbated, and generally loco, that the event had lost its significance. The last we saw of India, sliding through the locks into the outer harbor, was a wizened beggar signaling us frantically for baksheesh. When none was forthcoming, he threw aside his servile manner and, bounding beside our porthole, dynamically thumbed his nose at us until we outdistanced him. It was a touching, and somehow an apt, symbol of the amity between our two great nations, and it made us proud that, within our limited capabilities, Hirschfeld and I had done our share to broaden and implement it.

Four days out, my stomach and the Arabian Sea arrived at a *modus vivendi*; it was agreed that the ocean would do its own heaving and my viscera the same. I made my way feebly to the dining room and, between sips of gruel, took inventory of our fellow-travelers. They were an unexciting lot. With a few colorful exceptions, like a family of Filipino mestizos, an Indian textile magnate and his wife, three nuns of the order of the Little Sisters of the Poor, and a Chinese insurance man, they were the sort of people you could have encountered at a New Jersey milk farm—prosperous, dowdy, fiercely normal. The quintet at our table, though, was not without a certain gargoyle charm.

Mrs. Kubic, a spirited, full-blown Latvian from Shanghai, was en route to Lausanne to place her adolescent daughter, Faustine, in school. At an age when most women are content to lie back on the oars, she was still as coquettish and full of wanton wiles as a subdeb. In the presence of the opposite sex, her somewhat porcine face assumed the most terrifying ardor; she was continually directing languishing glances and melting smiles with lavish impartiality at the male passengers, deck stewards, officers, and foremast hands. The hoydenish Faustine, naturally, cramped her style a good deal, and her mother resorted to the most transparent devices to rid herself of the girl so she could exercise her blandishments. Mrs. Kubic's most winsome trait was an insistence on publicly airing her admiration for Hirschfeld's eyes in the poor chap's presence, likening them to those of a spaniel, and she succeeded in embarrassing him so completely that he kept them narrowed to mere slits whenever he ventured out of the cabin. The other lady at the table, a Mrs. Ledyard, was a flamboyant giantess in her fifties who owned a wire rope factory in Pawtucket, Rhode Island, and a roaring voice like the Bull of Bashan. Just why she was circumnavigating the globe she

never made clear; the only time I noticed her display any particular
enthusiasm was at Alexandria, when she caught sight of the rigging of
a merchant ship near by. "Look!" she cried out jubilantly, seizing my
arm in a paralyzing grip. "See that wire cable? It's our heavy-duty
Number Three Tiger-Strand Special, Best by Test—isn't it a sweetheart?"

Flanking these personalities at the table were two men—Gruber, an
energetic diamond importer with a sardonic manner and a huge store
of information about the East, mainly inaccurate, and a quondam foreign correspondent named Ramspeck. Roger Ramspeck was a chubby,
pompous youth who wore his hair aggressively *en brosse* and cultivated
the air of tired condescension peculiar to the recipient of a Princeton
sheepskin. For the preceding year he had been stationed in Nanking as
representative of an obscure American news magazine, in which ca-
pacity he had unearthed some sublimely uninteresting facts about
Chiang Kai-shek's boyhood. Ramspeck suffered from a common ail-
ment of the immature; he would sit quiescent, brooding over Chiang's
boyhood, then abruptly short-circuit the conversation with a remark
so rude that it would focus everyone's attention on him. Our very first
session together, he suddenly buried his face in his hands.

"Oh, God, how you all bore me!" he wailed. Mrs. Kubic and Mrs.
Ledyard stared at him horrified, refusing to credit their ears.

"Ah, don't pay any attention to him," Gruber advised them, "he
needs a good physic." Disregarding this excellent diagnosis, the ladies
promptly and indignantly told Ramspeck his shortcomings. He listened rapt, basking in their character analysis and drawing them on
with piecemeal disclosures about his unhappy love life. It was obviously not the first time he had employed shock as a social gambit, and
it was certainly not the last, for whenever the table talk showed signs
of becoming adult, Ramspeck could always be depended on to wrench
it toward himself. Before long, the rest of us gave up trying and contented ourselves with watching Ramspeck and Mrs. Kubic out-jockey
each other for the egomania sweepstakes.

The heat, which had relaxed a trifle between India and Africa, redoubled the moment we raised the Straits of Bab el Mandeb and started
into the Red Sea. Tongues lolling out, swollen with sunburn, we hung
over the rail scanning the furnacelike profile of French Somaliland,
surely the bleakest, most inhospitable coastline conceivable. Seven
days' steaming from Bombay, we entered Port Tewfik, the harbor of
Suez, and dropped anchor among the fleet of tankers lying there.
Hirschfeld and I had subscribed, along with fourteen other passengers,

for an overland tour to Cairo that would rejoin the ship at Alexandria
after it cleared the Suez Canal. As soon as landing formalities were
over—an interminable process of being chivvied by a couple of extremely bumbling, self-important, inefficient, and illiterate Egyptian
shamuses—our group was ferried ashore and loaded into four sedans.
It might be proper at this juncture to tender my respects to the Egyptian passport and customs service. Never, not even at the French
douane, whose officiousness and pettifoggery are proverbial, have I beheld such egregious insolence and obstructionism. From the outset the
wayfarer is treated to every possible humiliation a first-class bureauc-
racy can invent to bedevil him. He is assumed to be a gallows bird,
a smuggler, and an anarchist, and is dealt with accordingly. To expose yourself to the Egyptian border official is to invite certain apoplexy; it is a source of constant surprise to me that I was able to emerge
from the Nile Delta without blood on my hands. They can well hang
their heads, these gentry—preferably on a row of pikes along the
waterfront.

The trip across the desert to Cairo was as hot and exhausting as one
would reasonably have supposed it to be in mid-July; a few skinny
camels and the occasional rusted skeleton of an armored car or tank
were the only objects visible in the stony, blinding waste. The journey was made no shorter by the presence in our car of Mr. Kantharides, the travel agent who was playing Mother Carey to our flock of
diversified chickens. He was a stout, oily gentleman, clearly hyperthyroid and possessed of what he considered to be fatal magnetism. He
constantly kept kissing the ladies' hands, swapping heavy *double-
entendres* with the men, and doing his utmost to promote the sort of
sickly good-fellowship that prevails at a department-store clambake.
The only person among us who ruffled his good nature was Mr. Chung,
the Chinese insurance man. Chung, a very slow man with a piaster,
convinced himself early in the jaunt that Kantharides was overcharg-
ing him and took to questioning each small expenditure.

"Six piasters for the lemon soda?" he demanded heatedly. "In Swatow we get a big bottle, twice the size of that one, for five cents!"

"It costs more here than in Swatow," snapped Kantharides. "What
do you want, wholesale prices in the middle of the desert?"

"Ha-ha, you can't fool me," retorted Chung mockingly. "It all goes
in your pocket. Look at that lunch we just had—thirty piasters. Why,
in Swatow—"

"Swatow, Swatow!" screamed the infuriated Greek. "You're making
me crazy with your Swatow! Why don't you go back there and drop

dead?" He turned toward me, his face dark with passion, and I braced myself for a further outburst. Instead, in a perfectly matter-of-fact tone in which there was no trace of rancor, he remarked conversationally, "Some people just aren't reasonable, that's all."

Heliopolis, the great sprawling suburb of Cairo, sprang up unexpectedly around us in the fading dusk; there was something bizarre in these ornate villas and functional apartment houses blossoming without any preparation out of the arid plain. Bowling at breakneck speed past huge, crowded cafés and expensive shops, I felt for the first time the sense of Europe: the East was irretrievably behind us. It was not just the neon lights, the traffic, the purposefulness of the crowds on the boulevards, but a subtle acceleration of rhythm, the substitution of a wholly different scale of values. Our caravan drew up before the high terraced embankment of Shepheard's Hotel, and we straggled out on the sidewalk, parched, dusty, and irritable. Before we could stir a step, we were engulfed in a sea of dragomen, panders, peddlers, mendicants, fortunetellers, magicians, tumblers, fakirs, and assorted mountebanks, all screeching at the top of their voices. They trampled us, rent our clothing, showered us with beads, shawls, foul-smelling pocketbooks, swagger sticks, scarabs, horoscopes, alabaster funeral urns, and statuettes of Nefertiti, Horus, and Ammon Ra. Through their midst churned Kantharides, savagely boxing ears and calling down the most bloodthirsty imprecations. Slowly, inch by inch, hemmed in by a phalanx of porters garbed in fezzes and nightgowns and raining down gewgaws on the heads of our pursuers, we fought our way up to the hotel and safety.

In a late Victorian bedroom easily the size of the Hall of Mirrors at Versailles, furnished with gigantic brass bedsteads and papered a brooding crimson, Hirschfeld and I sprawled in the hot plush armchairs and caught our breath. A shred of sleazy muslin, torn from the burnoose of one of the importunate dragomen, dangled from the rim of my glasses; I disentangled it with the ponderous concentration of a man teetering on the edge of neurasthenia and let it drop. Together we watched it flutter dementedly to the floor. Then Hirschfeld expelled a deep, troubled sigh.

"Listen," he said, weighing every word, "this is a promise. If I ever get home again, I'm going to take every suitcase I own and burn it to ashes. Then I'm going to take a hammer and beat the ashes so that no ——— can ever make a suitcase out of them again."

"Promise me one thing more," I said. "Don't throw away the hammer."

"Why?"

"Because," I said with equal deliberation, "if I ever suggest, if I ever so much as *hint* at, a trip anywhere, even Jersey City, I want you to take that hammer and beat me to a powder." Hirschfeld arose and extended his hand, his eyes shining.

"Old man," he said emotionally, "it'll be a pleasure."

FORTY CENTURIES LOOK DOWN

THE CARBUNCULAR young Egyptian guide, his face lightly dappled with overexposure to the actinic ray and too many tourists, paused at the entrance of the passageway leading into the Great Pyramid at Gizeh and removed his fez. Extracting the monogrammed lawn handkerchief he had pilfered the day before from a wealthy Englishwoman, he unfolded it with excessive care, gave his forehead several dainty pats, tucked the handkerchief in his sleeve, and elegantly stifled a yawn. Without deigning to look at them, he knew that the three ancient attendants in the dirty white caftans, whose duty it was to conduct visitors through the maze of tunnels within, were watching him in respectful awe.

"What do you bring us today, our benefactor?" inquired one of the gaffers, lips skinned back over his gums in a particularly seductive smile.

"A bonanza, my father," returned the guide with self-satisfaction, "four nice pigeons ripe for the plucking—an Armenian, a Chinese, and two American journalists."

"In the name of Allah, effendi!" protested the old attendant. "Are you insane? Who can get baksheesh out of an Armenian?"

"Pooh!" spat another. "The Armenian is a philanthropist compared to the Chinese!"

"And the two journalists are worse than either," moaned the third. "Those scavengers will end up stealing our turbans. Woe unto us, brothers—take to the hills!"

"Button your lip!" snapped the guide. "Here come the infidels now, and remember, whosoever among you tries to hold out on me in the final divvy, him will I beat with a besom until his noggin rings. Now bestir yourselves, loafers, for I hear *el moola* (the moola) jingling in their pockets." He darted away down the steps and, as Hirschfeld puffed into view at the head of our little sightseeing party, grasped his elbow solicitously and hoisted him up the last tier of masonry.

It was scarcely more than a couple of hours since sunup, but already the massive blocks of stone against which we leaned to regain our breath burned to the touch. The four of us—Chung, the Chinese insurance man, Hirschfeld, myself, and Wickwire, a malaria-ridden State Department employee from Siam whom our guide inexplicably persisted in regarding as a Levantine—had driven out from Cairo for a morning's rubbernecking with several other passengers from the *President Polk*. With infinitely sounder judgment than ourselves, however, the rest had elected to proceed immediately to the Sphinx rather than burrow into the recesses of the pyramids, and now, aboard a drove of mangy camels, were jolting off into the shimmering heat. An icy hand clutched my heart as I watched them go; some inner voice warned me to eschew this harebrained adventure while there was still time. Before I could summon up enough moxie to bolt after them, unfortunately, the attendants herded us into Indian file and nudged us forward. Stifling my panic by the simple expedient of biting off the tip of my tongue, I plunged into the chilling darkness.

The memory of the next half hour will haunt my dreams for years to come. Doubled over in a half crouch, we groped our way along a gallery approximately the length of the Simplon tunnel, crawled up a backbreaking ninety-degree incline studded with slippery metal cleats, and then, on all fours, scrambled everlastingly through a Stygian channel no bigger than a rain-barrel and certainly not as fragrant. Throughout the ordeal (purely to pass the time, of course), I amused myself with a number of quaint conceits: decided that the pyramid was slowly settling down on me, pretended I was buried alive, convinced myself an embolus was loose in my aorta and my extremities had turned to stone, and altogether managed to enrich every existing medical concept of claustrophobia. To add to my manifold problems, Mr. Chung, who was evidently in a state of keen anxiety also, clung to my ankles as we inched forward and lost consciousness from time to time, so that I was obliged to pull his weight as well as my own. At last, from up ahead, the exhilarating word was passed that we had gained our goal, and smeared with cobwebs, maimed, and grimy, we rolled into a small dank vault illuminated by the flares of the attendants.

"The Queen's Chamber, gents," panted Hassan, our guide. "Very old." We stood about staring vacuously at the very old premises for a moment, hungering for an epochal revelation about its significance, but apparently Bubastis, the sacred cat, had Hassan's tongue. Finally he broke the painful silence with a discreet cough. "Excuse me, noble sirs, but I think the boys would like a little backsheesh."

"Oh, they would, would they?" rejoined Hirschfeld belligerently. "And what cooks if we don't give them any?"

"I think," said Hassan with a feline grin, "that it would be much sooner to get out if you did." I do not recall ever having heard a remark which carried so many interesting implications, and since the four of us were men of quick understanding, we grasped them all in a flash. Personally, I would have loved to spend the winter creeping through the complex network of passages and exploring the balance of the sarcophagi, but it would have been selfish to let personal considerations detain the other members of the party, and swallowing my chagrin, I promptly whacked up my share of the pay-off. We completed the return journey in jig time; some mysterious metamorphosis in the royal tomb had endowed me with the agility of a lizard, for I was out of the pyramid and gasping on the sand a full five minutes before Hirschfeld, Chung, and Wickwire emerged. Beyond the fact that we were breathing, the affair had only one compensating aspect—our guide's Promethean fury when he discovered that his new ball-point fountain pen, which he had been exhibiting pridefully all morning, had been heisted by the attendants. Taking advantage of the hullabaloo of splintered Arabic and heartrending lamentations that ensued, we hastily chartered a panel of burros and galloped off smartly to the Sphinx. The howl of the hyena is supposed to be the eeriest sound in the Libyan Desert, but I will match it with Hassan's scream of anguish as he realized that our donkey-boys had flimflammed him out of a fee.

There are, no doubt, individuals of such shining stoicism that they can stand face to face with the Sphinx in a July noonday sun, with the thermometer at 119 Fahrenheit and a plague of sand-flies assailing them, and derive from it the intellectual catharsis it is said to produce. I wish that I were one of them. As it was, all I bore away from the encounter was a nose burned the color of an eggplant and a fearsome case of bloat induced by drinking seven bottles of soda pop in quick succession. Some anonymous genius has had the inspiration to pitch a soft-drink stand a few hundred feet away, or possibly it was even part of the original statue; in any case, I never expect to recapture the gratitude I felt for that pitiful patch of shade. The next morning there arrived at the hotel a photograph of two goatish imbeciles, each mounted on a dromedary in front of a pyramid with his arm encircling the bust of a lady passenger, which the dragoman insisted Hirschfeld and I had posed for. It was sheer blackmail, naturally, because apart from the coincidence that the spalpeens were wearing our faces and clothes, they were quite dissimilar; but rather than create a fuss, we slipped the wretch a couple of thousand piasters, threatened to blacken his eye if he ever mentioned it, and sank the photograph in the Nile.

The tourist who hopes to get any valid impression of Cairo from a thirty-six-hour stay is, to put it mildly, fatuous, and the program of activities designed for us by Mr. Kantharides, our conductor, played heavily on this gullibility. By nightfall we had been hustled at dizzying speed through the Blue Mosque, the bazaars, the National Museum, and a score of jewelry shops we were positive the wily Greek operated under a multiplicity of assumed names. Any rational citizen would have had the grace to collapse after so punishing a day, but Hirschfeld and I had reached the stage of hypertension that recognizes no fatigue. Whipping into fresh tarbooshes, we charged off to an open-air vaudeville establishment to witness a celebrated muscle-dancer named Badia who was currently, so to speak, holding Cairo in the hollow of her navel. The lady was unquestionably gifted, as is anyone who can keep an audience of two thousand art-lovers enthralled with a repetition of the same basic pattern, yet there were moments, along about three-thirty in the morning, when one's attention flagged. Hirschfeld likewise noticed that our whistles and erotic moans were losing their first intensity; and ordering an usher to convey a floral horseshoe to the star (for which, stupidly enough, we neglected to give him the money), we sleepily wended our way back to Shepheard's.

At three o'clock the following afternoon, had you been dawdling around the ocean front at Alexandria ninety miles to the north, you would have glimpsed a scene to bring tears to the most jaundiced eye. My colleague and I, still streaked with coal-dust accumulated on the rigorous rail trip up from Cairo, were draped over a table in the Café Athenaeos, having just annihilated a quart of pistachio ice cream, four chocolate éclairs, three charlotte russes, and a little assorted pastry. A cool, delicious Mediterranean breeze ruffled our hair and fanned our fevered cheeks; no words can convey the measure of utter, blissful well-being that pervaded us. I am not at all sure our stomachs could have withstood a diet of pure carbohydrate longer than the few hours we luxuriated waiting for our steamer, but to nervous systems frazzled from months of tropical heat, the city seemed almost paradisiacal. Its people were cordial and colorful, its atmosphere civilized, and its climate soothing, and if anyone is disposed to link my name with the Alexandria Chamber of Commerce, he has another link coming. I am in love with a certain Mediterranean seaport and I don't care who knows it.

In the couple of days it took the *President Polk* to cover the distance between Alexandria and Naples, the passengers' spirits underwent a marked change. The idyllic weather and the exciting proximity of Europe generated a vigor and bonhomie that had been hitherto lacking; even I found myself showing a hundred little unaccustomed kindnesses, like presenting the purser with a box of wormy figs I had purchased from a leper in Colombo or refusing to read Hirschfeld's personal mail when he left it indiscreetly strewn about the cabin. The captain's dinner, the night preceding our arrival in Italy, aroused the strain of relentless whimsy latent in ocean travelers the world over. Eleven persons turned up dressed as sheikhs, and practically every female on board, except the stewardess and several old harridans too sunk in apathy to care, came as Oulëd Naïl girls. Mrs. Ledyard, the Amazon at our table who owned the wire cable factory in Rhode Island, felt it best to wear on her head an old-fashioned, befringed parlor lampshade. How she procured it nobody knew, and I can only infer that she must have portaged it all the way from Pawtucket for just such an occasion. At one point in the saturnalia, when the fun was at its grimmest, Mrs. Ledyard suddenly gave way to an excess of animal energy. She caught up a springy iron clapper, and, since I am always in the trajectory of people like that, fetched me a lethal blow on the sconce, causing a goose-egg. I overlooked it at the time, realizing the woman was in wine, but my salutation thereafter was the frostiest of nods and I suspect she gathered she had breached the canons of good taste.

It did not require an especially perceptive nature to sense from the moment we tied up at Naples the sadness and dilapidation of the city. Great stretches of dockside and industrial district were still in ruins, and the population, or what remnant was visible in the echoing, poorly lighted streets, seemed malnourished and despairing. Perhaps it was this heavy oppressiveness, aggravated by the rumor that the ship might be detained there, that stampeded me into joining the excursion I did. If I had suspected its true scope, or the complete naïveté of trying to cover a major portion of Italy in four days, I might have harkened to Hirschfeld and sailed with him to Genoa. But then, that would have been sagacious, and sagacity has never been my long suit.

On the surface, to one who had never been in the country, our itinerary appeared perfectly feasible—Pompeii, Rome, Siena, Florence, Pisa, and on to Genoa by the Italian Riviera. In the big red Fiat bus with me that sparkling morning went eight other innocents—Wickwire and Chung, the intrepid duo who had helped me solve the riddle of the Great Pyramid; Mr. Sabadhai, a pursy Indian textile magnate, and his wife; Azeez, a sniveling young Bengali on his way to Johns Hopkins to study dentistry; the Beavers, a well-heeled elderly couple from Lake Forest; and Miss Gorsline, a spinsterish New England schoolteacher. In charge of the flock, and none too elated with his assignment, was a peppery, disenchanted Neapolitan named Mr. Frascati, whose expression of choler hardly deserted him from the instant he saw us. He considered the expedition unmitigated lunar idiocy, and I must say nothing happened to disprove him.

We tore through Pompeii in a dog-trot, frantically snatching postcards and marveling dutifully at the reconstructions; anyone who showed a tendency to browse was quickly shooed along by Frascati, who made it clear the schedule allowed no time for giggling over erotica. By midday we were boiling through the Apennine hill towns at a terrifying rate, in our wake a series of moribund chickens and peasants screaming maledictions. The scenery was spectacular: endless rolling vineyards under full cultivation, medieval villages perched on the most outlandish crags, superb perspectives of cypresses and Lombardy poplars outlined against the sky. At Viterbo, a somnolent mountain hamlet out of a Shubert operetta, we dallied long enough to gulp down a flask of memorable white wine and allow a bullock to trample on my foot and thundered on. The havoc caused by bombs and shellfire, sporadic until now, became truly appalling at the Volturno. The destruction was so overwhelming that you wondered how men found the courage to face the task of rebuilding; and yet there, as everywhere along the Via Appia, were constant evidences of a tenacious, energetic rehabilitation. No monument or shrine I saw in central Italy, and I was fated to see nearly all of them, was half as impressive as the dogged industry with which the people were restoring their homes and workshops.

There is a pungent old Calabrian proverb, whose meaning I have forgotten if I ever knew it, which states that the human spinal column can stand a powerful lot of abuse. Mine certainly served as a whipping boy that day. Long after dark, spent and nerve-weary, I doddered into the foyer of a third-rate hotel in Rome, was fed as wretched a meal of rubbery veal and warmed-over spaghetti as a swindling management could confect on short notice, and was bivouacked in a disused storeroom. My slumber was a mite less than refreshing; Azeez, my Indian bunkmate, dreamt he was being crushed by the Juggernaut and howled like a timber wolf all night long. The next morning found us on the treadmill in earnest; paced by Frascati, we sprinted through the mile-long corridors of the Vatican, gaped at Michelangelo's murals in the Sistine Chapel, goggled at the immensity of St. Peter's. After lunch, Wickwire and I made a desperate attempt to vamoose, but the guide had been ordered to show us Rome and show it he did. Blubbering and begging for mercy, we were haled to the Borghese Gardens, the Roman Forum, the Colosseum, the Piazza Venezia, and the gigantic cheese fondant commemorating Victor Emmanuel. Somewhere in the midst of these architectural glories, my feet ceased to function as organs of locomotion and I finished the day *hors de combat,* numbly festooned over Frascati and Wickwire in the humiliating posture known as the fireman's carry. With admirable presence of mind, they dragged me to a small surgery on the Corso, where my jaws were pried open with a sharp stick and a shakerful of martinis introduced, and soon I was reeling back to my hotel, yodeling *La Traviata* as good as new.

It would serve no useful purpose to prolong the agonizing chronicle of our hegira; once established, the hallucinatory pattern intensified like that of a six-day bicycle race. Out of the nightmare I remember isolated highlights: a truly symphonic dish of green noodles in Siena, the panorama of Tuscan hills that was purest primitive painting, the theatrical splendor of Florence, the breathtaking Byzantine mosaics in the cathedral at Pisa, a lunch deserving of the Cordon Bleu in a tiny restaurant in Viareggio. Interthreaded through it is the recollection of unending heat and dust, of a blurred succession of churches, fountains, and largely hideous sculpture, and the tireless clack of Miss Gorsline's tongue as she annotated the wonders whirling by us. When we reached the Italian Riviera at last, the driver cast discretion to the winds and decided to give us a farewell *frisson.* All his southern Latin daredeviltry rose to the surface; throttle wide open, rocking and careering around horrid chasms, the bus hurtled down the precipitous coast past La Spezia and Rapallo as though Beelzebub himself were at the controls. Our homecoming created a minor sensation aboard the *President Polk* and provided touching proof, if any was necessary, of the esteem our mates felt for us. So sure had everyone been that we would never return alive that our effects had been auctioned off among the passengers. I consumed a whole day retrieving my wardrobe from other people's cabins and had many piquant adventures, none of them, however, pertinent to this narrative.

The lights of Genoa were vanishing astern that evening as Hirschfeld and I, languidly brushing from our cummerbunds the crumbs of our final dinner aboard the *Polk,* sauntered out on the promenade deck.

In the afterglow of the sunset the Mediterranean was dark and smoothly rippling; off on the horizon ahead, the faint jagged silhouette of the Côte d'Azur was fast taking shape. It was the poetic hour of twilight, the hushed diminuendo that concludes every Fitzpatrick Traveltalk, and it cried out for some cosmic reflection that would sum up man's tangled destiny and the quintessence of everything we had experienced thus far. Ever more attuned to the infinite than myself, Hirschfeld was the first to put it into words.

"It's a rum thing," he observed thoughtfully, "but in all the thousands of miles I've traveled and all the books I've read, I never heard of anybody catching beriberi in the Sixth Avenue Delicatessen."

"Come, come, man," I objected, "don't be an ingrate! Think of the people who'd like to be in your shoes right now."

"I am," he muttered, "and they're for rent from here in. Oh, well," he shrugged, flinging away his cheroot in a wide curving arc, "this trip's taught me one lesson anyway. You can't have your strudel and eat it too. See you in France." And he went below.

SEAMY SIDE UP

ON A SWELTERING Sunday evening in the closing days of July, the sleek reception clerk of the Hotel Negresco in Nice looked up from his ledger and beheld, approaching him across the lobby, a grotesque duo. Offhand, it appeared to be a team of tramp comedians, except that the make-up and costumes of the pair were, if anything, a shade too broad. The bearded half of the act, a villainous customer on the order of Mack Swain, was clad in a military raincoat, baby-blue shorts, shrunken white socks, and open-toed sandals. The other, bespectacled and snaffle-toothed, nervously scratching a chin you could hang a lantern on, wore a white twill fisherman's hat, a greasy bush jacket, khaki bathing trunks, and a pair of scuffies. A clerk with less aplomb might have yielded to a pardonable impulse to snatch up the cashbox, sound the alarm, and hide in the lavabo until the gendarmes came. Two considerations, however, gave this one pause: first, he had just received an excited phone call from the stationmaster, employing the Provençal word "halvies," informing him that a brace of eccentric American millionaires had tumbled off the Marseilles express, and second, his X-ray eye, trained to pick out a dead beat under the most flawless dinner coat, unerringly diagnosed the bulge in the gentlemen's waistbands as American Express checks. By the time, consequently, that the bearded type had begun identifying himself in the execrable French accent that had flunked him out of Principia High School in St. Louis, the clerk was way ahead of him.

"Mais certainement, mon cher M. Hirschfeld!" he cooed, vaulting over the desk and pinching our money-belts playfully. "The royal suite, the grand ballroom, the moon if you like! Jacques! Étienne! Carry in the baggage—and gently with that typewriter, idiot, don't you know platinum when you see it?" While we toiled over the police questionnaires, our Boniface smacked his lips over the room chart. Yes, he could let us share the fifth floor with the Nizam of Hyderabad, though man to man, he ought to warn us that facilities for mooring a yacht there were limited. His own recommendation was that we book the three top floors favored by the Aga Khan, unless, of course, we minded stabling our horses in the bridal suite. Eventually, we plucked the opium pipe from his teeth and brusquely demanded a double room and bath. The descent to reality was so abrupt that it left him speechless for an instant. As we shot skyward in the lift five minutes later, I could still hear him shrilly bombinating to the head porter. "Fakers, tinhorn sports!" he was choking. "I saw right through them, but *nom de Dieu*, what could I do? They held a gun against my ribs!"

Conditioned as we were to the noisome rabbit warrens that masquerade as hotel rooms in the East, our bedchamber at the Negresco seemed like heaven on the half shell. Granted the decor was pure marzipan, a riot of rosebuds, pink taffeta, and gilt; notwithstanding, there were real box springs, a bathtub big enough to float an LST, an infinity of towels. When we finally descended into the Promenade des Anglais for an aperitif, no feminine heads swiveled around to exclaim at our comeliness, but at least we had the merit of being reasonably clean. Fortified by a few Cinzanos, we sat at a café table on the esplanade and watched the vacation crowd undulating past. It had the same opulent, *sportif* air I remembered from my last visit thirteen years before, and yet I became increasingly aware of a profound change. Everyone was much more subdued; I saw little evidence of the effervescence, the explosive arguments, the gesticulation, and the exaggerated passion of old.

People's appearance, too, had undergone a definite transformation. Every other woman was a chemical blonde resolutely modeling herself on Veronica Lake or Lauren Bacall, and the men's clothes were indistinguishable from those on Mosholu Parkway and Michigan Boulevard. Probably the most distressing note in the scene to a couple of Francophiles was the prevalence of the American ice-cream cone. Baby, dowager, gigolo, and slippered pantaloon, all the world and his wife had their noses plunged in some form of popsicle or candied apple as they passed in review before us. We both understood to what depths France had sunk when a Chevalier of the Legion of Honor, sporting a monocle and a white imperial, trotted by munching an Eskimo Pie. Had Marcel Proust suddenly materialized with a mouthful of bubble gum, we could not have been more deeply disenchanted. "That tears it," snapped Hirschfeld, rising in disgust. "Come on, let's have dinner— and the way our luck is running, I bet it'll be corned beef hash."

His fears were superfluous; the meal proved to be magnificent, a work of such consummate artistry that it even assuaged the shock of the bill when it arrived. Perhaps two bottles of Beaune '23 and a demijohn of Calvados also helped to cushion the blow; in any case, we teetered out into the night airily impervious to the fact that we had pauperized ourselves in a single stroke. The ensuing events are a bit kaleidoscopic. I recall whirling along the Middle Corniche road in a rented Panhard-Levassor that must have steered itself, since the driver was seated with us in the tonneau harmonizing *"Auprès de Ma Blonde."* Superimposed on this are three or four zigzag flashes, technically akin to what are termed Vorkapich shots in Hollywood, of the Casino at Monte Carlo: a fiendish wooden rake darting at me like an adder and decimating my stack of counters; a vinegary cashier with the face of a bluebottle fly spurning my wrist watch as if it were infected; a short interregnum of Greco-Roman wrestling with a doorman; and the springy recoil of a privet hedge as I soared over a white marble balustrade and bounced into it. Evidently, however, one of us must have performed some act of gallantry deserving of public acclaim, because when I came back into focus, we were in a *boîte* called the Club Maxim receiving an ovation from a bevy of charming young maidens. We all seemed to be on a footing of the greatest cordiality. Hirschfeld, wearing one of the ladies' hats, was demonstrating his proficiency at the can-can, and I was serenading the company with an instrument on which I am something of a virtuoso, a piece of tissue paper stretched over a comb.

Never, I venture to say, has jollity been so spontaneous and unrehearsed, but it was getting late, and anxious not to disrupt the party, we essayed to steal out quietly through the kitchen. We learned then and there that you do not lightly flout the laws of French hospitality. With many good-natured sallies and a firm grasp on our coat collars, the manager escorted us back and presented us with a souvenir document solemnizing the occasion. I forget its exact wording, but after we finished acknowledging it, our throats were dry and our dependents doomed. It still hangs over the bar at Maxim's, framed as neatly as the manager knows how, and he certainly knows how.

At the end of forty-eight hours in Nice, our arteries and our resources were too brittle to withstand added stress, and ruthlessly deafening our ears to the siren song of the Midi, we struck out for Paris. We began to get an inkling of what conditions there might be from the dinner served en route in the Wagon-Lits restaurant. The roast (a purely formal designation) was microscopic, the vegetables a travesty, the bread well-nigh inedible, sugar, cream, and butter nonexistent— and this aboard a luxury train which before the war had prided itself on its posh cuisine. Another contrast to the good old days greeted us on disembarking at the Gare de Lyon the following morning. Instead of the crowd of importunate taxi drivers we expected, there was a queue of travelers a block long wrangling like fishwives for the infrequent cab that loitered by. Excluding pots, pans, and a tent, my colleague and I had managed in seven months' wandering to accumulate more gear than a gypsy caravan; and since we had thoughtlessly forgotten to stock a Conestoga wagon, we could think of no feasible way of spanning the five miles to our Left Bank hotel. Eventually, we made it in tortuous, roundabout fashion through the subway, aided by four porters groaning in the best safari tradition. We all became fast friends in the process, and to show their esteem, the men put on an impromptu decathlon in the lobby which consisted of beating their heads on the floor, kicking the luggage, and jumping up and down on our tips.

The character exists, unquestionably, who managed to have a riproaring time in Paris in the summer of 1947, but who he is, where he did so, and how he found the inclination, I cannot imagine. To my way of thinking, it was one of the more woeful locales west of Shanghai; the food scarcity was acute, the cost of living was astronomical, and a pall of futility and cynicism hung over the inhabitants, Physically, to be sure, the city was completely unchanged; it was still the most beautiful capital on earth, but it was mere architecture, a series of superb vistas forsaken by the spirit that had once animated it. There were streets, indeed, whole quarters, devoid of any sign of life and business appeared to be at a complete standstill. Everywhere you went, you sensed the apathy and bitterness of a people corroded by years of enemy occupation.

Under these melancholy circumstances, therefore, it may be appre-

ciated why the lengthy visit we had projected soon shrank to the dimensions of a condolence call. Out of some dim feeling of obligation,
we forced ourselves back to the cafés and restaurants we had frequented in the spacious twenties, only to reaffirm that there are far
cheerier pastimes than lingering in a haunted house. After ten o'clock
in Montparnasse, which used to be a fairly boisterous parish, the
prairie dogs came out of their holes; Montmartre was not half as iniqui-
tous as Barnegat, New Jersey, and considerably less charged with
glamour. The Café Flore, popularized by Jean-Paul Sartre and the
Existentialist coterie, drew together on its terrace a few unrecon-
structed Bohemians, but the only procurable drinks, synthetic grape
juice and venomous French beer, did not make for vivacity or sparkle.
Food was the constant preoccupation and, with the majority of persons
we met, the sole topic of conversation; the American tourist like ourselves, who symbolized prosperity and whose dollars ruled the world
economy, was popularly regarded as either a pigeon or a usurer. Altogether, the atmosphere was every whit as cheerless and unnerving as
our previous information had described it; and it was with a sensation
of exquisite relief that we finally threw in the sponge and entrained for
London. I had never felt that way before in leaving Paris, and I experienced a twinge of guilt that it should be possible. But this was not
the city I had known and really loved—it was a jarring echo out of
the past, a brief, disturbing episode I hoped to subordinate to rosier
memories.

The Channel crossing, a chore even under optimum conditions, was
aggravated in my case by an unforeseen affliction, a heroic-sized plaster
cast of the head of Buddha I was toting home to supplement the windy
after-dinner discourses I planned. I had acquired it in Paris; it was not
a very good head, but it cost only four dollars, which in my muddled
logic conclusively branded it a bargain. Done up in brown manila
paper in typically slapdash French fashion, it made a package about
the size of a Flexible Flyer. Early in the trip, I convinced myself that
someone would accidentally shatter it, so, hugging it fearfully to my
breast, I sat bolt upright all the way to Calais, sweating with panic each
time the railway carriage lurched. To increase my agitation, the bundle
seemed to possess a strange magnetic attraction for the other passengers, who constantly kept ricocheting into it, hooking it with their um-
brellas, and generally trying to demolish it. An appeal to their aesthetic sensibilities went for naught; various coarse innuendoes were
advanced, that I was disposing of an unwelcome mistress, trafficking
in white slaves, smuggling cocaine, and so on. Fortunately for my equi-

librium, the wretched thing disappeared somewhere on the Channel steamer, for had I had to play governess to a bagful of plaster the balance of the journey, there might well have been psychiatric repercussions.

If anybody would like a few facile platitudes about the English people from a man who spent twelve days in London, I have the largest stock of new and used generalizations in the business. They have two qualities in common: they are all glib and all equally shallow. With minor variations, they are the same fatuities an Englishman who has spent twelve days in New York would spout. Nevertheless, there were a couple of traits I observed often enough in my stay to believe that they must be basic national characteristics: courage and serenity. It needed plenty of both to have endured the rigors of the foregoing seven years and to face an extremely dubious future, and that they were still apparent struck me as nothing short of a miracle. Perhaps, coming from the despair and lethargy of Paris, the contrast was especially keen, but from the glimpse of postwar London I had, my admiration for British fortitude was unbounded.

There is an infallible test for detecting a tourist in any metropolis in the world—simply look for a man standing in front of a cutlery or luggage shop with his mouth ajar, gazing vacantly in at the manicure sets, razor strops, and collar-boxes and jingling the change in his pockets. Nine times out of ten, investigation will prove he hails from some point outside the city limits, be it Yakima, Nairobi, or Antofagasta. Hirschfeld and I adhered faithfully to the classic tradition, except that we broadened it to include every tobacconist's, bookstore, haberdashery, tailoring establishment, and bootmaker's in the West End. Before we wrote finis to a week of shopping, we had successfully slimmed down our purses to the vanishing point and amassed a weird profusion of phony Staffordshire, shooting sticks, brandy decanters, hand-tied flies suitable for whipping the streams off Times Square, tab-collar shirts that pinched our throats, and underslung pipes we had no intention of smoking. In a burst of affection, we also picked up a few paltry gifts for our families: tweed coats for our small daughters that would have fitted a Grenadier guardsman, a blow-gun with poisoned darts for my son, and some enchanting limp-leather diaries for our wives in which to jot down the household expenses. The latter, to be sure, was just a munificent gesture on our part, as neither of the girls, Lord love them, had ever learned to write, but we figured it was the sentiment rather than the keepsake that mattered.

London after dark we found to be on the whole not much more beguiling than Paris, although the theater was flourishing and, if you could readjust yourself to a curtain that rose at six-thirty, providing some brisk diversions. The outstanding, to our taste, was a revue starring a comedienne named Hermione Gingold, whose style may be loosely described as an amalgam of that of Groucho Marx and Tallulah Bankhead. Seen from the aisles where we rolled about freely on the three occasions we attended, the lady impressed us as the wittiest and most engaging performer in many a year. Her touch was consistently dextrous, whether she was depicting a musical comedy favorite of the 1900s, an elderly clublady delivering a dissertation on India, or the hapless subject of a cubist portrait painter. Following our last visit, we paid homage to her in her dressing room; I made a long, fervent address crammed with superlatives, enjoining her to do with our hearts as she saw fit. She was plainly overcome—blushed the color of a peony, modestly cast down her eyes, bathed us in ardent glances, and made repeated attempts to stanch my flow of eloquence. I learned later from a reliable source named Hirschfeld that Cary Grant had been standing directly behind me vainly trying to proffer his compliments, but I like to think they must have seemed pretty wooden after mine. That is what I like to think, and hell's bells, a man can think what he likes.

The thorniest problem we faced in London, and one that taxed our ingenuity to unravel, was the staggering cultural program we had outlined for ourselves, how to crowd a wealth of symphony concerts, art exhibits, and historic sites into the period preceding our sailing. We solved it in a rather effective manner, if I do say so, by merely tearing up the list we had prepared. We did, though, devote a morning to two places of prime aesthetic significance, Madame Tussaud's waxworks and Sherlock Holmes's chambers in Baker Street.

At the former, I had a trifling contretemps that robbed me of my appetite for a day or so; in the dimly lit Chamber of Horrors, I linked arms with a bearded party I supposed to be Hirschfeld and discovered somewhat belatedly that it was Henri Landru. Unluckily, a button on my sleeve got entangled in the manikin's vest, and by the time we were sorted out, Landru and my poise were in shreds. At 122-b Baker Street, we were dismayed to see that a grocery store occupied the great detective's diggings. The four stolid clerks insisted that nobody named Holmes had ever lived there. I maintained hotly that he, or rather his fictional self, most definitely had and, treating them to a scathing lecture on their ignorance, stormed out. Of course, I knew all along that Holmes's correct address was 221-b, as Hirschfeld triumphantly pointed out on checking up; I was only testing the clerks to puncture their middle-class smugness. It really astonishes one, traveling about the globe, to learn how little comprehension people have of their own literary background.

That a jubilee spirit hovered over one spot in London I can vouch for, and that was the platform at Waterloo Station the afternoon we caught the boat train for Southampton. The homeward-bound Americans were as merry as grigs (the Southern Railway had considerately furnished a box of grigs for purposes of comparison), and the English passengers were dewy-eyed with anticipation of the victuals awaiting them on the *Queen Mary*. Every man in sight had a brand-new suit of Glenurquhart plaid and a pigskin attaché case, twirled a cane bright with varnish, and puffed on a shiny briar; the womenfolk, parading those dove-gray tailleurs and furpieces they invariably don for the shortest train jump, were entwined with orchids. For our part, Hirschfeld and I betrayed not the slightest exuberance at leavetaking, beyond an occasional handspring or a shrill Comanche war whoop. The fact that we abandoned the train halfway and sprinted ahead, beating it into Southampton by half an hour, also meant nothing; we just felt the need for a bit of healthful exercise. I guess it was when my friend proposed that we bypass the steamer and swim to Newfoundland that I really began to suspect we were returning in the nick of time. But then, any fool could have told us as much—that is, any fool who could read a letter of credit.

HOME IS THE HUNTED

SILHOUETTED against the afterglow of the fiery red sun which had vanished a moment before over the Mid-Atlantic horizon, the chief officer of the *Queen Mary* paced the bridge, frowning into the gathering darkness. From the deck beneath his feet came the even, measured throb of the ship's pulse as she cleft the trackless deep, driving ever onward toward the shores of the New World. It had been a halcyon day; wind and water were favoring the voyage, passengers and crew alike were in a frame of high good humor, and all indications pointed to a smooth, uneventful run to Ambrose Channel sixty hours distant. And yet this vigilant watcher of the skies, on whose shoulders rested the responsibility for the leviathan and her cargo of four thousand souls, was oppressed by a vague disquiet. A feeling of remissness, as of some major obligation neglected, gnawed his conscience. Again and again he grappled with it, seeking to ferret out its source, but try as he would, the reason eluded him. At last, with a sigh of frustration, he threw open the door of the chartroom, entered, and addressed the young officer hunched over a set of calipers.

"Look here, ffoulis," he said abruptly, "a feeling of remissness, as of some major obligation neglected, has been gnawing my conscience. Can you give me any clue to this vague disquiet?"

"Why, yes, sir," said ffoulis, whose business it was to know everything, "perhaps it concerns that colorful pair of birds in Cabin 541 which their cognomens are Hirschfeld and Perelman and which they have for the last eight months been running the gamut of exotic climes from the frozen barrens of Manchuria to the sun-baked delta of the Nile."

"By Jove—of course!" exploded his senior. "Wonderful chaps—salt of the earth! I meant to have a drink with them, but I was too busy out there having my conscience gnawed. Tell me: has any stone been left unturned to provide for their animal comfort whilst aboard this here microcosm?"

"No, indeed, sir," said the other, "their fastidious palates have been tickled with our choicest viands, their tongues loosened with our rarest vintages, and their ears regaled with our most lilting dance harmonies."

"In short," nodded the chief, "they have been living like pigs in clover."

"I don't know about the clover part," admitted ffoulis, "but believe me, chief—"

"That will do, ffoulis," the chief interrupted sternly. "Where are these two arresting personalities at this instant?"

"Where they usually are," said the young man, "in the Pompeian bar getting fractured on Manhattans."

"Then we need not addle our pates anent them," said the chief, picking up the calipers and unfurling a map. "Come, let us put the chart before the course." And he fell to work with a will.

Actually, the junior's surmise as to our whereabouts was mistaken; at the moment we were seated in the ship's lounge in a state of dreamy absorption, listening to a string ensemble sawing Cécile Chaminade in half and wondering why we felt like a couple of characters in *Outward Bound*. For there was a definitely eerie quality about the vast salon with its glaring candelabra, its ghostly creak of woodwork, and its half-dozen cardiac cases slumbering in the overstuffed furniture. The stewards flitted soundlessly over the thick carpets, and frequently, when they passed between us and the light, a faint ectoplasmic glow seemed to outline their forms. Any minute you expected a grave but kindly messenger, impersonated by Edward Everett Horton or Claude Rains, to materialize to the muted sound of bells and beckon you into the hereafter.

The same sense of unreality, of other-worldliness, had in fact obsessed us ever since embarking on the *Mary* two days before at Southampton. Lost in her sheer magnitude, submerged in the endless swarms of passengers circulating through her myriad smoking rooms, restaurants, shopping galleries, verandas, and foyers, we found ourselves assuming an anonymous, wraithlike aspect. Our conversation was pitched in whispers and our normal gait slowed to a shuffle; we reported obediently at meals, queued up at the merest tinkle of a gong, salaamed in the most servile fashion to anyone wearing a wisp of gold braid. From the labels on our luggage and the occasional whiff of salt air that penetrated our porthole, we were dimly aware that we were at sea, but every artful device of modern hotel management had been employed to insulate us. Our cabin, a luxurious affair in brown and beige, was a marvel of compression, elevators inlaid in semi-precious stones whisked us from keel to topmast, and a host of barbers, tailors, masseurs, trainers, couriers, and assorted lackeys trembled at our whim. It was hemispheric travel on its loftiest level, and, to a couple of peasants like Hirschfeld and myself, unaccustomed to such splendors, a wholly spectral experience.

It was made even more so by the appearance at our table of a brace of citizens, Cozine by name, bizarre enough to unhinge the strongest reason. Wallace Cozine was a sallow, rumpled individual in tweeds and a pale red beard who modestly confessed at our only luncheon together that he was perhaps the world's foremost surrealist photographer. He and his wife, a gaunt, cavernous-eyed creature laden with quantities of abstract costume jewelry, had been visiting Paris the previous month in behalf of a small advance-guard magazine called *Umlaut!,* and there was no phase of French culture, politics, or cuisine they were not equipped to discuss in exhaustive detail and with absolute authority. It was obvious from the start that they had conceived a very low opinion of our taste, and they could not comprehend how we had passed through France without meeting the people who were doing the really challenging things.

"Who did you see there?" demanded Cozine. "Did you see Hans Raffia?"

"Who's that?" asked Hirschfeld.

"You mean to tell me you never heard of Hans Raffia?" hooted Cozine. "Why, the man's ceramics have practically revolutionized the whole conception of modern art!"

"We—er—we didn't get to look at much crockery," I faltered.

"Anybody who calls ceramics crockery is a boob, a barbarian, and a Yahoo," announced Cozine in a voice audible across the dining room. We accepted the classification with submissive smiles and pretended to be engrossed in our chicken patties. After a pause, his wife resumed the inquisition.

"What about Stanislaus Farkas?" she probed. "Did you see his show of non-objective horseshoes at the Galérie Frugl?"

"We . . . got there right after it closed," said Hirschfeld lamely. "The director was just putting up the shutters—"

"Aha," murmured Cozine cynically, "and I don't suppose you saw Serge Smetana's invisible ballet either."

"How could we if it was invisible?" I protested. "I mean—"

"*Nothing*'s invisible unless you close your mind to it," snapped Cozine, "but of course you couldn't have seen Smetana—he didn't give any recitals at the American Express Company." By the conclusion of the meal, they had so effectively demolished our self-esteem that we slunk off to the stateroom and thereafter had our food sent in on a tray. A day or two later, an envelope containing a picture postcard of the Eiffel Tower was slipped surreptitiously under the door. "Thought you'd like this," the note with it read. "Maybe it'll convince *somebody* you were in Paris, even if we don't think so." There was no clue to the sender, but the left-hand corner of the envelope bore the crisp legend "Umlaut! A Lance to Puncture Hypocrisy and Sham."

On the fourth morning, a new air of energy and purposefulness animated the ship; the bulletin boards bloomed with landing instructions, batteries of fountain pens scratched away at customs declarations, mountains of trunks choked the promenade decks. Caught up in the universal hysteria of homecoming, we pelted through the shops buying last-minute gifts that duplicated ones we already had and feverishly sent off dramatic cablegrams announcing our advent to families long oppressed by the fact. Then, loins girded, we attacked the job of winnowing from our baggage the exotic chaff the experts had insisted we take on the tour. Out through the porthole went the glass beads, red cloth, and Mother Hubbards we had planned to trade to savage tribes. After them went the maps of Tasmania, the Swahili dictionaries, the collapsible drinking cups, the Primus stoves, the underwater goggles, and the medical kit comprising every malaria specific, dysentery remedy, antivenin, vitamin, ointment, lotion, plaster, poultice, and powder known to hypochondria. Our knottiest problem was what to do with the score of empty leatherette folders which had contained our travelers' checks. We finally presented them to our cabin steward in lieu of a tip and the poor fellow's emotion as he realized the extent of our generosity was pitiful. He just stood there and fumbled for words, many of which I am sure were familiar to us, but we thought it kinder to leave him to his own salvation and tiptoed out.

The arrival of the *Queen Mary* in New York, far from being the noisy, vivid pageant we expected, was as fleeting and elusive as an episode in a Kafka novel. Stealthily, almost as if fate begrudged us the satisfaction of seeing the harbor and the skyline, we were wafted from the open sea one evening to a North River pier the following dawn. The whole process was a grotesque mixture of the ephemeral and the banal; we descended the gangplank with no more illusion of having spanned the Atlantic than as though we had commuted from Weehawken. It was only when our consorts and the fledglings streamed toward us from behind the barrier that our bewilderment abated. To say it disappeared entirely would be untrue; at one point in the resulting scrimmage, I discovered myself bussing a willowy showgirl under the impression that she was Hirschfeld's infant daughter, at another I was dandling a peppery old gentleman on my knee and quizzing him about his progress at school. At last, however, we managed to unsnarl our respective kinfolk, and after a breathless résumé of the fire, flood, and famine that had occurred in our absence, plunged into the ordeal of the customs examination.

Three quarters of an hour afterward, a fetching tableau might have presented itself to anyone sufficiently curious to invade the section bearing my initial. Knee-deep in a mound of shawls, brocades, bracelets, necklaces, purses, fans, and bric-a-brac resembling the contents of a thrift shop, three nonplused inspectors were attempting to calculate the duty I owed. My wife and I, our faces drawn, sat on the sidelines tonelessly discussing some practical solution to the dilemma—flight, a rubber check, a fifth mortgage on our home, selling the children. Under the circumstances, the last seemed the most feasible, inasmuch as they were loading the antique pistols I had bought them with percussion caps and discharging them into our eardrums. I am still not sure how I ever got off the hook, except that a few weeks afterward Hirschfeld showed me an I.O.U. with my name signed in a shaky scrawl. It was, needless to say, a blatant forgery and beneath contempt, but rather than see my friend victimized by some unscrupulous rascal, I shouldered the responsibility and settled with him for ten cents on the dollar.

Speeding across town from the pier to the family flat, I was dismayed to find hardly any civic recognition of our return; no bunting decked the buildings, almost no crowds clustered about the cab showering it with confetti and cheering hoarsely, and a minimum of brass bands lined the sidewalk before my residence. The sole member of the welcoming committee, a beery doorman chewing a half-dead cigar stump, eyed me with restrained enthusiasm as I sprang from the taxi. "Oh, *you're* back, are you?" he commented sourly. "Well, won't be long before I'll be carrying *you* upstairs four o'clock in the morning."

A similarly fervent salutation greeted me on entering our front door. The woolly little puppy I remembered cuddling in my arms, now grown to mastiff proportions, took one rapid sniff and zestfully sank his fangs into my ankle. By stroking him gently on the head with a length of chain, though, I won his confidence, and, dusting glass and shredded wallpaper from my shoulders, groped my way into the nest. Nothing was changed; the veneer on our installment furniture curled as crazily as ever and a disgruntled maid (not the one I recalled, but another equally morose) was stuffing herself with caviar and watering the whisky. Subsequently I observed her comparing me furtively with my photograph on the piano and shaking her head. "Don't try and tell *me* that's the same man," I overheard her declaring to the broom. Whoever I was, she obviously thought me worthy of respect, because from then on she seldom ventured into my presence without a bread-knife concealed under her apron.

For the next week I filled a dubious role in the family unit, a cross between that of Santa Claus and a second-story worker. I was never certain, when I came through a doorway, whether my relatives would overwhelm me with caresses or recoil as from a phantom. Conditioned to the idea that I was mousing around in Asia or Africa, my proximity unnerved them. Even inanimate objects seemed to resent my presence; my clothes-closets were jammed with bicycles, vacuum-cleaners, moth-proof bags, and corresponding household impedimenta that resisted any effort to dislodge them. The telephone rang constantly with what I supposed would be joyful greetings from friends but invariably proved to be the children's playmates and credit managers. Neither of the latter appeared to be enthralled by my adventures, and I finally decided that if they preferred to live in abysmal ignorance of the true state of the world, I personally had done my utmost by them.

No trip of the scope of ours, naturally, would have been complete without a motion-picture record, and Hirschfeld, an ardent cameraman, had exposed over four thousand feet of sixteen-millimeter film on the journey. On a brisk autumn evening in November, a select audience of two or three dozen friends crowded into my living room to witness the results. The party buzzed with anticipation; it was generally admitted that by all existing standards, this bade fair to be the outstanding travel picture of the decade. And in many respects it was. Though the greater part of it was upside down, backward, and out of focus, it had moments of breathtaking beauty—the traffic on Wilshire Boulevard in Los Angeles, the traffic on Hornby Road in Bombay, and the traffic in Leicester Square in London. In between were illimitable miles of shoreline in Siam and countless shots of monkeys picking fleas out of each other, interspersed here and there with gaudy sunsets. Unluckily for my commentary, I swallowed a poisoned highball halfway through it and confused many of the locales, a mischance that led to protracted bickering between the projectionist and myself. The audience tactfully muffled our squabble by yawning as loudly as it could, and everybody agreed that you would have to get up pretty early in the morning to find a more piquant film. Most of them were willing to try, nevertheless, and, since it was already way past nine o'clock, hurriedly took their leave. To show what degree of wanderlust the travelogue inspired, not a single one of those who saw it on that occasion was available for a second showing. They had all left town within forty-eight hours, and I can only assume they must have set forth immediately for the romantic places we had visited.

One year from the day on which our project to circle the globe had been hatched, Hirschfeld and I sat in a chophouse off Broadway and solemnly clinked glasses. Our pilgrimage was over. Behind us lay the twenty-five thousand miles of desert, sea, and jungle we had traversed; we had trod a perilous course through wars, revolutions, uprisings, and insurrections; we had undergone greater extremes of heat and cold, seen more underprivileged people, and eaten worse food than either of us had dreamed existed. And now, looking at the whole thing in retrospect, we saw with incredulity that we had come through our adventure absolutely unscathed. In our faces was none of that rich harvest of serenity and wisdom, that fund of mellow philosophy to lighten the daily burden, and that broad tolerance for human frailty guaranteed to shine forth from the countenance of the returned traveler. If anything, we were more crabbed, pettifogging, and ornery than before we had set off.

"Yes, sir," murmured Hirschfeld, leaning back in the booth with a sigh, "it's been a glorious year—and do you know what I'd say if anyone offered me a million dollars to go through it again?" The words had hardly left his lips when a portly, well-to-do individual in a black Homburg, pince-nez, white piping on his vest, and gold-headed cane, strode up to the table.

"Have I the honor of addressing Mr. Hirschfeld?" he inquired.

"You have," returned Hirschfeld steadily.

"Capital," said the stranger, spreading his coattails. "Then we need not waste time in idle formalities. I have been delegated by a group of powerful men whose identity I may not reveal to ask you to go around the world. Realizing, of course, that you have other commitments, we are prepared to offer you this trifling emolument." He withdrew his wallet and extended a certified check for a million dollars. Hirschfeld arose, took the check, and carefully tore it into a dozen tiny pieces.

"That, sir, is my answer," he said, flinging them in the astounded emissary's face. He turned toward me, proffering his arm. "Shall we stroll?" he suggested. "The air has a rather pleasant tang this afternoon, don't you think?" And with a courtly bow to our would-be benefactor, we brushed past him into the eddying mass of humanity in Times Square.

🌠 THE PANTS RECAPTURED

LAURE HAYMAN, "that strange courtesan colored with preciosity," doted on the young Proust, took him with her everywhere, and called him "Mon petit Marcel" or "Mon petit Saxe psychologique." When Paul Bourget made her the heroine of his novel, *Gladys Harvey*, she gave Marcel a copy, bound in the flowered silk from one of her own petticoats.

—*Proust: Portrait of a Genius,*
by André Maurois

IT WAS a quarter past one, and Nadine Sanger, torpid from her drugstore lunch of peanut butter on English muffin, apple strudel, and frosted chocolate, sat at the desk in Ezra Vedder's anteroom, listlessly staring at a four-act tragedy in blank verse based on the decline and fall of Montezuma. The play-script, two hundred pages long and a fraction under six pounds in weight, was the work of a young English instructor named Paepke at an obscure women's college outside Buffalo. In the unbiased judgment of the agent submitting it, Paepke was America's answer to Christopher Fry. Theatergoers, he asserted, were ravenous for historical tragedies in blank verse, especially Aztec ones, and if Vedder sponsored the piece, it would be the greatest smash in Broadway history. With the peddler's deep instinct for self-preservation, however, the agent managed in the same breath to disavow all enthusiasm, pointing out that his was only one man's opinion. Nadine yawned, thrust the masterwork into a filing cabinet full of similar potential hits, and got up. Her employer's buzzer had sounded—three short, imperious blasts that heralded the usual crisis. Vedder glowered at her as she opened his door.

"Where were you—in Ceylon?" he demanded pettishly. "Crissakes, I've been massaging this bell for an hour!" Knowing the futility of argument, Nadine countered with a bright maternal smile. A glance told her that while Ezra looked seedier than usual, nothing requiring a pulmotor had arisen. The upturned coatcollar, the rumpled hair above his lusterless black eyes, and the rime of Bromo-Seltzer around his lips were all intended, Nadine knew, to extract sympathy. "Who called?" he rasped.

"Nobody except Dazian's lawyer," she returned. "He said something I didn't catch about a two-timing little roach and he's bringing suit to recover the peach scene curtain. Oh, yes, and the Dramatists' Guild. They claim that Nungesser's back royalties now amount to—"

"Don't plague me with details," the producer interrupted. "Can't you see I haven't slept a wink all night?" He paused, stricken with an anguished nobility worthy of Bertha Kalich. "I was reading *The Splendid Guttersnipe*."

"Oh?" said Nadine, assuming a childlike innocence. She had read, and reveled in, the novel based on Ezra's artistic and emotional excesses, but she knew better than to admit it. "What's it about?"

"Lay off the chicken fat," said Ezra harshly. "You know damn well I'm the central character."

"Is that a fact?" she said wide-eyed. "I must get hold of a copy. I understand it's rather—clever."

"Well, I've got news for you," he snapped. "It's trash, and furthermore, it's the sneakiest job of character assassination since Martin Dies laid down his stiletto. If I wanted to stoop so low, I could drag that miserable hack into court and strip him of his last dime." Mingled with Ezra's indignation, Nadine detected a note of triumph that he should have been lampooned; manifestly, it established his prominence beyond doubt. He emitted a somber chuckle. "The louse certainly put in some legwork, though," he acknowledged. "He's even got me involved with a dame like Mrs. Haislip. I wonder how he tumbled to *that*."

"How could he avoid it? You march her into the Stork—"

"Strictly a one-night stand," said Vedder. "Discretion is the keynote with the lady you refer to. We frequent those French hideaways where the lights are low and the conversation is carried on in whispers."

"For all I care, you can run naked on the Mall," said his secretary. "It's her husband you better watch out for. According to *Town and Country*, he's a six-goal man, with muscles."

"That brisket of beef?" Vedder said contemptuously. "He don't know from nothing except sewage disposal bonds."

"O.K., I was just warning you," Nadine said with a shrug. "Look, today's the nineteenth. Your Equity settlement's three weeks overdue."

"Never mind that now," said Vedder. "I want you to run an errand. Krakauer, that Kraut bookbinder down on East Eleventh Street, is doing a rush job for me." He scribbled a note on a card. "Pick it up and take it to this address."

Nadine scanned the card and hesitated. "What happens if the cuckold himself answers the door?" she inquired. "Do I pretend I'm from the Visiting Nurses' Association?"

"Don't worry, you'll never get past the lobby," Vedder replied. "The joint is guarded like a medieval fort. Well, what are you waiting for?"

"Some money for Krakauer. He's an eccentric; he likes to be paid."

"Nonsense," said Vedder loftily. "The man works purely for the joy of creation, just as I do. However, if he starts caterwauling, send him a check in the mail tonight."

"On the level?" she asked in obvious disbelief.

"Sure," he said. "We can always run out of stamps temporarily, can't we?"

"Oh, brother," sighed Nadine. "Nine years here and you still freeze my blood." An amiable grin overspread his face as she clicked shut the door behind her.

The proprietor of the Astor Place Lunch flicked open the spigot of his coffee urn, drained off a cup, and set it down before Krakauer. With a perfunctory swish of the dishrag, he swept a few crumbs of pastry into the binder's lap, and resting on his elbows, resumed his discourse.

"How can anybody miss?" he demanded. "You feed 'em—they lay. The ones that don't lay, you sell for broilers. I tell you, it's a gold mine."

"Then why does this guy want to pull out?" Krakauer asked.

"His wife can't stand the winters in Jersey," said the other. "Besides, he's got an idea to raise chinchillas. There's big dough in chinchillas."

"Well, I don't blame you for looking around, Hagopian," said Krakauer. "If I was a younger man, I would too, the screwballs and phonies I have to contend with."

"You?" said Hagopian. "You got a well-established business."

"Yeah, me and the Consolidated Edison," retorted the bookbinder. "You want to know how I spent all day yesterday, for instance? Binding a book in a pair of men's underpants."

"You're kidding."

"You heard me," said Krakauer. "Regular cambric shorts, with a waistband and pearl buttons. A special order for a crackpot uptown. You should have seen his secretary's face when she called for it."

"Holy Jesus," his friend marveled. "How does anyone dream up such a notion?"

"That's what *I* asked him," said Krakauer. "He read about it in some French book—naturally."

"To think people would throw away their jack on a gag—"

"There's no gag about my fee," Krakauer assured him. "I'm getting a check in the morning mail."

"I surrender, dear," said Hagopian. "The more I hear about humanity, the better I like chickens."

"*Ganz richtig*," agreed Krakauer gloomily. "Maybe I'll go out with you Sunday and look over that poultry farm."

Hugo Haislip's head was slightly smaller than life-size, crowned by wheat-colored stubble, and joined to his body by a sturdy, columnar neck that flowed unbrokenly from shoulder to occiput. Owing to certain advantages of birth and a deeply ingrained self-satisfaction, Hugo carried it at an angle that enhanced its arrogance and caused many to regard him as insufferable. This view, of course, he did not share; indeed, as he stood lathering his face late next day in his bathroom, he experienced a lively sense of pleasure at the reflection in the shaving mirror. Plenty of character there, he thought—Patricia was a lucky girl, even if he did say so himself. Fortunately for his *amour propre*, Hugo had no inkling that his wife held a contrary opinion, one she was given to expressing graphically to her intimates after three Manhattans.

As Hugo gripped his left ear between thumb and forefinger and poised his razor, the ball-and-socket swivel supporting the mirror loosened and the glass tilted downward. With a grunt of annoyance, he looked around for some means of tightening the set-screw—scissors or a nail file. He opened the door of Patricia's bedroom and made a quick, impatient survey of her dressing table. The soap on his cheeks was drying momentarily and his temper mounting. Where the devil did she keep the countless manicure kits he had given her on birthdays and anniversaries? Fumbling vainly through bureau drawers crammed with lingerie, he was about to turn elsewhere when an object half hidden in a nest of stockings caught his attention. It was a book of some sort, bound in cloth tinted robin's-egg blue and outlined in white buttons. As one in a trance, Hugo extracted the book, sat down on the bed, and turned to the title page. Under the legend "The Splendid Guttersnipe by Roland Keyhoe" was an inscription in spidery handwriting. "To luscious-lipped Pat," it read, "this souvenir of a hundred mad moments. From her much-maligned but enraptured cavalier, Ezra Vedder."

Three-quarters of an hour afterward, Hugo, who had been assimilating the text with a speed none of his tutors at New Haven would have credited, rose decisively and started out. At the same moment, his wife, a sultry-eyed young matron in standard mink and diamonds, entered her boudoir. She had put in a grueling afternoon at a beauty salon followed by four Manhattans with a schoolmate, and she was counting on a snooze to fortify her against Hugo's dialogue at dinner. One glimpse of his face and the book in his hand told her that the fat was in the fire.

"Well, well," she said, instinctively aware that the best defense was offense. "So you've taken to rifling my bureau drawers, have you?"

"Drawers?" Hugo bellowed in a voice that rang welkins thirty blocks away. "You have the gall to talk to me about *drawers*?" He lifted a hand no larger than a peanut-fed ham and slowly crooked the fingers. "When I get through with that—that playmate of yours, I'll send you a souvenir too—from Reno! Where is he?"

"Find him," Patricia challenged.

"I will, baby, I will!" Hugo told her in an exultant shout, and vanished. His wife stood irresolute for an instant; then, her forehead puckered with anxiety, darted to the phone and hurriedly began dialing a number on the Longacre exchange.

"Be right with you, Miss Sanger." The butcher bobbed his head familiarly at Nadine and finished doling out change to another customer. Then he exhumed a small package from the refrigerator and bore it up the counter. "Pound and a half of beefsteak—that what you said on the phone?"

"Thanks," she said, extending a bill.

"You didn't have to come in yourself," he said. "I could have sent it over with the boy."

"Well, it wasn't for me exactly—I mean," she added with a lame smile, "I needed it in a hurry, so I just thought I'd stop by."

"My pleasure." He wedged the pencil more firmly under the band of his straw hat and bent forward confidentially. "Say, Miss Sanger, was Winchell leveling this morning? He said your boss and some socialite mixed it up last night at El Moroc—"

"Excuse me, Stanley, I've really got to run," Nadine apologized. She caught up her gloves and purse, in her mind's eye the image of Vedder in a darkened room grinding what remained of his teeth and awaiting succor.

"I guess you can't believe what you see in the columns," observed Stanley with infinite lingering regret.

"Not only in the columns, friend," said Nadine feelingly. "Sometimes I think I'm dreaming."

"Me too," Stanley agreed, eager, despite his calling, to assert his spiritual nature. "Nobody seems to know where they stand. Be seeing you." He picked up a cleaver and abstractedly began partitioning a crown rib roast. What a world, he reflected. If a man had any sense at all, he'd retire to a little place in Jersey and raise chickens. Or better yet, chinchillas. In a changing world, a person could still cling to one shibboleth. There was big dough in chinchillas.

☙ CLOUDLAND REVISITED: GREAT ACHES FROM LITTLE BOUDOIRS GROW

WHENEVER I STRETCH OUT before my incinerator, churchwarden in hand, and, staring reflectively into the dying embers, take inventory of my mottled past, I inevitably hark back to a period, in the spring of 1926, that in many ways was the most romantic of my life. I was, in that turbulent and frisky epoch, an artist of sorts, specializing in neo-primitive woodcuts of a heavily waggish nature that appeared with chilling infrequency in a moribund comic magazine. It was a hard dollar, but it allowed me to stay in bed until noon, and I was able to get by with half as many haircuts as my conventional friends above Fourteenth Street. My atelier was a second-floor rear bedroom in a handsome mansion on West Ninth Street, temporarily let out to respectable bachelors during the owner's absence abroad. In this sunny and reposeful chamber, I had set up my modest possessions: the draftsman's table and tools of my trade; a rack of costly Dunhills I never smoked; and a lamp made of a gigantic bottle, formerly an acid carboy, and trimmed with an opaque parchment shade that effectively blanketed any light it gave. After pinning up a fast batik or two, I lent further tone to the premises by shrouding the ceiling fixture with one of those prickly, polyhedral glass lampshades esteemed in the Village, a lethal contraption that was forever gouging furrows in my scalp. It met its Waterloo the evening a young person from the *Garrick Gaieties*, in a corybantic mood, swung into a cancan and executed a kick worthy of La Goulue. The crash is said to have been audible in Romany Marie's, six blocks away.

I had not been installed in my diggings very long before I found that they were not ideally suited to provide the tranquillity I had hoped for. My windows overlooked a refuge for unwed mothers operated by the Florence Crittenton League, and almost every morning between four and six the wail of newborn infants reverberated from the chimney pots. Occasionally, of an afternoon, I beheld one of the ill-starred girls on the roof, scowling at me in what I interpreted as an accusatory manner, and although I had in no way contributed to her downfall, I was forced to draw the blinds before I could regain a measure of composure. Far more disturbing, however, was the behavior of the clientele attracted by the tenant of the studio above mine, a fashionable Austrian portrait painter. This worthy, a fraudulent dauber who had parlayed an aptitude for copying Boldini and Philip de László into an income of six figures, was the current *Wunderkind* of Park Avenue; the socially prominent streamed to his dais like pilgrims to the Kaaba in Mecca. The curb in front of the house was always choked with sleek, custom-built Panhards and Fiats, and hordes of ravishing ladies, enveloped in sables and redolent of patchouli, ceaselessly surged past my door. What with the squeals and giggles that floated down from the upper landing, the smack of garters playfully snapped, and pretty objurgations stifled by kisses, I was in such a constant state of cacoëthes that I shrank to welterweight in a fortnight.

It would be unfair, though, to hold the painter entirely culpable for my condition; a good share of it was caused by a novel I was bewitched with at the time—Maxwell Bodenheim's *Replenishing Jessica*. Its publication, it will be recalled, aroused a major scandal hardly surpassed by *Lady Chatterley's Lover*. Determined efforts were made to suppress it, and it eventually gave rise to Jimmy Walker's celebrated dictum that no girl has ever been seduced by a book. Whether the *mot* was confirmed by medical testimony, I cannot remember, but in one immature reader, at least, *Replenishing Jessica* created all the symptoms of breakbone fever. So much so, in fact, that prior to a nostalgic reunion with it several days ago, I fortified myself with a half grain of codeine. I need not have bothered. Time, the great analgesic, had forestalled me.

To call the pattern of Mr. Bodenheim's story simple would be like referring to St. Peter's as roomy or Lake Huron as moist; "elementary" sums it up rather more succinctly. Condensed to its essence, *Replenishing Jessica* is an odyssey of the bedtime hazards of a young lady of fashion bent on exploring her potentialities. Jessica Maringold is the twenty-three-year-old daughter of a real-estate millionaire, willful, perverse, alternately racked by an impulse to bundle and a hankering for the arts. Without any tedious preliminaries, she weighs in on the very first page perched on a piano bench near a stockbroker named Theodore Purrel, for whom she is playing "one of Satie's light affairs." "She was a little above medium height, with a body that was quite plump between the hips and upper thighs," the author recounts, exhibiting a gusto for anatomical detail that often threatens to swamp his narrative. Purrel receives a similarly severe appraisal: "He was a tall man, just

above thirty years, and he had the body of an athlete beginning to de-
teriorate—the first sign of a paunch and too much fat on his legs."
With all this lard in proximity, it is preordained that high jinks will
ensue, and they do—cataclysmically. "His fingers enveloped the fullness of her breasts quite as a boy grasps soap-bubbles and marvels at
their intact resistance." The soap bubbles I grasped as a boy were not
distinguished for their elasticity, but they may have been more resilient
in Mr. Bodenheim's youth. Meanwhile, during these gymnastics Jessica
surrenders herself to typically girlish musings. "She remembered the
one night in which she had given herself to him. . . . She knew that Purrel would grasp her, and she reflected on some way of merrily repulsing
him, such as pulling his tie, wrenching his nose, tickling his ears." Unluckily, the delaying action had been futile, and Purrel managed to
exact his tribute. Now, however, he impresses her as a dull, self-confi-
dent libertine, an estimate borne out by his Philistine rejection of her intellect: "I wish you'd give this mind stuff a rest. . . . It doesn't take
much brains to smear a little paint on canvas and knock around with
a bunch of long-haired mutts. . . . I may not be a world-beater but I've
run up a fat bank account in the last eight years and you can't do *that*
on an empty head." The struggle between Theodore's animal appeal
and Jessica's spiritual nature is resolved fortuitously. "The frame of
the piano, below the keys, was pressing into her lower spine, like an absurd remonstrance that made her mood prosaic in the passing of a second," Bodenheim explains, adding with magisterial portentousness,
"The greatest love can be turned in a thrice [*sic*] to the silliest of frauds
by a breaking chair, or the prolonged creaking of a couch." When the
lust has blown away, Jessica is safe in her bedroom and her admirer
presumably on his way to a cold shower. "Purrel felt feverish and
thwarted without knowing why," says the text, though any reasonably
alert chimpanzee of three could have furnished him a working hypothesis.

Jessica's next sexual skirmish takes place at twilight the following
afternoon, in the studio of Kurt Salburg, a dour Alsatian painter who
addresses her as "*Liebchen*" and subjects her virtue, or what's left of
it, to a coarse, Teutonic onslaught. His brutal importunities, unac-
companied by the slightest appeal to her soul, provoke her into withholding her favors, but she confers them a scant twenty-four hours later
on Sydney Levine, a masterful criminal lawyer, who requisitions them
in the terse, direct fashion of an Army quartermaster ordering sixty
bags of mule feed. "I have wanted you for six months," Levine tells
her. "I have no lies or romantic pretenses to give you. My love for you

is entirely physical, and nothing except complete possession will satisfy it. . . . From now on, it would be impossible to control myself in your presence, and it will have to be everything or nothing." Their romp leaves Jessica remorseful and more frustrated than ever. Eschewing the opposite sex for three weeks, she stays glued to her easel, creating futuristic pictures apropos of which the author observes, "She had a moderate talent for painting." The sample he describes would appear to permit some room for discussion: ". . . two lavender pineapples, placed on each side of a slender, black and white vase, all of the articles standing on a dark red table that seemed about to fall on the cerise floor." Of course, there is always the possibility that Mr. Bodenheim is being sardonic, just as there is always the possibility that the Princess Igor Troubetzkoy is planning to leave me her stock in the five-and-ten-cent stores.

Ostensibly purified by her joust with the Muse, Jessica now retreads her steps to Salburg's studio to bedevil him a bit further. This time the lecherous Alsatian uses a more devious gambit to achieve his ends. He employs the infantile, or blubber-mouth, approach. " 'If you should refuse me now, I would never live again,' he said, in a low voice. 'Never, never . . . I am helpless and frightened, Jessica.' His words had a defenceless quiver that could not be disbelieved. . . . A disrobed and frantic boy was speaking his fear that she might whip his naked breast." Following a rough-and-tumble interlude, the participants spend the evening at a *Nachtlokal* with Purrel, whom Jessica pits against Salburg to keep things humming. In the resulting scrimmage, the stockbroker draws first claret; Jessica is repelled by the artist's craven behavior and, dismissing her flames as bullies and cowards, decides to pop over to Europe and see what beaux are available in England. There is a vignette of her, aboard ship, calculated to awake tender memories in the older girls: "She was dressed in dark purple organdy with white rosettes at the waist, stockings and shoes of the same purple hue, a long, thin cape of white velvet, and a pale straw turban trimmed with black satin." It is a coincidence worth recording that the young person from the *Garrick Gaieties* referred to earlier wore exactly this costume when she danced the cancan in my web. Naturally, she removed the long, thin cape of white velvet to facilitate her kick at the lamp, but in every other respect her ensemble was identical. Sort of spooky, when you come to think of it.

Having installed herself in an apartment in Chelsea, Jessica plunges intrepidly into the bohemian whirl of London, keeping a weather eye out for brainy males. At the 1919 Club, a rendezvous so named "in commemoration of a Russian revolution"—an aside that pricks your curiosity as to which one the author means—she encounters four. They are (disguised under impenetrable pseudonyms) Ramsay MacDonald, the Sitwell brothers, and Aldous Huxley, but, regrettable to say, no pyrotechnics of note occur. At last, the situation brightens. One evening, Jessica finds herself in her flat discussing Havelock Ellis with a personable ex-officer named Robert Chamberlain, ". . . and during the course of the talk Jessica partly unloosened her heliotrope blouse because of the warmness of the room, and sprawled at ease on a couch without a thought of sensual invitation." Innocent as the gesture is, Chamberlain in his crass, masculine way misconstrues it. "His confidently thoughtful mood was shattered, and for the first time he looked steadily at the tapering, disciplined curve of her legs, slowly losing their plumpness as their lines fell to her ankles, and half revealed by her raised, white skirt; and the sloping narrowness of her shoulders, and her small-lipped, impishly not quite round face that was glinting and tenuous in the moderated light of the room." But the foregoing is merely a feint on Bodenheim's part, and two months of interminable palaver are necessary before his creatures coalesce to make great music. The slow buildup plainly does much to intensify Chamberlain's fervor: "His mind changed to a fire that burned without glowing—a black heat—and his emotions were dervishes." Once the pair wind up in the percale division, the same old sense of disillusion begins gnawing at Jessica. A week of stormy bliss and she is off to New York again, hastily sandwiching in a last-minute affair with Joseph Israel, a London real-estate broker.

The concluding fifty pages of *Replenishing Jessica* cover a span of approximately six years and vibrate with the tension of high-speed oatmeal. Jessica passes through a succession of lovers (including poets, musical-comedy stars, and other migratory workers), marries and discards Purrel, and inherits four million dollars, zestfully described as composed of real estate, bonds, and cash. (Offhand, I cannot recall another novel in which the scarlet threads of sex and real estate are so inextricably interwoven. It's like a union of Fanny Hill and Bing & Bing.) All these stimulating experiences, nevertheless, are no more than "a few snatchings at stars that turned out to be cloth ones sewed to the blue top of a circus tent," though one suspects a handful of the spangles may have been negotiable. Tired of drifting about the capitals of Europe and unable to find a mate who offers the ideal blend of sensuality and savvy, she devotes herself to teaching children to paint at an East Side settlement house. Here, among the lavender pineapples she is midwifing, she meets a saintly, partially deformed type given to reading Flaubert and writing aesthetic critiques. His luxuriant brown beard, exalted eyes, and general Dostoevskian halo augur well, and as the flyleaves loom, Jessica's saga ends with a prolonged quaver reminiscent of a Jesse Crawford organ solo.

Every book of consequence ultimately produces lesser works that bear its influence, and *Replenishing Jessica* is no exception. As collateral reading, I can recommend a small semi-scientific monograph I myself recently helped to prepare. It concerns itself with the peculiar interaction of codeine and ennui on a white hysteroid male of forty-four exposed to a bookful of erotic fancies. Unlike the average hypnotic subject, the central character was fully conscious at all times, even while asleep. He ate a banana, flung the skin out of the window, flung the book after the skin, and was with difficulty restrained from following. It sounds technical but it really isn't. It's an absorbing document, and above all it's as clean as a whistle. Not a single bit of smooching in it from start to finish. I made certain of *that*.

❧ MANY A SLIP

SCENE: *A hotel room in Wilmington, Delaware. It is in a state of some disorder as the curtain rises—newspapers strewn about, service trays cluttered with coffee cups and half-eaten chicken sandwiches, several partially empty Scotch bottles and glasses, ash trays heaped with cigarette butts. On the davenport at left, hands interlaced behind his head and his eyes fixed unwinkingly on the ceiling, lies Costain, senior partner of Costain & Nudelman, lingerie manufacturers and sponsors of Cost-Nudel Creations. A day-old beard darkens his dyspeptic cheeks, and his nose is pinched with fatigue. Nudelman, his bald, hard-bitten associate, teeth clamped on a cigar, stands moodily staring out the window at a neon sign blinking on and off—an effect achieved by a stage-hand with an electric torch concealed in the wings. Over the room hangs the unmistakable air of apprehensiveness typical of an out-of-town tryout. (Note: This last effect may be a trifle more difficult to achieve, but a good stage manager can do anything.)*

NUDELMAN (*whirling around*): Holy cats, quit pacing up and down, can't you?

COSTAIN: Who's pacing? I've been lying on this sofa the last ten minutes!

NUDELMAN: Well, get off it. Pace up and down—do something, only stop looking like Svengali or Trilby or whoever it was. It's enough to turn a man's hair gray.

COSTAIN: You should worry, with that billiard ball *you've* got.

NUDELMAN (*darkly*): Now, look here, Costain, one more insinuendo about my scalp—

COSTAIN: All right, all right, skip it. We're both a little high-strung, I guess.

NUDELMAN: These tryouts are nothing but aggravation. The next underskirt I produce, we open cold in New York.

COSTAIN: Ah, that's what you always say. How can you find out what's wrong if you don't see it before an audience?

NUDELMAN: You call this bunch of rhubarb down here an audience?

COSTAIN: Well, they wear underwear, too. We're bound to get reactions.

NUDELMAN: Yeah, and strictly corny. They don't know from sophistication—the flounces, the eyelet embroidery, all the clever touches we beat our brains out to get into the script.

COSTAIN: Listen, that Noel Coward stuff never yet made a petticoat a smash. It's O.K. for the first-nighters in New York, but if you ask me, it's the meat-and-potatoes appeal—the old pull at the heartstrings—that'll put us over at the box office.

NUDELMAN (*gloomily*): Well, I wouldn't make book on these farmers. When our model gives with the pratfall on the dance floor and flashes her petticoat, they might figure it's an accident and yell.

COSTAIN: Just what we want—soften 'em up with some good rowdy slapstick. I remember I once broke in a pair of rompers in Cleveland—

NUDELMAN: Infants' wear is different. Young people go for low comedy.

COSTAIN: You can't be too broad. Look at Milady Underthins. They previewed three rayon slips in a row here in the Caprice Room and every one wowed the critics.

NUDELMAN: Theirs were all native-American folk slips—earthy, if you know what I mean. With an adaptation from the Hungarian, like ours, we should have opened in a more metropolitan pitch— Philly or New Haven.

COSTAIN (*hooting*): And have the whole wise mob from the needle trades there with their knives out? Those buzzards'd run right back to the Garment Center and spread the word we had a flop.

NUDELMAN (*consulting his watch*): I wish young Nirdlinger would get back here. I sent him downstairs to kind of mingle with the press and smell out how things are going.

COSTAIN: Say, I meant to speak to you about that boy. What makes him a press agent except the fact he's your nephew?

NUDELMAN: Just because the kid is only fifteen and wears knee pants—

COSTAIN: Oh, I know he's big for his age and all that—

NUDELMAN: You're damn right he is. He's been shaving for over two years.

COSTAIN: Still, it's a hundred and fifty a week on the payroll, and some of the backers are beginning to talk.

NUDELMAN: Let me ask you a question. Have you ever done the night spots with Teddy—the Stork, the Copa, the El Morocco?

COSTAIN: No, I can't say I have.

NUDELMAN: Well, if you want to see men fall all over theirselves, you just watch Lyons and Earl Wilson around Teddy. They're tongue-tied when he breezes in. He's like a god to them.

COSTAIN: Why?

NUDELMAN: Search me. Sheer personality, I suppose. All I know is, you never see little digs at Costain & Nudelman in their column, and to me that's worth the peanuts we pay him. Besides, show me another press agent who'll push a delivery truck in his spare time. I tell you, he's one in a million.

COSTAIN (*ungraciously*): Well, I wish somebody would tip him off that Edward Bernays don't wipe his nose on his sleeve. After all, how does it look for Cost-Nudel Creations—

NUDELMAN: That reminds me—I've been meaning to speak to you about something. Now, answer me honestly, Chick. Have I ever been unreasonable in my demands?

COSTAIN: I know that expression on your face. What are you driving at?

NUDELMAN: Time and again, I've given in to you, on the director, on casting—

COSTAIN: Come on, never mind the schmaltz. Spit it out.

NUDELMAN: It's the producing credit. I've had my ear to the ground lately and there's a definite resistance on the public's part to the name of the firm.

COSTAIN (*dangerously*): So you were wondering if it wouldn't have more bite, maybe, if we switched it to Nudel-Cost Creations—is that it?

NUDELMAN (*taken aback*): How did you know?

COSTAIN: I've been making a study of weasels ever since our first bankruptcy.

NUDELMAN: I don't get you. We're not in the fur business.

COSTAIN: O.K., I'll blueprint it for you. Someone was writing "Nudel-Cost," "Nost-Cudel," "Nude-Costel," and a lot of other variations on the blotter over there.

NUDELMAN (*quickly*): It wasn't me.

COSTAIN: No, probably the woman who cleans up. (*The telephone rings. Nudelman springs to it. The eager expectancy on his face turns sour as he listens.*)

NUDELMAN (*banging down the receiver*): The desk. The designer's on his way up.

COSTAIN: After the way he carried on at rehearsal about changing the buttons to a zipper, you'd think he'd be ashamed to show himself.

NUDELMAN: Chick, we might as well face it. Anspacher can handle a camisole or a frilly nightgown, but a petticoat's over his head.

COSTAIN: What we need is a fresh slant. He's too close to it.

NUDELMAN: Mind you, I'm no writer, but I see a hundred places where it could stand brightening up—over the yoke, around the waistband, in the seams . . .

COSTAIN: I hate to call in somebody to doctor it, though. Once the news gets around Sardi's you're in trouble, you're practically in the hands of the jobbers.

NUDELMAN: I don't mean anyone with a big rep—I'd like to give some unknown with promise a chance. (*casually*) For instance, I heard of a brilliant kid up on the West Side. So far, he's only fooled around with panties, and I bet we could get him for tinfoil.

COSTAIN (*suspiciously*): What's his name?

NUDELMAN: What difference does that make? Rukeyser, I think—I don't recall exactly . . .

COSTAIN: Seems to me your wife has a nephew by that name.

NUDELMAN: Why—er—I believe there *is* a Rukeyser who's a distant relative. Just a coincidence.

COSTAIN: Have you ever thought of adopting me as your nephew? Then it would all be in the family. (*A knock at the door. Anspacher, the designer, enters excitedly. A slight unsteadiness hints that he has taken a dram or two.*)

NUDELMAN (*anxiously*): What's happened? Any news?

ANSPACHER: But colossal! It's the biggest thing that ever hit Wilmington!

COSTAIN: You're kidding!

ANSPACHER: You never saw such an uproar. The scouts from Rochester are using words like "Kuppenheimer." The hotel even had to call the police!

NUDELMAN (*paling*): The police? What for?

ANSPACHER: Why, to take our leading lady to the cooler; they're booking her now. Oh, that girl's a sweetheart! She played it to the hilt—she got values I never dreamt existed!

COSTAIN: For God's sake, stop brumbling! We didn't figure on the cops!

ANSPACHER: Darn right you didn't. (*preening himself*) That took imagination. Once I stumbled on the gimmick, everything fell into place.

NUDELMAN (*outraged*): You deliberately stuck in a new piece of business without consulting us?

ANSPACHER: Yes sirree, and a dilly! I was knocking myself out for a twisteroo and it came to me in a flash before the performance— send her out in just the petticoat, with no dress at all!

NUDELMAN: It's madness! It violates every law of dramatic unity!

COSTAIN: And Delaware, too!

ANSPACHER: Wipe your chin, both of you. You've made sartorial history tonight and you don't know it.

NUDELMAN (*wringing his hands*): But laying it right in their laps like that . . . Where are the halftones, the shading, the Continental *soupçons* we're famous for?

ANSPACHER: Who cares? This is red-blooded, boffo entertainment for both sexes. You should have seen the men climbing on chairs to get a better view.

COSTAIN (*uneasily*): You—you say it really caused a sensation?

ANSPACHER: Terrific. You'll be all over the front page tomorrow, I guarantee you.

COSTAIN (*extracting a hat from closet*): Well, if it's as big as you say, I better bail out—I mean, I better get back to New York right away.

ANSPACHER: What for?

COSTAIN: To—to arrange additional financing. You know, for exploitation.

NUDELMAN (*following him to door*): Me, too. We don't want to get caught flat-footed with no exploitation.

ANSPACHER: But what am I supposed to do here?

NUDELMAN: You keep your eye on the creative angles. We'll tend to the business end.

ANSPACHER: Aren't you even going to wait for the reviews?

COSTAIN: No, no, you can phone 'em to us. Abba-dabba! (*They scurry out. Anspacher stares after them, then runs to door.*)

ANSPACHER: Hey! You forgot your suitcases! (*A pause. He turns back into room, pours himself a drink, and shrugs.*) Businessmen— huh!

CURTAIN

❧ SWISS FAMILY PERELMAN

RANCORS AWEIGH

SEVEN HUNDRED TONS of icy green water curled off the crest of the California ground swell and struck with malignant fury at the starboard plates of the *S. S. President Cleveland,* westbound out of San Francisco for Honolulu, Manila, and Hong Kong. Midway along its deserted promenade, huddled in a blanket, a solitary passenger sprawled in his deck chair, pondering between spasmodic intakes of breath the tangled web of circumstance that had enmeshed him. To even the most cursory eye—and there was no shortage of cursory eyes among the stewards hurrying past—it was instantly apparent that the man was exceptional, a *rara avis.* Under a brow purer than that of Michelangelo's David, capped by a handful of sparse and greasy hairs, brooded a pair of fiery orbs, glittering like zircons behind ten-cent-store spectacles. His superbly chiseled lips, ordinarily compressed in a grim line that bespoke indomitable will, at the moment hung open flaccidly, revealing row on row of pearly white teeth and a slim, patrician tongue. In the angle of the obdurate outthrust jaw, buckwheat-flecked from the morning meal, one read quenchless resolve, a nature scornful of compromise and dedicated to squeezing the last nickel out of any enterprise. The body of a Greek god, each powerful muscle the servant of his veriest whim, rippled beneath the blanket, stubbornly disputing every roll of the ship. And yet this man, who by sheer poise and magnetism had surmounted the handicap of almost ethereal beauty and whose name, whispered in any chancellery in Europe, was a talisman from Threadneedle Street to the Shanghai Bund, was prey to acute misery. What grotesque tale lurked behind that penetrable mask? What dark forces had moved to speed him on his desperate journey, what scarlet thread in Destiny's twisted skein?

It was a story of betrayal, of a woman's perfidy beside which the recidivism of Guy Fawkes, Major André, and the infamous Murrel paled to child's play. That the woman should have been my own wife was harrowing enough. More bitter than aloes, however, was the knowledge that as I lay supine in my deck chair, gasping out my life, the traitress herself sat complacently fifty feet below in the dining saloon, bolting the table d'hôte luncheon and lampooning me to my own children. Her brazen effrontery, her heartless rejection of one who for twenty years had worshiped her this side idolatry and consecrated himself to indulging her merest caprice, sent a shudder through my frame. Coarse peasant whom I had rescued from a Ukrainian wheat-field, equipped with shoes, and ennobled with my name, she had rewarded me with the Judas kiss. Reviewing for the hundredth time the horrid events leading up to my imbroglio, I scourged myself with her duplicity and groaned aloud.

The actual sellout had taken place one autumn evening three months before in New York. Weary of pub-crawling and eager to recapture the zest of courtship, we had stayed home to leaf over our library of bills, many of them first editions. As always, it was chock-full of delicious surprises: overdrafts, modistes' and milliners' statements my cosset had concealed from me, charge accounts unpaid since the Crusades. If I felt any vexation, however, I was far too cunning to admit it. Instead, I turned my pockets inside out to feign insolvency, smote my forehead distractedly in the tradition of the Yiddish theater, and quoted terse abstracts from the bankruptcy laws. But fiendish feminine intuition was not slow to divine my true feelings. Just as I had uncovered a bill from Hattie Carnegie for a brocaded bungalow apron and was brandishing it under her nose, my wife suddenly turned pettish.

"Sixteen dollars!" I was screaming. "Gold lamé you need yet! Who do you think you are, Catherine of Aragon? Why don't you rip up the foyer and pave it in malachite?" With a single dramatic gesture, I rent open my shirt. "Go ahead!" I shouted. "Milk me—drain me dry! Marshalsea prison! A pauper's grave!"

"Ease off before you perforate your ulcer," she enjoined. "You're waking up the children."

"You think sixteen dollars grows on trees?" I pleaded, seeking to arouse in her some elementary sense of shame. "*Corpo di Bacco*, for sixteen dollars a family like ours could live in Siam a whole year! With nine servants to boot!"

"And you're the boy who could boot 'em," my wife agreed. "Listen, ever since you and that other poolroom loafer, Hirschfeld, got back from your trip around the world last year, all I've heard is Siam, morning, noon, and night. Lover, let us not dissemble longer. *Je m'en fiche de Siam.*"

"Oh, is that so?" I roared. "Well, I wish I were back there this minute! Those gentle, courteous people, those age-old temples, those placid winding canals overhung with acacia—" Overhung with nostalgia and a little cordial I had taken to ward off a chill, I gave way to racking sobs. And then, when my defenses were down and I was at my most vulnerable, the woman threw off the veneer of civilization and struck like a puff adder.

"O.K.," she said briskly. "Let's go."

"Go?" I repeated stupidly. "Go where?"

"To Siam, of course," she returned. "Where'd you think I meant—Norumbega Park?" For a full fifteen seconds I stared at her, unable to encompass such treachery.

"Are you crazy?" I demanded, trembling. "How would I make a living there? What would we eat?"

"Those mangosteens and papayas you're always prating about," she replied. "If the breadfruit gives out, you're still spry enough to chop cotton."

"B-but the kiddies!" I whimpered, seeking to arouse her maternal sense. "What about their schooling—their clay and rhythms? Who'll teach them to blow glass and stain those repugnant tie-racks, all the basic techniques they need to grow up into decent, useful citizens?"

"I'll buy a book on it," she said carelessly.

"Yes, do," I urged, "and while you're at it, buy one on the snakes and lizards of Southeast Asia. Geckos under your pillow, cobras in the bathtub—not that there *are any* bathtubs—termites, ants, scorpions—"

"You'll cope with them," she asserted. "You did all right with that viper on Martha's Vineyard last summer. The one in the electric-blue swim-suit and the pancake make-up."

"I see no reason to drag personalities into this," I thundered. Deftly changing the subject, I explained as patiently as I could that Siam was a vast malarial marsh, oppressively hot and crowded with underprivileged folk scratching out a submarginal existence. "You and I would stifle there, darling," I went on. "It's a cultural Sahara. No theaters, no art shows, no symphony concerts—"

"By the way," she observed irrelevantly (women can never absorb generalities), "how was that symphony you attended Tuesday at the Copa? You were seen with another music-lover, a lynx-eyed mannequin in black sequins featuring a Lillian Russell balcony."

"I brand that as a lie," I said quietly, turning my back to remove a baseball constricting my larynx. "A dastardly, barefaced lie."

"Possibly," she shrugged. "We'll know better when the Wideawake Agency develops the negative. In any case, Buster, your next mail address is Bangkok." In vain to instance the strife and rebellion sweeping Asia, the plagues and political upheaval; with the literal-mindedness of her sex, the stubborn creature kept casting up some overwrought declaration I had made to the effect that there was not a subway or a psychoanalyst north of Singapore.

"No," I said savagely, "nor a pediatrician, an orthodontist, or a can of puréed spinach in a thousand miles."

"That's what I've been dreaming of," she murmured. "Keep talking. The more you say, the lovelier it sounds." At last, spars shot away and my guns silenced, I prepared to dip my ensign, but not without one final rapier thrust.

"Well, you've made your bed," I said cruelly. "I wash my hands. Bye-bye Martinis." The blow told; I saw her blanch and lunged home. "There's not a drop of French vermouth between San Francisco and Saint Tropez." For an instant, as she strove with the animal in her, my fate hung in the balance. Then, squaring her shoulders, her magnificent eyes blazing defiance, she flung the shaker into the grate, smashing it to smithereens.

"Anything you can do, I can do better," she said in a voice that rang like metal. "Fetch up the seven-league boots. Thailand, here I come."

Had the ex-Vicereine of India attended the Durbar in a G-string, it would have occasioned less tittle-tattle than the casual revelation to our circle that we were breaking camp to migrate to the Land of the White Elephant. "She dassen't show her face at the Colony," the tongues clacked. "They say he smokes two catties of yen shee gow before breakfast. *In Reno veritas.*" Rumors flew thick and fast. They ranged from sniggered allusions to the bar sinister to reports that we were actually bound for the leper colony at Molokai, the majority opinion holding that we were lamisters from the FBI. The more charitable among our friends took it upon themselves to scotch these old wives' tales. "He's merely had a nervous breakdown," they said loyally. "You can tell by the way he drums his fingers when she's talking." Our children, they added, were not real albinos, nor was it true I had been made contact man for a white slave ring in Saigon. I was much too yellow.

The reaction of the bairns was equally heart-warming. When the flash came that they were shortly transplanting to the Orient, they received it impassively. Adam, a sturdy lad of twelve, retired to his den, barricaded the door with a bureau, and hid under the bed with Flents in his ears in readiness for head-hunters. His sister Abby, whose geography at ten was still fairly embryonic, remained tractable until she discovered that Siam was not an annex of Macy's. She thereupon spread-eagled herself on the parquet and howled like a muezzin, her face tinted a terrifying blue. Toward evening the keening subsided and both were cajoled into taking a little nourishment through a tube. On discussing the matter tranquilly, I was gratified to find they had been laboring under a misapprehension. They had supposed we were going to discontinue their arithmetic and spelling, a situation they regarded as worse than death. When I convinced them that, on the contrary, they might do five hours of homework daily even en route, their jubilation was unbounded. They promptly contrived wax effigies of their parents and, puncturing them with pins, intoned a rubric in which the phrase "hole in the head" recurred from time to time.

Ignoring the tradesmen who, under the curious delusion that we were about to shoot the moon, crowded in to collect their accounts, we fell to work assembling the gear necessary for an extended stay out East. Perhaps my most difficult task was to dissuade the memsahib from taking along her eighty-six-piece Royal Doulton dinner service. I tried to explain that we would probably crouch on our hams in the dust and gnaw dried fish wrapped in a pandanus leaf, but you can sooner tame the typhoon than sway the bourgeois mentality. Within a week, our flat was waist-high in potato graters, pressure cookers, pop-up toasters, and poultry shears; to the whine of saws and clang of hammers, crews of carpenters boxed everything in sight, including the toilet, for shipment overseas. My wife's cronies, lured by the excitement like bears to wild honey, clustered about loading her with dress patterns, recipes for chowchow, and commissions for Shantung and rubies, while children scrambled about underfoot flourishing marlinspikes and igniting shipwreck flares. Through the press circulated my insurance broker, who had taken the bit in his teeth and was excitedly underwriting everyone against barratry and heartburn. Doctors bearing Martinis in one hand and hypodermics in the other immunized people at will; a caldron of noodles steamed in a corner and an enterprising Chinese barber worked apace shaving heads. The confusion was unnerving. You would have sworn some nomad tribe like the Torguts was on the move.

A lifelong gift of retaining my aplomb under stress, nevertheless, aided me to function smoothly and efficiently. Cucumber-cool and rocket-swift, canny as Sir Basil Zaharoff, I set about leasing our farm in the Delaware Valley and our New York apartment. The problem of securing responsible tenants was a thorny one, but I met it brilliantly.

The farm, naturally, was the easier to dispose of, there being a perennial demand for dank stone houses, well screened by poison sumac, moldering on an outcropping of red shale. Various inducements were forthcoming; at length, by paying a friend six hundred dollars and threatening to expose his extramarital capers, I gained his grudging consent to visit it occasionally. Disposing of our scatter in town, though, was rather more complex. The renting agents I consulted were blunt. The rooms were too large and sunny, they warned me; sublessees were not minded to run the risk of snow blindness. Washington Square, moreover, was deficient in traffic noise and monoxide, and in any event, the housing shortage had evaporated twelve minutes before. Of course, they would try, but it was a pity our place wasn't a warehouse. Everybody wanted warehouses.

The first prospects to appear were two rigidly corseted and excessively genteel beldames in caracul who tiptoed through the stash as gingerly as though it were a Raines Law hotel. It developed that they were scouts for a celebrated Hungarian pianist named Larczny, and their annoyance on learning that we owned no concert grand was marked. I observed amiably that inasmuch as Larczny had begun his career playing for throw money at Madame Rosebud's on Bienville Street, he might feel at home with the beer rings on our Minipiano. The door had hardly slammed shut before it was reopened by a quartet of behemoths from Georgia Tech. Wiping the residue of pot-likker from his chin with his sleeve, their spokesman offered to engage the premises as a bachelor apartment. The deal bogged down when I refused to furnish iron spiders for their fatback and worm gears for their still.

Interest the next couple of days was sporadic. A furtive gentleman, who kept the collar of his Chesterfield turned up during the interview, was definitely beguiled, but did not feel our floor would sustain the weight of a flat-bed press. He evidently ran some sort of small engraving business, cigar-store coupons as I understood it. Our hopes rose when Sir Hamish Sphincter, chief of the British delegation to United Nations, cabled from the *Queen Elizabeth* earmarking the rooms for his stay. Unfortunately, on arriving to inspect our digs, the baronet and his lady found them in a somewhat disordered state. Our janitor, in a hailstorm of plaster, was just demolishing the bathroom wall to get at a plumbing stoppage. By the time he dredged up the multiplication tables the children had cached there, Sir Hamish was bowling toward the Waldorf. We never actually met the person who rented the flat after our departure, but his manners were described as exquisite and his faro bank, until the law knocked it over, was said to be unrivaled in downtown Manhattan. I still wear on my watch-chain a .38 slug which creased the mantelpiece and one of his patrons, though not in the order named.

Dusk was settling down on Washington Square that early January afternoon and a chill wind soughed through the leafless trees as I marshaled our brave little band for the take-off. Trench-coated and Burberryed, festooned with binoculars, Rolleiflexes, sextants, hygrometers, and instruments for sounding the ocean floor, we were a formidable sight. The adults, their nerves honed to razor sharpness by weeks of barbital and bourbon, were as volatile as nitroglycerine; the slightest opposition flung them into apocalyptic rages followed by floods of tears. Without having covered a single parasang, the children had already accumulated more verdigris and grime than if they had traversed Cambodia on foot. The bandage on Adam's hand acquired in a last-minute chemistry experiment had unwound, but he was dexterously managing to engorge popcorn, read a comic, and maneuver an eel-spear at the same time. Abby, bent double under her three-quarter-size cello, snuffled as her current beau, a hatchet-faced sneak of eleven, pledged eternal fealty. Heaped by the curb were fourteen pieces of baggage exclusive of trunks; in the background, like figures in an antique frieze, stood the janitor, the handyman, and the elevator operators, their palms mutely extended. I could see that they were too choked with emotion to speak, these men who I know not at what cost to themselves had labored to withhold steam from us and jam our dumbwaiters with refuse. Finally one grizzled veteran, bolder than his fellows, stepped forward with an obsequious tug as his forelock.

"We won't forget this day, sir," the honest chap said, twisting his cap in his gnarled hands. "Will we, mates?" A low growl of assent ran round the circle. "Many's the time we've carried you through that lobby and a reek of juniper off you a man could smell five miles down wind. We've seen some strange sights in this house and we've handled some spectacular creeps; it's a kind of a microcosm like, you might say. But we want you to know that never, not even in the nitrate fields of Chile, the smelters of Nevada, or the sweatshops of the teeming East Side, has there been a man—" His voice broke and I stopped him gently.

"Friends," I said huskily, "I'm not rich in worldly goods, but let me say this—what little I have is mine. If you ever need anything, whether

jewels, money, or negotiable securities, remember these words: you're
barking up the wrong gee. Geronimo."

Their cheers were still ringing in my ears twenty minutes later as our
cab swerved down the ramp into Pennsylvania Station. Against the
hushed cacophony of the Map Room, I began to hear another and
more exotic theme, the tinkle of gamelans and the mounting whine of
the anopheles mosquito. The overture was ending. The first movement,
molto con citronella, had begun.

FIFTEEN DUTCH ON A RED MAN'S CHEST

EVERYBODY WAS BEING excessively kind, and kindest of all was Mr.
Smit. There were no limits to Mr. Smit's benevolence; waves of cordiality radiated from him like heat from a diaper-drier as he leaned forward across the rattan table and smoothly expounded to me the complex Indonesian political situation. Outside, in the dismal, sprawling
dock area of Macassar, principal port of the island of Celebes, the torrential rain of the west monsoon drummed on the godowns; from time
to time, a vicious gust rattled the windows of the ship's lounge, forcing
Mr. Smit to inflect more precisely, but his voice never lost its silky, insinuating purr.

"Suicide, sheer suicide," he was saying. "I tell you, my dear chap, on
the day these unfortunate natives are allowed to govern themselves,
you are going to witness the greatest catastrophe in history. My
heart—" he placed a large, plump, strangler's hand on his damp bosom
to indicate where that organ lay lurking—"my heart goes out to them."
Tears of compassion glistened in his pale Malemute eyes, and as the
familiar old glycerin bubbled forth, I began to experience the sense of
déjà vu which had obsessed me the past fortnight. It was the same litany
of persecution we had evoked from every Dutch colonial since entering
the archipelago—the black ingratitude of their subjects, the mendacity
and guile of the Republican leaders, the intolerable presumption of the
United Nations in obtruding itself into a domestic quarrel. It was crys-
tal-clear that if I were ever going to escape from Mr. Smit's hypnotic
mumble, I would have to resort to desperate measures. Under pretext
of refilling his glass with Bols, I dexterously upset the bottle in his lap
and we both sprang up, our foreheads colliding violently in mid-air.

"Look here, I'm most frightfully sorry," I apologized, retrieving the bottle and inadvertently spilling half of it on his shirt. "Let me get you a little ketchup or something to sprinkle on that before it stains."

"No, no, thank you," Mr. Smit protested, backing away. "It's nothing at all—I was going anyway—"

"Nonsense!" I interrupted. "Here's some soy-bean sauce on the sideboard—no, Worcestershire's better—" Holding on to his jacket and using his wrist as a lever, I wrestled him unobtrusively toward the accommodation ladder. As he backed down it, agitatedly assuring me that he would return to complete my political orientation, my wife and bairns sprinted across the quay from the customs barrier. Soaked to the skin, tingling with irritation and heat rash, they clawed their way up the ladder and inevitably became entangled with Mr. Smit. By the time the Laocoön group unscrambled itself and my family gained the deck, the mem was buzzing like a wasp.

"Who was that confounded idiot?" she sputtered, her magnificent bosom heaving in accordance with the laws governing the upheaval of magnificent bosoms.

"Oh, just another exposed nerve," I replied carelessly. "He controls all the copra in this bailiwick. He'd like to know just what we're doing out here."

"So would I," she said vengefully. "Listen, I've been in some pretty abysmal drops since I threw in my lot with yours, but of all the backward, stultified fleabags on earth—"

"Steady on, Cassandra," I soothed her. "The *Cinnabar* tied up an hour ago; we weigh tomorrow on the tide." The news that our exile in Macassar was ended produced the reaction I had anticipated. For the previous four days, we had been vegetating aboard the *Kochleffel* at the dockside, awaiting the small coasting steamer that would carry us into the Moluccas. The distractions of Macassar at any time, and particularly during the rainy season, are hardly such as to earn it the reputation of a spa. True, there is a famous old harbor where, by scaling a barbed-wire fence, you may catch a glimpse of some quaint native prahus, and for lovers of sixteenth-century Portuguese forts, there is a passable sixteenth-century Portuguese fort; but the town, a huddle of bleak and pungent alleys, does not twine itself around the heart and the population seemed merely an Asiatic version of a West Virginia mining community. As for the Dutch contingent, a cross-section of which we reveled with at a social club called the Harmonie, it was less than the gayest society in memory. Most of the men bore a chilling resemblance to either Baldur von Schirach or Himmler; their ladies, with minor exceptions, were cumbrous, hostile, and notably devoid of chic. Possibly it was the music, a series of Wiener waltzes danced with exuberance and no grace whatever, that gave the occasion a highly Germanic flavor, but Milady and I were forced, at the conclusion of the evening, to confess without prejudice that it had been one of the more loathsome of our lives.

It would be cheeky to suppose that our brief stay in Macassar enriched the folklore of that dingy outpost, and yet I think that nobody who was privileged to watch our removal from the *Kochleffel* to the *Cinnabar* will ever forget it. In the estimation of several waterfront loungers (whose opinion is always authoritative), it was the single greatest achievement since the construction of the Assouan Dam, the restoration of Angkor Wat, and the diversion of the Yellow River. When our trunks, satchels, hatboxes, duffel bags, baskets, portmanteaux, and parcels were finally piled on the deck of the *Cinnabar* by nine panting coolies, they formed a cone visible ten miles at sea. Predictions of disaster, naturally, flew thick and fast; it was pointed out that the ship had developed a dangerous list to port and Captain Versteegh, her master, gloomily prophesied that we would founder in the first blow, but fortunately for all concerned, most of our kit toppled over the side as soon as we got under way.

Whether the vessel would have caused a naval architect to throw his cap into the air is debatable; to my layman's eye, she appeared a marvel of compactness, comfort, and stability. Though displacing only two thousand tons, she carried four hundred passengers (the majority of them in deck class), thirty cows, three hundred chickens, a dozen pigs, and an impressive quantity of mixed cargo ranging from tractors to cold storage eggs. She was, in point of fact, an engaging combination of Toonerville Trolley and Noah's Ark, delivering mail, freight, and contract labor to the farther reaches of East Indonesia and gathering copra in return, and as a vehicle from which to observe some of the most breathtaking scenery in the Orient, she was unsurpassed.

The loveliness of the islands and the sense of enchantment with which they instill the traveler have been captured with such fidelity by Conrad, Maugham, and Tomlinson—as well as by Alfred Russel Wallace in his superb and ageless *The Malay Archipelago*—that any lesser artisan who tries to emulate them may well wind up gelding the lily. In my own case, I can testify that as the *Cinnabar* moved up the western rim of Celebes, tarrying briefly at obscure outposts like Pare-Pare, Donggala, Ternate, and Batjan, I was caught up in a mood of rapture and euphoria so intense that my family became actively concerned. I began rising at dawn, declaiming fragments of Pierre Loti to the setting sun, and studying astronomy; made plans to sever all ties with civilization, install myself on a coral reef, and rove the South Seas in an auxiliary yawl; and altogether comported myself in an exalted, swashbuckling fashion reminiscent of the senior Fairbanks or a schoolboy in love. The fever reached a crescendo one afternoon at Ternate as we stood on the tumble-down escarpment of an old Dutch fortification, giant coconut palms nodding gently about us and breakers pounding on the black volcanic beach below.

"Well, shipmates," I said, encompassing the scene with a dramatic, sweeping gesture, "It's been a long, weary search, but I've found it at last."

"Found what?" my wife glowered, disengaging a leech from her instep.

"The land of heart's desire," I said quietly, my noble profile silhouetted against the horizon like Robinson Jeffers'. "A safe anchorage from the storms and petty distractions of life. A snug eyrie where, as the sea birds sport ceaselessly overhead and the majestic diapason of the Pacific echoes in my ear, I can achieve that inner harmony to which Lao-tzu and Gautama Buddha point the way. Now the first thing we need," I said briskly, casting a shrewd, experienced glance about me, "is a rude shelter of some sort." Suiting the deed to the word, I extracted a gold penknife and started to hack down one of the palms. What was my chagrin, on turning a second later, to find that my kinsmen had taken a powder and were climbing back into our rented jeep.

"We're just nipping back to New York for a few supplies," my wife explained apologetically. "You know, corn meal and linsey-woolsey and stuff. You stay right here; we won't be a minute." Obviously I could not permit a woman and two small tots to drive unescorted through five miles of jungle terrain, and since the blade of my knife had snapped off in any case, partially sundering an artery in my wrist, I decided to accompany them back to the ship. My vigilance proved extremely farsighted, for I discovered subsequently that there was not a granule of marinated herring on Ternate, and had we settled there, we might have been exposed to untold hardships.

After the bile displayed by so many of the Dutch theretofore, Captain Versteegh's amiability and desire to please came as a heartening change; throughout the twenty-three-day voyage, he exhibited a solicitude for our welfare and a zeal in organizing tours, picnics, and similar diversions that made him an anomaly among his countrymen. Under his guidance, we saw much we would otherwise have missed—the villages of the Minahassa, the residences of the sultans of Ternate and Batjan, the sinister lake straight out of Edgar Allan Poe named Tanah Tinggalam which had swallowed up three native compounds when it was created by an earthquake, and the stupefying flora and fauna, the cockatoos, apes, and orchids, which flourish in those incredible islands. One of the more bizarre spectacles was a collection of two hundred Flying Fortresses and several thousand jeeps crumbling away in the bush at Morotai, the huge air base of the last war. This edifying sight, it should be noted, was shown us as an example of Yankee prodigality and waste; our cicerone, a Dutch subaltern, underscored it with footnotes on our dollar diplomacy and pharisaism distilled of purest snake venom. It was really quite awe-inspiring, as the trip progressed, to discover with what revulsion the United States was regarded by the Dutch in Indonesia. America, we found, occupied the curious dual role of skinflint and sucker, the usurer bent on exacting his pound of flesh and the hapless pigeon whose poke was a challenge to any smart grifter. The aversion assumed a thousand exotic shapes; whenever conversation flagged, some body-snatcher could always be depended on to conjecture when the next depression would engulf America or the atomic bomb obliterate New York. The most studied insult I heard of was directed at a young American missionary who journeyed with us from Ternate to Amboina. He was chatting one evening with a couple of Batjan planters and their wives when the subject of Hawaii's impending recognition as our forty-ninth state arose. One of the planters suddenly slapped his knee.

"That reminds me," he said, turning to his wife. "Did you tell the houseboy?"

"Tell him what?" she asked.

"Why, to sew another star on that American flag we use for a dishrag," he said with a feline grin. "After all, we can't lag behind the times, can we, gentlemen?" Our missionary friend was in something of a dilemma. His natural impulse to hang a mouse on the speaker's eye clashed with his clerical vows, and he felt moreover that his usefulness would be restricted in the cooler where the Dutch would most certainly have flung him. He therefore excused himself with a tortured smile and retired to his stateroom to reread certain admonitions on turning the other cheek—as striking an instance of Christian self-restraint as any in the revealed writings.

The gleam of the stiletto was nowhere as pronounced, perhaps, as at Sorong, the western tip of New Guinea, where we ran full tilt into the prettiest little case of industrial despotism imaginable. An oil company town complete with electrified fences, searchlights, armed guards, and all the standard appurtenances of the detention camp, Sorong will never dispute with Bar Harbor as the vacationist's choice, but it was the only contact we were having with New Guinea and I had hoped to see at least a bit of its fabulous jungle at first hand. The anchor chains had barely stopped quivering before I was disabused. An insufferably pompous, pear-shaped young Hollander boarded the *Cinnabar*, introduced himself as Van Wuppertal, public relations officer of the firm, and demanded my credentials. I presented my parole card from the Lewisburg Penitentiary, together with a certificate to the effect that I had been cured of mopery and drug addiction, and having scanned them minutely, he handed down a mandate from the front office. The management, he announced, had graciously consented to our landing at Sorong the following day for a period of two hours, when we would be taken on a tour of the oil installations.

"Please forgive me for sounding blasé," I returned, "but in the eleven years I spent in Southern California, I became reasonably browned off on high octane. My family and I would like to take a gander at the greenery. Capricious though it sounds, we ache to see a bird of paradise on the wing."

"The whim of the foreign journalist is not law in Sorong," retorted Van Wuppertal. "This is private territory, and you will be shown that portion of it we deem fit. Good morning." The notion that an oil concern had superseded the Dutch crown and was administering New Guinea was so captivating that I rounded up Captain Versteegh (who, of course, promptly blew a gasket), and we called on the assistant resident for a clarification of Sorong's status. This diplomat, lodged on an atoll offshore bearing the apposite name of the Island of Doom, also flew into a passion. New Guinea was ours to come and go as we pleased, he thundered; heads would roll in the sand if any man moved to gainsay us. He urged us to proceed on the double into Sorong, he would show those beggars who was master here, but at the same time, he disavowed any responsibility for our safety. In short, he gave a splendid imitation of a man badly frightened by an oil well.

The next morning, accordingly, the four of us, chaperoned by the captain in his snowiest drill, piled into the latter's gig and made for the mainland. Van Wuppertal must have been observing our sortie through a spyglass, because he was waiting on the jetty in a state of considerable perturbation. Apparently our intransigence had created a situation.

"E-excuse me, ladies and gentlemen," he puffed, "but this is all highly irregular. Where are you going?"

"To the jungle, Mac," spoke up my first-born, squaring his jaw, "and we don't want any of your chicken-fat, savvy?" Checking a violent impulse to kick a small boy in the sweetbreads, Van Wuppertal feverishly bade the rest of the party wait and rushed me to his superior's office. The company's Number Two man was a museum specimen, a knifelike Junker whose quartz eyes and pitiless mouth would have endeared him to the *Herrenvolk*. In a tone that beautifully blended contempt with condescension, he made it evident that he ranked my profession between that of an iguana and a poor-box thief. The company, he snapped, had suffered some slight annoyance at the hands of an Australian pen-pusher who had published damaging reports about labor conditions in Sorong. He wanted it understood that his personnel was supremely content with its lot, and, he added significantly, he hoped I was not one of these snoopers and troublemakers. I assured him that next to the Magna Carta, I worshiped the stockholder's dividend more than life itself; no muckraker I, but a vapid little tomtit writing elegiacs about temple bells and lepidoptera. Thanks to my beguiling bourgeois aspect and the fact that I was accompanied by my family, his suspicions were allayed, and in Van Wuppertal's custody, we were permitted to venture fifteen kilometers into the forest.

Presumably the birds of paradise, the Papuans, and the giant butterflies had also been warned of our advent and had stampeded, for all we saw in the end was impenetrable timber, a gravel road flanked by a pipeline, and a series of roadblocks at which our identities were methodically rechecked. The coup de grâce, though, awaited us on our return to the jetty. We were about to leave Sorong to her rosy future of development by the termite and Dutch capital when Van Wuppertal drew me aside.

"There is just one more detail," he said. "Before you publish anything on what you have seen here, you will first submit a copy to the company for approval."

"Would you mind repeating that rather more slowly?" I asked, cupping my ear. "I have a feeling that you have just said something quite epochal."

"Certainly," he answered. "You must show us whatever you write before it is printed. So we can judge whether it is suitable for public consumption."

"You wouldn't be trying to tamper with Mummy's prose by any

chance, would you?" I inquired. "You know, we have a nasty name for that sort of thing in the States."

"I am not interested in the States," said Van Wuppertal loftily. "We are in New Guinea at the moment."

"That we are, Peaches," I agreed, "and I'll tell you what you can do with it." I told him, and when I had finished, I left New Guinea. If he is still standing there as I last saw him, they'll never need a lighthouse in Sorong.

A hundred and twenty miles southeast of Amboina in the vast and lonely tropical sea lies a microscopic cluster of islands known as the Banda group. From them, in 1604, stemmed the rich spice trade which became the cornerstone of Dutch imperial power; even today, the reputation of their nutmeg and mace is unrivaled among gourmets and those exacting folk who pride themselves on their condiments. As the political importance of spice and the Netherlands declined across the centuries, however, the Banda group was forgotten; and since they are almost entirely inaccessible, offer no facilities to the wayfarer, are reputed to be malarial, and contain a population of minor anthropological interest, their appeal nowadays is fairly negligible. Why, consequently, I should have bamboozled myself into visiting them, at the price of abandoning my family and pitting myself against one of the world's most treacherous oceans in an antiquated, greasy launch manned by a bunch of untrained Indonesian sailors, was something of a conundrum. Exactly who did I think I was anyway, Captain Joshua Slocum? And what kind of insane romantic compulsion possessed a sedentary, diffident taxpayer of forty-five to suddenly start behaving like Vasco da Gama? These and a host of equally wintry reflections surged through my mind as I stood on the stringpiece at Amboina in the gathering dusk and watched the *Cinnabar* back slowly into midstream. The faces of my wife and children began growing indistinct; in a few moments, the handkerchiefs they waved were no longer discernible against the blurred bulk of the ship. The native boy assigned to conduct me aboard the *Sembilan* touched my arm respectfully. I handed down my gear into his dinghy, scrambled after him, and we rocked away toward the buoy where the launch lay moored.

"Tuan mengerti Inggris?" I asked him in my execrable Berlitz Malay, which was to say, Do you understand English, Jack?

"Tidak, Tuan," he replied, shaking his head.

"Good," I said, relieved. "Because then I can make a promise without any fear you'll hold me to it. If I ever so much as budge off the island of Manhattan, I want you to take an outsize baseball bat . . ." I gave him quite a lengthy set of instructions before I was through, and I do hope he was telling me the truth. I'd hate to think I had misplaced my confidence.

PART III

1950–1958

THERE IS, *as far as I know, no concise and felicitous word in our language for the sportive essay. The English, who developed such masters of the form as Beerbohm and E. M. Forster, refer to it as a "middle," a vague and deprecatory term that implies it is used to interlard material of real substance. In this country, we are more forthright and less exact; we tend to classify writers like Ade, Lardner, and Benchley as humorists, conjuring up neuralgic images of a jackanapes with upturned hatbrim chewing his cigar and relentlessly spouting yocks.* The New Yorker, *in whose pages most of the following items appeared, calls them casuals, which is obviously a convenient solecism to describe a particular brand of merchandise in its shop. Unsurprisingly, the French come closest to it. If I were to apply for a library card in Paris, I would subscribe myself as a* feuilletoniste, *that is to say, a writer of little leaves. I may be in error, but the word seems to me to carry a hint of endearment rather than patronage.*

In whatever case, and despite my conviction that the pasquinade will soon be as extinct in America as the naphtha launch

431

*and the diavolo, I should like to affirm my loyalty to it as a
medium. The handful of chumps who still practice it are as
lonely as the survivors of Fort Zinderneuf; a few more assaults
by television and picture journalism and we might as well post
their bodies on the ramparts, pray for togetherness, and kneel
for the final annihilation. Until then, so long and don't take any
wooden rhetoric.*

❦ UP THE CLOSE AND DOWN THE STAIR

I'M NO BLOODY HERO, and when the Princess Pats stood at Passchendaele in '17, I was damned careful to be twelve years old and three thousand miles to the rear, selling Domes of Silence after school to the housewives of Crescent Park, Rhode Island. I never go out of my way to borrow trouble, but if it comes, I pride myself I can face up to it as well as the average Johnny. I once spent a night in a third-class carriage in the F.M.S. with seventy-odd indentured Chinese out of Swatow and Amoy bound upcountry for the tin mines at Ipoh. Blasted engine broke a coupling, way up the back of beyond in Negri Sembilan, and there we sat, rain pelting through the roof, not a cup of tea to be had, and every mother's son of them smoking chandoo and tucking in rice mixed with *trassi*, compared to which even the durian is attar of roses. Worse luck, the coolie in the berth over mine kept munching bananas and dropping the skins on me; half a dozen times, you'd have sworn a cobra or a Russell's viper was loose in your bed. Touch and go, as they say, but I bit on the bullet and the old buckram carried me through. Another time, down Amboina way in the Moluccas, a chap buying *bêche-de-mer* and shell in the Kai and Aru groups southeast of Ceram offered me a lift as far as Banda Neira in his prahu. A filthy scow she was, thirty-five tons, with a poop deck and double sweeps, manned by a crew of Bugi who'd slip a kris into you at the drop of a diphthong. Well, you know the Banda Sea at the turn of the monsoon, treacherous as a woman, waves thirty feet high one minute and flat calm the next, wind howling like a thousand devils and sharks all over the ruddy place. Thinks I, weighing the beggar's proposal in the bar in Amboina, steady on, old son, better have another drink on it. We'd a second bottle of *genever* and a third, till I could almost feel the eyes start out of my blooming head. Lord knows how I managed to stick it, but she sailed without me and that was the last ever heard of the lot of them. I probably would have heard more, except I had to rush back to New York to see about my Social Security.

Yes, the going has to be pretty rugged before I show the white feather, and when it comes along, I'm willing to own up to it. A couple of weeks ago, business called me up to town from my Pennsylvania retreat and I stayed alone overnight at our flat in Greenwich Village. This much I'll say: I've knocked about a bit and I've taken the rough with the smooth, but I wouldn't duplicate that experience for all the rubies in the Shwe Dagon Pagoda. Just in a manner of speaking, that is. If anybody wants to talk a deal, I can be in Rangoon in two days.

Maybe, since the circumstances were special, I ought to sketch in the background. Last December, deferring to my wife's prejudice against sleeping on subway gratings, I moved the family into a hand-some old brownstone on West Ninth Street. It was a charming house, its brick front weathered a soft rose under the ivy, with a cool, spacious stair well and a curving walnut balustrade worn smooth by the hands of many a defaulting tenant. Determined to apportion the charm among the greatest possible number of people, the owner had cut up the prem-ises into eight apartments, and the top floors in particular into two minute duplexes, the rear one of which we invested. It commanded an unbroken view of a health-food shop on Eighth Street, and of a dismal winter afternoon it was heartening to watch the dyspeptics totter out carrying pails of blackstrap molasses and wheat germ, their faces ex-alted with the gospel of Gayelord Hauser. The services, to be candid, were deplorable. The hot-water taps supplied a brown viscous fluid similar to cocoa, the radiators beat an unending tomtom like the Royal Watusi Drums, and the refrigerator poached our food instead of chill-ing it, but the mem and I didn't care a fig. We were living graciously; we could breathe. We thanked our lucky stars we weren't cooped up in one of those great uniform apartments on Park Avenue, full of stall showers and gas ranges that work, and all kinds of depressing gadgets.

About a month after moving in, I learned a beguiling fact from an-other tenant; viz., that three decades before, the house had been the scene of an audacious heist. To recap the affair briefly: One Sunday afternoon in April, 1922, Mr. and Mrs. Frederick Gorsline, the wealthy elderly couple who occupied the mansion, were enjoying a siesta when five yeggs, led by a French high-binder once employed there as relief butler, gained entrance. They overpowered the householders and their staff of eight, locked them in a wine vault in the basement, and fled, bearing gems and silver worth approximately eighty thousand dollars. That the prisoners escaped from the vault alive was due solely to the sangfroid and enterprise of its seventy-three-year-old owner; working in total darkness with a penknife and a ten-cent piece, he succeeded after two hours in loosening the screws that held the combination in place, and opened the door. He then expended seven years and a sizable part of his bundle tracking down the culprits, the last of whom, the ringleader, was apprehended in France and transported to Devil's Island.

I, naturally, lost no time in making a close scrutiny of the vault with a wax taper, or something the man at the hardware store assured me was a wax taper, and convinced myself of the veracity of the story. I even found a dime embedded in a crack in the floor; it was dated 1936, but I filed off the final numerals and worked up a rather effective account of my role in the case, which folks used to clamor for at our parties this past spring. It was funny the way they'd clamor for it, sometimes without even opening their mouths. They'd just stand there and sort of *yearn*, and being host, of course, I'd have to oblige. But all that is by the way. You're clamoring to hear about the night I put in alone there.

Well, I got downtown about six of a Friday evening, pretty well bushed, no engagements on hand. (Curious the way they'd rather stay home and wash their hair than accept a date at the last minute. I never will understand it.) As I say, I was done up and looking forward to a quiet session with Gibbon or Trevelyan, eleven hours of shut-eye, and an early start back to Pennsylvania in the morning. One of our neighbors, a young fellow who poses for those Bronzini neckwear ads of people with their torsos transfixed by a dirk, was loading a portable sewing machine and a nest of salad bowls into the back of his MG. "Huddo," he said, startled. "I thought you-all had cleared out." I explained my presence and he shuddered. "Too ghastly. Everyone in the house is away. The Cadmuses drove off this minute to their haunt in Bucks. Even Benno Troglodeit's gone to the beach, and you know what an old stick-in-the-mud *he* is."

"Solitude don't make no never-mind to me," I said loftily. "When one's kicked around the far places of the earth as much as I have, he becomes pretty self-sufficient. I recall one time in Trebizond—" The roar of his powerful little engine drowned out the remainder of my sentence, and with a flick of his wrist he was speeding down Ninth Street. Sensational acceleration, those MGs.

I watched him out of sight, then slowly went upstairs. Somehow—I couldn't have said why—a puzzling change of mood had overtaken me, a vague and indescribable malaise. The house, too, seemed to have altered mysteriously; the stair well was nowhere as cool or spacious as it had been in the past. The air smelled stagnant and oppressive, as though it had been filtered through hot plush, and I imagined some unspeakable secret behind each doorway I passed. Fumbling the key into the lock of our apartment, the distorted, waxen faces of Andrew and Abby Borden rose up before me; with a galvanic twitch, I flung open the door, darted inside, and bolted it fast. By the weak rays of light struggling through the drawn Venetian blinds, I took careful stock of the living room, its floor devoid of carpets and the furniture shrouded in dust covers. Nothing appeared amiss, but I decided to double-check. I licked my lips and spoke in a soft, placating tone that made it clear I wouldn't give offense to a dog. "Is anybody home?" I inquired. It goes without saying that had a reply been vouchsafed, I was prepared to drop dead instantly. Satisfied no corporeal intruders were astir, I stole on padded feet upstairs to the bedrooms—trekking through the jungles of southern Siam long ago taught me how to move without disturbing a twig—and made a routine tour of the closets.

Just as I was feeling around gingerly among the topcoats for any unauthorized bodies, the telephone gave a sudden, nerve-shattering peal. I sprang out and flattened myself against the wall near the instrument, every faculty tensed. Something very, very unsavory was afoot; I distinctly remembered having canceled the service myself a month before. Ought I answer or play for time? Trying to envision the face at the other end, the twisted smile and the narrow, baleful eyes, I felt perspiration ooze from my scalp. Then equilibrium returned; better to know my enemy than succumb to this nameless, creeping horror. I picked up the receiver. "Grand Central Roach Control," I said tonelessly. "Leonard Vesey speaking." There was a watchful pause, and, realizing the full stature of his adversary, the unknown hung up discomfited.

The first round was mine, but from now on my only safety lay in extreme vigilance. With a view toward sharpening my sensibilities to razor edge, I decided to toss off two fingers of brandy neat. A search of the kitchen cupboards failed to elicit any such restorative; I did, however, turn up a can of warm tomato juice whose top I finally breached with an apple corer. Five or six gauze pads soon dried the trifling gash in my wrist, and, stripping down to my shorts (for I was not minded to carry excess poundage if an emergency arose), I opened my Gibbon to the campaigns of Diocletian.

How noble a spirit infuses those stately periods, what sapience and celestial calm! Musing on the paltriness of latter-day historians, I fell into a gentle reverie that must have lasted close to four hours.

Shortly after midnight, I came awake with the ineradicable conviction that I had neglected some vital obligation. I lay rigid, struggling to recapture it, and suddenly it flashed over me. In the hustle and bustle of moving last fall, I had forgotten to tip the janitor of our new quarters at Christmastime. Suppose, for argument's sake, that he had been brooding over the slight. Suppose that his bitterness had developed into a persecution mania that demanded my extinction, that he had seen me enter the house alone tonight, had seized the chance to put me out of the way, and, at this very moment, was tiptoeing stealthily up the stairs, cleaver in hand. I saw myself cruelly dismembered, my head in a hatbox as in *Night Must Fall*, my extremities wrapped in burlap and dispersed through a dozen railway checkrooms. Tears of self-pity welled up in my eyes; I was too young to die in such meaningless fashion, victim of a madman's whim. What would become of my brood in Pennsylvania, waiting for the paternal hug and the sweetmeats that never came? I resolved to sell my life as dearly as possible. Grimly rolling up my figurative sleeves, I was about to burrow under the quilt when a muffled clang from below turned me to stone.

In that awful instant, all the details of the Gorsline robbery reverted with diamond clarity, and the whole hideous truth dawned on me. The police, despite their rodomontade, had never really regained the loot; the brains of the mob had hidden it somewhere in the building, and now, after twenty-nine years in the hell of French Guiana, had come back to exhume it and settle old scores. Like Jonathan Small in *The Sign of Four*, returning to Pondicherry Lodge from the Andamans to claim the Agra Treasure, he was a beast unchained, and in slamming the door of the vault he was notifying the occupants of the house that their hour had struck. All that remained was the stab of the poisoned thorn and the last convulsive agony. Ten minutes hence, my features frozen in the dreadful *risus sardonicus*, I would be indistinguishable from Bartholomew Sholto. I was a gone coon.

And yet, such is the complexity of the human spirit, and especially one molded in the crucible of the East, not a muscle flickered in my lean cheek. Instead, I was filled with a vast, consuming anger; I was determined to invade the vault and purge society of this loathsome scourge if it meant annihilation. I routed out the wax taper, boldly flung open the door, and descended the stairs with catlike tread. Just as I neared the first-floor landing, a feminine voice, taut with a terrible urgency, drifted up to me from below.

"Put your back into it," it was saying harshly. "We've got to crack it tonight, I tell you." I repressed an involuntary snort of triumph. So that was it; a woman was mixed up in it—indubitably had engineered the entire caper, as I had suspected from the beginning. Pressed close to the balustrade, I worked myself down along it with infinite caution and peered around the stairhead.

The sight that met my eyes was one calculated to unsettle the most magnificent aplomb. Clad in a flowered kimono that ill concealed her generous charms, Mrs. Purdy Woolwine, the first-floor tenant, knelt by a galvanized rubbish can, striving to anchor it to the floor. Her gleaming coiffure was disordered and her face contorted like that of a wrestler in a Japanese print. At her side, a small, sallow man, whom I dimly recognized as Woolwine, had driven a screwdriver under the lid with the aid of a hammer and was desperately trying to prise it off, obviously bent on disposing of a wastebasket heaped high with bottles and fruit rinds. Neither of them was aware of my existence, nor would they ever have discovered it but for an unbearable compulsion to sneeze. As my wild "Kerchow!" rang out, they wheeled convulsively and beheld me, bone-naked in my shorts and taper in hand, agape on the landing. With an eerie screech that shook the Piranesi reproductions off the walls, Mrs. Woolwine half rose and toppled sidewise in a dead faint.

Fantastic how people deliberately misconstrue the most innocent occurrence. Damn my eyes if I wasn't two hours explaining away the affair to those chuckleheads from the Eighth Precinct. They'd got the wind up, don't you see, had to find a scapegoat and all that frightful rot. You'd have thought I was Harvey Hawley Crippen, the way they mucked about with their sobriety tests and their argle-bargle about Peeping Toms and God knows what all. Ah, well, it's over and done with now, thank goodness. I spend most of my time these days down in Pennsylvania, and, come autumn, we'll probably find digs more suited to the family needs. Might even go out East again, between you and me. I've had my fill of gracious living and cocktail kit-kit and hysteroids named Mrs. Purdy Woolwine. I breathe better in some place like Amboina, where nobody asks any questions, where all you need is a twist of cotton around your loins and a pinch of rice, and a man's past is his own.

❧ THE HAND THAT CRADLES THE ROCK

PARDON ME, friends, but would you mind if I borrowed a corner of this lawn to faint dead away on? Go ahead with whatever you're doing; I just want to conk out until this roaring in my ears subsides. It's the damnedest sensation—somewhat as though I'd been pumped full of helium, tossed in a blanket, and shot through a wind tunnel. If I could only get these extremities to stop twitching. . . . There, that's better. Christopher! Serves me right. I should have known what'd happen if I tangled, even remotely, with Fleur Fenton Cowles, today's editorial thunderhead and the most dynamic personality in the postwar publishing world. At least, that's the way someone named Mort Weisinger, billed as the editor of *Superman*, classifies her in the leading article of *The Writer's 1950 Year Book*, and if long intimacy with cloudborne genius means anything, the man certainly knows what he's talking about.

Mr. Weisinger's portrait of the versatile directress of *Look, Quick*, and *Flair*, whom no amount of keelhauling will persuade me to address by his emetic term of "boss-lady," depicts her as a high-voltage executive in whose personality a Kansas cyclone has been successfully wedded to Devonshire clotted cream. The vignette that introduces her and describes her accession to the throne of *Look* three years ago has a distinctly medieval tinkle:

"Behind a huge horseshoe-shaped desk in an office high above Fifth Avenue's sidewalks sat a straw-haired, sleekly groomed woman. Before her, on the luxurious carpet, stood three ranks of high-priced editorial and advertising brains. There was silence in the room while everyone waited for the slender, fragile woman to start talking. Deliberately, coolly, she let them wait, flipped the pages of a magazine dummy on her desk. When her right wrist moved, an eye-catching bracelet studded with pearls, rubies, and diamonds glittered in the sunlight. She spoke in a soft, gentle voice which almost cooed: 'It's been two weeks since I came to work on this magazine,' she began. 'You've all been sweet—too sweet—flattering me, buttering me up. I want you all to know that I've been in this game a long, long time. I've got a job to do here, and you're all going to help me. If not, heads will roll and fingers will be lopped off. That's all!' "

The whole scene is undeniably Florentine in feeling. The analogy is fortified a bit later when the author remarks, apropos of his subject's taste in jewels: "She is never without a huge one-inch Russian emerald ring. 'It's my trademark, it's me, it's Fleur—rough, uncut, vigorous,' *Time* magazine reports she said."

Enthralling as is the narrative of Fleur Cowles' meteoric climb to fame—copy writer, columnist, advertising-agency head, and vicereine of a publishing empire—it is Weisinger's account of her distinctive personal gifts that sets the thrushes singing in the reader's belly. "Fleur Cowles has a fantastic memory and her mnemonic powers would do credit to a Dunninger," reports her biographer. "Possibly because of her own uncanny memory, Fleur makes short shrift of hirelings whose retentive talents are not so prodigious. She is reputed to have fired a secretary who forgot to wind her office alarm clock, causing Fleur to miss an important engagement." A few lines later, Weisinger careers into another exceptional knack of Fleur's. "Fleur says she can breeze through a normal 120-page issue of *Time* in a half hour," he states, completely unaware that I myself hold the world's record of twenty-two seconds.

The roster of Fleur's accomplishments—her incessant travel, entertaining, and extracurricular activities—is an impressive one; I cull only two small blooms from Weisinger's nosegay as samples: "A former aviatrix with hundreds of hours in the air to her credit, Fleur has given up piloting, although she still holds a license. . . . Fleur paints a little, designs every stitch of her own clothes, designs her own jewelry, and even her glasses. 'I'm just a generally creative person,' she says modestly." The same stubborn honesty that prevents her from blinking her creative endowment emerges constantly at the office. "When she rejects a layout, a cover, or a project," says Weisinger, "she is apt to express her scorn with the fury of a hard-boiled city editor in a Hollywood front-page movie. 'Oh, I know I'm horribly blunt,' she admits. 'But if I think an idea is poor, I can't help coming right out and saying it's lousy. Yes, I'm direct.' " And again: "By the same token, she will fire an incompetent at the drop of a semicolon. 'I guess I'm just professionally intolerant of stupid people,' she confesses. 'I despise slow-witted persons, particularly in the creative fields. It's one of my biggest faults, but I can't help it.' " Could pitiless self-analysis go any further? Geez, it's like the *Confessions* of Jean-Jacques Rousseau.

The specific idiosyncrasy of Fleur's that crimps the heart into a waffle, however, is the exaggerated distrust Weisinger claims she displays toward her associates. "Because she is the wife of the Big Boss," he says, "Fleur Cowles has a fixation about being yessed to death by sycophantic staffers. To test their sincerity, she is always planning deliberate traps. At her conferences she will intentionally offer mediocre ideas of her own, invite criticisms. Employees who have the gumption to pooh-pooh these booby traps win her confidence." If I interpret the foregoing rightly (and if I interpret it wrongly, I couldn't be more contrite), the pressure in a certain editorial sanctum must be roughly equivalent to that in the Mindanao Deep. I have been asking myself, between decreasing spells of vertigo, what life on such capricious levels is like. In the following morality, a webfooted attempt to approximate it, it should be borne in mind that the heroine is patterned after no actual boss-lady, living or dead. Like the immortal Topsy, she sprang full-blown from the forehead of Zeus. I'm just a generally creative person.

SCENE: *The office of Hyacinth Beddoes Laffoon, queen-pin of the pulp oligarchy embracing* Gory Story, Sanguinary Love, Popular Dissolution, *and* Spicy Mortician. *Hyacinth, poised and chic in a chiffon dress for which she herself spun the silk this morning, sits behind a gumshoe-shaped desk leafing through a copy of* Shroud, *her latest fictional brain child. Standing alertly at attention before her, their Adam's apples moving up and down in unison, are Bunce, Van Lennep, Hagedorn, and Vishnu, her four editorial assistants.*

HYACINTH (*looking up abstractedly*): What's that chattering sound?
BUNCE (*eagerly*): It's Hagedorn's teeth, Mrs. Laffoon. I've been meaning to squeal on him the first opening I got. Gosh, you ought to hear the noise he makes over the partition! A man can hardly concentrate—
HYACINTH: Oh, you have trouble concentrating, do you?
BUNCE: No, no, no—it'd take a lot more than that to upset *me*! Why, I could work in a boiler factory!
HYACINTH: You may yet, the way you've been delivering around here. Meanwhile, Hagedorn, let's have those choppers out before the next conference. That is, if you last that long.
HAGEDORN (*quietly*): They'll be out right after lunch hour, Chief. You won't have to mention it again.
HYACINTH: Splendid. Now, then, I've had my ear to the ground re-

cently and I get the impression some of you disagree with my
policy on *Shroud*.

VAN LENNEP: Hell's bells, Hyacinth! Where'd you ever pick up that
idea?

HYACINTH: From the dictaphone I had instilled in the water cooler.
(*reading from a typed report*) "Just give the old windbag enough
rope. You wait, the public'll pin back her ears." Does that sound
familiar, Van Lennep?

VAN LENNEP (*squirming*): I—I was talking about Miss Lovibond,
who solicits those ads for bust developers and lost manhood. You
said yourself we needed more tone.

HYACINTH: Well, all right, you twisted out of that one, but watch your
step. I'm sentimental enough to think this organization can't
function without one-hundred-per-cent loyalty.

VISHNU: And you've got it, Mrs. Laffoon. We worship the ground—

HYACINTH: At the same time, I won't stand for any soft soap or hogwash when I come up with a notion. The fact that Mr. Laffoon
has ninety-three million dollars and owns all the real estate on
Wacker Drive is beside the point. I want honest, sturdy, independent reactions—is that clear?

OMNES: Like crystal. . . . Gee, I wish I could express myself so forcefully! . . . Boy, what an editor! . . . etc.

HYACINTH: O.K. Well, I've just had a couple of hunches for brightening up *Shroud* that I'd like to try out on you. (*quickly*) Oh, I
know what you're going to say, that they *might* be feasible or that
they *could* work—

HAGEDORN: No sirree, I can tell already they're world-beaters! A kind
of a glow shines out of your face whenever you're on the beam.

HYACINTH: First, these covers we've been running. They're namby-
pamby, no more punch than in a textbook. Look at this one—a
naked girl tied to a bedpost and a chimpanzee brandishing a
knout.

BUNCE: I see the structural weakness. It demands too much of the
reader.

HYACINTH: Correct. We've got to drill him right between the eyes.
Now, I visualize a cover with an aperture and a real revolver
barrel protruding from it. With an acrid wisp of smoke curling
out. Imagine that confronting you on a newsstand!

VISHNU: Where would the smoke be engendered?

HYACINTH: In a mechanism hinged to the back cover. To be sure, it's a trifle bulky and we might fall afoul of the smog ordinance in some areas—

VAN LENNEP (*ecstatically*): Nah, that can all be worked out! Baby, what a brain wave. It'll knock Publishers' Row right back on its heels!

HYACINTH: You think it's got undertow?

VAN LENNEP: Ho-ho, I can almost hear those dimes and nickels showering down!

HYACINTH: You bet you can; it's the cashier counting your severance pay. So long, Van Lennep, it's been nice knowing you. (*sadly, as he leaves*) He just wouldn't learn. There's no room at Laffoon for a toady.

VISHNU: I knew it was a come-on from the start, Hyacinth. Did you notice how I gave a negative little shrug?

BUNCE: Me, too. I had difficulty in repressing a smile.

HAGEDORN: Smoke boxes on the back cover! Man, that was rich!

HYACINTH: Well, let's see how the next one appeals to you. You know, more and more of our younger readers are leaning toward marijuana, and I was wondering if we couldn't insert a complimentary sack in the body of the magazine, along with a trial book of cigarette papers. Might even approach Max Schling or some high-class florist to sponsor a special blend for us.

BUNCE: Mmm, that's a provocative slant. Trouble is it stirs me and yet it kind of leaves me cold. Thermally, it's ambivalent.

VISHNU: Ditto. I want to throw my arms around it but something indefinable holds me back.

HYACINTH: You, Hagedorn?

HAGEDORN: Straight from the shoulder, Mrs. Laffoon, it's as broad as it is long. How— How do you feel about it yourself?

HYACINTH: Well, naturally, it's my own idea—

VISHNU: Yes, and you can afford to crow. I know I'd be proud of it.

HYACINTH: I suspected you would. Personally, I think it's all wet.

VISHNU (*thoughtfully*): Um. Maybe, if I hurry, I can ride down in the elevator with Van Lennep.

HYACINTH: Take your time—you've got oodles. (*He goes.*) There was just one other wrinkle that occurred to me, boys, but it's so idiotic I hesitate to mention it.

BUNCE: Aw, come on, Mrs. Laffoon. No matter how—er—amorphous it is, it might fire us—I mean it might lead to another angle.

HYACINTH: Well, it's this. Would there be any promotional value if we inserted several facsimile twenty-dollar bills into the binding, to serve as a blueprint for out-of-town readers who have to make their money at home?

BUNCE: I—ah—don't cotton to it, Hyacinth. We'd be accused of competing with *Popular Mechanics*.

HAGEDORN: It's basically a rural pitch. You'd expect to find it in *Capper's Weekly*.

HYACINTH: Yes, you're absolutely right. Thanks, men. It took plenty of guts to voice your frank, unvarnished opinion. (*They smirk.*) Still, if there was the teeniest chance it might benefit the magazine, we shouldn't block it with our pigheadedness, should we?

HAGEDORN (*paling*): We're not dead set against it— I say give it a whirl—

HYACINTH (*regretfully*): No. Deep down, there'd always be the lurking sense of guilt, the knowledge that we deliberately imperiled a valuable publishing property with our timidity. Sorry, gentlemen, it was my fault. I'll have to stay and face the music.

BUNCE: We could help you forget—

HYACINTH: It's white of you, but there are some burdens a woman must carry alone. Goodbye. (*They exit. Velvet dusk veils the office, softening the lonely figure at the desk into a fragile, ghostly moth. Then, with a muted sigh, Hyacinth switches on her reading lamp, picks up a box of paper clips, and patiently begins constructing a linotype machine.*)

CURTAIN

✿ IS THERE A DOCTOR IN THE CAST?

HE HAS A TRUE humanist's care for the wholeness—the mental and physical health—of individuals. . . . It is not surprising, therefore, that in his youth Mr. Kaye wanted to be a doctor. . . . That childhood ambition has, indeed, remained with him, but reduced to its necessary proportion. Interest in healing is a sideline with him, though a sideline for which he cares intensely. . . . He is neither frightened nor repelled by disease; and his interest in it, and in its cure, is no more morbid than a doctor's.

An extraordinary incident—without precedent, surely, in the history of the London Palladium—occurred in Mr. Kaye's dressing room last Saturday night. It occurred shortly before ten o'clock—about ten minutes before he was due to appear in the second house. At such moments, most entertainers must be undisturbed; many of them are "bundles of nerves."

Mr. Kaye had begun to put on his make-up. Suddenly his door burst open. A man rushed in, crying, "Hey, Danny! Can you do anything for Louis? He's very bad." He dragged in a dancer, in stage costume, whose face was gray and agonized. He was suffering, he said, from a migraine-type headache.

"Sit down," said Mr. Kaye, standing behind a chair. "Rest your head against my body." He then went to work on the man's neck and face and scalp, in the manner of an osteopath. In perhaps three or four minutes the job was done: the man still looked unwell, but he said that the pain was gone. Mr. Kaye only remarked, "Let me know a bit earlier next time"; went on making up; and was on stage on time.—*From an article on Danny Kaye in* The New Statesman & Nation.

NEW YORK, SEPTEMBER 12

I FEEL such a sense of guilt—can it really be two months since I made the last entry in these pages? How strange that every time I temporarily desert show business, the same thing should happen. The moment I take some noxious little job to keep myself going between parts, my

ego deflates and I can't bear to face my diary. The reason's perfectly
obvious, of course; the theater is my whole life, and while the name of
Bruce Menafee on a marquee right now wouldn't draw flies, one day
it'll be up there with the greats like Maurice Barrymore, Maurice
Evans, and Maurice Schwartz. Still, you can get pretty discouraged in
these wretched doldrum periods, when you're reduced to posing for
mail-order catalogues, ushering at the Music Hall, or working as night
watchman at an embalmer's, frantically making the rounds of the managers' offices meanwhile. This last break of mine was typical. I was all
ready to go back to Antioch and teach Freshman Drama, to marry
some vapid booby and resign myself to perpetuating the human race.
Then, out of the blue, Alec Fragonard, who played the second leper in
the road company of *Father Damien's Chickens* last season, called up
to say there was a bit in *On You It Looks Good*, which had just started
rehearsals Monday. I hotfooted right over, auditioned for Ronnie
Castlemaine, the director, and, wondrous to relate, was chosen from
among thirty applicants. The pay is scale and the role isn't especially
large, but I do think it's rather impressive histrionicwise. I make my
first entrance in white flannels, carrying a tennis racket with rhinestone
strings, in an ensemble number called "Forte Love" that introduces
Louella Grope, our female lead. I next appear in the Newport house-
party scene, impersonating a tipsy English butler; not much dialogue
here except trifles like "Hic" or "Shay, Countess, lesh you and me
dansh," but I'm confident I can work out some amusing horseplay.
My real chance to shine is the Casbah sequence halfway through the
second act, where I come on as Osmani el Fatoom, an Arab soothsayer
who unwittingly unites the lovers. It's a ticklish characterization in
that I'm not supposed to know I'm doing it and neither are they—kind
of a mystic slant, with overtones of "The Passing of the Third Floor
Back." As yet, I haven't quite got my teeth into it, but I plan to contact
the author and have him build up the precise nuances I have in mind.

Thus far, there's nobody in the cast, with one exception, whom I'd
describe as particularly *simpatico*. Fletcher Kumyss, our star, is a
pompous ass who's forever flexing his biceps at the showgirls, one of
those standard romantic leads whose semicircular canals are deafened
by the sound of his own voice. Louella Grope, who plays opposite him,
is a real torn-down piece from Memphis, all moonlight and magnolias
on the surface but pure brimstone underneath. The rest of the company
is routine, either wide-eyed worshipers of Stanislavski or hopheads.
The only person with any sensitivity, I'd say, is Rags Meiklejohn. He's
a tall, dreamy chap, with a poetic face in which you sense enormous

compassion, a connoisseur of beauty and an omnivorous reader. Unlike the others, who drug themselves with comic books, he spends every spare moment poring through Huysmans, Cabell, Firbank, and Anatole France (he's supposed to have read *Jocasta and the Famished Cat* four times). I was surprised to learn, though, that his real preoccupation is medicine. From earliest youth, he confessed to me the other morning, he has yearned to be a healer, to assuage bodily and emotional distress. "Funny, isn't it?" he reflected, with a wry smile. "Here I am in jester's motley, distilling yocks out of exploding cigars and pratfalls, when deep down and basically I'd give everything to be another Schweitzer, to don an operating gown and rehabilitate my fellow man."

I commented on his long, sensitive fingers—better suited to wield a scalpel, I ventured, than the traditional pig bladder of the buffoon. "Who knows?" I speculated. "You might have been a world-famed surgeon had the opportunity arisen."

"It still may, Menafee," he said, his eyes gone pensive. "After all, is there any man jack amongst us, basically speaking, which he can prognose what the future holds in store?"

An unusual personality, Meiklejohn—more than a touch of the visionary in his make-up. I've a curious feeling there was something prophetic about his words.

NEW YORK, SEPTEMBER 15

My instinct was right; Meiklejohn *is* psychic. Scarcely twenty-four hours after our conversation, he got a chance to use his therapeutic gift and rose to it nobly. It happened day before yesterday during the Andalusian scene. Fletcher Kumyss—who, for plot purposes, is disguised at this point in the show as Louella's chaperon, though she and the audience are unaware of it—was perched on a stepladder being serenaded by Jackie Renoir, the second lead. I guess the director's attention was elsewhere, but at any rate our ballerina, Gemze de Lapidari, did a sudden *tour jeté* downstage, accidentally grazed against the ladder, and over went Fletcher into the orchestra pit. There was a simply appalling crash as he struck the music stands; it sounded exactly like my Uncle Ned backing through the wrong end of our garage the time he got drunk on zinfandel. Well, all hell instantly broke loose. Everybody was milling around, shouting advice and scrambling for smelling salts, when Rags Meiklejohn stepped into the breach.

"Keep cool, folks!" he sang out. "Nothing wrong with Mr. Kumyss —just a little stunned, that's all. The main thing is to restore his circulation right away. Here, someone help me get him back on his feet."

There was an immediate outcry, a number of the company protesting that it was risky to move the man before determining whether he had a spinal injury. An old wives' tale, rejoined Rags crisply; overwhelming medical evidence showed that the sooner you became ambulatory following an accident, the better, and that any delay might result in the direst consequences. He spoke with such authority that opposition melted at once. Fletcher, disheveled and mumbling, was assisted off to his dressing room, and the rehearsal continued. Somewhat later, however, he unaccountably lapsed into a dead faint, and our producer, Mr. Finsterwald, decided to implement Meiklejohn's opinion with a professional one. The doctor he called in—derisively referred to by Rags as a quack from a nearby theatrical hotel—promptly dispatched Fletcher to the Polyclinic Hospital, where his X-rays revealed a dislocated collarbone, three broken ribs, and a fractured spleen.

"Moonshine!" snorted Rags when I approached him for an explanation. "Didn't have a scratch at the time I examined him. Between you and me, the ambulance probably hit a lamppost on the way to the clinic."

Have decided that for the nonce, at least until the show opens out of town, I shall hang on to my night-watchman job at the Golgotha Funeral Home. The duties aren't too onerous, and I've been able to put in some concentrated work on the role of the Arab soothsayer. I expect to use the merest soupçon of a French accent, with an inscrutable smile flickering around my lips—somewhat the expression Tony Glaucoma wore when he played the second goldsmith in *Father Cellini's Chickens*. With a black Vandyke and pale olive make-up, it ought to be quite effective.

NEW YORK, SEPTEMBER 22

This has been a fairly momentous week, fraught with tension and portents that our dramatic craft may encounter squalls before it arrives safe in port. The first came when Ronnie Castlemaine, irritated by Louella's Southern accent, acidly requested her to take the boll weevils out of her mouth, whereupon she threw a container of coffee in his face. Fortunately, it was cold, and other than momentarily blinding him, caused no irreparable damage. Just the same, it took hours to smooth everyone's ruffled plumage, and, knowing Louella's vengeful nature, I doubt she'll ever wholly forgive Ronnie. A much more ominous complication, though, has been the mounting antagonism between

Mr. Finsterwald and Rags Meiklejohn. Rags—animated by what are plainly the most altruistic motives—has been treating the cast for various minor ailments like colds and sprains; in fact, he has converted the prop room into an informal dispensary and busies himself between scenes cauterizing abrasions, massaging pulled tendons, and rendering all manner of first aid. While the majority of his cases have responded beautifully, two or three have developed puzzling symptoms such as traumatic shock, gangrene, etc., which have necessitated Mr. Finsterwald's replacing them on very short notice. His exasperation with Rags reached a pitch yesterday when two showgirls in the Aztec ballet, after receiving medication for heartburn arising from pastrami sandwiches, fell into a near-epileptic state and had to be removed on stretchers. Thus far, Mr. Finsterwald has avoided any public denunciation, but to judge from his labored breathing and phrases one overhears through the flats, like "You and your goddam chemistry kit!", managerial ire is aflame.

Basil Clingstone, last seen locally as the second sculptor in *Father Praxiteles' Chickens*, has taken over Fletcher Kumyss' role. Though less incisive dictionwise, Clingstone is a more cerebral actor than Fletcher, and his cleft palate gives his portrayal of the stalwart Canadian Mountie who dares all for love an interesting added dimension. My conception of the Arab soothsayer, by the way, is also fast taking on light and shade; I intend to sport a monocle and an amber cigarette holder, and to space my words so deliberately that the audience must needs hang on every syllable. "Towering above his mediocre colleagues, Bruce Menafee gave a sharply etched performance—vibrant, witty, dynamic. Not since John Carradine has a personality held us so spellbound. . . ." Daydreams, perhaps, and yet some small inner voice bids me have faith in my destiny. Next week, Philadelphia.

PHILADELPHIA, SEPTEMBER 29

It may be too soon to make predictions, but *On You It Looks Good* does not seem slated for an easy success. Four of the five critics who attended our opening here Monday ranged from lukewarm to negative, deeming the production "a nightmare," "three hours of unmitigated cretinism," and "the most noisome swill since *Bertha, the Sewing-Machine Girl*." The fifth reported that a handful of taxpayers had inadvisedly sought refuge from a rainstorm at our attraction the previous evening, a classic example of leaping from the frying pan into the fire. Mr. Finsterwald nevertheless refused to be disheartened; he immediately ousted the author, composer, and lyricist, imported several television writers from New York, and the show is now being revamped into a Mormon folk operetta. Inasmuch as some of our parts have not yet been changed—I still appear in my burnous in the Salt Lake Tabernacle, but speak the English butler's lines—the audience must be a whit confused. Luckily, we have been drawing moderately small houses during this transition period, so the confusion has had no chance to spread.

Apropos of opening night, we almost had a crisis—averted, in the nick of time, by Rags Meiklejohn's quick-wittedness. One of the Conquistadors, Norman Trebizond, was unable to remove his helmet while making a change; evidently it had lodged over his ears, constricting the blood supply, and the poor man was in mortal agony. Just as the stagehands were struggling to loosen it, Rags came by and instantly diagnosed the trouble as a slipped casque. He commandeered a hammer, gave the helmet a few expert taps, and in a twinkling Norman was free. Ultimately, malicious rumors got around that he developed a concussion as a result, but when I queried Rags, he seemed unperturbed. "Quite possible," he said, looking up abstractedly from his copy of *The Skin Around Us*. "That's what we practitioners call a calculated risk. After all and basically, we don't pretend to be miracle men, you know."

Mr. Finsterwald has turned the most alarming color lately—a deep Burgundy shade with streaks of purple—and the cigars he gnashes between his teeth rustle like cornstalks. I fear he is not at all well.

BOSTON, OCTOBER 11

The past few days have been exceptionally trying ones, so much so that it demands every ounce of fortitude to chronicle them in any logical order. Following Mr. Finsterwald's sudden decision to move to the Hub City, our company was sent up here in three buses, and we rehearsed madly in the laundry of the Hotel Touraine while the scenery was being hung. Thanks to the clouds of steam and the wet wash brushing against their faces, most of the singers came down with laryngitis and croaked like a chorus of frogs at the première last night. From the moment the overture struck up, in fact, it was evident that a hoodoo was pursuing the show. A couple of Conestoga wagons someone had hoisted into the flies to conserve space came unstuck, raining spokes and whiffletrees on the musicians with such force that three of them were knocked senseless. In the meantime, a truly shattering incident was taking place backstage. A trained bear, which I understand was scheduled to appear in a new gypsy sequence in Act II, somehow worked out of its cage, grabbed hold of Basil Clingstone, and began waltzing him about, trampling the sets to matchwood. The crew clobbered the animal unmercifully with fire extinguishers and brooms, but by the time he relaxed his hold, Basil was in hysterics and his understudy had to go on. Everything considered, it was amazing our performance got the reviews it did. Mergenthaler of the *Globe*, who can be devastating if he dislikes a play, gave us only two onions and a leek, and the *Post* hailed us as "indispensable mulch for a bounteous theatrical season."

As regards my personal status, the future does not engender optimism. I now appear but twice, first as a Sioux hostage who declines to disclose the whereabouts of his tribe, and later as a Trappist monk, which, as I took occasion to point out to Mr. Finsterwald today, reduces me entirely to pantomime. His answer was rather incoherent, possibly because he had just surprised Rags in process of giving Basil Clingstone a tetanus shot, but it was something to the effect that trains left Back Bay Station hourly for New York. I think I acquitted myself with laudable dignity. I extracted my monocle and screwed it into my eye, surveyed him with the same withering scorn Yankel Frobisher displayed as the second plenipotentiary in *Father Metternich's Chickens*, and stalked away. When he shows up in my dressing room tonight, groveling and stammering apologies, I shall be austere, reserved, faintly sardonic. "Yes, Mr. Finsterwald, I will continue in your wormy little attraction," I envision myself saying, "but first let us discuss salary and billing. Here is my ultimatum. . . ."

NEW YORK, OCTOBER 14

What a sense of utter calm enshrouds the Golgotha Funeral Home at this hour; except for the measured ticking of the clock and the faint, pervasive scent of formaldehyde, one might well fancy himself on some remote South Sea island. Candidly, I did not anticipate returning here quite so soon, but circumstances beyond my control made it obligatory. Suffice to say they have been referred to an attorney who will teach a certain producer that actors cannot be booted down a circular iron stairway with impunity. Sawdust puppets though we are considered, some of us *do* have feelings.

Ran into Rags Meiklejohn on Sixth Avenue this morning as I was emerging from a cruller shop. Oddly enough, he, too, is at liberty, though he confided that interests outside the greenroom increasingly claim his attention; indeed, he was just en route to the New York

Academy of Medicine to read a paper. He tapped the stethoscope protruding from his pocket with a mischievous smile. "On me it looks good," he observed archly. An engaging cuss, Meiklejohn, and a rare specimen of the *genus homo*. The stage lost a great personality when he took up medicine.

❧ CLOUDLAND REVISITED: WHY, DOCTOR, WHAT BIG GREEN EYES YOU HAVE!

HALFWAY THROUGH the summer of 1916, I was living on the rim of Narragansett Bay, a fur-bearing adolescent with cheeks as yet unscarred by my first Durham Duplex razor, when I read a book that exerted a considerable influence on my bedtime habits. Up to then, I had slept in normal twelve-year-old fashion, with the lights full on, a blanket muffling my head from succubi and afreets, a chair wedged under the doorknob, and a complex network of strings stretched across the room in a way scientifically designed to entrap any trespasser, corporeal or not. On finishing the romance in question, however, I realized that the protection I had been relying on was woefully inadequate and that I had merely been crowding my luck. Every night thereafter, before retiring, I spent an extra half hour barricading the door with a chest of drawers, sprinkling tacks along the window sills, and strewing crumpled newspapers about the floor to warn me of approaching footsteps. As a minor added precaution, I slept under the bed, a ruse that did not make for refreshing slumber but at least threw my enemies off the scent. Whether it was constant vigilance or natural stamina, I somehow survived, and, indeed, received a surprising number of compliments on my appearance when I returned to grammar school that fall. I guess nobody in those parts had ever seen a boy with snow-white hair and a green skin.

Perhaps the hobgoblins who plagued me in that Rhode Island beach cottage were no more virulent than the reader's own childhood favorites, but the particular one I was introduced to in the book I've mentioned could hold up his head in any concourse of fiends. Even after thirty-five years, the lines that ushered him onstage still cause an involuntary shudder:

"Imagine a person, tall, lean and feline, high-shouldered, with a brow like Shakespeare and a face like Satan, a close-shaven skull, and long, magnetic eyes of the true cat-green. Invest him with all the cruel cunning of an entire Eastern race, accumulated in one giant intellect, with all the resources of science, past and present, with all the resources, if you will, of a wealthy government—which, however, already has denied all knowledge of his existence. . . . This man, whether a fanatic or a duly appointed agent, is, unquestionably, the most malign and formidable personality existing in the world today. He is a linguist who speaks with almost equal facility in any of the civilized languages, and in most of the barbaric. He is an adept in all the arts and sciences which a great university could teach him. He also is an adept in certain obscure arts and sciences which *no* university of today can teach. He has the brains of any three men of genius. . . . Imagine that awful being, and you have a mental picture of Dr. Fu-Manchu, the yellow peril incarnate in one man."

Yes, it is the reptilian Doctor himself, one of the most sinister figures ever to slither out of a novelist's cranium, and many a present-day comic book, if the truth were told, is indebted to his machinations, his underground laboratories, carnivorous orchids, rare Oriental poisons, dacoits, and stranglers. An authentic vampire in the great tradition, Fu-Manchu horrified the popular imagination in a long series of best sellers by Sax Rohmer, passed through several profitable reincarnations in Hollywood, and (I thought) retired to the limbo of the second-hand bookshop, remembered only by a few slippered pantaloons like me. Some while ago, though, a casual reference by my daughter to Thuggee over her morning oatmeal made me prick up my ears. On close questioning, I found she had been bedeviling herself with *The Mystery of Dr. Fu-Manchu*, the very volume that had induced my youthful fantods. I delivered a hypocritical little lecture, worthy of Pecksniff, in which I pointed out that Laurence Hope's *Indian Love* was far more suitable for her age level, and, confiscating the book, holed up for a retrospective look at it. I see now how phlegmatic I have become with advancing age. Apart from causing me to cry out occasionally in my sleep and populating my pillow with a swarm of nonexistent spiders, Rohmer's thriller was as abrasive to the nerves as a cup of Ovaltine.

The plot of *The Mystery of Dr. Fu-Manchu* is at once engagingly simple and monstrously confused. In essence, it is a duel of wits between the malevolent Celestial, who dreams of a world dominated by his countrymen, and Commissioner Nayland Smith, a purportedly brilliant sleuth, whose confidant, Dr. Petrie, serves as narrator. Fu-Manchu comes to England bent on the extermination of half a dozen distinguished Foreign Office servants, Orientalists, and other buttin-skies privy to his scheme; Smith and Petrie constantly scud about in a webfooted attempt to warn the prey, who are usually defunct by the time they arrive, or busy themselves with being waylaid, sandbagged, drugged, kidnaped, poisoned, or garroted by Fu-Manchu's deputies. These assaults, however, are never downright lethal, for regularly, at the eleventh hour, a beautiful slave of Fu-Manchu named Kâramanèh betrays her master and delivers the pair from jeopardy. The story, consequently, has somewhat the same porous texture as a Pearl White serial. An episode may end with Smith and Petrie plummeting through a trap door to nameless horrors below; the next opens on them comfortably sipping whisky-and-soda in their chambers, analyzing their hairdbreadth escape and speculating about the adversary's next move. To synopsize this kind of ectoplasmic yarn with any degree of fidelity would be to connive at criminal boredom, and I have no intention of doing so, but it might be fruitful to dip a spoon into the curry at random to gain some notion of its flavor.

Lest doubt prevail at the outset as to the utter malignancy of Fu-Manchu, the author catapults Nayland Smith into Petrie's rooms in the dead of night with the following portentous declaration of his purpose: "Petrie, I have traveled from Burma not in the interests of the British government merely, but in the interest of the entire white race, and I honestly believe—though I pray I may be wrong—that its survival depends largely on the success of my mission." Can Petrie, demands Smith, spare a few days from his medical duties for "the strangest business, I promise you, that ever was recorded in fact or fiction"? He gets the expected answer: "I agreed readily enough, for, unfortunately, my professional duties were not onerous." The alacrity with which doctors of that epoch deserted their practice has never ceased to impress me. Holmes had only to crook his finger and Watson went bowling away in a four-wheeler, leaving his patients to fend for themselves. If the foregoing is at all indicative, the mortality rate of London in the nineteen hundreds must have been appalling; the average physician seems to have spent much less time in diagnosis than in tiptoeing around Wapping Old Stairs with a dark lantern. The white race, apparently, was a lot tougher than one would suspect.

At any rate, the duo hasten forthwith to caution a worthy named Sir Crichton Davey that his life is in peril, and, predictably, discover him already cheesed off. His death, it develops, stemmed from a giant red centipede, lowered down the chimney of his study by Fu-Manchu's dacoits, regarding whom Smith makes the charmingly offhand state-

ment "Oh, dacoity, though quiescent, is by no means extinct." Smith
also seizes the opportunity to expatiate on the archcriminal in some
delicious double-talk: "As to his mission among men. Why did M.
Jules Furneaux fall dead in a Paris opera house? Because of heart
failure? No! Because his last speech had shown that he held the key
to the secret of Tongking. What became of the Grand Duke Stanislaus?
Elopement? Suicide? Nothing of the kind. He alone was fully alive to
Russia's growing peril. He alone knew the truth about Mongolia. Why
was Sir Crichton Davey murdered? Because, had the work he was engaged upon ever seen the light, it would have shown him to be the only
living Englishman who understood the importance of the Tibetan fron-
tiers." In between these rhetorical flourishes, Petrie is accosted by
Kâramanèh, Fu-Manchu's houri, who is bearing a deadly perfumed
letter intended to destroy Smith. The device fails, but the encounter
begets a romantic interest that saves Petrie's neck on his next excursion. Disguised as rough seafaring men, he and Smith have tracked
down Fu-Manchu at Singapore Charlie's, an opium shop on the
Thames dockside. Here, for the first time, Petrie gets a good hinge at
the monster's eyes: ". . . their unique horror lay in a certain filminess
(it made me think of the *membrana nictitans* in a bird) which, obscuring them as I threw wide the door, seemed to lift as I actually passed
the threshold, revealing the eyes in all their brilliant viridescence." Before he can polish his ornithological metaphor, however, Petrie is
plunged through a trap door into the river, the den goes up in flames,
and it looks like curtains for the adventurous physician. But Providence, in the form of a hideous old Chinese, intervenes. Stripping off
his ugly, grinning mask, he discloses himself as Kâramanèh; she ex-
tends her false pigtail to Petrie and, after pulling him to safety, melts
into the night. It is at approximately this juncture that one begins to
appreciate how lightly the laws of probability weighed on Sax Rohmer.
Once you step with him into Never-Never Land, the grave's the limit,
and no character is deemed extinct until you can use his skull as a
paperweight.

Impatient at the snail's pace with which his conspiracy is maturing,
Fu-Manchu now takes the buttons off the foils. He tries to abduct a
missionary who has flummoxed his plans in China, but succeeds only
in slaying the latter's collie and destroying his manservant's memory—
on the whole, a pretty footling morning's work. He then pumps chlo-
rine gas into a sarcophagus belonging to Sir Lionel Barton, a bothersome explorer, with correspondingly disappointing results; this time the

bag is another collie—sorry, a coolie—and a no-account ginzo secretary.

The villain's next foray is more heartening. He manages to overpower Smith and Petrie by some unspecified means (undoubtedly the
"rather rare essential oil" that Smith says he has met with before,
"though never in Europe") and chains them up in his noisome cellars.
The scene wherein he twits his captives has a nice poetic lilt: "A mar-
moset landed on the shoulder of Dr. Fu-Manchu and peered gro-
tesquely into the dreadful yellow face. The Doctor raised his bony hand
and fondled the little creature, crooning to it. 'One of my pets, Mr.
Smith,' he said, suddenly opening his eyes fully so that they blazed like
green lamps. 'I have others, equally useful. My scorpions—have you
met my scorpions? No? My pythons and hamadryads? Then there are
my fungi and my tiny allies, the bacilli. I have a collection in my laboratory quite unique. Have you ever visited Molokai, the leper island,
Doctor? No? But Mr. Nayland Smith will be familiar with the asylum
at Rangoon! And we must not forget my black spiders, with their diamond eyes—my spiders, that sit in the dark and watch—then leap!' "
Yet, having labored to create so auspicious a buildup, the author inexplicably cheats his suspense and lets it go for naught. No sooner has
Fu-Manchu turned his back to attend to a poisoned soufflé in the oven
than Kâramanèh pops up and strikes off the prisoners' gyves, and the
whole grisly quadrille starts all over again. Smith and Petrie, without so
much as a change of deerstalker hats, nip away to warn another prospective victim, and run full tilt into a covey of *phansigars*, the religious
stranglers familiar to devotees of the *American Weekly* as Thugs. They
outwit them, to be sure, but the pace is beginning to tell on Petrie, who
observes ruefully, "In retrospect, that restless time offers a chaotic
prospect, with few peaceful spots amid its turmoils." Frankly, I don't
know what Petrie is beefing about. My compassion goes out, rather, to
his patients, whom I envision by now as driven by default to extracting
their own tonsils and quarrying each other's gallstones. *They're* the
ones who need sympathy, Petrie, old boy.

With puff adders, tarantulas, and highbinders blooming in every
hedgerow, the hole-and-corner pursuit of Fu-Manchu drums along
through the next hundred pages at about the same tempo, resolutely
shying away from climaxes like Hindus from meat. Even the episode
in which Smith and Petrie, through the good offices of Kâramanèh,
eventually hold the Doctor at gun point aboard his floating laboratory
in the Thames proves just a pretext for further bombination about

those filmy greenish eyes; a shower of adjectives explodes in the reader's face, and he is whisked off on a hunt for certain stolen plans of an aero-torpedo, an interlude that veers dangerously close to the exploits of the indomitable Tom Swift. The sequence that follows, as rich in voodoo as it is innocent of logic, is heavily fraught with hypnosis, Fu-Manchu having unaccountably imprisoned a peer named Lord Southery and Kâramanèh's brother Aziz in a cataleptic trance. They are finally revived by injections of a specific called the Golden Elixir— a few drops of which I myself could have used to advantage at this point—and the story sashays fuzzily into its penultimate phase. Accompanied by a sizable police detail, Smith, Petrie, and a Scotland Yard inspector surprise Fu-Manchu in an opium sleep at his hideout. A denouement seems unavoidable, but if there was one branch of literary hopscotch Rohmer excelled in, it was avoiding denouements. When the three leaders of the party recover consciousness (yes, the indispensable trap door again, now on a wholesale basis), they lie bound and gagged in a subterranean vault, watching their captor sacrifice their subordinates by pelting them with poisonous toadstools. The prose rises to an almost lyrical pitch: "Like powdered snow the white spores fell from the roof, frosting the writhing shapes of the already poisoned men. Before my horrified gaze, *the fungus grew*; it spread from the head to the feet of those it touched; it enveloped them as in glittering shrouds. 'They die like flies!' screamed Fu-Manchu, with a sudden febrile excitement; and I felt assured of something I had long suspected: that that magnificent, perverted brain was the brain of a homicidal maniac—though Smith would never accept the theory." Since no hint is given of what theory Smith preferred, we have to fall back on conjecture. More than likely, he smiled indulgently under his gag and dismissed the whole escapade as the prankishness of a spoiled, self-indulgent child.

The ensuing events, while gaudy, are altogether too labyrinthine to unravel. As a matter of fact they puzzled Rohmer, too. He says helplessly, "Any curiosity with which this narrative may leave the reader burdened is shared by the writer." After reading that, my curiosity shrank to the vanishing point; I certainly wasn't going to beat my brains out over a riddle the author himself did not pretend to understand. With a superhuman effort, I rallied just enough inquisitiveness to turn to the last page for some clue to Fu-Manchu's end. It takes place, as nearly as I could gather, in a blazing cottage outside London, and the note he addresses to his antagonists clears the way for plenty of sequels. "To Mr. Commissioner Nayland Smith and Dr. Petrie—

Greeting! I am recalled home by One who may not be denied. In much that I came to do I have failed. Much that I have done I would undo; some little I have undone. Out of fire I came—the smoldering fire of a thing one day to be a consuming flame; in fire I go. Seek not my ashes. I am the lord of the fires! Farewell. Fu-Manchu."

I daresay it was the combination of this passage, the cheery hearth in front of which I reread it, and my underwrought condition, but I thought I detected in the Doctor's valedictory an unmistakable mandate. Rising stealthily, I tiptoed up to my daughter's bedchamber and peered in. A shaft of moonlight picked out her ankles protruding from beneath the bed, where she lay peacefully sleeping, secure from dacoity and Thuggee. Obviously, it would take more than a little crackle of the flames below to arouse her. I slipped downstairs and, loosening the binding of *The Mystery of Dr. Fu-Manchu* to insure a good supply of oxygen, consigned the lord of the fires to his native element. As he crumbled into ash, I could have sworn I smelled a rather rare essential oil and felt a pair of baleful green eyes fixed on me from the staircase. It was probably the cat, though I really didn't take the trouble to check. I just strolled into the kitchen, made sure there was no trap door under the icebox, and curled up for the night. That's how phlegmatic a chap gets in later life.

❧ NO STARCH IN THE DHOTI, S'IL VOUS PLAÎT

UP UNTIL RECENTLY, I had always believed that nobody on earth could deliver a throwaway line with quite the sang-froid of a certain comedian I worked for in Hollywood during the thirties. You probably don't recall the chap, but his hallmark was a big black mustache, a cigar, and a loping gait, and his three brothers, also in the act, impersonated with varying degrees of success a mute, an Italian, and a clean-cut boy. My respect for Julio (to cloak his identity partially) stemmed from a number of pearls that fell from his lips during our association, notably one inspired by an argument over dietary customs. We were having dinner at an off-Broadway hotel, in the noisiest locale imaginable outside the annual fair at Nizhnii Novgorod. There were at least a dozen people in the party—lawyers, producers, agents, brokers, astrologers, tipsters, and various assorted sycophants—for, like all celebrated theatrical personages, my man liked to travel with a retinue. The dining room was jammed, some paid-up ghoul from Local 802 was interpreting the "Habanera" on an electric organ over the uproar, and, just to insure dyspepsia, a pair of adagio dancers were flinging themselves with abandon in and out of our food. I was seated next to Julio, who was discoursing learnedly to me on his favorite subject, anatomical deviations among showgirls. Halfway through the meal, we abruptly became aware of a dispute across the table between several of our companions.

"It is *not* just religious!" one was declaring hotly. "They knew a damn sight more about hygiene than you think in those Biblical days!"

"That still don't answer my question!" shouted the man he had addressed. "If they allow veal and mutton and beef, why do they forbid pork?"

"Because it's unclean, you dummy," the other rasped. "I'm trying to tell you—the pig is an unclean animal!"

"What's that?" demanded Julio, his voice slicing through the altercation. "The pig an unclean animal?" He rose from his chair and repeated the charge to be certain everyone within fifty feet was listening.

"The pig an unclean animal? Why, the pig is the cleanest animal there is—except my father, of course." And dropped like a falcon back into his chow mein.

As I say, I'd gone along for years considering Julio pre-eminent in tossing off this kind of grenade, and then one Sunday a few weeks ago, in the *Times* Magazine, I stumbled across an item that leaves no doubt he has been deposed. The new champ is Robert Trumbull, the former Indian correspondent of the paper and a most affable bird with whom I once spent an afternoon crawling around the Qutb Minar, outside New Delhi. In the course of an article called "Portrait of a Symbol Named Nehru," Mr. Trumbull had the following to say: "Nehru is accused of having a congenital distaste for Americans because of their all too frequent habit of bragging and of being patronizing when in unfamiliar surroundings. It is said that in the luxurious and gracious house of his father, the late Pandit Motilal Nehru—who sent his laundry to Paris—the young Jawaharlal's British nurse used to make caustic remarks to the impressionable boy about the table manners of his father's American guests."

It was, of course, the utter nonchalance of the phrase "who sent his laundry to Paris" that knocked me galley-west. Obviously, Trumbull wasn't referring to one isolated occasion; he meant that the Pandit made a practice of consigning his laundry to the post, the way one used to under the academic elms. But this was no callow sophomore shipping his wash home to save money. A man willful and wealthy enough to have it shuttled from one hemisphere to another could hardly have been prompted by considerations of thrift. He must have been a consummate perfectionist, a fussbudget who wanted every last pleat in order, and, remembering my own Homeric wrangles with laundrymen just around the corner, I blenched at the complications his overseas dispatch must have entailed. Conducted long before there was any air service between India and Europe, it would have involved posting the stuff by sea—a minimum of three weeks in each direction, in addition to the time it took for processing. Each trip would have created problems of customs examination, valuation, duty (unless Nehru senior got friends to take it through for him, which was improbable; most people detest transporting laundry across the world, even their own). The old gentleman had evidently had a limitless wardrobe, to be able to dispense with portions of it for three months at a time.

The major headache, as I saw it, though, would have been coping with the *blanchisseur* himself. How did Pandit Motilal get any service or redress out of him at such long range? There were the countless vexations that always arise: the missing sock, the half-pulverized button, the insistence on petrifying everything with starch despite the most detailed instructions. The more I thought about it, the clearer it became that he must have been enmeshed in an unending correspondence with the laundry owner. I suggest, accordingly, that while the exact nature of his letters can only be guessed at, it might be useful—or, by the same token, useless—to reconstruct a few, together with the replies they evoked. Even if they accomplish nothing else, they should help widen the breach between East and West.

ALLAHABAD,
UNITED PROVINCES,
JUNE 7, 1903

Pleurniche et Cie.,
124, Avenue de la Grande Armée, Paris.
MY DEAR M. PLEURNICHE:

You may be interested to learn—though I doubt that anything would stir you out of your vegetable torpor—that your pompous, florid, and illiterate scrawl of the 27th arrived here with insufficient postage, forcing me to disgorge one rupee three annas to the mailman. How symbolic of your character, how magnificently consistent! Not content with impugning the quality of the cambric in my drawers, you contrive to make me *pay* for the insult. That transcends mere nastiness, you know. If an international award for odium is ever projected, have no fear of the outcome as far as India is concerned. You can rely on my support.

And apropos of symbols, there is something approaching genius in the one that graces your letterhead, the golden fleece. Could any trademark be more apt for a type who charges six francs to wash a cummerbund? I realize that appealing to your sense of logic is like whistling an aria to the deaf, but I paid half that for it originally, and the Muslim who sold it to me was the worst thief in the bazaar. Enlighten me, my dear fellow, since I have never been a tradesman myself—what passes through your head when you mulct a customer in this outrageous fashion? Is it glee? Triumph? Self-approbation at the cunning with which you have swindled your betters? I ask altogether without malice, solely from a desire to fathom the dark intricacies of the human mind.

To revert now to the subject of the drawers. It will do you no good to bombinate endlessly about sleazy material, deterioration from pounding on stones, etc. That they were immersed in an acid bath powerful enough to corrode a zinc plate, that they were wrenched through a mangle with utmost ferocity, that they were deliberately spattered with grease and kicked about the floor of your establishment, and, finally, that a white-hot iron was appliquéd on their seat—the whole sordid tale of maltreatment is writ there for anybody to see. The motive, however, is far less apparent, and I have speculated for hours on why I should be the target of vandalism. Only one explanation fits the facts. Quite clearly, for all your extortionate rates, you underpay your workmen, and one of them, seeking to revenge himself, wreaked his spite on my undergarment. While I sympathize with the poor rascal's plight, I wish it understood that I hold you responsible to the very last sou. I therefore deduct from the enclosed draft nine francs fifty, which will hardly compensate me for the damage to my raiment and my nerves, and remain, with the most transitory assurances of my regard,

Sincerely yours,
PANDIT MOTILAL NEHRU

PARIS,
July 18, 1903

Pandit Motilal Nehru,
Allahabad, U.P., India.
DEAR PANDIT MOTILAL:

I am desolated beyond words at the pique I sense between the lines in your recent letter, and I affirm to you on my wife's honor that in the six generations the family has conducted this business, yours is the first complaint we have ever received. Were I to list the illustrious clients we have satisfied—Robespierre, the Duc d'Enghien, Saint-Saëns, Coquelin, Mérimée, Bouguereau, and Dr. Pasteur, to name but a handful—it would read like a roll call of the immortals. Only yesterday, Marcel Proust, an author you will hear more of one of these days, called at our *établissement* (establishment) to felicitate us in person. The work we do for him is peculiarly exacting; due to his penchant for making notes on his cuffs, we must observe the greatest discretion in selecting which to launder. In fine, our function is as much editorial as sanitary, and he stated unreservedly that he holds our literary judgment in the highest esteem. I ask you, could a firm with traditions like these stoop to the pettiness you imply?

You can be sure, however, that if our staff has been guilty of any oversight, it will not be repeated. Between ourselves, we have been zealously weeding out a Socialist element among the employees, malcontents who seek to inflame them with vicious nonsense about an eleven-hour day and compulsory ventilation. Our firm refusal to compromise one iota has borne fruit; we now have a hard core of loyal and spiritless drudges, many of them so lackluster that they do not even pause for lunch, which means a substantial time saving and consequently much speedier service for the customer. As you see, my dear Pandit Motilal, efficiency and devotion to our clientele dominate every waking thought at Pleurniche.

As regards your last consignment, all seems to be in order; I ask leave, though, to beg one trifling favor that will help us execute your work more rapidly in future. Would you request whoever mails the laundry to make certain it contains no living organisms? When the current order was unpacked, a small yellow-black serpent, scarcely larger than a pencil but quite dynamic, wriggled out of one of your *dhotis* and spread terror in the workroom. We succeeded in decapitating it after a modicum of trouble and bore it to the Jardin d'Acclimatation, where the curator identified it as a krait, the most lethal of your indigenous snakes. Mind you, I personally thought M. Ratisborn an alarmist—the little émigré impressed me as a rather cunning fellow, vivacious, intelligent, and capable of transformation into a household pet if one had leisure. Unfortunately, we have none, so fervent is our desire to accelerate your shipments, and you will aid us materially by a hint in the right quarter, if you will. Accept, I implore of you, my salutations the most distinguished.

Yours cordially,
OCTAVE-HIPPOLYTE PLEURNICHE

ALLAHABAD, U.P.,
SEPTEMBER 11, 1903

DEAR M. PLEURNICHE:

If I were a hothead, I might be tempted to horsewhip a Yahoo who has the effrontery to set himself up as a patron of letters; if a humanitarian, to garrote him and earn the gratitude of the miserable wretches under his heel. As I am neither, but simply an idealist fatuous enough to believe he is entitled to what he pays for, I have a favor to ask of you, in turn. Spare me, I pray, your turgid rhetoric and bootlicking protestations, and be equally sparing of the bleach you use on my shirts. After a single baptism in your vats, my sky-blue *jibbahs* faded to a ghastly greenish-white and the fabric evaporates under one's touch. Merciful God, whence springs this compulsion to eliminate every trace of color from my dress? Have you now become arbiters of fashion as well as littérateurs?

In your anxiety to ingratiate yourselves, incidentally, you have exposed me to as repugnant an experience as I can remember. Five or six days ago, a verminous individual named Champignon arrived here from Pondichéry, asserting that he was your nephew, delegated by you to expedite my household laundry problems. The blend of unction and cheek he displayed, reminiscent of a process server, should have warned me to beware, but, tenderhearted ninny that I am, I obeyed our Brahmin laws of hospitality and permitted him to remain the night. Needless to say, he distinguished himself. After a show of gluttony to dismay Falstaff, he proceeded to regale the dinner table with a disquisition on the art of love, bolstering it with quotations from the Kama-sutra so coarse that one of the ladies present fainted dead away. Somewhat later, I surprised him in the kitchen tickling a female servant, and when I demurred, he rudely advised me to stick to my rope trick and stay out of matters that did not concern me. He was gone before daylight, accompanied by a Jaipur enamel necklace of incalculable value and all our silver. I felt it was a trivial price to be rid of him. Nevertheless, I question your wisdom, from a commercial standpoint, in employing such emissaries. Is it not safer to rob the customer in the old humdrum fashion, a franc here and a franc there, than to stake everything on a youth's judgment and risk possible disaster? I subscribe myself, as always,

> Your well-wisher,
> PANDIT MOTILAL NEHRU

> PARIS,
> OCTOBER 25, 1903

DEAR PANDIT MOTILAL:

We trust that you have received the bundle shipped five weeks since and that our work continues to gratify. It is also pleasing to learn that our relative M. Champignon called on you and managed to be of assistance. If there is any further way he can serve you, do not hesitate to notify him.

I enclose herewith a cutting which possibly needs a brief explanation. As you see, it is a newspaper advertisement embodying your photograph and a text woven out of laudatory remarks culled from your letters to us. Knowing you would gladly concur, I took the liberty of altering a word or two in places to clarify the meaning and underline the regard you hold us in. This dramatic license, so to speak, in no way vitiates the sense of what you wrote; it is quite usual in theatrical advertising to touch up critical opinion, and to judge from comment I have already heard, you will enjoy publicity throughout the continent

of Europe for years to come. Believe us, dear Pandit, your eternal
debtor, and allow me to remain

Yours fraternally,
OCTAVE-HIPPOLYTE PLEURNICHE

ALLAHABAD,
NOVEMBER 14, 1903

DEAR M. PLEURNICHE:

The barristers I retained immediately on perusing your letter—
Messrs. Bulstrode & Hawfinch, of Covent Garden, a firm you will hear
more of one of these days—have cautioned me not to communicate
with you henceforth, but the urge to speak one final word is irresistible.
After all, when their suit for a million francs breaks over you like a
thunderclap, when the bailiffs seize your business and you are reduced
to sleeping along the *quais* and subsisting on the carrot greens you pick
up around Les Halles, you may mistakenly attribute your predicament
to my malignity, to voodoo, djinns, etc. Nothing of the sort, my dear
chap. Using me to publicize your filthy little concern is only a secondary factor in your downfall. What doomed you from the start was the
bumbling incompetence, the ingrained slovenliness, that characterizes
everyone in your calling. A man too indolent to replace the snaps he
tears from a waistcoat or expunge the rust he sprinkles on a brand-new
Kashmiri shawl is obviously capable of any infamy, and it ill becomes
him to snivel when retribution overtakes him in the end.

Adieu, then, *mon brave*, and try to exhibit in the dock at least the
dignity you have failed to heretofore. With every good wish and the
certainty that nothing I have said has made the slightest possible impression on a brain addled by steam, I am,

Compassionately,
PANDIT MOTILAL NEHRU

GENUFLECTION IN THE SUN

I AM NOT A TEETOTALER and enjoy a good snort as well as the next one, but for sheer delight and ecstasy in the region of the tonsils none of them can even begin to compare with that strange combination of syrup, ice cream and carbonated water skillfully proportioned and compounded by some Master Dispenser at my favorite Liggett fountain.

I can see him now, this delicate and brilliant chemist, his head tilted forward slightly as his ear reaches for my order—"All black, please."

"All black!" Already his hand has whisked a large-sized tumbler whose narrowed round bottom was scientifically designed to aid the magical blending of all the weird component parts of the soda. Under the chocolate syrup faucet it goes. See how the rich, dark brown goo covers a third of the bottom of the glass, clinging lovingly to the side.

Now a splash of cream and the first of a series of wonderful amalgams has taken place. The dark chocolate is lighter in tone, more fluid, better prepared for the life infusion that follows—the fizzer.

Here is surely the secret of this nectar for the Gods of America, the genius touch of this unknown benefactor of mankind. The Master Dispenser is all concentration now, for this is a solemn moment, the aerating of the milk and chocolate mixture with the wire-thin stream of vital and living fizz. It hisses into the glass as he turns it carefully to all points of the compass. Under the impulse of this injection, the liquid suddenly begins to bubble and boil and heave, seething with a new and inner life of its own. Whereas a moment ago it was somber and viscous, now it is light, merry, purposeful, and gay.

Plop! Into its joyously heaving bosom is dropped a rounded gobbet of smooth, rich ice cream.

Now the Master Dispenser approaches the climax. Infected by his own artistry, he swings the glass and turns on the soda faucet, his eye keen to the task of producing perfection. As the charged water joins the composition, great, luscious brown bubbles begin to rise in the glass. Higher and higher under the watchful gaze of the Super Dispenser. Not yet . . . not yet . . . NOW! A corona of pure aerated chocolate flavor stands an inch high above the glass, a crown of sweet nothing, too superb in texture and flavor for words. A spoon, two straws, and there it is vibrant, pulsating—ready. . . .

Ah, Ye Gods of Gluttony! That first taste, the mouthful of froth, the sweet of the chocolate, the brisk tang of the soda, the ecstasy of the now-you-have-it, now-you-haven't, which sends you on for fulfillment into the first bite of ice cream irrigated with the lovely fluid of the soda.

Rich though these rewards be, they are nothing to the grand finale, the climax of enjoyment, when with froth gone, ice cream gone, you discard the straws, lift the glass, tilt back your head and subject your tonsils to the first superb shock of the pure Ichor of the soda, syrup, bubble water, water, melted ice cream, all blended into one Ambrosia of flavor, action and chill.

What is there to match it? Where is it to be found? Who, oh, who, is the great, great man who thought it all up for the likes of you and me?—*From a Liggett menu.*

Two MILES south of Corona del Mar, I saw looming up ahead the Piggy-Wig Drive-In they had told me in Balboa to watch for. Narrowly missing a Hupmobile driven by an old harpy in curlers, who interpreted my left-hand signal as an invitation to sleep with her, I swerved off the Coast Highway and pulled up alongside it. A heavy miasma of frying lard and barbecued ribs drifted across the wheel of asphalt radiating from the structure; somewhere inside, the sepulchral voice of Patti Page sniveled a plaint about a doggie in a window. Three lymphatic carhops, manifestly chosen for their resemblance to porkers, were seated under a bong tree made of papier-mâché, and as one languidly rose and undulated toward me, I noticed a curled pink celluloid tail protruding from her scientifically designed narrowed round bottom, which bobbled as she moved.

"Villa Jacaranda?" she repeated, swallowing a yawn. "What is it—a motel?" I explained I was looking for the residence of Willard Inchcape, the writer. "I wouldn't know, I'm sure," she returned with disdain. "There's some bohemians up that dirt road there. They all sculp or weave or something."

I thanked her and, resisting an impulse to order a slice of quince to see whether it came with a runcible spoon, a form of cutlery that has always pricked my curiosity, drove on. The road straggled into the foothills past a cluster of aggressive ranch-style homes—each equipped with an incinerator adapted for those murders in which Southern California seems to excel—and terminated at a high wall of white-washed brick. Over the massive gate was a chemically aged plastic shingle bearing the legend "Villa Jacaranda" in Carborundum Old Style. I pushed the gate open and stepped down into a garden choked with poinsettias. Their foliage was so lush that it veiled the outlines of the house beyond, but in a patch of greensward at the far end there was visible a woman laboring at a sculptor's table. As I approached, she turned and I beheld a portly matron of fifty-odd in a green smock, with an uncompromising henna bob and Hashimura Togo spectacles.

"Mrs. Inchcape?" I asked. "I phoned from Los Angeles."

"Oh, yes," she said energetically. "You're the man who wanted to talk to Willard. Come in." She laid her graving tool on the stand, a gesture that automatically drew my eye to the object she was modeling. It was the head of a Scotch collie, carved from a block of castile soap with such fidelity to nature that I had no difficulty repressing a start.

"Aha," I commented with a portentous frown, aware that she was watching me closely. "Er—is that an actual portrait or more of an idealized conception, as it were?"

"Half and half," said Mrs. Inchcape. "I based it on our Timmy. He passed on several years ago."

"You don't say," I murmured, attempting to mingle respect for her bereavement with a note of philosophic fatalism.

"Yes, he's buried right where you're standing." I jerked sidewise, remorseful at having desecrated a tomb. "Do you like it?"

I cocked my head and nodded emphatically. "You certainly got him down cold," I said. Then, conscious of the ambiguity of my critique, I added hurriedly, "What I mean is you sure got him dead to rights." I felt the perspiration start on my forehead. "Of course, I never knew Timmy—"

"You bet you didn't," said Mrs. Inchcape. "If he were alive, you'd never be in this garden. He'd have torn you limb from limb."

"Well, well," I said, feigning admiration for her pet's loyalty. "I guess his death was a real loss."

"I can't imagine to whom," she returned. "He bit everybody, right up to the man who chloroformed him. But I suppose you're one of those people who get sentimental about animals."

It impressed me as singular that she should be immortalizing a beast she abhorred, but I decided not to pry. "Is Mr. Inchcape home?" I asked, looking around. "I wouldn't like to disturb him if he's working."

"Don't get fidgety, he'll be along in a minute," she said, motioning toward a bench. "Sit down while I clean up this mess. Did you ever hear of Daniel Chester French?"

"The sculptor?"

"Well, I certainly don't mean Daniel Chester French the upholsterer," she said with asperity. "The one who did the statue of 'Memory' at the Metropolitan. I studied with him for two years, and let me tell you, young man, there wasn't a mean bone in his body." I tried to recall anything discreditable I had ever heard about French, and failed. "Your ears remind me of his. The way they're articulated to the head."

"Gee," I said, feeling it was incumbent on me to exhibit some sign of elation. "I've never been told that before. You—ah— It must have been a great privilege to know Mr. French."

"That depends on how you look at it," said Mrs. Inchcape acidly. She lapsed into a tight-lipped silence, dusting chips of soap from the stand and casting me an occasional suspicious glance.

Suddenly a man's voice, tremulous with excitement, resounded through the shrubbery. "Rowena!" it called. "Where are you—in the patio?" Her hail of response, easily audible in Mazatlán, flushed up my quarry, a leathery old gentleman with an Armagnac nose, a black velvet tam, and a smoking jacket. In one hand he clenched a Tyrolean porcelain pipe fluttering a pair of green tassels and in the other a typewritten sheet that bristled with interlineations. "Just listen to this, honey bun!" he crowed. "It's the copy for Mother Stentorian's Fish Kebabs, and if I do say so, it's a sockdolager. I couldn't get the exact poetic throb at first—"

"This geezer here's waiting for you," said his wife laconically.

"Well, he's got a stomach—let him hear it, too!" said Inchcape jovially. He rotated toward me. "You the party called me about my ice-cream-soda tribute?"

"I am, sir," I said, extending my hand, "and I've come to tell you it's the finest thing since Baudelaire's *Flowers of Evil.* I just wanted to pay my respects to a great poet."

"Thank you, son, thank you," he replied, his face suffused with pleasure. "But if you think *that* was good, get ready for a real treat." He adjusted a pince-nez secured to his lapel by a silver chain, cleared his throat, and began declaiming in a rich, fruity baritone: " 'Up from the silent, sunless depths of the seven seas into Mother Stentorian's spotless antiseptic kitchens come the hake, the scrod, the plaice, the fluke, the cream of the finny tribe, briny-fresh and jam-packed with succulent vitamins, to tickle the gourmet palate. Man alive, watch these yumdingers, these dorsal dainties, tumble from the nets in silver iridescence, splendid largess from Nature's treasure-trove, yearning to sputter in butter and ravish the jaded esophagus! Here in this hygienic temple of the culinary art, under the watchful yet kindly eye of Mother Stentorian, they are portioned into appetizing mouth-size chunks, sprinkled with mace, dill, rape, capsicum, and rose leaves, and precooked on skewers over aromatic fires of specially processed driftwood imported from faraway Armenia.' "

"Jiminetty," I ejaculated as he paused for breath. "That's inspired, Mr. Inchcape! You can almost taste the crisp, savory—"

"Wait, you haven't heard anything yet," he broke in. "I'm just warming up. 'Then each individual kebab, its delectable goodness sealed in, is wrapped in gleaming chlorophane—cellophane from which all harmful chlorophyll has been extracted—by deft-fingered, full-bosomed girls pledged to change their uniforms every hour. Now comes the most vital phase in the preparation of Mother Stentorian's Matchless Fish Kebabs. Science has discovered that these fishy shasliks—or, more properly, fishliks—acquire a mysterious added tang when impregnated with the folk songs of Asia Minor. Consequently, before your personalized package of kebabs is handi-packed, it is locked into a special tone chamber—a musical autoclave, so to speak—where it is saturated with rollicking airs like "The Well-Tufted Ottoman," "Sohrab and Rustum Were Lovers," and "Sister, Shake That Amphigouri." Why deny yourself any longer the color and enchantment of the Near East you've always secretly hungered for? Simply perfume your house with the odor of cold mutton fat, heat up a box of Mother Stentorian's Genuine Fish Kebabs, and become part of the world's most ancient culture. As you squat on your hams greedily engorging these zestful tidbits, you, too, will be at one with Shadrach, Meshach, and Abednego, with Nineveh and Tyre.' "

Mrs. Inchcape was the first to break the silence when her husband had concluded. "Will he be staying for lunch?" she demanded, nodding in my direction.

"Why, I can't really say," hesitated Inchcape, obviously derailed. "We haven't had a chance—"

"No, no, thank you," I said hastily. "I'm bound for La Jolla. I'll be leaving very soon."

"Then I'll just make a soybean *pizza* for two," Mrs. Inchcape announced, departing. "Come when I call you, now. It's no good cold."

The bard looked so stricken that first aid was indicated at once. "Mr. Inchcape," I said, "this may sound insincere, but when you were reading that, you brought a lump to my throat. It's tremendous. Absolutely symphonic."

"You think it jells, do you?" he asked eagerly.

"Good heavens, man, it sings!" I said. "They'll be quoting you in advertising circles for years to come. The lyricism—the imagery! It's a downright classic, I promise you."

"Oh, shucks, it's only a pastiche," said Inchcape, buffing his nails on his sleeve. "I mean with a theme as limited as kebabs you don't have the scope, naturally. Now, the ice-cream soda—there I had material to work with. I employed a kind of a cosmic approach, if you noticed."

"It struck me right away," I confessed. "First the syrup, then the cream, then the fizz. Like architecture."

"Each symbolizing a step in the universal creative process," he pointed out. "Fire, earth, and water, all uniting to produce bliss everlasting, or, in the wider sense, the Promethean spark."

"And the whole compounded by a Master Dispenser," I recalled. "Yes, the mystical analogy was perfect. Did you ever get any figures from Liggett's? Were there many conversions?"

"You mean abstainers who took up ice-cream soda as a result?" queried Inchcape. "Frankly, it *was* rather impressive; in fact, for a while they considered having prayers with the sandwiches, but the customers balked." He shrugged. "Ah, well, between you and me, I was shooting at the aesthetic angle more than the religious."

"You hit the bull's-eye, in any case," I declared. "Tell me, how did you happen to get into inspirational writing?"

He pondered for a moment before replying. "Well, it was sort of a call," he said reflectively. "I had my own business up in Hollywood, a few doors from Grauman's Egyptian, on the Boulevard. We eternalized baby shoes—you know, dipped them in bronze for ash trays and souvenirs. The work was creative, but somehow I felt I wasn't realizing my potentialities. Then one day I came across a copy of Elbert Hubbard's magazine, *The Philistine*, and his style reacted on me like a long, cold drink of sauerkraut juice. Right there, I made up my mind to follow in the footsteps of the Sage of East Aurora, and I never deviated one hair from my resolve. Which I'm thankful to say that Rowena— that's Mrs. Inchcape—has always been my shield and my buckler, urging me on and giving unselfishly of her artistic judgment. She's a very gifted woman, as you can see for yourself."

"And a very gracious one," I agreed. "Well, I must be moving on,

Mr. Inchcape. Much obliged for the preview of Mother Stentorian's Fish Kebabs. I'll be on the lookout for them."

"Yes, I hear they're quite tasty," he said. "Sure you won't stay and take potluck with us? Rowena can fix you a mock omelet or some toasted dates or something."

"No, thanks a million," I said, backing through the poinsettias. "Well, goodbye, sir, and long may you flourish." I got into my rented convertible, switched on a commercial for atomic laxatives, and drove down to the coast road. As I passed the Piggy-Wig Drive-In, I saw two persons costumed as an owl and a pussycat dancing hand in hand on the edge of the asphalt. At least, I thought I saw them, but it may have been only a mirage. That Southern California sunlight can be pretty tricky at times.

❦ A GIRL AND A BOY ANTHROPOID WERE DANCING

THERE IS MANY a justly celebrated name in the pantheon of show business, but last Saturday, looking over a small pantheon I keep handy so I can get at it in a hurry, I was struck by one omission. In the subsection enshrining strip-teasers, I found no mention of Rozina Carlomusto. All the others were there: dazzling Lili St. Cyr, who electrified Las Vegas a while back by peeling down to the ultimate rosette, jettisoning that, and landing in quod, an exploit that boosted her salary to five thousand dollars a week; Sherry Britten of the flamboyant torso, sometimes likened to a human acetylene torch; the immortal Gypsy Rose, Georgia Sothern, Hinda Wasau, Margie Hart, Ann Corio, and others too numerous to list. But of Rozina not a whisper, not even a footnote to remind posterity of her sensational performance with a stuffed gorilla which made theatrical history two short months ago.

The exact nature of the lady's specialty is not altogether clear; it seems to have been a cross between jujitsu and a gavotte, from which her partner invariably emerged victor. The ensuing chaotic account of the act and its repercussions appeared in the New York *Daily News*:

> CALUMET CITY, ILL., Oct. 9 (UP)—Justice of the Peace Ted Styka today tossed out the case against dancer Rozina Carlomusto, accused of staging a lewd wrestling match with a stuffed gorilla in a night club. "Insufficient evidence," Styka ruled, even though authorities had claimed that Miss Carlomusto always lost the fall to the gorilla. The police said it appeared that the gorilla completed a seduction of the dancer during the act . . . It (the gorilla) is still in the hands of the State's Attorney's office as evidence. Last month the dancer gave a command performance in court so that Styka could judge for himself whether the act was "lewd and lascivious" as charged. She stripped to the bare essentials in chambers and went into an animated tussle with the stuffed beast. Sure enough, the gorilla won, pinning Rozina in 10 minutes flat. "This is a work of art," she said. "I've performed

the same show hundreds of times in Panama and before soldiers in U.S.O. shows. This is the first time anybody questioned the dance."

What the poor, bewildered kid doesn't realize, of course, is that she is a victim of the same quidnuncs and busybodies who have plagued every artist from Zola and D. H. Lawrence to Joyce Hawley. Here is a girl quietly wrestling away with a gorilla in a spotlight, enriching the cultural life of her community and impinging on nobody's livelihood. You can depend on some salvation-happy bluenose, with a paid-up annuity in Paradise, to begin reading things into it. I don't want to borrow trouble, but once such folk get the upper hand, we are finished —*ausgespielt*. It will no longer be possible for your daughter and mine to disrobe on a night-club floor and juggle a pair of doves or plastic bubbles, and before you know it, all the calendars will be featuring depressing snow scenes and collies instead of voluptuous maidens in black net curled around a telephone. If we aren't heading into the most repressive era since Cromwell, I'm a Chinaman.

The thing that really riles me, though, is the aura of secrecy surrounding Rozina's demonstration in court. We are told that "she stripped to the bare essentials in chambers and went into an animated tussle with the stuffed beast." Does Mr. Styka suppose for a moment that he can dismiss an enormously complex legal process in so bald a fashion? No matter how incurious the reader may be, his mind is flooded with a host of questions. Who else witnessed these star-chamber proceedings? Any disinterested zoophile or art connoisseur qualified to advise the justice? Any other gorillas? What assurance have we, indeed, that the exhibition took place in an atmosphere free of prejudice toward the lower order of primates? Lacking a court record or similar certified testimony, one is forced to reconstruct the circumstances as a paleontologist does a Brontosaurus, from a single, ossified splinter. In my own restoration, which follows, none of the characters represent real persons, Midwestern or otherwise. The ape, however, is modeled after Ngonga, a young Lowlands gorilla with whom I conducted a half-hearted love affair last summer at the San Diego Zoo. And to her, in memory of what might have been, I dedicate it.

SCENE: *The private chambers of Milo Usufruct, a justice of the peace. A cheerless room dominated by a rolltop desk overflowing with writs, torts, and estoppels. A Globe-Wernicke sectional bookcase at left contains half a dozen moldy law books and a greenish pair of arctics. On the walls, two steel engravings, one of Blackstone*

*and the other of a stag beleaguered by wolves. At rise, Usufruct
is bent over a venerable, table-type Victor talking machine,
fiddling at it with a screwdriver. He is a thin, bald radish of a
man with watery, protuberant eyes. Miss Ripperger, his secretary and a woman polarized to attract every catastrophe, is un-
wrapping several phonograph records.*

USUFRUCT (*peevishly*): Something's scraping inside. There was nothing wrong with it when I put it away thirty years ago.

MISS RIPPERGER: It's probably all corroded. Or else somebody dropped
it and smashed the mechanism.

USUFRUCT: If the mechanism was smashed, the turntable wouldn't
revolve.

MISS RIPPERGER: You better not fool with that thing. You're liable to
cut your finger and get blood poisoning. A nephew of mine—

USUFRUCT: Yes, yes. How about the records I wanted?

MISS RIPPERGER: They don't have any African tomtom numbers.

USUFRUCT: Well, then, did you ask for wrestling music, like I told you?

MISS RIPPERGER: He said he never heard of any special songs a person
could wrestle to. He gave me some Sousa marches—here's "Under
the Double Eagle"—

USUFRUCT: Never mind, they'll do. That's all for now.

MISS RIPPERGER: If you'd give me more of an idea what it was for, I
could try one of the big record stores downtown.

USUFRUCT (*evasively*): Just a hearing I've called—doesn't matter.
Now look, you go to lunch, and take an extra hour. I'm expecting
a party, a Miss LaFlange.

MISS RIPPERGER: Is she the one in the Ziegler assault case?

USUFRUCT: Er—no, no, some theatrical mixup. Go on, run along.
(*She exits. Her employer burrows into a desk drawer, produces
a pocket mirror and comb, and trains a few filaments of hair
across his scalp. He has seated himself and joined his fingertips
judicially when a light knock sounds at the door. Opal LaFlange
enters, carrying a fiber sample case. She is a statuesque blonde
clad in tomato-colored satin. A trifle steatopygous and endowed
with what the poet Herrick has felicitously described as "that
brave vibration each way free." Her flaxen hair, worn long over
her shoulders, and milk-white skin recall to mind the pneumatic
nudes who used to be portrayed on jackknives.*)

OPAL (*in a childish treble*): Hill-oo-oo! How are yoo-oo?

USUFRUCT: Ah, good morning! And how is our—ahem—little trans-
gressor today?

OPAL: Just finely, judge. My, what a darling office! Is this where you
do all your studying and stuff?

USUFRUCT: Yes, I—er—I'm a bug on privacy. You see, in my type
work I have to get off by my lonesome and ponder over the—uh—
briefs, so to speak. Do you like it?

OPAL: Oh, it's adorable! So snug and well—sort of anteem, if you
know what I mean.

USUFRUCT: Precisely. No meddlers around to distract—(*He starts
as Opal zips open her dress and begins pulling it over her head.*)
Hey, what are you doing there?

OPAL: Why, getting ready for my routine with Bombo. I thought you
wanted to see the way we work in the clubs.

USUFRUCT (*scuttling to the door and shooting the bolt*): Sure, but
after all, people might misunderstand. A man in my position
can't be too careful.

OPAL: You can say that again, brother. (*She discards her slip.*) If
anyone broke down that door right now, you'd have a hell of a
time explaining.

USUFRUCT: L-listen, maybe we ought to skip it for the time being. I—
I've got to run over to the Board of Estimate. I'll see your act
at the Tropics tonight.

OPAL: Not unless you're a mind reader you won't. The coppers pad-
locked the joint three days ago.

USUFRUCT: Then we'll put it on in a field somewhere—at the Elks
Clubhouse—

OPAL: Gorgeous, when I strip down to dance, I dance. Here, help me
blow up Bombo. (*She draws an inert bundle of fur and a bicycle
pump from the sample case, hands him the pump.*) This lousy
valve in his belly button, it never did work right. . . . There. Now
come on, lover, put your back into it.

USUFRUCT (*panting*): I . . . I'm doing the best I can . . . phew . . .

OPAL: Keep at it—the chest has to come out a whole foot yet. (*She
spots the phonograph.*) Say, don't tell me! Got any fast tempo
tunes—"Cow-Cow Boogie" or anything like that?

USUFRUCT (*the veins in his forehead bulging*): Uh . . . just those there.
. . . Look, I'm getting winded. . . .

OPAL: "The Stars and Stripes Forever." "Semper Fidelis." "Washington Post March." Jeez, what cornball picked these out? (*The*

*gorilla, a remarkable simulacrum with bared fangs, towers menac-
ingly over Usufruct, who instinctively cowers away from it. A
resounding blare of brass issues from the phonograph.*)

USUFRUCT: Good grief, are you crazy? Turn that noise down—we'll
have the whole building in here!

OPAL: O.K., O.K., keep your girdle on. (*She mutes the music, de-
taches the pump, and twines the gorilla's arms about her.*) Well,
here we go. Opening announcement, green dimmers on the lights,
and we're on. (*She and Bombo rock across the floor, pantomiming a struggle to capsize each other. Suddenly, as Usufruct stares
openmouthed, a sharp knocking at the door is heard.*)

USUFRUCT (*aghast*): Oh, my God. . . . Turn it off—*stop!*

OPAL: I can't—he's crushing me in his mighty arms—spare me,
Bombo—

USUFRUCT (*babbling to himself*): I'm locked in here with a mental
case. (*He snaps off the phonograph, and with a strength born of
desperation, wrenches apart Opal and Bombo.*)

OPAL: Take your hands off me, you popeyed little shrimp!

USUFRUCT: Sh-h-h! Get in the closet there, quick—your petticoat—
no, no, don't put it on—wait a minute, the satchel too—(*As he
thrusts her through the door and slams it, the knocking grows
more insistent. In an agony of apprehension, he steals to the door
and opens it. Flitcraft, the town's leading banker, and Zeugma, a
retired merchant and pillar of the church, appear on the threshold. They exhibit obvious concern.*)

FLITCRAFT: Are you all right, Milo? We heard some sort of struggle—
a crash—

ZEUGMA: We were afraid you had a seizure—apoplexy or something—

USUFRUCT (*with a ghastly attempt at jauntiness*): Who, me? Ah ha
ha ha. . . .

ZEUGMA: Well, you do look kind of shaky, doesn't he, Simeon? Look
at the cold sweat on his forehead.

USUFRUCT: I—I was trying to repair the ape—I mean, the apparatus
—that is, the Victrola there. (*sponging his brow*) Gentlemen, if
you could come back in an hour—

FLITCRAFT (*entering*): Tell the truth, Milo, this is rather important;
we'd like to have a little chin with you right now.

ZEUGMA: Yes, indeed. (*grimly*) There are some very, very peculiar
things going on in Tigris County, my friend. The sooner we put
them right, the better. (*Usufruct twitches uncontrollably as his
callers dispose themselves in chairs.*)

FLITCRAFT: Let's not beat around the bush, Milo. The political administration in this town is rotten to the core. You know who runs it? A lot of crooked gamblers, racketeers, and gorillas. (*Usufruct reacts, dislodges a phonograph record which shatters on the floor.*) My word, man, you're nervous today. What's wrong?

ZEUGMA: Shouldn't wonder he's coming down with the grippe.

FLITCRAFT: Yes, plenty of it around. Well, anyway, speaking for the law-abiding element in the community, Zeugma and I say they've made a monkey of us long enough.

USUFRUCT (*faintly*): Fellows, I feel a bit feverish. I—I believe I'll go on home and lie down for a spell.

FLITCRAFT: A very good idea, but first, tell me—have you ever thought of running for public office?

ZEUGMA: We need a decent, upright citizen to clean house. Throw the rascals out, that's my motto.

FLITCRAFT: Just so. Now, Milo, we've been over your record and your life is an open book. (*He breaks off, his eyes pinned on the closet door.*) Say, that's funny. What's that hanging out of there?

USUFRUCT (*teeth chattering*): A fur rug—a lap robe. You know, to cover up when you're driving in a sleigh. It b-belonged to my grandfather.

FLITCRAFT: Hmm. (*rising*) If you don't mind, I'd like to see the rest of that robe. (*As he starts toward it, Usufruct frantically interposes himself.*)

USUFRUCT: Simeon, you've known me thirty years! I swear on everything holy that I never—

MISS RIPPERGER (*entering*): Mr. Flitcraft! Mr. Flitcraft!

FLITCRAFT: What is it?

MISS RIPPERGER: They just held up the bank—three men in a Buick coop! The police are chasing them down Wentworth Avenue!

FLITCRAFT: Great Scott! (*He runs out, followed by Zeugma. As they exit, Usufruct's knees buckle and he goes horizontal. Miss Ripperger hurries to him, and kneeling, begins to chafe his wrists.*)

MISS RIPPERGER: Oh . . . Oh . . . I just knew something was going to happen when I got up this morning! (*She raises her eyes inquiringly as the closet door opens.*)

CURTAIN

❦ CLOUDLAND REVISITED: ROCK-A-BYE, VISCOUNT, IN THE TREETOP

A COUPLE OF MONTHS BACK, the firm of Bramhall & Rixey, Ltd., a shipping concern on lower Broadway operating a string of freighters to West African ports, received an unusual communication. It was inscribed in pencil on both sides of a sheet of lined yellow paper of the sort commonly employed in secondary schools, and its numerous erasures and interlineations attested to the care that had gone into its composition. The correspondent identified himself as a prominent New York sportsman and big-game hunter who was contemplating a safari into the heart of the Dark Continent (Africa, he explained in a helpful aside). Without going into wearisome detail, he was in a position to assure Bramhall & Rixey that the expedition would eclipse anything of the kind on record. Not only was he planning to bring back a number of leopards, man-eating lions, and comparably gaudy fauna but, if time allowed, he proposed to search out King Solomon's mines and corroborate the existence of a mysterious white goddess ruling a vast empire of blacks in the Cameroons. Obviously, any wide-awake shipping company could appreciate what enormous publicity must accrue to it if chosen to transport such an enterprise. Should Bramhall & Rixey agree to carry the party—without charge, of course—the sportsman thought he might prevail on his associates to assent, though he warned that they rather favored a rival fleet. Stressing the need for an immediate decision, due to the impending monsoon rains (whether in Manhattan or Africa he did not specify), the writer enclosed a self-addressed postal for a speedy reply.

My first reaction when I came across a postal in my morning mail several days ago with the terse admonition "Wipe your nose, bub," signed by Bramhall & Rixey, was one of spontaneous irritation. I caught up the phone, forgetting for the moment that my fourteen-year-old son had been enthralled this past summer by a book called *Tarzan of the Apes* and that he had been treating the family to a sustained panegyric on Africa. "I'll teach you whose nose to wipe!" I shouted into it. "I've half a mind to come down and cane you people publicly in

Beaver Street!" Fortunately, they were spared the humiliation, as, in my wrath, I forgot to dial their number, and by the time I tumbled to the probable culprit and documented his guilt, I was able to take a much more lenient view of the incident. The fact of the matter is that back in 1918, the year I myself first encountered Edgar Rice Burroughs' electrifying fable, it exercised a similarly hypnotic effect on me. Insofar as the topography of Rhode Island and my physique permitted, I modeled myself so closely on Tarzan that I drove the community to the brink of collapse. I flung spears at the neighbors' laundry, exacerbated their watchdogs, swung around their piazzas gibbering and thumping my chest, made reply only in half-human grunts interspersed with unearthly howls, and took great pains generally to qualify as a stench in the civic nostril. The hallucination passed as abruptly as it had set in; one morning I awoke with an overwhelming ennui for everything related to Africa, weak but lucid. My kinsfolk were distrustful for a while, but as soon as they saw me constructing a catamaran in which to explore the Everglades, they knew I was rational again.

Curious as to why Tarzan had enraptured two generations and begotten so many sequels, movie serials, and comics, I commandeered my son's copy of the novel and my wife's chaise longue and staged a reunion. Like most sentimental excursions into the past, it was faintly tinged with disillusion. Across the decades, Burroughs' erstwhile jaunty narrative had developed countless crow's-feet and wrinkles; passages that I remembered outracing Barney Oldfield now seemed to puff and wheeze like a donkey engine. The comparison was aided by a donkey engine puffing directly outside my window, and frequently, in all honesty, its rhythmic snoring was amplified by my own. Nevertheless, I got the gist of the story, and for gist-lovers who prefer to sniff the candy at long range, that little may suffice.

Strictly speaking, the tale begins in the African forest with the adoption by a female anthropoid ape of an English baby of lofty lineage, but to render this association feasible, if not palatable, some valiant exposition is required. Lord and Lady Greystoke, outward bound on the barkentine *Fuwalda* from Freetown in the summer of 1888, are en route "to make a peculiarly delicate investigation of conditions" in a British West Coast colony when mutiny breaks out among the crew. Considering that the captain and his mates are forever emptying revolvers into the men and felling them with belaying pins, Burroughs' appraisal of the situation is dazzlingly understated: "There was in the whole atmosphere of the craft that undefinable something which presages disaster." The lid ultimately blows off, and a lamentable scene ensues: "Both sides were cursing and swearing in a frightful manner, which, together with the reports of the firearms and the screams and groans of the wounded, turned the deck of the *Fuwalda* to the likeness of a madhouse." Lord Greystoke, however, behaves with the coolness one expects of a British peer; through it all, he "stood leaning carelessly beside the companionway puffing meditatively upon his pipe as though he had been but watching an indifferent cricket match." After the mutineers have disposed of authority, the fate of the couple trembles briefly in the balance. Then Black Michael, the ringleader, intercedes for them and persuades his colleagues to maroon the Greystokes in a secluded spot. The speech transmitting this decision somehow recalls the rhetoric of Gilbert and Sullivan's magnanimous scalawags. "You may be all right," he explains kindly, "but it would be a hard matter to land you in civilization without a lot o' questions being asked, and none o' us here has any very convincin' answers up our sleeves."

To skim over the rest of the prologue, the blue bloods survive the immediate rigors of life in the bush; Greystoke, exhibiting a virtuosity rarely met with in castaways and almost never in the House of Lords, builds a stuccoed log cabin furnished with cozy appurtenances like bamboo curtains and bookcases, and his wife, materially aiding the story line, presents him with a male child. But all unbeknownst to the patrician pair, their hourglass is already running out. Her Ladyship, badly frightened by a marauding ape, expires on the boy's first birthday, and as her husband sits stricken at the deathbed, a band of apes bent on stealing his rifle invade the cabin and kill him. Among them is Kala, a female whose own babe has just been destroyed by the king of the tribe. Obeying what Burroughs reverently terms "the call of universal motherhood within her wild breast," and the even greater urgency for a gimmick to set the narrative rolling, she snatches up the English tot, deposits her lifeless one in its cradle, and streaks into the greenery. The blueprint is now technically complete, but the author, ever a man to juggle complications, contrives an extra, masterly touch. Since the cabin contains the schoolbooks from which the lad will learn to read eventually, as well as his father's diary—capriciously written in French—proving his identity, it must be preserved intact. The king ape, therefore, accidentally discharges Greystoke's gun and, fleeing in terror, slams the door shut. Burroughs may foozle his prose on occasion, but when it comes to mortising a plot, he is Foxy Grandpa himself.

It would serve no useful purpose to retrace the arduous youthhood and adolescence of Tarzan (whose name, incidentally, means "White-Skin," there being no equivalent for Greystoke in ape language), his sanguinary triumphs over a long roster of enemies like leopards, pythons, and boars, and his easy emergence as undisputed boss of the jungle. Superior heredity, of course, gives "the aristocratic scion of an old English house" a vast edge over his primitive associates. Thanks to the invaluable schoolbooks in the cabin, he instinctively learns to read and write—not without hardship, for, says Burroughs, "of the meaning and use of the articles and conjunctions, verbs and adverbs and pronouns, he had but the faintest and haziest conception." But he perseveres, and along with literacy come further civilized attributes. He bathes assiduously, covers his nakedness with pelts, and, out of some dim recess of his consciousness, produces a really definitive method of distinguishing himself from brute creation: "Almost daily, he whetted his keen knife and scraped and whittled at his young beard to eradicate this degrading emblem of apehood. And so he learned to shave—rudely and painfully, it is true—but, nevertheless, effectively." No reasonably astute reader needs to be told twice that when the hero of a popular novel, whether he is Willie Baxter or an ape man, starts shaving, a pair of mischievous blue eyes are right around the corner. However astute, though, no reader could possibly anticipate a simp of the proportions of Jane Porter, or the quartet of frowzy vaudeville stereotypes that now bumble into the picture.

The newcomers, it appears, are a party of treasure-seekers hailing from Baltimore, headed by an absent-minded pedagogue called Professor Archimedes Q. Porter, complete with frock coat and shiny plug hat. In his retinue are Samuel T. Philander, an elderly fusspot secretary straight from the pages of *Puck*; Esmeralda, a corpulent Negro maid aquiver with fear and malapropisms; his daughter Jane, whose beauty ravishes the senses; and, finally, Charley-horsing the long arm of coincidence, Tarzan's own cousin and the incumbent Lord Greystoke, William Cecil Clayton. They, too, have just been involved in a ship's mutiny—Burroughs' favorite literary calamity, evidently—and are now marooned in Tarzan's very parish. Using these piquant ingredients for all they are worth, the author hereupon proceeds to stir up the most delirious chowder of larceny, homicide, aboriginal passion, and haphazard skulduggery ever assembled outside the Newgate calendar. In all this, Tarzan plays the role of the Admirable Crichton, snatching each of the characters, in turn, from the jaws of death and, in-

evitably, turning Jane Porter's head. The section in which she betrays
her partiality for him is sheer poetry. Tarzan is putting the kayo on
Terkoz, a bull ape who has abducted Jane: "As the great muscles of
the man's back and shoulders knotted beneath the tension of his efforts,
and the huge biceps and forearm held at bay those mighty tusks, the
veil of centuries of civilization and culture was swept from the blurred
vision of the Baltimore girl. When the long knife drank deep a dozen
times of Terkoz's heart's blood, and the great carcass rolled lifeless
upon the ground, it was a primeval woman who sprang forward with
outstretched arms toward the primeval man who had fought for her
and won her. And Tarzan? He did what no red-blooded man needs
lessons in doing. He took his woman in his arms and smothered her
upturned, panting lips with kisses. For a moment Jane Porter lay there
with half-closed eyes. . . . But as suddenly as the veil had been withdrawn it dropped again, and an outraged conscience suffused her face
with its scarlet mantle, and a mortified woman thrust Tarzan of the
Apes from her and buried her face in her hands. . . . She turned upon
him like a tigress, striking his great breast with her tiny hands. Tarzan
could not understand it." If Tarzan, who was so intimately involved,
was baffled, you can imagine my own bewilderment, especially with
a donkey engine puffing in my ear. Had the yarn not been so compel-
ling and the chaise longue so comfortable, I would have abandoned
both, bearded the Baltimore Chamber of Commerce, and given them
my opinion of such a heartless flirt.

While one properly expects major characters as vital as Tarzan and
Jane to dominate the canvas, it would be grossly unfair to ignore the
figures in the background. Professor Archimedes Q. Porter and his
secretary carry the burden of the comic relief, and their sidesplitting
misadventures evoke chuckles galore. Herewith, for example, is the
Professor's tart rejoinder when Philander nervously informs him they
are being stalked by a lion: " 'Tut, tut, Mr. Philander,' he chided.
'How often must I ask you to seek that absolute concentration of your
mental faculties which alone may permit you to bring to bear the highest powers of intellectuality upon the momentous problems which naturally fall to the lot of great minds? And now I find you guilty of a
most flagrant breach of courtesy in interrupting my learned discourse
to call attention to a mere quadruped of the genus *Felis*. . . . Never, Mr.
Philander, never before have I known one of these animals to be permitted to roam at large from its cage. I shall most certainly report this
outrageous breach of ethics to the directors of the adjacent zoological

garden.' " Can you tie that? The poor boob's so absent-minded he
doesn't even realize he's in *Africa.* An equally rich humorous conceit
is Esmeralda, the maid, who is constantly "disgranulated" by all the
"gorilephants" and "hipponocerouses" about her. I doubt if Amos 'n'
Andy at their most inventive have ever surpassed her attempt to soothe
Jane at a moment of crisis: "Yas'm, honey, now you-all go right to
sleep. Yo' nerves am all on aidge. What wif all dese ripotamuses and
man eaten geniuses dat Marse Philander been a-tellin' about—laws, it
ain't no wonder we all get nervous prosecution."

Indeed it ain't, and while the subject of nerves is on the tapis, I suspect that at this point in the action Burroughs himself became a trifle
discombobulated. With two-thirds of the piece behind him, he still had
to unravel Tarzan's complex genealogy, resolve the love story, account
for the Professor's treasure (lost and found half a dozen times throughout), and return his puppets intact to everyday life. Accordingly, he
introduces a French cruiser to rescue the Baltimoreans and Clayton,
and, once they are safely over the horizon, begins untangling the labyrinthine threads that remain. An officer of the vessel, one D'Arnot, has
fallen into the clutches of some local cannibals; Tarzan saves the captive and, in return, is taught French, an accomplishment that enables
him to translate his father's diary and legally prove himself the real
Lord Greystoke. Armed with the proofs, he hurries to America to
claim his mate, but Burroughs is just ahead of him, piling up barriers
faster than Tarzan can surmount them. Before he can clasp Jane in his
arms, he is compelled to rescue her from a Wisconsin forest fire and
eliminate her current fiancé, a Scrooge who financed her father's expedition. The minor matter of the treasure is washed up with a check
for two hundred and forty-one thousand dollars, which, the ape man
fluently explains to Professor Porter, is its market value. And then,
as the lovers' last obstacle vanishes, the author, consummate magician
that he is, yanks a final bunny from his hat. Jane jilts Tarzan for his
cousin, William Cecil Clayton, and Tarzan, placing her happiness
above all, deliberately conceals his true identity. There may be scenes
of self-renunciation in Tolstoy that lacerate the heart, but none, I contend, as devastatingly bittersweet as the closing one between the two
Greystoke cousins: " 'I say, old man,' cried Clayton. 'I haven't had a
chance to thank you for all you've done for us. It seems as though you
had your hands full saving our lives in Africa and here. . . . We must
get better acquainted. . . . If it's any of my business, how the devil did
you ever get into that bally jungle?' 'I was born there,' said Tarzan

quietly. 'My mother was an Ape, and of course, she couldn't tell me much about it. I never knew who my father was.' "

Ordinarily, my fleeting sojourn in such an equatorial mishmash might have had no worse consequences than myopia and a pronounced revulsion from all noble savages thereafter. As luck would have it, though, the Venetian blind above me slipped its moorings as I finished the romance, and, doubtless overstimulated by Tarzan's gymnastics, I climbed up to restore it. Halfway through the process, the cornice gave way and I was left hanging by my fingernails from the picture molding that encircles the room. At this juncture, a certain fourteen-year-old busybody, who has no better means of employing his time than sending postals to shipowners, came snooping into the room. His pitiless gaze traveled slowly from my pendant form to his copy of *Tarzan of the Apes*. "Watch out, Buster, you'll strain your milk!" he cautioned. "Better leave that stuff to Weissmuller." Yes, sir, it's pretty disheartening. You lie on your back all day worrying about the junk your children read, you hang from moldings, and that's the thanks you get. It's regusting.

❧ NESSELRODE TO JEOPARDY

CITY CRACKS DOWN ON RESTAURANTS

IN HOLLANDAISE SAUCE CLEAN-UP

"The sauce is loaded with dynamite when carelessly prepared," a Health Department spokesman declared yesterday. "It has become one of the bureau's worst headaches. . . ."

Many temperamental chefs, it was learned, resent the Health Department's infringement on their culinary art. One chef, for example, refused to tell an inspector how he made the sauce because it was a "secret technique" that he had learned in France.

Several weeks later, five persons contracted food poisoning at the restaurant because of the hollandaise. The Health Department then demanded to know the chef's secret and found that his technique consisted of straining the sauce through a cheesecloth bag that must be squeezed with the hands.—*The Times.*

WHENEVER I turn over the whole grotesque affair in my mind, trying to rationalize the baffling complex of events that overtook me on the French Riviera this autumn, I always ask myself the same questions. What would have happened if Destiny, unpredictable jade, had drawn my laggard feet to some hotel other than the Villa Heliotrope? What if Anglo-Saxon shyness had sealed Colin Rentschler's lips and he had not impulsively come to the aid of a fellow-American in hazard? Would I ever have met that elegant assassin, Colonel Firdausi of the Turkish secret police, or cowered in the hold of a rusty Greek steamer bound for the Piraeus, or given chase at midnight to a music-hall juggler over the roofs of Montparnasse? In short, why should I, timid recluse, have been wantonly singled out for a supporting role in a nightmare as fantastic as the riddle of the cheesecloth bag, a problem to shame the wildest conceits of an Eric Ambler or a Carol Reed? And why—except that it is highly traditional—do I ask these questions all over again when I should be getting on with my story?

To begin at the beginning, I'd been down at Fez, in North Africa, all summer, working on a book of favorite recipes of famous people like

Tennessee Williams, Paul Bowles, Truman Capote, and Speed Lamkin, and my nerves were at sixes and sevens. I felt completely drained, used up; I'd pretty well exhausted my emotional bank balance doing the necessary research, and I knew it was touch and go unless I immured myself in some quiet pied-à-terre where I could slough off superficialities and organize my material. I shan't burden you with tedious autobiographical details, but perhaps I ought to explain that my people (poor bourgeois dears) left me a goodish bit of money. Praise be to Allah—and the automobile wax my father invented—I don't have to fret excessively about the sordid aspects of life, and hence I've applied myself to living graciously, which I do think is all that matters, really. I mean I sometimes wonder if a properly chilled Gibson or a superb *coq au vin* isn't basically more important than these grubby wars and revolutions everyone's being so hopelssly neurotic about. Not that money's actually vital to my existence, mind you; one art I've mastered is how to make do with the absolute minimum. Given fair seats at the ballet, half a dozen friends with country houses from whom I can scrounge weekends, a few custom-tailored suits, some decent hand-lasted shoes—it's weakness, I know, but I'm fixated on good leather—and three months a year at Montreux or Bordighera, and I can live in a hole in the wall at the Crillon and rub along on a gigot and a crisp salad.

Anyhow, I'd finally fetched up at the Villa Heliotrope, a modest little establishment on the Estérel coast west of Cannes, and everything was proving utterly ideal. The cuisine wasn't too repugnant, and if *Madame la Patronne* occasionally used overmuch musk on her embonpoint, she at least rationed it in her seasoning. Well, one evening I came in to dinner with a truly pagan appetite (ardent sun-worshiper that I am, I'd spent the entire day on the *plage*, baking a glorious golden brown). I had just dispatched Madame's creditable *rôti* and was attacking the dessert when the chap at the next table cleared his throat.

"Easy does it," he said abruptly. "I wouldn't bolt that Nesselrode if I were you."

"Why the devil not?" I snapped, glaring around at him. Bolting's sort of a sacrament with me, I suppose, and I didn't much fancy the highhanded line he'd taken.

"Because it's lumpy," he said. "They forgot to strain it." I tasted a soupçon and found he was right. I turned back for another look at my neighbor. His lean, dark face showed good bone structure, and there was something about his trench coat and the gravy on his hat that bespoke the inspector of a metropolitan health department.

"Look here," I said, mystified. "You knew that pudding was lumpy?"

"It's my business to know things like that, friend," he said with an opaque smile. As he rose and passed me, a card fluttered down beside my plate. It bore the legend "Colin Rentschler," and, below, "Inspector, New York Health Department." I was pretty thoughtful the rest of the meal. Something curious was shaping up, and while I'm not especially intuitive, I felt Colin Rentschler might have some connection with it.

I was seated on the terrace that evening, sipping a final pousse-café before turning in, when his loose-jointed figure settled into the adjoining chair. After a rather watchful silence, he made some inconsequential remark about the écru-colored sky's portending the advent of the mistral, the dry northerly wind characteristic of Provence. "Odd écru-colored sky, that," he observed. "Shouldn't wonder if it portends the advent of the mistral, the dry northerly wind characteristic of Provence."

"Yes," I agreed. "Sinister shade, isn't it? It reminds me of—well, of hollandaise sauce that's gone a trifle bad."

I heard the sharp, sudden intake of his breath, followed by a little click as he expelled it. When he spoke again, it was in a tight, strangled whisper that put shudders up my spine. "Then you know," he said. He glanced quickly over his shoulder and leaned forward, his eyes merciless as snails. "Listen. Pierre Moustique has been seen in Istanbul."

"Good God!" I murmured. Like everyone else, of course, I knew that New York gourmets were in a grip of terror due to a wave of hollandaise poisoning, and that Moustique, the chef who had betrayed his secret technique of squeezing the sauce through a cheescloth bag with his bare hands, had escaped to Canada in a hamper of towels, but in the shimmering heat of Morocco I had lost touch with later developments, and my allusion to the evening sky had been made in all innocence. Before I could extricate myself, nonetheless, Fate, in the guise of a health inspector, had altered my future with a single decisive stroke.

"It's incredible—" Rentschler shrugged—"but then so is life. Last Thursday afternoon, Anna Popescu, a Moldavian seamstress in the Kadikoy quarter of Istanbul bearing a Nansen passport, reported that a chef closely resembling Moustique had approached her to repair a rent in a cheesecloth bag, offering ninety piasters. When she hesitated, he fled." His harsh voice stabbed at me, insistent as the cicadas in the Mediterranean night. "Schneider, until we can lay Moustique by the heels and analyze that bag which its poisoned meshes spell finis for unwary epicures, death will lurk in every frond of broccoli. I have two tickets on the morning plane for Istanbul. Are you the man to share a desperate adventure?"

I picked up my glass and, twirling the stem meditatively, swallowed it in a single gulp. A mad, foolhardy errand, I thought, and still the challenge to gamble for consummate stakes awoke a tocsin in my blood. I spat out a spicule of glass, arose, and extended my hand. "Done and done, Rentschler," I said coolly. "I've always taken my liquor mixed and my peril neat, and I see no reason to switch now. Next stop, the Golden Horn!"

Colonel Firdausi, deputy director of the Turkish secret police, hoisted a polished cordovan boot to the edge of his desk and, extracting the monocle from his eye, carefully scraped a bit of *shish kebab* from the sole. As he dusted his delicate, saurian hands with a handkerchief strongly redolent of attar of roses, motes of halvah danced in the slanting beam of sunlight above his head.

"This is a very interesting tale you tell me, gentlemen," he said with a smile. Colonel Firdausi's smile could have refrigerated a whole chain of Turkish frozen-food stores. "But I do not see precisely why you come to me. Surely you do not imply Pierre Moustique is still in Istanbul?"

"I imply that and more." Rentschler's left forefinger traced what was seemingly an idle pattern on the dusty arm of his chair, and then I realized with a start that he was scribbling a message to me. "Watch this man's mouth," it read, in Italian. "It is willful, sensual, that of a sybarite who will not cavil at resorting to violence if he is bilked." My colleague chuckled thinly, his steady gaze meeting Firdausi's square. "I imply, my dear Colonel, that he is in this selfsame room at the moment."

"You cease to amuse me, Monsieur." The Turkish official rapped the bell before him peremptorily. "The interview is ended. My secretary—"

"One second," cut in Rentschler. "Have you ever heard of the Club Libido, in Pera? No? Allow me to refresh your memory. The principal chanteuse at the Libido is Marie Farkas, a naturalized Transylvanian traveling under a League of Nations passport."

"Neither you nor Marie could possibly hope to surprise me," returned Firdausi icily. "I have been sleeping with the lady fifteen years."

"And therefore enjoy considerable seniority over me," admitted Rentschler. "Nevertheless, she has been fickle enough to confide that on your last two nuptial flights you wore a chef's cap, with the name of Pierre Moustique inscribed on the headband in indelible pencil."

"Inconstancy, thy name is woman," reflected Firdausi. "Ah, well, there is no use dissembling with such adversaries." Reaching into his tunic, he withdrew a green cheesecloth bag and tossed it pettishly on the blotter. "Is this what you are looking for?" As Rentschler's hand shot forward, it struck the ice-blue barrel of the Colonel's automatic. "Tchk, tchk, impetuous boy," chided Firdausi. "Be so good, both of you, as to lace your fingers over your heads. Thank you. Now, Messieurs, exposition is wearisome, so I will be succinct."

"I will be succincter," Rentschler put in. "The real Colonel Firdausi is reposing at this instant in the Bosporus, in a burlap sack weighted with stale nougat. You are about to bind us back to back in a similar pouch and deposit us alongside him, as a warning to meddlers not to interfere in matters that do not concern them. Need I point out, though, Moustique, that you cannot possibly hope to get away with it?"

"Of course not," agreed the other, withdrawing from his tunic a capacious burlap sack. "Still, in the brisk interplay of Near Eastern intrigue, these little—ah—involutions are mandatory. *Au 'voir*, gentlemen."

Forty-five minutes later, trussed up in the sack, we were jolting in a dray over the cobblestones fringing the waterside. Despite our extreme discomfort and the danger confronting us, however, my companion exhibited no hint of the disquiet that pervaded me. Listening to his tranquil comparison of the respective merits of the pickles obtainable at Lindy's and the Russian Tea Room, one might easily have imagined him in his own club. At length, my endurance crumbled.

"Dash it all, man!" I burst forth. "Here's one pickle your precious department won't get us out of!"

"No, but Victor Hugo will," he said evenly. "I take it you've read *Les Misérables*?"

"This is hardly the time for a literary quiz," I interjected.

"You will recall," said Rentschler imperturbably, "that at an equally crucial pass Jean Valjean confounded Papa Thenardier and his gang by sawing through his bonds with a watch spring concealed in a penny. Tug manfully at your wrists." I complied, and, to my stupefaction, found myself liberated. The next thing I knew, Rentschler and I were racing through a maze of warehouses and cranes; I remember a ship's gangway clangorous with roustabouts shifting cargo, a lightning descent into a labyrinth of hatches, and, over the bellow of the siren, my colleague's unruffled explanation that we were stowaways aboard the *Thessalonian Welterweight*, bound for the Piraeus and Trieste. Actually, we never went to either; a few hours later, Rentschler nudged me and we stole back on land. The whole thing had been a clever feint, for, as he pointed out, nobody was chasing us and there was no reason to slip out of the country illicitly. That night, seated in the aircraft droning toward London, I dully wondered what fresh complications lay in wait for us. But Fate and the stewardess, a shapely Philadelphian named Dougherty traveling under a nylon bust support, gave me back only an inscrutable smile.

Thin fingers of fog drifted across the West India Dock Road, tracing an eerie filigree across the street lamp under which Rentschler and I stood shivering in our mackintoshes. From time to time, almond-eyed devotees of the poppy, furtively hugging poppy-seed rolls, slid past us in their bast shoes, bent on heaven knows what baleful missions. For more than three hours, we had been breathlessly watching the draper's shop across the way, and I still had no clue as to why. Rentschler, shrewd judge of human foibles that he was, must have sensed my perplexity, for at last he broke silence.

"In the split second you saw that bag of Moustique's, Schneider," he queried, "did any thought occur to you?"

"Why, yes," I said, surprised. "I remember thinking there was only one shop in Europe that handles cheesecloth of that type—Arthur Maggot's Sons, in the West India Dock Road. But I still can't fathom why we've spent three hours casing it."

"No particular reason," he rejoined. "It's just the kind of patient, plodding labor the public never gives one credit for in this profession. Come on, let's move in."

Bartholomew Maggot shrugged his vulpine shoulders irascibly and, applying a pinch of Copenhagen snuff to his nostril, opened the cash register and sneezed into it. A half hour's questioning had merely aggravated his normally waspish temper, and it was dishearteningly plain that we had reached an impasse. Rentschler, notwithstanding, refused to yield.

"This man who asked you to appraise his cheesecloth bag yesterday," he persisted. "You say he was hooded and smelled of attar of roses, but surely you must have noticed something unusual about him."

"No, sir, I did not," growled the draper. "Wait a bit, though, there *was* something. His lapel had a few grains of rice powder on it—the sort those French music-hall artistes wear."

"You've a sharp pair of eyes in your head, Maggot," complimented the inspector. "It's a pity we don't know where they came from."

"Why, this one came from Harrod's," explained Maggot, removing it. "It's glass, as you see, and has a little Union Jack in it. The other—"

"No, no, the grains," Rentschler interrupted testily. "Haven't you any idea which music hall uses that type of powder?"

"Let me see," said Maggot slowly. "The cove was carrying a theatrical valise with the name of Pierre Moustiqu , Bobino Théâtre, Rue de la Gaîté, Paris, France, painted on it in white letters, but I didn't really pay much mind."

"Humph," muttered Rentschler. His quick, deductive mind had caught something of importance in the other's words. "A very good evening to you, Mr. Maggot, and now, Schneider, to Paris *en grande vitesse*. Are you hungry? I think I can promise a ragout spiced with melodrama and served piping hot." I have often thought the world lost a major poet when Colin Rentschler joined the New York Health Department.

The mingled scent of caporal, cheap perfume, and garlic hung like a pall over the motley audience jamming the stalls of the Bobino, the Left Bank's most popular vaudeville. A succession of weight-lifters, trained dogs, diseuses, and trick cyclists had displayed their enchantments, and now, as the curtain rose on the final turn and M. l'Inconnu, the masked juggler, strode into the glare of the footlights, my heart began beating like a trip hammer. Those delicate, saurian hands, the heavy odor of attar of roses—I racked my memory vainly, trying to recollect where I had met them before. A buzz of excited speculation rose from the patrons surrounding us; humor ran rife that l'Inconnu was an unfrocked chef from New York, a quondam Turkish police official, a recent arrival from Limehouse, but none knew for sure. Yet some sixth sense told me that Rentschler, his hawk's profile taut in the darkness beside me, was close to the answer.

"*Messieurs et dames!*" The guttural voice of Pierre Moustique suddenly set my every nerve atingle. "I now attempt a feat to dizzy the imagination, keeping *trois boules* [three balls] suspended in the air simultaneously!" From the depths of his cape, he brought forth a green cheesecloth bag and spun three mothballs into swift rotating motion.

Rentschler sprang up with a choked cry. "*Gobe-mouche* that I am! Blockhead!" he exclaimed. "Don't you see, Schneider? That's why the hollandaise laid those diners low—he used that very bag to squeeze the sauce, indifferent to the fact that it had contained mothballs! Seal the exits! Stop that man!" But it was too late; with a snarled imprecation, Moustique sprang toward the wings. In the shrill hubbub that ensued, I inexplicably found myself dancing a java with a comely grisette; then Rentschler, flinging people aside like ninepins, was pulling me through a skylight and we were hurtling across the rooftops after our quarry. In reality, my associate explained as we hurtled, Moustique had left the Bobino in a cab, but protocol precluded our following him in any such mundane fashion.

"He's heading for the Ritz," panted the inspector. "A group of asparagus connoisseurs are holding their annual feed there tonight, which the columns of *Le Figaro* have been full of it for a week. Superfluous to add that if this blackguard, who is cooking for them under a nom de plume, compounds his lethal dressing, why the poor bastards will be stretched out in windrows. I've a pretty—good—hunch, though," he panted on, clearing the Rue du Cherche-Midi with a bound, "that we're about to tie a kink in his mayonnaise whip."

Well, we didn't. Two minutes afterward, Rentschler tripped over a loose gargoyle and dashed out his brains in the Quai Voltaire. I pressed on to the Ritz, but I must have crept in through the wrong dormer, because I wound up at a too, too marvelous gala at the Vicomtesse de Noailles'. Edith and Osbert and Sacheverell were there, and they gave me a simply divine recipe for my book. It's called Continental Upside-Down Chowchow, and here's what you do. You take a double handful of exotic locales . . .

CHEWIES THE GOAT BUT FLICKS NEED HYPO

IT APPEARS TO BE more than a rumor that *Variety*, that reliable and colorful barometer of show business, may shortly change its name. According to my source (a papaya-juice vender on West Forty-sixth Street, whose identity I cannot disclose for fear of reprisals), the editors plan, by the simple expedient of altering three letters, to rechristen their paper *Anxiety*, a title more suited to its contents these days. This decision, between ourselves, comes as no surprise to me. Every Wednesday of late, skimming through *Variety*'s picture grosses and film chatter, I have run into palpitations and anguish not normally aired outside the *American Journal of Orthopsychiatry*. To judge from these bedside reports, the movie business is clearly *in extremis*; bats and mice are daily replacing audiences in theaters across the land, cobwebs are forming on the ushers, and exhibitors, hysterically accusing television, politics, substandard product, and even sunspots, have succumbed to panic. The most Talmudic reasons have been adduced to explain the decline in the box office, and it was inevitable that before long some Hawkshaw would try to pin the rap on that old whipping boy, the human stomach.

By the human stomach, of course, I refer in a broad, generic sense to the goodies—the caramel popcorn, molasses chews, coconut bars, and similar delicacies—sold in cinema lobbies. The suspicion has been gaining ground among showmen, says *Variety*, that "the annoyance of other customers' munch-crunch and the emphasis some houses are putting on selling of sweets" underlie the crisis. It quotes in support a conversation overheard by a member of the Allied Theater Owners of Indiana. Four women sitting at the table next to him in a restaurant, he reported, "all agreed with one of the ladies, who said very emphatically that her family never attended the ————— theater any more because they were tired of all the efforts made there to sell concessions, all the people in the audience munching during the show, and, most of all, having to sit through advertising trailers telling about how delicious were the concession-stand wares. Is it possible that theater-lobby merchandising can be a factor why people are staying away from the movies, and is it worth a little restudy?"

Restudy, if I may make so bold, is not only indicated here; it is downright mandatory. The plain truth is that the Allied Theater Owners of Indiana, and exhibitors generally, are staggering under a tremendous burden of mistaken, self-imposed guilt. As their patrons dwindle, keening about the pressures exerted on them to purchase sweets, the poor simps neurotically look inward for the reason instead of westward. The real culprit, I submit, is Hollywood itself. The industry has been locked too long in its ivory tower, too long preoccupied with artistic considerations better left to highbrows like Johnny Ruskin or Walt Pater. What the situation cries out for is pictures that will tell a gripping story and at the same time subtly sell the eatables in the lounge. With the aid of a small hand loom, I have woven a few necessary elements into an action-packed, down-to-earth yarn that may serve as a model, appealing to the gustatory as well as the visual instinct. It may not wheedle customers into the show shop, but at least it will act as a tourniquet.

We fade in on the porte-cochere of a mansion ablaze with lights, and, as sleek motors laden with impeccably groomed men of aristocratic visage and women garbed in the *dernier cri* from Paris disgorge their human freight, establish that this is the home of Monica, Lady Beltravers, arbiter of Bombay society. Monica, an Irene Dunne-type chatelaine that is the very essence of the chicly poised British gentlewoman, loiters on the stoop greeting her guests. "Sir Cyprian Chetwynd—what a surprise!" she exclaims cordially to one imperious, hawk-nosed oldster as he alights from his equipage. "I certainly never expected the Home Secretary himself at my ball, crowning event of the social season albeit it is!" To another arrival, a swarthy potentate in whose turban glows a single magnificent ruby, she observes laughingly, "Well, Hara Singh, I guess we will not be having to press our crystal chandelier into service, now that the Star of Assam is shedding its beam on the courtly throng!" From hints like the foregoing, it is blueprinted that her Ladyship's annual rout is the smartest affair in the Punjab, and that even the Viceroy would count himself lucky to get the nod from her. Monica, the cynosure of all eyes, wears on her queenly head the famous Beltravers tiara, and as we truck indoors with her through the assemblage, we garner numerous startled reactions. (The reactions are startled not because she is wearing the tiara on her head, where it should be, but because of its splendor.) Everybody thinks she is goofy to display so costly a bauble, for is it not an open secret that Tony Pickering, the most elusive international-society jewel thief in the Empire, is somewhere in the area, pledged to steal it from under the fair owner's nose? Monica, notwithstanding, snaps her pretty fingers at the ravens who croak disaster, graciously urging them to sample the lavish feed arrayed on the sideboard—turkey, tongue in aspic, slaw, and suchlike viands. And right here, without slackening pace, is an ideal spot to slip in an offbeat allusion to the comestibles available to moviegoers in the lobby.

"Bless me, Monica, what a toothsome collation," remarks one of the dowagers, enviously scanning it through her lorgnette.

"Thanks, Baroness," Lady Beltravers replies. "And, speaking of matters edible, the fans watching this need not fall prey to the green-eyed monster, for adjacent to their chairs they will lamp a pleasing selection of mint drops, chocolate creams, and candied apples to beguile themselves stomach-wise." Needless to say, I am not writing dialogue, just spitballing to indicate how smoothly the pitch blends in with the action.

To pick up our story thread: Unsuspected by the merrymakers, Tony Pickering, a debonair figure in flawless tails (Randolph Scott), saunters nonchalantly amid the waltzing couples. The Beltravers tiara is almost within his grasp. Suddenly, he comes face to face with Sandra Thrale (Greer Garson), the second-most-elusive society jewel thief in the Empire. A sardonic situation, fraught with boffs—two devil-may-care tricksters bent on the same perilous mission. Who will emerge victor? The lovers (for so they soon prove to be, despite their mutual antagonism) strike a bargain, snatch the prize in some ingenious fashion as yet to be devised, and show their pursuers a clean pair of heels. Sprinkled through the chase I see a couple of knockabout Hindu comics, on the order of Karl Dane and George K. Arthur, whose uproarious antics constantly land them in hot water and reap a rich harvest of laffs. This concludes the first sequence, a high-octane mixture of suspense, comedy, and romance guaranteed to keep people on the edge of their seats but still not allow them full mobility.

Sidi-Bel-Abbès, headquarters of the French Foreign Legion. Sand . . . heat . . . primitive passions fanned into flame by a word, a look. Into this port of nameless men drifts the flotsam of many races, asking only one thing—to forget. And with it, seeking salvation under the remorseless African sun, has come Tony Pickering. He and Sandra, after a senseless quarrel in Rome, during which she cast the tiara into the Tiber in a fit of pique, have broken. We iris down on him idling through the bazaars shortly before his regiment leaves for El Kébir, a remote desert outpost. A vivid background and a perfect opportunity to insinuate a timely message to the savages out front.

"Look, *mon capitaine*," a merchant whines, plucking at Tony's sleeve. "Splendid fresh figs, succulent as a Bedouin maid."

"Yes, and just as tricky," comments Pickering acidly. "That's where folks buying peanuts in their neighborhood flicks have the jump on us creatures of the silver screen. Those tasty goobers, warranted bacteria-free, speed directly from the roaster into sanitized glassine bags and thence to grateful palates. Boy, I could eat a slew of them." In other words, rather than hit the patrons over the head with a crass commercial, we actually use it to further the narrative. From now on, every man, woman, and child in the building is psychologically primed to rush out and give his taste buds a treat, except that the action is moving so fast he dassn't tear himself away.

We now deliver a surprise twist, a terrific sock that nobody but a clairvoyant could anticipate. In the ordinary scenario, the next scene would portray El Kébir beleaguered by tribesmen; Tony and brutal Sergeant Lepic (Brod Crawford), the only survivors in the fort, have propped their dead comrades on the parapet with rifles in their hands to hoodwink the attackers when a relief column led by Sandra (who has followed her swain unbeknownst to Algeria) raises the siege. Instead of this tepid denouement, which would merely generate yawns, we dissolve to a hunting lodge in the Canadian Rockies, where Sandra's wealthy father (Charles Coburn) has taken her to cure her infatuation for Tony. Since their spat in Rome, the girl has paid her debt to society and become a brilliant woman psychiatrist, a leader in her profession. Yet—irony of ironies—she, who brings happiness to others, is denied it herself, for Cupid has laid waste her heart. She cannot decide between Tony, now a world-famed construction engineer, and Jim Stafford (John Wayne), New York's most outstanding criminal lawyer. As father and daughter breakfast in their mountain retreat, unaware that a consuming forest fire rages toward them, the kindly old millionaire is concerned anent her birdlike appetite.

"You haven't eaten a crumb, sweet," Thrale chides her. "Try one of these speckled beauties which I captured it with rod and reel outside our door this morning."

"They *are* scrumptious, Daddy," she makes wistful reply, "but you'll never know bliss till you tackle Frosticles, the jet-powered ice-cream sensation." Thrale's curiosity is piqued, as anyone's would be, and he inquires where the confection may be obtained, whereupon Sandra enlightens him. The scene can be made doubly effective by dispatching candy-butchers down the aisle on cue, shouting "Frosticles!" They should, however, be cautioned against shouting so loud that the audience loses the thread. Once that happens, the jig is up.

The framework of the story being elastic, we now have two possibilities to milk for a climax. In one, Tony and Jim, who have renounced their careers to be near Sandra and are loggers in a lumber camp close by, fight a sensational watery duel for her hand with peaveys. The flames soon bring them to their senses and, good-naturedly laying aside their rivalry, they race to save the trapped pair, but they arrive too late. Since this line is a little on the defeatist side, it might be better to develop the other, a device that gives the plot a neat switch. We lap-dissolve to a primitive raft becalmed in the South Pacific and plant that Tony, Jim, and four Norwegian buddies have all but given up hope for the success of their expedition. Tony has staked his reputation as a world-famous anthologist to prove that certain old-time Peruvians migrated to Tahiti on a raft made of balsam logs. The gallant sextet's provisions have run short, and in his delirium each man dreams longingly of his favorite dish on terra firma. If only he could feel the icy trickle of a cola drink between his parched lips, muses Tony, or nibble the delectable taffy that even the humblest filmgoer has at his beck and call. The various dainties pass in review in balloons over his head, to hammer the point home to the most obtuse. And then we belt into a sizzling washup. A typhoon strikes the frail craft, the seafarers are drenched to the bone, and one of the Norwegians is revealed to be Sandra, who has renounced her psychiatric career to be near Tony. As they joyfully nestle in each other's arms, the cry of "Polynesia ho!" echoes from the yardarm. Tony's scientific thesis is vindicated, Jim sportingly acknowledges him the better man, and we squeeze on a tag wherein the couple sails homeward to the strains of "Aloha Oe." By then, the projectionist can breeze right into "Coming Attractions," for the patrons will be streaking toward the lobby to gorge themselves or apply for refunds, as the case may be.

Well, there it is—no *Intolerance* or *Gone with the Wind*, I grant you, but a nice, sound program film that'll hold up its end on any double bill and yield a good many TV residuals after the run is finished. I've even written a score for it, containing half a dozen songs of "Hit Parade" caliber, and if Hammerstein's fee is excessive, I'll throw in a hatful of lyrics for good measure. The main thing is to release it pronto and get rid of all that glucose in the lobby before the mice get at it. You don't want sagebrush growing in your bathtub, do you, Mr. Selznick?

❦ *PERSONNE ICI EXCEPT US CHICKENS*

YES, IT WAS FANTASTIC, inconceivable, illogical, but no more so than lots of things that happen nowadays. One sunny forenoon along about the middle of March, the man whose teeth I brush every morning (although there is less and less left to brush of late) was seated on the top step of a country post office in eastern Pennsylvania, immersed in a recent issue of *Harper's Bazaar*. It was a peaceful scene and one that would have quickened the step of any painter—the feathery pale green of the willows mirrored in the placid bosom of the canal, the darker green of the man's face suspended above the magazine, the rainbow pastel of steam escaping from his nostrils as he warmed to its pages. I had just skimmed the Paris openings and was sampling an essay on estrogenic face creams when Rufe Hillpot slid down beside me. Rufe is a fibrous little poultryman of sixty-odd whose solvency is as questionable as that of Prudential Life and who has forgotten more about baby chicks than *Harper's Bazaar* will ever know. Not that this sleek publication ordinarily concerns itself with anything so mundane, but spread out on the page before me was a photograph of seven cheeping Leghorn chicks pecking straw, seductively captioned "And Even the Chickens Work for Beauty."

"What's that book?" demanded Rufe, professional curiosity finally conquering his deep-rooted conviction that anything in print is a ruse to extract money from the unwary. I told him it was a gazette of the bon ton chiefly devoted to feminine fashion and Milady's loveliness. "You read that?" he asked with a quick, suspicious glance. "Why?"

"Well—er—I like to look at the patterns," I said lamely, and then flushed scarlet. "I mean my wife's in the garment trades—that is, she trades one garment for another—" Fortunately, Rufe's interest had shifted to the photograph of the chicks, and I hastily followed up the advantage. "Listen to this, Rufe," I said with a deep, booming laugh that scotched any hint of androgyny. "Right up your alley." I read off the caption to him in a manly bass. " 'All Paris is talking about a new beauty product called Retzoderme that is supposed to be death on wrinkles. "It comes from chickens," women scream to each other over

501

the lunch table, and so it does, for its manufacturers call it an embryonic juice extracted from eggs at the moment when the embryo's cells are reproducing most rapidly. It is sealed in glass ampoules and rushed, fresh, to the lady's dressing table. Parisiennes swear that they can see results after only a few days' use, especially on the crepy skin of the neck. The Leghorn farm and laboratory where the product is made is on the outskirts of Paris near the Forest of Marly. And there we photographed these baby chicks destined for a long career of egg-laying solely in the interests of beauty. Sorry, there's no Retzoderme in America—as yet.' "

"You know," remarked Rufe, thoughtfully rubbing his grizzled chin, "if a feller played his cards right, that could turn into a nice sideline."

"Darn tooting," I said, humoring him. "A hatchery the size of yours, he'd be on Easy Street in no time. Of course, he'd have to nip over to the old country and see how they do it."

"You hit the nail on the head, son," said Rufe. "When do we start?"

"Now, hold your horses, Rufe," I said indulgently. "You don't really believe this works, do you?"

"Why not?" he snapped. "Says so in the paper, don't it?"

"Sure, sure," I said, "but you've got to understand about the cosmetic industry." I made a short, incisive talk, not one word of which he heard, explaining how the journalistic peony thrives in the rich humus of publicity and advertising, and, at the end of it, reluctantly consented to lend him the magazine overnight. There was a feverish glint in his eye when I dropped him off at his barn, and I did not like the glib *"Oui, m'zoo"* with which he acknowledged my parting injunction to stick to his last.

Early the next morning, as I was cross-pollinating the ageratum (I always like to cross-pollinate the ageratum before the linnets get into it), Rufe excitedly sped up the lane in his Winton Six and collared me. His kin had discussed the commercial potentialities of the rejuvenator and were prepared to underwrite an immediate trip abroad to scout its validity and production technique. They felt, furthermore, that if I could be persuaded to accompany Rufe, my familiarity with France would be invaluable in smoothing his way.

"Won't cost you a dime," he said forcefully. "All expenses paid—in a thing as big as this, a man can't afford to be a piker. Just say the word and I'll phone down to Philly for the plane tickets."

"Wait a minute, friend," I protested. "I wouldn't mind a week or two in Paris, but I've got a family to think of."

"It'd be a marvelous rest for them while you're gone," he pointed out coaxingly. "Tell you what, I'll throw in a Maggy Rouff ensemble for the Missis. How's that?"

"You're certainly picking up the idiom fast," I commented.

"I always keep abreast of the times," Rufe said coolly. "Well, what's the verdict—yes or no?"

"Jeekers!" I began, my thoughts in a whirl. "You act as if this were a trip to Allentown. You'd have to get a passport and—"

Rufe looked over his shoulder at a pair of robins scrutinizing us narrowly from a nearby herbaceous border and lowered his voice. "I know a Red in the State Department who can fix anything," he confided. "Now, how much applejack will we need?"

The task of justifying a spontaneous trip overseas to my wife was not easy, but once she grasped the importance of our errand and the magnitude of the stakes involved, her misgivings vanished. The realization that she would have a free hand with the household chores, the dishwashing and scrubbing that I had selfishly appropriated as my special domain, more than compensated for the crêpes Suzette and vintage champagne I was slated to enjoy. Chief among the problems confronting Rufe and me in the hurly-burly of leave-taking was the question of wardrobe. It was my colleague's opinion, and I heartily concurred, that our native overalls and galluses would excite derision in the *beau monde*; we wished, understandably, to mingle inconspicuously on soigné levels without the imputation of "hayseed" being thrown at us. I therefore procured, after some searching, a couple of Prince Albert coats and silk toppers with conical crowns, of the sort worn by those legendary stereotypes, Alphonse and Gaston. The effect was Frenchy in the extreme, and it was obvious from the deference with which everyone at Idlewild gave way to us that we would have no difficulty in passing as *flâneurs* just off the Grands Boulevards.

Twenty-three hours after the moment the giant airliner soared up from the runway, Rufe and I were seated before Byrrh Cassis at Fouquet's, on the Champs-Elysées, our eyes drinking in the colorful panorama eddying about us. Ever and anon, saucy midinettes with hatboxes twinkled past, their silken ankles a target for the ardent glances of gendarmes twirling spiked mustaches and muttering appreciative ooh-la-las. Flower-sellers hawked their wares—i.e., sold their flowers— amid the undulating throng; furtive apaches from Montmartre in gooseneck sweaters and caps, bent on who knows what sinister missions, slunk by, now and then violently repulsing their importunate drabs; and everywhere on the terrace elegantly gowned women in the latest creations from Paris flaunted their plumage and shrilly exchanged beauty recipes.

"You don't see anything like this in Plumsteadville, do you?" I observed jokingly. "Keep your ears open, Rufe; if that chicken juice is really meritorious, these gals'll know the score." Hardly had the words left my lips when I heard a high-pitched feminine voice behind me. *"Ça vient des poulets!"* it was screaming. "It comes from chickens! It's *merveilleux, épatant, incroyable!"* I nudged Rufe significantly and we craned around to obtain a better view of the speaker. She was a handsome *femme du monde* in her early forties, superbly hatted, gloved, and shod by the most exclusive couturiers of the Rue de la Paix, and every detail, from her heaving embonpoint down to her diavolo heels, was a testimonial to Gallic chic. She had distended the erstwhile crepy skin of her neck for the inspection of her companion, an equally modish lady, and was exhibiting the miraculous change wrought by the ampoule before them on the table. "But eet ees like suède, *votre peau* [your skin]!" the other woman exclaimed rapturously, unscrewing a watchmaker's glass from her eye. *"Ma foi,* this unparalleled extract of embryonic fowls should prove a boon to countless women which they are distraught by crow's-feet and similar inroads of senility!"

"You hear that?" whispered Rufe triumphantly. "I bet this is going on all over town, like the paper said." And, indeed, loath as I was to spring to conclusions, a circuit of various haunts of fashion—the Steam Room of the Ritz, Weber's, the Crémaillère, and the Ambassadeurs—corroborated his belief. Wherever smart society forgathered, the magic wrinkle-remover was the topic of the moment; Dior and Balenciaga, quick to sense a trend, had seized on poultry as the leitmotiv of their spring collections, and *Cracked Corn,* the nude revue at the Bal Tabarin, was in its eighth smash week. Satisfied that *Harper's Bazaar* had not exaggerated the furor caused by the cream, Rufe proposed that we address ourselves to the task of eliciting its formula. He was all for a bold frontal attack, suggesting that we invade the laboratory, lay our pasteboards on the table, and negotiate for American manufacturing rights. The time had now come, I felt, to reveal to my partner the fruit of certain inquiries I had been developing privately.

"Rufe," I said, choosing my words carefully, "you must first be apprised that the White Russian syndicate that controls this process—former Czarist officers and unscrupulous men, as you will shortly comprehend—has no earthly intention of relinquishing a secret worth, by conservative estimate, many millions of francs. Worse yet, by approaching them as you indicate, you will fall into the very trap they have prepared for you."

"What's that? What's that?" he exclaimed agitatedly. "Do they know we're here?"

"Know?" I permitted myself a thin smile. "They *lured* you here, man. What if I were to tell you that they printed that one special copy of *Harper's Bazaar*, with its caption designed to inflame your poultryman's cupidity, just to entice you away from Pennsylvania?"

"But—but I don't follow," Rufe faltered. "Why should they do that?"

"So they could buy your hatchery at a fraction of its value," I said. "They desperately needed your chicks and your reputation to capture the American market, and with a ruthlessness unmatched in modern criminal annals, they will stick at nothing to attain their ends. Here is a cable from your son, who fortunately did not yield to the blandishments of their agents and wired me in time."

"I knew there was suthin' fishy from the start," said Rufe slowly. "When did you cotton on to these sarpints?"

"When I detected one of their creatures tailing us from Orly airport," I replied. "This morning, while you were still in the arms of Morpheus, I drove to the Forest of Marly, entered the laboratory by forcing a sash, and established their guilt from the documents hidden in a disused autoclave."

"I'll teach those plausible Rooshians to trifle with a Yankee farmer," he declared, bristling like a turkey cock. "We're taking the next plane."

"Steady on, Rufe," I calmed him. "We can still turn the tables and get that formula, if you've nerve enough. Listen . . ."

Four hours later, the two of us crouched in the bedroom closet of a luxurious apartment on the Avenue Hoche tenanted by Gaby Delorme, the star of *Cracked Corn* and reigning toast of Paris. In a few terse whispers, I sketched in complexities I had hitherto withheld from my companion—how Grimalkin, head of the White Russian syndicate and Gaby's lover, had been deceiving the fair songstress with other women and how, by cleverly playing on her jealousy, I had influenced her to betray the formula to us.

"Why can't she betray it to us on the phone?" asked Rufe querulously. "What fer do we have to skulk in here like a passel of raccoons?"

"Sh-h-h!" I cautioned. "That's the way things are done over here." Applying my eye to the keyhole, I made out Grimalkin, tipsily sprawled on a chaise longue, downing repeated goblets of Pol Roger while the beauteous Gaby, in a revealing peignoir, murmured endearments in his ear. The Muscovite's tongue was loosened and it was manifest that he was on the point of divulging the information we sought when events took a singularly unexpected turn. A peremptory knock sounded at the bedroom door and Gaby sprang up, her face ashen.

"*Mon Doo*, my 'usband!" she gasped. "If 'e finds you 'ere, *chéri*, 'e weel keel you!"

"Name of a name!" exploded Grimalkin. "Why have I never heard of this husband before?"

"Ze exposition was too extensive to plant 'is existence," she hissed. " 'Ide queek—no, not under ze bed; in ze closet!" Before Rufe and I could scramble behind the racks of costly gowns and furs, the closet door flew open and Grimalkin landed in our midst. I clapped a hand over his mouth to prevent his crying out, but luckily the wine had fuddled his senses and after a brief, unavailing struggle he grew passive.

Aeons passed as we cowered there expecting momentary discovery and humiliation; then the door reopened softly and Gaby, in an expressive pantomime signifying that her husband was reassured, conducted Rufe and me to a waiting fiacre. What became of the sodden Grimalkin, I cannot state with certainty, though the fact that there was a second fiacre, waiting behind ours, spoke volumes for Gaby's resourcefulness. Indeed, eight or ten fiacres were standing by, and I wondered fleetingly what the rest of her closets contained, but in the bustle of departure I thought it best not to pry.

One week afterward, I sat again on the top step of our rural Pennsylvania post office, idly watching the willow fronds sway in the warm breeze as I waited for the mail to be sorted. The benign sunshine had wafted me into semi-consciousness when an object similar to a rolled-up periodical dropped into my lap. As I straightened up with a start, I descried a familiar figure dwindling in the distance.

"Hi there, Rufe!" I sang after him. "What's your hurry, stranger? I never see you around any more!" He shouted something evasive about the egg business taking up most of his time. "Say, look here!" I called, holding up the newly arrived *Harper's Bazaar*. "Here's the latest issue of that magazine! Don't you want to borrow it?" To my surprise, he broke into a run as I started toward him, and vanished across the fields. I still can't figure out his motive; probably associated me with some frustration in his past, but Lord knows what. I tell you, just try and fathom these country people. *Ils sont absolument biscuit.* (They're absolutely crackers.)

🌿 DE GUSTIBUS AIN'T WHAT DEY USED TO BE

A GIRL and the four walls she lives in can get mighty tired of each other. Especially in midwinter. Well, here are twenty-five transfusions which, with a minimum investment of time and money, will repay sparkling dividends. They're as effective as the dozen roses someone once sent you just for fun, as easy as a birthday telephone call. Most of them don't even demand that you roll up your sleeves.

1. Invest in eight small white pots of ivy to range on your window sills. 2. *Paint* a gaily fringed rug on a wooden floor. 3. Rent an original picture from a painting rental library. (Between $2 and $35 will let you live with a masterpiece for two months.) 4. Put a bowl of glittering goldfish on your coffee table. 5. Partition a room with fish-net running on a ceiling track. 6. Get a kitten. 7. Cover your throw pillows with polka-dot cotton—perhaps white dots on black, black dots on white—variously sized and spaced. 8. Get a mobile to grace your room with motion—or better, make one yourself. 9. Slip cover your couch in dark denim—navy, brown or charcoal, maybe—depending on your color scheme. 10. If your living room walls are plain —on a Sunday, wallpaper just one wall. 11. Give houseroom to a *tree* in a big wooden tub. 12. Paste golden notary seals in an all-over design on your white window shades. 13. Wallpaper the insides of your cabinets and drawers with a flower print. 14. Have a favorite drawing photostated up as big as they'll make it; then hang it on your wall. 15. Forget polishing forever and spray all your metal surfaces with a new plastic preservative. 16. Buy a new shower curtain—and make it SILLY. 17. Make a new tablecloth out of irresistible cotton yard goods. 18. Draw outline pictures of your kitchen utensils on the wall right where each should hang. 19. Dye your mother's white damask tablecloths in brilliant shades. If they're huge, cut the surplus up into squares and hem them for napkins. 20. Put silk fringe along the bottoms of window shades. 21. Get yards of fake leopard skin to throw over your studio couch. 22. Make a cork bulletin board. 23. Cover your lampshades in wallpaper to match your papered walls.

24. Find some cutlery boxes to keep your jewelry lucid in the drawers. 25. Invest in flowered china or glass doorknobs.

. . . And if you're still yearning for a change: Spend an evening by candlelight.

—*Glamour.*

SCENE: *A one-room apartment in Manhattan occupied by April Monkhood, a young career woman. At some time prior to rise, April and her four walls have tired of each other, and she has called in Fussfeld, a neighborhood decorator, to give the premises the twenty-five transfusions recommended above. Fussfeld, a lineal descendant of Brigadier General Sir Harvey Fussfeld-Gorgas, the genius who pacified the Sudan, has attacked the assignment with the same zeal that characterized his famous relative. He has placed at stage center a magnificent specimen of Bechtel's flowering crab, the boughs of which are so massive that it has been necessary to stay them with cables and turnbuckles. This has perforce complicated the problem of the fish-net partitions on their ceiling tracks, but, fortunately, most of these have ripped off and now depend from the branches, supplying a romantic effect akin to that of Spanish moss. What with the hodgepodge of damask, yard goods, fake leopard skin, floral wallpaper, silk fringe, and notary seals, it is difficult at first to distinguish any animate object. Finally, though, the eye picks out a rather scrawny kitten, licking its lips by an overturned goldfish bowl. A moment later, April Monkhood enters from the kitchenette, practically on all fours. She is a vivacious brownette in knee-hugging poltroons, with a retroussé nose which she wears in a horsetail. Behind her comes Fussfeld, a small, haggard gentleman with a monocle he affects for chic. However, since he is constantly losing it in the décor and scrabbling about for it, he fails to achieve any impressive degree of sang-froid.*

FUSSFELD (*dubiously*): I'm not so sure it's advisable, dusting spangles over the gas stove like that. The pilot light—

APRIL: Now, Mr. Feldpot, don't be an old fuss— I mean stop worrying, will you? It's gay, it's chintzy. It's a whiff of Mardi Gras and the storied Vieux Carré of New Orleans.

FUSSFELD (*with a shrug*): Listen, if *you* want to run down a fire escape in your nightgown, that's your privilege. (*looking around*) Well, does the job suit you O.K.?

APRIL: Mad about it, my dear—simply transported. Of course, it doesn't quite have a feeling of being lived in . . .

FUSSFELD: I'd sprinkle around a few periodicals, or a can of salted peanuts or so. Anyway, a place gets more homey after your friends drop around.

APRIL: Golly, I can't wait to have my housewarming. Can you imagine when people step off the dumbwaiter and see this room by candlelight?

FUSSFELD (*faintly*): You—er—you're hoisting them up here?

APRIL: How else? We'll be using the stairs outside to eat on.

FUSSFELD: M-m-m. I'm trying to visualize it.

APRIL: I thought of Basque place mats, two on each stair, and sweet little favors made of putty. Don't you think that would be amusing?

FUSSFELD: Oh, great, great. (*Produces a statement.*) I got everything itemized here except what you owe the paperhanger. When he gets out of Bloomingdale, he'll send you a separate bill.

APRIL (*frowning*): Sixteen hundred and ninety-three dollars. Frankly, it's a bit more than I expected.

FUSSFELD: Well, after all, you can't pick up this kind of stuff for a song. Those notary seals, for instance. We used nine dozen at fifty cents apiece. The guy at the stationery store had to witness each one.

APRIL: I know, but you list four hundred dollars for structural work.

FUSSFELD: We had to raise the ceiling to squeeze in the tree. The plumber was here three days changing the pipes around.

APRIL (*gaily tossing aside the bill*): Ah, well, it's only money. I'll mail you a check shortly.

FUSSFELD: No hurry—any time in the next forty-eight hours. (*carelessly*) You still work for the same concern, don't you?

APRIL: Certainly. Why?

FUSSFELD: In case I have to garnishee your pay. (*A knock at the door. April crosses to it, admits Cyprian Voles. The associate editor of a pharmaceutical trade journal, he is a rabbity, diffident young man with vague literary aspirations. He is at present compiling* The Pleasures of Shag, *an anthology of essays relative to smoking, which will contain excerpts from Barrie's* My Lady Nicotine, *Machen's* The Anatomy of Tobacco, *etc., and which will be remaindered within thirty days of publication.*)

CYPRIAN: Am I too early? You said six-thirty.

APRIL: Of course not, dear. Cyprian, this is my decorative-relations
counsel, Mr. Fussfeld—Mr. Voles.

FUSSFELD: Likewise. Well, I got to be running along, Miss Monkhood. About that check—

APRIL: Just as soon as my ship comes in.

FUSSFELD: I'll be studying the maritime news. (*Exits. Cyprian, meanwhile, has backed into a mobile of fish and chips suspended overhead and is desperately fighting to disengage it from his hat.*)

APRIL (*thirsting for approval*): Isn't the flat delectable? Have you
ever in your whole life seen anything so cozy?

CYPRIAN: Yes, it—it's stunning. It's really *you*—it captures the inner
essence—that is, the outer inwardness—

APRIL: You don't think it's overdone, do you?

CYPRIAN: Overdone? Why, it's stark! You couldn't omit one detail
without damaging the whole composition.

APRIL (*hugging him*): You old sorcerer. You know just the words to
thaw a woman's heart. Now, I've an inspiration. Instead of going
out for dinner, let's have powdered snails and a bottle of Old
Rabbinical under the crab.

CYPRIAN (*fingering his collar*): Er—to tell you the truth, I—I find it
a little close in here. You see, I fell into a grain elevator one time
when I was small—

APRIL: Nonsense, it'll be heaps of fun. I loathe those big, expensive
restaurants. Sit ye doon while I mix us an apéritif. (*She thrusts
him backward onto the studio couch, almost decapitating him
with a guy wire, then whisks a bottle from a cabinet.*) Who do
you suppose called me today? My husband, of all people.

CYPRIAN: Hanh? You never told me you were married.

APRIL: Oh, Sensualdo and I've been separated for years. He's a monster—an absolute fiend.

CYPRIAN: Is he a Mexican?

APRIL: Uh-uh—Peruvian. One of those insanely jealous types, always
opening your mail and accusing you of carrying on with his
friends. He tried to stab a man I was having a Coke with. That's
what broke up our marriage.

CYPRIAN: W-where is he now?

APRIL: Right here in New York. His lawyers are trumping up evidence
for a divorce— What's the matter?

CYPRIAN (*he has risen and sways dangerously*): I feel faint . . . spots
before the eyes . . .

APRIL: Lie down. I'll get you some water—

CYPRIAN (*panting*): No, no. I've got to get out of here. The walls are closing in. (*He becomes entangled in a pile of mill-end remnants and flounders hopelessly. Simultaneously, a peremptory knock at door.*)

VOICE (*off scene*): Open up there!

CYPRIAN (*in an agonized whisper*): Who's *that*?

APRIL: I don't know, unless—

ANOTHER VOICE (*off scene*): Open the door, you tramp, else we break eet down!

APRIL (*biting her lip*): Damnation. It's Sensualdo. (*grabbing Cyprian's arm*) Quick, into the bathroom—no, wait a second, stand over there! (*She snatches a handful of notary seals from a shelf, and, moistening them, begins pasting them at random on his face.*)

CYPRIAN (*struggling*): What are you doing?

APRIL: Sh-h-h, never mind—help me! Stick them on your clothes—anywhere! (*Pandemonium at the door as Sensualdo attempts to kick in the panels. April, in the meantime, has found a heavy iron ring—conveniently included in the props by the stage manager—and now arranges it to dangle from Cyprian's outstretched hand.*) There. Now lean forward and try to look like a hitching post. That's perfect—don't budge! (*She runs to the door, yanks it open. Sensualdo, an overwrought Latin in the world's most expensive vicuña coat, erupts in, flanked by two private detectives.*)

SENSUALDO (*roaring*): Where is thees animal which he is defiling my home? (*He and his aides halt in stupefaction as they behold the apartment.*)

APRIL: Get out! How dare you barge in without a warrant? Help! Police!

FIRST SHAMUS (*ignoring her*): Holy cow! What kind of a joint is this?

SECOND DITTO: It's a thrift shop. Look at that statue with a ring in its hand.

FIRST SHAMUS (*to Sensualdo*): Hey, Bright Eyes, we didn't hire out to break in no store. I'm takin' a powder.

SENSUALDO: Eet's a trick! Search in the closets, the bathroom—

SECOND SHAMUS: And lay in the workhouse ninety days? No sirree. Come on, Havemeyer. (*The pair exit. Sensualdo, his hood engorged with venom, turns on April.*)

SENSUALDO: You leetle devil. One day you go too far.

APRIL (*tremulously*): Oh, darling, don't—you mustn't. I'm so vulnerable when you look at me like that.

SENSUALDO (*seizing her roughly*) : Do not play pelota weeth my heart, woman. You mean you are still caring for me?

APRIL: Passionately, joyously. With every fiber of my being. Take me, hold me, fold me. (*Her eyeballs capsize.*) To kiss anyone else is like a mustache without salt.

SENSUALDO: Ah-h-h, *Madre de Dios*, how you set my blood on fire anew. Let me take you out of all thees—to a hilltop in Cuzco, to the eternal snows of the Andes—

APRIL (*simply*) : Geography don't matter, sugar. With you I could be happy in a hallway. (*They depart, absorbed in each other. Cyprian holds his pose a few seconds, and then, straightening, tiptoes after them as warily as the goldfish bowl on his foot permits. His face at the moment is inscrutable, but, broadly speaking, he has the look of a man hellbent on completing an anthology on the joys of the weed.*)

CURTAIN

❧ CLOUDLAND REVISITED: ANTIC HEY-HEY

PERHAPS the saltiest observation Max Beerbohm made in *Seven Men*, a book whose saline content has remained as high and delightful as it was on its appearance thirty years ago, occurs in that matchless story of a literary vendetta, "Hilary Maltby and Stephen Braxton." Writing about the preoccupation of contemporary novelists with sprites and woodland gods—Maltby, it will be recalled, was the author of *Ariel in Mayfair* and Braxton of *A Faun in the Cotswolds*—Beerbohm remarked, "From the time of Nathaniel Hawthorne to the outbreak of the war, current literature did not suffer from any lack of fauns." I suppose this reflection has always struck me as especially astute because when I originally encountered it, back in 1923, I happened to be in a milieu where satyrs and dryads, Silenus and Bacchic revels, were as common as cattails in a Jersey swamp. Its impact was heightened, moreover, by the fact that I was just convalescing (although for a while my reason was despaired of) from the effects of a tumultuous, beauty-bound best seller of the period called *Wife of the Centaur*, by Cyril Hume.

The place was Brown University, and the particular focus of all this mythological activity was a literary magazine by the name of *Casements*, on whose staff I had a brief, precarious toehold as assistant art editor. At least three-quarters of the text of *Casements* each month was made up of villanelles, rondels, pantoums, and ballades in which Pan pursued laughing nymphs through leafy bowers, and it was my job to provide decorative headings and tailpieces to complement them. Fortunately, I had a steady hand and an adequate supply of tracing paper, and if my superiors had not accidentally stumbled on the two albums of Aubrey Beardsley I was cribbing my drawings from, I might have earned an enviable reputation.

My short and brilliant tenure had one positive result, however; I finally discovered what was inspiring the Arcadian jingles I illustrated. One afternoon, while dawdling around the dormitory room of our chief troubadour and waiting for him to shellac a madrigal about cloven hoofs in the boscage, I picked up a novel bound in orange and gold and read a passage he had underscored. "Ho!" it ran. "The centaur is born! Child's body and colt's body, birth-wet and asprawl in the ferns. What mother will nourish this wild thing? Who will foster this beast-god? Where will he grow? In what strange cavern will he make his bed, dreaming his amazing dreams? What shaggy tutor will teach him as he lolls with his head on nature's breast? What mortal maid will he carry away to his upland pastures in terror and delight?"

"Hot puppies!" I burst out excitedly. "This isn't prose—it's frozen music! The gink who wrote this is the bee's knees!"

"Yes, yes," said the poet guiltily, plucking the book out of my hands. "I—er—I haven't read it myself, but I guess it's had a wide influence." It was a Freudian slip on his part, which some instinct told me was worth investigating, and when I did, my suspicions were confirmed. Not only he but practically every bard on *Casements* had been using *Wife of the Centaur* as a water hole. The opportunities for blackmail were, of course, illimitable, and had my own nose been clean (the Beardsley complication was just breaking), I might have taken advantage of them. The truth is, though, that on reading the book I succumbed to its witchery so completely that I, too, began writing villanelles and pantoums in the same idiom. Sad to say, they never saw printer's ink; my colleagues, jealous of the applause the verses might excite, stopped publishing *Casements* altogether, and overnight a potential Wordsworth again became a drab little sophomore.

A week or so ago, standing with nostrils atwitch and a pocketful of rusty change over the bargain table of a Fifty-ninth Street bookstore, I spotted a copy of Mr. Hume's chef-d'oeuvre and, unable to resist a cut-rate sentimental pilgrimage into the past, gave it a home. Its effect, after a lapse of twenty-seven years, was not quite as dynamic as I had anticipated. Rather than quickening me to an orgy of spondees and dactyls, it slowed down my heartbeat to that of a turtle's and enveloped me in a profound slumber under a grape arbor, where I narrowly escaped being consumed by a colony of ants. It may sound unfair to suggest that they were attracted by the rich and sticky imagery of the book, but from now on I plan to restrict my open-air reading to the *World Almanac*, with a Flit gun cocked across my knee to repel browsers.

Since *Wife of the Centaur* is the tale of a sensitive boy who grows up to be a poet, it quite properly begins with a salvo of rapturous and yeasty verse to help you adjust your emotional sights. The following, one of several quatrains introducing a fifty-page pastiche of Jeffrey Dwyer's childhood, gives a hasty but reliable preview of the feature picture:

The centaurs awoke! they aroused from their beds of pine,
Their long flanks hoary with dew, and their eyes deep-drowned
In the primal slumber of stones, stirred bright to the shine!
And they stamped with their hooves, and their gallop abased the
  ground!

Jeffrey, it is shortly established, is an infant centaur, in what might be described as cushy circumstances; he attends an exclusive private school in Connecticut, preparing for Yale, and, when not saturating himself in *The Oxford Book of English Verse*, struggles tormentedly under the lash of awakening sex. The description of the process discloses him to be a pretty full-blooded lad: "Lean desire wrapped his body in taut coils, oppressing him like pain. . . . Lust was a blind force, immeasurable, overwhelming, irresistible as a toppling wall of black water. . . . And desire, the gaunt beast, buffeted and shook him. . . . 'God! God!' . . . The air was a voice that hissed hot promises of forbidden mysteries, the trees were erotic minstrels singing old songs of shameful loves." Luckily for Jeffrey, if not for the reader, his adolescent libido is channeled into writing verse before it lays waste the Nutmeg State, and while the samples furnished are hardly calculated to set the Housatonic on fire—packed as they are with fantasies of whitely radiant madonnas with golden coils of hair and cherry-red lips moving in strange benedictions—it is clear that Calliope has destined the youngster for the business end of a quill.

The heroine of the book, a conventional maiden named Joan Converse, in the same affluent social stratum, now makes her advent with a clash of cymbals and another fifty pages of adolescent background. Joan's sexual yearnings do not seem quite as turbulent as Jeffrey's, but she gets a symbolical sendoff just as rousing: "Ohé hamadryad, lurking in yon covert of ruddy sumac, are your cheeks red with remembered dreaming? Hark! Hark, little maid with the limbs of a slim cascade— hark, for the young centaur tramples and neighs along the wooded hillside, no longer far away. And you do not flee, little maid with your rose-petal cheeks? Ah, the centaur! Ho, hamadryad!" It is futile to begin slavering and speculating on the explosion the two will eventually create, though, because their paths do not converge for years, and by the time they do, at a Long Island house party, the third leg of the

triangle is already in place. Jeffrey, during the interval, has been distinguishing himself at Yale as a poet and tosspot, and is currently dangling after Inez Martin, a heartless flirt whose eyes range from clear
gray to transparent green with her varying moods. "She's a willow beside a brook of running water, and the sun on both," the poet epito-
mizes her to Joan, brokenly recounting the indignities Inez has subjected him to. Irksome as the maternal role is, Joan sensibly bides her
time and is rewarded in the Easter vacation, when Jeffrey buckles under
her own glamour in the rear seat of a Stutz. He kisses her roughly,
impetuously; as she goes faint at the contact of his slim, strong hands,
she notices that "they seemed to have an eager, fine life of their own.
Tense and flexible and swift as blood horses." Much to Joan's chagrin,
alas, it is merely a routine workout for the ponies. Reining them in
before they can bolt, Jeffrey warns her that something horrible might
have happened, that she must never let anyone again kiss her in such
abandoned fashion. " 'Me least of all,' he said harshly. Then he bent
down and kissed the cool palm of her hand." And so, in a bittersweet
dying fall that combines echoes of Havre de Grace, Jergens Lotion,
and the code of a Yale gentleman, is born the romance of Joan Converse, occupation hamadryad, and Jeffrey Dwyer, jongleur and centaur.

Actually, despite all the preliminary huffing and puffing, nothing concrete develops between them in the ensuing third of the story, for
Jeffrey still has to fight the First World War and purge Inez from his
system. He cleans up the first, and obviously easier, assignment in a
brisk ten pages, throws himself into a journalistic career, and makes a
superhuman but fruitless pitch for Joan's rival. How greatly she dis-
turbs him may be gauged from this saucy vignette: "Her blouse was
deeply opened at the neck, showing a long V of glowing flesh with a
faint shadow at the point. One foot was drawn up under her and
Jeffrey caught a glimpse of a rosy knee with the stocking rolled below
it. . . . Happiness pierced him suddenly like a flaming sword. His pulses
beat to the rhythm of a wild prothalamion. . . . He! For him! He was to
explore the shrouded mysteries that dwelt behind her eyes. Her Venus
body and the youth of it, the promises he read in the sultry curves of
her mouth . . . these were his to take and hold like a cup, to drink deep.
. . ." The goodies, maddeningly, remain just out of reach; Inez has
pledged herself to a wastrel named Jack Todd, and, sick with disillusion, Jeffrey plunges into a stormy cycle of wenching and boozing
that climaxes in the arms of a lady of the town. Slowly and painfully,
his equilibrium returns, a salvage operation that calls forth fresh flights
of lyricism: "Now is the centaur weary of men and men's ways. . . .

Centaur, is your beast's spirit broken? Is your man's heart crushed utterly? No! For now the centaur shouts anew his loud defiance! . . . I will go back again to taste the bright hill-water of my colthood and my nostrils shall know as of old the thin air of my mountain realms. I shall lie upon a bed of ferns under familiar constellations. . . . In the still of the night, in an hour when quiet comes upon the crickets and all the little creatures of the dark, I shall reach up with my hand and pluck that round honeycomb, the moon, out of the sky to feed my hunger."

Reduced to prosaic, taxpayer's lingo, this means that Jeffrey goes back to his prep school, engages in a purifying bull session with the headmaster, sobers up, finishes a novel called "Squads Right About" debunking war, and publishes it to wide critical acclaim. Joan, who meanwhile has lain obligingly dormant for a hundred pages waiting for her swain to unsnarl his glands, hereupon pops back into view. Just why she and Jeffrey should plight their troth at the Museum of Natural History, I was unable to fathom, except that it affords the hero an opportunity to indulge in some verbal pyrotechnics on science—or, rather, his conception of it. "Geology, Joan!" he exclaims. "God, but I love geology! Astronomy! The gorgeous tremendousness of it! Science for gods! . . . Your mind goes tramping through space like a hobo in spring, with spiral nebulas trailing at its ankles like gobs of cobwebs. You want to howl and kick suns around because then you realize that the human mind is the greatest created thing." At any rate, after a plethora of similar brainy generalizations, Jeffrey providentially runs out of saliva, and the two dissolve into an embrace that leads to the altar and the next movement of the symphony, a section stylishly entitled "Lilith's Garden."

"Lilith's Garden" is ecstasy unconfined by whalebone, chaperone, or censor, a honeymoon that makes most other fictional ones I can recall seem vapid by comparison. The newlyweds spend it at a seaside cottage on Long Island, whooping around the dunes and behaving in a thoroughly heathen and unfettered fashion: "At night on the beach, he would suddenly make a horrible face and howl, 'I'm a remora!' or 'I'm a mandrake!' or even 'I'm a Calvinist!' Then he would growl and come after her in great fantastic leaps, flinging out his arms and legs and she would squeal and try to double back to the deserted steamer rug." The proximity of salt water, naturally, brings on a whole new rush of metaphor, and the hamadryad switches into a mermaid: "And when he kissed her mouth he tasted the brine of the deep places where her home was; and her dipping arms crept around his neck to draw him under and carry him down forever to a palace of pale coral where fish darted like birds in a garden." As if these quincelike frivolities were already not sufficient to pucker up one's lips, they are punctuated by scolding comments from an old Irish retainer of Joan's playfully known as Madsy, a dialectician of the school of Harrigan and Hart: "Didn't I hear the both of yez on the beach last night carryin' on like wild pagan creatures? Half the night you was up behavin' scandleous and un-daicent as though there wasn't that much of a Christian soul between yez! . . . When you might better have been in your bed you was out on the sand there schreechin' like a pair of unredeemed catamounts. . . . Then *you*, Mr. Dwyer, takes and carries her upstairs, with the pair of yez drippin' like Tim Connel's ghost and him just after drownin' him-self for havin' hit Father Mulligan a skelp wid an axe." Alanna, and 'tis with a sigh of relief and the divil's own skippin' of pages that you finally claw your way out of the tunnel of love.

The culmination of *Wife of the Centaur* may be one of the mildest in letters, but I was never so glad to see a culmination in my life. It is, of course, Inez, the girl with the chameleon eyes, who motivates it; Jeffrey has barely settled down on a Connecticut hilltop with his bride when the enchantress slinks back into the plot and everything goes hay-wire again. Night after night, the harassed poet patrols the countryside, waging a losing fight against her allure and addressing rhetorical ques-tions to the heavens: "Must all true metal be tempered in flame? Is every birth a long agony? *Designer infinite. . . . Ah! must Thou char the wood ere Thou canst limn with it?*" Then, at very long last, comes blessed deliverance for all hands. Amid melting snows and adjectives, Jeffrey finds that the dross has burned away, and in a single burst of renewed creativeness composes two hundred and sixty lines of a saga called "The Brook." "God, Joan! I've never written anything like it in my life before! It's poetry . . . it's great poetry!" But whether it is or not will forever rest a secret, because at this juncture the reader is swept up on a mountainous comber boiling with allusions to Botticelli, Pallas Athene, and the old surefire thunder of centaur hoofs, and is washed up, weak as a kitten, in the end papers.

The reaction of a forty-five-year-old stomach to twenty-five-year-old brandy is a physiological certainty, but surprisingly little information exists on how that organ responds to novels of the same vintage. My subsequent history, therefore, may have a trifling clinical value. For thirty-six hours after completing *Wife of the Centaur*, I experienced intermittent queasiness, a tendency to howl "I'm a Philistine!" and an exaggerated revulsion for the printed page. A day or two later, while emptying a wheelbarrow of old books into a gully near my home, I saw (or thought I saw) a stout, bearded individual with four feet chasing a scantily clad maenad along a ridge. I returned home on the double and, having notified the local game warden, busied myself with indoor matters. Ever since, I have been hearing reedy sounds from the ridge, as of someone playing a rustic set of pipes. More than likely, the game warden got himself mixed up in a three-handed saturnalia and they're looking for a fourth. One of these evenings, as soon as I can get myself shod, I really must gallop up there and see.

🌾 HELL HATH NO FURY . . . AND SAKS NO BRAKE

TELL A WOMAN SHE CAN'T HAVE SOMETHING AND SEE WHAT HAPPENS.
. . . Not so long ago we heard about a fine perfume that women are not permitted to buy. Just men. The only way a woman can get the perfume is to be given some. This struck us as being a unique and wonderful idea. So—we looked into Chaqueneau-K . . . smelled it . . . liked it . . . and were convinced you would, too. . . . Thus, we offer Chaqueneau-K to you. For, within an astonishingly short time it has become a sort of legend. Clark Gable buys Chaqueneau-K . . . and Henry Ford II and Angier Biddle Duke and ever so many others whose taste is beyond question . . . to whom gift-giving is an art rather than an obligation. After all, there ought to be something a man can buy for a woman that *she* can't *buy for herself*. Chaqueneau-K will never be sold to a woman.
                                          —*Saks Fifth Avenue brochure.*

MRS. HECTOR SEAFORTH PATROON, Park Avenue socialite, prominent Bermuda hostess, and spouse of the chairman of the American Roller Towel Corporation, was in high dudgeon. Stamping her aristocratic foot, shod by Palter DeLiso, she drew her ankle-length Revillon Frères sable coat closer about a statuesque figure sculptured by Lily of France, snapped shut the emerald clasp of her handbag, and glared down majestically at the clerk behind the perfume counter. "Young man," she said with freezing scorn, "do you know, by any remote chance, who you're talking to?"

"Perfectly, Mrs. Patroon," he replied, bowing courteously. "Whether captivating every eye in her ringside box at the Horse Show or bandying persiflage with other celebs at Gotham's gilded '21' Club, the uncrowned queen of the champagne set is class personified, part and parcel of the metropolitan élite. Indeed, 'tis rumored by wiseacres that without her portrait to grace their pages, *Vogue* and *Harper's Bazaar* would long ago be floundering on their derrière."

521

"Very well, then," retorted the lady, her arctic reserve thawing under his flattery. "Give us a large flacon of Chaqueneau-K and let me have no more ridiculous chin music about you do not cater same to the frail sex."

"I'm sorry, Madam," apologized the clerk. "Those, regrettably, are my orders, that their infraction is punishable by summary dismissal."

"This is the last straw," declared Mrs. Patroon, who was not accustomed to receiving sauce from myrmidons. "Close my charge accounts as of date, and, I assure you, me and mine will drop dead ere I set another foot in your precious emporium."

As Mrs. Patroon sailed out, head held high, a grizzled old cattleman close by, who had overheard the interchange, chuckled amusedly. "Purty riled, warn't she?" he observed, stroking his tobacco-stained mustache. "Down on the south fork of the Bravos, where I hail from, we know how to curb them fillies." He stripped off a picturesque cowboy gauntlet and extended a gnarled finger. "Here, sonny, reckon my missis'd cotton to this—how d'ye call it—Chaknoo?"

"Oh, yes, sir," the clerk said, concealing a smile at the old stager's inept pronunciation. "It's delightfully feminine, a little bit heady—never boring. And she can't buy it for herself, you know—not for a million dollars."

"Pussonally, I'd ruther sniff the ozone a-blowin' through the mesquite than all this fool loco-juice," growled his customer, producing a wad of crumpled bills. "Howsomever, the wimminfolks set rich store by sich fiddledeedee, so I'll be obleeged if ye'll jest draw me off a Mason jar of thet thar shemale nonsense, pardner." The clerk complied with alacrity and, the transaction effected, waved adieu as the patriarch hobbled off on bowed legs. With true Western hospitality, the latter had tendered the salesman his card and a hearty invitation to visit Amarillo. "Maw kin allus bed ye down with the cowpokes, even if'n they don't smell as purty as these dudes," he had cackled, slapping his thigh. The young fellow scanned the card carelessly and was on the verge of pocketing it when a sickening realization smote him. Engraved on it was no homely Lone Star cognomen but the chill legend "The Falcon." A strangled cry burst from his lips. The elusive, mocking creature who had consecrated herself to flouting the pledge that Chaqueneau-K would never be sold to a woman had scored another coup.

"Stop that man—I mean that woman!" the clerk shouted, bounding into the aisle. But it was too late; already the phantom had melted into the crowd, a female David victor once again over the mighty department-store Goliath.

Robsjohn Cropsey, head of the internal-security division of Saks Fifth Avenue, stood at the window of his private sanctum, his lean, saturnine countenance a grim cameo against the twilight. Those who knew him well—and they were few, for the gaunt, loose-jointed Cropsey discouraged intimacy, living only for his work and his daughter Faustine, a graduate student at Columbia U.—might have discerned something almost pantherlike in the man at the moment, the look of a great jungle cat poised to spring. Nor would they have erred; there was a truly feral gleam in his eyes as he wheeled toward the man cringing beside the desk.

"Now, then, Mr. Freytag," he purred. "My dossier reveals that yesterday forenoon you entered our haberdashery and attempted to purchase an Allen Solly cardigan and some Izod hosiery."

"I—I had the money," whimpered Freytag, his face gray with fear.

"That's irrelevant," Cropsey snapped. "You knew these articles were exclusive with Saks, that they were intended for the discriminating few who appreciate the finer things of life." The other nodded miserably. "Other than sheer snobbery, what made you, social cipher and Yahoo that you are, think you had any right to the vestments described?"

Freytag licked his lips. "I wanted to be a big shot," he whined. "I saw Fred Astaire wearing them in a movie, and I figured to be spruce and nobby like him, and—well, I guess I thought I could get away with it." Head in hands, he cowered away from the pitiless gaze and broke into tortured sobs.

"An exterminator," Cropsey lashed him remorselessly. "For this, men herd sheep on the lonely barrens of the Hebrides, women in thatched cottages card and spin their wool, copy writers distill winged words from their hearts' blood—all this so that a vermifuge peddler may pass for Fred Astaire. Well, Freytag, you've gambled and lost. Take him away, boys."

As the luckless wretch was removed by two impersonal operatives in trench coats, condemned to shop at Bamberger's and Loeser's for five long years, Cropsey sank into his chair with a sigh. Always the same, he thought wearily, an unending procession of petty chiselers spawning equally grubby crimes. When would he meet a foeman worthy of his steel? As if in answer to his prayer, Darryl Blauvelt, his second in command and a lad keen as mustard, entered with an aura of suppressed excitement.

"I gleam an aura of suppressed excitement, Blauvelt," noted Cropsey, thoughtfully packing shad into his odorous briar. "Out with it, boy." In a few maladroit words, Blauvelt sketched in the salient details of the atrocity at the perfume counter. The scent of burning fish suffused the room as his superior pulled austerely on his pipe. A harsh sound that was less mirth than epiglottal outrage escaped him. "I knew it, by Jove!" he exclaimed triumphantly, squirting a drop of ink into the pipe bowl to extinguish the coals. "Listen—you remember what the clerk told us about Clark Gable, Henry Ford II, and Angier Biddle Duke?"

"Why, yes," said Blauvelt, racking his memory. "He noticed that Gable wore a domino mask and Inverness cape when he came in, that Mr. Ford had a billycock hat and muttonchop whiskers, and that Duke was sporting burnt-cork make-up and a rhinestone vest. We thought it was odd at the time—"

"Odd!" exploded Cropsey. "Great Scott, man, don't you see? Impostors all! It was the Falcon, now revealed to be a past-mistress of disguise, who fobbed off her bogus charge plates! Do we have snaps of the trio to check my conjecture?"

"We do, sir," confirmed the other, extracting them instanter from a drawer cunningly concealed in the wall. "The average public would be floored to learn that our files are as comprehensive as Scotland Yard's." A single glance corroborated the chief's deduction; except for the hirsute appendage edging the film star's lip, the three were clean-cut men of distinction, devoid of ostentatious garb.

A muscle twitched in Cropsey's cheek and a dangerous yellow light shone in his gritted teeth. "A crafty adversary, this, Blauvelt," he rapped out. "Somewhere in that vast beehive of humanity, the Falcon has gone to earth, storing up venom for another pounce. We've got to match her woman's guile with the very snare she used on us. Attend me carefully. . . ."

Faustine Cropsey stirred her tea dreamily and, lowering the newspaper that shielded her piquant face, cast a wary glance around the restaurant. Save for two or three matrons hissing confidences over their jelly rolls, and the waitress yawning nearby, the Forty-sixth Street Schrafft's was deserted. She nervously consulted her watch, wondering what mischance could have delayed her contact. Through office and factory, library and rehearsal hall, word had sped from one woman to another in the network of the L.C.M.S.—the League to Combat Male Supremacy—that the Falcon was in peril and was to receive briefing at the third table along the north wall of the tearoom at five-fifteen that afternoon. Considering their devious routing, the tidings had traveled with amazing speed. They could have been telephoned to her just as easily, but then, reflected Faustine, the machinery of conspiracy always functions ponderously. She had cause to know. It had been whilst penning her thesis on the machinery of conspiracy at Columbia that Chaqueneau-K had hurled its defi at her sex. The insolent mandate proscribing the scent had lashed Faustine to fury; in a flash of resentment, the idea of the avenging sisterhood was born. Fanned by general indignation, it had grown overnight into a widespread cabal that enabled its leader, under the *nom de guerre* of the Falcon, to execute her intrepid forays. All Manhattan was agiggle at the sham Texan who had circumvented the edict, yet some vague premonition, a fear that she had overreached herself, was chewing at Faustine.

"Chicken giblets with orange snow, and a small pandowdy." The words, uttered in a swift undertone, cut sharply into her reverie. It was the password; unperceived by Faustine, her contact had slipped into the chair behind. As the waitress scribbled the order and moved off, Faustine, lips barely moving, whispered the countersign: "Pandowdy, Roger, and over."

"You are the Falcon?"

"I am known by that name. I have others."

"I caught a glimpse of your profile when I sat down. Your hair's terribly unattractive."

"You're no bargain yourself. What message do you bring?"

"I speak through a doily. Pay close heed. A perfume exists at the vigil counter."

"Is the message in code?" asked Faustine. "I don't follow. Repeat, please."

"Sorry. A vigil exists at the perfume counter. Tread softly; gins and pitfalls are being prepared. Swoop with care, Falcon. More I may not say."

"Why not?"

"My mouth is full of corn bread. Wait till I swallow."

The organization was becoming unwieldy, Faustine decided. Instructions would have to be issued to contacts to do their eating off duty. Aloud, she said, "Anything else?"

"Yes." Desperate urgency underlined the other's voice. "It is like thrusting your head into the lion's maw to venture into that store, even to one of your cool bravado who her aplomb might well be ruffled by scores of dicks subjecting you to their pitiless scrutiny."

"Hmm." Faustine's mouth tightened. "You are certain nobody followed you here?"

"They may have. Some fresh egg in the subway kept pinching me, but he got off at Columbus Circle."

"That's all." Her chieftain withdrew into her paper. "You can go now."

"What about my giblets?"

"They seem normal," said the Falcon cryptically, "but if I were you, I'd consult a physician about my adenoids."

"Can you direct me to the perfume counter, please?" The speaker, a swarthy, autocratic individual in flowing burnoose, whose curled black beard, snowy turban, and bejeweled yataghan bespoke the baking deserts of Trans-Jordan, stood irresolute in the turmoil of the brassière section. The salesgirl at his elbow, though inured to the grotesque by her environment, blinked in momentary surprise.

"Oh, yes, sir. Two aisles over and left," she said, and smiled coquettishly. "You speak surprisingly good English for a lint-head."

"Thanks," the man acknowledged with Old World gallantry. "On account of my governor was well off, I was senior wrangler at Brasenose. *Salaam aleikum.*" He strode off, spurs jangling, amid a battery of languishing glances. As he gained his objective, several workmen who had been deployed about polishing showcases and spearing excelsior abandoned their labors and drifted nearer.

"A dozen bottles of Chaqueneau-K, my good woman," the Arab said to the angular spinster in black behind the counter, "and do not spare full measure, lest the gazelles in my harem accuse me of favoritism."

The saleswoman surveyed him coolly out of a lean, saturnine countenance, removed the briar from between her teeth, and signaled the workmen to hold themselves at the ready. "Well, Falcon, we meet at last," she said, in the rasping Cropsey nasal that had spelled curtains to many a trickster's career. "Nab her, men!" In a trice, Cropsey's aides had closed in, pinioned their prize, and borne the captive, kicking and struggling, into the freight elevator. So deftly was the incident staged that not a head turned to remark it, most of the shoppers dismissing it merely as a strenuous preparation for the midseason white sales.

Half an hour later, Cropsey, feet on desk and shad in pipe, reviewed the affair for his admiring subordinate in half a dozen broad strokes.

"The Falcon, emboldened by success, was cock-a-hoop," he explained negligently. "Hence, foolhardiness and concomitant disaster. It was child's play."

"I know, sir," cut in Blauvelt, "but the thing is, I'm afraid we pinched the wrong—"

"Don't interrupt," reproved Cropsey. "I was observing that my modest knowledge of criminal psychology—"

"Please, sir," the younger man persisted. "I feel I've got to tell you. That sheik was legit. We tried to rip his beard off, but all we have is a lawsuit." As his dumbstruck senior goggled at him, there was an insistent knocking on the door. Blauvelt peered out and engaged in a low-pitched colloquy. "No, no, he's tied up," he said with finality. "You what? . . . From where? . . . Well, I'll see." He looked uncertainly over his shoulder at Cropsey, sunk in a blue funk. "There's a—a Mennonite gentleman here, from Lancaster County, sir. He says it's something urgent—about Chaqueneau-K."

Cropsey beckoned abstractedly. A small, plump figure clad in the sober raiment of the Pennsylvania sect, his beaver hat shading a visage set off by a luxuriant chin whisker, insinuated himself into the room. Rubicund cheeks glowing like Winesaps with embarrassment, he laid a gift-wrapped bottle on the blotter.

"You take back from me this perfume, not?" he implored. "I will be so grateful. My wife will bake for you a shoo-fly pie—"

"Blauvelt! Who is this man?" Cropsey half rose. "We don't make refunds here!"

"*Nein, nein*, you shall have it as a present," the visitor said doggedly. "Keep it for a souvenir. Give it to your daughter."

"Souvenir?" Cropsey grated. "Daughter? What do you know of my daughter?"

"Ha-ha!" his vis-à-vis rejoined, with a sly grin. "I know one thing, old smearcase. She has a *Dummkopf* for a father."

"Damn your impudence, sir!" Cropsey went white with passion and snatched a penang-lawyer from the wall. "I'll teach hayseeds to come in here and insult me!" His hand recoiled from the intruder's collar as a mocking feminine voice rang out from beneath the beaver hat.

"Not so fast, Daddy," it warned. "Two can play at that game!" With a dexterous movement, the Mennonite swept off hat and beard, shook out a mop of honey-colored hair, and disclosed to the electrified sleuth his treasured offspring.

"Faustine!" choked her sire. "You—the Falcon?"

"The same," returned the girl, violet orbs flashing defiance. "Just a normal, spunky miss pitting her wiles against consuming odds to deflate the bumptious masculine ego."

"Well, I'll be—jiggered!" gasped Darryl, thoroughly flabbergasted. "She certainly took me in."

"And me, too," concurred Cropsey, his sportsman's code bowing to the inevitable. "This has been a good lesson to all concerned that male chauvinism is un-American to the core. From here in, Blauvelt," he announced inflexibly, "this store will stand as a bastion against sexual niggling, freely retailing Chaqueneau-K to every gender."

"Dear old Dad!" approved Faustine, enveloping him in a bear hug. "I really believe you knew the Falcon's identity from the start, you old fox."

"Well, best leave sleeping dogs lie," Cropsey twinkled. "As for you two young scalawags, do not imagine I have been blind to the sheep's eyes exchanged behind my back, and the furtive smooching. She's yours, my boy," he told Blauvelt as the blushing pair sought each other's arms. "And now, if you will excuse me, I will buzz on down to the Gamecock and buy a glass of oblivion for a suspicious frog in my throat." The lovers stood clasped in the gloaming and watched him go. He turned with a whimsical smile on the threshold. "After all," he said, and for an instant elf overrode detective, "there ought to be something a man can buy for a frog that a frog can't buy for itself." And he shut the door very carefully.

❧ AND THOU BESIDE ME, YACKETING
   IN THE WILDERNESS

IF I EVER sit down like a retired Scotland Yard inspector to write my memoirs, which I have provisionally entitled "Forty Years a Boob," one of the episodes I plan to gloze over is the night of pub-crawling I spent in Hollywood last summer with a beautiful, Amazonian extra player named, for purposes of this indiscretion, Audrey Merridew. For nine tumultuous hours, her destiny and mine were interwoven. (No more than our destinies, I hasten to add; we never even progressed to the point of lacing fingers.) The encounter was so brief, our lack of rapport so conclusive, that when I received a postcard from her recently—an aerial view of San Bernardino, with a tiny shrunken lemon wired to it—I could not recall the creature for a few seconds. Then the whole gruesome affair came back, and I realized with an uprush of pique that the card had an ulterior significance. So I was a wizened little fruit long past its prime, was I? That was feminine gratitude for you; you danced attendance on them, flattered their vanity, listened to their preposterous confidences, subordinated everything to their whims, and in return they made you a laughingstock across the country. Standing at my rural-delivery box in the Pennsylvania bush, I could hear the personnel of the entire postal system, from coast to coast, guffawing at the gibe. Well, I thought as I flung the postcard into the weeds, it's damn lucky a continent lies between us, or I'd hang a shiner on Audrey's eye, for all the eight inches she towers over me. When my dander's up, I lash out irrespective of size or sex.

I got embroiled in the thing through Norman Spindrift, a budding producer at Metro who entered show business by the back door as a dice hustler at Las Vegas. He had taken me to lunch at his commissary and devoted most of it to soliciting my opinion of Frank Harris's *My Life and Loves* as a potential movie. "How can it miss?" he kept demanding. "It's got girls, situation, jeopardy—everything."

"That it has," I conceded. "But why not try something more current in the same vein—the new Kinsey, for instance? You could get boffs out of those statistics if you animated them."

Norman contemplated the tip of a panatela he had exhumed from its cedarwood coffin. "Not a bad idea," he said thoughtfully. "Assuming it could be cleared legalwise, would you be interested in an assignment like that?"

"Hell, I'm just opening a can of kumquats," I said. "I believe in giving a man the handle bars and letting him ride the bicycle."

"Well, it's worth a fast mull," he said, his eyes narrowed. "Look, walk me back to my office and let's see if we can't synthetize our thinking."

We had traversed an expanse of burning concrete fully the length of an airstrip when Norman abruptly broke off his speculations and propelled me toward the door of a sound stage. "Mind if I check on this unit a second?" he asked. "I got a company here doing a ballroom sequence." Molelike in the pitch dark, I followed him through a labyrinth of cables and props to the set, a dazzling affair of chromium staircases and tufted leather that exactly simulated, said my companion, the lounge of the Reform Club in London. A sizable crowd of dress extras in the last stages of tedium loitered about waiting for the technical crew to complete a setup, and while Norman engaged in a colloquy with the director, I picked up a script and updated my glossary of Hollywood subjunctives. A minute or two later, he returned, looking, I thought, unbearably arch.

"Listen," he said, in a guarded tone. "Is the little woman in town with you?" I explained that the two of us had been unable to fit into a roomette on the Chief but that I wrote her daily copious letters that would give anyone the illusion of being in the movie capital. "Yes, yes," he said impatiently. "Well, I know how lonely a man can get in this burg, so I got you a date for tonight. Now, don't start giving me that Nujol," he said, hushing my objections. "She's a hep dame, a million laughs, good-looking, just your type. And, what's more, not a gold digger. Take her out, buy her the blue plate, a couple of drinks—you can *talk* to Audrey. She isn't one of these china dolls." Since the man had obviously gone to considerable trouble in my behalf, I yielded, and accompanied him around the rear of the set to meet the lady. She was undeniably striking—a bold, wide-eyed brunette, with dimples and a smoldering quality, who reminded me somehow of one of my early screen deities, Priscilla Dean. Her white evening gown, accented at the bodice with pompons, appeared at first glance to have been improvised from a candlewick bedspread, though it admittedly complemented her olive skin and pneumatic *balcon*. She did not rise from the camp chair

she was seated in but extended her hand in a fashion, at once comradely and languorous, that won me.

"Why hasn't Norman brought you around before?" she asked re-
proachfully. A long-time partisan of contraltos, I recognized at once
that hers was instinct with moonlight and camellias. "I love people
from the East," she went on. "There's so much more *to* them." Uncertain whether I was supposed to hail from Jubbulpore or Newark, I decided to play it safe and adopted an inscrutable global expression.
Audrey—our matchmaker had instantly put us on a first-name basis—
jotted down her home address, where I was sweetly enjoined to call
for her no later than seven, and stood up in response to the assistant's
whistle. My inscrutability curled around the edges when I saw she was
a good head and a half taller than me.

"Pretty slick, eh?" Norman commented as she waved adieu. "You're
in solid, man. I can tell."

I seemed to have a frog in my throat temporarily. "Tall girl, isn't
she?" I wheezed. "I mean sitting down she gives the impression—"

"I told you she wasn't any china doll, for Crissake," he snapped.
"What's the matter—you afraid to trust yourself with a real woman?"
I countered with some hearty masculine ribaldry, vitiated, unfortunately, by my falling over a guy wire, and had to endure the humiliation
of being assisted to my feet and brushed off. Norman wanted to hale
me to the studio infirmary to have my shins dressed, and even spoke
darkly of preventive tetanus shots, but I pooh-poohed his solicitude
and left with assurances that we would meet again soon to resume our
assay of Kinsey.

I was staying at the time with friends in Bel-Air, and they must have
suspected I was pleasure-bent that evening, because while nothing in
my speech or demeanor betokened exhilaration, I surprised my hostess
discreetly removing some crystal epergnes from her foyer. True, I *had*
borrowed her husband's brilliantine and inquired several times where
people were wont to rumba nowadays; however, I happen to feel that
the well-behaved guest does not burden his friends—and his wife's—
with confidences, and I did not expatiate.

The section Audrey lived in was easily ten miles distant, south of
Hollywood off Olympic Boulevard, and I consumed a good hour blun-
dering around unfamiliar streets in my rented convertible, flashing its
headlights up driveways and sending watchdogs into paroxysms. Just
before eight o'clock, I drew up before a two-story house of peach-color
stucco exhibiting a marked Spanish influence. Its entrance was flanked

with dagger cacti, maguey plants, and similar lethal vegetation, so dimly lit that I lacerated my hands unmercifully groping for the bell. As the chimes within subsided, Audrey, her face transfigured with a smile of almost painful radiance, opened the door. She was wearing a black organza dress and some extremely becoming costume jewelry, and, to my uncritical eye, looked very chic, but for the second time that day I was oppressed by her size. The girl really loomed in the doorway.

"My fault for not giving you directions," she cooed, stemming my apologies. "Matter of fact, we didn't finish shooting till late, so I went ahead and had dinner with Mommy. Come in and meet her." Before I could find words to express my signal gaucherie with mothers, I was swept into a baronial hall that might have served as audience chamber for Queen Isabella. A gigantic hooded fireplace bearing the arms of Castile dominated the far end of the room; eight or nine thrones, council chairs, and pews upholstered in red damask and embossed with brass studs were ranged about the tiled floor; and wherever a visitor might want to drop his casque or mailed gloves there was a quartered-oak table or a *prie-dieu*. Seated by a lamp whose parchment-and-mica shade depicted the poop of a galleon was a prim-faced elderly woman in what I took to be a chasuble of flowered cotton. Somehow the work-basket in her lap seemed out of character. I expected her to be holding a mace.

"Do sit down, Mr. Parmalee," she said when Audrey had ceased bellowing my name into her ear. "I've heard so much about you." It occurred to me I was being confused with the transfer people, but instinct warned me to dummy up until I was besought to wrangle a trunk. While Audrey busied herself pouring out two ponies of Chartreuse, Mrs. Merridew embarked on a short review of the advantages of Southern California—notably its abundance of flora and paucity of unions. She herself, she signified, was descended from one of the finest families in Georgia and had migrated hither at great personal sacrifice to further her daughter's career. She now feared, though, that an undesirable foreign element was creeping into the picture industry, exposure to which might have a malign effect on Audrey. "Honey, do your Goldwyn imitation," she begged her daughter. "I declare, Mr. Parmalee, it's better than a show." Alluring as was the prospect of a dialect lampoon, I felt the time had come to depart. The ladies exchanged kisses as protracted as though Audrey and I were setting off on a four-year whaling cruise, and in short order I was tooling my date toward a club celebrated for its jazz virtuosi. Audrey adored jazz; in fact, she said, giving me a coquettish nudge that almost capsized our vehicle, next to Easterners there was nothing she loved more than barrelhouse tempered with a couple of mild highballs.

As it developed, the star turn at the club was one of the great modern masters, the incomparable Jess Alexandria Stacy, of Cape Girardeau, Missouri. His keyboard was bewitched that night; never has there been such a rolling bass, such superb arpeggios. I was in a transport—destined, I should have known, to rank as the world's briefest. The moment Audrey's tongue touched bourbon, it began wagging in a key just resonant enough to drown out the music. Had I ever heard Carmen Cavallero play "The Flight of the Bumblebee"?

Yes, I admitted, we had been shipmates en route to Hawaii once, and for a whole blessed week—

Hawaii! She was ecstatic about the South Seas. Had I seen Esther Williams and Howard Keel in *Pagan Love Song*? The shots of Tahiti were ravishing. One day, she and Mommy were going to Tahiti, if it was the last thing they ever did. George Sanders had gone there in that picture about the artist who deserted his family and cut off his ear—she couldn't remember his name, but he had leprosy in the last reel. She understood they had found a new cure for leprosy; it was in the *Reader's Digest*, which she hoped I liked as much as she did, because it was practically her bible. As for artists, she had a particular kinship with them, her onetime girl friend having espoused a man who was in the paint business in Monrovia. Desperately trying to stanch her rhetoric and at the same time pay homage to Stacy, who was doing a transcendent version of "Back Home in Indiana," I made the fatal error of ordering double whiskeys. Under their influence, Audrey not only became more garrulous but beat time on her glass with a muddler. A party of cats in the next booth, who had been giving us frigid glances, started to mutter like the sans-culottes in a novel by Baroness Orczy. When Stacy stopped dead in the middle of "Riverboat Shuffle" and swung around ominously on his stool, I knew that jigwise, all was up.

"Judas priest!" I said, smiting my forehead. "I nearly forgot—Kid Ory's at the Beverly Cavern, with his whole ensemble! They're syncopation plus—let's go!" Luckily, Audrey's mood was still pliant. With a bright, detached smile, she fumbled together her gear and lurched after me.

In the next hour or two, we canvassed every snug on Beverly Boulevard from Figueroa Street to the Sunset Strip, an area comparable in size to Upper Assam. We were in grogshops where the patrons wore turtleneck sweaters and billycocks reminiscent of Chimmie Fadden, in juke joints, bodegas, rathskellers, and even sukiyaki parlors, but nowhere could we find a trace of the Kid and his golden horn. Despite my entreaties, Audrey insisted on pausing frequently for a chota peg, and finally, in a clangorous spot called the Dixieland, she took her stand and refused to continue. Nevertheless, she remained as articulate as ever, chattering away with such verve about her girlhood in the South and race relations there that the Negro bandsmen had to labor to make themselves audible.

At the conflux of Santa Monica and Wilshire boulevards, or hard by, there stands, as it has stood from time immemorial, a restaurant dedicated to serving the world's most succulent hot cakes. I speak of it wistfully—from a threshold acquaintance, as it were, for Audrey chose that point as a central and showy one in which to crumple. Happily, the lobby was crowded with people, many of whom I knew quite well and who were kind enough to avert their faces. The management also reflected admirable restraint by overlooking a philodendron snapped off at the base, and supplied me with native bearers to convey Audrey to the parking lot. On the way home, as I was pondering some means of delivering her short of a block and fall, she suddenly revived. Instead of husbanding her strength, however, she clamored that I must come home and let her prepare us hamburgers. In vain I pleaded that I was a vegetarian and a dyspeptic, that my presence in the house would compromise her, that I had an early appointment with my astrologer. Her insistence became so heated at last that I feared she might do me physical violence, and I pretended to submit. Actually, an easy solution had occurred to me.

"Let's have a bracer first," I whispered conspiratorially, herding her up the walk. "Where does Mommy hide the Chartreuse?" As she careered off into the dark in quest of it, I headed for the kitchen, figuring I could escape by the side door, but my evil star was in the ascendant, and I wound up in a cul-de-sac, a dismal cement patio fenced breast-high with woven paling. To swarm over it in my weakened condition without provoking a hue and cry was manifestly impossible. I was done for, trapped. I sank into a chair and, head in hands, reviled Norman Spindrift and all his issue from hell to breakfast. A few moments later, the odor of frying meat pervaded the air, and out bustled Audrey, sporting a bungalow apron. By some inexplicable process, she had known all along where I was; perhaps her beaux instinctively made for the patio, as eels seek out the Bahama Banks. From then on, the outlines began to shift and blur. I remember Audrey silhouetted against the eucalyptus tops, passionately declaiming fragments of Ella Wheeler Wilcox while I sat by in frozen despair. Through the torpor gradually enveloping me flashed a realization of the hopelessness of my position. I was enmeshed in a monstrous fairy tale, doomed to listen to this giantess until madness set me free. And then, out of the blue—or, rather, the Gray—came my reprieve. The voice of Mrs. Merridew, pure boll-weevil but more melodious to my ears than Galli-Curci's, cut across her daughter's. "Audrey!" it called from above. "It's five o'clock! You hush your bazoo and come to bed!"

A sob of gratitude constricted my larynx, and by the time it relaxed, I was roaring west on Pico Boulevard, jumping every light and singing "The Battle Hymn of the Republic." That I ran out of gas on Copa de Oro Road in Bel-Air and had to finish the journey on foot didn't upset me in the least. I bounced in just as the Japanese gardener was turning on the revolving sprinkler. He inclined his head gravely and I inclined back. We didn't exchange a word. As I always say, the deepest thoughts are those that are left unsaid.

🌿 THE FROSTING'S ON THE DRY GOODS, THE CUSTOMER'S IN SHOCK

FOR THE BENEFIT of anyone puzzled by the eerie purr, like that of a Himalayan snow leopard, issuing from the headquarters of the Burlington Hosiery Company on Fifth Avenue, I can offer a crumb of enlightenment that may be useful later this fall. I thought at first it was looms fashioning the colorful plaid socks the firm prides itself on, but I was wrong—it's self-satisfaction. The hosiers have been gloating in ever-widening circles over a promotional coup, first revealed in the New York *World-Telegram & Sun* and subsequently trumpeted in impressive full-color advertisements in *The New Yorker* and other periodicals. The coup was to persuade the Duke of Argyll himself to ballyhoo the socks named after his house. Besides authenticating every pair with his signature—a job that could chain him to his escritoire for some time to come—the Duke has thrown in his warrant as Master of the Royal Household of Scotland, Keeper of the Great Seal, Admiral of the Western Coasts and Isles, Hereditary Sheriff of Argyll, and Hereditary Keeper of the Royal Castles of Dunoon, Dunstaffnage, Tarbert, and Carrick for use in counter cards, brochures, and similar teasers, and he will presently materialize on these shores to meet the press and retail merchants. The latter are jubilant, it develops, "because they recognize the Duke as a richly laden symbol of tradition with plenty of consumer appeal." Their regard undoubtedly springs from a billet-doux he sent them a while ago, which began, "Gentlemen: I am writing to you from my castle at Inveraray in the heart of the country of Argyll in Scotland. As Duke of Argyll and head of the Clan Campbell, I was greatly pleased when representatives of the great Burlington Hosiery Co. visited me to ask for my comments and advice on their new Argyll socks for the fall."

Though every knee, however rheumatic, will bend when the distinguished laird stumps this country in behalf of his ancestral socks, the account is disappointing in one respect: it omits to tell us how the Duke's compeers feel about it. Many a Briton whose family has been immortalized in apparel must have stiffened as the word spread through

536

St. James's, and, it is reasonable to conjecture, bit the end off his fragrant Havana with a touch of spleen. To get some inkling of the repercussions, suppose we link arms and ascend the crumbling stairs of the Asphodel, the most exclusive male stronghold in Pall Mall. Fracturing the laws of probability into flinders, assume that nobody stops us in the entresol and that we've penetrated to the upper floor.

SCENE: *The library of the club, a tenebrous chamber some seventy-five feet long and eighteen wide. Glowering from the niches that relieve the rows of Bulwer-Lytton are busts of bygone members who quelled their countrymen or the heathen, all of them with a uniformly supercilious expression. There are the usual newspaper racks, a pedestaled globe showing the Empire as Lord Kitchener left it, and several placards demanding silence, to which a grandfather's clock pays no heed. The room's only occupant at rise is Oscar Norfolk, the Earl of Chantry, asleep in an armchair. He wears the belted jacket his forebears popularized during the reign of Edward, and his complexion, the result of a lifetime of salmon fishing and superior port, gleams like a well-worn saddle. After an interval, Mullet, the head porter, enters, discreetly twitches the Earl's sleeve.*

MULLET: It's three o'clock, Your Grace.
NORFOLK (*indistinctly*): Careful with that howitzer, damn it. . . . Good-oh, Steelyard, now we can enfilade the beggars. . . . Ready? One—two—
MULLET: Beg pardon, sir, but you left word to be called.
NORFOLK: What's that? . . . Oh, yes—yes, of course. (*squinting around*) Anybody here yet?
MULLET: Lord Balbriggan's downstairs, sir. The rest of the gentlemen will be along directly.
NORFOLK (*querulously*): What's the delay? Have trouble in reaching 'em?
MULLET: Not the slightest. (*producing a notebook*) Viscount Tattersall wasn't sure he could get away, but one of the other hairdressers agreed to substitute for him.
NORFOLK: What about Inverness?
MULLET: It's a half holiday at Fortnum's, sir; none of the doormen are working. The Duke of Ulster and Lord Cardigan—
NORFOLK: What time do they finish lunch at the Ivy?
MULLET: They'll be here as soon as their tables are straightened up.

NORFOLK: Splendid. Remember, we're not to be disturbed under any circumstances. (*Clad in the celebrated underwear that bears his name—though it is invisible for the most part—Lord Balbriggan enters. He is accompanied by Tattersall, in his jaunty and characteristic vest, and a person whose bulky layered cape would identify him anywhere as Vyvyan, Baron Inverness.*)

TATTERSALL (*as Mullet goes*): Ah there, Oscar—glad to see you looking so fit. How's Phylloxera?

NORFOLK: Mountainous. Put on two stone since she went to work for that pork butcher in Cheapside.

TATTERSALL (*archly*): She's certainly bringing home the bacon, what?

NORFOLK: You're pretty cocky, considering this news about Argyll.

BALBRIGGAN: Yes, do you realize what the fellow's done, with his letter to those confounded shopkeepers and singeing all their hosiery?

TATTERSALL: He's not singeing it—he's *signing* it.

BALBRIGGAN: Shilly-shallying. Whatever he's at, he's let us all down.

INVERNESS: Betrayed his class, by gad. The man must be starkers.

BALBRIGGAN: This can spell ruination for every mother's son of us. What are we going to do about it?

NORFOLK: Hold a council of war, for one thing. That's why I called you together. (*Ulster and Cardigan enter. They are not easy to differentiate, since the latter sports an ulster and the former a cardigan, but their views are reciprocal and vehement.*)

ULSTER (*explosively*): Paper towels in the lav—it's an outrage, sir!

CARDIGAN: The handwriting on the wall. The Yankees are everywhere. (*Quotes ominously.*) "The huckster's cry from street to street/ Will weave old England's winding sheet."

NORFOLK: You're batting the wrong wicket, Cardigan. We're here to discuss the Argyll crisis.

CARDIGAN: Don't make a pennorth of difference. The principle's the same.

ULSTER: I absolutely concur. Take a strong line with the bleeders. If we falter, we're finished.

NORFOLK: We all see eye to eye, I take it. (*His colleagues growl assent.*) Very well, then, let's frame a letter to the *Times*. . . . "Sirs: It is indeed a sorry state of affairs—"

TATTERSALL (*cutting him short*): Too late for that, chaps. I've already been approached.

NORFOLK: Approached? By whom?

TATTERSALL: Big clothing wallah from Rochester, the capital of New

York. Wants me to sponsor my family waistcoat—tour the provinces, appear on the wireless, hell's own amount of handshaking.

NORFOLK: You threw the offer in his face, of course.

TATTERSALL: We-ell, not squarely. There's a rather cozy stipend attached.

ULSTER (*explosively*): The cheek! You should have horsewhipped the swine.

CARDIGAN: Bastinadoed him. Still—just out of curiosity, Simon—what was the *quid pro quo*?

TATTERSALL: Eleven hundred guineas.

CARDIGAN (*sleekly*): I was offered seventeen, deposited in Tangier. Naturally, my endorsement's worth more, what with the sweater in "My Fair Lady" packing the stalls.

BALBRIGGAN: A transitory fad, old boy. According to an impartial survey I've been asked to vet, balbriggans have been in use overseas longer than any other garment.

INVERNESS: Longer than the Inverness cape, I suppose?

BALBRIGGAN: The figures speak for themselves. I have no reason to distrust my agency.

INVERNESS: Well, you go to your agency and I'll go to mine. Furthermore, any time you'd like to debate the issue publicly when we get there—

NORFOLK: Come, come, Vyvyan, this is the Asphodel, not a bear garden. . . . Obviously, gentlemen, a concerted drive's under way to extort our patronage. (*evasively*) I myself haven't been solicited, except through a relative in Cheapside—

TATTERSALL: You will, Oscar, you will.

NORFOLK: I pray I may be equal to it. The Moloch seeking to devour us is crafty, his resources incalculable. We must not waver or tergiversate.

ULSTER: I advocate a minimum of ten thousand pounds for our services!

BALBRIGGAN: You mean all together or individually?

ULSTER: Either way. (*inspired*) And if the bounders refuse, we'll get up our own company, junket through the States, and warn the public they've been had!

OMNES: Hear, hear . . . Masterly idea . . . Stroke of genius . . . Good old Ulster, etc. (*A sudden sneeze from the grandfather's clock arrests the babble. As all turn, transfixed, its case opens and a buoyant individual with a crew cut and Madison Avenue regimentals emerges.*)

STRANGER: Greetings, friends. Permit me to introduce myself—Gordon Alewife of the J. Walter Juggernaut organization. I couldn't help overhearing your brain wave.

NORFOLK: How the devil did you get in here?

ALEWIFE: Very simply. I happen to be the nephew of Mullet, your head porter. I also happen to know a few things about his past.

CARDIGAN: That's blackmail, sir!

ALEWIFE (*sunnily*): So's your little dodge, confidentially, but we're prepared for it. A troupe of character actors, the exact doubles of each of you, is standing by at the Lambs in New York, ready to grease the sales mechanism the minute they get the nod.

TATTERSALL: Damn your impudence, you wouldn't dare . . .

INVERNESS: No matter how benighted his countrymen are, they can tell a blue blood from an impostor.

ALEWIFE: They won't be able to, after they read our medical plugs. (*hastily*) But we're not trying to sell haberdashery, gentlemen— far from it. We merely want to present you—the flower of the peerage, the men who helped King John forge a nation that historic day at Runnymede—to the American consumer in a fitting and dignified manner.

BALBRIGGAN: Well, I've always looked on 'em as cousins, in a way.

ULSTER: My kennelman's elder daughter married a Chicagoan. Very sound chap.

NORFOLK: Harumph. Whilst I welcome a closer understanding between ourselves and the colonies—

ALEWIFE: Let me finish, Your Grace. For that high honor, that privilege of saluting your prestige, my associates propose to recompense you handsomely.

NORFOLK: You have some—ah—cash honorarium to suggest?

ALEWIFE: Even better. An unlimited expense account, all your transportation, fountain pens, et cetera, and a nickel royalty on every gross of merchandise you move.

INVERNESS: How much would that come to? I'm not frightfully keen at mathematics.

ALEWIFE: In your case, it could mean a very substantial amount. I forget how many tweed capes we sell annually, but it's staggering.

NORFOLK: Well, that doesn't seem ungenerous. . . . Tell you what, Alewife. Put up fifty pounds apiece so we'll have something to jingle in our pockets, and it's a bargain.

ALEWIFE (*instantly*): You've got a deal. (*They clasp hands as the peers exchange gratified winks at the outcome.*) And now, gentlemen, if you'll just crowd in around this escutcheon over the mantel, we'll take a group shot for the slicks.

BALBRIGGAN: Completely out of the question, young man. The interior of the Asphodel's never been photographed.

ALEWIFE: That's what you think. Come on out, Chuck. (*He taps the pedestaled globe, and a minion armed with a portable television camera pops out.*) We've also got a sound track on this whole shindy, haven't we, Chuck?

CHUCK (*in typical New Yorkese*): You're damn tootin', boss.

NORFOLK (*flummoxed*): Well, I give up. You can't beat these Sammies for enterprise and initiative. (*As he and his fellow-peers ruefully pose themselves before the hearth—*)

CURTAIN

❧ *I AM NOT NOW, NOR HAVE I EVER BEEN, A MATRIX OF LEAN MEAT*

I AWOKE with a violent, shuddering start, so abruptly that I felt the sudden ache behind the eyeballs one experiences after bolting an ice-cream soda or ascending too recklessly from the ocean floor. The house was utterly still; except for the tumult of the creek in the pasture, swollen with melting snow, a silence as awesome as that of Fatehpur Sikri, the abandoned citadel of the Moguls, shrouded the farm. Almost instantly, I was filled with an immense inquietude, an anxiety of such proportions that I quailed. The radium dial of the alarm clock read two-thirty: the exact moment, I realized with a tremor, that I had become involved the night before in the affair of the Boneless Veal Steaks. The Boneless Veal Steaks—it had the same prosaic yet grisly implications as the Five Orange Pips or the Adventure of the Engineer's Thumb. Propped up on one elbow and staring into the velvet dark, I reviewed as coherently as I could the events of the preceding night.

I had awakened around two and, after thrashing about in my kip like a dying tautog, had lit and smoked the cork tip of a cigarette until I was nauseated. I thereupon woke up my wife, who apparently thought she could shirk her responsibilities by sleeping, and filed a brief résumé of the disasters—financial, political, and emotional—threatening us. When she began upbraiding me, in the altogether illogical way women do, I did not succumb to justifiable anger but pacifically withdrew to the kitchen for a snack. As I was extricating a turkey wing from the tangle of leftovers in the icebox (amazing how badly the average housewife organizes her realm; no man would tolerate such inefficiency in business), my attention was drawn by a limp package labeled "Gilbert's Frozen Boneless Veal Steaks." Stapled to the exterior was a printed appeal that had the lugubrious intimacy of a Freudian case history. "Dear Chef," it said. "I've lost my character. I used to have sinews, then I met a butcher at Gilbert's. He robbed me of my powers of resistance by cutting out some of the things that hold me together. I am a matrix of lean meat with my trimmings ground and worked back into me. Please be kind. Pick me up with a pancake turner or a spatula, don't grab me by the edges with a fork. Because of all I've been through I'm more fragile than others you've known. Please be gentle lest you tear me apart. Tillie the Tender."

The revelation that food had become articulate at long last, that henceforth I was changed from consumer to father confessor, so unmanned me that I let go the turkey wing; with a loud "Mrkgnao" she obviously had learned from reading *Ulysses*, the cat straightway pounced on it. I must have been in a real stupor, because I just stood there gawking at her, my brain in a turmoil. What floored me, actually, wasn't that the veal had found a way to communicate—a more or less inevitable development, once you accepted the basic premise of Elsie, the Borden cow—but rather its smarmy and masochistic pitch. Here, for the first time in human experience, a supposedly inanimate object, a cutlet, had broken through the barrier and revealed itself as a creature with feelings and desires. Did it signalize its liberation with ecstasy, cry out some exultant word of deliverance, or even underplay it with a quiet request like "Mr. Watson, come here. I want you"? No; the whole message reeked of self-pity, of invalidism, of humbug. It was a sniveling, eunuchoid plea for special privilege, a milepost of Pecksniffery. It was disgusting.

In the same instant, however, I saw both the futility of moral indignation and an augury of things to come. Before long, the other victuals in the icebox, their tongues loosened by some refrigerative hocus-pocus as yet unknown to science, would undoubtedly emulate Tillie and demand similar coddling. Two courses presented themselves; I could either scream the house down and prepare it for the contingency, or I could bear the brunt singlehanded—i.e., get back into bed and let things take their course. The latter plainly being the coward's way, I adopted it at once. Between various distractions, I neglected to check the icebox the next morning, but now, as I lay there sleepless, I knew that every second of delay was calamitous. With the stealth of a Comanche, I swung my feet over the side of the bed and stood up on a standard apricot poodle who happened to be dozing there. He emitted a needle-sharp yelp.

"Shut up, damn you," I hissed through my teeth, immediately tempering it with a placatory "Good boy, good boy." The brute subsided, or pretended to, until I closed the bedroom door behind me; then, convinced I was sneaking off on a coon hunt or some other excursion without him, he started excitedly clawing the panels. I permitted him to follow and, when we were well out of earshot of his mistress, gave him a kick in the belly to teach him obedience. The moment I opened the refrigerator door, I sensed mischief was afoot. Clipped to an earthenware bowl of rice pudding was a note scrawled in a shaky, nearly illegible hand. "Dear Chef," it said breathlessly. "You're living in a fool's paradise. You wouldn't believe some of the things that go on in this box—the calumny, the envy, the trickery. They're all against me because I have raisins. Ish ka bibble—I had raisins when that Nova Scotia salmon in the upper tier was a fingerling in the Bay of Fundy. But don't take my word, just look around for yourself. Nuf sed. A Friend."

A quick scrutiny of the various compartments revealed that something was indeed very much awry. Two bunches of celery had worked their way out of the freezer, where they normally lay, and stood jammed in a cluster of milk bottles. A mayonnaise jar had been emptied of its rightful contents and was half-filled with goose fat, hinting at the possibility of foul play. It wasn't any one single factor—the shreds of icy vapor or the saucer of frozen gravy, as bleak as Lake Baikal—but the interior was filled with a premonitory hush of the sort that precedes a cyclone or a jail break. All of a sudden, as I racked my wits for some clandestine method of eliciting the true state of affairs, the perfect solution hit me—my tape recorder. I could secrete it in the adjacent kitchen cabinet, run the microphone inside disguised as a potato knish, and overnight astound the world with its first documentary on talking groceries. The thought of the millions I was scheduled to make in royalties, the *brouhaha* in the press and the acclaim of learned societies, and the chagrin of my enemies when I was elevated to a niche beside that of Steinmetz so dizzied me that I had to drink a split of Dr. Dadirrian's Zoolak to recover. True, I felt a bit anthropophagous as I swallowed it, and I half expected a gurgled Levantine outcry, but nothing more dramatic than a slight attack of double vision ensued, and within minutes I had the mechanism hooked up and ready to function.

"Now, then," I ordered the poodle, flicking on the switch, "back to the hay we go. Better be up bright and early before someone finds this and misinterprets it."

"Applesauce," he retorted. "It's your recorder, isn't it?"

"Sure," I said, "but you know how silly peop— *What did you say?*" Of course, he dried up then, not another word out of him, and you'd have thought the cat had his tongue.

I got to bed pretty perplexed about the whole thing and, what with fear lest I oversleep and worry at the quantity of current the machine was using, fell into a wretched slumber that terminated around daylight. Hastening to the kitchen, I downed some black coffee, and rewound the spool of tape to get the playback. The first few revolutions were unproductive of anything but conspiratorial whispers and an occasional word too jumbled to decipher. Then, all at once, I heard a low-pitched voice in the background, oily and yet pompous, stiff with disdain.

"Beggars on horseback," it was saying contemptuously. "Strictly keeping up appearances. I spotted him and the Missis right away the day they came into the delicatessen. She was wearing an old Persian-lamb coat, remodeled. 'Something in the way of a cocktail snack, Greengrass,' she says, yawning like she's Mrs. T. Markoe Robertson. 'I'll take a two-ounce jar of that domestic caviar.' Then she turns to her husband, which he's nervously jingling the change in his pants, and she says, 'Dear, don't you think it would be amusing to have a slice or two of Novy for our guests?' Well, the poor *shmendrick* turned all different colors when the boss weighed me on the scales. Five cents more and he'd have had to walk home in the rain like a Hemingway hero."

"Listen," rejoined a grumpy bass voice that unmistakably proceeded from a forsaken bottle of horseradish. "Stick around as long as I have and nothing these people do will surprise you. Why, one time we had a rack of lamb in here seven weeks. The plumber had to cut it out with a blowtorch."

A mincing, rather overbred voice, of the sort usually associated with Harvard beets, chimed agreement. "There's one thing that doesn't get stale here, though," it said. "Club soda. How long can he last on that liquid diet of his?"

"Forever, if he don't fall down and cut himself," the lox replied with a coarse guffaw.

"Can't you make less noise, please?" put in a hateful, meaching soprano. "I haven't closed an eye. I'm just a bundle of nerves ever since my operation—"

"Pssst, there goes Tillie again," warned the horseradish. "Pipe down or she'll write him another note. The little sneak repeats everything you say." A hubbub of maledictions and recriminations broke out, the upshot of which I never heard. Quivering with fury, I stripped the tape off the reel, ran into the living room, and flung it on the embers in the hearth. Specks of assorted hues swam before my eyes; it was unendurable that I should have nourished such vipers in my bosom. Drastic steps were indicated, and I was the boy who could take them. As I flew back to the refrigerator, bent on evicting the whole kit and caboodle without mercy, I caromed off my wife, huddled in a plain wrapper for all the world like a copy of *Lady Chatterley's Lover*, gaping at the recorder.

"Wh-what happened?" she stammered. "What are you doing with that microphone in the icebox?"

Well, I learned one lesson from the episode; suavity is lost on women. There isn't a blessed one, from the Colonel's Lady to Judy O'Grady, capable of dealing with abstract ideas, and if you try a civilized, worldly approach, it just antagonizes them. Can you imagine a person getting so huffy that she barricades herself in a henhouse and refuses to breakfast with her own husband? I made a meal off a few odds and ends—a grapefruit and a couple of eggs—but I can't say much for their dialogue. You need someone you can really talk to.

CLOUDLAND REVISITED: WHEN TO THE SESSIONS OF SWEET SILENT FILMS . . .

ON A SLUMBEROUS AFTERNOON in the autumn of 1919, the shop-keepers along Weybosset Street in Providence, Rhode Island, were nonplused by a mysterious blinding flash. Simultaneously, they heard a sound like a gigantic champagne cork being sucked out of a bottle, and their windows bulged inward as though Dario Resta's Peugeot had passed, traveling at incalculable speed. Erupting from their bazaars, they saw a puny figure streaking in the direction of the Victory, the town's leading cinema. The first report, that anarchists had blown the cupola off the state capitol, swiftly yielded to a second, that a gopher mob had knocked over the vault of the Mercers' & Pursers' Trust Co. Before either rumor could be checked, a bystander appeared with a green baize bag dropped by the fugitive, establishing him as a sopho-more at the Classical High School. Among its contents were a copy of Caesar's Gallic commentaries, a half-eaten jelly sandwich, and a news-paper advertisement announcing the première that afternoon at the Victory of Cecil B. De Mille's newest epic, *Male and Female*, starring Thomas Meighan, Gloria Swanson, and Lila Lee.

By the time the foregoing had been pieced together, of course, the sophomore in question—whose measurements coincided exactly with my own—was hanging out of a balcony seat at the Victory in a cata-tonic state, impervious to everything but the photoplay dancing on the screen. My absorption was fortunate, for at regular intervals the ushers circulated through the aisles, spraying the audience with an orange scent that practically ate away the mucous membrane. Whether this was intended to stimulate the libido or inhibit it, I never found out, but twenty years later, when I met Mr. De Mille in Hollywood, I could have sworn he exuded the same fragrance. The fact that we met in an orange grove, while relevant, did not materially alter my conviction.

Male and Female, as moviegoers of that epoch will recall, was based on James M. Barrie's *The Admirable Crichton*, a play that derided caste and sought to demonstrate how a family of *hochgeboren* snobs, marooned on a desert island, was salvaged physically and spiritually

by its butler. That so special a problem could enthrall a youth living on
a New England chicken farm might seem unlikely, but it did, and to
such a degree that I saw the picture twice over again on the spot. The
silken luxury of its settings, the worldliness and bon ton of the characters, and their harrowing privations held me spellbound. I was bewitched in particular by the butler as portrayed by Thomas Meighan.
His devastating aplomb, the cool, quiet authority with which he administered his island kingdom and subdued the spitfire Lady Mary
Lasenby, played by Miss Swanson, displaced every previous matinée
idol from my heart. For weeks afterward, while toting mash to the hens
or fumigating their perches, I would fall into noble attitudes and apos-
trophize the flock with lines like "One cannot tell what may be in a
man, Milady. If all were to return to Nature tomorrow, the same man
might not be master, nor the same man servant. Shall I serve the ices
in the conservatory?" The consequences of this sort of lallygagging soon
made themselves felt. There was a sharp decline in egg production,
followed almost immediately by word from the Classical High School
that I had achieved the lowest grade ever recorded in second-year Latin.

Quite recently, through the good offices of the Museum of Modern
Art, I was enabled to re-examine the masterwork that gave me so profound a catharsis. It was a reassuring experience; I discovered that although the world is topsy-turvy, De Mille still remains the same. His
latest pictures display the same baroque pomp, the same good old five-
cent philosophy, and the same lofty disregard for sense. *Male and Female* could be remade today with equal success at the box office. All I
ask in return for the suggestion is that prior to its release I be given
twenty-four hours' head start.

The film begins with a pious explanation that its title is derived
from the passage in Genesis "Male and female created He them," and
first introduces a scullery maid named Tweeny, in the person of Lila
Lee. Tweeny is employed at fashionable Loam House, in London,
where she nurses a violent, unreciprocated passion for its major-domo,
Crichton. We now meet, in a series of keyhole shots, the various members of the Loam family as they appear to an impudent pageboy delivering their boots. They are, respectively, the Earl (Theodore Roberts),
his silly-ass cousin Ernest (Raymond Hatton), and his daughters,
Lady Mary and Lady Agatha. Miss Swanson, the former, reclines on
a couch worthy of the Serpent of the Nile, having her nails and hair
done by a pair of maids. This lovely sybarite is to learn, says an acid
subtitle, that "hands are not only to be manicured but to work with,

heads not only to dress but to think with, hearts not only to beat but to love with." Her sister, a languid wraith engaged in scrutinizing her cosmetic mask, fares no more kindly: "Lady Agatha, who is to find like most beauties that the condition of her face is less important than to learn to face conditions." There follows a piquant scene wherein Miss Swanson dons a peekaboo negligee, sinuously peels to enter a sunken marble tub, and sluices down in a shower containing a spigot marked "Toilet Water." Emerging, she finds a box of long-stemmed roses sent by an admirer named Lord Brocklehurst. The accompanying card read (as I thought), "My Lady of the Roses: I am coming over to show you something interesting for the slim white finger of your slim third hand," but this seemed so Surrealist in mood that I had the projectionist run it again. The actual phrase, "slim third finger of your slim white hand," is pretty humdrum by comparison.

Depicted next is the ritual of Lady Mary's breakfast, served by three underlings and presided over by Crichton. "The toast is spoiled," declares his mistress capriciously. "It's entirely too soft." Ever the flower of courtesy, Crichton pinks her neatly in the ego with a deadpan riposte: "Are you sure, Milady, that the toast is the only thing that is spoiled?" Leaving her to gnash her teeth on the soggy toast, he descends to the library, where Tweeny is dusting, and proceeds to read aloud, for no cogent reason, a dollop of poesy by William Ernest Henley beginning, "I was a King in Babylon and you were a Christian slave." The scullery maid, eyes swimming with adoration, furtively strokes his instep. "I wouldn't be nobody's slave, I wouldn't," she murmurs. "Unless maybe your slave." Lady Mary, who by a spooky coincidence has been reading the very same book earlier, now enters just in time to hear Crichton declaiming, "I saw, I took, I cast you by, I gently broke your pride." The delicious spectacle of varlets pretending to understand poetry evokes her patrician mirth, and, imperiously requisitioning the book, she goes to greet Lord Brocklehurst, her suitor.

Brocklehurst, by and large, is an inconsequential character in the drama—merely a lay figure dragged in to spice the budding romance between Lady Mary and Crichton. The plot, which has been betraying definite symptoms of rigor mortis, comes alive about teatime, when the Loams, frantic with ennui, determine to cruise to the South Seas in their yacht. As they animatedly begin studying maps, a confidante of Lady Mary's, Lady Eileen Duncraigie, drops in to consult her about a glandular dilemma. She is infatuated with her chauffeur—one of those typical crushes that followed in the wake of the internal-combustion engine—and wonders whether she stands any chance of happiness. Lady Mary smiles commiseratingly. Indicating a bird cage nearby, she poses a searching zoological parallel: "Would you put a jackdaw and a bird of paradise in the same cage? It's *kind to kind*, Eileen, and you and I can never change it." Well, sir, you know what happens to people who run off at the mouth like that. It's even money La Belle Swanson will be eating crow before the turn of the monsoon, and the cinematic bobbin shuttles madly back and forth as it starts weaving her comeuppance.

Dissolving to the Loam yacht at sea, we observe our principals leading the same unregenerate existence—squabbling endlessly and being coddled by Crichton, whose insteps, in turn, are being dogged by Tweeny. In a newspaper presumably flown to her by albatross, Lady Mary reads of her friend's marriage to her chauffeur. "I suppose," waggishly remarks Ernest, "that if one married a chauffeur, one would soon *tire* of him—get it?" Lady Mary haughtily rejoins that the whole affair is ridiculous—exactly as if she were to marry Crichton. The latter's face freezes as he overhears the slur, and when Thomas Meighan's face, already icy to begin with, froze, it looked like Christmas at Crawford Notch. "And there," explains a crunchy caption, "it might have ended had they not been blown by the Winds of Chance into uncharted Tropic Seas with Destiny smiling at the wheel." Which, draining away the schmaltz, is to say that the yacht runs aground, the crew obligingly perishes, and the Loams, plus their retinue, are washed up intact. The shot that gave one the old *frisson* in 1919, of course, was Meighan carrying Miss Swanson, more dead than alive and more naked than not, out of the surf. It is still gripping, and for those who are curious about its effect on Meighan—inasmuch as there is no clue to be found in his features—the succeeding title is helpful: "Suddenly, like mist melting before the sun, she was no longer a great lady to him, but just a woman, a very helpless and beautiful woman." Brother, they don't write subtitles like that any more. The fellows who dream up the scenarios nowadays are daffy enough, to be sure, but there's no *poetry* in them.

It takes approximately a reel and a half of celluloid and some of the most cumbersome foolery since the retirement of Louise Fazenda to reunite the shipwrecked party. The Earl, who has landed in a dressing gown and yachting cap, chewing the celebrated Theodore Roberts cigar, becomes embroiled in various comic misadventures, such as nestling against a turtle he mistakes for a boulder and disputing possession of a coconut with some chimpanzees. The mishmash of fauna on

the island, by the way, would confound any naturalist past the age of
twelve; I doubt whether Alfred Russel Wallace, either in the depths of
the Malay Archipelago or malarial fever, ever saw apes and mountain
goats, wild boars and leopards, sharing a Pacific atoll. When noses are
finally counted, the survivors number seven—the four Loams, Crichton and Tweeny, and an unidentified young minister whose presence
is never quite explained but whom De Mille was doubtless limbering
up for one of his later Biblical productions. Crichton borrows the
padre's watch crystal to light a fire, allots various chores to the group,
and in short order manages to arouse Lady Mary's anger. When he
proposes to use her gold lace stole as a fish net, she rebels openly and
talks the others into seceding, but the revolt soon collapses. One by
one, the insurgents sneak back to Crichton's fire and his kettle of seaweed broth, leaving her impenitent and alone. Then she too weakens,
for, as the subtitle puts it, "You may resist hunger, you may resist cold,
but the fear of the unseen can break the strongest will." The unseen in
this case takes the form of a moth-eaten cheetah rented from Charlie
Gay's lion farm in El Monte. As he noses through the undergrowth,
Lady Mary's nerve cracks and she scurries to Crichton for protection.
Ultimately, after much digging of her toe awkwardly in the hot sand,
or what used to be known as the Charlie Ray school of acting, she
knocks under and ponies up the gold lace stole. The sequence, or the
round, or whatever it is, ends with both breathing hard but not the least
bit winded—considerably more, goodness knows, than can be said for
the spectator.

    "Under the whiplash of necessity," the narrative continues son-
orously, "they come to find that the wilderness is cruel only to the
drone, that her grassy slopes may clothe the ragged, her wild boar feed
the hungry, her wild goats slake their thirst." Two years, we discover,
have wrought substantial changes in the castaways. They have fashioned themselves a nobby compound, domesticated everything in sight
but the chiggers, and dwell contentedly under a benevolent despotism
set up by Crichton. Lady Mary and Lady Agatha, in play suits of
woven bark and in Robinson Crusoe hats, skip over the savannas hunting wild fowl with bow and arrow; the Earl, still chewing the same
cigar stump, hauls lobster pots on the lagoon; Ernest and the anonymous divine milk goats in a corral; Tweeny, whose status nothing apparently can alter, stirs a caldron of poi in the kitchen; and Crichton,
garbed in a tunic resembling a Roman centurion's made of palm
fronds, labors in his study on a Boob McNutt contraption designed to
ignite a rescue flare on the cliffs. His new eminence is illustrated at

mealtime that evening, when he is revealed dining in splendid isolation, fanned by a punkah that is operated by Lady Mary. Henley's poems, providentially saved from the wreck, are propped up before him, and he is rereading "I was a King in Babylon," the eternal references to which were beginning to give me a dull pain in the base of my scullery. It presently develops that the greedy old Earl has eaten some figs earmarked for Crichton's dessert, and Lady Mary hurries to pick more. Learning she has gone to "the drinking place of the leopards," Crichton hastens after her and transfixes one of the beasts as it attacks. She gratefully flings herself into his arms, and confesses her belief that he is the reincarnation of a king in Babylon. "Then you were a Christian slave," he says with sudden understanding, turning her face up to his. The action thereupon pauses for what is unquestionably the snazziest flashback that has ever emerged from silver nitrate. Meighan, duked out as a Semitic tyrant on the order of Ashurbanipal, receives from a vassal a tigerish, scantily clad slave girl—i.e., Miss Swanson—who repays his tentative caresses by biting him in the wrist. With a cruel sneer, he promises to tame her, and she is borne off snarling defiance in the classic tradition. In due time, she re-enters on a palanquin powered by Nubians, clothed in sequins and wearing on her head a triumph of the taxidermist's art, a stuffed white peacock. "Bring forth the sacred lions of Ishtar," Meighan commands, gesturing toward an arena installed meanwhile by the studio carpenters. "Choose thine own fate. Yield to me willingly or thou shalt know the fitting cage built for thee, O Tiger Woman." Secure in her long-term contract, Miss Swanson proudly elevates her chin. "Through lives and lives you shall pay, O King," she predicts, and advances into the pit. As the episode concludes, we are back on the island, with Crichton telling Lady Mary, in mettlesome spondees, "I know I've paid through lives and lives, but I loved you then as I love you now." A Zbyszko hammer lock, and at long last their lips, parched with rhetoric, meet in a lingering kiss.

The note of implied finality, however, is only a ruse; if the fable is to come full circle, its characters must show the effect of their sojourn away from civilization. Just as the pair are being united by the preacher, a ship appears on the horizon. Lady Mary tries to dissuade her chieftain from signaling for help, but he knows the code and gallantly bows to it. "Babylon has fallen and Crichton must play the game," he announces, gently unyoking her arms and yoking the metaphors.

Transported back to England in an agile dissolve, master and servant promptly revert to type. Lady Mary agrees to wed Lord Brocklehurst, though she reveals her heartbreak to Lady Eileen, whose marriage to her chauffeur has spelled social obloquy. Crichton retaliates by proposing to Tweeny, and, in a penultimate scene, we see them between kisses, operating an Australian sheep farm. For the tag, or washup, De Mille chose a bittersweet dying fall. On the lawn of a vast country house, amid drifting petals, Lady Mary toys with her parasol and dreams of what might have been. The title reads, "You may break, you may shatter, the vase if you will, but the scent of the roses will hang around her still. Thus does the great sacrifice shed its fragrance over a lifetime." Enter a beflanneled Brocklehurst, who stands regarding her with doglike devotion. "I understand, my dear, why you postponed our marriage," he declares, manfully sweeping up the loose exposition. "You loved Crichton, the admirable Crichton. I'll be waiting for you at the judgment day." He raises her hand to his lips, Lady Mary's eyes under her picture hat fill with tears, and, to use a very apt technical term, we squeeze.

I suspect that a lot of people in my generation, the kind of romantics who blubber at the sight of a Maxfield Parrish print or a Jordan roadster, would not have withstood my sentimental excursion as gracefully as I did, and would have wound up fractured at the Jumble Shop, harmonizing "The Japanese Sandman." Matter of fact, I ran into a couple of these romantics *at* the Jumble Shop, strangely enough, right after seeing *Male and Female*. We got to talking, and darned if they hadn't seen it too as kids. Well, we had a bite of supper, took in the ice show at the Hotel New Yorker, and then, armed with plenty of ratchets, started back to the Museum about midnight so I could screen the picture for them. Luckily, their car hit a hydrant en route and I managed to slip away unnoticed. If I hadn't kept my wits about me, though, the whole day might have ended with much worse than eyestrain. As a middle-aged movie fan, I've learned one lesson: Lay off that nostalgia, cousin. It's lethal.

❧ THE SAUCIER'S APPRENTICE

THE LAST PLACE I would have expected to run into Marcel Riboflavin, *sous-inspecteur* of the Police Judiciaire—which is to say, the Sûreté—was the Sunday-morning bird market in Paris, but then Marcel's vagaries have long since ceased to surprise me. Stoop to tie your shoelace in Baton Rouge or Bombay, in Dublin or Dar es Salaam, and like as not you will find Marcel confronting you with an owlish eye and nibbling a meditative praline. Where he gets all those meditative pralines from—or why, since they attract a veritable canopy of flies—the Lord only knows; nonetheless, there he is in rusty bourgeois black, patiently following up some infinitesimal clue, or like as not just nibbling a praline. I was standing in the hurly-burly of the bird market three Sundays ago, lost in admiration of two little doves in georgette blouses who would have rounded out any boy's aviary, when an unmistakable voice sounded in my ear.

"*Doucement, mon vieux*," it warned. "We old roosters must be cautious. Don't try to outwit your arteries."

Startled, I turned to behold Marcel, an indulgent smirk on his face, wagging his forefinger at me. It was quite apparent what he was thinking, and I hastened to disabuse him. "The fact is," I explained, "the smaller of that pair—the helpless-looking one—reminds me of a teacher of mine at grammar school, a Miss Floggerty. She had taffy-colored hair, as I recall—"

"*Bien sûr, bien sûr*," he said sympathetically. "I, too, have those symptoms of senility. Tragic but inescapable. Come, let us link arms and stroll through the complex of alleys fringing the Quartier Latin." As we linked arms and strolled, genially updating each other on our activities since our last meeting, I noticed a strangely familiar magazine protruding from my friend's coat pocket.

"You have symptoms of gentility also," I remarked. "Since when have you taken to reading *Harper's Bazaar*? Or do your investigations extend into the gilded salons of the *haute couture*?"

Marcel's face, or at least that portion of it visible through the flies,

554

suddenly became cryptic. "In my post, one is called on to unravel many tangled skeins," he said evasively. "By the way, this café we are nearing is reputed to have the worst anisette in Paris. Shall we try it?" We did, and it was unspeakable. After a moment, Marcel withdrew a praline from a recess in his clothing and nibbled it meditatively. I am not overly intuitive, but I have learned that when sub-inspectors of the Sûreté with dicky fashion magazines protruding from their pockets invite one to share an apéritif, curious stories ofttimes unfold, and so it proved.

"As you are doubtless aware," began Marcel, drawing on his praline, "*Harper's Bazaar* not only prognosticates the mode but frequently publishes news of consuming interest—you will pardon the play on words—to gourmets. Such was the arresting article you see here." He spread out the periodical and indicated a piece entitled "Sauces from the Source," by Rosamund Frost. At first glance, it did not seem particularly cataclysmic. Maxim's, the celebrated Paris restaurant, had confected five basic frozen sauces calculated to tease the American palate. It was the secrecy attending their manufacture, however, and the abnormal precautions adopted to guard the creators, that riveted my attention. "Seat of the production," wrote Miss Frost, conspiratorially turning up the collar of her typewriter, "is Seabrook Farms in New Jersey, the well-known purveyors of frozen fruit and vegetables. But because M. and Madame Vaudable, owners of the Paris Maxim's, have a deep distrust of American cooking methods, they have evolved their own system of preparation. For each large batch of sauces, a head chef, an assistant, and several *sauciers* are flown over from Paris, to be held virtually incommunicado in New Jersey until the batch is finished. They are then flown home before they have had any chance to be contaminated by such ill practices as thickening with flour."

I lifted my eyes slowly to Marcel's, the question I was almost afraid to put into words muted to a whisper. "You mean . . ." I asked.

"Precisely," he said, dislodging a grain of sugar from his denture. "Scarcely a month after this information appeared, the chief of our Bureau Culinaire, the section specializing in food outrages, sent for me in a state of pronounced agitation. A few nights earlier, faint but indisputable traces of flour had been detected in a pipkin of sauce béarnaise served at Maxim's."

"It could have been pure coincidence," I objected. "A harassed scullion, a sudden avalanche of orders—"

"In France," Marcel said with wintry dignity, "accidents occur in the bedroom, not the kitchen. No, it was all too plain that this was a deliberate, predetermined *coup de main*, a perfidious assault on the very citadel of our national cuisine. The victim of the atrocity, it appeared, was a distinguished artist of the Comédie-Française and one of its foremost tragedians, Isidor Bassinet. Providentially, Bassinet realized the implications of his discovery in time to avert a panic that might easily have wrought havoc among the clientele. Summoning the maître d'hôtel, he cuttingly suggested that the sauce was more suitable for calking a boat, tweaked the man's nose, and retired. The headwaiter, of course, relayed the gibe to the chef, who instituted a probe forthwith and immediately gave us the alert."

"I hesitate to denigrate an actor," I said, hesitating almost a full second, "but might not Bassinet himself have insinuated flour into the sauce as the pretext for a histrionic outburst?"

"We did not discount the possibility," said Marcel. "A clandestine search was made of his rooms that yielded naught incriminating gravy-wise; his erotic photomurals, his collection of whips, and the jar of candied hashish by his bedside could have belonged to any floorwalker in the Bon Marché. The longer I pondered the problem, the more convinced I became it was an inside job. Someone on the kitchen force— whether a madman or a cold, diabolic intelligence I was not yet prepared to say—had engineered the deed, and I knew that, encouraged by success, he would strike again. My theory was vindicated all too swiftly. Two evenings later, Alexander Satyriasis, the Greek shipping magnate, was dining at Maxim's with his wife and his mistress. The occasion was their silver wedding anniversary, and Satyriasis, an epicurean, had left no spit unturned to insure a gastronomical triumph. The hors d'oeuvres, the soup, the roast—all were transcendent. Then, as the trio expectantly attacked the salad, Paradise crumbled about their ears. Under their forks lay the ultimate annihilation, the final obscenity—a canned pear stuffed with cream cheese and walnuts, garnished with cole slaw and Russian dressing."

"Good God!" I exclaimed. "At the Fig 'n Thistle, yes; at the Mumble Shop and a thousand Stygian tearooms, yes; but in the Rue Royale—"

Marcel repressed an involuntary shudder. "It was appalling," he admitted. "When I got there, the table was cordoned off and Satyriasis had not yet recovered consciousness. He came around eventually, but, *entre nous*, the man will never be the same. I instantly fell to work and grilled the entire personnel, from the head sommelier down to the doorman. Nobody would even hazard a guess at the origin of the salads; apparently they had been slipped onto the service tray while the waiter's back was turned, and beyond that not a vestige of a clue. Those were dark days, I can tell you," Marcel went on somberly. "The knowledge that we were powerless to combat him exhilarated our mysterious adversary, spurring him on to new and more gruesome excesses. Under the management's very nose, patrons were assailed with baked grapefruit topped with maraschino cherries, fried clams encapsulated in deep fat, mashed potatoes pullulating with marshmallow whip. The nadir of bestiality was reached one night when cards were surreptitiously pinned to the menu inviting diners to have their tea leaves read by a gypsy palmist."

"Forgive me for underscoring the obvious," I said. "Surely it must have occurred to you that a woman, and patently an American, was at the bottom of all this?"

"Naturally," said Marcel with a shade of impatience. "The crucial question, though, was where was she and how was she effecting her depredations? Five of the restaurant's employees, as you saw from the magazine account, had been flown to New Jersey and held there incommunicado. Plainly, one of their number—younger and more impressionable than the rest—had evaded his custodians and succumbed to some harpy who had lured the fatuous boy to a drive-in like those Howard Monsoon places that line your roads, and there, befuddled by viscous malted drinks and chicken-in-the-basket, he had been persuaded to betray his birthright. In all likelihood, I reasoned, the seductress had followed him to Paris to gloat over her handiwork; perhaps, if I could ferret out the cat's-paw, he might lead me to her. Acting on my presentiment, I at once attached myself to the kitchen in the guise of an assistant pastry chef and proceeded to elicit what I could about the quintet who had been overseas."

"And your hypothesis bore fruit?"

"In a fashion I never anticipated," replied Marcel. "Four of them were prosaic, stodgy types, family men whose world revolved around their thimbleful of Pernod and their game of bowls. The youngest, however, was an altogether different piece of work. A mere novice entrusted with handling condiments, he was a shy, secretive lad with long eyelashes and a curiously girlish aspect. Whenever the badinage among his mates grew ribald, he flushed deeply and made himself scarce, and once or twice I surprised him examining his complexion in a compact. The conviction that our little colleague was a masquerader emboldened me to experiment. Utilizing the test that had unmasked Huckleberry Finn, I casually asked the youth to thread a needle: As I expected, he brought the thread to the needle instead of vice versa. Then I shied an egg beater at him without warning—that is, without warning that I was shying an egg beater at him—and, sure enough, he automatically spread the knees under his apron to form a lap. The evidence was too damning to be ignored. That night, when my suspect let himself into his modest furnished room in the Saint-Germain-des-Prés quarter, stripped off his mess jacket, and disclosed a brassière, I emerged from an armoire and sprang the trap."

"You might have waited a moment or two for confirmation," I remonstrated.

"As a reader of *Harper's Bazaar*, I am reasonably *au courant* with the subject," said Marcel tartly. "Besides, I had all the proof necessary to stamp the creature as the perpetrator of the crimes. Simmering on the gas stove was a dish of salmon croquettes flanked by carrots and peas, and, in the oven beneath, a graham-cracker pie. Overcome by remorse, yet grateful that the suspense had ended, the fair culprit dissolved in tears. Her name, she confessed, was Gristede Feigenspan, and she was a feature writer for *Effluvia*, a periodical circulated gratis by supermarkets in your country. To dramatize the pre-eminence of American cookery, her editors had abducted the youngest member of the French contingent, had substituted Gristede, and were planning to publicize her exploits under the title 'I Was a Fake Saucier at Maxim's.' "

I drew a long breath. "A singular tale," I commented. "I take it she paid the inevitable price for her audacity?"

"That," said Marcel, with an enigmatic smile, "is a matter of opinion." He hoisted himself cumbrously to his feet as a dynamic young woman in black jodhpurs, with a bag slung over her shoulder, gravitated toward our table. "I don't think you know my wife," he said. "Gristede, allow me to present an old *copain* from the States—a journalist, like yourself."

"Too, too fantastic," she trilled, extending her hand. "How long are you staying in Paris? You must come to dinner."

"I—er—I'm just en route to Beirut," I stammered. "I mean I'm off to a fiesta in Trieste—"

"Don't be an Airedale," she said forcefully. "We'll give you a real home-cooked meal. Hasn't Marcel told you about my noodles Yankee Doodle, smothered in peanut butter and mayonnaise?"

I looked at Marcel, but his face, flies and all, had turned to stone. That's the trouble with these garrulous French detectives—they're unpredictable. One moment they wring their dossiers inside out for you, and then—*pouf!*—they shut up like a clam.

🌿 *A HEPCAT MAY LOOK AT A KING*

MICHAEL TODD'S PEEP SHOW, a revue in two acts and twenty-two scenes, staged and lighted by Hassard Short. Music and lyrics by Bhumibol (King of Thailand), Prince Chakraband, Sammy Fain, Herb Magidson, etc., etc.—*From a drama review in the* Herald Tribune.

SCENE: *The Central European branch of Savacool & Thaumaturge, Ltd., theatrical bookers and artists' representatives, in Lausanne, Switzerland. The portion of the offices observable at rise consists of a somewhat bleak anteroom furnished with half a dozen spavined chairs and a spittoon, separated by a low-railed partition from a switchboard and receptionist's desk. Typing away busily at the desk is Sibyl Hinshaw, a thin, atrabilious girl on whom years of contact with show folk have acted like an olive press and whose features, together with those of Anna Held and Bernhardt on the walls, have long since become part of the fixtures. The occupants of the anteroom, two in number, offer a marked contrast to its shabby décor. The portly gentleman yawning through a copy of* Variety, *who wears a magnificent turban blazing with jewels and a chestful of military orders, bears more than a passing resemblance to the Maharajah of Kapurthala. His companion, more conservatively clad in a frock coat tailored of cloth of gold and trimmed with aigrettes, would not be mistaken east of Suez for anyone but the Nawab of Bhopal. The latter's fingers, incidentally, are so thickly incrusted with emeralds that he is having some difficulty paring his nails. An accordion and a couple of black fiber suitcases, of the sort customarily used by vaudeville performers, lie at their feet.*

BHOPAL: Mind you, I won't say this Bhumibol ain't an able administrator, but he don't know a beguine from a cakewalk. The kid is absolutely devoid of rhythm.

560

KAPURTHALA: He's a Buddhist, that's why. A downbeat don't mean a thing to a Buddhist.

BHOPAL: I'm surprised a showman like Todd would fall for that type air.

KAPURTHALA: Eight to five he's a Buddhist, too. All those guys stick together.

BHOPAL (*carefully lowering his voice*): Well, I heard a story which it may not be gospel but I'll pass it on. You know the skinny monarch who plays the traps at the Café Schlagober? He claims Bhumibol can only write his tunes in the key of C. He's got a little colored fellow in Bangkok that transposes 'em.

KAPURTHALA: Yeah, and I bet he pays him off in fried rice, the chiseler.

BHOPAL: There must be something to it. Why should anybody that their real name is Phumiphon Aduldet suddenly turn around and start calling themselves Bhumibol?

KAPURTHALA: I'll tell you why. So if he gets sued for plagiarism, he's judgment-proof. They're all alike, those kings. The minute they click on Broadway, all they care about is angles.

BHOPAL: I know, but *Bhumibol*—it sounds like a sleeping tablet. If it was Hoagy Bhumibol, or even Blumenthal, you could understand.

KAPURTHALA (*with a shrug*): Go figure out a Siamese. . . . Say, girlie, who do you have to be around here to see Savacool—Genghis Khan? We been waiting an hour.

SIBYL: I've told you already—he's over at the recording studio, cutting a platter.

BHOPAL: Of who?

SIBYL: The Sultan of Morocco, I believe.

BHOPAL: Huh, that groaner! Cliff Edwards in a tarboosh.

KAPURTHALA: Well, there's one thing. Savacool don't have to worry about running out of wax with *that* greaseball around.

BHOPAL: Hey, that's not bad. Maybe we could work it into our routine.

KAPURTHALA: Where we going to play it after we do—at our boarding-house? The bookings Savacool's been getting us, we're lucky to pick up a split week between Antwerp and Kurdistan.

BHOPAL: Look, face facts. The act needs a hypo and there's nothing like dames. Instead of that bit where we jump over our own legs and make with the Indian clubs, I'd like to see some breezy cross-fire with a pair of good-looking babes.

KAPURTHALA (*dangerously*): Are you still trying to unload that ten-cent harem of yours?

BHOPAL: Well, after all, they're sitting around the Punjab eating their heads off, and I thought—

KAPURTHALA: Listen, I don't want any of those Goddamned gazelle-eyed relatives of yours on my payroll, do you hear me?

BHOPAL: Watch that big mouth, brother. They're *my* concubines, and for two rupees I'd knock those betel-stained teeth right down—

SIBYL: Stop it, both of you! No wonder the managers cancel you left and right! You don't need a hypo; you need a referee.

BHOPAL (*with a growl*): Well, nobody talks to *me* like that. My family descends in an unbroken line—

KAPURTHALA: Descends is right. Sponging as they go.

BHOPAL (*seizing him by the throat*): You'll eat those words, you big pail of ghee! (*He releases his grip precipitately as Savacool, a smooth homuncule embodying the less attractive characteristics of Uriah Heep and Simon Legree, enters. He is accompanied by a swarthy young man with liquid eyes, who is dressed in the resplendent uniform of a field marshal.*)

SAVACOOL: Here, here, you two, what's cooking?

KAPURTHALA: Nothing—nothing at all. We were just rehearsing a new pratfall.

SAVACOOL: Well, throw it away. I got you a real break at last—the Hedgehog Room of the Piccadilly, in New York!

BHOPAL: What's that?

SAVACOOL: It's the Wedgwood Room in spades, the place where all the big-shot producers and movie execs hang out. They call it the Showcase of Stars. Once they catch you boys there, you can write your own ticket!

BHOPAL: Does Mike Todd go in there?

SAVACOOL: Go *in* there—he practically sleeps there! I guarantee you, the minute he sees that mind-reading act of yours—

KAPURTHALA: But we do a juggling specialty and nipups.

SAVACOOL: Not any more you don't. From now on, you're high-class Hindu mystics. You know, reading the serial number on people's watches, guessing where they left their umbrella—that is, when you're not waiting on table, of course.

KAPURTHALA (*picking up his accordion*): Well, you can suit yourself, Bhopal, but I'll take the Vale of Kashmir.

SAVACOOL (*quickly*): Who runs that?

KAPURTHALA: It's a kind of a Moslem version of Grossinger's.

SAVACOOL: Oh, playing cozy, eh? Well, remember this, bright eyes—whatever it is, I'm entitled to ten per cent commission.

BHOPAL: Good luck. We'll see you in the small-claims court. (*They exit.*)

SAVACOOL (*bitterly*): That's human nature. You run yourself ragged for a couple of hams, and as soon as the wrinkles are out of their cummerbunds, they spit on you. . . . Oh, well. Have a seat, Riza, be with you in a jiffy. Any calls, Sibyl?

SIBYL: Yes. One of the Soong brothers—T.V., I think. He says they're stranded in Liverpool with that plate-balancing act of theirs.

SAVACOOL: I know, I know. And they need money because the Chinaman's holding their laundry.

SIBYL: No, he won't even do it. He doesn't approve of their politics.

SAVACOOL: Well, what am I supposed to do, fly over and wash it for them?

SIBYL: I couldn't tell. The connection was poor and he insisted on talking in the Mandarin dialect.

SAVACOOL: It's pretty fishy. How can T. V. Soong, that he's one of the wealthiest men in the world, be stranded in Liverpool?

SIBYL: You can't fathom those Orientals. They're a race apart. (*under her breath*) Who's that over there, a Hapsburg?

SAVACOOL: No, the Shah of Iran. He was laying for me on the sidewalk with a note from Shapiro, Bernstein in New York.

SIBYL: Shall I ask him to leave his ballads and you'll contact him?

SAVACOOL (*magnanimously*): Nah, I'll give him a quick shake. Who knows, maybe the poor *nebich* has something we can peddle. (*returning to the anteroom*) O. K., Excellency, you're on the air. Just hum over the lyrics of that novelty you mentioned on the stairs.

SHAH: What do you mean—without a piano or anything?

SAVACOOL: Correct. I'll fill in the sharps and flats in my head.

SHAH: But how can you appreciate all the—well, the tempo and the *lilt* of the song?

SAVACOOL: By instinct, bud—the same way you know if a prime minister is shortchanging you. There's tricks in every trade. Come on, I'll beat time with my foot.

SHAH (*dubiously*): All right, but it's a shame to louse it up. (*He unfurls a roll of music and clears his throat.*)

> *'Way down yonder in Khorramshahr,*
> *That's where singing and dancing are,*
> *It's a pleasure to browse there,*
> *Or so I'm told.*
> *Persian mamas with shapely gams,*
> *Lips as sweet as Southern yams—*

SIBYL (*breaking in*): Sorry, Mr. Savacool. Leopold of Belgium on the wire.

SAVACOOL: I'll call him back in his dressing room.

SIBYL: He's in some sort of jam; his trunks went astray.

SAVACOOL: Holy cats! (*jumping up*) Go on humming, Riza. I'm listening to every word. (*into phone*) Yep, speaking. . . . What? . . . You mean with all the trapeze equipment and everything? . . . Oh, *those* trunks. (*with relief*) What the hell, Leo, you can go on without tights, especially at the matinée. . . . Well, then, borrow a pair of shorts from the stage manager. . . . Positively, by air mail. So long.

SHAH (*continuing undaunted*):

> *Take me back to those dreamy glades,*
> *Let me revel with sloe-eyed maids,*
> *'Way down yonder in Khorramshahr.*

(*anxiously*) How does it strike you, Mr. Savacool?

SAVACOOL: You want my honest reaction, Riza? It's too sophisticated. The average person don't know from the Persian Gulf.

SHAH: Would it be more believable if I made it North Africa? Like:

> *'Way down yonder in Marrakech*
> *That's the place which it gives me a letch.*

SAVACOOL (*concentrating*): No-o-o, I'm groping for some spot—it's on the tip of my tongue. . . . Wait, I got it! What about " 'Way down yonder in New Orleans"?

SHAH: Gee, that'd be sensational!

(*During the foregoing, two individuals swathed in burnooses, but not so heavily as to obscure the fact that they are Ibn-Saud and his son Faisal, have come in. They seat themselves unobtrusively and, realizing they will be forced to wait, draw out a sheep and begin roasting it on a charcoal brazier. Captivated by its delicious odor, Savacool moves toward them like a somnambulist.*)

SAVACOOL: Yes? What can I do for you gents?

IBN-SAUD: Well, it's like this. My boy and I, we've been hashing up a comedy skit. The way we estimate, we have a hundred and fourteen boffs, fifty-six bellies, and twenty-two yocks.

SAVACOOL: Why don't we step into my private office and discuss it over lunch?

FAISAL: We don't want to interrupt you if you're busy.

SAVACOOL (*gaily*): Neighbor, I'm never busy when two guys bust in with a red-hot idea. Here, let me help you carry that stove.

SHAH: Uh—getting back to my lyric, Mr. Savacool, what becomes of the dervish line in the vamp if I make it New Orleans?

SAVACOOL: Yes, yes, work it out along those lines. (*escorting his new clients off*) You know, I might just have an opening for two Arab comics in the Hedgehog Room.

SIBYL (*compassionately, as the Shah stands woebegone*): Cheer up, Your Highness. Remember, there's no business like show business.

SHAH: What did you say? Would you mind repeating that? (*She does. An expression of almost insupportable glee invades his face.*) *Yowzer!* Have I got a terrific theme for a song!

CURTAIN

❧ *WHO STOLE MY GOLDEN METAPHOR?*

I HAD A SUIT over my arm and was heading west down Eighth Street, debating whether to take it to one of those 24-hour dry-cleaning establishments or a Same-Day Cleaner or even a place that might return it before I left it, when I ran smack into Vernon Equinox in front of the Waffle Shop. Fair weather or foul, Vernon can usually be found along there between MacDougal Street and Sixth Avenue, scanning the bargain Jung in the corner bookshop or disparaging the fake Negro primitive masks at the stationery store. His gaunt, greenish-white face, edged in the whiskers once characteristic of fisherfolk and stage Irishmen and now favored by Existentialist poets, his dungarees flecked with paint, and his huaraches and massive turquoise rings clearly stamp Vernon as a practitioner of the arts, though which one is doubtful. The fact is that he favors them all impartially. He writes an occasional diatribe for magazines called *Neurotica* and *Ichor*, paints violent canvases portraying one's sensations under mescaline, dabbles in wire sculpture, and composes music for abstract films as yet unphotographed. He derives his sustenance, if any, from a minuscule shop on Christopher Street, where he designs and fashions copper sconces and jewelry, but since the place is open only from six-thirty in the evening until eight, its revenue is nominal. It has been whispered, late at night in Alex's Borsch Bowl, that Vernon holds a Black Mass now and again in his shop. How he can get a naked woman and a goat into that tiny store, though—let alone himself—is a puzzle.

Anyway, there he was outside the Waffle, staring at the three rows of Dolly Madison ice-cream cones slowly revolving in the window before a background of prisms, and his contempt was magnificent to behold. It was a pretty unnerving display, actually; the ice cream was so obviously pink-tinted cotton and the cones themselves made of the plywood used in orange crates that you instinctively shuddered at the oral damage they could inflict. As he turned away from the window with an almost audible snarl, Vernon caught sight of me.

"Look there," he said furiously, pointing at the multiple rosy reflections shimmering in the glass. "That's what you're up against. Is it any wonder Modigliani died at thirty-three?" I stood transfixed, seeking to fathom the connection between Dolly Madison and the ill-starred Italian painter, but Vernon had already hurdled his rhetorical question. "I give up! I throw in the towel!" he proclaimed. "You spend your whole life trying to imprison a moment of beauty, and they go for borax like that. Gad!"

"When did you get back?" I asked placatingly. There was nothing in his appearance to indicate that he had been away at all, or even exposed to direct sunlight for the past six months; still, it seemed a reasonably safe gambit.

"End of January," he said with a morose backward look at the window.

"Er—how did you like Haiti?" I asked. That too was a wild stab, but I dimly remembered being waylaid outside the Bamboo Forest in an icy wind and told of up-country voodoo rites.

"Haiti?" Vernon repeated, with such withering scorn that two passers-by veered toward the curb. "That tourist drop? Nobody goes there any more. I was in Oaxaca. Not Oaxaca proper, mind you," he corrected, anxious to scotch the impression that he frequented resorts, "a tiny village about sixty miles north, San Juan Doloroso. Completely unspoiled—Elspeth and I lived there for three pesos a day."

"Oh, yes," I said fluently. "Henry Miller mentions it in *Tropic of Capricorn*." From the quick look Vernon gave me, I knew I had planted the seeds of a sleepless night. "Well, old boy," I inquired, giving his shoulder an encouraging clap, "what are you up to these days? When are we going to see a show of those nereids made out of pipe-cleaners?"

"I'm through with that dilettante stuff," said Vernon. "I've been designing some nonobjective puppets. It's a combination of dance and mime. Schoenberg wants to do the music."

"I'd let him," I recommended. "It sounds exciting. Tip me off before the recital, won't you?"

"There isn't going to be any," he said. "The puppets are suspended in zones of light and the music comes over. That is, it's superimposed. We're trying to establish a mood."

"Very definitely," I agreed. "I'm sure it'll work out. Well, good luck, and—"

"I'd have finished it months ago if Truman Capote hadn't sabotaged me," Vernon went on irascibly. "The aggravation I suffered from that episode—well, never mind. Why burden you?"

Arrested by the bitterness in his tone, I turned back. "What do you mean?" I asked. "What did he do?"

"Come in here and I'll show you," said Vernon, propelling me into a coffeepot a few doors away. After extensive byplay with the counter-man involving the preparation of a muffin, obviously calculated to heighten the suspense, he drew a clipping from his wallet. "Did you read this interview with Capote by Harvey Breit? It came out in the *Times Book Review* around a year ago."

"Why, yes," I said vaguely, scanning the text. "It was rather tiptoe, but then, most of the publicity about him is. I didn't notice anything special."

"Nothing except that the little creep helped himself to my whole style," said Vernon with rancor. "Things I said at different parties. It's the most barefaced—"

"Wait a minute," I interrupted. "Those are blunt words, neighbor. You sure of your facts?"

"Ha *ha*!" Vernon emitted a savage cackle. "I just happen to have about two hundred witnesses, that's all! People who were there! Look at this, for instance." He ran his forefinger down a column. "Breit asked Capote to describe himself, and what do you think he said? 'I'm about as tall as a shotgun—and just as noisy. I think I have rather heated eyes.' "

"He's rumored to have ball-and-claw feet too, like a Queen Anne dresser," I returned, "but why should *you* get worked up?"

"Because it's a straight paraphrase of a thumbnail sketch I gave of myself," said Vernon tigerishly. "You know Robin Nankivel, the ceramist—the girl who does the caricatures in porcelain? Well, it was in her studio, next to the Cherry Lane Theater. I remember the whole thing plainly. They were all milling around Capote, making a big fuss. He was wearing a chameleon silk vest and blue tennis sneakers; I could draw you a picture of him. Arpad Fustian, the rug-chandler, and Polly Entrail and I were over in a corner, discussing how we visualized ourselves, and I said I was about as tall as an Osage bow and just as relentless. Right then I happened to look over, and there was Capote looking at me."

"I guess his eyes *are* really heated, though," I said. "The only time I ever saw him, in the balcony of Loew's Valencia, they glowed in the dark like a carnation."

"At first," continued Vernon, too full of his grievance to encompass anything outside it, "I didn't associate this puling little simile of his with my remark. But after I read on further, where he analyzes his voice and features for Breit, I nearly dropped dead. My entire idiom! The same unique, highly individual way I express myself! Here it is—the end of the paragraph. 'Let's see,' he (Capote) said. 'I have a very sassy voice. I like my nose but you can't see it because I wear these thick glasses. If you looked at my face from both sides, you'd see they were completely different. (Mr. Capote demonstrated.) It's sort of a changeling face.' "

I studied the photograph imbedded in the letterpress. "A changeling," I said, thinking out loud, "is a child supposed to have been secretly substituted for another by elves. Does he mean he's not really Truman Capote?"

"Of course he is," said Vernon irritably, "but read the rest—"

"Hold on," I said. "We may have uncovered something pretty peculiar here. This party admits in so many words that he's not legit. How do we know that he hasn't done away with the real Capote—dissolved him in corrosive sublimate or buried him under a floor someplace—and is impersonating him? He's certainly talking funny."

"God damn it, let me finish, will you?" Vernon implored. "It's this last part where he copied my stuff bodily. Listen: 'Do you want to know the real reason why I push my hair down on my forehead? Because I have two cowlicks. If I didn't push my hair forward it would make me look as though I had two feathery horns.' "

"Great Scott!" I exclaimed, a light suddenly dawning. "Don't you see who's talking? It's not Capote at all—it's *Pan*. The feathery horns, the ball-and-claw feet—it all ties together!"

"He can be the Grand Mufti of Jerusalem for all I care," snapped Vernon. "All I know is that I was having brunch at Lee Chumley's one Sunday with Karen Nudnic, the choreographer, and she was wearing a bang. I said she looked like one of those impish little satyrs of Aubrey Beardsley's, and that just for kicks she ought to do up her hair in points to accentuate it. Well, I don't have to tell you who was in the next booth with his ear flapping. Of course, I never thought anything of it at the time."

"It's open and shut," I said. "The jury wouldn't even leave the box."

"Ah, why sue a guy like that?" he replied disgustedly. "So I'd expose him publicly and get six cents in damages. Would that recompense me for my humiliation?"

I tried not to appear obtuse, but the odds were against me. "I don't quite understand how he hurt you," I said. "Did any of your friends spot this—er—similarity between Capote's dialogue and your own?"

"No-o-o, not until I wised them up," admitted Vernon.

"Well, did they avoid you subsequently, or did you lose any customers as a result of it?"

"What?" he shouted. "You think that twirp could make the slightest difference in my life? You must have a lousy opinion of my—"

"Hey, you in the back!" sang out the counterman. "Pipe down! This ain't Webster Hall!"

"No, and it's not Voisin's either!" Vernon snarled. "The coffee here's pure slop. Who are you paying off down at the Board of Health?"

As the two of them, spitting like tomcats, converged from opposite ends of the bar and joyfully began exchanging abuse, I recovered my suit and squirmed out into Eighth Street. The Dolly Madison cones were still revolving turgidly in the Waffle Shop, and a light spring rain fell on the just and the unjust alike. All at once, the fatuity of dry-cleaning a garment that would only become soiled again overcame me. How much more sensible to put the money into some sound cultural investment, such as a copy of *Other Voices, Other Rooms,* for instance, thereby enriching both its talented author and one's own psyche. I instantly directed my steps toward the corner bookshop, but as luck would have it, halfway there I ran into a young bard I know named T. S. Heliogabalus. The story that kid told me!

CLOUDLAND REVISITED: ROLL ON, THOU DEEP AND DARK SCENARIO, ROLL

One August morning during the third summer of the First World War, Manuel Da Costa, a Portuguese eel fisherman at Bullock's Cove, near Narragansett Bay, was calking a dory drawn up beside his shack when he witnessed a remarkable exploit. From around a nearby boathouse appeared a bumpkin named Piggy Westervelt, with a head indistinguishable from an Edam cheese, lugging a bicycle pump and a coil of rubber hose. Behind him, with dragging footsteps, because of the quantities of scrap iron stuffed into his boots, came another stripling, indistinguishable from the present writer at the age of twelve, encased in a diving helmet that was improvised from a metal lard pail. As Da Costa watched with fascinated attention, Piggy ceremoniously conducted me to the water's edge, helped me kneel, and started securing the hose to my casque.

"Can you breathe in there all right?" he called out anxiously. There was some basis for his concern, since, in the zeal of creation, we had neglected to supply a hinge for my visor, and between lack of oxygen and the reek of hot lard my eyes were beginning to extrude like muscat grapes. I signaled Piggy to hurry up and start pumping, but he became unaccountably angry. "How many hands do you think I got?" he bawled. "If you don't like the way I'm doing it, get somebody else!" Realizing my life hung on a lunatic's caprice, I adopted the only rational attitude, that of the sacrificial ox, and shallowed my breathing. Finally, just as the old mitral valve was about to close forever, a few puffs of fetid air straggled through the tube and I shakily prepared to submerge. My objective was an ancient weedy hull thirty feet offshore, where the infamous Edward Teach, popularly known as Blackbeard, was reputed to have foundered with a cargo of bullion and plate. Neither of us had the remotest idea what bullion and plate were, but they sounded eminently useful. I was also to keep a sharp lookout for ambergris, lumps of which were constantly being picked up by wide-awake boys and found to be worth forty thousand dollars. The prospects, viewed from whatever angle, were pretty rosy.

They began to dim the second I disappeared below the surface. By that time, the hose had sprung half a dozen leaks, and Piggy, in a frenzy of misdirected co-operation, had pumped my helmet full of water. Had I not been awash in the pail, I might have been able to squirm out of my boots, but as it was, I was firmly anchored in the ooze and a definite candidate for Davy Jones's locker when an unexpected savior turned up in the person of Manuel Da Costa. Quickly sculling overhead, he captured the hose with a boat hook, dragged me inboard, and pounded the water out of my lungs. The first sight I saw, as I lay gasping in the scuppers, was Manuel towering over me like the Colossus of Rhodes, arms compressed and lips akimbo. His salutation finished me forever as an undersea explorer. "Who the hell do you think you are?" he demanded, outraged. "Captain Nemo?"

That a Rhode Island fisherman should invoke anyone so recherché as the hero of Jules Verne's submarine saga may seem extraordinary, but actually there was every justification for it. All through the preceding fortnight, a movie version of *Twenty Thousand Leagues Under the Sea* had been playing to packed houses at a local peepshow, engendering almost as much excitement as the Black Tom explosion. Everyone who saw it was dumfounded—less, I suspect, by its subaqueous marvels than by its hallucinatory plot and characters—but nobody besides Piggy and me, fortunately, was barmy enough to emulate it. In general, I experienced no untoward effects from my adventure. It did, however, prejudice me unreasonably against salt water, and for years I never mentioned the ocean floor save with a sneer.

Some weeks ago, rummaging through the film library of the Museum of Modern Art, I discovered among its goodies a print of the very production of *Twenty Thousand Leagues* that had mesmerized me in 1916, and, by ceaseless nagging, bedeviled the indulgent custodians into screening it for me. Within twenty minutes, I realized that I was watching one of the really great cinema nightmares, a *cauchemar* beside which *King Kong*, *The Tiger Man*, and *The Cat People* were as staid as so many quilting bees. True, it did not have the sublime irrelevance of *The Sex Maniac*, a masterpiece of Krafft-Ebing symbolism I saw in Los Angeles whose laboratory monkeyshines climaxed in a scene where two Picassoesque giantesses, armed with baseball bats, beat each other to pulp in a cellar. On the other hand, it more than equaled the all-time stowage record set by D. W. Griffith's *Intolerance*, managing to combine in one picture three unrelated plots—*Twenty Thousand Leagues*, *The Mysterious Island*, and *Five Weeks in a Balloon*—and a sanguinary tale of betrayal and murder in a native

Indian state that must have fallen into the developing fluid by mistake. To make the whole thing even more perplexing, not one member of the cast was identified—much as if all the actors in the picture had been slain on its completion and all references to them expunged. I daresay that if Stuart Paton, its director, were functioning today, the votaries of the Surrealist film who sibilate around the Little Carnegie and the Fifth Avenue Playhouse would be weaving garlands for his hair. That man could make a cryptogram out of Mother Goose.

The premise of *Twenty Thousand Leagues*, in a series of quick nut-shells, is that the Navy, dismayed by reports of a gigantic sea serpent preying on our merchant marine, dispatches an expedition to exterminate it. Included in the party are Professor Aronnax, a French scientist with luxuriant crepe hair and heavy eye make-up who looks like a phrenologist out of the funny papers; his daughter, a kittenish ingénue all corkscrew curls and maidenly simpers; and the latter's heartbeat, a broth of a boy identified as Ned Land, Prince of Harpooners. Their quarry proves, of course, to be the submarine *Nautilus*, commanded by the redoubtable Captain Nemo, which sinks their vessel and takes them prisoner. Nemo is Melville's Captain Ahab with French dressing, as bizarre a mariner as ever trod on a weevil. He has a profile like Garibaldi's, set off by a white goatee; wears a Santa Claus suit and a turban made out of a huck towel; and smokes a churchwarden pipe. Most submarine commanders, as a rule, busy themselves checking gauges and twiddling the periscope, but Nemo spends all his time smiting his forehead and vowing revenge, though on whom it is not made clear. The décor of the *Nautilus*, obviously inspired by a Turkish cozy corner, is pure early Matisse; Oriental rugs, hassocks, and mother-of-pearl taborets abound, and in one shot I thought I detected a parlor floor lamp with a fringed shade, which must have been a problem in dirty weather. In all justice, however, Paton's conception of a submarine interior was no more florid than Jules Verne's. Among the ship's accouterments, I find on consulting the great romancer, he lists a library containing twelve thousand volumes, a dining room with oak sideboards, and a thirty-foot drawing room full of Old Masters, tapestry, and sculpture.

Apparently, the front office figured that so straightforward a narrative would never be credible, because complications now really begin piling up. "About this time," a subtitle announces, "Lieutenant Bond and four Union Army scouts, frustrated in an attempt to destroy their balloon, are carried out to sea." A long and murky sequence full of lightning, falling sandbags, and disheveled character actors occupies the next few minutes, the upshot being that the cloud-borne quintet is stranded on a remote key called Mysterious Island. One of its more mysterious aspects is an unchaperoned young person in a leopardskin sarong, who dwells in the trees and mutters gibberish to herself. The castaways find this tropical Ophelia in a pit they have dug to ward off prowling beasts, and Lieutenant Bond, who obviously has been out of touch with women since he was weaned, loses his heart to her. To achieve greater obscurity, the foregoing is intercut with limitless footage of Captain Nemo and his hostages goggling at the wonders of the deep through a window in the side of the submarine. What they see is approximately what anybody might who has quaffed too much sacramental wine and is peering into a home aquarium, but, after all, tedium is a relative matter. When you come right down to it, a closeup of scup feeding around a coral arch is no more static than one of Robert Taylor.

At this juncture, a completely new element enters the plot to further befuddle it, in the form of one Charles Denver, "a retired ocean trader in a distant land." Twelve years earlier, a flashback reveals, Denver had got a skinful of lager and tried to ravish an Indian maharani called Princess Daaker. The lady had thereupon plunged a dagger into her thorax, and Denver, possibly finding the furniture too heavy, had stolen her eight-year-old daughter. We see him now in a mood of remorse approaching that of Macbeth, drunkenly clawing his collar and reviling the phantoms who plague him—one of them, by the way, a rather engaging Mephistopheles of the sort depicted in advertisements for quick-drying varnish. To avoid losing his mind, the trader boards his yacht and sets off for Mysterious Island, a very peculiar choice indeed, for if ever there was a convocation of loonies anywhere, it is there. Captain Nemo is fluthering around in the lagoon, wrestling with an inflated rubber octopus; Lieutenant Bond and the leopard girl (who, it presently emerges, is Princess Daaker's daughter, left there to die) are spooning on the cliffs; and, just to enliven things, one of Bond's scouts is planning to supplant him as leader and abduct the maiden.

Arriving at the island, Denver puts on a pippin of a costume, consisting of a deerstalker cap, a Prince Albert coat, and hip boots, and goes ashore to seek the girl he marooned. He has just vanished into the saw grass, declaiming away like Dion Boucicault, when the screen suddenly blacks out, or at least it did the day I saw the picture. I sprang up buoyantly, hoping that perhaps the film had caught fire and provided a solution for everybody's dilemma, but it had merely slipped off the sprocket. By the time it was readjusted, I, too, had slipped off, consumed a flagon or two, and was back in my chair waiting alertly for the payoff. I soon realized my blunder. I should have stayed in the rathskeller and had the projectionist phone it to me.

Denver becomes lost in the jungle very shortly, and when he fails to return to the yacht, two of the crew go in search of him. They meet Lieutenant Bond's scout, who has meanwhile made indecent overtures to the leopard girl and been declared a pariah by his fellows. The trio rescue Denver, but, for reasons that defy analysis, get plastered and plot to seize the yacht and sail away with the girl.

During all this katzenjammer, divers from the *Nautilus* have been reconnoitering around the craft to learn the identity of its owner, which presumably is emblazoned on its keel, inasmuch as one of them hastens to Nemo at top speed to announce with a flourish, "I have the honor to report that the yacht is owned by Charles Denver." The Captain forthwith stages a display of vindictive triumph that would have left Boris Thomashefsky, the great Yiddish tragedian, sick with envy; Denver, he apprises his companions, is the man against whom he has sworn undying vengeance. In the meantime (everything in *Twenty Thousand Leagues* happens in the meantime; the characters don't even sneeze consecutively), the villains kidnap the girl, are pursued to the yacht by Bond, and engage him in a fight to the death. At the psychological moment, a torpedo from the *Nautilus* blows up the whole shebang, extraneous characters are eliminated, and as the couple are hauled aboard the submarine, the big dramatic twist unfolds: Nemo is Prince Daaker and the girl his daughter. Any moviemaker with elementary decency would have recognized this as the saturation point and quit, but not the producer of *Twenty Thousand Leagues*. The picture bumbles on into a fantastically long-winded flashback of Nemo reviewing the whole Indian episode and relentlessly chewing the scenery to bits, and culminates with his demise and a strong suspicion in the onlooker that he has talked himself to death. His undersea burial, it must be admitted, has an authentic grisly charm. The efforts of the funeral party, clad in sober diving habit, to dig a grave in the ocean bed finally meet with defeat, and, pettishly tossing the coffin into a clump of sea anemones, they stagger off. It seemed to me a bit disrespectful not to blow "Taps" over the deceased, but I suppose nobody had a watertight bugle.

An hour after quitting the Museum, I was convalescing on a bench in Central Park when a brandy-nosed individual approached me with a remarkable tale of woe. He was, he declared, a by-blow of Prince Felix Youssoupoff, the assassin of Rasputin, and had been reared by Transylvanian gypsies. Successively a circus aerialist, a mosaic worker, a diamond cutter, and a gigolo, he had fought (or at least argued) with Wingate's Raiders, crossed Outer Mongolia on foot, spent two years in a Buddhist monastery, helped organize the Indonesian resistance, and become one of the financial titans of Lombard Street. A woman, he confided huskily, had been his undoing—a woman so illustrious that the mere mention of her name made Cabinets totter. His present financial embarrassment, however, was a purely temporary phase. Seversky had imported him to the States to design a new helicopter, and if I could advance him a dime to phone the designer that he had arrived, I would be amply reimbursed. As he vanished into oblivion cheerily jingling my two nickels, the old lady sharing my bench put down her knitting with a snort.

"Tommyrot!" she snapped. "Hunh, you must be a simpleton. That's the most preposterous balderdash I ever heard of."

"I *am* a simpleton, Madam," I returned with dignity, "but you don't know beans about balderdash. Let me tell you a movie I just saw." No sooner had I started to recapitulate it than her face turned ashen, and without a word of explanation she bolted into the shrubbery. An old screwbox, obviously. Oh, well, you can't account for anything nowadays. Some of the stuff that goes on, it's right out of a novel by Jules Verne.

❦ HEAT YEGGS IN VESSEL AND SPRINKLE WITH HAZARD

For 57 years Macy's Taster has rarely sat down to a quiet meal at home. For he's always coming or going . . . scouting this country and Europe for better, rarer, more exotic delicacies. Part Sherlock, part Escoffier, he's flown so many air miles he may be more bird than man. For 38 of his 57 years as Macy's Taster, he has made regular trips across the Atlantic . . . always on the track of another discovery: an especially fiery mustard in Dijon, an unusual oatmeal in Ireland, a particularly pristine olive oil in Italy.—*Adv. in the* Times.

Italian Spaghetti a la Toffenetti . . . with Mushroom Sauce. The sauce is made from a treasured recipe of old, discovered by Mrs. Toffenetti in archives among the ruins of the ancient Castle of the Count of Bonpensier in Bologna.—*From a Toffenetti menu.*

Romeo Salta, owner of the restaurant which is such a favorite with lovers of Italian food, goes to unusual lengths to stock his larder with the finest delicacies. He travels all over the world to sample new dishes, and thinks nothing of having his breadsticks flown over daily from Italy, his lemons from Cuba.—*Dorothy Kilgallen in the* Journal-American.

IT WAS on the boat train from Paris to Le Havre that I met Norman Popenoe, though come to think of it, I first saw him, prior to boarding the train, in the buffet of the Gare Saint-Lazare. I was dallying over a farewell *café crème*, unable to realize that my brief European idyl was over and that inside a fortnight I should again be an anonymous librarian in Wichita, when the man at my left turned toward me. A bulky old duffer in a broad-brimmed panama, he reminded me fleetingly of the late Sydney Greenstreet, until I had a closer look at his face. His fantastic hawk's nose, flanked by hooded, quartzlike eyes, brought to mind a grotesque bird of prey, yet his mouth was that of an

577

epicure, one who had sampled every vintage and kickshaw of the gourmet's art.

"Forgive the liberty," he said, "but what did you think of the lobster bisque at Prunier's? A bit on the viscous side, perhaps?"

"I beg your pardon?" I said, not quite sure I had heard aright.

"And the *foie gras* at the Périgourdine," he continued blandly. "Far too much seasoning, between ourselves. After all, the mission of the herb is to accentuate rather than impregnate, *n'est-ce pas?*"

I stared at the fellow utterly nonplused, trying to place him. It was true I'd just emptied my purse in a final gastronomical debauch, but I didn't recall seeing him at either of the places he named. "Have we met somewhere?" I blurted out, feeling uncommonly sheepish.

"Never saw you before in my life," he averred. "I needn't have, though—these stains on your sleeve tell the story. D'ye mind if I corroborate?" Without biding for an answer, he bent over, gave the fabric a delicate, expert sniff, and straightened up. "Quite," he said with a benign smile. "You've also been to Le Chien Qui Fume, but you chose wrong. You should have had their *gigot en potpourri à la Provençale*—a classic experience. Good morning." He inclined his head civilly and, retrieving a stick and dispatch case from the zinc, vanished into the horde of passengers milling around the concourse. So sudden was the encounter and so inexplicable that I was still recovering a quarter of an hour later as my train rattled through the outer suburbs. There seemed to be no rational explanation. The man was a trickster, I supposed—and a clever one, for his guesses had been uncanny—but maybe overeating had led me into byways of fantasy. I gave up speculating and retired into the autumn issue of the *Hibbert Journal*.

Between its somniferous prose and the vibration of the carriage, I must have lapsed into a doze, because I came to with the abrupt sensation of being watched. Seated opposite, his basilisk eyes fixed on mine, was my neighbor of the buffet. He emitted a chuckle obviously designed to reassure me.

"I owe you an apology," he said, extending a card. "No doubt you were shaken by that display of my olfactory powers. People frequently are." The card bore the name of Norman Popenoe and beneath it that of Milwaukee's renowned department store, Passedoit, Vavasour & Munch. Mr. Popenoe shrugged self-deprecatingly. "Nothing spooky or inspired about it," he confessed. "My nose is my job, as it were; I'm senior taster of the firm. I buzz around the globe rooting out tidbits for the discerning—baby squid and sea urchins from Livorno, stewed iguana from Yucatán, fried locusts from Somaliland, anything that contributes to gracious living."

I introduced myself in turn. "I envy your footloose existence," I remarked, "but isn't it rather hard on your family?"

"Haven't sat down to a quiet meal at home for forty-three years," he admitted. "However, that's no loss. My wife's the worst cook in Christendom."

"Well, she has a tough assignment," I said. "Virtuosity like yours would make anyone self-conscious."

"Thank you," he said, visibly pleased. "You flatter me. We're to be shipmates on the Dyspepsia, I take it?"

His conjecture verified, we exchanged a few inanities about travel, and Mr. Popenoe, for all his vulturine exterior, soon proved a most companionable soul. His calling, I learned, was marked by ferocious competition; tasters would resort to any extreme, not excluding mayhem, to bag a more odoriferous Stilton, a gummier caviar, or a less palatable health bread. He spoke also of his past, of his novitiate in the bloater and sprat division of Filene's in Boston, his triumphs at Scruggs-Vandervoort-Barney's in St. Louis—where he had introduced the first macadamia nuts, Canadian muskrat, and crystallized violets eaten in the Midwest—and the nightmare years in Los Angeles preceding his current post. "Barbarism," he said with a shudder. "The indigenes are worse than Australian bushmen. All they care about is passion fruit and jumbo malteds."

In the turmoil of embarkation, I lost sight of Popenoe, but at the cocktail hour he waylaid me in the ship's bar. Excusing his officiousness, he offered to have me placed at the captain's table. The prospect of its superior fare conquered my diffidence, and I was not disappointed. Captain Lovibond, a myopic dumpling of a man with tinted spectacles and a luxuriant red beard, was a host who left no serviette unturned to please us. He threw the table d'hôte to the winds, interrogating us painstakingly on our whims and satisfying them with every delicacy at his command. The reason for his solicitude emerged presently. Our two tablemates were, like Popenoe, experts on cuisine, and both, coincidentally, restaurateurs in New York. Mrs. Fettucini was a handsome, overblown creature, mascaraed like Clara Kimball Young and twice as grandiloquent, whose slightest gesture released clouds of scent from her massive, rigidly corseted embonpoint. In repose her face tended to be sullen, but occasionally she broke into an inscrutable smile implying that she harbored some momentous secret. Mr. Balderdacci, portly and volcanic, radiated a similar theatricality;

several times during the meal, I expected him to spray the dining room with gems from *The Barber of Seville,* but luckily he forbore. The two, it transpired, had been scouring Italy for piquancies to enhance their menus, and very shortly they began to boast of their acquisitions and taunt each other.

"You'll soon be back selling charcoal, Balderdacci," the lady chortled. "My new recipe for gnocchi is going to blast you out of business. It is worth its weight in gold."

"Banana oil," he jeered. "Wait till you see the reviews of the green peppers I found in Milan." He blew an ecstatic kiss. "I got six downstairs under lock and key. Starting next Tuesday," he announced portentously, "special couriers in trench coats like Cesar Romero will bring them over to me every night. That's how I treat *my* customers."

"Where'd you discover this recipe of yours, Madame?" the captain asked.

"Oh, in some dusty old archives in Lasagna," she said evasively.

"Which archives?" Balderdacci demanded, jealous. "I combed through all of them, but I didn't see anything about gnocchi."

Mrs. Fettucini hesitated, then complacency overrode her caution. "In the ruins under the ancient castle of the Marchesa di Rigmarole," she gloated. Balderdacci was effectively demolished; that was the one place, he admitted, chopfallen, he had neglected to look. Captain Lovibond stroked his beard manifestly disquieted.

"I shouldn't leave it lying around my stateroom," he counseled. "Let me put it in the purser's safe for you, Mrs. Fettucini. That goes for the peppers as well. I'd feel better if I could keep an eye on them."

"Oh, come, come," Popenoe interjected in a curiously silky tone. "Surely there's no danger of their being purloined? Who'd be foolhardy enough to attempt it—in mid-ocean, under our very noses?" He was regarding the captain steadily, an expression on his face I couldn't quite fathom.

"As master of this ship, sir, it's my duty to forestall any eventuality," said Lovibond with a touch of frost. "However, if you people take adequate precautions, nothing untoward can happen. And now, would you all join me for a cognac in the lounge?"

Popenoe's estimate of our fellow-passengers after we dispersed was not cluttered by magnanimity. He likened Mrs. Fettucini to the faded meringues one instinctively avoids in pastry shops, and hinted that her colleague's operatic gusto cloaked a devious and crafty nature. Deeming his tartness professional jaundice, I paid little heed, but I had cause to recollect it the following evening. Mrs. Fettucini arrived at dinner fizzing like a Catherine wheel; when she finally subsided, it was to inform us that the recipe was gone. The details left no doubt that the circumstances were deliberate and nefarious. Whoever ransacked her cabin had ignored a tempting quantity of jewels and cash, intent only on the gustatory prize he knew was there.

"Well, that rules out a sneak thief," said the captain bluntly. "This is the work of someone with a motive." He stared at Mrs. Fettucini's embonpoint, reluctant to meet her gaze. "Did anybody else on board know about the recipe?" She shook her head. There was an uncomfortable pause. Balderdacci cleared his throat as if to speak, then thought better of it. A cold drop that was not vichyssoise rolled down my temple. Popenoe unexpectedly broke the silence.

"Let's not jump to conclusions, folks," he purred. "Any one of us might have done it—myself included. As this gentleman's aware—" he nodded toward me—"we often split ethics in my profession to land an exceptional dainty. A delectable gnocchi would be worth a mint to Passedoit, Vavasour & Munch, I assure you."

Constrained as the atmosphere was already, his cocky avowal made it well-nigh stifling. The meal became interminable; conversation was minimal and furtive, fits of coughing epidemic. Weighing Balderdacci as the prime suspect, I decided he was too chickenhearted. Then I tried to divine Popenoe's reason for incriminating himself, but got nowhere. The words he uttered as we left the room made his behavior even more enigmatic.

"If I were Balderdacci," he said with a conspiratorial wink, "I'd keep a chair against my door tonight. There's many a slip between the peppers and the lip, *amigo*."

"Why, what do you mean?" I queried, startled.

"Oh, nothing—nothing at all," he tittered. "Just that daylight may bring fresh surprises. A diverting voyage, no? Well, pleasant dreams." He strode off whistling into the darkness, leaving me to disentangle a hopelessly twisted skein. Baffled, I made for my berth and the relative lucidity of *Finnegans Wake*.

The tragic mask Balderdacci brought to luncheon the next day told us unmistakably what was amiss. The unknown marauder had struck again, filching his peppers from a seemingly impregnable wardrobe trunk. Livid with anguish, the victim rocked to and fro. "I was saving them for Kilgallen personally," he wailed. "How can I face her and the other critics—Clementine Paddleford, Nickerson . . ."

"Pull yourself together, man," Captain Lovibond snapped. "You'll panic the rest of the passengers. We must proceed warily. Above all, remain calm."

"Calm! Calm!" burst out Mrs. Fettucini. She flung a venomous nod toward Popenoe. "Ask *him* where he was last night! He said he could use my recipe, didn't he?"

The mockery in Popenoe's eyes yielded to a dangerous glint, and he arose. "*Dolce, Signora, dolce*," he said, satin menace in his tone. "It would be wanton folly to lodge any accusations you couldn't support." He touched my shoulder. "Might we have a word in private, my boy?"

In a secluded corner of the hurricane deck, my companion, speaking with marked urgency, drove to the point at once. While it was premature to confide anything, he said, events had reached a critical stage. He vitally needed an ally to help him further a plan; could he count on my co-operation?

"Of course," I said, bewildered. "But I don't understand—"

"You will ere long," he promised. "Now listen, closely. At dinner tonight, I shall entrust to your safekeeping, with a tedious preface about its value, a canister of Irish oatmeal I discovered in Maynooth. Express misgivings, shun the responsibility, but acquiesce. Then take it to your cabin, put out the lights, and lie doggo till I arrive." He stopped on a hesitant note. "I should warn you there's an element of danger," he said. "The person we're dealing with will stick at nothing to get that cereal."

"Librarians' muscles aren't as stringy as they seem," I said quietly. "We lift some pretty heavy folios out in Wichita."

"Good show," he said, pleased. "*Au 'voir*, then, and remember—follow my instructions to the letter."

By mealtime, I would gladly have withdrawn my pledge had pride allowed, and it took a stiff vermouth to gird myself for the role thrust on me. Despite the gloomy suspicion enveloping the table, however, and the Italians' threnody about their plight, all went off as outlined. I accepted Popenoe's canister after much protest, hurried it to my quarters, and sat down with pounding heart to await him. Within ten minutes, he slipped into the darkened cabin, wheezing audibly.

"Was that all right?" I whispered.

"Capital," he said with elation. "A few seconds and our bird will flutter into the snare. Don't move."

"Did you see Mrs. Fettucini react to the oatmeal? Her eyes glistened like black olives."

"Sh-h-h!" he hissed, and clutched my arm. "I hear footsteps—douse your cigarette!"

We crouched immobile, straining our ears; the footsteps drew closer, receded. Aeons passed. At length I heard the click of a key in the lock and saw a shadowy figure illuminated on the threshold. As it entered stealthily, Popenoe sprang for the electric switch. Blinking in the sudden glare, a guilty flush dyeing his cheeks, stood Captain Lovibond.

"Looking for some Maynooth porridge, Captain?" inquired Popenoe in a honeyed voice. "I wouldn't blame you. It's priceless."

"I— I only wanted to make sure it was safe," our caller stammered.

"Most considerate of you," Popenoe granted, "but I'm afraid your little imposture has run its course." With a lightning gesture, he ripped off the other's beard and glasses. "So, Pachyderm," he said exultantly. "We meet at last, do we?"

"Who is this man?" I asked, my jaw dropping.

"Rory Pachyderm, of Springer, Uris & Bodkin's in Cleveland," he said, each word the knell of doom. "One of the most unscrupulous tasters in the annals of retail merchandising. The diabolic and twisted genius behind every culinary snatch of our time, a Moriarty so devoid of conscience that he would heist a child's onion from its Martini or a cripple's anchovy paste if it served his ends."

"Curse you for a meddling swine, Popenoe," snarled Pachyderm. "I'll square accounts with you one day, mark my words."

His nemesis measured him coolly. "Take him away, girls," he ordered the two burly stewardesses, armed with boat hooks, who had appeared meanwhile. "And I think that if you search the chartroom closet, you will find your true skipper, trussed up as neatly as a fowl, where this rascal has impounded him."

"But how on earth did you ever penetrate his disguise?" I demanded as Pachyderm was borne away fuming. "Don't tell me you recognized him."

"Never saw him before in my life," said Popenoe. "However, in my job the trained ear is just as essential as the nose. That first night at dinner, I heard our *soi-disant* captain refer to the ship's funnels as chimneys and the hold as the basement. One rarely employs such terms at sea."

"Nor does one pretend guilt, as you did, to rid society of a scourge," I replied with unconcealed respect. "You took a long chance, Popenoe. You might have been rewarded with a sharp pain in your tripes, like a stiletto."

"I still may be," he replied jovially. "Would you join me for a triple cognac in the lounge?"

❧ ON ME IT LOOKS WIZARD

You know the Fifth Avenue lobby of the Plaza, facing the golden miss in the Fountain of Abundance? And the circular banquette that dominates it? Of course you do; many's the time you've fumed there, I'll wager, waiting for some popsy who never showed up, or who was so visibly jingled when she did that you knew you'd been supplanted. Anyway, if your head size happens to be seven and an eighth and you can contrive to stop by there next Monday morning, you'll stumble into a Klondike. Just bring along three dollars in unmarked bills and hand them to the narrator, and he'll hand you a brand-new English hat—an absolute beauty. It's not every day a man runs into merchandise like this—a genuine import with almost no mileage on it, finest quality felt, smartly styled in dark green, and guaranteed to harmonize with anything in one's kit. No, sir, you don't have to worry about *this* hat. I've already done it for you.

The circumstances date back, broadly, to a cocktail party I attended about a year ago, at which some befuddled guest (or klepto, more likely) abstracted a hat I'd owned since 1947. I shan't weary you with any panegyrics on this hat other than to say that it had certain associations. When I settled it on my head, I was reminded of how we had crossed the raging Salween together during the monsoon rains, of how I had doffed it one winter's day in Shanhaikwan, overcome with emotion at my first sight of the Great Wall of China. Wadded into a ball, it had been my pillow aboard a dhow named the Triumph of Sensuality en route to Zanzibar, a missile to deter Balinese pye-dogs from their nocturnal howling, and a flail to combat *Anopheles* in the saw grass of the Albert Nile. I had drunk water from it in the burning wastes of Kenya's Northern Frontier District, sheepishly twisted it as I besought understanding from odalisques in Hollywood and unfriendly finance companies on Lexington Avenue. In short, that hat wasn't just headgear, if you dig me; it was folks—or, in the inexpressibly more tangy phrase of Lindy's, *mishpocha*.

The hat my host forced on me in exchange (there was a torrential downpour in progress) was a greasy black affair of the sort generally

584

affected by sculptors—or, rather, sculptors in Shubert musicals. Saturated with rain and limply sagging over my ears, it made me look like some flyblown poseur out of "Bubu de Montparnasse," and the taxi-driver's oblique appraisal, when I eventually found a cab, confirmed my fears. "Where to, Doc?" he asked, with a familiar wink. "One of them poetry pads down on MacDougal Street?" The next day, I made a valiant and utterly bootless attempt to recover my property. Nobody at the party recalled it; indeed, several people swore I had worn the sepulchral black number on arrival, and wondered why I was belatedly aping Maurice Maeterlinck. With a heavy heart, I resigned myself to the loss of my old talisman, and, abandoning the bohemian makeshift in an areaway, set out to procure a substitute.

The second I entered the hat department of the Madison Avenue outfitters I patronize, I was dumfounded by the change it had undergone in the brief intervening decade. The place was lit up like a delicatessen, and the palsied octogenarians who had served me from boyhood had all been replaced by whippersnappers with exophthalmos and white carnations, who, quite obviously, were dedicated to one goal only—to sell as many hats as possible. Bursting with self-satisfaction, the beefiest and most florid swept down on me.

"Let's see," he said, giving me a diagnostician's frown. "We'd like something on the sporty side—velours with a feather in the back, eh?"

"Where'd you get that idea?" I asked, making a mental note to buy the store at the earliest opportunity and banish him to the stockroom.

"Your head type," he said complacently. "You've a broad, knobby cranium there, friend—what we call brachycephalic."

"With fairly prominent ears," I bade him observe. I amended my earlier note; instead of demotion, I would fire him and reduce his whole family to penury.

"Oh, they're not *too* bad," he said with the clear implication that Ichabod Crane's were worse. "Anyway, we'll dig up something to distract attention from them. Step over here."

In the ensuing half hour, I tried on every kind of headdress, from billycocks to lumberjack toques—trilbies, telescopic little beanies that transformed me into a Mittel-Europan gigolo, cattlemen's sombreros, minute sports caps with adjustable belts, even the astrakhan tarboosh that Muscovite travelers wear in sleighs pursued by wolves. All of them, without exception, seemed alien to my features; not one had the panache, the verve my old hat had acquired in the brine of the Banda Sea and the snows of Kilimanjaro. The salesman's glib small talk dried up into a series of impatient snorts as he strove abortively to pierce my indifference. At last, having vetoed a beret and a raffish tweed whim-wham popularized by Rex Harrison, I reluctantly consented to a chocolate-brown Homburg made in England. Its lofty conical crown, almost seven inches tall, gave me a rather Foreign Office aspect. The only knock was that the brim refused to snap down—a shortcoming that filled me with anguish. Nevertheless, with repeated steaming and kneading, we managed to achieve the debonair effect I felt was vital, and, amid oily reassurances that the hat would swiftly adapt to its new owner, I bore it away.

For a week or so, the Homburg behaved itself and, I was pleased to note, measurably raised my status in the community. Our newsdealer, under the illusion that I had turned financier, whipped out the Wall Street closing at the sight of me. My wife, with a prefatory spoonful of Karo to the effect that men over forty looked well in Chesterfields, began needling me to discard the shopping bag I use as a portfolio and buy an attaché case. Then, as though actuated by a Poltergeist, the wretched hat started to carry on in the most capricious, spiteful manner. The brim flew up, and thereafter, defying all attempts to press it flat with bookends, a typewriter, and an andiron, invariably sprang back to its original position. With the brim upturned, the thing was ludicrous; I looked shifty, full of stratagems, a third-rate grifter casing prospects for the handkerchief switch outside the Hotel Dixie. I hastened back to the store to complain to the salesman, but he was on vacation—lolling at Montego Bay, obviously on the commission from my Homburg—and I had to visit my aggravation on the floorwalker.

"You see," I said patiently, "my original hat, the one I had in Burma but lost at the party—that is, if it *was* lost, which I very much doubt—had a soft brim, unlike this one—"

"Yes, yes," the floorwalker cut in. "Now, look, it's all very simple. Has this hat ever been out in the rain?"

"Certainly," I said, "but I always protect it with a cellophane bag—you know, so I'll be mistaken for an osteopath or a New Jersey chicken farmer."

"Quite," he said uncertainly. "Well, the difficulty is that the ribbon around the edge here has shrunk, and that causes the brim to pop up."

"O.K.," I said. "Then suppose you replace it."

"Can't," he said, with unconcealed satisfaction. "The English ribbon's an altogether different shade from ours." I asked if he could conceivably send for a piece, and was informed that the hat itself must be shipped overseas, necessitating a lapse of two months. The most feasible solution, in his view, was to have the repair made on my next trip to Britain, where the hatmakers might appreciate the dimensions of the problem. "Usually happens with a round, flat head like yours," he consoled me. "The way your temples bulge, it's bound to force the average hat out of shape."

"They only bulge this way when I come in here," I began heatedly. "I never had any troub—"

"How old are you?" he queried. I told him, and he smiled compassionately. "Better see a specialist, old sock," he said. "You need a cardiogram, not a snap-brim. Excuse me, won't you? I can't stand here jawing all day."

It was well-nigh seven months before I got to London and the modest shop in Jermyn Street whose signboard advised the passerby that Farquhar & Petrie had been hatters here by royal patent since Wat Tyler's Rebellion. Its tranquil interior, untainted by the wolfish commercialism I was used to, inspired confidence; the Regency pier glasses, the few discreet hatboxes in the cupboards, and the decorous help in their dove-gray dusters all proclaimed an outpost—perhaps the last—of craftsmanship. I could have embraced the kindly old clerk who greeted me so civilly. His sweet, saintly face reminded me of Alec Francis in the movies, and his seamed cheeks glowed like pippins.

"Ah, yes, sir," he said sympathetically as I poured out my tale. "We had a similar complaint from a Wyoming gentleman some years ago, except that his brim refused to stay up. Jackson's Hole—is that anywhere near your lodge?" I unsnarled his geography and led him gently back to my dilemma. "You know," he observed after due examination of my Homburg, "there's nothing amiss with the ribbon. The crown's been wrenched out of shape. Of course you keep it on a form whilst using your other hats?"

"I—er— Which other ones?" I hedged, playing for time. "Offhand, I don't recall—I mean I'd have to ask my valet—"

His saintly old face hardened. "But this is a town hat, you must be aware," he said, in a pained voice. "Surely you haven't worn it in the country, sir—for rough shooting or beagling?"

"Good heavens, no!" I assured him, forcing a grisly simulacrum of a chuckle. "I daresay the stewardess dented it aboard the aircraft. . . . Those low rafters at the Cheshire Cheese . . ."

"I daresay," he returned, his lips compressed. Drawing me out of earshot of the other clients, he explained that it was mandatory to rotate hats, like shoes. If the wearer was not a downright vag, his headgear needed intervals of rest on a made-to-order facsimile. He would strongly suggest that I order three or four such from him without delay. "Chap in Manchester carves them for us in pearwood," he confided. "A bit steep at thirty-six guineas, but they'll pay for themselves handsomely over the years to come."

"Well—um—all right," I said feebly. "Put me down for three. But how about this hat? Can't you possibly fix it so the brim stays down?"

"I'll mail it off to our Nottingham works posthaste," he promised. "We should get a report in a fortnight or two. Now, then," he said briskly, "we've got to find you something to wear in the interval. What sort of bowler did you have in mind?"

My destiny was already so intertwined with Farquhar & Petrie that I knew protest was futile. Pliant as a lynchee doll, I let myself be dragooned into trying on two-thirds of their stock. Just as the staff was collapsing in frustration, they discovered from a chance remark that I had a peripheral connection with show business. Ten minutes later, I emerged from the shop in a dashing green pork pie reminiscent of Sherwood Forest—the exact duplicate, according to the clerks, of one they had supplied to my confrere Sir John Gielgud. I have telegraphed Sir John twice recently, offering to let him in on a bargain, but thus far he has vouchsafed no reply. Unless he turns up at the Plaza Monday with cash in hand, it'll be first come, first served; I'm closing out this merchandise lock, stock, and barrel. I'm also sacrificing three lovely pearwood hatstands, which cost eighty-eight guineas originally, as well as a dark-brown Homburg with an iron brim, but we can talk about that later. Right now it's much too painful.

🌸 *THE YANKS ARE COMING, IN FIVE BREATHLESS COLORS*

IF, AT THE MOMENT, you're intent on piloting a wire carriage across a supermarket, or a plane through the overcast, or a cartel through reorganization, I don't want to rattle you, and please don't abandon the controls for anything. If, however, you're basking before the hearth with a siphon handy and Rosy Fahrleit playing over your face, and are convinced that life isn't so insupportable after all, you're exhibiting symptoms of *hubris* and I have the very corrective you need. It's to be taken externally, in the form of a letter received by several publishers around town from an outfit in Dallas called the Lake Park Research Specialists, W. D. Cross, President:

> DEAR SIR:
>
> We are living today in a nation which surely must be man's nearest approach to the proverbial "Land of Milk and Honey." Certainly, huge fortunes have been amassed in other lands and in other times but never have so many hundreds of thousands of families, in one nation, had the means to buy the finest products available, regardless of price.
>
> The truth of the above statement has been brought home to me many times in my regular work of forecasting the growth of cities, and the telephone market, for the Southwestern Bell Telephone Company. It is a well established fact that the standard of living is on a long term upward trend. This means that not only can more families afford many of the available luxuries, many others are becoming interested in them.
>
> On this premise we are compiling a book to illustrate and describe several hundred of the most outstanding and costly products regularly available on the American market. These products fall into categories ranging from wearing apparel and home furnishings to sports equipment and pets. We believe the unique and interesting aspect of our book will be the wide diversity of the luxuries included. . . .

589

The products in this *Almanach de Gotha* of merchandise, ranging from a $4.95 can of pretzels to an airplane costing $540,000, are to be colorfully illustrated and will carry short, enticing descriptions, regarding which Mr. Cross observes, in a singularly artless aside, "The text . . . will not conflict with the advertising policy of the companies represented since it is to be largely based on copy furnished by them." Among these companies, and to exemplify the catholicity of the subject matter, are Rolls-Royce, I. Magnin, Royal Crown Derby, Mr. John, Schmieg & Kotzian, Poodles Inc., Bronzini, Dorothy Gray, Bachman Bakeries, and Fiddler's Green, all of whom have responded vibrantly to the tocsin. There is also appended a list of eighty-six assorted products, which includes such bijoux as "Breakfront—$6,000," "Four Postage Stamps—$2,850," "Beef Roast—$27.50," "Mink Coat—$12,980," "Kitten—$200," "Needlework Carpet (sq. yd.)— $495," and "Tub and Shower Controls—$240." Got the picture?

One could blithely shrug off Mr. Cross and reach for the siphon and Rosy except that the proposal has another, and far more baleful, aspect. After declaring that the gift of this book would imply the recipient to be a person of discrimination—a rather carefree assumption— its advocate continues with true Texan buoyancy, "It has also been suggested to me that the State Department might buy copies for overseas libraries to illustrate the rewards held out to the more successful under our system of free enterprise." As the stanchest adherent of free enterprise since Collis P. Huntington, I shall labor unceasingly to propagate it as long as the breath whistles in my lungs. I do feel, notwithstanding, that Mr. Cross's export scheme deserves extremely sober reflection before barging into it. There are certain far-flung locales where his book may have an unintended impact, and I think that since forecasting is his métier, he might usefully try some in this direction—or better yet, permit us to. Let's adjourn, therefore, to Tanganyika, in British East Africa, and see what cooks there. Careful where you sit, bub; those blasted sisal plants are needle-sharp.

SCENE: *A Masai encampment in the shadow of Mount Kilimanjaro— a huddle of twelve or fifteen earth-and-wattle mounds inside a thorn fence contrived to discourage marauding lions. Seated before a mound atop which a broken Pepsi-Cola bottle proclaims its administrative status is Undaprivolo, headman of the camp. He is a magnificent specimen, tall and lissome as one of the golden acacias painted on the backdrop, and his poll, thickly pomaded with zebra fat, glistens in the afterglow. He is endeav-*

oring, with scant success, to read a tattered magazine. From within his hive issues a discord of women's voices raised in execration and laughter.

UNDAPRIVOLO (*shouting into the interior*): Hey, you in there! How do you expect a man to concentrate? (*The noise subsides abruptly. As he returns to his periodical, No'Valuta, another Masai chieftain, enters bearing his tribal spear, shield, and fly whisk.*) Oh, hello, No'Valuta. What brings you over this way?

No'VALUTA: Just the nomad instinct. As you know, we Masai are herdsmen; we have no fixed place of abode.

UNDAPRIVOLO: Yes, ours is a marginal existence, subsisting as we do on a mixture of blood and milk and frequently decimated by the ravages of the tsetse fly.

No'VALUTA: Well, I guess that pretty well cleans up the exposition. What are you perusing there with such interest?

UNDAPRIVOLO: An American organ of show biz y-clept *Variety*, which it ofttimes contains stray nuggets of info pertaining to these climes. Do you recall a stocky little chap, an author, who was on safari hereabouts a while ago?

No'VALUTA: The Serengeti's been full of stocky authors the past few years. Hemingway . . . Ruark . . . Buchwald . . .

UNDAPRIVOLO: Ruark—that's the name. We got him a couple of rhino, all right, but it sure took plenty of typewriter ribbon. Well, he's just bagged some more. It says here that M-G-M paid three hundred grand for his tome *Something of Value*.

No'VALUTA: Boy, that ain't sisal. How much is a grand?

UNDAPRIVOLO: I don't know exactly, but I think about two dollars.

No'VALUTA: Those Yankees certainly throw it around. I was in Arusha, buying some mint to hang on my spear, when that all-girl safari came through. Do you know that every blessed one of them had their own individual toothbrush?

UNDAPRIVOLO: True, but the whole bevy of fifteen had only one author betwixt them. A nearsighted coot with ginger-colored mustaches—named Pebbleman, some name like that.

No'VALUTA: Still, one gracious personality like him is worth a dozen of your average scriveners, in my view.

UNDAPRIVOLO: Agreed. And speaking of the unusual, have you seen the catalogue of American luxury wares available under their free-enterprise system?

No'VALUTA: You mean the one assembled by a Texan soothsayer that his job is predicting the growth of cities, and the telephone market, for Southwestern Bell? No, I haven't, old man.

UNDAPRIVOLO (*extracting a volume from his toga*): Well, here is a mint copy I brought home on my spear from the U.S.I.S. Library in Nairobi.

NO'VALUTA: A classy piece of bookmaking. I note that the dust jacket reproduces in full color an orchid, a 1913 Mercer Raceabout, a barbecue wagon, jeweled glass frames, and a yacht. What is the connection between these?

UNDAPRIVOLO: Tenuous, but I glean that anybody with enough initiative over there can have all of them if he wants.

NO'VALUTA: Anybody who doesn't must be a resident of Queer Street.

UNDAPRIVOLO: Or a subversive. (*opening the book*) Look at this pair of curtains priced at $4,080, for instance. What housewife so blasé that she could resist their shimmer? Her spouse would certainly be top dog if she flaunted them in their picture window.

NO'VALUTA: Would he not be more avid for this fishing reel at $645, or the beer stein opposite at $300?

UNDAPRIVOLO: There is something here for every taste, including Fido's—viz., a poodle sweater priced at $20 that will effectively shield his soft underbelly from drafts. Here is a group of mechanical birds for $300, or an animated Santa Claus display for $3,000, warranted to make Baby crow with delight. Junior, depending on his age, can choose between a child's toy car, $595, and a foreign one, $21,745, whilst Sister, seated at her vanity and bench, $1,020, is lost in dreams of a $2,250 bridal gown. At eventide, I envision the family united at the $3,500 dining table, ready to partake of pheasant at $14 a brace or rattlesnake meat, $2 the 5-oz. can, heated on an $1,195 range, and after a tunefest around the $4,585 piano, dossing down in their $1,600 beds.

NO'VALUTA: Hmm, this is all very fine, Undaprivolo, but does it follow that acquisitions like these insure happiness?

UNDAPRIVOLO: Why, of course. The more cattle, wives, and pelf a man has, the more serene he is—that's rudimentary. The Americans are the happiest folk on earth.

NO'VALUTA (*thoughtfully*): I wonder. The other day I was over at my headshrinker's in Moshi—

UNDAPRIVOLO: I didn't know you were having problems.

NO'VALUTA: I don't. This fellow is preparing a couple of trophies for my hut—Wakamba tribesmen.

UNDAPRIVOLO: Is Eudora redecorating again? It beats me where you people get the money.

No'VALUTA: Let's not go into *that*. Well, as I say, I was chewing some fat with him when this tourist couple passed by. She was a real long-stemmed American Beauty—hair like spun gold, skin like a magnolia petal—

UNDAPRIVOLO: Not African magnolias. Their petals look like skin.

No'VALUTA (*impatiently*): Anyway, she was a lulu, and you could see she had more shekels than the U.S. Mint.

UNDAPRIVOLO: The thought of the Mint transfixes me like a spear.

No'VALUTA: Me, too. Well, the man with her was a pasty-faced little runt, dark-complected, a cipher. The shrinker told me he's an Italian noble that her family bought for her, but she cries herself to sleep every night at the hotel.

UNDAPRIVOLO: Pah. He's been reading too much Henry James.

No'VALUTA: Just the same, it shows that money isn't everything. I'd have taken her away from him if I didn't have a houseful already. . . . Well, abba dabba.

UNDAPRIVOLO: Where are you going?

No'VALUTA: Oh, anywhere that instinct dictates. We nomads are restless, you know.

UNDAPRIVOLO: Won't Eudora be worried about you?

No'VALUTA: No, she's off in the scrub, as usual, playing knucklebones with her ladies.

UNDAPRIVOLO: Then why don't you stay for supper? We can always rustle up an extra wildebeest chop.

No'VALUTA: You're sure I won't crowd you in there? I'm kind of rangy.

UNDAPRIVOLO: Nonsense, my dear boy. (*lifting door flap*) Now, remember, you mustn't expect too much. It's only an unpretentious mound without any $750 tablecloth or $4,150 silver service, but we like it.

No'VALUTA (*gallantly*): Better a dinner of herbs where love is than the stalled ox.

UNDAPRIVOLO: Could be you'll get both. If I know my womenfolk, the ox may be there, too. (*As they vanish into his burrow, and W. D. Cross*, Deo volente, *vanishes into his*—)

CURTAIN

❦ CLOUDLAND REVISITED: VINTAGE SWINE

SOME HOLLYWOOD FLACK, in a burst of inspiration, dubbed him the Man You Love to Hate. He was a short man, almost squat, with a vulpine smirk that told you, the moment his image flashed upon the screen, that no wife or bank roll must be left unguarded. The clean-shaven bullethead, the glittering monocle, and the ramrod back (kept rigid by a corset, it was whispered) were as familiar and as dear to the moviegoing public as the Pickford curls or Eugene O'Brien's pompadour. No matter what the background of the picture was—an English drawing room, a compartment on the Orient Express, the legation quarter of Peiping—he always wore tight-fitting military tunics, flaunted an ivory cigarette holder, and kissed ladies' hands profusely, betraying them in the next breath with utter impartiality. For sheer menace, he made even topnotch vipers like Lew Cody, Ivan Lebedeff, and Rockliffe Fellowes seem rank stumblebums by comparison. He was the ace of cads, a man without a single redeeming feature, the embodiment of Prussian Junkerism, and the greatest heavy of the silent film, and his name, of course, was Erich von Stroheim.

I first saw him in a tempestuous drama, presented by Carl Laemmle in 1919, called *Blind Husbands*, which von Stroheim, with cyclonic energy, had adapted into a photoplay, and directed, from *The Pinnacle*, a novel he had also written. Actually, I must have seen him three years earlier as the Second Pharisee in the Judean movement of *Intolerance*, wearing a fright wig and a gaudy toga and heckling the Nazarene, but there was so much Biblical flapdoodle flying around that I was too confused to peg him.

The picture that definitely canonized von Stroheim for me, though, was *Foolish Wives*, a gripping exposé of the swindlers who were popularly supposed to prey on rich Americans in Monte Carlo. In this 1922 chef-d'oeuvre, he impersonated a spurious Russian noble named Ladislaw Sergius Von Karamzin, as ornery a skunk as ever flicked a riding crop against a boot. Everything about him seemed to me touched with enchantment: his stiff-necked swagger, his cynical contempt for the

594

women he misused, and, above all, his dandyism—the monogrammed
cigarettes, the dressing gowns with silk lapels, the musk he sprayed himself with to heighten his allure. For six months afterward, I exhibited
a maddening tendency to click my heels and murmur *"Bitte?"* along
with a twitch as though a monocle were screwed into my eye. The mannerisms finally abated, but not until the Dean of Brown University had
taken me aside and confided that if I wanted to transfer to Heidelberg,
the faculty would not stand in my way.

Not long ago, the Museum of Modern Art graciously permitted me
to run its copy of *Foolish Wives*, on condition that if I became overstimulated or mushy, I would not pick the veneer off the chairs or kiss
the projectionist. Such fears, it presently turned out, were baseless.
The showing roused me to neither vandalism nor affection; in fact, it
begot such lassitude that I had to be given artificial respiration and
sent home in a wheelbarrow. Ordinarily, I would incline to put the
blame on my faulty metabolism, but this time I knew what the trouble
was. A certain satanic *Schweinhund* hadn't blitzed me as he used to
thirty years ago.

Foolish Wives upsets precedent by first investigating the seamy side
of Monte Carlo instead of its glamour. We fade in on a milieu brimful
of plot—the tenebrous hovel of an aged counterfeiter named Ventucci. A visit from his principal client, Count Karamzin, establishes
that the latter is using Ventucci's green goods to support an opulent
villa as a front for his stratagems. During their colloquy, the Count's
jaded appetite is whetted by his host's nineteen-year-old daughter, a
poor daft creature fondling a rag doll. The old man stiffens. "She is my
only treasure," he snaps at von Stroheim, unsheathing a stiletto. "If
anyone should harm her . . ." Leaving this promissory note to be hon-
ored at whatever point von Stroheim has run his gamut, the action
shifts to an exclusive hotel near the casino. Here we meet an overripe
young matron with a face like a matzoth pancake, all bee-stung lips
and mascara, the wife of an American millionaire called (*sic*) Howard
Hughes, and played by a sluggish *Rheinmaedchen* identified in the cast
of characters only as Miss Dupont. Von Stroheim ogles the lady, who
seems complaisant, gets himself presented to her, and, baiting his hook
with a sermon about the pitfalls of Monte Carlo, offers to introduce
her to his cousins the Princesses Olga and Vera Petchnikoff. He furthermore assures her, brazenly squinting down her bodice, that they—
and, of course, he—would be enraptured to act as her social sponsors.
Mrs. Hughes, understandably, is *bouleversée*, and, consenting to accompany him to a water carnival several nights thence, lumbers away

to loosen her stays and recover her wits. Whether she has any of either is debatable; both her figure and her deportment are so flabby that one cannot work up much moral indignation against von Stroheim. The man is earning a very hard dollar.

Disclosed next is the Villa Amorosa, the seaside lair of the Count and his confederates, Princess Olga (Maude George) and Princess Vera (Mae Busch). For my money, Mae Busch never possessed the spidery, ghoulish fascination of that consummate she-devil Jetta Goudal, but she ranked high as a delineator of adventuresses and Eurasian spies. At any rate, the two lady tricksters, far from being von Stroheim's cousins, live in what appears to be a languid state of concubinage, switching about in negligees and exchanging feline gibes. Over breakfast, the three agree on the *modus operandi* standard among movie blackmailers, whereby the Princesses are to divert Mr. Hughes while von Stroheim compromises his wife. Ventucci, meanwhile, bustles into focus in the crisp, matter-of-fact fashion of a milkman, trailed by his daughter and bringing a satchel of fresh queer just off the press. He gives off ominous rumblings when the Count behaves familiarly with the girl, but nothing more consequential than glowering results. The same is true of the water carnival that evening. Mr. Hughes, a silver-haired, phlegmatic wowser, whose civilian name escaped me in the credits, betrays mild pique at the sight of his wife paddling around the studio tank and pelting von Stroheim with artificial roses but, after a few heavy sarcasms, relapses into coma. Had the tempo not quickened in the ensuing scene, the picture might have ended right there for me. What with the whir of the projector and the weight of my eyelids, it took every bit of buckram I had, plus frequent pulls at a Benzedrine inhaler, to keep from sliding into the abyss.

Whittled down to essentials, the purport of the scene is that the Count takes Mrs. Hughes on an afternoon excursion, pretends to get lost in a thunderstorm, and steers her to a sinister house of assignation run by a crone called Mother Gervaise. The sole function of this unsavory character, as far as I could tell, was to persuade the young matron to doff her wet shimmy, so that von Stroheim, who has made a great show of turning his back, can stealthily appraise her in a pocket mirror—as neat a sample of voyeurism, I may add, as any ever reported by Wilhelm Stekel. After endless chin music calculated to allay her trepidation, von Stroheim has just maneuvered his sweetmeat into the horizontal when a wild-eyed anchorite reels in, ululating for shelter. Who this holy man is the picture never explains, but his scowls put a quietus on the high jinks, and Mrs. Hughes regains her hotel next

morning shopworn but chaste. Inexplicably enough, the Count does
not use the incident to shake down her husband—indeed, he has
Princess Vera affirm that Mrs. Hughes spent the night with her—and
the whole affair mystifyingly trails off with nobody the wiser, least
of all the audience.

Up to now, the element of gambling has been so ruthlessly slighted
in the story that the locale might as well have been a Scottish tabernacle or the annual dance festival at Jacob's Pillow. Suddenly, however, Lady Luck rears her head beside that of Sex. In addition to his
other *chinoiserie*, von Stroheim has been shacking up with a bedraggled
maiden named Malishka, a servant at the villa, whom he has glibly
promised to wed as soon as the Bolsheviki are deposed. To still her
importunities, the Count cooks up a pitiable tale of insolvency and
borrows her life savings, which he loses at roulette. Mrs. Hughes, who
is also having a flutter at the wheel, observes his despair and lends him
her pile of counters—a gesture that abruptly changes his luck. Strong
though the temptation is to pocket his winnings, he craftily relinquishes
them to his benefactress, and then, a few hours later, lures her to the
Villa Amorosa with a plea that his life and honor are at stake. The
rendezvous takes place in a tower room. Outside the door, Malishka
crouches in a fever of jealousy, and this time generates sparks in a
quite literal sense. Infuriated by her lover's endearments to Mrs.
Hughes prior to easing her of ninety thousand francs, the maid locks
the pair in and sets fire to the stairs. They take refuge on an exterior
balcony, from which they shout appeals for help, but the other guests
at the villa are absorbed in being fleeced at baccarat by the Princesses
and fail to respond. Hughes, meanwhile, has become increasingly
worried about his wife's absence, pantomiming his solicitude by sitting
on the edge of his bed and thoughtfully scratching his chin. Eventually,
the Monte Carlo Fire Department, which has been snoozing under the
bulldog edition of *Le Petit Monégasque*, bestirs itself, and, dashing to
the scene, spreads a net under the balcony. Von Stroheim gallantly
knees his companion aside and jumps first. Mrs. Hughes follows, almost hurtling through the roof of the limousine in which her husband
has just driven up. Apart from the indignity of the *pompiers'* catching
a glimpse of her bloomers, though, she sustains no perceptible damage,
and the episode peters out, like all those preceding it, with Morpheus,
the patron saint of the scenario, drowsily sharpening his quill for the
next sequence.

Low as were the price of film and the salaries of actors in 1922, Mr.
Laemmle and his aides must nevertheless have decided at this point in

Foolish Wives that the consumer's patience was finite, and ordered the curtain down. The last reel, therefore, begins with Hughes's discovery, in his wife's corsage (while hunting for his pipe or a pair of shoe trees, I got the impression), of the note by which the Count had enticed her to his villa. He seeks out von Stroheim, knocks him down, and exposes his activities to the police. The Princesses are apprehended on the verge of flight, and unmasked as a couple of actresses named Maude George and Mae Busch, and now all that early scaffolding about Ventucci and his fey daughter comes in handy. Von Stroheim, in a stormy Dostoevskian finish, sneaks back to the coiner's hovel, ravishes the girl, is disemboweled by her father, and winds up being stuffed into a cistern. The concluding shot shows the Hugheses reunited—if two pieces of strudel can be said to be en rapport—lying in bed and reading, from a volume entitled *Foolish Wives*, the passage "And thus it happened that disillusionment came finally to a foolish wife who found in her husband that nobility she had sought for in—a counterfeit."

The vehicle creaks and possibly should have been left to molder in the carriage loft, yet it confirmed one opinion I had treasured for three decades. Whatever von Stroheim's shortcomings were as an artist, he was consistent. When he set out to limn a louse, he put his back into it. He never palliated his villainy, never helped old ladies across the street to show that he was a sweet kid *au fond* or prated about his Oedipus complex like the Percy boys who portray heavies today. I remember Grover Jones, a scenarist of long experience, once coaching me in Hollywood in the proper method of characterizing the menace in a horse opera. "The minute he pulls in on the Overland Stage," expounded Jones, "he should dismount and kick the nearest dog." Von Stroheim not only kicked the dog; he kicked the owner and the S.P.C.A. for good measure. With the things he has on his conscience, I don't suppose the man ever slept a wink. But after all, nobody needs a whole lot of sleep to keep going. You can always drop off for a jiffy—especially if there's a projector and a can of old film around.

❦ AND DID YOU ONCE SEE IRVING PLAIN?

When Hollywood nabobs forgather in their knotty-pine libraries beside the murmurous Pacific and, as the cigar smoke wreathes their Renoirs, wax nostalgic over the past, one name invariably produces a hush—that of Irving Thalberg. Of all the comets who have streaked across the movie firmament, Thalberg is held to be the one truly authentic genius; in his sway at M-G-M, the dividends sprouted like honeysuckle and such demigods as Gable and Garbo, Joan Crawford and Wallace Beery arose to dazzle the multitude. The legends of his munificence rival those of Lorenzo de' Medici, his wisdom that of Spinoza. Perhaps the most striking instance of the latter was his evaluation of the role of the scenarist in films. "The writer," he declared with Mosaic profundity, "is a necessary evil." The assertion that he said "weevil" appears to have no foundation in fact.

What was this exceptional showman like? To describe any colossus in a phrase is patently impossible, but as it happens, I worked for the man briefly circa 1937, and I spent a good many weeks trying to get to know him. Herewith, and visibly impeded by a lump in my throat the size of a matzo-ball, are my memories of that signal experience.

ON A SUNNY November afternoon in 1936, the Japanese gardener pruning the bougainvillaea that entwined Villa 12 at the Garden of Allah in Hollywood inadvertently glanced into its bedroom window and saw a sight that caused him to drop his shears. Sprawled on the bed, my irises glazed like Staffordshire ware, I lay snuffing uncontrollably into the counterpane. A 130-page manuscript labeled *Greenwich Village* had just fallen from my nerveless hand, and the realization that hunger might compel me and my wife to distill from it a vehicle for Joan Crawford contorted my face with a despair only Hieronymus Bosch could depict.

The circumstances underlying our plight were all too prosaic. Of the small bundle of loot we had accumulated the previous winter in Hollywood there remained only a frayed elastic band, and by mid-

September my wife and I were again back on the Coast, feverishly importuning our agent for an assignment. The latter, a frog-faced individual named Kolodny clad entirely in suède even down to his underthings, assured us there was nothing to worry about. The studios were crying for writers, he declared buoyantly; in a week or two at the utmost, he would have us established, at a princely salary, with one of the titans of the industry. The week had grown into nine, and the manager of the hotel bubbled like a percolator every time he saw us, when Kolodny phoned in a lather. Irving Thalberg, a producer whose name was uttered only in cathedral whispers, universally acknowledged the top genius of celluloid, had expressed interest in us and was sending over a story for our inspection. True, the *quid pro quo* was paltry but, Kolodny added quickly, the luster of associating with Thalberg, the patina we would gain in his orbit, would cinch our position forever in Hollywood.

My wife's reaction to *Greenwich Village*, if somewhat less volcanic than mine, was one of vast incredulity. "He *can't* be in earnest about this," she said after thumbing through it. "Why, it's pure parody, all these roistering poets, the painters in their picturesque smocks, that motherly old bag in the boardinghouse with the capacious bosom and the heart of gold. They'll hoot it out of the theaters. What made him pick us to work on it?"

"Our background, it seems," I said. "Kolodny told him we lived near Washington Square once. I gather he described us as dead ringers for e.e. cummings and Edna Millay."

"Well, there's no sense fighting our custard," she declared with brisk feminine acumen. "God knows it isn't Flaubert, but it's better than picking lettuce in the Imperial Valley. How fast can we get on the payroll?"

The answer to her query was soon forthcoming. Before the sun gilded the steeples of the Pacific Finance Company, the agent had transmitted our conviction that the property was a bewitching blend of *Trilby* and *La Bohème*, and we were ordered to report for duty at M-G-M the next morning. Kolodny was jubilant. Henceforth, he announced, we belonged to the aristocracy of filmdom. In a burst of clairvoyance, he foresaw us occupying *palazzos* in Coldwater Canyon, lolling in Bentleys, hobnobbing with the élite at Palm Springs. The story editor at Metro next day, while not quite so rapturous, expatiated similarly on our good fortune.

"I hope you appreciate the break you're getting," he said, as he led us to the structure, colloquially known as the Triangle Shirtwaist

Factory, where writers were housed. "I know people in this town who'd give half of their salary to work under the aegis of Irving Thalberg."

"You're looking at two of them, Jack," I confided.

"Well, just wait till you meet him," he said. "I've dealt with some pretty brainy men in my time, from L. B. Mayer down, but between you and me, Thalberg is the greatest intellect we have. And cheek by jowl with it goes a wonderful candid humility which reminds you of Abe Lincoln. The most simple, unaffected person you can imagine."

"Gee, that's swell," said my wife. "Listen, if it isn't violating any secret, how much did they pay for this—this original we're supposed to adapt?"

"Somewhere in the neighborhood of seventy-five grand," he replied. "A humdinger, isn't it?"

"A peachamaroot," she agreed. She looked around the gloomy little chamber we were to occupy, furnished with a worm-eaten desk, two gumwood chairs and a spavined divan. It was a pity, she observed mildly, that the studio's prodigality did not extend to its décor.

Our cicerone, nettled, retorted that the office had harbored a series of distinguished authors, none of whom had voiced any complaint. The most recent, it appeared, was a celebrated lady playwright much in vogue then, who had spent the past fourteen months there—in vain, he added, since nobody had come up with a story worthy of her stature. Curious to learn how she had beguiled the time, I made a quick inventory of the desk the moment the door closed behind him. The only memento of her tenancy was a pair of highly intricate doilies, created by braiding together narrow strips of yellow typewriting paper. Assuming she had received fifteen hundred dollars a week—a modest estimate for anyone of her attainments—it followed that the mats had cost the corporation roughly forty-two thousand dollars apiece: a heartwarming example of craftsmanship adequately rewarded.

From the air of immediacy surrounding our project, we figured it would be all of noontime before Thalberg summoned us to impart his hopes and dreams for the script. When three days elapsed with no manifestation, however, I grew restive and phoned. His secretary reassured me at length. Our picture was high on the agenda, but Mr. T. had two in production and was working around the clock; she would advise us the instant he was free. Since it was fatuous to proceed without some clue to what he wanted, we settled down resignedly to wait. Inside of a week, the tedium was well-nigh claustrophobic. Even by reading the trade papers, Louella Parsons' column, and Dostoevsky's prison memoirs, we barely got through the mornings, and the antlike industry of our colleagues discouraged fraternization. Possibly the most consecrated was a writer just across the hall, whose creative habits seemed to derive from science fiction. He customarily wore on his head, while dictating into the mouthpiece of an Ediphone, a scalp vibrator resembling a metal cocktail shaker, which oscillated so busily that you wondered what his dialogue would sound like when transcribed. I subsequently saw the movie he worked on and can testify that I left the theater deeply shaken.

Languishing through our fourth week, I again rang up Thalberg's office and again was counseled patience; the audience was just around the corner. Our agent, Kolodny, who checked us at intervals like a lobsterman visiting his pots, scolded me roundly for fidgeting. He besought us to lie doggo, collect the weekly stipend, and thank our lucky stars that we were eating. That night, on our way home from the jute mill, my wife stopped off in Westwood and bought an ambitious needlepoint design and a dozen hanks of yarn. I ransacked the stores for a narwhal tusk or a bit of whalebone wherewith to execute some scrimshaw work, but none being available, compromised on a set of Boswell and a handbook of chess problems.

Some two weeks later as I was emerging from the studio commissary, I ran into a Broadway acquaintance named Reifsneider. At our last encounter five years before, he had been the choreographer of some thimblerig musical I was embroiled in. Now transformed into a scenario writer for no visible reason, he drew me into the oubliette where he had been laboring the past fifteen months on a screenplay of *Edwin Drood* and began recounting his woes.

"It's a witch," he lamented. "I can't seem to figure out an ending for it." I remarked consolingly that Dickens hadn't been able to think of a finish, either, and to cheer him up, told him of our impasse. He emitted a cluck of pity at my naïveté. Nobody, even the most eminent of playwrights, had ever succeeded in conferring with Thalberg, he asserted, and went on to relate the chronicle of George Kelly. Imported at an astronomical fee from the East, the author of *The Show-Off* and *Craig's Wife* had been shown every courtesy, installed in a luxurious office, and left to await Thalberg's convenience. After two months of futile telephoning, Kelly sent the producer word that he was departing for New York in twenty-four hours unless he was given an interview. He was put off with fervent promises, and finally, embittered, shook the dust of Culver City from his feet. About six weeks later, though, other business recalled him to Hollywood and he drove out to M-G-M to pick up his mail. Neatly crisscrossed on his desk were six envelopes containing salary checks for the period of his absence. In a rather somnambulistic state, Kelly pocketed the checks and withdrew. Just as he was rounding a sound stage, he came face to face with Thalberg. The producer, his face remorseful, caught his sleeve.

"Forgive me, old boy," Thalberg apologized. "I know I've been neglecting you, but this time you have my word as a gentleman. I'll see you tomorrow—tomorrow afternoon. Four o'clock at the very latest."

As another ten days dragged by, my wife and I seriously began to question whether Thalberg even existed, whether he might not be a solar myth or a deity concocted by the front office to garner prestige. If few had ever actually beheld the man, however, there was no lack of legends about his idiosyncrasies. One of the more memorable, vouched for by Ivan Lebedeff, the actor, concerned a Russian officer he knew. A veteran of the Foreign Legion with a brilliant record in the North African campaigns, Major Peshkov had written a book around his exploits called *The Bugle Sounds* and was promptly hustled to California by Thalberg to translate it to film. Meeting each other one day at Metro, the fellow countrymen held a joyous reunion over a stoup of borsch, and Lebedeff asked how his friend's venture was progressing.

"To tell the truth, I'm a little worried," Peshkov admitted. "I've been trying to discuss the story the last two months, but Mr. Thalberg always puts me off. Mind you, he's been the soul of courtesy—gave me a fine office, a lovely blond secretary——"

With cynicism born of long experience, Lebedeff allayed his fears. This was standard Hollywood conduct, he explained. Thalberg would eventually materialize; meanwhile, there was the steady honorarium, an excellent commissary and, above all, the beautiful blonde. At their next meeting, a month or two later, Peshkov betrayed distinct agitation. He announced that a man of his temperament, accustomed to the Sahara, could not brook such inactivity and confinement. If Thalberg persisted in avoiding him, he said through his teeth . . . Lebedeff urged self-control, reminded him of the discipline and fortitude he had shown in his arduous military career. The wars with the Bedouin, retorted Peshkov darkly, had been child's play compared to what he was undergoing in Culver City. He would hang on a little longer, but only because he hesitated to reflect dishonor on the Legion. It was a good ten weeks afterward that Lebedeff saw him again, and he instantly detected a change in the other's bearing, a new air of decision.

"The die is cast," declared Peshkov. "I am returning to Morocco tomorrow and nothing on earth can dissuade me. I have just wired Mr. Thalberg that I shall call on him at four today to settle our accounts."

The nature of the interview puzzled Lebedeff until he heard it from his friend's own lips in Paris several years later. On the stroke of four, Peshkov had entered Thalberg's suite, brushed aside his secretary and invaded the sanctum. Tersely introducing himself, he sought indulgence for bungling his mission, adding that had he done so in the Legion, he would have been shot.

"But look here," said Thalberg, perplexed. "You couldn't be more mistaken. We're completely satisfied with you—in fact, we're picking up your option. You and I'll sit down together one of these days——"

"No, no," said Peshkov. "It's too late." He withdrew an itemized list and laid it on the desk. "I believe you will find this accurate," he said. "My salary for eight months at $750 a week—$24,000. Steamship, rail, and hotel charges en route from Morocco—$915. Incidentals, $360. And here," he continued, extending a slip of paper, "is my check for the total. I can only ask you to forgive me for abusing your trust."

Thalberg stared at him uncomprehending for a few moments, and then, with a shrug, flicked up the key of his Dictograph. "Suit yourself, Major," he said. "I don't know what your game is, but if you won't talk to me, you'll talk to Loophole, my attorney. Good afternoon, sir."

It may have been the unsettling effect of such stories or merely slow attrition, but three weeks later my wife and I decided we had reached the breaking point, and spitting on each other's hands, began work on the screenplay of *Greenwich Village*. After all, we reasoned, we could hardly be accused of insubordination when we'd waited so long in vain for orders. We were waist-deep in clichés one morning, portraying Joan Crawford's anguish at the onslaught of a lecherous etcher, when Thalberg's secretary phoned: we were to present ourselves instanter at his bungalow. Thunderstruck and wrangling over how best to comport ourselves, we hastened toward the Palladian stucco edifice that contained his unit. Cooling their heels in the anteroom were a dozen literary artisans of note like Sidney Howard and Robert Sherwood, George S. Kaufman, Marc Connelly, S. N. Behrman and Donald Ogden Stewart. The epigrams inspired by such a galaxy may well be imagined, but by winnowing them, I discovered that everybody there had been seeking Thalberg's ear without success and was seething. In a few moments, the door of his lair opened, someone of the caliber of

Pirandello or Molnar emerged, and to our intense surprise, the secretary waved us in. The resulting epigrams may well be imagined. I forget what they were, but they made my cheeks flame at the time.

The room in which we found ourselves was very long, bathed in shadow and reminiscent of an advertisement for Duo-Art Pianos. Picked out in a single beam of light at the far end was a frail gentleman with intense eyes which he kept fixed unwinkingly on us during our trip to his desk, barely a matter of two minutes. After routine salutations, he inquired if we saw any possibilities in *Greenwich Village*. I replied that they were limitless and that we were already busily at work on the screenplay.

"Oh, you are, are you?" said Thalberg with marked displeasure. "Well, you can stop right now. I don't want a word on paper—I repeat, not a single word—until we've found the answer to the question."

"The question?" I repeated uncertainly.

"That's right," he said. "The all-important question your story raises —namely, should a woman tell?"

There was a short, pregnant silence, approximately long enough to consume a slice of poppyseed strudel, and my wife leaned forward. "Should a woman tell what?" she asked with almost Japanese delicacy.

"Why, the truth about her past," returned Thalberg, like one addressing a child. "In short, should a beautiful, sophisticated woman confess her premarital indiscretions to her fiancé?"

Before the beautiful, sophisticated woman beside me could confess that this was her first inkling of any such problem in the story, she was saved by the Dictograph. Some Olympian personality, whose voice contained enough gravel to pave the Cahuenga Pass, was calling to borrow a cupful of proxies, and halfway through his plea, word arrived from Miss Garbo that Western civilization would collapse unless Thalberg hastened on the double to Stage 9. The next my wife and I knew, we were blinking in the sunlight outside the building, the same suspicion burgeoning in our breasts. Neither of us put it into words, but we were both right. At suppertime that evening, Kolodny phoned to say that we could sleep as late as we wished the following morning. *Greenwich Village* had been shelved and we were back on the auction block. I toyed with the idea of driving over to pick up the needlepoint and the set of Boswell, and then, on due reflection, abandoned it. I also abandoned, even more speedily, the notion of emulating Peshkov and returning the loot. Strong as was my sense of *noblesse oblige*, I had enough headaches without the honor of the Foreign Legion.

♻ PULSE RAPID, RESPIRATION LEAN, NO MUSTARD

> "Espresso" wrist. A large number of espresso coffee bars have sprung up in the last year or two. Dr. Kessel, an orthopedist, has described a wrist complication in those who operate the coffee dispensers. For each cup of coffee poured out, three to four strong movements of the wrist into full radial deviation have to be carried out, and in the average day several thousand such maneuvers are often made. Bartenders are not so affected, because beer is drawn with the wrist held stiffly, the elbow being flexed.—*Journal of the American Medical Association.*

THE NOTE stapled to the grocery bill was explicit and minatory, and as Dresden Binswanger read it, her heartbeat quickened perceptibly. Mr. Brunschweig had always extended the widest latitude to customers, and professional men in particular—his own two sons were lawyers, he recalled pointedly—but his patience was exhausted. Unless the account was settled in five days, he would attach Dr. Binswanger's chattels down to the very last centrifuge and roll of medicated gauze. Dresden squared her attractive shoulders, traversed the corridor that led to her husband's consulting room, and, in response to the indistinct mumble within, thrust open the door. Bent over a portable, his head wreathed in smoke, Webster Binswanger was laboriously pecking interlineations on a page of typescript. Though he was barely thirty, a sallow complexion and receding hairline made him seem older, and he was cultivating a mustache to augment his dignity, but it would be years before anyone mistook him for a healer. He greeted the intrusion with visible annoyance.

"What it is now?" he queried. "You see I'm busy, don't you?"

"The market," said Dresden in a metallic voice. "Brunschweig's on the warpath again—says he's going to court. Listen, Webster," she added urgently, "I think he really means it this time."

"Not so loud, for Pete's sake," Binswanger cautioned. "The whole anteroom can hear you."

"There's nobody out there and you know it," his wife retorted. "And what's more, there hasn't been since you hung up your shingle."

"That's *my* fault," he snapped. "It's my fault three other doctors moved into the neighborhood after I did. Men with established practices."

"No, but you could show some initiative—"

"How?" he demanded aggrievedly. "Stand outside with a sandwich board?"

"Don't ask me," said Dresden. "I'll tell you one thing, though. I won't borrow one cent more from the family."

"Here it comes," Binswanger rumbled. "I wondered what was holding it up. Go ahead, remind me how generous your father was to set me up, to pay for my equipment . . ."

Familiar with its explosive content, Dresden sidestepped the challenge. "Look, honey, we both know it's a long pull," she said pacifically. "If there was only a little coming in meanwhile."

"There will be—honest," he assured her, taking her hand. "Wait till I finish this. I guarantee you can snap your fingers at Brunschweig and all of 'em. Once the public gets a taste of these stories, we'll be in clover."

"But mysteries," she said dubiously. "Everybody writes whodunits."

"Not with characters like mine," Binswanger exulted. "An English sleuth with a razor-sharp intellect, relentless, a human thinking machine. His loyal, stodgy colleague, a former Army doctor. And the background of Victorian London—hansom cabs, bumbling police inspectors, the flavor of a bygone era. You mark my words, baby: these tales may yet become immortal."

She had hardly marked them when the unfamiliar whine of the buzzer sounded from the anteroom. The two stared at each other, disbelieving. "A *patient*!" Dresden hissed in an ecstatic whisper. Electrified, Binswanger swept his handiwork into a drawer, interred the portable, and, while his wife frantically tidied the desk, struggled into a rubber laboratory apron. A half minute later, an X-ray in hand and an apologetic smile on his face, he emerged from the office. His caller, a fattish individual radiating almost palpable anxiety, extricated himself from a tubular chair.

"Sorry to keep you waiting, Mr.—ah—"

"Lebkuchen," the patient supplied. "Howard Lebkuchen."

"Come in, won't you?" said Binswanger pleasantly. "I was just checking this photograph—the heart chamber of one of my patients. It may interest you. The shadowy area here, surrounding the bulge."

"Is that bad?" Lebkuchen faltered.

"No-o-o, not necessarily," said the Doctor in a tone of bright determined optimism. "However, one can't drink three cups of coffee a day without some result. Ah, well," he broke off, "I'm sure you don't do anything so foolish. . . . Now, then, sir, have a seat and tell me all about it."

Grateful for a sympathetic ear, Lebkuchen proceeded to bend it. He prefaced his symptoms with a biography, from whose irrelevancies Binswanger gleaned he was a counterman in a nearby Sixth Avenue tavern, had two gifted children, and dwelt in Flushing, and at last he disclosed his affliction—a recurrent and fiendish twinge in the right knee. Having disposed in a routine catechism of arthritis, sprain, and faulty footgear, Binswanger bade the sufferer articulate the contiguous bones, but he could discover nothing irregular.

"You notice the pain chiefly on duty," he reviewed thoughtfully. "Think a minute, now. Do you always observe a set pattern in your movements—I mean when you dish out the meatballs or dice the cole slaw or whatever you do?"

"I specialize in sandwiches," Lebkuchen said in the accents of the Quai d'Orsay. "There's a man for the platters, like the veal cutlets or so, and a dessert man—"

"Yes, yes," Binswanger cut in. "What I'm getting at is do you always follow the same procedure in making your sandwiches? Show me just how you function."

Lebkuchen blinked and, arising, demonstrated the technique. Protracted by his lengthy footnotes on how fat was trimmed away, the performance consumed fully three minutes, but the Doctor did not curtail it. He scratched his chin reflectively.

"Very significant," he remarked. "Well, Mr. Lebkuchen, no need to be alarmed, I think. Pending the confirmation we'll want, of course, I'd say you were down with a mild attack of corned-beef knee."

"W-what's that?" the counterman quavered.

"Nothing serious—don't get upset," Binswanger soothed him. "It's a minor industrial complaint found among people in your craft. I've read about it in the literature but never actually have seen a case."

"Then how can you be sure?" asked Lebkuchen piteously. "Maybe we should have another opinion."

"I'm afraid it's unmistakable," said the other with compassion. "You see, when you fold the bread over the meat that way—"

"We don't use bread so much. Mostly seed rolls."

"The ingredients are immaterial," Binswanger interjected. "The point is that in doing so you execute a half twist like a gymnast, throwing the weight of your torso onto the right leg. The constant flexion of the knee, which pivots as you turn, inevitably produces clonic spasm, or, as you laymen call it, cramp."

His forebodings affirmed, Lebkuchen relinquished what little aplomb he still clung to. He could ill afford therapy, he whimpered, and to cease work was out of the question. Perhaps an elastic bandage . . .

Nimbly reversing the cloud, the Doctor displayed its silver lining. Despite his anguish, Lebkuchen was not incapacitated; let him resume work until the diagnosis was verified, until Binswanger beheld him *in situ* and decided whether any pertinent factor had been overlooked.

"You couldn't drop in this noon, I suppose?" his patient implored. "I know how busy you are, but if you had a chance between calls—"

"I do have a fairly tight schedule," Binswanger admitted, flicking through a snowy engagement pad. "Mrs. Moodie's pancreas at eleven-thirty . . . A tonsillectomy at two . . . Very well, I'll try. Chin up, now," he counseled on the threshold. "Just let me shoulder your burdens."

"You can have 'em," Lebkuchen replied wanly. "I wish you were behind that counter instead of me."

Binswanger scrutinized him afresh. "Yes," he said abstractedly. "That would be useful, wouldn't it?" For some time after the visitor had left, he stood lost in reverie. When Dresden glanced up from the hillock of macaroni and tuna fish she was evolving into what the recipe whimsically called "Bohemian steak," her husband's step was springy and he was whistling.

By two-fifteen, a measure of sanity had returned to the interior of the Beehive Bar & Grill. The last wave of housewives, torpid with cheesecake, had receded into Fourteenth Street to purchase Roto-Broils on easy credit, the jars of toothpicks had been replenished, and an infinity of Formica and chrome glistened under the blinding neon. Closeted in a rear booth, Binswanger and Lebkuchen pondered a solution to the latter's dilemma.

"The one thing I can say with certainty," said the Doctor with certainty, "is that you're playing with fire. The leg must be immobilized—period."

"How l-long on the average does corned-beef knee take to cure?" the victim asked forlornly.

"Nine weeks, unless caught in time," said Binswanger. "We *have* found, though, that care at the onset yields surprising relief." He paused, ruminating. "Look here, Lebkuchen," he said. "As a physician, I'd like to make a controlled experiment—study the malady under actual conditions, as it were. Perhaps, if I were to substitute for you a day or two—"

"Gee whiz, Doc, that would be a lifesaver!" breathed the counterman. "Even a few hours off my feet— But how about your practice in the meantime?"

"One's livelihood can wait, where science is concerned," said Binswanger, wrapping himself in the mantle of Pasteur. "Maybe you'd have to give me some pointers on carving, though. To implement my surgical training."

"Nothing to it—it's a pipe," averred Lebkuchen. He half rose, quickly scanned the establishment. "Old man Huysmans is out, and anyway he knows from nothing," he confided. "Come around the showcase. I won't keep you five minutes." The briefing, as prophesied, was simple, and Lebkuchen's eyes were moist when he finished. "I can't tell you what you're doing for me," he said fervently. "The pain feels a hundred per cent better already."

"Yes, that often happens," Binswanger agreed. "I often say, the deeper I penetrate into medicine, the less I know. . . . Now, just one more detail. In slicing Huysmans' brisket, does one go with or against the grain?"

"Vistas I never dreamed of." Binswanger's voice was shaky, and the coffee cup he was holding rattled as his wife refilled it. "I tell you, Dresden, it's overwhelming. Six weeks ago I was a nobody, an obscure little practitioner, desperate—and now I can't even catch my breath between appointments—"

"You're overtensed, darling," she warned him. "You've got to slow down."

"How can I?" he demanded feverishly. "The anteroom's full this minute. Ever since Lebkuchen raved about me at his union meeting, the phone hasn't stopped ringing. And the variety, the complexity, of their ailments!" he added, gulping down the coffee. "Fellow in here an hour ago with an open-and-shut case of digitrophia—hardening of the fingers. We finally traced it to the ice-cream scoop he uses for mashed potatoes."

"You should do a paper for the *Journal of the American Medical Association,*" said Dresden, aglow.

"A paper?" he said with scorn. "A whole book! Why, the possibilities are infinite. There's pastrami elbow, the sciatic result of the pressure employed in anchoring the meat; skin pucker, which may or may not stem from excessive salinity in pickles—Lord knows *what* else."

"Well, I mustn't keep you," said Dresden, rising as the buzzer punctuated his words. "Now, remember, no more patients after six. We have to dress for the theater."

"I'm reading you, kid," he said ebulliently. He waved adieu, opened the door to the anteroom, and beckoned a client with a burly neck into the office. "Come in, Mr. Papakadis," he invited. "Sit down, old man. How are the insteps today?"

"They're killing me, Doctor," Papakadis groaned. "If I don't get some relief real soon—"

"You will, don't worry," Binswanger soothed him. "It's too early to tell, but I have every reason to believe your trouble is occupational." Joining his fingertips, he assumed a sweet-and-sour gravity that would have done credit to a Harley Street specialist. "Have you ever heard of salami foot, or, as it's sometimes called, veal heel?"

❦ CUCKOOS NESTING—DO NOT DISTURB

IT'S A SOBERING THOUGHT, but I guess I'd never have known how Lady Diana Cooper, third daughter of the eighth Duke of Rutland and widow of Alfred Duff Cooper, first Viscount Norwich, feels about picnics if a London bootmaker had chosen excelsior to wrap a shoe he was mailing overseas not long ago. The shoe in question, which has the paradoxical distinction of being one of the best-traveled and least-worn on earth, had been shuttling across the Atlantic all winter between the two of us, attended by a correspondence almost as voluminous as the Shaw-Terry letters. There was still some crippling defect in the instep, however, and as I wrote Mr. Shenstone, perhaps a bit floridly, I was fed up with stumping around on the backs of my hands like a confounded gorilla. Instead of taking advantage of such an ideal opening, he simply replied that he was returning my valued order, with alterations as discussed, by surface post, and begged to remain my faithful servant, etc., etc.

In any case, it was from a page of the Kemsley newspaper, the *Sunday Times*, which he used to pack the shoe in, that I gleaned my insight into Lady Diana's repugnance for conventional picnics and the scope and splendor of her own. Beginning a series of reminiscences entitled "The Pleasures of Living," she issues a rather superfluous caveat against dining in cemeteries and along arterial roads, and enjoins the reader to avoid as picnic companions such kill-joys as "the easily sunburnt," "the intolerant wasp-panicker," and "the fly-attracter." Presumably the English have some sort of litmus test to determine whether a chap is fly-prone, so that you may cut him dead in Rotten Row well in advance, but Lady Diana doesn't particularize. Instead, she launches into a philippic against the yahoos who desecrate picnic sites —specifically, it turns out, those who mommixed up Belvoir, her family seat, in days gone by. "They tumbled from charabancs, sprawled themselves on terrace and slope, took off their boots, let fall their waist-long hair and spread their picnics," she wrathfully recalls. "They tucked into cold beef and doorsteps, cold dumplings, water-

cress and jam puffs and sluiced it all down with bottled beer." No
doubt the lady is justified in disliking folk who ate her ancestral doorsteps; I do think, nevertheless, that anybody who could masticate one
was hardly eccentric if he washed it down with a little beer.

In lofty contrast to the foregoing, Lady Diana cites two memorable
junkets she herself participated in, one at Chantilly and the other on
the island of Ischia. The latter was truly *bon ton*, an exotic affair staged
around a bonfire on a mountaintop, where the guests consumed "salami, gorgonzola, pizza and finocchio, raisins in vineleaves, figs and
raw ham, and cascades of Chianti from the straw-jacketed fiaschi . . .
while the muleteers sang island laments and fought over our crumbs
on the precipice against the moon." After which, I gather, the muleteers, engorged with crumbs and voting the party the best ever, conveyed the revelers down the mountain, taking extreme care not to push
any of them into chasms. It was the Chantilly excursion, though, and
its blithe revelation of what unlimited means and monumental gall can
achieve, that pinioned my interest. Some ten miles from her home
there, Lady Diana had spotted a deserted château in whose park was
a lake, surrounded by classical statues, containing a folly boathouse.
The owner was an "unknown Baron" who, in her arch phrase, "hadn't
said yes—though he hadn't said no—to my request two years before
to be allowed to trespass." Accordingly, she and a friend drove over
one Sunday morning in a station wagon "loaded with dining-room
chairs (nothing of the camping order), a carpet, pictures, flowers,
china, glass, cutlery, silver and best tablecloth (an abandoned table
for ten was already there), soups and chickens, cheeses and cake and
peaches and wine and ice (in an icebox)." As they were installing
these Spartan indispensables, the interlopers were startled by a report,
and learned from the gatekeeper that the baron was shooting that day.
Braving the chance of a load of buckshot in the ancestral seat, they
completed their arrangements and stole away. Later in the day, Lady
Diana lured her luncheon guests to the estate, hoodwinked them into
thinking they had stumbled on the baron's shooting lunch, and persuaded them to hijack it. Several cornballs in the group, afflicted with
ingrown scruples, made ineffectual protest but were overruled, and,
Lady Diana gleefully concludes, "there was one who believed to the
very end that we were poachers and he in a fairy tale."

Ordinarily, such rogueries would throw me into a state of lacquered
composure, except that by a strange quirk of circumstance they clarify
an experience that has puzzled me ever since I underwent it last spring.

One Saturday in mid-April, after a nine weeks' absence from my Pennsylvania freehold, I wheedled our Wills-Ste. Claire out of its New York garage and drove down to see whether the mice there had enough to eat, the paint was scaling off the woodwork on schedule, and the basement flooded properly. It was a glorious day, sunshine and fleecy clouds, and the prospect of a serene, leisurely afternoon of chipping rust and emptying drains, with no sound to break the stillness but my own labored breathing, made me slightly heady. I hummed a stave from *The Vagabond King* as I swung into our lane. Halfway up it, I was stricken by an obscure intuition that something was agley. Drawn up before the barn and on the surrounding grass was a whole flotilla of cars—Cadillacs, Jaguars, Volkswagen buses, foreign sports cars innumerable. A couple of them, I observed as I drew closer, were parked squarely on top of some prize peonies I had been nurturing, doubtless to shade them from the sun. The next thing I observed was that the upper door of the barn, communicating with the hayloft, hung open, and that a young lady in clam-digger pants and a yellow halter was lolling out of it, a cigarette lazily dangling from her lips. As anyone who is reasonably *au courant* knows, clam-digger pants are hideously inflammable, and the thought of the holocaust they might touch off hit me right in the solar plexus. I sprang from behind the wheel like the Mameluke bey.

"Hey, what are you doing up there?" I shouted.

"Taking a sunbath," the baggage replied brightly. "The rest of them are down at the house. You go in through that gate—by those lilac bushes."

"The *rest* of them?" I repeated. "The rest of whom?" Before she could reply, I became aware of a confused uproar in the yard, of laughter and a babble of voices, but the shrubbery along the fence impeded my view of the lawn. I headed back toward the front gate. Before I had got midway, a chauffeur in spruce green livery intercepted me.

"Here, better move that heap of yours," he directed crisply. "My boss wants the driveway kept clear, in case she needs any last-minute stuff for the picnic." His boss, and hostess of the occasion, I managed to elicit, was a Mrs. Knatchbull, who was supervising matters somewhere within, and I went full tilt in search of her. The grounds, to dignify the quarter acre of dandelions and crab grass contiguous to the house, were *en gala* to a degree undreamed of in my twenty-five years of residence. A striped marquee housing a bar had been pitched in a convenient flower bed, and around it milled a festive group in sports clothes, exchanging noisy badinage. A few yards away, by the grape arbor, a hearty soul in a chef's cap and apron was doling out *shish kebabs*, hamburgers, and other succulents from a portable barbecue. I overheard him as I passed call out an appeal for more kindling, and an assistant, who had just wrenched free one of the uprights of the arbor, began splintering it into firewood. Most of the jollification, though, centered about the screened porch, which had been pressed into service as backstop for an archery butt. The marksmen engaged in trying to hit it were fairly inept, and half their arrows lodged in the screens, but it evidently made little difference, for gales of merriment and good-natured persiflage attested to their sportsmanship. It was a scene to warp the cockles of one's heart.

Once I got into the kitchen, I realized that what I had supposed was an informal al-fresco affair was something quite different. Amid an almost deafening racket, four or five upper-case characters of a type not usually visible around the scullery were partitioning cold fowls, blending salads, and ladling out jellied soups and vichyssoise. My petition for Mrs. Knatchbull went unheeded as they ransacked the cupboards for seasoning and utensils. A similar bustle of activity was in progress in the dining room, except that it seemed more orderly. Several young matrons, under the watchful eye of an imposing, dowagerlike party, were unloading china, cutlery, and silver from hampers and setting the table. Our pictures had been taken down and replaced with chic canvases by I. Rice Pereira and Morris Graves. Sensing that the overseer with the majestic bosom was the lady I sought, I cleared my throat to speak. As if forewarned, a Weimaraner curled up under the sideboard arose, sniffed my leg, and emitted a bloodcurdling growl.

"Dagobert—lie down!" the dowager snapped. "Leave that man alone!" She turned back to me, eyebrows raised in an anticipatory smile. "You finally found us, did you? So glad you could come. You're that friend of Boots Paleologue—what's the name? Fippinger, that's it—Milton Fippinger. Well, Mr. Fippinger," she went on briskly, "now you're here, suppose you make yourself useful. You might clear the hall closet so we'll have a place for our coats."

"Couldn't he adjust the heat first, Lydia?" one of her helpers pleaded. "It's stifling in here. We fiddled with the thermostat, but the wretched thing pulled right out of the wall."

At that moment, the phone on the sideboard rang, and I automatically started to answer it. Mrs. Knatchbull snatched the instrument from my hand.

"Good heavens, don't touch that!" she said apprehensively. She had merely borrowed the premises, she explained, without going through the red tape of consulting the owner; nonetheless, since he was known to be *in absentia*, whoever was calling might wax suspicious. Assuring her I was an uncanny mimic and knew the local dialect as though I dwelt in the neighborhood, I overrode her qualms and took the receiver. It was the farmer adjacent, mystified by the concentration of vehicles around our barn and somewhat piqued because he had not been invited to the funeral. I satisfied him that we were all in robust health and that he would be alerted if there was any spring planting, and, commending him for his solicitude, sent him back to his churn. Mrs. Knatchbull was clearly impressed with my fluency.

"You certainly handled that beautifully, Milton," she marveled. "I swear, you sounded like the owner himself. Just the same, we'd better begin lunch before anyone else comes sniffing around." She was handing me a dinner bell to summon the guests when her chauffeur bolted in, concern evident on his face. "I hate to bother you, Mrs. Knatchbull, but I thought you ought to know," he panted. "Something's wrong with the barn. There's a big cloud of smoke pouring out of it."

"Oh, *blast!*" she said pettishly. "This would happen to me just as my party was starting. What in the world shall we do?"

"M-maybe the smoke would blow away if you opened all the barn doors," I heard myself saying from a great distance. "Or better yet— why not simply close them so it doesn't show?"

Mrs. Knatchbull, *triste* as only one persecuted by the Fates can be, shook her head. "No, no, the whole picnic's ruined," she said inconsolably. "The next thing you know, the place'll be swarming with volunteer firemen and all sorts of impossible rustics." Then her lips tightened in sudden decision. "Get everybody back in the cars, Wohlgemuth," she ordered her chauffeur. "Come on, girls—we're all going to the Pavillon, where we can dine graciously instead of like a pack of squirrels. I've never known it to fail. These country excursions always end disastrously."

A quarter of an hour later, the entire company and its paraphernalia had vanished like one of Prince Florizel's soirées in *The New Arabian Nights*. They did leave behind, however, a galantine of chicken, a Smithfield ham, and half a case of Taittinger '37, which looked pretty good to the firemen by the time they finished working on the barn. As for myself, thus far I haven't figured out exactly where I stand on the afternoon. I still have two Pennsylvania Dutch stone gables with the original hex signs, and an I. Rice Pereira abstraction that ought to fetch a cool fifty dollars if I can find the right connoisseur. The affair taught me one thing, though, and that is to stay in the city, where I belong. It doesn't pay to go poking your nose into your own business.

❧ CLOUDLAND REVISITED: THE WICKEDEST WOMAN IN LARCHMONT

IF YOU WERE BORN anywhere near the beginning of the century and had access at any time during the winter of 1914–15 to thirty-five cents in cash, the chances are that after a legitimate deduction for non-pareils you blew in the balance on a movie called *A Fool There Was*. What gave the picture significance, assuming that it had any, was neither its story, which was paltry, nor its acting, which was aboriginal, but a pyrogenic half pint by the name of Theda Bara, who immortalized the vamp just as Little Egypt, at the World's Fair in 1893, had the hoochie-coochie. My own discovery of Miss Bara dates back to the sixth grade at grammar school and was due to a boy named Raymond Bugbee, a detestable bully who sat at the desk behind mine. Bugbee was a fiend incarnate, a hulking evil-faced youth related on both sides of his family to Torquemada and dedicated to making my life insupportable. He had perfected a technique of catapulting BB shot through his teeth with such force that some of them are still imbedded in my poll, causing a sensation like *tic douloureux* when it rains. Day after day, under threat of the most ghastly reprisals if I squealed, I was pinched, gouged, and nicked with paper clips, spitballs, and rubber bands. Too wispy to stand up to my oppressor, I took refuge in a subdued blubbering, which soon abraded the teacher's nerves and earned me the reputation of being refractory. One day, Bugbee finally overreached himself. Attaching a steel pen point to the welt of his shoe, he jabbed it upward into my posterior. I rose into the air caterwauling and, in the attendant ruckus, was condemned to stay after school and clap erasers. Late that afternoon, as I was numbly toiling away in a cloud of chalk dust, I accidentally got my first intimation of Miss Bara from a couple of teachers excitedly discussing her.

"If you rearrange the letters in her name, they spell 'Arab Death,' " one of them was saying, with a delicious shudder. "I've never seen an actress kiss the way she does. She just sort of glues herself onto a man and drains the strength out of him."

"I know—isn't it revolting?" sighed the other rapturously. "Let's go

618

see her again tonight!" Needless to add, I was in the theater before either of them, and my reaction was no less fervent. For a full month afterward, I gave myself up to fantasies in which I lay with my head pillowed in the seductress's lap, intoxicated by coal-black eyes smoldering with belladonna. At her bidding, I eschewed family, social position, my brilliant career—a rather hazy combination of African explorer and private sleuth—to follow her to the ends of the earth. I saw myself, oblivious of everything but the nectar of her lips, being cashiered for cheating at cards (I was also a major in the Horse Dragoons), descending to drugs, and ultimately winding up as a beachcomber in the South Seas, with a saintly, ascetic face like H. B. Warner's. Between Bugbee's persecutions that winter and the moral quicksands I floundered into as a result of *A Fool There Was*, it's a wonder I ever lived through to Arbor Day.

A week or so ago, seeking to ascertain whether my inflammability to Miss Bara had lessened over the years, I had a retrospective look at her early triumph. Unfortunately, I could not duplicate the original conditions under which I had seen her, since the Museum of Modern Art projection room is roach-free and lacks those powerful candy-vending machines on the chairs that kicked like a Colt .45. Nonetheless, I managed to glean a fairly comprehensive idea of what used to accelerate the juices in 1915, and anyone who'd like a taste is welcome to step up to the tureen and skim off a cupful.

Produced by William Fox and based on the play by Porter Emerson Browne, *A Fool There Was* maunders through a good sixth of its footage establishing a whole spiral nebula of minor characters before it centers down on its two luminaries, the Vampire and the Fool. As succinctly as I can put it, the supporting players are the latter's wife Kate, an ambulatory laundry bag played by Mabel Frenyear; their daughter, an implacably arch young hoyden of nine, unidentified; Kate's sister (May Allison); her beau, a corpulent slob, also anonymous; and a headlong butler seemingly afflicted with locomotor ataxia. All these inhabit a depressing chalet in Larchmont, where, as far as I could discover, they do nothing but shake hands effusively. A tremendous amount of handshaking, by the way, distinguished the flicks in their infancy; no director worth his whipcord breeches would have dreamed of beginning a plot before everybody had exchanged greetings like a French wedding party entering a café. In any case, the orgy of salutation has just begun to die down when John Schuyler, the Fool, arrives by yacht to join his kin, and the handshaking starts all

over again. Schuyler (Edward José), a florid, beefy lawyer in a high
Belmont collar, is hardly what you would envision as passion's plaything, but I imagine it took stamina to be a leading man for Theda
Bara—someone she could get her teeth into, so to speak. We now rico-
chet to the Vampire and her current victim, Parmalee (Victor Benoit),
strolling on a grassy sward nearby. The siren, in billowing draperies
and a period hat, carries almost as much sail as the Golden Hind, making it a bit difficult to assess her charms; however, they seem to have unmanned the young ne'er-do-well with her to the point where he is unable to light the Zira he is fumbling with. Their affair, it appears, has
burned itself out, and Parmalee, wallowing in self-pity, is being given
the frappé. Midway through his reproaches, a chauffeur-driven Sim-
plex, sparkling with brass, pulls alongside, Miss Bara shoves him impatiently into it, and the pair whisk off screen. These turgid formalities
completed, the picture settles down to business, and high time. In another moment, I myself would have been shaking hands and manumit-
ting the projectionist to the ball game I was keeping him from.

In a telegram from the President (Woodrow Wilson presumably
chose his envoys in an extremely haphazard manner), Schuyler is ordered to England on some delicate mission, such as fixing the impost
on crumpets, and makes ready to leave. He expects to be accompanied
by Kate and his daughter, but just prior to sailing, his sister-in-law
clumsily falls out of the tonneau of her speedster, and Kate remains
behind to nurse her. The Vampire reads of Schuyler's appointment,
and decides to cross on the same vessel and enmesh him in her toils.
As she enters the pier, an aged derelict accosts her, observing mourn-
fully, "See what you have made of me—and still you prosper, you hellcat." Meanwhile, Parmalee, learning of her desertion from a Japanese
servant whose eyelids are taped back with two pieces of court plaster,
smashes all the bric-a-brac and ferns in their love nest, tears down the
portieres, and hastens to intercept her. The derelict waylays him at the
gangplank. "I might have known you'd follow her, Parmalee," he
croaks. "Our predecessor, Van Diemen, rots in prison for her." The
plea to desist from his folly falls on deaf ears; Parmalee sequesters his
Circe on the promenade deck and, clapping a pistol to his temple, declares his intention of destroying himself if she abandons him. She
smilingly flicks it aside with a rose and a line of dialogue that is unquestionably one of the most hallowed in dramaturgy: "Kiss me, my
fool." Willful boy that he is, however, Parmalee must have his own
way and shoots himself dead. The gesture, sad to say, is wasted, exciting only desultory interest. The body is hustled off the ship, a steward

briskly mops up the deck, and by the time the *Gigantic* has cleared
Sandy Hook, Theda and her new conquest are making googly eyes and
preparing to fracture the Seventh Commandment by sending their
laundry to the same *blanchisseuse* in Paris.

A time lapse of two months, and in a hideaway on the Italian Riviera
choked with rubber plants and jardinieres, the lovers play amorous
tag like Dido and Aeneas, and nibble languidly on each other's ears.
Although everything seems to be leeches and cream, a distinct undercurrent of tension is discernible between them; Schuyler dreams be-
times of Suburbia, his dusky cook who used to make such good flap-
jacks, and when Theda jealously tears up a letter from his wife, acri-
mony ensues. Soon after, while registering at a hotel, Schuyler is recognized by acquaintances, who, much to his anguish, recoil as from an
adder. Back in Westchester, Kate has learned of his peccadilloes
through a gossip sheet. She confronts Schuyler's law partner and, with
typical feminine chauvinism, lambastes the innocent fellow: "You
men shield each other's sins, but if the woman were at fault, how
quick you'd be to condemn her!" Mrs. Schuyler's behavior, in fact, does
little to ingratiate her. Not content with barging into a busy law office
and disrupting its routine, she then runs home and poisons a child's
mind against its father. "Mama," inquires her daughter, looking up
from one of Schuyler's letters, "is a cross a sign for love?" "Yes,"
Kate retorts spitefully, "and love often means a cross." The fair sex
(God bless them) can be really extraordinary at times.

In our next glimpse of the lotus-eaters, in London, Schuyler has already begun paying the piper; his eyes are berimmed with kohl, his
step is palsied, and his hair is covered with flour. Theda, contrariwise,
is thriving like the green bay tree, still tearing up his correspondence
and wrestling him into embraces that char the woodwork. Their idyl
is abruptly cut short by a waspish cable from the Secretary of State,
which reads, in a code easily decipherable to the audience, "ON AC-
COUNT OF YOUR DISGRACEFUL CONDUCT, YOU ARE HEREBY DISMISSED."
Remorse and *Heimweh*, those twin powerful antibiotics, temporarily
dispel the kissing bug that has laid Schuyler low. He returns to the
States determined to rid himself of his incubus, but she clings and
forces him to install her in a Fifth Avenue mansion. Humiliations mul-
tiply as she insists on attending the opera with him in a blaze of aigrettes, and there is an affecting scene when their phaeton is overtaken
by his wife's auto near the Public Library and his daughter entreats
him, "Papa, dear, I want you." But the call of the wild is too potent,
and despite pressure from in-laws and colleagues alike, Schuyler sinks

deeper into debauchery. Kate, meanwhile, is keening away amid a houseful of relatives, all of them shaking hands as dementedly as ever and proffering unsound advice. There is such a hollering and a rending of garments and a tohubohu in the joint that you can't really blame Schuyler for staying away. When a man has worn himself down to the rubber struggling in a vampire's toils, he wants to come home to a place where he can read his paper in peace, not a loony bin.

Six months of revelry and an overzealous make-up man have left their stamp on the Fool when we again see him; the poor chap is shipping water fast. He reels around the mansion squirting seltzer at the help and boxing with double-exposure phantoms, and Theda, whose interest in her admirers wanes at the drop of a security, is already stalking a new meatball. Apprised of the situation, Kate goes to her husband bearing an olive branch, but their reunion is thwarted by his mistress, who unexpectedly checks in and kisses him back into submission. The action now grows staccato; Schuyler stages a monumental jamboree, at which his guests drink carboys of champagne and dance the bunny hug very fast, and then, overcome by delirium tremens, he violently expels them into the night. Kate, in the meantime, has decided to take his daughter to him as a last appeal. Preceded by her sister's beau (the Slob), the pair arrive at the mansion to find Schuyler in parlous shape. The child throws herself on him—a dubious service to anyone suffering from the horrors—and the adults beseech the wastrel to come home and, one infers, be committed to a nice, quiet milieu where his expenditures can be regulated. His dilemma is resolved by the reappearance of Theda; Schuyler grovels before her, eradicating any doubt as to his fealty, and the folks exit checkmated. The last few seconds of the picture, in a somber key unmatched outside the tragedies of D'Annunzio, depict the Fool, obsessed by a montage of his sins, squirming on his belly through an openwork balustrade and collapsing in a vestibule. "So some of him lived," comments a final sepulchral title, "but the soul of him died." And over what remains, there appears a grinning presentment of Miss Bara, impenitent and sleek in black velvet and pearls, strewing rose petals as we fade out.

For all its bathos and musty histrionics, *A Fool There Was*, I am convinced, still retains some mysterious moral sachet, if the experience I had after seeing it is at all indicative. As I was quietly recuperating in a West Side snug over a thimble of sherry and the poems of St. John Perse, a young woman who was manifestly no better than she should be slid into the banquette adjoining mine. So absorbed was I in the poet's meter that it was almost two minutes before I detected her wanton gaze straying toward me in unmistakable invitation. I removed my spectacles and carefully placed them in their shagreen case. "Mademoiselle," I said, "the flirtation you propose, while ostensibly harmless, could develop unless checked into a dangerous liaison. I am a full-blooded man, and one who does not do things by halves. Were I to set foot on the primrose path, scenes of carnival and license to shame Petronius might well ensue. No, my dear young lady," I said, draining my glass and rising, "succulent morsel though you are, I have no desire to end my days like John Schuyler, crawling through balustrades and being sprinkled with blooms." As luck would have it, her escort, whose existence I had somehow neglected to allow for, materialized behind me at this juncture and, pinioning me, questioned my motives. I gave him a brief résumé of *A Fool There Was* to amplify my position, but he acted as though I had invented the whole thing. Maybe I have. Still, who could have made up Theda Bara?

🌿 I'LL ALWAYS CALL YOU SCHNORRER, MY AFRICAN EXPLORER

BORNE ON THE NORTHEAST GALE that had whipped Narragansett Bay into icy froth all through a February night in 1916, a freezing rain beat down relentlessly on Westminster Street, main artery and Rue de la Paix of Providence, Rhode Island. Inside the box office of the Keith-Albee Theater, the town's principal vaudeville stand, the house manager gnawed his nails and stared glumly at a rackful of unsold tickets. It was almost three o'clock; there were seventeen patrons out front, five of them cuffed in on Annie Oakleys, and the curtain had been up half an hour on the most disastrous matinée in the history of show business. Just as he was preparing to issue forth to Farcher's Drugstore and end it all with two minims of prussic acid, a curious homuncule scurried into the lobby. He wore a reach-me-down Mackinaw, a pair of mismated overshoes, and a yellow sou'wester by courtesy of Scott's Emulsion, and his twelve-year-old-face—if, indeed, it could be so dignified—was beef-red with excitement.

"The holley had a trot-box!" he panted. "I mean, the trolley had a hatbox—I had to run all the way from Chalkstone Avenue! Are they on yet?"

"Is who on?" growled the manager, surreptitiously burning a pastille to neutralize any infection around his wicket.

"The head-hunters," the other babbled. "I mean, the headliners—the Four Marx Brothers in their sidesplitting extravaganza, *Home Again,* a funfest for young and old." Before the showman could produce his vouchsafer and vouchsafe a reply, the youth had fumbled a knotted bandanna from his jumper and spilled out a cache of greasy nickels. Then, snatching a ticket, he bounded up the stairs to the peanut gallery.

To recall with any degree of clarity the acts I saw on gaining my balcony perch would, of course, be impossible across the gulf of thirty-six years. Out of the haze of memory, however, I remember Fink's Trained Mules, Willie West & McGinty in their deathless housebuilding routine, Lieutenant Gitz-Rice declaiming "Mandalay" through a

624

pharynx swollen with emotion and coryza, and that liveliest of night-
ingales, Grace Larue. All these, though, were mere appetizers for
the roast. The *mise en scène* of the Marx Brothers piece was the Cu-
nard docks in New York, an illusion conveyed by four battered satchels
and a sleazy backdrop purportedly representing the gangway of the
Britannic. Garbed in his time-honored claw-hammer coat, his eyes
shifting lickerishly behind his specs and an unlit perfecto in his teeth,
Groucho irrupted onstage accompanied by his presumptive wife, a
scraggy termagant in a feather boa. Behind him came Gummo, impersonating his cocksure son, and Harpo and Chico, a pair of ship-
board cronies. Groucho's initial speech set the flavor of the proceedings.

"Well, friends," he observed, stifling a belch, "next time I cross the
ocean, I'll take a train. I'm certainly glad to set my feet on terra firma.
Now I know that when I eat something, I won't see it again." This
earthy confidence, understandably, evoked a paroxysm from the audience (a small paroxysm, to be sure, in view of its size), and Groucho
began to expand on his trip abroad. Heckled at almost every turn by
Gummo, he at length remarked waspishly, "Nowadays you don't know
how much you know until your children grow up and tell you how
much you don't know." According to Groucho, no pundit has ever
been able to explain exactly what the foregoing meant or why it always
elicited cheers and applause; apparently the customers sensed some
deep undercurrent of folk wisdom he himself was unaware of. At any
rate, after considerable horseplay in which Harpo disgorged the entire ship's cutlery from his sleeves and inspected the lingerie of several
zoftick fellow-passengers, Chico approached Groucho with hand extended.

"I'd like-a to say goombye to your wife," he proposed, in what was
unquestionably the paltriest dialect ever heard off Mulberry Street.

"Who wouldn't?" riposted his brother. This boffo ushered in the
second scene, laid without any tiresome logical transition at Groucho's
villa on the Hudson. The plot structure, to be candid, was sheerest
gossamer; vague reference was made to a stolen chafing dish, necessitating a vigorous search by Harpo of the corsages of two showgirls
drifting unaccountably about the premises, but on the whole there
were few nuances. Following a rather soupy rendition of "The World
Is Waiting for the Sunrise" by Harpo, Chico played "Chopsticks" on
the piano with grueling archness, and the pair exited rear stage left in
a papier-mâché boat on wheels, knocking down three members of the
troupe. Those who remained thereupon joined in a stylish chorale en-

titled "Over the Alpine Mountains E'er So Far Away," and, as the orchestra segued into von Suppé's "Light Cavalry Overture" to herald the acrobats, I descended to Farcher's Drugstore for a double banana split with maxixe cherries.

The years slipped away in their usual fleet fashion, leaving an impressive residue of silver in the hair and none whatever in the pocket. I heard no more of Groucho and his tatterdemalion crew, and I assumed they had drifted into some other field where their inadequacies handicapped them less. What was my surprise, therefore, to receive a long-distance call not long ago from Groucho in Hollywood.

"Well, well," I said encouragingly, "and what are you doing now? Working in some sort of restaurant or garage?"

"The deuce I am," he sneered. "I'm on Main Street now. I'm making a flick with William Bendix and Marie Wilson, and what's more," he added boastfully, "I've got my own radio and television show."

"Of course you have," I said soothingly. "What's afoot?"

"Well," he said. "I was just thinking it's time you came out of your shell. You're bored, restless, fed up with civilization and its hollow pretense—right?" I had to admit he had divined my mood. "Then why not fly out for a couple of days with me—at your own expense, of course? If you want to see unspoiled, primitive people, we've got some here who've just begun to walk erect."

"M-m-m," I said reflectively. "It does sound appealing, but I can't get away. There's my secretary, for one thing." I'd acquired an absolute whiz of a typist shortly before, kind of a younger Boots Mallory, and the problem of how to keep the child off my lap wrung my withers, word of honor.

"Couldn't you stand up and dump her off?" he suggested. It was typical of the man's audacious imagination, his refusal to bow to convention, that he should go straight to the core of things. Within forty-eight hours I had severed my obligations and was disembarking at the Los Angeles airport, and within another twenty-four, had reached the film colony. Slightly unsteadied by a cup of puréed avocado and a chickenfurter, I betook myself to R-K-O, where Marx was filming *A Girl in Every Port*. The set to which I was directed, a faithful replica of a battleship, hummed with activity; hordes of extras in navy blue were absorbed in scratch sheets, electricians on all sides feverishly worked to draw inside straights, and high on a camera parallel, two associate producers, arms clasped about each other, were busily examining their pelts for fleas. Groucho, as was his wont, was in the very thick of the melee. He was sprawled blissfully in a director's chair,

having his vertebrae massaged by Marie Wilson, a young lady whose
natural endowment caused a perceptible singing in the ears. I promptly
drew up a chair next to her and confided that I too was suffering from
a touch of sacroiliac, but the fair masseuse appeared to be hard of
hearing.

"Did you bring any coffee with you?" demanded Groucho abruptly.
I asked whether he realized that I had just flown across the country.
He countered with a peevish snort. "That's neither here nor there," he
snapped. "Anybody with an ounce of decency would have brought
me a cup of coffee from Lindy's. The stuff out here's pure slop."

"Then why do you stay here?"

"Where else can you get Marie Wilson to rub your back?" he asked.
"A little lower down, dear—there, that's better."

"I haven't met the young lady yet," I remarked pointedly.

"No, and you're not likely to, you sneak," he retorted. "I know
when I'm well off. Well, what's the chatter on Broadway?" In a few
incisive phrases, I summed up recent developments there, such as
Olga Nethersole's resounding success in *Sappho*, the razing of Hammerstein's Victoria, and the emergence of A. Toxen Worm as leading
drama critic, and, to bolster his spirits, revealed that Milton Berle's
TV show had a much larger following than his own. He was visibly
pleased. "Let's get together before you leave town," he said, wringing
my hand warmly. "I'd like you to poison some moles in my lawn." At
this juncture, the lunch gong pealed, and leaving an effigy of himself
with Miss Wilson to rub until his return, Groucho bore me off to the
commissary. His outsize corona and eyeglasses were somewhat at vari-
ance with his nautical dress, but he lent a maritime tang to the meal by
snarling out an occasional "Belay there, ye scut" and dancing a hornpipe with the waitress. Bendix, also clad in sailor suit, spent the lunch
chewing meditatively on the foreleg of an Angus steer. He is a hearty
trencherman, as befits a man of his girth, and has been known to consume a firkin of butter and a hectare of gherkins in less time than it
takes to say "Bo" to a goose.

"You know, Mr. Bendix," I said enviously. "It must be hilarious,
making a movie with a topflight comedian."

"Yeah," he agreed. "I'd love to do it some day."

"But I—I don't understand," I persisted. "You must roll on the
floor when he gets off those repartees of his."

"Who's that?" he queried, detaching his eyes slowly from the steer.
I indicated his co-star. He masticated pensively for a moment. "It's a
living," he grunted. During our exchange, Groucho had seized the op-

portunity to couple his check with mine. On my expostulating, he unleashed such a torrent of sniveling and abuse that I finally paid in disgust. The mercurial temperament thrives on petty triumphs; at once he became ardent, solicitous of my welfare, determined to accord me every hospitality.

"Now listen," he said forcefully. "From here in, it's strictly my treat. What about dinner at my place and a night ball game afterward?" I agreed readily, and he pondered. "Where are your grips?"

"I left them with the cop at the main gate."

"Good," he said. "I've got a big, roomy house out in Beverly. Pick up the bags and take them to Schwabacher's used-car lot on Exposition Boulevard. You can sleep for nothing in one of their old jalopies."

"I have to clean up, take a shower," I protested feebly.

"Who takes a shower to go to a ball game?" he asked with irritation. "Lot of cheap swank." He scribbled on a card. "O.K., give this to my maid and she'll let you in the bathroom, but take it easy on the hot water—I'm not made of money. Did you bring a towel?"

"Only a fiber one I muckled from the plane."

"We-e-ll," he said grudgingly, "I guess we can loan you one, providing you sign for it. See you later, then; dinner at seven sharp." As I moved toward the door of the commissary, I felt myself the cynosure of countless envying eyes. A great star had bared his heart to me. What idiosyncrasies, what foibles I could divulge were I not bound by the journalist's sacred code. But my lips were sealed, and if Groucho's cuisine was as toxic as I anticipated, it would be worth my life to open them even a fraction.

At seven-thirty that evening, in the playroom of a repossessed hacienda on Hillcrest Drive, a couple of middle-aged gallants racked with sciatica descended painfully from their bar stools and linked arms with two statuesque actresses. The mood of the quartet was distinctly festive; tongues loosened by copious draughts of loganberry cocktails, their flushed cheeks and sparkling eyes marked them incontrovertibly as devotees of Bacchus.

"Shay, Groucho," I hiccoughed. "Thish a grea' party. Le'sh not go ball game; le'sh have s'more logleberry cocktails. Wha' shay, girls?" My host quickly snatched an aquarium from my path and threw open the door of the dining room.

"Bring him in here and we'll get some grub into him," he directed. "Watch out—he's scraping the piano."

"That's not all he's scraping," muttered my partner, disentangling my arm from her waist. "Where'd you find this crumb, anyway?"

"On the old Fall River Line," said Groucho plausibly. "Used to be a whitewing, I think. I gave him a lavish tip and he's been bleeding me ever since." He propped me up in a chair and retired to a side table to carve the roast. Inwardly I smiled a small, secret smile. My ruse was working perfectly; beneath a seemingly tipsy exterior, I was razor-keen, studying them as objectively as specimens under a microscope.

"You're too softhearted, Groucho," chided Queenie, the more buxom of the duo, thoughtfully crumbling her roll. "Silly boy, why do you leave grifters like this milk you? You need a woman to take care of you." Groucho was immediately all ears, so much so that he almost sliced one of them off.

"That's what I was just thinking," he said, swiftly circling the table. "What did you have in mind?"

"Oh, I don't know," she said coyly.

"You *don't*?" he demanded, rounding on her. "Then what do you mean by teasing me to the brink of madness, mocking me with a smile like a scimitar?" He flung aside his knife with a bitter laugh. "Do you know what it means to stand here night after night, sawing away at a cheap pot roast and thirsting for a coquette's kisses?"

"Hey, this meat is awful dry," complained Chiquita, our other dryad. "Isn't there any gravy?"

"Gravy, gravy!" shouted Groucho. "Everybody wants gravy! Did those six poor slobs on the *Kon-Tiki* have any gravy? Did Scipio's legions, deep in the burning African waste, have gravy? Did Fanny Hill?"

"Did Fanny Hill what?" I asked.

"Never mind, you cad," he threw at me. "I'm sick to death of in-nuendo, brittle small talk, the sly, silken rustle of feminine under-things. I want to sit in a ball park with the wind in my hair and breathe cold, clean popcorn into my lungs. I want to hear the crack of seasoned ash on horsehide, the roar of the hydra-headed crowd, the umpire's deep-throated 'Play ball!' " So graphically had he limned the color and excitement of the game that the three of us hung there with shining eyes, too rapt even to spurn the paper-thin, parsimonious slices of meat he had served us.

"Golly!" breathed Chiquita. "I feel like as though I had really wit-nessed the game!"

"So do I," said Groucho, yawning, "and I'm pooped. I'll thank you two harpies to clear out and take that lush with you. I've got to be on the set at eight." Courtly as one of George Cable's antebellum planters, he stood in the doorway and waved us farewell. I turned from the curb for a last glimpse of him, and somehow it seemed to me his gesture of parting had a peculiar tremulous quality. I looked again; yes, he was scratching himself. I called to him, but already his thoughts were far away, intent on the copy of the *Partisan Review* with which he invariably concluded his day. Softly I tiptoed out into the smog.

"All right, settle down, everybody—this is a take!" bawled the director. "Hit the wind machine, and remember, Groucho, bend down into his ear and plead with him." A hush fell over the turbulent sound stage, technicians exchanged a last crisp monosyllable, and the transparency screen behind the set lit up to reveal half a dozen race horses plunging toward us. In front of them, in jockey's silks, sat Marx and Bendix on two amazingly lifelike steeds molded of rubber. As the machinery underneath them began churning, the horses came alive; their necks elongated, manes and tails streamed in the breeze, muscles rippled in their flanks and bellies. The riders plied their mounts with whip and endearments, straining forward into the camera to steal the scene from each other.

"Cost twenty-five grand to build those bang-tails," the producer confided to me in the darkness. "We rent the pair of 'em for five hundred a day. But it's worth it. When they go to see the picture, they'll swear it's a real horse race."

"What happens if they don't go to see the picture?" I asked, fascinated. He turned deathly pale, and excusing himself, stumbled off to the studio psychiatrist. A few minutes afterward, rid of his make-up and in jaunty spirits, Groucho met me at the door of his dressing room. The picture was finished, and he was at last free to resume his passionate avocation, the collecting and cross-fertilization of various kinds of money. To celebrate its completion, he had suggested a final lunch at Romanoff's. Over our risotto, I inquired about his future plans.

"Who knows?" His smile was charming, and seeing his teeth, one would have sworn they were real. "I shall, of course, travel; I do think travel tends to broaden, don't you? Marriage? No, I hardly think so. Babies? No, I hardly think so."

"Chutney?" put in the waiter.

"No, I hardly think so," said Groucho. "Wait a minute—that comes with the *plat du jour*. Give me a double portion, and I'll take some home in a bag."

"What advice would you give a young person just starting out in the theater?" I asked.

He ruminated awhile, and his face softened.

"You know what I'd say?" he mused. "I'd take that young girl by the shoulders, I honestly would, and I'd say, 'Honey——' " He looked up alertly as Marilyn Monroe, in a diaphanous pink blouse, passed the table bound for a rear booth. There was a sudden uprush of air beside me, and a scant fifty minutes later he returned, wry bewilderment on his countenance. "Talk about coincidence," he marveled. "It seems that kid was just starting out in the theater, too, and she asked me the very same thing."

"What did you tell her?"

"Oh, just trivialities." He coughed. "Naturally, in so brief an encounter, I didn't get a chance to grapple with her particular problems. We're meeting at the Mocambo tonight to discuss them further."

"Well, Groucho," I said huskily, reaching for my hat, "it may sound fulsome, but I can testify you've got a heart as big as all outdoors. If you ever come to Bucks County, there'll always be an extra bed for you at the George S. Kaufmans'."

"My boy," he said, and his voice shook slightly, "a very wise old man once said that there are two things money cannot buy—nostalgia and friendship. He died in the poorhouse. Don't forget to square that tab on the way out." He gripped my hand hard and was gone, a gallant freebooter who had made his rendezvous with Destiny. As his skulking, predatory figure faded from view, I bowed my head in tribute. "Adieu, Quackenbush," I whispered. "Adieu, Captain Spaulding. No man ever buckled a better swash." Then, through a mist of tears, I soberly signed his name to the check and went forth to a workaday world.

🌿 *THIS LITTLE PIGGY WENT TO MARKET*

I WAS A FIRST-BORN (there were forty of us in that first year of my mother's maturity), she was eight years old at the time if I remember rightly. Swinging high and joyously in my lofty cradle—feeling myself grow and grow; basking in the sunlight, loving my green satin coat, I grew the fastest and was handsomer and bigger than all the rest.

Like all families we have our troubles, a bit of hardship during the hot dry season (thirsty and all that), and wretched coconut beetles who do their best to bore into our supports. When the typhoons come, wind and rain tear through our house, the palm leaves whip straight out! Plunk! Thud! Children drop out of their cradles.

When I was old enough to lean safely over the edge of my cradle, I had lots of fun watching the world below. The clumsy man animals sorting the fallen; stacking them in piles to await the coming of the carabao and his creaking cart. They'd grab a coconut and crash it down on a spike they had wedged in the ground. A couple of twists, presto! A coat torn off and a victim thrown aside. . . . Afterwards, a whack of the bolo and the poor things were split wide open and left to dry! One gets hardened to such things, and too, it was someone else's life, which makes the difference.

One day as I was watching the spectacle below I felt my stem give —an instant later, I was hurtling through space! Those awful seconds! Me there on the ground . . . exhausted, fear in my heart! What would be my fate? Lose my shiny green coat? A swift bolo baring my inner self to the sun?

I smile now at that poor innocent! My fate was never in doubt. My very size and perfection was a guarantee. I was placed in a seed bed for propagation, *of course*! Side by side with the elect of our species I was left to drowse and dream, and wait. . . .

Nice coconuts go into syrup and candy kettles, into beauty creams, and fragrant soaps, and of course, into vegetable shortening.—*From "Autobiography of a Coconut," a leaflet advertising Mandalay Coconut Syrup.*

HONESTLY, it's enough to make you blow the cover off your jar, the way some coconuts run off at the mouth. You'd think nobody else had ever done anything significant or exciting, and coming from your own sister, it's twice as provoking. She always was stuck on herself, even when the clump of us used to sway out there in the Philippines, and now, since she managed to break into print, she's intolerable. Well, I've got news for her: I've had ten times the career she's had. I've traveled, I've rubbed elbows with cosmopolitan, glamorous people—or been rubbed on their elbows, which amounts to the same thing—and I'll bet I've had more weird, hair-raising experiences, ounce for ounce, than any beauty cream with a coconut-oil base *she* could name. But you be the judge; I'll just put it down as I recall it, and if it brings a blush to the unsophisticated cheek, so much the better. After all, that's why I was compounded in the first place, *n'est-ce pas?*

My earliest recollections, after being sundered, squeezed, and boiled, are naturally vague; I was swirling around turbidly, deep in the hold of this freighter, part of a glutinous white purée consigned to a wholesale cosmetics firm in New York. Then a confused interval—grim-faced customs inspectors rummaging through me for opium, the rough persiflage of roustabouts and truckmen, and, finally, a scrubby loft in the West Thirties full of noise and commotion. When I eventually got my bearings, the establishment proved to be a fly-by-night laboratory styling itself La Pulchrituda Lotions, operated by two grifters named Victor Spatula and Morty Krisp. They were both sallow, ulcerous dwarfs, treacherous as quicksand, ever on the *qui vive* to fleece the public and each other. Spatula, whose previous scientific experience had been confined to adulterating bourbon, was officially head chemist of the concern; Krisp, the one-man sales force, scurried about town hawking their products to hairdressers and department stores. I well remember the afternoon they originated me—in my present form, that is. Amid half a dozen other ingredients chosen at random, like capsicum, sage, oil of cinnamon, and buckwheat flour, I had been revolved a few hasty seconds in a centrifuge and decanted into a number of small opaque jars. Just as I was settling, I overheard the partners conferring.

"What'll we call this gunk?" asked Spatula. "We already used every name there is—Stimulose, Velveena Nose Unguent, Rejuvenola . . ."

"Wait, I thought of one yesterday," said Krisp, pondering. "How about Monadnoid Cream? It's a combo of hormone and adenoid."

"Say, that sounds beneficial," the other assented. "It lacks feminine appeal, though. How about Monadnoid Youthifonium Cream?"

"The greatest!" exulted Krisp. "I'll go ask the printer to knock out the labels on spec. Here, give me a couple of jars for his wife."

The contrast between their squalid hive and my next home was refreshing. Less than a week later, I was the apex of a window display in a chic little salon on East Fifty-fourth Street, lording it over a whole phalanx of gilt nail polish and costly wrinkle removers. It was enthralling to study the women who paused to stare in at us—pert secretaries and models with hatboxes, basilisk-eyed dowagers, housewives bearing rib roasts, *poules de luxe*. Invariably, their nostrils dilated when they saw my legend, and they yearned toward me like iron filings in a magnetic field, but they were either too busy or too timid to gratify their longing, because I remained where I was. The dogs resident in the neighborhood behaved even more curiously. Impossible to drag them past; there was always a poodle, a boxer, or a Bedlington gazing through the plate glass in stupefaction, sniffing and whimpering feverishly. I presume that Spatula, in his creative frenzy, must have unwittingly included some element in my formula, like beef extract, that aroused their desire. At any rate, one midmorning I was plucked from the window by the proprietress, a highly synthetic Parisienne, and exhibited with a flourish to a young lady. She was a vivid, shapely brunette in expensive sports clothes, with sloe eyes and the kind of mouth traditionally referred to as a scarlet wound.

"You really recommend this?" she asked hesitantly. "You see, I have a special problem with my skin. It's as tender as a baby's."

"But *mais certainement!*" the shopkeeper effervesced. "Zis is *absolument* miraculous—astringent but not harsh, oily but not greasy. Eet supplies the very essential Mademoiselle needs." She lowered her voice portentously. "Eet comes from an old Aztec recipe."

The tiny flat in the upper Seventies that Jasmine Lispenard took me home to was, I shortly deduced, typical of those occupied by most career girls, though I never quite ascertained what Jasmine's career was. She had evidently been married at one time, to judge by her frequent appeals to her lawyers, Howells & Imprecation, to collect back alimony. Once or twice, I heard devout resolutions about a course in Greek drama at Hunter, a television appearance, and some abstract jewelry Jasmine meant to design, but they dissipated along with her hangovers. From eleven, when she awoke, she clung like a limpet to the phone, relaying gossip, arranging dates with beaux and playing them off against each other, and analyzing their potentialities to her girl-friends. The apartment was usually in disorder, except on the day the maid came in, when it became a shambles. The latter, a Hungarian lady afflicted with *folie de grandeur*, fiercely disdained the chores expected of her and did nothing but dust the neo-Calder mobile, scream vilification at the cat, and read her employer's mail. As a result, the place was ankle-deep in old theater programs and tangerine peels, discarded stockings, and crumpled Kleenex. Fresh from an elegant shop window off Park Avenue, it required time to accustom myself to this informal atmosphere. Nonetheless, I soon adapted to the clutter on Jasmine's vanity—the pots of mascara, the eyebrow pencils, and the manifold skin tonics and bracers—and, indeed, found it a quite cheery *ambiance*.

My chatelaine's single attempt to use me was, I fear, rather disastrous. One evening, her amatory scheming misfired; three of her cavaliers canceled out, and, willy-nilly, she was forced into the kip at nine o'clock. Placing a volume of Turgenev on the night table and me on top of it, she got into bed and opened the *Journal-American*. As she thoughtfully digested Cholly Knickerbocker, chewing a salami sandwich the while, she massaged me on her forehead and cheeks. Suddenly, she emitted a choked cry, sprang out of bed, and caught up a hand mirror. A chain of horrifying red welts had risen on her face, giving her the uncanny aspect of one of those old-time testimonials for Poslam Ointment. I vanished forthwith into the wastebasket, where I sojourned for three days until the maid, piecing together a letter of Jasmine's, discovered me. My label obviously intrigued her, and she applied me in quantity to her jowls, studying the effect critically in the mirror. Then, yielding to her ungovernable inclination to identify herself with the *haut monde*, she procured an evening cape from the closet, wrapped it about her, and paraded languidly before the vanity.

"How do you do, Mrs. Astorbilt?" she drawled in a haughty, aristocratic voice. "So divine to see you again since we had tea together in your cabaña at Newport. Tell me, how is dear Reggie? Is he still coining money hand over fist down there in Wall Street?"

When she had departed, leaving me on the vanity with my cover askew, the cat reappeared and prowled around, stalking me with intense curiosity. He managed to insinuate his paw and extract a dab, but the taste plainly revolted him, for he arched his back, spat, and withdrew under the bed.

Life in the apartment pursued its uneven tenor for a while thereafter. Absorbed in a new and unusually promising conquest, Jasmine forgot my existence, and I made myself as inconspicuous as possible. The latest admirer, it appeared from reports to her intimates, was a big advertising executive—no less than the copy chief of Phlebotomy,

Stinch & Mercer, she told them carelessly. His name was Raoul Paltry, and according to Jasmine he was criminally good-looking, even if his hair had begun to thin out and he *was* a trifle heavy in the seat. Raoul's manners were exquisite; he wore the most beautiful suits—dispatched from Savile Row, he had confided to her, in dozen lots semiannually—and his largess in places like the Chambord and Le Pavillon was legendary. As she reconstructed it, his wife, a withered crone, had not kept pace with his rise to success, but Jasmine understood him fully. To her, he was just a small boy who had lost his way.

From the outset, it was a stormy romance, if the skirmishes over the phone, the duplicity, and the recriminations were at all indicative. To fan Raoul's ardor, Jasmine invented a rival named Don Carlos Morales y Muñoz Carvalho, heir to Brazil's greatest coffee fortune and a Neronian spendthrift. She tortured Raoul by the hour with inventories of Don Carlo's toys—his Rolls-Royces and Ferraris, his yachts, planes, and shooting boxes—and his mulish insistence on plying her with gifts. No morning dawned, she asserted, without some new bauble from Winston's or Olga Tritt's, which, to be sure, she instantly returned out of principle, but the strain was driving her to the edge of neurasthenia. I went liquid as she retailed scenes of Latin jealousy, bloodcurdling threats Carlos had made to disembowel Raoul on sight. The latter, caught between his wife, his analyst, and Jasmine, must have led a dog's life; one could visualize the poor devil striving to compose elegiacs to shoe polish or laxatives while disentangling his emotional problems. With the affair gaining momentum daily, I grew increasingly concerned for the man and most eager to see him, for as yet he had never set foot on the premises. What pretexts Jasmine used to hold him at bay I cannot imagine, but the hour of reckoning arrived at last. Late one night, I heard her unlock the outer door and engage in a protracted debate too muffled to comprehend.

"Oh, all *right*, Raoul," she said impatiently, after a bit. "But remember, just one drink and off to your beddie-byes. Promise?"

The promise was forthcoming, in an unsteady basso; there then ensued a series of predictable sounds—the slam of the icebox door, the tinkle of ice cubes, a glass crash. From my situation on the vanity, I could follow the succeeding dialogue only imperfectly, and the record-player did not help matters, but I gathered Raoul sought the conventional return on his investment and Jasmine was proving obdurate.

"What do you mean, I'll think less of you?" His voice, hitherto cajoling, contained a note of exasperation. "I'll think *more* of you!

After all, you're a man—that is, I'm a man and you're a woman, and when two people—"

"Look out, for God's sake. You're dislocating my arm!" she protested. "Now, go on, dear, fly away home. You have to finish that exciting advertisement you were telling me about."

"Aw, sugar, this is no time to bring up linoleum," Raoul whined. "Listen, why don't you slip into something like a negligee?"

"Yes, and you slip into something like the Pelham local," she retorted. "Let me *go*, I said!"

In the next breath, the two of them were framed in the doorway, Jasmine struggling manfully to escape her suitor's clasp. She kicked out at his ankle and, as he jumped back, broke away. Then, seizing the weapon closest to hand, she whisked me off the vanity and shied me at Raoul's head. I landed square on his right temple. With a peculiar sobbing intake of breath, he collapsed over a Hitchcock chair and sprawled on the floor, out for the count. Immediately, Jasmine's whole mood changed. She ran to him, uttering little broken moans of contrition, loosened his collar, bathed his forehead with a washcloth, hysterically begged his forgiveness. Within the minute, Raoul had revived and they were babbling assurances of mutual esteem couched in the most repugnant baby talk.

As for me, I've been on pretty much of a retired basis since then. Jasmine's circumstances improved strikingly soon afterward, and she moved to a far roomier apartment on Central Park South. Along with a spavined Venetian blind and innumerable soda bottles, I was transferred to the janitor's quarters in the basement, where his wife has earmarked me for future experiment. Ah, welladay, life's a whirligig. I may be ousted from this jar to make room for a handful of bobby pins or I may wind up greasing a window cord, but at least I haven't stagnated. That's more than I can say for a certain gasbag of a coconut out in the Philippines. No need to mention names. Maybe, if she's so goddam adept at writing, she can also read.

❧ NIRVANA SMALL BY A WATERFALL

WITH BARELY POTABLE SPIRITS fetching a king's ransom these days, and the price of barbiturates indistinguishable from that of gold dust, it ought to interest anyone looking for a little fast surcease that the best fifteen-cent nepenthe in town is still Louella Parsons' monthly column in *Modern Screen*. Slick though the testimonial may sound, I have been using the lady's feed-box gossip (in moderation, naturally) over the past twelvemonth and I can honestly say that it has been a boon. Once your system adjusts to her syntax, and the initial impulse to scream or scale a tree wears off, it has a wonderfully emollient effect, somewhat like sliding into a tub of lukewarm oatmeal. It slows down the heartbeat to turtle pace, irons out those corduroy furrows in the forehead, and sets up a pleasurable tingling in the Malpighian layer. I cannot for the life of me understand why the medical profession has shown no inclination to adopt it as an all-purpose anodyne. True, the back numbers of the *National Geographic* in the general practitioner's waiting room have an undeniably narcotic value, but for a real charge Lollie stands alone. The next time you feel prompted to bolt to your healer, seek out the nearest newsstand. You don't even need a prescription.

The title of the column, "Louella Parsons' Good News," is a largely arbitrary designation; most of the glad tidings seem to consist of tempestuous divorces and the unerring instinct of Homo Hollywood to mismate. "What a month of headlines!" exclaims the fair conductress, opening her March article with a catalogue of current rifts in the households of Barbara Stanwyck, Elizabeth Taylor, and Judy Garland. "Whew! Never can I remember so many important stories from movietown breaking so close together—and, frankly, never can I remember working so hard batting out my scoops and 'inside' yarns on wot hoppen." An appealing vignette this, the veteran hunched over her typewriter in the turbulent city room, eyeshade askew and corn-cob ablaze, pecking out bulletins and gulping coffee from a cardboard container. Not all of Louella's dispatches, to be sure, are couched in such breakneck Hildy Johnson tempo; she normally favors a gelatinous, sorghum-sweetened idiom in which archness, bonhomie, and vinegar struggle for mastery. Her antennae are quick to detect subterranean marital discord or the broken heart skillfully concealed. Last September, for instance, she remarked clairvoyantly, "I can't help feeling that Joan Fontaine is unhappy. Yes, I know she is a famous actress with beautiful clothes, admiring fans, a lovely home—all that goes with stardom. But, every time I see her she seems so wistful. It is also my idea," she continued, displaying her matchless talent for sucking honey from nonexistent flowers, "that she is NOT carrying a torch for good-looking agent, Charlie Feldman, her ex-husband Bill Dozier, or any other gent." A cast into troubled waters the previous April brought forth another cupcake frosted with custard and strychnine. Commenting on Jennifer Jones's renewed radiance since marrying David Selznick, she observed, "During their engagement, they battled continually and usually staged their biggest tiffs at parties. One or the other of them would leave in a huff. But at Nadya and Reggie's [a buffet supper *chez* Reginald Gardiner], all was sweetness and light between the Selznicks." Evidently this heavenly rapport acted like wine on the correspondent, for the same party produced two added sugar-plums. Joan Bennett, she reported, "was saying she spent a fortune educating her daughter—who is now using that education to raise grapes in Imperial Valley! 'She is happiest,' said Joan, referring to Diana, her eldest, married daughter—'when dashing about in a red jeep, seeing how the grapes are coming on.' " Of the state of the grapes —whether they had agreed to disagree—there was no indication; forthwith, the spotlight turned on Mrs. Tyrone Power: "Linda Christian Power, who dramatizes everything, gave us a blow-by-blow account of her robbery in Mexico City—and what a difficult time her brother's wife had when her baby was born. All the time the fascinating and volatile Linda was telling us these tidbits, she was also modeling her new Italian gown and showing us her French purse—the latter giving me an idea. I have a top just like the little jade mouse on her handbag that I could use as a clasp—only my top is composed of elephants." Under these booming non sequiturs, hypertension falls away, the reader's jaw relaxes, and he is transported, beyond reach of internal revenue and nuclear fission, onto the seventh astral plane.

If I were bullied into choosing the story in which Miss Parsons comes closest to artistry, I would vote unhesitatingly for her report, this March, of starlet Ruth Roman's adventures in housekeeping with her husband, Mortimer Hall:

Ruth met Morty when she was in New York last September. She was lunching at "21" Club with a girl-friend who introduced her to the good-looking young millionaire sitting at an adjoining table. "So you are Ruth Roman," said the handsome gent she was to marry within three months. "I'm coming to the Coast soon to manage my mother's network out there. (His mother is Mrs. Dorothy Schiff, publisher of the New York *Post* and owner of KLAC radio station.) I was told to look you up." . . . A few days after they returned from their 24-hour honeymoon Morty said to her: "How much money do you need to run the house?" "Money?" said Ruth. "I don't need it. I can take care of the household expenses." "Not on your life," said the head of the family, shoving a wad of bills into her hand. "I'M paying all the bills. You're a married woman now, baby." After he bolted out the door, Ruth just sat there and cried. . . . Morty also insisted that Ruth move out of her house and into his. He is firmly convinced that a wife shouldn't remain in the domicile where she has lived as a bachelor girl. Nobody knows this—but Ruth's "wonderful guy" is so sold on this idea—he wouldn't even move in her house for the few days she needed to pack and move out. For three days—the newlyweds lived in separate houses! The reason Ruth couldn't move in immediately is that she has two dogs and two cats—and a runway had to be fixed at Mr. Hall's house before Mrs. Hall could move in with her private zoo.

The trials and tribulations of the Halls in launching their matrimonial bark are doubly absorbing because they parallel, in many respects, those of Rhonda St. Cyr and Stewart Fels-Natchez, another pair of newlyweds in the screen colony. Miss St. Cyr, it will be recalled, played the role of the pretty hourglass vender in "Fly by Noon" and the lady neurologist in "Schizoids Three," and her madcap elopement to Las Vegas with the playboy Ohioan set the film capital by the ears. The following playlet, based on tape recordings made by friends after their return, as a post-nuptial gift, might be dubbed a semi-documentary. However dubbed, it is an indisputable slice of life and, in common with all organic matter (including gossip columns), should be kept in a refrigerator until ready to serve.

SCENE: *The living room of Stewart Fels-Natchez' palatial salt box in Beverly Hills. The basic décor is Arabian and, to judge from the quantity of massive earthenware jars on view, might easily be the headquarters of Ali Baba, but the Pennsylvania Dutch dough tray and spatter floor, Queen Anne highboy, and chromium bar*

*upholstered in okapi hide proclaim its owner a connoisseur who
can afford to indulge his taste. Bookshelves filled with priceless
literary treasures—Avon, Bantam, the cream of the world's great
abridgments—also stamp him an inveterate reader. As the curtain rises, Pargeter, a dignified English manservant in butler's
apron, is surprised before the fireplace consigning an armload
of cabinet photographs to the flames and brushing up the exposition.*

PARGETER (*aloud*): Ah, well, there's the last of the master's youthful
indiscretions, bless him for a high-spirited colt. Now that connubial bliss is his, you—ahem!—young persons will only foul up
the premises, so away with you. They do say that ever since Mr.
Stewart met Miss St. Cyr, he's forsworn his flibbertigibbet ways.
I don't doubt she'll be the making of the boy. Hello—I think I
hear his supercharged Alfa-Romeo crunching up the driveway.
This is where I scuttle off belowstairs, so as not to be under the
feet of the doting honeymooners. (*He exits. The door opens
boisterously, and Stewart strides in, bearing Rhonda in his arms.
There is a sheen about them.*)

RHONDA (*gazing about, enraptured*): Stooky! It's divoon!

STEWART: Like it, lover?

RHONDA: Oh, lambie, leave me down out of your importunate arms,
as I must browse around and drink my fill of everything. (*clapping her hands*) An aquarium! How darling! Here, fishie-fishie!

STEWART: They don't know you yet. I mean you're still a stranger to
them.

RHONDA: You watch, we'll be friends in no time. I'm a regular bug
on ichthyology.

STEWART: Queer, I sort of sensed it. When two persons are very
deeply in love, sometimes they can commune without words.

RHONDA: I wish I could express myself like you. I think that's what first
enthused me anent a certain Mr. Stewart Fels-Natchez. That and
the funny, crinkly laughter lines around his eyes.

STEWART (*ardently*): Gee, I could gobble you up in one bite!

RHONDA: Now, stop it, naughty boy, you're loosening all the cherries
on my hat. Is that our pool out there in the patio?

STEWART: No, that's the servants' pool. Ours is in the bedroom upstairs.

RHONDA (*looking up*): Doesn't it leak down through the plaster?

STEWART: Uh-uh. I had tar paper laid between the beams.

RHONDA: You shouldn't have went to all the expense, precious.

STEWART: Well, after all, it would sting a chap's pride to have his snookums laying down here with moisture dripping on top of her unruly head.

RHONDA: Honest, I sometimes think you must be a Latin to understand women the way you do. (*They kiss hungrily.*) What is that strange crisscross door sawed in the wall there?

STEWART: Never mind, you will be apprised in due course. First off, how are you fixed for cash to run our domicile?

RHONDA: Oh, I have scads. We mummers earn a goodly stipend, you know.

STEWART: Silly, impractical angel! Henceforward, Madam, I foot the bills and no sass. Here is a bundle of scratch to grease the skids, and should you at any time need largess for the bird that delivers the bottled water or so, simply let out a holler.

RHONDA (*through a mist of tears*): Nobody ever had such a thoughtful hubby. Prince Charming was an ignatz alongside of you.

STEWART: Your lips set my brain on fire—

RHONDA (*evading him*): But I don't think you really trust me, else you would wise me up as to the function of that door.

STEWART: Don't be nosy, honey. Remember what happened to Mrs. Bluebeard.

RHONDA: If you hadn't been so nosy at the Sump Room in Chicago, we wouldn't of met. I was eating a *shashlik* off a flaming spear and you couldn't keep your eyes off me.

STEWART: You know why? The night prior, I caught your personal appearance at the Mastbaum in Philly, and you were alike as two peas. It was fantastic.

RHONDA: I'll never forget when my secretary introduced us. You said, "So this is Rhonda St. Cyr. Well, my old man has more kale than anybody in Ashtabula. He's got bakeries and lubritoriums and wet-wash laundries, and I'm going to lavish it all on you."

STEWART (*fondly*): Was that when you definitely started to care?

RHONDA: No. I could never be taken by storm. I was intrigued when you did over that Glendale theater lobby in chinchilla for my preview.

STEWART: I had a trick idea the time you went to Honolulu. I was going to rent a Piper Cub to strew orchids on your ship over the Golden Gate.

RHONDA: I'm glad you didn't. I hate garishness. (*pouting*) Stooky, dear, mayn't I have just one bitty peek behind that door?

STEWART (*relenting*): Oh, well, you were bound to sooner or later. (*opening it*) It's a runway.

RHONDA (*ecstatically*): A *runway!*

STEWART: Yes, for your private zoo. Knowing your oft-expressed kinship for your animal chums, I moved mountains to bring them in arm's reach. Come on, fellows! (*A puma, closely followed by a gibbon and a llama, plummet in and leap distractedly about their mistress.*)

RHONDA (*cuddling them joyfully*): Did ever a bride's cup brim over like yours truly's? Sweetheart, I fear it's some marvelous golden dream.

STEWART: Your woman's intuition tells you true. Who do you think is lodged in this closet, biding my signal to erupt on the scene?

RHONDA: My—my numerologist?

STEWART: No, our lawyers. (*soberly*) Rhonda, we must be brave. Our marriage has drifted on the rocks. The both of us are living a lie.

RHONDA (*dully*): I—felt something had snapped, too.

STEWART: Ever since our union forty-eight hours ago, I sensed it was doomed. Deep down, you rebelled against my dating other bimbos and squiring them to the niteries.

RHONDA: It's nobody's fault, Stewart. People with careers like ours aren't fated to love.

STEWART: You'll always remain a shrine in my memory. No matter how many ears I whisper sweet nothings in, your dear face will rise to haunt me.

RHONDA: Likewise, darling. (*Her voice breaks.*) If only—oh, if only Louella or Hedda Hopper were here to share our unhappiness!

STEWART: They are, dearest—and Skolsky, too. (*Neatly synchronized with his words, the celebrated trio rise from the earthenware jars at rear, whisk open notebooks, and clamor for details of the property settlement, division of yachts, etc. Rhonda silences them with a gesture.*)

RHONDA: One moment, please. We want you three to be the first to know. We're going on a second honeymoon. We've found each other again. (*sensation*) Thanks to a loyal mate which he was tireless to anticipate my every wish, we have wrote finis to conjugal strife. In her next vehicle, the fans will see a new, more mature Rhonda St. Cyr, mellowed by suffering and compassion.

STEWART (*softly*): To be followed, I may divulge, by a chubby little sequel, with Stewart Fels-Natchez, quondam playboy, listed as the associate producer.

PARSONS, HOPPER, AND SKOLSKY (*exhaling*): Judas Priest, what a story! (*As they scatter to alert the wire services, the couple embrace, the gibbon showers them with confetti, the puma lies down with the llama, and the lawyers quietly smother in the closet.*)

CURTAIN

🌺 CLOUDLAND REVISITED: IT TAKES TWO TO TANGO, BUT ONLY ONE TO SQUIRM

BY CURRENT STANDARDS, the needs of a young man-about-town in Providence, Rhode Island, in 1921 were few—an occasional pack of straw-tipped Melachrinos, an evening of canoeing on the Ten Mile River, with its concomitant aphrodisiac, a pail of chocolate creams, and a mandatory thirty-five cents daily for admission to the movies. My fluctuating resources (most of the family's money evaporated in visionary schemes like a Yiddish musical-comedy production of *The Heart of Midlothian*) often forced me to abjure tobacco and amour, but I would sooner have parted with a lung than missed such epochal attractions as *Tol'able David* or Rudolph Valentino in *The Four Horsemen of the Apocalypse*, and I worked at some very odd jobs indeed to feed my addiction to the cinema. One of them, I recall, was electroplating radiators in a small, dismal factory that turned out automobile parts. It was an inferno of dirt and noise; half a dozen presses, operated by as many scorbutic girls whose only diet seemed to be pork pies, were kept busy turning out the honeycomb radiators used in several cars at that time, and it was my task to baptize these artifacts in a huge vat filled with boiling acid. The fumes that rose from the immersion were so noisome that within a month I lost eleven pounds and developed nightmares during which I shrieked like a brain-fever bird. Compelled under parental pressure to resign, I wheedled a job as clerk at the baked-goods counter of Shepard's, a department store that dealt in fancy groceries. Overnight, my anemia magically vanished. Cramming myself with cinnamon buns, broken cookies, jelly doughnuts, ladyfingers, brownies, macaroons—anything I could filch while the floorwalker's back was turned—I blew up to fearful proportions. When not folding boxes or discomposing customers, I transported fresh stock from the bakery on the top floor of the building, a function that eventually led to my downfall. One afternoon, spying a beguiling tureen, I snatched a heaping ladleful of what I thought was whipped

645

cream but which proved to be marshmallow. Just as I was gagging horribly, I heard behind me the agonized whisper, "Cheese it, here comes Mr. Madigan!" and the floorwalker appeared, his mustache aquiver. He treated me to a baleful scrutiny, inquired whether I was subject to fits, and made a notation on his cuff. The following payday, my envelope contained a slip with a brief, unemotional dispatch. It stated that due to a country-wide shortage of aprons, the company was requisitioning mine and returning me to civilian life.

After a fortnight of leisure, my bloat had disappeared but so had my savings, and, unable to wangle credit or passes from the picture houses, I reluctantly took a job selling vacuum cleaners from door to door. The equipment that graced my particular model must have weighed easily three hundred pounds, and I spent a hideous day struggling on and off streetcars with it and beseeching suburban matrons to hold still for a demonstration. I was met everywhere by a vast apathy, if not open hostility; several prospects, in fact, saw fit to pursue me with brooms. Finally, a young Swedish housewife, too recent an immigrant to peg a tyro, allowed me to enter her bungalow. How I managed to blow all the fuses and scorch her curtains, I have no idea, but it happened in an *Augenblick*. The next thing I knew, I was fleeing through an azalea bed under a hail of Scandinavian cusswords, desperately hugging my appliances and coils of hose. The coup de grâce came upon my return to the warehouse. It transpired I had lost a nozzle and various couplings, elbows, and flanges, the cost of which I had to make good by pawning the household samovar.

It was more or less inevitable these early travails should return from limbo when, as happened recently, I settled myself into a projection room at the Museum of Modern Art with a print of *The Four Horsemen of the Apocalypse*. Actually, I would have much preferred to reinspect another vehicle of Valentino's called *Blood and Sand*, which co-starred Nita Naldi, down whom it used to be my boyhood ambition to coast on a Flexible Flyer, but the ravages of time had overtaken it. (Miss Naldi, *mirabile dictu*, is as symmetrical as ever.) *The Four Horsemen*, however, provided the great lover with a full gamut for his histrionic talents, and a notable supporting cast, containing, among others, Alice Terry, Wallace Beery, Alan Hale, Stuart Holmes, Joseph Swickard, and Nigel de Brulier. It was difficult to believe that only thirty-two years before—only yesterday, really, I told myself comfortingly—it had kept me on the edge of my chair. Ah, well, the chairs were narrower in those days. You positively get lost in the ones at the Museum.

The Four Horsemen, as any nonagenarian will remember, was based on Vicente Blasco Ibáñez's best seller. It was released on the heels of the First World War, and its pacifist theme was unquestionably responsible for a measure of its success, but Valentino's reptilian charm, his alliances with Winifred Hudnut and Natacha Rambova, the *brouhaha* about his excesses and idiosyncrasies were the real box-office lure. An interminable, narcotic genealogy precedes his appearance in the film, establishing a complex hierarchy of ranchers in the Argentine dominated by his maternal grandfather, an autocratic Spanish hidalgo. Julio Desnoyers (Valentino) is French on his father's side and the patriarch's favorite; he has German cousins being groomed as legatees of the family fortune, and the sequence pullulates with murky domestic intrigue. Petted and indulged by the old man, Julio grows up into a sleek-haired finale hopper who tangos sinuously, puffs smoke into the bodices of singsong girls, and generally qualifies as a libertine. In the fullness of time, or roughly six hundred feet of minutiae that remain a secret between the cameraman and the cutter, Julio's mother inherits half the estate and removes her son, daughter, and husband to Paris, where they take up residence in a Gallic facsimile of Kaliski & Gabay's auction rooms. Julio dabbles at painting—at least, we behold him before an easel in the manner of those penny-arcade tableaux called "What the Butler Saw Through the Keyhole," sighting off lickerishly at some models dressed in cheesecloth—and, in more serious vein, applies himself to seducing Marguerite Laurier (Alice Terry), the wife of a French senator. The role must have been a nerve-racking one for Valentino. Not only did he have to keep an eye peeled for the senator but the production was being directed by Miss Terry's husband-to-be, Rex Ingram. No wonder the poor cuss fell apart when he did.

To provide Valentino with a setting for his adagios, the affair gets under way at a fashionable temple of the dance called the Tango Palace, packed with gigolos and ladies in feathered turbans swaying orgiastically; then Marguerite, apprehensive of gossip, makes surreptitious visits to her lover's atelier. He, intent on steam-rollering her into the Turkish corner, is oblivious of all else, and there is a portentous moment, embroidering the favorite movie thesis that mankind always exhibits unbridled sensuality just prior to Armageddon, when his male secretary tries to show him a newspaper headline reading,

"ARCHDUKE FERDINAND ASSASSINATED AT SARAJEVO," only to have
Julio petulantly brush it aside. The symbolism now starts to pile up
thick and fast. The secretary, croaking ominously, exits to consult a
mysterious bearded philosopher in a Russian tunic (Nigel de Brulier),
who, it has been planted, dwells upstairs. No reliable clue to this
character's identity is anywhere given, but he seems to be a mélange
of Prince Myshkin, Savonarola, and Dean Inge, possesses the gift of
tongues, and is definitely supernatural. His reaction to the murder is
much more immediate, possibly because he doesn't have a girl in his
room. "This is the beginning of the end," he declares somberly. "The
brand that will set the world ablaze." Downstairs, meanwhile, Marguerite's scruples are melting like hot marzipan under Julio's caresses,
and it is manifest that she is breaking up fast. The camera thereupon cuts back to the oracle extracting an apple from a bowl of fruit.
"Do you not wonder that the apple, with its coloring, was chosen to
represent the forbidden fruit?" he asks the secretary, with a cryptic
smile. "But, when peeled, how like woman without her cloak of virtue!" I don't know how this brand of rhetoric affected other people
of my generation, but it used to make me whinny. I secretly compared
it to the insupportable sweetness of a thousand violins.

Before very long, Marguerite's husband ferrets out her peccadillo,
wrathfully announces his intention of divorcing her, and challenges
Julio to a duel. The scandal never eventuates, happily; in response to
a general mobilization order, the senator joins his regiment, the Fifth
Calvados Fusiliers, and his wife, seeking to make atonement for her
guilt, enrolls as a nurse. "The flames of war had singed the butterfly's
wings," explains a Lardnerian subtitle, "and in its place there was—a
woman, awakening to the call of France." Excused from military service because of his nationality, Julio dawdles around Paris making an
apathetic pitch for Marguerite, which she priggishly rejects on the
ground that venery is unseemly while the caissons roll—a view dia-
metrically opposed to that of another nurse in the same conflict described in *A Farewell to Arms*. Throughout the preceding, the soothsayer in the attic has been relentlessly conjuring up double-exposure
shots of the apocalyptic horsemen and their sinister baggage, and a
funereal pall descends on the action—not that it has been a Mardi
Gras thus far, by any means. Julio's father (Joseph Swickard) has
been taken prisoner at his country house by a detachment of uhlans
commanded by Wallace Beery, who proceeds to stage one of those
classic Hearst-Sunday-supplement revels with bemonocled Prussians
singing *"Ach, du lieber Augustin,"* girls running around in their ted-

dies, etc. At the height of the debauch, a frosty-eyed general (Stuart Holmes) enters and is revealed as Desnoyers' own nephew; i.e., a cousin of Julio's from the Argentine. Touched by the old man's plight, the officer displays unusual clemency and has him confined to a small, airy dungeon all his own; then, unbuckling his sword, he broaches an especially choice jeroboam of his uncle's champagne for the staff. Julio and Marguerite, in the meantime, continue their marathon renunciation in, of all places, the grotto at Lourdes, where she is nursing her husband, now blind and, of course, totally unaware of her identity. With a tenacity verging on monomania, Julio still hopes to con his sweetheart back to the ostermoor, but she is adamant. At length, he sickens of the whole enterprise—a process one has anticipated him in by a good half hour—castigates himself as a coward unworthy of her love, and rushes off to enlist. And just in the nick, it may be added, for what scenery hasn't been blasted by the foe has been chewed beyond recognition by the actors. Next to Mary Miles Minter laundering a kitten, nobody in the history of the silent screen could induce mal-de-mer as expertly as Valentino when he bit his knuckles to portray heartbreak.

The ensuing sequence is a bit choppy, occupying itself with Julio's heroism under fire and his parents' vicissitudes, though the only indication we get of the former is a shot of him, in a poilu helmet, fondling a monkey at a first-aid station. (However, the animal may conceivably have been afflicted with rabies.) Papa Desnoyers eludes his captors and visits the young man at the front with news that Marguerite pines for him but is devoting herself unsparingly to the senator, which can hardly be classified as an ingenious plot twist. There obviously remains but one situation to be milked to dramatize the irony of war—a battlefield encounter between Julio and his German cousin —and, blithely skipping over the mechanics of how a general falls into a shell hole in No Man's Land, the scenario maneuvers the relatives into a death grapple. I rather suspect that at this point a hurried story conference was called on the set to debate the propriety of allowing Valentino to be strangled. No doubt it was argued that the spectacle might cause mixed emotions in the audience, and a compromise was evolved wherein, before the outcome is resolved, we whisk to Marguerite's bedroom as she prepares to abandon her husband for Julio. Suddenly her lover's image materializes, suffused with an unearthly radiance, and she realizes the issue is academic. The rest of the picture is a lugubrious wash-up of the incidentals, climaxed by a graveside meeting between the elder Desnoyers and Julio's former upstairs neighbor, the apparition in the fright wig. Their conclusion, as I understood it, was that things were going to be a great deal worse before they became any better, but confidentially I found it hard to keep from whistling as I raced the projectionist to a *bourbonnerie*, around the corner from the Museum. After all, come sunshine or sorrow, it was extremely unlikely I would ever have to see *The Four Horsemen of the Apocalypse* a third time.

With the fatuity of middle age, I imagined I had exorcised the ghost of Valentino for keeps, but in some inexplicable fashion his aura must have clung to my person or otherwise put a hex on me. An evening or so later, my wife exhumed from the attic a Spanish shawl and several filigree combs she had been hoarding until she could get the right offer from a thrift shop. As she was executing an impromptu fandango to the strains of "Siboney," employing a pair of coasters as castanets, I was jealously impelled to demonstrate my superior co-ordination. "Watch this, everybody!" I sang out, flourishing a roll of shelf paper. "My impression of a matador winding himself in his sash, as created by the immortal Rudy Valentino in *Blood and Sand*!" I wrapped one end of the paper around my midriff, ordered a teen-age vassal to pay out some twenty feet and steady the roll, and, with a wild *"Ole!"* spun gyroscopically in her direction. Halfway, I ran full tilt into a peculiar blizzard of white specks and, to weather it, grabbed at a student lamp for support.

I got the lamp, all right, and plenty of time to regret my impetuosity. Lazing around the house with my tweezers, subsequently, probing for slivers of glass, it occurred to me all at once that maybe Valentino used a double in moments of hazard. Maybe I should have, beginning way back around 1921.

ABOUT THE AUTHOR

S. J. PERELMAN *was born in New York, attended Brown University, and began his professional career as an artist and writer for* Judge *and* College Humor. *Subsequently, as a scenario writer, he worked for the Marx brothers and most recently for Michael Todd on* Around the World in Eighty Days. *He has written several plays produced on Broadway, notably* One Touch of Venus (*with Ogden Nash and Kurt Weill*). *He is a member of The National Institute of Arts and Letters. He resides at Erwinna, Bucks County, Pennsylvania.*